AN IRISH READER IN MORAL THEOLOGY

Edited by Enda McDonagh and Vincent MacNamara

An Irish Reader in
Moral Theology

Volume II: Sex, Marriage and the Family

the columba press

First published in 2011 by
the columba press
55A Spruce Avenue, Stillorgan Industrial Park,
Blackrock, Co Dublin

Cover by Bill Bolger
Origination by The Columba Press
Printed by
Martins The Printers, Berwick-on-Tweed
ISBN 978 1 85607 739 2

Acknowledgements

In the preparation of this second volume, ranging over fifty years of Irish publications, we were fortunate to have in Catherine KilBride a friend experienced in writing and publishing. She volunteered to retrieve all the early material and prepare it for publication, while making important editorial suggestions. She also supervised the final proof-reading. Without her generous assistance this volume would not have been ready for publication for quite some time yet.

In the early development of the Reader project we were greatly assisted both in research and editorial work by, at that time, two Ph D students at Maynooth. They were also of considerable help in the production of this second volume. We owe them a debt of gratitude.

We also wish to thank Mary O'Malley for skilled secretarial work and the staff at Columba Press, our very co-operative publishers.

Contents

Biographies

WILLIAM BINCHY is Regius Professor of Laws in Trinity College, Dublin. He lectures and has written widely in the areas of family and constitutional law. A former Research Counsellor to the Law Reform, he is currently a member of the Irish Human Rights Commission.

PETER CONNOLLY was Professor of English Literature at St Patrick's College, Maynooth. He was also a well-known film critic and for many years wrote film reviews for *The Furrow*. He died in 1987.

WILLIAM COSGRAVE received his doctorate in moral theology at St Patrick's College, Maynooth. He lectured in moral theology at St Peter's College, Wexford. He is Parish Priest of Monageer, Co Wexford and the author of *Christian Living Today* and of many theological articles.

MARIE COLLINS has campaigned for justice for survivors of clerical sexual abuse in the Dublin Archdiocese for many years. She was subjected to this abuse while a patient in a Dublin children's hospital. She assisted the Archdiocese in the setting up of their Child Protection Office in 2003. Along with other survivors, Marie lobbied the government for the setting up of the Dublin Archdiocese Commission of Investigation (the Murphy Commission). Marie has been married for thirty-five years and has one son.

EOIN DE BHALDRAITHE joined the Cistercians in 1956. Since 1965 he has lived at Bolton Abbey, Co Kildare where he has filled various roles: prior, abbot, farm manager, guest master. He writes on many ecumenical issues, being particularly interested in the latest ARCIC agreement on Mary

EAMONN CONWAY is a priest of the Tuam diocese and currently professor of theology at Mary Immaculate College, University of Limerick. His recent publications include 'Die katholische Kirche Irlands und sexuelle Gewalt gegen minderjaehrige - Beschreibung der Krise und Entwurf einer theologischen Agenda' in Michael Albus and Ludwig Brueggeman, *Haende Weg! Sexuelle Gewalt in der Kirche* (2011), 'Broken Hearts and not Just Torn Garments – Beginning the Discussion about Forgiveness and Healing' in John Littleton & Eamon Maher (Eds), *The Dublin/Murphy Report: A Watershed for Irish Catholicism* (2010), 'Rahner's "Tough Love" for the Church – Structural Change in the Church as Task and Opportunity' in Padraic Conway and Fainche Ryan (eds), *Karl Rahner: Theologian for the Twenty-first Century* (2010).

DONAL DORR is a member of St Patrick's Missionary Society (Kiltegan). He has written extensively on issues of spirituality and international social justice. His latest book is *Spirituality, Our Deepest Heart's Desire* (2008).

ÁILÍN DOYLE has a background in law and theology. She has practised as a solicitor and has taught moral theology at Milltown Institute for a number of years. She has written numerous articles on sexuality and bioethics and is a member of several medical ethics committees. She is married with an adult family.

ORAN DOYLE is a member of the Law School and a Fellow of Trinity College, Dublin where he lectures in jurisprudence and constitutional law. He has written widely on issues of constitutional law and jurisprudence particularly as they concern equality.

GARRET FITZGERALD is a former Taoiseach (Prime Minister) of Ireland. He is a member of the Council of State and former Chancellor of the National University of Ireland. A well-known lecturer and author, his most recent book is *Just Garret* (2010). He died in May 2011.

RAPHAEL GALLAGHER, an Irish Redemptorist, is currently Visiting Professor at the Alphonsian Academy, Rome. He is co-author of *History and Conscience: Studies in Honour of Fr Sean O'Riordan* (1989) and author of *Understanding the Homosexual* (1985) and *Sean O'Riordan: A Theologian of Development* (1988).

PATRICK HANNON is Professor Emeritus of Moral Theology at St Patrick's College, Maynooth. He is the author of *Church, State, Morality and Law* (1992), *Moral Decision Making* (2005), *Moral Theology: A Reader* (2006), and *Right or Wrong: Essays in Moral Theology* (2009).

WILFRID HARRINGTON OP is Professor Emeritus at the Milltown Institute and Visiting Lecturer at the Church of Ireland Theological College.

BRENDAN HOBAN is a priest of Killala diocese and at present Parish Priest of Ballina, Co Mayo. A regular contributor to the print and electronic media at local and national level, in 2010 he was a co-founder of the Association of

Catholic Priests. His latest book, *Turbulent Diocese, The Killala Troubles, 1798-1848*, will be published at Easter by Banley House

MICHAEL HURLEY taught theology at the Jesuit Theological Faculty in Dublin from 1958 until 1970. He founded the Irish School of Ecumenics in 1970 and remained as Director until 1980. In 1983 he founded the residential Columbanus Community of Reconciliation in Belfast and remained a member until 1993. His publications include *Church and Eucharist* (ed 1966), *Theology of Ecumenism* (1969), *Irish Anglicanism* (ed.1970), *Reconciliation in Religion and Society* (ed 1994), *Church Unity: an Ecumenical Second Spring* (1998). He died in April 2011.

MARIE KEENAN is a psychotherapist and lecturer at the School of Applied Social Science UCD and a member of the Advisory Board of the UCD Institute of Criminology. She is chairperson of the Family Therapy Association of Ireland. Her book *Child Sexual Abuse and the Catholic Church: Gender, Power, Organizational Culture* is to be published by Oxford University Press, New York in September.

URSULA KILKELLY is a member of the Law Faculty in University College, Cork. She has lectured and published widely on children's rights, the European Convention on Human Rights and juvenile justice. She is a member of the Board of the Irish Penal Reform Trust and a founder member of the Irish Youth Justice Alliance.

BERNADETTE (BEN) KIMMERLING is an occasional writer and group facilitator. She lives at School House Bay, Foxford, Co Mayo.

MICHAEL G. LAWLER, Professor Emeritus of Catholic Theology at Creighton University in Omaha, received his training in theology in Dublin, Rome and St Louis. He has published 21 books and some 150 scholarly essays on topics related to sacraments, marriage, and sexuality. His most recent book, *The Sexual Person: Towards a Renewed Catholic Anthropology*, won first prize from the Catholic Press Association as the best theology book of 2009. He is married with three adult children.

JOHN MCAREAVY was ordained a priest of Dromore diocese in 1973. He was Professor of Canon Law at St Patrick's College, Maynooth from 1988 to 1999. He has been Bishop of Dromore since 1999.

ENDA MCDONAGH was Professor of Moral Theology at St Patrick's College, Maynooth from 1958 to 1995. He is the author of numerous publications, including *Immersed in Mystery: En Route to Theology* (2007) and *Theology in Winter Light* (2010).

VINCENT MACNAMARA has published several articles and books in the areas of morality and spirituality. His most recent book is *The Call to be Human: Making Sense of Morality* (2010).

BARRY MCMILLAN is a theological ethicist. His research interests include feminist theological ethics, sexual ethics, and contemporary culture. He lectures in theology and ethics at Galway-Mayo Institute of Technology (GMIT).

SÉAMUS MURPHY SJ worked at the Jesuit Centre for Faith and Justice, Dublin from 1987 to 1990. He has taught philosophy at Milltown Institute of Theology and Philosophy for many years up to 2008. He currently teaches philosophy at Loyola University Chicago.

CATHY MOLLOY is a part-time staff member of the Jesuit Centre for Faith and Justice. She completed a Licentiate in Theology at Milltown Institute where she was an associate lecturer for several years. She is the author of *Marriage: Theology and Reality* (1996) and of several articles on marriage, church and Catholic social teaching.

SUZANNE MULLIGAN is a graduate of the Pontifical University, Maynooth. She lectures in the Department of Moral Theology at Milltown Institute, Dublin. From 2006 to 2009 she held the Finlay Post-Doctoral Fellowship in Theology awarded by the Irish Province of the Jesuits. She is the author of *Confronting the Challenge: Poverty Gender and HIV in South Africa* (2010) and of numerous articles in theological journals.

DENIS O'CALLAGHAN has had long and varied experience in academic and pastoral life over half a century. A former professor of moral theology at St Patrick's College, Maynooth, he was a frequent contributor to theological journals in Ireland and abroad. He is the author of *Putting Hand to the Plough* (2007) and *Gone Fishing: Anecdotes of an Angler* (2008).

FERGAL O'CONNOR OP was for many years Lecturer in Ethics and Politics at University College, Dublin. He died in 2005

GERARD O'HANLON is a staff member of the Jesuit Centre for Faith and Justice and Associate Professor of Systematic Theology at the Milltown Institute. His most recent publication is *A New Vision for the Catholic Church: A View from Ireland* (2011).

THOMAS O'LOUGHLIN is Professor of Historical Theology at the University of Nottingham. Among his many publications are *Teachers and Code-Breakers:*

The Latin Genesis Tradition (1998), *Celtic Theology: Humanity, World and God in Early Irish Writings* (2000), *Adomnan and the Holy Places: The Perceptions of an Insular Monk on the Location of the Biblical Drama* (2007), *The Didache: A Window on the Earliest Christians* (2010).

SÉAMUS RYAN was educated at Maynooth and at the University of Münster where his professors included Joseph Ratzinger, Walter Kasper and Karl Rahner. He has taught theology at St Patrick's College, Thurles. He is a former President of the National Council of Priests of Ireland. He is currently Parish Priest of St Matthew Parish, Ballyfermot, Dublin.

ANNE THURSTON is currently on the PhD register of ISE / Trinity College Dublin. She is the author of numerous articles and of the following books: *Because of Her Testimony: the Word in Female Experience* (1995); *Knowing her Place: Women and the Gospels* (1998) and *A Time of Waiting* (2004)

DAVID WOODWORTH was Church of Ireland Rector in Bandon at the time of writing this article. He died in 1994.

General Introduction

A colleague on the way to a theological forum in the heady days after Vatican II picked up a farmer whose tractor had broken down. In the course of the conversation he asked his passenger how farming was doing. The answer: 'Agriculture is thriving but farming is gone to h...'. My colleague recounted this story to his audience while asking if theology might be thriving while religion was gone to h... Over forty years on, the questions might merit a double negative. It is hard to see that either theology or religion/ faith is thriving. As some service to the return of thriving in both, the editors undertook some years ago to recall and record the theological work of Irish theologians in the area of moral theology over the last half-century. They quickly realised what a major task it would be, given the extent of published material and the variety of topic, viewpoint, standard and sources of so much published work. An early decision settled on at least two volumes, later extended to three and, at last count, to four. As this is only the second volume, the life-and-publication-expectancy of the editors may be unduly optimistic

In the general introduction to Volume I, I attempted to justify the whole enterprise by emphasising the theological energy of the previous fifty years, not just in moral theology and not just among students for the priesthood or religious life. This, as indicated earlier, was mainly due to the impact of Vatican II. In recognition of this wider theological and church context the volume was launched at a seminar discussing *Fifty Years of Theology in Ireland*, involving scripture scholars and systematic/dogmatic theologians, religious, clerical and lay, women and men, Catholic and Protestant. As so much of all this was influenced, even inspired, by theology and theologians outside the island, the participants in the seminar did not confine themselves to Irish activity or just to the past. Indeed Volume I was dedicated to future generations of Irish (moral) theologians. One of the underlying aims of the enterprise was to enable the past to surprise and perhaps inspire the future.

In that extended general introduction some of the earlier history of moral theology in Ireland, from the latter half of the nineteenth century to the latter half of the twentieth, was dealt with somewhat summarily. Catholic theology could not operate in Ireland from the sixteenth to the nineteenth century and the Reformed traditions, including Anglicanism, did not have a formal discipline of moral theology. The introduction did, however, underline a couple of

14

distinctively Irish moral issues particularly in the social and political sphere such as just war, revolution and hunger strike in the national struggle for independence and various campaigns for fair rent and secure land tenure such as boycott of individual landlords and the more systematic 'Plan of Campaign'. In these and other social issues there was intense and often divisive moral debate among theologians and among bishops. Although the background to these debates were socio-political and the diverse views were frequently influenced by the socio-political stance of individual protagonists, this did not eliminate the serious moral content of the arguments. This has always been so, at least in this sphere of public and political morality. But these are mainly the concerns of later volumes.

This volume which concentrates on 'Sex, Marriage and the Family' has its own social and political dimensions in relation to society as a whole and internally to what one might call church politics, the relations of truth and power and their various promoters. The church's internal debate moving towards conflict is expressed firstly in more general terms lest it be reduced too easily to a Pope and bishops versus theologians struggle, as if both or either of these groups were always unanimous on all such matters, or even on a particular one such as contraception, which has long divided bishops among themselves, if more silently than the divided theologians. Of course there are large groups of informed church members active in such debates who are neither bishops nor theologians.

The truth of power and the power of truth have seldom coincided within any of these divided groupings. In these matters further reductionisms threaten as the gospel message is dominated by concern for sexual morality within the church itself and the church is perceived in the wider world as obsessed with sexual morality. The intensity of the Irish and wider church debates on contraception, divorce and homosexuality has few parallels in such areas as justice or peace.

It is in the midst of such a simmering civil war among Christians of all denominations, and not just Catholics or Anglicans, that we have undertaken to present this volume of material on 'Sex, Marriage and the Family' published by Irish theologians over the last fifty years. Confined as we were by our programme to already published work, we could only guarantee such quality and balance as already existed there. We had hoped to include some articles by moral theologian Sean Fagan SM but 'due to circumstances outside our control' this was not possible. Given our experience of last minute ecclesiastical interference with the publication of Volume I, *Foundations*, and our consequent need to find an alternative publisher, it is hard to believe that this volume will escape some controversy. If the criticism is presented fairly and, above all, openly, allowing for genuine debate, then truth, moral theology and the Church can only benefit.

We are offering a view of theological writing in the past fifty years. In fairness to the authors, the reader should note the original date of the various contributions. Some authors of earlier articles wished to give an update. Such additions are noted as 'Update' in the relevant articles. We have also had, for a variety of reasons – mainly reasons of space – to ask some authors to allow us to include extracts rather than whole chapters or articles. We regret that this was necessary. We thank them for their willingness.

Enda McDonagh

Introduction to Volume II

Is there any area of morality that has so divided people as much as the morality of sexuality? Is there any in which there is a greater gap between the stance of Christian churches and the rest of society? Is there any that has led to so much anger among church adherents? Any in which moralists have felt more keenly that they were walking on eggshells? Probably not.

It is hardly any wonder. All religions and cultures have found sex a troubling issue. The theologian has to recognise that. So that a first question might be: what are we talking about when we talk about sexuality – in any religion or culture? Where would you begin if you wished to engage it theologically? The sciences, through the ages, have sought to analyse our human experience. But which of them would you turn to? Anthropology, sociology, psychology, philosophy, medicine? Or all of them? There are different approaches and different contributions. It is taken for granted now that moralists need to dialogue seriously with the sciences: we can expect to see more of that.

It is interesting to take a historical approach. Which is just what this volume does. I think it was Pius XI who said that we are all spiritually Jews. You might wonder, as you read the history here, if we have been, through the centuries, spiritually Stoics or Manichaeans or Gnostics. The general, often unconscious, sense of sexuality, which was current in any age, determined its moral norms. It is part of the task of the theologian always to stand in critical appraisal of what has been handed down and why, to have a hermeneutic of suspicion. That is ongoing – life builds on life, decade builds on decade, thought builds on thought. This volume is witness to the development of thought in the Christian community. It is in some instances also witness to the development of the individual authors. So, it is only fair to them and to the ages past to keep that in mind: we have therefore been careful to note the date of each article.

'Like other religious and cultural traditions the teachings within the Christian tradition regarding human sexuality are complex, subject to multiple outside influences, and expressive of change and development through succeeding generations of Christians.' (Farley)[1] So we tread our way. As Christianity spread from being a sect to being a religious institution and sought to systematise itself, it found itself in a world of bewildering thought-patterns. It was coloured by strange theories of good and evil forces, even of good and evil gods, of world-denying attitudes, of suspicion of pleasure and desire, even

17

sometimes of life and the handing on of life – not infrequently leading to quite contradictory stances, to a denial of sexual pleasure or an insouciant abandonment to it. Worse, thought about sexuality was curiously enmeshed in a powerfully influential notion of original sin. Sin, concupiscence and human generation were conspirators. The human person was thought to be so swamped, so damaged, so prone to wayward passion that it was hard to think how sexual intercourse could ever be justified: it was so inimical to reason as always to carry a suspicion of evil. Procreation became the shaky justification for it. Though it is hardly very uplifting, that the formula which emerged was *malo bene utitur* – marital intercourse was a good use of something evil. The much-maligned Augustine fought, against diverse adversaries, to maintain that marriage is a natural good, but the fact that he too, on occasion, had recourse to the *malo bene utitur* formula cast a long shadow.

All that is worth recalling, and it is recalled here, when we look at the tortuous thought-journey of Christianity. The middle ages were still dominated by many of the same ideas. If there was one attribute of humans that delighted medievals it was the conviction that 'the light of your countenance is shined upon us O Lord' – a testimony, as Aquinas had it, that we are sharers in the reason of God. How could one justify the dangerous pleasure of intercourse, which could dull the sharp light of reason? By procreation, of course. But was it morally lawful to seek or enjoy the pleasure accompanying intercourse? And even if one did have the best of intentions, did the very experience of pleasure taint one in some way – so that one needed cleansing of some kind? Could one receive the Eucharist the day after sexual intercourse – look at the Penitentials in which we Irish specialised. Was the sacred event of child-bearing itself not in some way tainted, so that 'churching' was at times understood as a kind of ritual cleansing? (Part I)

Two factors encompassed theological thought: the purpose or end of sexuality in God's plan; and the manner of sexual intercourse which respected such a purpose. The subjective intent to procreate and the objective possibility of procreation were equally critical. The act had to be open to procreation. The argument that developed around it, although its origins are found in Greek thought, rested on the thesis that morality can be derived from the physical structure of the human person, with its faculties and ends. There, it was argued, one could read the plan of God. That there might be other elements in the sexual experience just as surely 'intended by God', was not something that easily forced itself into the light of thought or practice. It was not entirely absent – it may come as some surprise that, as one of our articles suggests, the love-theme of Vatican II is not quite as new as we might have accepted. But, other articles here remind us that there was, famously, a subordination of ends. Marriage was a contract in which the parties handed over to each other the right to acts *per se* apt for generation, as the 1917 Code of Canon Law had it. That was the primary end: anything else was subordinate to that.

That is part of the story. There were also more subtle influences. In morality generally we have come to recognise the pervasive effect of culture, the conditionality of moral thought. We know about the social construction of reality, about the fact that moral notions and mores are considerably affected by non-moral facts: so that it is difficult to understand the moral orthodoxy of any age without a sense of its thought-background. You cannot leap out of culture into the clear and abiding moral law. That, we have seen, for centuries affected notions relevant to sexual morality such as reason and emotion, pleasure and ascesis, spirit and flesh, life and death. It also had deleterious effects in gender issues. The place of women was determined by the powerful ones, by men: it was out of their conviction about social roles and their experience of their own sexuality that norms were established. Women had only a limited latitude; their sexual identity was dictated by culture. The whole notion of sexual relations, in effect of marriage, was at times coloured by cultural ideas of family, property and clan. We know how, particularly in Christian thought, this led to the narrowing exaltation of motherhood and family, to the expectation of woman as domestic and submissive – a woman should devote her attention to children, husband and family (*Casti Connubii*, 26, 74-6) – but at the same time, curiously, carrying responsibility for the salvation of men. We know about the 'right' to the marital act. Cultural ideas change: conceptions of marriage, among other things, are culture and time bound: it is a different human reality from one age to another. Moralities must take account of that.

I think it will be accepted that there is no simple way of dealing with, of moralising about, or of legislating for sexuality. It is a complex experience, involving basic instinct, biological urge, relationship, intimacy, tenderness, pleasure, eroticism, procreation. Points of view range from the thesis that sex should have no other significance than pleasure and that it is obnoxious to have it burdened with 'meaning',[2] to John Paul II's statement that couples by contraception degrade human sexuality, and with it themselves and their married partner, by altering its value of 'total' self-giving,[3] to the suggestion that the ultimate meaning of carnal desire is Unity, the need for God.[4] Ricoeur puts it interestingly: 'We have learned from Freud – principally from *Three Essays in Sexuality* – that sexuality is not simple and that the integration of its multiple components is an unending task … [it] remains perhaps basically impermeable to reflection and inaccessible to human mastery. Ultimately, when two beings embrace, they don't know what they are doing, they don't know what they want, they don't know what they are looking for, they don't know what they are finding.'[5]

Sexual desire is mysterious, and the sexual history of each one is individual and unique. A theology that is not aware of its multiple components will be inadequate. But how can one encompass such a complex issue in morality or discipline? How can one find a way between frightened rigidity and mindless licence. Certainly not through crude notions of 'normal' and 'abnormal', 'natural' and 'unnatural', nor in a simplistic concentration on one element, which would filter out all other elements of the experience. Nor in blunt, unyielding absolutes. Nor in condemnations that are deaf to the particularity of situations. Thankfully, we do now know more about its heterosexual, homosexual, bisexual forms. The sciences of psychology and psychiatry and the witness of brave individuals have mercifully opened us to an acknowledgment of that. What is important is listening openly to the variety of experiences and not extrapolating from one form of sexuality to another. And if, as *Familiaris Consortio* recognises, sexuality is such an intimate part of the human person, what is one to make of sexuality and the single life? And can we have a better context for the particular form of sexuality that is celibacy? All such matters come in for consideration here. (Parts VII, IX)

And what is one to say about the frightening phenomenon with which we have been confronted in recent times – the attraction of some of our fellow human beings to sex with children. It has caused deep confusion, deep anger, deep shame. No current consideration of morality could ignore that. As a society we deplore it but have not yet gone any distance in understanding it. The times are raw, but one must listen both to survivors and perpetrators if there is to be cleansing. There is work to be done for sociologists, psychologists and moralists. We thought it appropriate to include in this section also a valuable essay, a critique of pornography in literature, that touches on another widespread form of abuse. (Part VIII)

Where are we going? Good things have happened. If we have become somewhat wiser about the nature of sexuality, we have also lived through subtle changes in the understanding of morality. The disembodied morality of the crude versions of natural law has had to yield some ground to a more personal view of the moral subject. The centrality of such a notion as 'flourishing' as a hermeneutic key to what is morally desirable, has brought to prominence elements such as love, relationship, pleasure, wholeness: they have come to be accepted as at least some part of the normative meaning of sex. That requires a re-imagining of the tension between such considerations and that of procreation.

A particular aspect of this has been recourse to the notion of sexuality as language, and by extension a new emphasis on the body as our human way of expressing ourselves – not least in the writings of John Paul II, although not everybody has been impressed by that. It fans out into consideration of the relationship between sex, commitment and fidelity. The stress on commitment-language is important but it creates problems as well as solving them. It is now an accepted approach in official church teaching, but the implications of it for pre-ceremonial relationship, for example, have not been faced. How often now does a priest find that those who present themselves for marriage have already

been living together, having made and expressed a commitment to one another? Does official teaching have anything to say to that, and what? Entwined
here are questions about the moral weight that is to be given not just to church
teaching but to its discipline, and the difficult matter of their relationship. Some
of that morality / discipline purports to affect the nature of marriage (the validity, if you will, although that is a strange way of speaking about a covenant of
mutual love, whatever about a contract) – the form of marriage, the meaning
of 'married in church', diriment ecclesiastical impediments, such as celibacy,
and re-admission to sacraments after breakdown. The downside of the stress
on body and language is the fear, which you sometimes hear expressed, that
emphasis on the relationship aspect has led to an unreal romanticising of sexuality and marriage – one remembers the well-known story of the old woman
who, on hearing a sermon on marriage from the young priest, quipped, 'God
love him, I wish I knew as little about it as he does.' (Parts IV, V)

Equally important have been developments in rethinking sexual morality
not in terms of biological functions but of a richer appreciation of the person
based on freedom, mutuality, respect and justice. This has been particularly
helpful in efforts to elaborate a morality which shakes off the accretions which
derive from a distorted view of the place of women in relationship, in family,
in culture and in society. It means allowing the woman to emerge as an equal
partner with desires and aspirations equally deserving of a hearing. (Part I)

It would be unfair to suggest that official teaching has been untouched by
such developments. I once heard a student say, echoing what is often said about
its justice teaching, that the church's teaching on sexuality is its best-kept secret.
I presume he was thinking of such statements as the following. 'Marriage is the
reciprocal gift of self; husband and wife tend towards the communion of their
beings; love is fully human ... of the senses and of the spirit at the same time'
(*Humanae Vitae* 8, 9). 'Sexuality, by which human beings give themselves to
each other in physical acts, concerns the innermost being of the person ... conjugal love involves a totality in which all the elements of the person enter – appeal of the body and instinct, power of feeling and affectivity, aspiration of the
spirit and of will' (*Familiaris Consortio*, 11, 13). 'That love ennobles the expressions of body and mind as special ingredients and signs of the friendship distinctive of marriage; that love is uniquely expressed and perfected through the
marital act; these actions signify and promote that mutual self-giving by which
the spouses enrich each other' (*Gaudium et Spes*, 49). 'The body is a constitutive
part of the person who manifests and expresses him / herself through it ... the
spouses mutually express their personal love in the "language of the body"'
(*Donum Vitae*, pp 8, 27). It is a long, long way from Augustine and Jerome and
the text-books and spiritualities of the 18th and 19th centuries, and perhaps
from popular conceptions of church morality. And yet it has some way to go.
Despite a modification of the traditional view of the ends of marriage, tension

still remains between the teaching on love/ relationship and that on contraception. One often has the feeling that official teaching is not always consistent, sometimes at odds with itself. (It is interesting to note, among other things, the conflicting views on the nature of marriage in the Roman Rota after Vatican II: Paul VI felt it necessary to come down on the side of marriage as a juridical entity, diminishing the Council's stress on marriage as a covenant of love.)

Nobody does morality in a vacuum. Christians do morality as Christians. How do the biblical vision and the core tradition, with their high ideals, colour one's understanding today? Christian worldviews in the past were inevitably infected by surrounding cultures and prejudices. But there were seams of gold there in the religious culture. As in so many other areas, a church must ever be renewed, seeking ever more clearly how the 'saving mystery' bears on the 'human reality'. It is a matter of constructing a morality that is open to dialogue on the human significance of sexuality, that is rooted in realism, that preserves the best insights of the past but sheds its cultural, social and gender distortions. A morality that recognises that a care for sexuality involves, among other things, a care for the social condition of people. The status of women in many countries makes a mockery of some of the high-flown rhetoric of official statements. (Parts I, II)

There is scope for strong and imaginative re-thinking. Experience is not decisive on its own, but if, as is generally accepted now, experience is a crucial part of moral thought, one can only hope that the experience of people generally, and of changing constructions of family life, will be allowed to inform the morality of the future. A willingness on the part of the clerical church to learn rather than to pronounce might be in order. It is not a matter of being nice to the laity but a foundational matter of how to proceed in morals and of recognising the paths to collective wisdom. There is a widespread acceptance that there is a yawning gap between official teaching and the practice of people – on divorce, contraception, admission to sacraments, homosexual acts, pre-marital relationships That is not a healthy situation. (Part III)

Our first volume was dedicated to the theologians of the future. The present volume shows that there is plenty of work for them to do. If sexuality is so central to human life, if it 'concerns the innermost being of the person' , if it carries so much possibility for good and ill, for happiness and unhappiness – for couples, families, society, and the common good – it must be a concern for an institution like the church that purports to care for human well-being.

Vincent MacNamara

Notes:

1. Farley, Margaret, 'Sexual Ethics' in Warren T. Reich, *An Encyclopedia of Bioethics*, first edition, vol 2, p 1578.

2. Ehrenheich, Hess and Jacobs, quoted Mary D. Pellauer in James B. Nelson and Sandra Longfellow, *Sexuality and the Sacred*, Louisville, Westminster/John Knox Press, 1993, p 168

3. *Familiaris Consortio*, n 32.

4. 'If people were told: what makes carnal desire imperious in you is not its pure carnal element. It is the fact that you put into it the essential part of yourself – the need for Unity, the need for God – they wouldn't believe you.' Simone Weil, *First and Last Notebooks*, quoted Sam Keen, *The Passionate Life*, New York, Harper Collins, 1964, frontpiece.

5. Paul Ricoeur, 'Wonder, Eroticism and Enigma', *Cross Currents*, Spring 1964.

6. Edward Schillebeeckx, *Marriage: Human Reality and Saving Mystery*, London, Sheed and Ward, 1965.

Part One
Sexuality

1   A church silence in sexual moral discourse?

Raphael Gallagher

(Amelia Fleming (ed), *Contemporary Irish Moral Discourse: Essays in Honour of Patrick Hannon*, Dublin: Columba Press, 2007, pp 53-65)

There is no end of conversation about sex in Ireland, and indeed about sexual morality. Silence begins to descend when Catholic sexual morality emerges as a topic: there may be some shouting and cross-talk, but hardly a conversation. The row dies down, and there is silence until the next spat. It is a curious sort of silence, somewhere between embarrassment and lack of interest. Trying to explain this silence demands some hypothesis. Mine is that there is a vacuum in Catholic Irish society, and thus in public forms of discourse, due to the way we have inherited and appropriated our religious legal system. Historically, the native Irish distrusted the English, including their public law. A lack of respect for public law did not necessarily mean that the natives were savages, quite the contrary. There were customs accepted at local level and a substratum

of beliefs that had a profoundly civilising effect. The fact that the Renaissance had minimal effect in Ireland, however, exacerbated the vacuum when the English legal writ no longer held sway. Such Irish as could be classified as Renaissance people, like John Toland, usually lived abroad. When the state was founded the Catholic Church, unconsciously using a legal mindset that was more mediaeval than modern, filled the vacuum in public discourse. A country anxious to forge an identity and provide a forum for public exchange on moral

issues readily accepted the legal presentation of Catholic doctrine. That mindset is no longer shared, hence the move towards silence on Catholic sexual morality as a public debating item.

Before the silence
The legal roots of Catholic sexual morality are not as narrow as sometimes portrayed. The Western legal tradition has its origin in the papal legal reform of the tenth and eleventh centuries. From the church point of view, law came to be seen as the essence of faith: God himself is law and therefore the law is dear to him. This view, taken from the *Sachsenspiegel*, the prototype book of German law published in 1220, helps to understand the sacred reverence given to church law. Law was part of fulfilling the mission of the church on earth. While

the subordinate position of secular law was implied, it was the church as a visible legal entity that was meant to control people for the next world by ensuring proper behaviour in the essential matters of this world. Church law be-

AN IRISH READER IN MORAL THEOLOGY

came a means of reforming the world. This legal system provided the establishment of an external forum to balance the internal forum that already existed in the sacrament of penance.

The jurisdiction of the church was of such import that Thomas Becket was prepared to die for it instead of allowing King Henry II to interfere with what Becket considered essential to the freedom of the faith under the pope. No one would have argued that the canon law was perfect, since it was a human formulation, but it was as close as one could get to natural law and divine law. If the universe is subject to law, and this would have been agreed by all, then the supreme law should reflect as closely as possible God's design for the world. This explains why the church would have insisted on the supremacy of canon law over all other forms of law.

It is dangerous to summarise something so complex as the mediaeval papal revolution in so few words.[1] Easily forgotten could be the subtlety involved in the interpretation of canon law, and this was done by some of the most brilliant schoolmen of the age. Law was administered in the classic Roman mode, with a sense of equity: exceptions could be dealt with. The summary could also give the impression that other forms of law such as feudal law, mercantile law or royal law had no importance. They had, and often co-existed with canon law. But on one point there was no doubt allowed: canon law, because of its closer connection with natural and divine law, was supremely better because it guided the soul to heaven.

This may seem a long way from the silence about sexual morality of a Catholic type in Ireland. Let me return to my hypothesis. If Ireland, at the time of the foundation of the state, had no legal memory, so to speak, except to be 'against the foreigner's law', there was an obvious vacuum. Different types of legal systems had developed in Europe after the collapse of papal power (such as the rational, traditional or charismatic forms, to use Weber's classification). If they had any influence in Ireland, it was through the rule of the foreigner, and thus entirely suspect. With the disappearance of the foreigner's rule, their legal mindset was also set aside. The categories of discourse implied in the canon law of the church took over this vacuum and, though this too was a foreign code of law, it was acceptable to a people who had suffered 'for the sake of the Roman faith'.

Central to my hypothesis is the widespread acceptance of these canonical categories for the interpretation of life. Just as the political unification of the Catholic Church under a system of law governed by papal authority could not have taken place in the middle ages without a grassroots acceptance by the people, so too in Ireland after independence. I would not interpret this as a supine attitude before a powerful hierarchy. The language made sense, not simply *faute de mieux*, but because it could be seen as coherent, once one accepted the basic premises. Canon law covered the essentials necessary for a good life, and it did so working with theological categories that gave a judgement on this life, and the next. Sexual morality was not simply couched in legal terms: these legal terms had a theological background that gave them legitimacy in the eyes of God. Without the fear of hell, the worry about purgatory and the hope of heaven, it is impossible to understand the origins of the Western legal tradition in general or the reason why a revived form of it, in canon law, had such a powerful effect in Ireland. The promulgation of the Code of Canon Law in 1917 and the achievement of a partial independence some five years later may not be coincidental in explaining how a particular Catholic legal system filled a vacuum in terms of sexual morality.

If all of life, including its sexual aspect, can be both controlled and interpreted through canon law, then the rejection of its powers has a far-reaching effect. That is the hypothesis I propose about the inability of the church to speak publicly now, with conviction, on sexual matters in Ireland. Other categories have taken over, the language of human rights being the most obvious one. The world of sexuality interpreted though a medieval conception of law, and underpinned by a particular theology of heaven, hell and purgatory, no longer convinces. There are other ways of explaining sexuality, and the problem for the church is in coming to understand these new languages. Meanwhile there is a silence because the new language is foreign to the heritage of an Irish church formed by canon law with its roots in a medieval conception of heaven, hell and purgatory.

A contemporary complication

There is a complicating factor, however. I presume that public conversations on Catholic sexual morality would at least acknowledge that such a morality has a religious component. The collapse of the canonical ways of dealing with sexuality coincides, in Ireland, with the growth of the view that religious based discourse is no longer proper in the public square. The emergence of this view has its own historical roots. The modern states, which took form in the seventeenth and eighteenth centuries after the bitter wars of religion, were in varying degrees philosophically conceived and practically arranged so that religion would not be considered part of political life. The secularisation of politics has had long-term effects. They are not to be seen in the immediate aftermath of the foundation of the Irish state, but it seems that they shape the current prevailing view. Politics is politics, and religion is religion: the two should not be mixed. While there was a mode of public conversation on sexual matters during the period where canon law held sway, the collapse of this mode has occurred precisely at an historical period where religious-based views are considered to be private matters, and thus not proper for a public conversation. This argument rests on the assumption that while religion may be deeply significant to people's personal lives it does not necessarily have public consequences.[2] The world can be understood in terms of economic policies, political arrangements, military strategies and social procedures to regulate democracies. These are the stuff of public discourse, but not religion. This does not seem to me to be very wise, but such is the current general perception. It is not very wise: the world flashpoints of the last decade, from terrorism to fundamentalism, are proving intractable precisely because politics has lost the art of public discourse about religious-based values. Though not wise, it is the prevailing view of public life. Thus, even when the church in Ireland wishes to speak publicly about Catholic sexual morality, it is doing so within a society that is not convinced that religious-based views are public debating points.

Are we condemned to be silent?

The omens are clearly not good for a public conversation about Catholic sexual morality given my hypothesis that the collapse of a canonically based view has coincided with an epoch when religious-based views are not particularly welcome in the public political forum. The impasse on Catholic sexual morality will be broken only by a closer analysis of the basis of how Catholic moral norms are given a foundation. This will have the advantage of moving the debating point from the public forum, at least initially, to its more proper home: a consideration of what is good for the human person in the first place. Following Charles Taylor,[3] this difficulty in giving a foundation for morality can be interpreted as a divergence about moral sources, or the constitutive goods, which form the modern moral person. I take the sources of morality to mean, in this context, those values which are at the basis of our moral ideals and practical actions. Traditionally, these sources were seen as exterior to the individual person: that is true of the philosophic systems of Plato and Aristotle as it is clearly also true of the revealed sources of morality developed by Christianity.

What is novel, and broadly coincident with the problems I have indicated in Ireland, is that the sources for morality are now considered to be internal to the human person. Typically, the contemporary person does not seek the sources for a good moral life outside themselves, but within. This happens in two different ways. One way of seeking an internal source for the moral life, which obviously includes our sexual options, is to see our human intelligence as a practical instrument that helps us to calculate what choices to make in life. A second line of internal searching, no less important than the first, is to look into our interior lives and decide on the basis of what is likely to be the most fulfilling choice in terms of being true to myself. Both these forms of placing the sources of morality within ourselves, as distinct from reliance on outside sources, deserve a comment in terms of the current difficulties for the church on sexual morality in public debate.

Take the first view, where human intelligence is seen as a personal instrument to shape one's life. The problem is not with having a high view of the gift of intelligence: the debating point, for this essay, is whether this intelligence is simply subject to its own internal laws. I think there is substantial evidence, in the sexual area, to show that this is what is generally accepted. If something can be done, without harming others intentionally, then go and do it. I am not so much thinking of a hedonistic view of life, however problematic that may be too, so much as the impact of technology on sexual patterns of behaviour. It is now possible to control fertility, and to avoid sexually transmitted diseases, if one thinks about it. In advance. Behaviour is not dictated by norms imposed from outside, but by a prior perception of what is good for myself. If I use my intelligence, I can control my body, and my body is my own to control. Clearly the cosmological worldview of a canon law based on theological presumptions about heaven, hell and purgatory does not enter this type of equation.

In the second view, the search for an internal sourcing of sexual morality is even more obvious. The important thing in life is to be true to my own feelings and to be authentic in the sense that the choices I make in life are mine, and no one else's. Once again, I do not think we should take issue with the importance of being aware of and accepting our own choices in life. That seems fundamental. What is novel, however, is the view that the moral criteria (or the sources of morality) are entirely to be found in the realm of my personal sentiments and feelings.

What is interesting, in considering a public language for Catholic sexual morality, is that these new forms of interiorising the sources of moral judgement may be in conflict with themselves as well as obviously not consonant with traditional views. The utilitarian view (my body is my own and I am intelligent enough to know what to with it) does not sit easily with the post-romantic view (my body is the source of my feelings and I must listen attentively to what it is telling me). But the point they have in common, a greater respect for the individual person as a moral subject, may be more fruitful territory for public conversations than at first appears. The breakdown of the externally imposed common language of the canonical books may be providential after all.

The inability to hold public conversations about Catholic sexual morality thus emerges as a problem of competing languages. The attempts at debate degenerate into shouting games because there is not a shared language. I have identified three variants. There is a residual language from the canon law tradition, and this usually identifies sexual morality as a question of norms and codes. Two new competing voices have emerged, one stressing the technological view of sex and the other more reliant on an emotional interpretation of what is considered good behaviour. Because the new voices are subjective, in the sense that the sources on which their arguments are based are interior to the individual, they are impatient with the normative language of the Catholic Church that is seen as an outside intrusion on personal freedom. Even the up-

AN IRISH READER IN MORAL THEOLOGY

holders of normative religious views on sexual matters would grant that there is more to be discussed than legal codes, but they have lost the language to communicate in an Ireland no longer religiously shaped by canon law. Their silence is thus the silence of strangers in a foreign land, speaking a language the natives do not know.

What is there to talk about?

I grant that people representing the new sources for morality are probably quite happy that the church is no longer interfering, or at least that its interventions are kept to the margins. How can I justify the recovery of a public voice?

This can be justified only on the basis of excluding certain positions. There can be no return to the view that Catholic moral norms should dictate the law of the land. Catholicism cannot function, either in theory or in practice, as a shared moral source for sexual morality in a culturally diverse Ireland. That point is clearly established theologically, and it has political consequences.[4] It has to be some form of shared moral reasoning, and not the fact that some actions are forbidden by the church, which provides the authority to establish public sexual norms. But this could beg the question: can we not have this form of shared moral reasoning without recourse to the Catholic tradition of arguing in moral matters? Though I have acknowledged that the current view in Ireland seems to favour an exclusion of religious based views from public debate, I have also entered a caveat that I do not think it is a very wise position. This deserves a further comment.

It is interesting that John Rawls, certainly an articulate exponent of a theory of liberal democracy organised on rational criteria, now seems more open to the possibility of religious considerations being a proper part of public debate in liberal democratic states.[5] He does so with a proviso. If a religious inspired view is being proposed as a suitable basis for social organisation, it must be accompanied by what he calls appropriate public reasons. Religious arguments are not *per se* excluded, according to Rawls in his later views, but only those religious reasons may be put forward which are capable of being communicated through the rules of public rational debate. This is an important clarification. The Catholic Church could claim a voice in public debate on sexual morality in Ireland if we followed through on this suggestion. The basis of any argument proposed would not be that such and such is the teaching of the church, but that sexual mores have public consequences which can be identified independently of the views of church authority. There would have to be agreement on what these consequences might be: one could propose the general common good of society, a respectful tolerance for the views of others and adequate care for the support of family-based institutions. This is clearly a limited list, and obviously is not meant as an agenda. I use it as an example. There are aspects of sexual morality, such as these three, which are a core concern of the general social fabric. The Catholic Church has views on these, and when such views are presented in terms of the issues themselves (thus, not on the basis of church teaching or authority claims) the public debate could be enhanced. To do this, however, will demand a substantial shift in the presentation of Catholic sexual morality. What has collapsed in Ireland, in the sense of not being welcomed in the public forum, is the normative residue of the canon law tradition on sexual morality.[6] Irish society has its own reasons for this rejection. It is my view that the rejection is not the great disaster it seems to many because sexual discourse cannot be reduced to conversations about norms and laws. The fabric of sexual identity and the tortuous path of sexual development are far too complex to be boxed into normative conversations. The recovery of a voice for the Catholic Church, more or less following the criteria of Rawls, will thus depend on the ability of the church to present its sexual moral views in a more inclusive way than has been the case.

To whom are we talking?

Getting to this position will not be easy. The collapse of a canonically based form of sexual norms left a void primarily within the church, and only then in Irish society given the prominent place of the church. I have the impression that the church, aware of the unresolved tensions about sexual morality within its own community, then tried to rely on political strategies to ensure the imposition of views consonant with its traditional teaching. The reversal of this trend means that the first partners for public dialogue should be within the church. If this conversation yields significant results it will be possible to see what aspects of sexual morality are germane to public political debate, and which are not. It will also ensure a measure of coherence between church morality and its contribution to the public debate: too often there is an impression of double-speak in this regard.

The question to be addressed, on an internal church level, is the correlation between norms and experience. The significance of sexuality is in proportion to its perceived significance. Of course, sexuality involves bodily desires that we can analyse on their own terms: equally, sexuality can be formulated in a normative way that can also be the subject of further considerations. The deeper meaning of sexuality, however, is shaped by the grammar, syntax and linguistic context in which bodily desires and normative formulae find their home. This is the heart of the matter. We have momentarily lost the ability to use an inclusive grammar of sexuality; its meaning is reduced either to the swirling plane of physical desires or the colder corner of normative formulations. It is no solution to urge, as Lady Bennerley did,[7] that the only way to be happy is to forget our body and then time passes quickly without further anxiety. The normative or legal way of dealing with the question is just as unpromising. The paradox here is that the liberalisation of sexual norms and laws, as has been the case in Ireland, still reduces the complex world of sexuality to a level of flatness where chastity may be seen as no more a virtue than malnutrition. The vacuum thus reveals itself for what it is: the lack of a symbolic language for sexuality. Rollo May's observation is pertinent: people can have so much sex but so little meaning in their lives. We need to recover the lost voices of the Catholic tradition if we are to escape from the reduction of sexual talk to a normative level. This was always problematic, but even more so when the consensus on the norms has gone.[8]

The grammar of our public language

I started with the hypothesis that one cause of the church's inability to engage in fruitful public debate on sexual morality is associated with the way a particular legal tradition of Catholicism took root in the nascent Irish state. The thesis I propose is that the alienation that this provoked in the long term could be addressed by a grammar of sexuality that is inclusive in its scope and integrative in its application. This involves a journey of retrieval: behind the canonical norms what was there, besides the particular notions of heaven, hell and purgatory that I alluded to?

The original vision is one where the allied aspects of sexuality, human loneliness and the natural desire for children, are integrated. In the twin accounts of the Book of Genesis the earlier Yahwist tradition (circa 950 BC) alludes to the linkage between our sexual nature and our inner emptiness: it is not good that the human person be alone (Gen 2:24). The later Priestly tradition (circa 550 BC), possibly reflecting a warrior agricultural nation's need for a workforce and soldiers, stressed the social role of our sexual nature: be fruitful and multiply (Gen 1:18). The retrieval has to be a full retrieval; otherwise the public discourse of the church on sexuality will continue its alienating path. The perception that the church has reduced the tradition to norms about procreation alone is well known: another strand in the tradition, more obvious in recent times, is the reduction of sexual desire to what is pleasurable and thus a way of lessening our loneliness. The starting point of the public grammar of sexual discourse is a retrieval of the fuller originating vision.

Complementing this retrieval, the grammar will then demand a mode of confronting the residue of the two forms of reductionism just mentioned. Reducing sex to procreation only, or simply to pleasure, is personally alienating: it leads logically to an alienated society given that we cannot understand the human person except as one who is constitutively social. The aspect of the social alienation that is most obvious is the influence of technology on sexual mores. I am not merely thinking of contraception or the now easy access to pornography. The influence is deeper and more corrosive. The technological mode of thinking, linked to the utilitarian sourcing of morality that I referred to, typically sees sex as a thing to be done, another performance that will ensure our identity. 'Having sex' strikes me as a most curious combination of ideas, as if it were the equivalent of having a job or a meal. It is interesting that Masters and Johnson, not known defenders of the Catholic moral tradition, share the same reservation: 'Sex, like work, becomes a matter of performance. There is always a goal in view, ejaculation for the man, and orgasm for the woman. If these goals are achieved, the job has been satisfactorily performed … sex for them is not a way of being, a way of expressing identity or feeling or a way of nourishing a commitment. It is always a single incident, an occasion, an accomplishment … goal-oriented sex is self-defeating. Sex interest is soon lost as a result of the performance demand.'[9]

The grammar of sex must be capable of addressing these issues. A reduction of that grammar to canonical norms has clearly failed in Ireland. What has filled the ensuing vacuum needs to be examined. It is not my agenda to suggest a reduction of sexual language to religious language: those days of the primitive religions, where the two great mysteries of life were intertwined to the extent that the sex life of the gods was a key myth, are of interest but hardly of moral relevance now. My concern is to suggest that the religious language and sexual language could be re-united. The competing voices in Irish society may seem unpropitious territory for this to happen.

Perhaps we are being too hasty in dismissing the new voices? The sexual and sacral worlds can be close, not in the sense of primitive religions, but in the light of our search for interpersonal comprehension. The public linkage between sexual and religious questions is easily demonstrable in the excesses of sexist language: if God is portrayed in a straitjacket patriarchal uniform, it is logical that our presentation of revelation and church teaching will be similarly flawed.

And what are they talking about?

The recovery of a public voice for the church in sexual debates thus indicates a surprising possibility. The talk will be less about sex than about religion as a persistent phenomenon in society. How the church deals with sexual morality among its own members will be a matter for the church community in the light of its own doctrine. The surprise is how the foundations for this doctrine, the sacred scriptures, have little to say about sexual morality but much to say about how society could benefit morally from a covenanted view of life where particular social values (such as love, mercy, forgiveness, solidarity with the stranger) could shape the way we relate to each other, including sexually.

An example may be useful before I offer my conclusion. Living together before marriage is largely accepted in Ireland, a clear rejection of the previous canonical prohibition to do so. There is some debate about this in theological journals,[10] but little public conversation in the church community. Yet, surely,

AN IRISH READER IN MORAL THEOLOGY

it is an issue that affects not just church doctrine but how Irish society is being shaped. We could be going through a cultural period when the definition of marriage, both theologically and socially, needs to be reformulated. This, surely, is an example where the public voice of the church should be heard, not to impose a particular moral view, but to contribute towards the construction of a new social consensus on key issues that affect family structures. Facing such issues I am in agreement with Octavio Paz: 'Every time a society finds itself in crisis it instinctively turns its eyes towards its origins and looks there for a sign.'[11] The remote origins of the canonical approach to sexual morality, whose collapse provoked the silence of the church, could be a useful debating point with the voices that have dominated since that collapse. The silence of the church on sexual questions is worrying, not because it is a sexual silence, but because it is symptomatic of the church's inability to explain the significance of a religious approach to life.

Notes:

1. A fuller account, on which my remarks are largely based, can be found in Harold J. Berman, *Law and Revolution. The Formation of the Western Legal Tradition*, Harvard University Press, Cambridge (Mass), 1983.
2. This argument is more fully examined in Heather Windows, 'Religion as a Moral Source: Can religion function as a shared source of moral authority in a liberal democracy?', *Heythrop Theological Journal* XLV (2004), 197-208.
3. Especially his classic book *Sources of the Self*, Harvard University Press, Cambridge (Mass), 1989.
4. Patrick Hannon, *Church, State, Morality and Law*, Gill and Macmillan, Dublin, 1992.
5. Compare the views of John Rawls in *The Law of Peoples*, Harvard University Press, Cambridge (Mass), 1999 with his earlier views as expressed in *A Theory of Justice*, Harvard University Press, Cambridge (Mass), 1971.
6. The process is documented in Tom Inglis, *Moral Monopoly. The Catholic Church in Modern Irish Society*, Gill and Macmillan, Dublin, 1987 (1st edition).
7. A minor character in D. H. Lawrence, *Lady Chatterley's Lover*, London, 1928.
8. The question is wider than sexual morality: the root question is a religious one. Confer Patrick Riordan, 'Permission to speak: Religious arguments in public reason', *Heythrop Theological Journal* XLV (2004), 178-196.
9. William Masters and Virginia Johnston, *Sex isn't that simple*, Strauss and Giroux, New York, 1974, 90.
10. An example is the exchange of views between Lisa S. Cahill and Michael G. Lawler on the theological interpretation of cohabitation in *Theological Studies* 64 (2003), 78-105 (Cahill's views) and *Theological Studies* 65 (2004), 623-629 (Lawler's views).
11. Octavio Paz, 'Reflections: Mexico and the United States', *The New Yorker*, 17 September 1979, 153.

2 Love and Justice: in God and Church, in Sexuality and Society

Enda McDonagh

(Julian Filochowski and Peter Stanford (eds), *Opening Up: Speaking Out in the Church*, London: Darton, Longman and Todd, 2005, pp 30-40)

Neil Astley's second major anthology of modern poetry, *Being Alive* (2004), sequel to *Staying Alive* (2002), opens with a poem by Elma Mitchell simply entitled 'This Poem' and it reads:

This poem is dangerous; it should not be left
Within the reach of children, or even of adults
Who might swallow it whole, with possibly
Undesirable side-effects. If you come across
An unattended, unidentified poem
In a public place, do not attempt to tackle it
Yourself. Send it (preferably, in a sealed container)
To the nearest centre of learning, where it will be rendered
Harmless, by experts. Even the simplest poem
May destroy your immunity to human emotions.
All poems must carry a Government warning. Words
Can seriously affect your heart.

The friend who gave me this volume as a present suggested that 'theology' might well be substituted for 'poem' as 'dangerous' to children or to adults if 'swallowed whole'. The simplest theology 'May destroy your immunity to human emotions' and 'seriously affect your heart'. Of course it too may be 'rendered harmless by experts' at 'the nearest centre of learning'.

If all this seems an over-elaborate introduction to a theological essay on 'Love and Justice' in honour of a friend, at least it helps underline the dangers any theologian faces as would-be poet or would-be expert in reflecting on the divine and human mysteries of Christian faith. The poem, the poet and the friend offer not only timely warning but loving support in facing these dangers. Too much theology lacks the human warmth of friendship, human friendship modelled on that of Jesus and his human friends, and on the love of God and neighbour, the primary characteristic of Christian life and thought. And the blessed justice seekers of Jesus' Sermon on the Mount (a truly dangerous poem) might learn something of the searching demands of justice from the poet's search for the *mot juste*, the word that 'can seriously affect your heart'. All this applies more sharply to a moral theologian, particularly in his efforts to relate love and justice across the spectrum of God, church, sexuality and society.

Liberating Moral Theology

The manuals of moral theology which dominated Catholic moral teaching from about 1600 to 1960 had very limited, legal perspectives on justice and sexuality and completely ignored love/friendship. With their scholastic background they might have been more mindful of their ultimate ancestor Aristotle and his discussion of friendship in the *Ethics*, and of their primary Christian teacher Aquinas and his much broader virtue approach to morality and in particular his insight that charity/love was the form of all the virtues. Intended as handbooks for training confessors in the wake of the reforms of the Council of Trent, they concentrated on sins as violations of a legally formulated code of morality and gave sexual morality a very negative bias, while restricting justice issues almost entirely to issues of exchange between individuals. From 1960 and particularly after Vatican II, a much broader and richer view of moral theology as a theology of Christian and human life began to address these limitations with at least some success. However, the task of such a moral theology is far from complete and, given the historical and eschatological character of Christian and human life, it never will be.

In many ways moral theology has made its most significant recent progress in areas of justice. This may be most effectively illustrated by comparing church attitudes to human rights in the late nineteenth century, when it firmly rejected them, to the current enthusiasm for them at the highest level. Indeed the Catholic Church and the late Pope John Paul II count among human rights' strongest defenders on a global scale. This does not mean that church authorities or moral theologians agree among themselves or still less with the wider world about particular public claims as human rights. The bitter divisions over abortion are proof enough of this and there are many other examples, some of which will surface later. More problematic and controversial still is the 'western' tendency to translate all moral issues into 'rights language', offering a new version perhaps of the legal codes of the old manuals and with many of their reductionist consequences. While human rights are an integral part of justice discourse and so have a role in developing a morality of love/friendship, justice and sexuality, they should not exclude other approaches to a fuller moral understanding of these and other issues.

Justice and Love

While justice and sex may have been restricted and distorted in the manuals of moral theology, love or charity, like its companion friendship, was completely ignored except for a strange and brief treatment of 'the sins against', such as scandal or co-operation in the sins of another. This undoubtedly related to the manuals' role as guides for confessors and confession of sins, but was more deeply based on the split between moral theology and the rest of theology, particularly the study of scripture. Vatican II's recall of moral theology to its scriptural base, which had already been initiated by various scholars, restored charity/love to the primacy that was its by New Testament right and which it had enjoyed in the seminal writings of theologians such as Augustine and Aquinas. Gerard Gilleman's *The Primacy of Charity in Moral Theology*, published in the late fifties, provided a crucial anticipation of the Council's ambition. At the same time inside and outside the Council, debates and documents such as John XXIII's *Pacem in terris*, Paul VI's *Populorum progressio* and the Council's *Gaudium et spes* expanded and deepened the understanding of justice in its personal and social senses. Although it did not become a primary concern of Catholic moral theologians then or later, the relation between justice and love is critical to any authentic theology of Christian living or moral theology.

Love and Justice in God

In many spheres of discourse, religious and secular, academic and popular, love and justice have been sharply opposed. At the extremes of theological discourse the God of the Old Testament, Yahweh, was contrasted with the God of the New, Abba, as a God of Justice opposed to a God of Love. More careful biblical scholarship and more sophisticated theological analysis revealed the critical love dimension of Yahweh, God of Israel, and the critical justice dimension of Abba, God of Jesus Christ and of Israel.

Distinguishing but not separating or opposing justice (*sedeqah/mispat*, Hebrew Bible) and love (*hesed/ahab*, HB; *agape*, NT) is the true message of the Hebrew and Christian scriptures. Jesus' exchange on the greatest commandment of the Law (*mispat*), clearly referring to the inherited Law, asks 'How do you read'. His interlocutor's reply, 'Thou shalt love [*agape*] the Lord your God with your whole heart and your whole soul and your neighbour as yourself', offers, as Jesus confirms, a true life-summary for the justice seekers who are listed in the charter of discipleship, the Beatitudes of the Sermon on the Mount.

The unity of love and justice in the Godhead and in the divine creative and re-creative activity recorded in the Old and New Testaments reflects the mysterious unity and simplicity of Godself. How this unity and simplicity are combined with three distinct persons has taxed the intellectual endeavours of the greatest theological minds in the tradition from Augustine and Aquinas to the Barths and Rahners of the twentieth century. Yet the divine diversity in unity and simplicity can illuminate the meaning of both love and justice between Creator and Creation and within creation itself, as well as the interrelation of love and justice internal to the divine and human spheres. Indeed it is in and through the interactions of God with human beings, history and society in the life, death and resurrection of Jesus Christ, that the tri-unity in God becomes known. These interactions in turn, from the overshadowing of Mary by the Holy Spirit at pregnancy through the distinctive roles of Father, Son and Holy Spirit at Jesus' baptism to the integral drama of Jesus' death into the hands of

AN IRISH READER IN MORAL THEOLOGY

the Father, his resurrection and sending of the Spirit at Pentecost bear the indelible marks of divine Love and Justice in face of human sinfulness and lovableness. The God, who so loved the world as to send his only Son to give his life as redemption for many, was in him reconciling the world with Godself. And God completed that work of justification, restoring just relations in love-reconciliation (Paul's words) by sending God's Spirit of reconciliation to call and enable Christ's disciples to be ambassadors of reconciliation in turn.

The Trinity as Unity of Love and Justice

The Mystery of the Triune God surpasses all human understanding. Yet as it creates and nourishes all human existence, personal and social, it challenges that understanding to trace God's image and likeness in human person and community. The *vestigia Dei Creantis et Trinitatis* in cosmos and humanity have fascinated theologians and contemplatives for millennia. In recent times theologians such as Jürgen Moltmann have concentrated on the Trinitarian shape of human community. A sharper, if less ambitious, analogy might seek to relate love and justice as analysed in human experience to the life of the Trinity as indicated in scripture and described by some mystics.

The differentiation of Father and Son, of the First and Second Persons of the Triune God, is by name and by the analogy of creation reflected in the relationship of human father and son, the relationship of two human beings. (The gender language may be laid aside for the time being.) At the divine and human levels such differentiation involves recognition and respect. ('This is my beloved Son in whom I am well pleased'; 'Into thy hands Father I commend my Spirit.') Such recognition of identity and otherness is the basis for justice in relationship, what the moral tradition following Aquinas called *debitum ad alterum*, what is due to the other. And it is only on the basis of such difference, recognition and respect that love and true communion or unity are possible. It is that love between divine Father and Son which constitutes the third mysterious person of the Trinity and in its distinctiveness receives the recognition and respect in justice/equality of the first two persons as it completes their unity in love. Human differentiation involving recognition and respect in justice as basis for (comm)unity in love is ultimately rooted in the tri-personal life of God, however crudely it reflects it.

In the Community of Disciples: The Church

Love and justice in the community of disciples operate at a number of levels. At the level of the Body of Christ, the theological and mystical substance of the community, love and justice come together as distinct, yet unified, as in the Godhead itself. As we have just seen, the love which unites Father and Son and issues in the Holy Spirit respects the otherness of each divine person in the ideal of justice. So with the church as founded in that divine reality through the mediation of Christ, each member is to hold every other in the bonds of love and the differentiation of justice.

That is the gift and call of membership of Christ's Body, of the graced sharing in the Trinitarian divine life in its unity in difference, of the baptismal insertion into the communion of saints. History, however, makes clear that the communion of saints is also a communion of sinners. Love and justice are engaged in a struggle with each other and with a range of other incomplete virtues in the individual and ecclesial life of Christians. It is in this incomplete historical era that the church seeks, in hope rather than certainty, for the fuller expression of the love and justice for which it was founded, both within its own life and structures and in the wider society. Only in the eschatological fulfilment of the reign of God will love and justice coincide and prevail. Such fulfilment is the final stage of the human, indeed cosmic, embodiment of divine justice and love.

In the aftermath of the death of Pope John Paul II and the impact of his funeral it is clear that he contributed powerfully to love and justice in the world. His striking message on developing a 'civilisation of love' and his range of encyclicals on justice in the world, as well as his travels, particularly to the poorer regions around the globe, gave eloquent testimony of this. Internally to the church many Catholics were less enthusiastic about his exercise of justice in different areas, from theology to the role of women to the treatment of gay and lesbian people. In most of this John Paul was carrying on the tradition of his immediate predecessors so it would be unfair to single out his papacy as the only or even the primary culprit. The internal structures, attitudes and activities of the institutions of church have failed for centuries to match, in varying degrees, the love and justice which ought always to characterise the church as people of God and body of Christ.

These failures have been failures in theology, in the understanding of faith–hope–love as much as in the practice of kingdom values such as justice. How the first apostolic community, the company of Jesus' friends and followers, assumed over the centuries the present, centralised juridical structures is too long and complex a story to recount here. Much of this may have been justified in particular contexts as the Christian community sought survival or faced unusual challenges of growth or decline. And the efforts at evangelical reform from time to time did not always meet with widespread acceptance. Here it is necessary to concentrate on love and justice and their understanding and practice within the church.

The Trinitarian insight of the distinction and equality of persons remains primary. Only the recognition and respect for others as equals in their otherness enables them at once to be given their due in justice and to be bonded in love and communion. The radical equality of Christians in communion rests on their baptism into Christ, which then becomes through the gift of the Spirit their call and capacity to love one another as Christ has loved them. Only equality in difference permits true community and the love and justice which it embodies. The call to particular ministry in that community to guard and guide it must be fashioned after the particular model of the serving Christ and not the model of the lording gentiles. In this context baptism maintains its primacy over ordination and the people of God over its clerical and episcopal ministers, as Vatican II tried to express. The neglect of these insights has resulted in unloving and unjust treatment, even exclusion of various individuals and groups within the church. And it has prevented many from making the contribution to faith-understanding and practice. Theology and other faith initiatives have suffered over the centuries from the absence of lay experience, skills and energy, perhaps particularly those of women, because of male clerical dominance and distrust. This has frequently been manifest in poor Christian understanding of the 'secular' worlds of civil society and sexual community/relationships.

Love and Justice in Sexual Relationships
In the liberation of moral theology referred to earlier, the theology of marriage was moved out of constraints of a contract in canon law to the more humane and Christian category of a community of love open to life. This allowed for a much more personal view of marriage and of sexual relationships as primarily loving rather than as primarily reproductive. This development has presented its own difficulties but it has been a powerful liberation in Catholic moral discourse just the same. No longer are sexuality and sexual relationships to be treated as either exclusively directed to reproduction or otherwise demeaning, even dirty, but as vehicles in the right circumstances of the highest Christian value, that of love. Of course the right circumstances are very important and sometimes highly disputable. In resolving the potential disputes, the justice dimension of love will be a key element.

Pope John Paul II's understanding and promotion of 'a civilisation of love', including sexual love, had all the hard qualities of justice, which always involves a certain equality. That equality in sexual relations operates first of all in consent, in the equal capacity to consent so that paedophilia is excluded, for example. But the equality required also excludes the kind of power play and exploitation in which one party intimidates or blackmails the other. The violence of rape is not only opposed to justice but to love also. Equal or just consent is not simply a matter of the freedom of both parties but also of their maturity and commitment to each other. In biological, social as well as phenomenological terms, the intimacy of bodily union betokens a mutual and continuing acceptance which one-night stands or deliberately short-term relationships do not express. Exclusivity and fidelity are part of just sexual loving.

Sexual differentiation and openness to procreation are traditional and crucial parts of sexual relationships. It has, however, been accepted in many traditions, including the Christian, that an infertile or childless relationship can be a moral and real marriage. The recognition of the woman's infertile period as a way of regulating procreation for Catholics from the time of Pope Pius XII has, despite the encyclical *Humanae vitae* of Paul VI, persuaded many theologians and married couples that other means of birth regulation are acceptable and in a further step that sexual loving may not be irrevocably confined to just heterosexual relationships. However, such other relationships between people of the same sex would have to satisfy the same just requirements as those between people of different sexes. Equality in capacity to consent, in commitment and so in fidelity and exclusivity would be clear demands of homosexual as of heterosexual loving. In sexual relations, heterosexual or homosexual, as already emphasised for members of Christ's body, each partner is to hold the other in the bonds of love and the differentiation of justice.

A Christian blessing of such love and justice, without involving the sacramental character of Christian marriage, could be appropriate to faithful disciples, if not generally accepted as yet. More urgent may be legal protection of gay citizens and partnerships from various kinds of discrimination, although also belonging to the following and final section on love and justice in civil society and culture.

In the long journey of humanity and Christianity to a fuller understanding and living of love and justice in sexual relations as in other areas of life, the concept and reality of friendship with God and one another will bear much revisiting. In such prayerful and reflective revisiting the love and justice inherent in God and manifest in Jesus will enrich our understanding and correct some of our inevitable mistakes.

Love and Justice in Civil Society and Culture
John Paul II's call for 'a civilisation of love' might be regarded as sentimental tosh, if he had not shown the world in deed, word and symbol his commitment to freedom, justice and peace, crucial characteristics of love. A brief digression on the Pope's achievements in the world might confirm the power of his words. His contribution to the liberation of Poland and other countries under the tyranny of the USSR witness his regard for political freedom, as does his later promotion of human rights. In the later part of his pontificate, his encyclicals *Laborem exercens, Sollicitudo rei socialis* and *Centesimus annus,* celebrating the centenary of the first social encyclical, included criticism of free market capitalism as well as Marxism. Together with his visits to the poorer countries and his pleas for debt cancellation for the poorest and for fair trading regulations, the Pope proved one of the major advocates of the global anti-war campaign. In his final years his anti-war stance became more pronounced, as evident in his persistent opposition to the war in Iraq.

However, love and justice in society and culture belong to a much older and broader tradition, Christian and secular, than that represented by the era of John Paul II. And we must not forget his overlooking some of the achievements of the enlightenment and democracy, particularly in the western world. The relations between religion, morality and law are indeed more complex in the present mixed democracies than the Pope seemed to realise. And the witness of the church to the truth, as it sees it, may not be simply imposed by the church on the democratic state, where other visions of the truth have a claim on voters and legislators. The interplay of love and justice, of the preaching and promotion of the reign of God and its values, tasks for the church, do not readily translate into political choices and civil legislation. Recent documents and regulations on the responsibilities of Catholic legislators, in the United States of America for example, failed to recognise the dangers, to the church itself as well as to the state, of attempting to restrict unduly the freedom of voters and legislators, and to turn complex political programmes into one or two issue agendas, with heavy emphasis on gender and sexual matters. The exclusion of some Catholic politicians from the Eucharist on the basis of their distinguishing between their private moral conviction on abortion and their acceptance of the law of the land at this point, did not really exemplify either love or justice. Such ecclesial behaviour was further undermined by particular church authorities ignoring the positions of other candidates on the legitimacy of capital punishment or of the war in Iraq, equally condemned by the highest authority in the church.

In response to the deprived and exploited, to the poor and the sick, many church leaders and agencies gave both powerful witness and effective help in a striking combination of love and justice. That too has a long Christian history. In recent decades, as the poor of the world became more visible and audible through mission and media, the mutual inhabitation of love and justice exercised a significantly transformative effect on ecclesial and indeed political aid programmes. It is in this area that the Christian insight, that love without justice is ineffectual and justice without love inhuman, is so important.

Among the many spheres in which such insight might be pursued, a neglected one is that of artistic achievement, the realm of what is sometimes grandly described as 'high culture'. Without the space, the technical (pictorial) equipment or the competence to pursue this at any great length or depth, one might reflect on love and justice in the form and matter of a single poem. As hinted in the introduction, ethics, moral theology and theology in general have been diminished by their distance from artistic creativity and aesthetic analysis. This applies in particular to ethical dimensions of love and justice in all human relationships and communities.

The poem selected here is by an Irish and Cork poet, Seán Dunne, who died prematurely in the 1990s before he was forty. In its free yet disciplined form, it reveals even in the abbreviated version quoted here what Yeats described poetry as: 'truth seen with passion', in word, image and rhythm. Its combination of practical love and sense of injustice needs no prosaic commentary.

Refugees at Cobh
We were sick of seeing the liners leave
With our own day in, day out, so when
When the boats edged with refugees to Cobh
It was worth the fare to travel
From Cork to glimpse on railed decks.

They hadn't a word of English but we gave
What we could: sheets and rationed tea,
Sweets, blankets, bread, bottles of stout.
The night they sang for hours

And then moonlight fell on silence.

So strange to see emigrants to Ireland

It was our Ellis Island: hunched
Lines of foreigners with bundles

In time we turned them away. Most stood
As still as cattle when the ship drew out
And the pilot boats trailed after it.

Still we turn them away, we Irish who depended for so long on not being turned away. The love which gave what it could in Cobh is still active in Ireland as elsewhere but it lacks the sustenance and substance of justice in dealing with the new refugees, asylum seekers and immigrants. Poets and artists often see further and deeper than politicians and church leaders, would-be guardians respectively of justice and love in the world. Love and justice with their associates, human rights, freedom and peace, belong together in a truly human society, its politics and economics, but have to be worked out in detail in their structures and practices.

Such talk, like 'This Poem', is dangerous. And the danger reaches back to the biblical poem of Genesis 1-3 and the first creative act of God. The risks taken in that divine initiative involved deeper risks still as finally God sent his own Son. His execution did not stay the divine hand and the sending of the Spirit inaugurated the New Creation, the reign of God preached by Jesus. That reign or kingdom is still in the making, in its dangerous making. A theology which would serve it cannot avoid the danger and the risk and yet it must attempt in its ham-fisted way to reflect and promote the love and justice intrinsic to the Triune God. Above all the words of that God, the poem that is that God can and should seriously affect your heart.

3 Sexuality and the Good of Human Relationships

Suzanne Mulligan

(*Human Trafficking, Prostitution, and Sexuality,* Dublin: APT, 2010, pp 53-60 [extract])

It has been argued elsewhere that a new way of thinking about sexuality and sexual relationship is needed,[1] and that at the heart of that 'new way' ought to be the recognition of the equal dignity of women. The idea of justice provides us with a starting point from which to critique the various sexual, social and economic abuses that support the sex industry, but we need to understand our relationships beyond the minimum requirements of justice. The way in which we think and talk about sexuality ought to affirm the dignity of the person as well as promote human well-being and human flourishing. In other words, our sexual ethic ought to be life-giving and life-enhancing.[2] Thus, at the heart of that ethic must be an understanding of the good of human relationships. So what sort of framework might we construct in our efforts to promote a life-giving and life-enhancing sexuality? What are the values or principles that promote such an ethic? We will discuss a number of key principles that it is believed ought to govern a more just and meaningful sexual ethic.[3] So what norms ought to govern a life-affirming and life-sustaining sexual ethic?

Do No Harm

The norm 'do no harm' ought to govern all relationships but it is particularly relevant for our sexual lives. In that context, the commitment to do no harm to the other is a commitment not to sexually exploit or harm other people and not to treat them as simply a means to an end. It is a commitment to, at the very least, treat individuals as ends in themselves, ends that are worthy of respect. Otherwise we see people simply as commodities to be utilised and discarded as we deem fit. The harm we can cause to others takes many forms, of course. It can be physical, psychological, or spiritual harm. We possibly identify the physical harm that is perpetrated in the sex industry most immediately: sexual violation can often be accompanied by physical aggressiveness. In some cases women and girls have to endure beatings from their pimps and clients, starvation and malnutrition, and forced drug abuse.

The principle 'do no harm', it could be argued, is especially important in sexual relationships because in those relationships we make ourselves vulnerable in a special way. There is always a degree of vulnerability in any relationship – there is an element of trust involved and we know that that trust can be violated. But the damage caused by betraying trust in the sexual sphere can be more difficult to overcome. 'Eros, the desire for another, the passion that accompanies the wish for sexual expression, makes one vulnerable … capable of being wounded.'[4] In instances where sexual harm does in fact occur, there is need for a special type of healing. As Seamus Heaney reminds us, 'Human beings suffer, they get hurt and they get hard.' Overcoming sexual hurt may take a considerable amount of time, a lifetime perhaps. And when that hurt takes place in the context of violent and forced sex, specialised services and facilities are likely to be needed in order to help individuals recover and heal.

Thus, 'do no harm' is perhaps the most basic starting point in any attempt at constructing a framework for a just sexual ethic. But that norm is not enough on its own. For it points only to the minimum that is expected of us in our relationships. Positive, healthy, affirming sexual relationships are built on much more than the requirement 'do no harm'. When we think of the ways in which we flourish, and the ways in which our sexuality contributes to that flourishing, we think of the maximum that might be achieved in our sexual lives. And so we must consider several other criteria before we can be satisfied that ours is a positive sexual ethic.

Free Consent
Just as the 'do no harm' principle is a very basic requirement in any sexual ethic, the idea of free consent is a fundamental condition. As with any relationship or agreement entered into, both parties must freely agree to the terms of the relationship. There are many ways in which one's freedom can be diminished or taken away completely. Various psychological factors might be at play, fear and intimidation can influence our decisions, and poverty very often forces individuals into high-risk situations. Instances of rape, sexual exploitation, forced participation in pornography all obviously violate the norm of free consent. Within the Christian tradition, free consent was emphasised at the point of entering marriage – the marriage contract/covenant had to be entered into freely and knowingly otherwise it could be deemed null and void. Unfortunately, less attention was given to an individual's freedom after that point, particularly a woman's freedom. Although the 'right' of both spouses to each other's bodies was acknowledged, that was usually interpreted as a husband's right to demand his conjugal rights from his wife. Human trafficking and the sex industry are just two examples of how sexual freedom is denied to a person. Free consent is so important that its absence seriously calls into question the appropriateness of the sexual activity or sexual relationship in question.

Respect and Responsibility
Having considered briefly these two very fundamental norms we are now directed towards the principles of respect and responsibility. Respect suggests that we identify others as ends in themselves rather than mere commodities. Our sexual conduct ought to promote and protect human dignity. And respect, as we shall see below, is intimately connected with equality.

46   AN IRISH READER IN MORAL THEOLOGY

Furthermore, responsibility is closely associated with respect. Responsibility must be exercised in our sexual relationships, and it implies both freedom and knowledge. Couples are called to make free and equal decisions regarding their relationship. We have a great responsibility to care for each other, and in that regard we must be honest when determining to what extent my relationship is good for the other. Am I/are we in a healthy relationship? Am I being true to my commitment to my partner? Being responsible demands a high degree of honesty and openness. Responsibility may not always be an easy thing to exercise in our sexual lives, and it requires a certain level of moral maturity. But it is an integral part of being able to live out our sexuality in a positive manner.

Mutuality and Equality

Thankfully we no longer think of our sexual activity in terms of one active partner and one receptive partner. Women were (and still are in some places) thought of as the sexually submissive partner; in many parts of the world women are expected to be submissive and unquestioning, and have little say over the type or frequency of sex they engage in. It is frightening how many men continue to understand their sexual relationships in that way. Gender roles and stereotypes can often impact negatively on our sexual lives. Speaking about the problem of rape in South Africa, Rachel Jewkes and Naeema Abrahams argue that the problem 'has to be understood within the context of the very substantial gender power inequalities which pervade society. Rape, like domestic violence, is both a manifestation of male dominance over women and an assertion of that position ... Both sexual and physical violence against women form part of a repertoire of strategies of control.'[5] But of course gender stereotypes affect how women see *themselves* too. A study carried out in Cape Town in 2005 suggests that many women thought of themselves as the submissive and obedient partner in a relationship. Of those surveyed (from both sexes) 27 per cent believed that rape results from something that a woman says, 18 per cent said that some cases of rape involve a women who wants to have sex, and 29 per cent agreed that rape is often a woman's fault.[6] The authors of the survey say that 'With regard to gender roles, we expected and found that men often viewed women as passive, subservient, and as fulfilling traditional gender roles. This finding is consistent with previous research that suggests South African women are expected to fulfill a stereotypical female gender role by being docile, especially in sexual relationships. However, we found that women endorsed these attitudes at rates that generally did not differ from men.'[7] But a truly just sexual relationship must include mutuality, both mutuality of desires and of what Farley calls embodied union.[8] It is no longer acceptable to think of women as the passive partner – mutual participation and decision-making confirm the equality and dignity of both partners, and in turn contributes to greater responsibility in the sexual relationship.

Of course, attaining mutuality in one's sexual relationships implies that there is equality in those relationships. We know that women's inequality (be it social, economic, or sexual) often places them at danger of trafficking and HIV infection. Therefore, equality should not simply be understood in terms of affirming the equal dignity of women – important and all as that is. There is need to promote *equality of power* also.[9]

Commitment

It is true to say that a just sexual ethic ought to incorporate the idea of commitment. Fidelity to one's marriage covenant has been a central part of Christian sexual teaching, but the living out of the principle of commitment (particularly in western culture) has changed somewhat over the past 30 years or so. We have witnessed increasing numbers of couples now choosing to live together before marriage. But it would be unfair to interpret that as a rejection of commitment – it is, rather, a different manifestation of the norm. However we understand and apply it today, our sexual relationships ought to incorporate some degree of commitment to the other. Otherwise, we risk seeing others only as a means and not as an end in their own right. Although casual sex is more common today, many have questioned to what extent these casual sexual encounters satisfy the person, in the long-term at least. Casual sex is just that – it is casual, no strings attached. But we generally long for something more meaningful and fulfilling in our lives. 'Sexual desire without interpersonal love leads to disappointment and a growing disillusionment. The other side of this conclusion is that sexuality is an expression of something beyond itself. Its power is a power for union, and its desire is a desire for intimacy.'[10]

Life-Giving and Life-Enhancing

For a great deal of the Christian tradition sexual intercourse was justified or excused because it had the potential to bring forth new life. For much of that tradition procreation was seen as the 'primary end' of marriage, while other dimensions such as the fostering of love between the spouses were thought of as 'secondary ends'. We have thankfully moved away from those rather forced categories, and although the raising of children is given special place in the Christian understanding of marriage it is not at the expense of what we might call the other 'fruits of marriage' – the fostering and nurturing of love between two people, the support and friendship that is enjoyed within marriage, and the fulfilment/completeness that can be experienced by that couple. We might call these the life-giving and life-enhancing aspects of sexuality. These terms are used here in a broad sense, and not confined to the procreative dimension of sexual activity. The life-enhancing aspect of intimate relationships is one that perhaps needs to be promoted more in contemporary Catholic teaching. Our relationships can bear fruit in many ways: they can enhance our lives, make us happier and more fulfilled people. Our sexual relationships should be no different in that respect.

Social Justice
And finally the norm of social justice has a profound relevance for sexual ethics. At first glance that norm may seem a little out of place until we consider the ways in which our sexual choices impact on society. It is true to say that there is a social dimension to our sexual activity and so social justice ought to be a guiding principle in any sexual ethic. For too long we thought about our sexual relationships as having little to do with so-called 'public morality'. But we are becoming increasingly aware of the fact that there are indeed social repercussions to sex. As Farley remarks, 'A social justice norm in the context of sexual ethics relates not specifically to the justice between sexual partners. It points to the kind of justice that everyone in a community or a society is obligated to affirm for its members as sexual beings.'[11]

Furthermore, social justice demands that couples take responsibility for the consequences of their love and sexual activity. That certainly includes bearing responsibility for any children that may result from intercourse, but it must also include other social dimensions of our sexual lives. Increasing levels of sexual and domestic abuse in society demand a re-evaluation of our sexual mores. Tough questions have to be faced with honesty and determination. Are we the kind of society that tolerates the subordination of women? Are we the kind of society that tolerates the abuse of women and children (physical or sexual)? Do we tolerate the establishment of lap-dancing clubs and accept the frequenting of such clubs as a normal part of societal life? Are we serious about eradicating gender inequality? Do we accept gender stereotypes that place both men and women at risk of sexual harm? Are we serious about tackling the problem of human trafficking in our own country? Any attempt to answer these questions will require public debate involving a variety of groups. But that debate must be critical, honest and open if we are to confront the sexual challenges of our society.

The Youth of Today
But are these ideals appealing to young people? I would suggest that the justice dimension of sexual ethics provides an excellent starting point for discourse with younger people. Other ideals – for example, that our sexual relationships ought to be life-enhancing – are ideals that most people can relate to, irrespective of age. Despite the often voiced lament that 'the youth of today' have no sexual morality, it seems to me that many young people have very high sexual ideals indeed. And these sexual ideals tend to relate to the kind of justice issues that we have been discussing. Rigid, cold sexual moralism will not do. That will simply turn people away from the important conversations about sexuality

that must take place. The many sexual injustices that are being perpetrated in our communities and homes need serious, critical analysis. But we need to find a language, indeed a way of conversing, that is inclusive rather than exclusive. What is needed instead is a creative, imaginative, and meaningful sexual ethic that offers hope and inspiration.

Notes:
1. See my article 'Sexuality and Justice' in APT, *Human Trafficking, Prostitution, and Sexuality*, (Dublin, 2010).
2. 'Life-giving' and 'life-enhancing' are not understood here in a strictly procreative way. Rather, they point to the ways in which healthy sexual relationships enhance our lives more generally.
3. For a more comprehensive account of these norms see Margaret Farley, *Just Love: A Framework for Christian Sexual Ethics*, (New York: Continuum, 2006). Kevin Kelly proposes a number of similar principles. See *New Directions in Sexual Ethics*, (London: Geoffrey Chapman, 1998), 139.
4. Margaret Farley, *Just Love: A Framework for Christian Sexual Ethics*, (New York: Continuum, 2006), 217. Farley is citing Karen Lebacqz here.
5. Rachel Jewkes and Naeema Abrahams, 'The epidemiology of rape and sexual coercion in South Africa: and overview', *Social Science and Medicine*, 55 (2002), 1238.
6. See Seth Kalichman, Leickness Simbayi, Michelle Kaufman, Demetria Cherry, Cain Chauncey, Sean Jooste, and Vuyisile Mathiti, 'Gender Attitudes, Sexual Violence, and HIV/AIDS Risks Among Men and Women in Cape Town, South Africa', *The Journal of Sex Research*, 42 (2005), 303.
7. Kalichman, Simbayi, Kaufman, Cherry, Chauncey, Jooste, and Mathiti, 'Gender Attitudes, Sexual Violence, and HIV/AIDS Risks Among Men and Women in Cape Town, South Africa', 304.
8. See Farley, *Just Love*, 221-22 on this point.
9. Farley, *Just Love*, 223.
10. Farley, *Just love*, 225.
11. Farley, *Just Love*, 228.

Part Two
Marriage

4   Marriage in Scripture

Wilfrid Harrington

(Enda McDonagh (ed), *The Meaning of Christian Marriage: Papers of Maynooth Union Summer School, 1962*, Dublin: Gill & Son in assoc with The Furrow Trust, 1963, pp 14-35)

My theme may be described, in a general fashion, as the biblical theology of marriage, but by way of introduction it is well to treat briefly of marriage as an institution within the society of Israel. This outline, following the historical pattern, will be concerned with monogamous marriage, whether as an ideal or in practice.[1]

Marriage in Israel

Already in the tenth century, at latest, the Yahwistic creation narrative proposes monogamous marriage as the will of the Creator.[2] In that same context the patriarchs of the line of Seth are presented as monogamous and polygamy made its appearance in the rejected line of Cain.[3] But later, in historical times, things have changed. True, Abraham had only one wife, Sarah, for Hagar was not his wife and he married Keturah only after the death of Sarah;[4] but Jacob married two sisters and Esau had three wives.[5] At the time of the Judges we learn that Gideon had 'many wives'.[6] Finally, bigamy was recognised in law.[7]

Despite these and other undoubted examples of polygamy, it appears that monogamy was the normal practice in Israel, apart from the royal family where a large harem was a matter of prestige. It is remarkable, for instance, that the books of Samuel and Kings, which cover the whole period of the monarchy, record only one case of bigamy among commoners and that very early: the father of Samuel.[8] Similarly, the sapiential books, which give us a picture of the society of their age, do not consider polygamy, and the many passages which regard the ideal wife are most readily understood in the atmosphere of a strictly monogamous family.[9] The book of Tobias, a family story, is concerned with monogamous families only. And it is in the image of a monogamous marriage that the prophets depict Israel as the only spouse of the one God. If Ezechiel does compare the relations of Yahweh with Samaria and Judea to a marriage with two sisters,[10] that is because he has developed the metaphor into an allegory and has adapted it to suit the political situation. Taking it all in all, it appears that at an early stage in Israel's history the monogamous concept of marriage prevailed, and long before New Testament times it had been accepted as the rule.

So much for the form; now to consider the implications of the institution. By marriage the wife became subject to her husband: he is her *ba'al*, her 'master', just as he is the *ba'al* of a house or field,[11] and a married woman is the 'possession' of a *ba'al*.[12] Does this mean that the wife was regarded as strictly the property of her husband, a mere chattel? The terminology would appear to imply as much; and, added to that, the custom of the *mohar* would seem to indicate that she had been purchased by him. The *mohar* is, ordinarily, a sum of money which the fiancé had to pay to the father of the girl.[13] The amount varied according to the demands of the father[14] or the social position of the family.[15] The payment of the *mohar* could be substituted by a term of work, as for the marriages of Jacob,[16] or by a service rendered, as for the marriage of David with Michal.[17]

The obligation to pay a sum of money, or its equivalent, to the family of the fiancée obviously gives Israelite marriage the appearance of a purchase.

But the *mohar* seems to be not so much the price paid for the woman as a compensation given to the family, and, in spite of the apparent resemblance, in law this is a different consideration. The future husband thereby acquires a right over the woman, but the woman herself is not bought or sold.[18]

The difference becomes clear when the marriage with payment of *mohar* is compared with another type of union which was indeed a purchase: a girl could be sold by her father to a man who wanted her as a concubine for himself or for his son[19] – she was a slave and not a wife.

If it is clear that marriage was normally monogamous, there is, on the other hand, the question of divorce. In Israel divorce was permitted; a husband could repudiate his wife. The motive accepted by Deuteronomy is: 'Because he has found some indecency in her.'[20] The expression is very general and in rabbinical times there were the widely divergent views of the rigoristic school of Shammai which would admit only adultery and misconduct as valid motives, and of the broad school of Hillel which would admit even futile reasons – that a meal had been badly prepared or that another woman was more attractive. The formality of divorce was uncomplicated; the husband made a declaration contrary to that which had concluded the marriage: 'She is not my wife and I am not her husband.'[21] Besides, he had to give the woman a bill of repudiation[22] which would allow her to remarry.[23]

Though the law placed few restrictions on a husband's right of divorce, it does not seem that the right was widely exercised. The Wisdom writings praise conjugal fidelity,[24] and Malachi teaches that, because marriage has made one being of the two partners, the husband should guard the fidelity sworn to his wife: 'I hate divorce, says Yahweh the God of Israel.'[25] It is only a step to the unequivocal proclamation of the indissolubility of marriage made by Christ[26] who invoked the same argument used by Malachi: 'What God has joined, man must not separate', and referred back to the same text of Genesis.[27] It is to Genesis that we now likewise turn.

The prototype of marriage

Though it really should not surprise us, it is at least thought-provoking that the essential doctrine of marriage is presented in the opening chapters of the Bible. The subject comes up quite naturally, because the two accounts of creation in Genesis chapters 1 and 2, though differing in many respects, agree in laying notable emphasis on the formation of man. They make the point, each in its distinctive way, that this creature is unlike all others, that he is made in God's image. But they also insist, just as emphatically, that the difference of sex was intended by God in view of marriage, that it is an integral part of the divine plan for mankind.

We shall start with chapter 2 of Genesis because this, the Yahwistic narrative, going back at latest to the tenth century, is the earliest biblical account of the creation of man and woman. It first describes, vividly but briefly, the formation of man and then depicts, at much greater length, the fashioning of woman.

Then Yahweh God formed man of dust from the ground, and breathed into his nostrils the breath of life; and man became a living being.[28]

The 'dust from the ground' is fine potter's clay and the divine Potter shaped it into a human form; then he breathed into that lifeless figure a breath of life and the figure became a man. The animals, too, the narrative relates, were moulded by Yahweh and became living beings, but they were not stirred to life by the divine breath. At a later date, in the Priestly version, the reality that underlies this animation by the breath of Yahweh will be described as the making of man to the image of God. Then follows, in the text, a brief description of the garden of Eden, the first home of man, and the author goes on to the emergence of woman.

Then Yahweh God said: 'It is not good that the man should be alone: I will make him a helper fit for him.'

But such a helper was not found among the animals.

So Yahweh God caused a deep sleep to fall upon the man, and while he slept took one of his ribs and closed up its place with flesh; and the rib which Yahweh God had taken from the man he made into a woman and brought her to the man. Then the man said: 'This at last is bone of my bones and flesh of my flesh; she shall be called woman, because she was taken out of man.' Therefore a man leaves his father and his mother and cleaves to his wife, and they become one flesh.[29]

To a superficial eye the Yahwistic narrative (the passage just quoted is a typical example) seems hopelessly na ve. Nothing could be further from the truth. It uses figurative language, indeed, but it is at the same time a profoundly theological work which faces and answers fundamental problems. This is just what it does here.

Philosophers tell us that man is a social animal; the Bible puts it more simply and with greater feeling: 'It is not good that man should be alone.' But the inspired writer has in mind something more specific than man's gregarious instinct; he is thinking rather of man's deep-felt need for another being like himself, one of the same nature as he, yet not quite himself. He does not find such a being among the animals. Though all these creatures have been fashioned, as he was, from clay he is unable to find one among them that can share his life, that can hold converse with him, for he alone has been livened by the divine breath.

Yahweh is still determined to provide a suitable helpmate. The fact that men and animals are made from a common clay has not sufficed to establish any real bond between them; man's helpmate must be more intimately bound to him: she will be formed from part of him. This alone will ensure the desired conformity between them. So Yahweh plunges the man into a deep sleep – the Hebrew noun *tardemah* means a profound and extraordinary sleep sent by God. While he slept Yahweh, now turned surgeon, removed one of his ribs and proceeded to build up that rib into a woman.

This description, apparently so artless, really presents a viewpoint that is nothing less than revolutionary, especially in view of the early date of the tradition. There was a widespread tendency, particularly notable among Semites – and prevalent in Israel too despite correctives – to regard woman as a chattel and to consider her as a being definitely inferior to man. In those days it was decidedly a man's world, and the mere fact that the author took the trouble to deal specially and specifically with the creation of woman is itself significant. But he goes further than that. By describing her, in purely figurative language of course, as made from man he presents her as a being of the same nature as man, his equal – a truth which man is made to acknowledge openly.[30] She is, therefore, in the fullest sense his helper, one entirely suited to him, particularly by her union with him in marriage, in which both become one flesh.[31]

When Yahweh introduces this new creature to him, as she stands before his delighted gaze, the man bursts into song – the first love-song! Here at last is his heart's desire, a being just like himself, one who can understand him and share his life to the full. He calls her by his own name, merely giving it a feminine form: *ishsha* from *ish*. The following verse is a comment on his words. It is because they were made for each other from the beginning that man and woman will break all other ties and join in marriage. Centuries later a greater one than the inspired writer of Genesis will add his comment and bring out the fuller implication of the earlier text: 'So they are no longer two but one flesh. What therefore God has joined together, let no man put asunder.'[32]

The account of creation given in chapter one of Genesis is some five centuries later than the other and is presented from the distinctive viewpoint and in the distinctive style of the Priestly narrative:

Then God said: Let us make man in our image, after our likeness; and let them have dominion over the fish of the sea, and over the birds of the air, and over the cattle, and over all the earth, and over every creeping thing that creeps upon the earth.

> So God created man in his image,
> In the image of God he created him;
> Male and female he created them.

And God blessed them and God said to them: Be fruitful and multiply and fill the earth and subdue it; and have dominion over the fish of the sea and over the birds of the air and over every living creature that moves upon the earth.[33]

At v. 27 the staid Priestly writer has a surprise in store for us: most uncharacteristically, he too breaks into song! With the account of the creation of man he has reached the climax of his creation narrative, and even he is carried away by the sublimity of this last work; at any rate, these few lines are in verse. Man, in this account a collective noun, is created male and female, both sexes in the image of God, both set on an equal footing. Thus, much more economically, and just as effectively, he has made the same point as the Yahwistic author: woman is man's equal in nature and was created so from the beginning.

Here, too, marriage is in view. It should be noted that the phrase, 'Be fruitful and multiply', is a blessing, not a command.

> The man and woman are blessed not only in that fruitful union by which they are to fill the earth and which will give birth to the human family, but also in that union, fruitful too in its own way, by which they will *together* make the earth minister to their needs. Thus in every respect the blessing is not an individual but a common one. It is a man and woman, *by their joint activity*, who will be masters of the 'house' bestowed by God on their race. In this way too the blessing appears once more as a correlative of creation. What has been made in the image of God to occupy the earth and bring it into subjection is a man and a woman, not isolated one from another but together. The context of the thought here, for creation as for blessing, is that of marriage and the home.[34]

The divine blessing imparted to the first pair that they may be fruitful and multiply makes it evident, once again, that the sexes are complementary and that marriage is of divine institution. It is no wonder, in view of the doctrine of these chapters, that Israel's attitude to sex and marriage was fundamentally healthy. Failures there were, because man is frail – and fallen – but moral standards remained and were exacting. It is rather the whole atmosphere that is refreshing because the thoughtful Israelite never forgot that at the end of this work God saw that it was 'very good'.

AN IRISH READER IN MORAL THEOLOGY

In the marriage of Adam and Eve we have the human prototype of marriage. The neighbours of Israel, who had created their gods in their own image, had evolved their myths to explain the origin of human relationships; and so they had their gods, and especially their goddesses of love and fertility. Israel, with its faith in one only God, could not find in him the model of human marriage; but they did believe that the Creator-God had himself instituted marriage when he created man. It is remarkable, in fact, that already in the tenth century, when polygamy was still common, it is monogamous marriage that was proposed as the model directly established by God. This is, evidently, the consequence of revelation. It remained for the full revelation of the New Testament to show how the human prototype had, after all, a divine archetype.[35]

The prophetic image

A foreshadowing of the ultimate New Testament doctrine appears already in a prophetical theme which seems to have originated with Hosea and was, indeed, developed by him. He it was who for the first time represented the covenant relation of God with his people as a marriage. It would, of course, have seemed natural enough, that the covenant, a treaty between God and Israel, might have been likened to the marriage contract between man and wife. The singular fact is that it is not the contract aspect that was exploited but, instead, the love aspect and especially the love of a husband for his wife.

It is well to have a clear idea of the prophetical imagery and what it involves. The prophet did not hold up the marriage of Yahweh and Israel as the archetype of marriage nor did he develop his theme with the intention of casting new light on marriage. What he did was to visualise and to represent the covenant relation of Yahweh and his people as a marriage union because he had learned that the image brought out in a striking way the personal character of the relationship. It is imagery, compelling imagery, but, at least as the prophet understood it, it is no more than that. Inevitably, though, it must have added new depth to the concept of human marriage.

It was out of his own personal experience that the marriage image came to Hosea and that he realised its aptness in describing the relations between Yahweh and Israel. The prophet has given us a sketch of his painful family life in chapters 1 and 3 of his book and the general picture conjured up by these descriptions is remarkably vivid, even though it is not easy to reconcile the two accounts.[36] According to the first narrative he was bidden to take 'a wife of harlotry' and have 'children of harlotry' – who stand for faithless Israel and the children of Israel given over to idolatry. In the second account Hosea is bidden: 'Go again, love a woman who is beloved of a paramour and is an adulteress.'[37] He might have delivered the woman over to death, in accordance with the law, but, instead, he bought her back and kept her shut off from her former lovers until she turned to him; it is thus that Yahweh will treat Israel. All in all, it is best to see here two parallel recensions of the one marriage, the marriage of the prophet with Gomer.

In the second chapter the symbolism of this marriage is worked out and it is seen that the psychology of human love can wonderfully illustrate the mystery of God's relation with men, the reality and depth of his love.[38] The divine husband has been betrayed by his wife who has given herself to adultery and prostitution. Yet he seeks only to win her again to him, and if he chastises her, it is with that sole end in view. As a last resort he determines to bring her back once more to the conditions of the Exodus, the honeymoon period of their love.

> Therefore, behold, I will allure her,
> and bring her into the wilderness,
> and speak tenderly to her …
> And there she shall answer as in the days of her youth,
> as at the time when she came out of the land of Egypt.
> And in that day, says Yahweh, you will call me 'my husband'.[39]

In fact, he ultimately goes beyond this and promises to bring her into the harmony of a new garden of Eden[40] where their love will be the crowning and fulfilment of the mutual love of the first human couple:

> And I will betroth you to me forever; I will betroth you to me in righteousness and in justice, in steadfast love, and in mercy. I will betroth you to me in faithfulness; and you shall know Yahweh.[41]

The theme of God's love for his people is already fully developed in Hosea, and later prophets do little more than ring the changes on it. The first presentation of the image in Jeremiah[42] opens with the poignant recall of a promising beginning:

> I remember the devotion of your youth,
> your love as a bride,
> how you followed me in the wilderness,
> in a land not sown.[43]

The rest is a sad catalogue of perversities interspersed with the impassioned pleadings of a loving God. But his tenderest words are reserved for the moment of despair when the people, deaf to his warnings and blind to his guidance, have rushed unheedingly into disaster and now find themselves exiles from a ravaged homeland. Now is the moment when he utters words of loving consolation:

> I have loved you with an everlasting love;
> therefore I have continued my faithfulness to you.
> Again I will build you and you shall be built,
> O virgin Israel![44]

AN IRISH READER IN MORAL THEOLOGY

He has remained faithful, unchanging, in spite of everything. And in the end he gently chides his people for their tardiness in realising that he loves them still and that he is welcoming them back to him:

Return, O virgin Israel,
return to these your cities,
How long will you waver,
O faithless daughter?
For Yahweh has created a new thing on the earth,
the woman seeks her husband.[45]

The return of Israel to her husband will be a 'new thing', a miracle of grace. That return is to be seen in the perspective of the new covenant foretold in the same chapter of Jeremiah.[46] It is within this new covenant that marriage, too, will come into its own and, now a source of grace, will sanctify men and women of the new Israel and lead them to their God.[47]

Personal values

We cannot measure to what extent the prophetical marriage image influenced the approach to marriage in Israel; perhaps the effect of it was less than we should have imagined. The prophetical theme had been current for centuries when the Priestly creation-narrative was edited, yet in its teaching on marriage it has no reference to mutual love, the aspect exploited by the prophets. Instead, the divine blessing imparted on the first human couple has in view the fruitfulness of their union; we are back in the main flow of biblical tradition. For few matters in the Old Testament are more evident than the desire, among all classes of Israelites, for a posterity, and sterility was always regarded as a reproach, even in New Testament times as, for instance, in the case of Elizabeth.[48] This constant preoccupation explains the prominence of genealogies throughout scripture. It might seem to lead to a rather one-sided conception of husband and wife relations in which mutual love and tenderness would find little part.

If this ever had been so it is certain that the balance was eventually restored. But, indeed, we catch stray glimpses of tenderness even at an early date: Jacob and Rachel,[49] Michal and David,[50] and Elkanah the father of Samuel who comforted his barren wife: 'Hannah, why do you weep? And why do you not eat? And why is your heart sad? Am I not more to you than ten sons?'[51]

For, if the fruitfulness of marriage is the aspect of it that is principally stressed, the personal relations of love and affection which bind husband and wife are an integral part of it. The reaction of the first man when confronted with his partner was one of spontaneous joy – it was literally love at first sight. It is not only to bear children that man and woman will break all other ties and, as the Genesis text implies, live together for a lifetime. The love that is normally an ingredient of married life, and which ought to be present at all times, is part of the work that God has made and has called very good.

Now this aspect of marriage, which tended to be minimised, is the special theme of a book that has too often been misinterpreted. Here we may point to a constant danger in our approach to scripture – the urge to impose on it our ways of thought. Perhaps unconsciously, we are tempted to set up our own criteria of what befits the word of God. It is hard to be quite rid of prejudice and we are still told, we may even think along the same lines ourselves, that the theme of human love – the love of man and woman – is unworthy of scripture; or, at least, that it is unlikely, even unseemly, that a biblical writing should be wholly dedicated to it. This outlook, it seems to me, quite misses the true significance of scripture. The Bible is the word of God, certainly, but, we may ask, to whom is that word addressed? God has not written this work just for his own pleasure, but has destined it for the human race which he had created. It is he who has made them, men and women; it is he who has implanted in them, deep in their natures, the mutual attraction that is destined to culminate in marriage. Like all the gifts of God this too may be abused; but, in the divine intention, the love that so strongly draws young people, that moves them to dedicate, each of them, his life to the other, and that later enables them, together, to support inevitable cares and troubles, is a good thing – it is part of the work which God himself has called very good. It is eminently worthy of special treatment in the Bible, that word of God *to men*.

The Canticle of Canticles takes its place in the Bible as the celebration of human love.[52] Whether it is a poem, or a collection of love songs, it is certainly lyrical; as such, it does not 'teach', it has no 'doctrine' to propound – it is the expression of a state of mind. It is concerned with the mutual love of two young people who, quite obviously, contemplate marriage; if, indeed, they are not already married. The language of it, throughout, is the language of love. If it seems daring, perhaps at times even shocking, in its realism, that is because it is the product of another culture; and even today, in these matters, convention varies considerably from people to people. And if we are a little shocked by the boldness of the language, is it not a singular expedient to refer the same language and sentiments directly to God? The biblical writers have not been guilty of such a *gaffe*. When they have in fact spoken of Yahweh and his people in marital terms, they have displayed an obvious restraint and have set very definite limits to the imagery.

We cannot here go into the problem of the interpretation of the Canticle except, perhaps, to assert that there is no real problem, apart from some matters of detail. The Canticle was never meant to be an allegory of the love of Yahweh and Israel,[53] because this is a prophetical theme, and the Canticle belongs to the Wisdom literature; besides, the earliest evidence of such interpretation is in the second century AD. We are not quite sure when the book originated, but it was certainly edited by Wisdom writers after the Exile, most likely in the fourth century BC, and one of the editorial additions makes it abundantly clear that these editors understood it in its original sense:

AN IRISH READER IN MORAL THEOLOGY

Love is as strong as death,
jealousy is cruel as the grave.
Its flashes are flashes of fire,
a most vehement flame.
Many waters cannot quench love
neither can floods drown it.
If a man offered for love
all the wealth of his house,
it would be utterly scorned.

Language such as that is reminiscent of Proverbs or Ecclesiasticus and orientates the Canticle in the traditional direction of Wisdom literature,[56] and it was only when the sapiential tradition had died out that the writing was reinterpreted in terms of the mutual love of Yahweh and Israel; but this was after the book has taken its place in the canon. The growing tendency among Catholic scholars to read the Canticle according to its obvious sense is due, in large measure, to a better understanding of the true background of the writing. The theme of human love is no more out of place in the Wisdom literature than is the theme of human wisdom in Proverbs.

A feature of the Canticle that often occasions surprise is the absence of the divine name. What should surprise is the absence of any allusion to a god or goddess of love. Israel did indeed feel the strong attraction of the Ashtaroth cult and did fall under the spell of the fertility cults, but Israel itself never divinised love, it never even personified love. The explanation of this fact, a fact which is truly remarkable when viewed in historical perspective, is to be found in the second chapter of Genesis. There too we find the reason why the Canticle is intrinsically religious: it is a practical act of thanksgiving to the Creator. For there is no essential difference between the admiration that attracted the first man to the first woman[57] and the mutual wonder of the young couple of the Canticle. There is little difference between the reflection of the editor of Genesis who commented: 'Therefore a man leaves his father and his mother, and cleaves to his wife, and they become one flesh',[58] and the reflection of the editor of the Canticle: 'For love is as strong as death … If a man offered for love all the wealth of his house, it would be utterly scorned.'[59] Both texts bear witness to the same attitude in face of the same human experience. Marital love belongs to the order of things created by God from the beginning; it is one of the wonders of God which should evoke admiration and gratitude.[60]

It is arguable that the Canticle was originally a collection of espousal songs or songs of the wedding feast; at very least it has been inspired and coloured by such songs. This explains the atmosphere of it, the spring-time joy, the companions, and the young couple immersed in each other. The whole is, admittedly, on a natural plane, but is there anything very strange in that? Love is normally awakened by physical beauty, by very human qualities, and God has made man's body as well as his soul. It would be unrealistic, to say the least of it, to wish to ignore all this; logically it should lead one to a denial of the role of sex in marriage – which would be inconvenient! Besides, and this is more to the point, such an attitude is entirely unbiblical.

The charming story of Tobias and Sarah forms a fitting pendant to the Canticle. Here, too, the love theme is very much to the fore; indeed Tobias loved his future wife even before he had set eyes on her. The angel had told him of Sarah and indicated that they had been destined for each other from eternity and 'when Tobias heard these things, he fell in love with her and yearned deeply for her'.[61] He was really in love, in the best sense, and the writer takes pains to put the matter beyond doubt. He tells us that on the wedding night Tobias was formally led, by the parents of Sarah, to the bridal chamber where his bride awaited him. And straightaway,

> when the door was shut and the two were alone, Tobias got up from the bed and said: Sister, get up, and let us pray that the Lord may have mercy upon us. And Tobias began to pray:
> Blessed art thou, O God of our fathers,
> and blessed be thy holy and glorious name forever.
> Let the heavens and all of thy creatures bless thee.
> Thou madest Adam and gavest him Eve his wife as a helper and support.
> From them the race of mankind has sprung.
> Thou didst say: It is not good that the man should be alone;
> Let us make a helper for him like himself.
> And now, O Lord, I am not taking this sister of mine because of lust but with sincerity. Grant that I may find mercy and may grow old together with her. And she said with him: Amen. Then they both went to sleep for the night.[62]

It is not surprising that our marriage liturgy is coloured by the book of Tobias, for Tobias and Sarah do indeed stand as an example to Christian husbands and wives. And it is against the background of such a faith that the Canticle of Canticles must be viewed and judged because it, too, in its final form, is a product of the same post-Exilic Israelite society.[63]

The archetype of Christian marriage
Uncompromisingly monogamous, personal values respected, the importance of mutual love recognised – the Jewish marriage institution, on the threshold of the New Testament, reflected its prototype with laudable fidelity; yet the coming of Christ was to transform it utterly. Henceforth the model of marriage is no longer that first, perfect, marriage of man and woman but something infinitely more sublime: the supernatural union of Christ and his church. It is to St Paul that we owe this doctrine, this vision. Undoubtedly there is already a

AN IRISH READER IN MORAL THEOLOGY

preparation for the Pauline concept in the prophetical theme of the marriage of Yahweh and Israel but it is nonetheless significant that the apostle, in elaborating his teaching, does not refer at all to the Old Testament image. His doctrine, though quite in harmony with the older idea, is essentially something new. Perhaps we have said all that can be said when we assert that Paul has shown us the meaning of *Christian* marriage.

In his epistle to the Colossians St Paul has, among a series of exhortations on family and social relations, a few words of practical advice for husbands and wives:

> Wives, be subject to your husbands, as is fitting in the Lord.
> Husbands, love your wives, and do not be harsh with them.[64]

Then in Ephesians, that finest synthesis of his thought which was written shortly after Colossians and along the same lines, but in a very much more tranquil frame of mind, he takes up the same theme. Now, however, from practical advice it is transformed into theology, the theology of Christian marriage.

The text of Ephesians 5:21-33 is the beginning of a long passage devoted to family relations, quite like Colossians. The opening verse is a general exhortation: 'Be subject to one another out of reverence for Christ',[65] and the following verse is exactly the same as in the earlier epistle: 'Wives, be subject to your husbands, as to the Lord.'[66] But at this point in Ephesians a motive for the subjection is added:

> For the husband is the head of the wife as Christ is the head of the church, his body, and is himself its saviour. As the church is subject to Christ, so let wives also be subject in everything to their husbands.[67]

Here, first of all, we encounter the fundamental idea of the Body of Christ. We learn later in the passage that the members of this Body are Christians whom Christ incorporates by the purifying and sanctifying action of baptism;[69] for Christians, all together, form the Body which Christ has saved and the church which he has baptised.[70] As the Body of Christ, the church is intimately attached to him; yet he, as head, remains distinct and the church is subject to him in loving obedience, thus becoming the model of that obedience which every wife owes to her husband. For Paul has realised that the marriage image most forcibly expresses the intimate union of Christ and his church. So he has set up a parallel between the husband-wife relationship and the relationship of Christ and his church; husband and wife, in their marriage, verify this union and make it manifest by their personal relations. The Christ-church relationship is thus the archetype of Christian marriage and it is precisely in view of this archetype, he explains, that the wife must be subject to her husband in all things. Of course, the human couple cannot really measure up to the divine model, and already the essential difference is manifest: Christ is the *saviour* of the Church.[71]

The Apostle then turns to husbands, urging them to love their wives, and again adds the reason for that love:

> Husbands, love your wives as Christ loved the church and gave himself up for her, that he might sanctify her, having cleansed her by the washing of water with the word, that the church might be presented before him in splendour, without spot or wrinkle or any such thing, that she might be holy and without blemish.[72]

The statement that wives must be subject to their husbands may, at first – and especially to modern ears – strike a disturbing note, but the example of the church's subjection to Christ, and the reference to him as Saviour, should already set the recommendation in proper perspective. More forcibly, the parallel exhortation to husbands makes it very clear that there is nothing humiliating about such subjection, for husbands are exhorted to love their wives, not in any fashion, but after the manner of Christ. And Christ loved his church and gave himself up for her that he might sanctify her; he purified her by washing her clean of every stain in the nuptial bath of baptism and presented her to himself as his spotless bride. Against this background the subjection of the wife – a loving subjection needless to say – is offset, and even quite outweighed by the love of her husband.

St Paul next passes to a new thought, one that sprang to mind when he recalled the text of Genesis 2:24. It suggests to him another reason why husbands ought to love their wives.

> Even so, husbands should love their wives as their own bodies. He who loves his wife loves himself. For no man ever hates his own flesh but nourishes and cherishes it, as Christ does the church, because we are members of his body. For this reason a man shall leave his father and mother and be joined to his wife, and the two shall become one flesh.[73]

It is, obviously, a truism that a man will look after his own body. But, according to the text of Genesis, which establishes the divine institution of marriage, man and wife form one being; therefore in loving his wife a man is only loving himself. This argument, admittedly banal, is lifted to a new level by the further observation that Christ, too, nourishes and cherishes his church, which is his Body, as it is his Bride. Nor is this St Paul's last word for he adds, again with reference to the Genesis text: 'This is a great mystery, and I take it to mean Christ and the church.'[74]

The argument of the apostle in the section vv. 28-32 comes to this:[75] Husbands should love their wives as they love their own bodies. Everyone loves his own flesh; so also Christ loves the church, his Body. This is the meaning of Genesis 2:24 when one sees there a type of Christ and the church. For Paul has in mind, not the marriage relationship in general, but the human prototype of marriage, that of Adam and Eve; and Adam, who cleaves to his wife is, in his view, a type of Christ who loves his church. That is precisely the great mystery

AN IRISH READER IN MORAL THEOLOGY

of which he speaks – great, not because of its mysteriousness but because of its sublimity. Adam and Eve, precisely in their relationship of husband and wife – for that is the sense of Genesis 2:24 – are types of Christ and his church. And in the measure in which each earthly marriage of man and woman reflects the mystery of the marriage of Christ and his church, it shares in that mystery. Here, in one breath, are associated the archetype and prototype of marriage, and the marriages in which these ideals are more or less realised. It is obvious that only Christian marriage, which is truly such, can hope to reproduce with any fidelity the perfect lines of the archetype.

Coming after this, the last verse sounds like an anti-climax; instead, it strikingly brings out the essentially practical nature of Christianity. Christians may have their eyes raised to heaven, but they must strive to give flesh and bone to sublime ideals in a world that is the home of men and not of angels. Thus, the parting admonition of the apostle, immediately after he has conjured up the divine archetype, is not banal, but shows a spirit of realism and an appreciation of actual conditions that signally set off the foregoing teaching.

Husbands, let each of you love his wife as himself, and let the wife see that she respects her husband.[76]

Once again, as at the beginning, love is recommended to the husband and reverence to the wife. For on both of these, on love and on the reverence of obedience, is marriage founded and by means of these it reflects the prototype already sketched in Genesis 2:24, that mysterious image of the marriage of Christ and his church.

It is, however, in heaven that the marriage-feast of Christ is celebrated because only there will his church appear glorious and without blemish 'as a bride adorned for her husband'.[77] Before she can come to that she has to be purified by him, cleansed of every stain; it is still the time of purification, yet she knows that she is his chosen one. But the church is no vague personification, it is a living organism made up of men and women, of beings who are not only human but fallen and whose fallen state is especially evident in the rebellion of their sex instincts. Yet it is before such men and women that scripture has set a standard that was progressively raised to match the development of revelation: monogamous marriage, the marriage-image of Yahweh and Israel, the marriage-type of Christ and his church. It is to the ultimate ideal that Christian husbands and wives must lift their eyes and must seek to reproduce in their lives the lines of that perfect union. It is by sanctifying their married life that they can win for themselves a place at the 'marriage supper of the Lamb'[78] when they, husbands and wives, with all the elect will be, not guests, but all together, the spotless Bride of Christ.

Notes:

1. This summary is based on R. de Vaux, *Les Institutions de l'Ancien Testament*, I, Paris

1958, 45-49, 60-62. E. tr.: Ancient Israel, London 1961, 24-27, 34-36.

2. Gen. 2:21-24.

3. 4:19.

4. 25:1.

5. 29:15-30; 26:34; 28:9.

6. Jdg 8:30.

7. Deut 21:15-17.

8. 1 Sam 1:2.

9. Cf Prov 5:15-19; Eccles 9:9; Eccles.26:1-4; Prov 31:10-31.

10. Ez 23.

11. Ex 21:3, 22; 2 Sam 11:26; Prov 12.

12. Gen 20:3; Deut 22:22.

13. Gen 34:12; Ex 22:16; 1 Sam 18:25.

14. Gen 34:12.

15. 18:23.

16. 29:15-30.

17. 1 Sam 18:25-27.

18. R. de Vaux, op. cit., 27.

19. Ex 21:7-11.

20. 24:1. All biblical citations are from the Revised Standard Version.

21. Hos 2:2.

22. Deut 24:1, 3; Is 50:1; Jer 3:8.

23. Deut 24:2.

24. Prov 5:15-19; Eccles 9:9.

25. Mal 2:16. 'Yahweh' is substituted for 'the Lord' of the RSV throughout.

26. Cf This author's chapter, 'Jesus' Attitude towards Divorce', pp 186ff.

27. 2:24.

28. 2:7.

29. 2:18, 21-24.

30. V.22.

31. V.24.

32. Mt 19:6. 'Flesh' is added after the Greek. Cf RSV margin.

33. 1:26-28.

34. J.-P. Audet, 'Love and Marriage in the Old Testament', *Scripture* 10 (1958), 74.

35. Cf P. Grelot, *Le couple humain dans l'Ecriture*, Paris 1962, 34-36.

36. P. Grelot, op. cit., 53.

37. 3:1.

38. P. Grelot, op. cit., 54.

39. 2:14-16.

40. 2:18.

41. 2:19-20.

42. 2:1-4.

43. 2:2.

44. 31:3-4.

45. 31:21-22. RSV: 'a woman protects a man'. I have followed the *Bible de Jérusalem* rendering: 'la Femme recherche son Mari'.

46. 31:31-34.

47. For the prophetical image see also Is 54:1-19; 62:1-12. Ezechiel has developed the theme in two long allegories: Ez 16 and 23.

48. Lk 1:25.

49. Gen 29:18-20.

50. 1 Sam 18-20

51. 1:8.

52. A.-M. Dubarle, 'L'Amour humain dans le Cantique des Cantiques', R.B. 61 (1954), 67-86; J.-P. Audet, 'Le sens du Cantique des Cantiques', R.B. 62 (1955), 197-221; 'Love and Marriage in the Old Testament', *Scripture* 10 (1958), 79-83. J. Winandy, *Le Cantique des Cantiques*, Ed. De Maredsous 1960.

53. The most notable recent attempts to explain the Canticle as an allegory are those of A. Robert, *Le Cantique des Cantiques* (B.J.), Paris 1958, and A. Feuillet, *Le Cantique des Cantiques*, Paris 1953. See the other authors just quoted for a telling criticism of this approach.

54. J.-P. Audet, 'Le sens du Cantique des Cantiques', 200-203; 'Love and Marriage in the Old Testament', 81.

55. 8:6b-7.

56. For the theme of the Canticle see Prov 5:15-19; 31:10-31; Ecclus 25:13-26:18.

57. Gen 2:23.

58. 2:24.

59. Cant 8:6-7.

60. J.-P. Audet, 'Le sens du Cantique des Cantiques', 219-220.

61. Tob 6:17.

62. 8:4-6.

63. It is an important fact that a biblical writing should have extolled the tender love of a young couple; it not only restores the balance of marriage, but has its place in the development of revelation. It plays its part in the transformation of the essentially communitary covenant of Sinai into the new Covenant foretold by Jeremiah (31:31-34) in which the standing and dignity of each individual are explicitly affirmed. For, when love had been acknowledged as a constitutive element in marriage, side by side with the establishment of a family, the individual had ceased to be absorbed in the group. It was a decisive step towards the recognition of the dignity of every man and woman. Cf A.-M. Dubarle, op. cit., 84.

64. 3:18-19.

65. 5:21.

66. 5:22; cf Col 3:18.

67. 5:23-24.

68. P. Benoit, 'Corps, tête et plérôme dans les ép tres de la captivité', RB 63(1956), 28-29.

69. vv. 30, 26.

70. vv. 23, 26.

71. H. Schlier, *Der Brief an die Epheser*, Düsseldorf 1957, 253.

72. 5:25-27.

73. 5:28-31.

74. 5:32.

75. H. Schlier, op. cit., 262.

76. 5:33.

77. Apoc 21:2; cf 19:7-8.

78. 19:9.

5 The Sacrament of Marriage: History
The Age of the Fathers

Michael G. Lawler

(Michael G. Lawler, *Marriage and Sacrament: A Theology of Christian Marriage*, Minnesota: Liturgical Press, 1993, pp 41-53 [extract])

The doctrine about sexuality and marriage in both Old and New Testaments was a Jewish doctrine, developed in the originating Jewish culture of the Christian movement. The developing Christian Church soon moved out of that Jewish culture into a Greco-Roman one in which Greek and Latin Fathers of the church shaped the biblical doctrine about marriage and sexuality within their own cultural contexts and established the Catholic approach to sexuality and sexual morality as marital morality. To understand fully the Christian tradition about sexuality and marriage that came down to our day, we must seek to understand not only their teaching but also the socio-historical situation in which it developed. In the Bible, there was no systematic and full treatment of either sexuality or marriage as a social and Christian institution. The Fathers' teaching was almost exclusively a defence of marriage and marital sexuality against certain errors which threatened both its Christian value and its future. The majority of these errors had Gnostic sources, and it will be to our benefit to consider, however briefly, the Gnosticism from which they came.

Gnosticism, a Hellenistic religious philosophy characterised by the doctrine that salvation is achieved through a special knowledge (*gnosis*), antedated Christianity and exercised a great influence on many Christian communities in the Mediterranean basin. Christian Gnostics looked upon themselves as the only faithful interpreters of the Jesus movement. They disagreed with orthodox Christian teaching on two major points: first, they preached predestination, denying free will to humans in either salvation or damnation; secondly, they preached a dualistic and pessimistic view of the world, a view in which good and evil are equally real. Both of these views affected their attitude toward sexuality and marriage and, therefore, the Fathers' expositions on them in response. Because matter, and therefore sexuality and marriage with their very material bodily intercourse and bodily outcome, was essentially evil, Gnostics believed, it could not have been created by a good God. That meant they had to revise the classic Jewish approach to creation, a task that was accomplished by Marcion. He taught there had to be two gods, one who created evil, the other who created good. The god who created evil is Yahweh, the god of the Old Testament; the god who created good is the Father of Jesus, who alone reveals him. The Old Testament, therefore, should be rejected along with all its doctrines and its laws. Among these doctrines is the one that men, women, sexuality, and marriage were created good by God; among such laws are those that legislate the relationships of men and women and their mutual sexual activity. Such attitudes generated, on the one hand, a negative, ascetic approach to sexuality and marriage and, on the other hand, a licentious, permissive approach, known as antinomianism. The second and third century Fathers had to defend marriage against attacks on both these fronts.

By the middle of the second century of the Christian era, Alexandria had become established as the intellectual capital of the Hellenistic world. We would expect to find powerful Gnostics there, and our expectation is verified via the writings of Clement, the Bishop of Alexandria. He tells us of the two kinds of Gnostics we have noted, namely, the ascetics who abstained from marriage and sexual intercourse because they believed them to be evil, and the antinomians who believed they are saved by their special *gnosis* no matter what and are, therefore, above any law regarding sexuality and marriage.[1] He tells us of the ascetic Julius Cassianus whose work *On Continence* he cites. 'Let no one say that because we have these members, that because the female is structured this way and the male that way, the one to give the seed and the other to receive it, that the custom of sexual intercourse is allowed by God. For if this structure were from God, toward whom we tend, he would not have pronounced blessed those who are eunuchs.'[2] We might note in passing the false biology in Cassianus' statement, a biology shared by the majority of thinkers of the time: the man is the one who gives 'seed', the woman is but the 'ground' or the 'field' in which the seed is sown.[3] The woman has no active part in procreation.

Clement declares the opinion of Cassianus 'impious' and responds with a simple argument. There is only one God, and that God is good; sexuality and marriage were created by the one God and, therefore, are good from their origin. 'If marriage according to the law is sinful,' he argues, 'I do not see how anyone can say he knows God, and say that sin was commanded by God. But if the law is holy, marriage is holy. The apostle, therefore, refers this mystery to Christ and the church.'[4] Irenaeus of Lyons employs this same argument in his extensive refutation of the Gnostics. He mentions Marcion and Saturnius, 'who are called the continent,' and accuses them of frustrating the ancient plan of God and of finding fault with him 'who made both male and female for the begetting of men.'[5] Marriage is primarily for procreation,[6] and for two other things secondarily. It is for a wife to bring help to her husband in the funding of his household, particularly in his sickness and old age,[7] and it is a union for a pious wife to seek 'to persuade her husband, if she can, to be a companion to her in those things that lead to salvation.'[8]

The early Greek Christian understanding of the nature of sexuality resembles that of the Stoic philosophers, represented in a statement from the Christian African, Lactantius. 'Just as God gave us eyes, not that we might look upon and desire pleasure, but that we might see those actions that pertain to the necessity of life, so also we have received the genital part of the body for no other purpose than the begetting of offspring, as the very name itself teaches. This divine law is to be obeyed with the greatest of devotion.'[9] This was a commonly accepted teaching, which carried with it several conclusions. First, by its very nature sexual intercourse is for the procreation of children; second, any such intercourse for purposes other than procreation is a violation of nature and, therefore, immoral; and third, any sexual intercourse when conception is impossible is similarly immoral. From this established position Christian Fathers would argue that Gnostics, or anyone else, engaging in sexual intercourse for any purpose other than procreation, love-making, for instance, or pleasure, were in violation of nature. It is an argument Latin church Fathers continued to make into the twenty-first century.

Already in the second century, in his apology for Christians, Justin had replied to Roman accusations about the sexual immorality of Christians by insisting that 'either we marry only to have children or, if we do not marry, we are continent always.'[10] But Clement goes much further, arguing that the only purpose for sexual intercourse is to beget a child and that any other purpose must be excluded. 'A man who marries for the procreation of children,' he argues, 'must exercise continence, lest he desire his wife whom he ought to love, and so that he may beget children with chaste and moderated will. For we are not children of desire but of will.'[11] Origen, his fellow Alexandrian, is just as clear, arguing that the man who has sexual intercourse only with his wife, 'and with her only at certain legitimate times and only for the sake of children,' is truly circumcised.[12] He underscores what he means by legitimate times, insisting that once a wife has conceived, intercourse is no longer good. Those who indulge in sexual intercourse with their own wives after they are already pregnant are worse than beasts, 'for even beasts know that, once they have conceived, they do not indulge their mates with their largesse.'[13] So ruthlessly consistent was Origen in his belief that sexual activity was only for procreation in marriage that, having decided not to marry, he castrated himself.[14]

Tertullian also argued that abstinence from sexual activity is the surest way to the grace of God. Commenting on Paul's 'It is better to marry than to burn with passion' (1 Cor 7:9), Tertullian adds that 'It is better neither to marry nor to burn with passion.'[15] Virgins, he goes on, have 'full holiness' because 'continence is more glorious' than marriage.[16] Tertullian seems to have been the first to make this evaluation of virginity as holier than marriage but, in the fourth century, that theological judgement was concretised in a new ascetic practice, the rejection of marriage and the embracing of virginity as a way to live a Christ-like, holy life. It was not that the Fathers of the time were opposed to marriage; they were not. It was rather the way they expressed their preference for virginity in their Greek rhetorical styles that made marriage look less than good.[17] Tertullian can argue that Paul permits marriage as a concession and that something good needs no concession.[18] Athanasius can say both 'blessed is the man who in his youth is joined in marriage for the procreation of children' and 'there are two ways in life, one inferior and vulgar, namely marriage, the other angelic and supreme above all, namely, virginity.'[19] John Chrysostom can say 'I believe that virginity is a long way better than marriage, not because marriage is evil, for to those who would use it correctly [for procreation] it is the doorway to continence.'[20] The same Chrysostom can also argue that 'Whoever denigrates marriage also diminishes the glory of virginity ... What appears good only in comparison with evil would not be particularly good. It is something better than what is admitted to be good that is the most excellent good.'[21] Basil also affirms the goodness of sexual intercourse in marriage which is 'entered into according to the sacred scriptures and legitimately,' that is, for procreation, but he also excoriates marital intercourse sought for pleasure.[22]

Marriage is good, especially when sought for procreation; it has to be good since God created it. But virginity is better. This ambiguity about the goodness of sexuality and marriage, introduced early into the Catholic tradition, perdures to the present time. Writing an apostolic exhortation *On the Family*, John Paul II, citing Chrysostom as above, removes any ambiguity about the church's position. '[T]he church throughout her history has always defended the superiority of this charism [virginity] to that of marriage, by reason of the wholly singular link which it has with the kingdom of God.'[23] When it comes to a comparison of sexual intercourse and marriage with virginity, one could say that John Paul has removed the Greek ambiguity.

Two Latin Fathers advanced the church's thinking on sexuality and marriage and left both with a theology that became a given in Christian thinking ever afterwards. The lesser one is Tertullian who wrote about marriage in both the orthodox Catholic and heretical Montanist periods of his life. In his first book, *To a Wife*, he exhibits the same ambivalence to sexuality and marriage that we have seen already in Origen. He grants that in the beginning marriage was necessary to populate the earth but argues that, when the end of the world is near (note his socio-historical assumption), there is no need for such activity. Paul may have allowed marriage as an antidote to desire, but Tertullian is in no doubt: 'How much better it is neither to marry nor to burn [with concupiscence].' He will not even allow that marriage can be called good, for 'what is *allowed* is not good ... nor is anything good just because it is not evil.'[24] One would be excused for thinking that Tertullian has no time for marriage and the sexual intercourse it legitimates. This same man, however, who is so pessimistic about marriage in his first book, in a second book under the same title writes the most beautiful lines on Christian marriage that one could ever hope to find. 'What a bond is that of two faithful who are of one hope, one discipline, one service; both are siblings, both are servants ... They are truly two in one flesh, and where there is one flesh there is also one spirit. They pray together, they sleep together, they fast together, teaching one another, exhorting one another, sustaining one another.'[25] It would seem that between the first and second books Tertullian had found a wonderful wife. When he became a Montanist, however, he regressed to his earlier judgement that Paul had simply allowed marriage and the sexual activity it encompasses which is, though not a sin, none the less a blot on a perfect Christian life.[26]

Augustine

When we reach Augustine, the great Bishop of Hippo, we reach the systematic insight into sexual morality and marriage that was to mould and control the doctrine of the Latin church down to our own day, so much so that Augustine is frequently called the doctor of Christian marriage. His influence is always present in Catholic talk about marriage. Pius XI, for instance, in the opening of his influential encyclical on Christian marriage, *Casti Connubii*, turned to him as to the wellspring of the truths about Christian marriage to which the Catholic Church adheres. The Second Vatican Council also turned to him, developing its teaching about marriage within the schema of the threefold good of marriage as he described it.[27] Since Augustine's influence on the doctrine of marriage is beyond doubt, we must look closely at it. His teaching too must be viewed in its socio-historical context, a context which is again largely a defence against attack. As the Alexandrians defended sexuality and marriage against the attacks of the Gnostics, so did Augustine defend them against the attacks of the Manichees, who at root were Gnostics, and Pelagians. We need to say a word, therefore, about these two.

The Manichees took their name from their founder, Mani, born in Babylonia about the year 216 CE. Mani claimed to have received from an angel, at ages twelve and twenty-four, the definitive revelation about the nature of the world and of history. Here we need to consider only those aspects of Manichaeism which impinge on its teaching on sexuality and marriage. First, it is a dualistic system, the dual opposites being, as always, good and evil, light and darkness, spirit and matter. Sexuality is listed among the dark and evil realities, along with wine and meat. Secondly, since Mani was looked upon as the ultimate prophet in the line of Jesus, he was said to have completed the latter's teachings and to have organised the ultimate church. That church had two kinds of members, a group of the perfect and a group of auditors, those we would call today catechumens. The perfect always abstained from wine, meat, and sexual activity; the auditors abstained only on Sundays. It is not difficult to imagine the Manichean approach to sexuality and marriage. Both were evil in themselves and, therefore, to be avoided. Against this approach Augustine repeated the argument of Clement and Irenaeus: sexuality and marriage, created by God, must be essentially good.

Pelagianism derived its name from a Briton, Pelagius, who lived in Rome around the year 380, though the Pelagian debate with Augustine was led more by Pelagius' disciple, Julian, Bishop of Eclanum. The debate centred around the extent of Adam's original fall from grace. Augustine taught that the original sin seriously impaired human nature, so that after the Fall men and women could not do without grace what they had been able to do without it before the Fall. Pelagius, on the contrary, taught that the Fall left human nature unimpaired, so that men and women could do after the Fall what they had been capable of doing prior to the Fall without any help from grace. Against the Pelagians Augustine taught that the results of the Fall make it very difficult to avoid sin in sexual intercourse, even in marriage. Pelagians, therefore, accused him of being a Manichee and of teaching that marriage and sexual intercourse are necessarily sinful.[28] They will be followed in this by many a modern writer who adverts only to Augustine's anti-Pelagian writings. For such a complex writer, caught in the crossfire of two opposing heresies, that is too simple a procedure to be correct.

Augustine's basic statement about sexuality and marriage is ubiquitous, firm, and clear. Contrary to those Manichee heretics who hold that sexuality is evil and who condemn and prohibit marriage and sexual intercourse, he states that sexuality and marriage were created good by a good God and cannot lose that intrinsic goodness.[29] He specifies the good of marriage as threefold and insists that even after the Fall the marriages of Christians still contain this threefold good: fidelity, offspring, sacrament. 'It is expected that in fidelity neither partner will indulge in sexual activity outside of marriage; that offspring will be lovingly accepted, kindly nurtured, and religiously educated; that in sacrament the marriage will not be dissolved and that neither partner will be dismissed to marry another, not even for the sake of offspring.'[30] In this triple good Augustine intends the mutual fidelity of the spouses, the procreation of children, and indissolubility. Procreation has priority because 'from this derives the propagation of the human race in which a living community is a great good.'[31] And yet, to some extent, the good of sacrament is valued above the good of procreation, for he insists, as we have just seen, that a marriage cannot be dissolved, 'not even for the sake of offspring.' There may be here the seed of a Christian attitude toward marriage that moves away from the priority of procreation to the priority of communion between the spouses, in the image of the communion between Yahweh and Israel and between Christ and the church. These two priorities have been given quite different weights at different times in Roman Catholic history. In the contemporary Roman Catholic approach they are given equal weights.

Alongside the tradition of the threefold good of marriage, Augustine advances yet another good, that of friendship between the sexes. In *The Good of Marriage*, after asserting that marriage is good he gives an interesting explication of why it is good. 'It does not seem to me to be good only because of the procreation of children, but also because of the natural companionship between the sexes. Otherwise, we could not speak of marriage in the case of old people, especially if they had either lost their children or had begotten none at all.'[32] Later in the same work he returns to that idea. 'God gives us some goods which are to be sought for their own sake, such as wisdom, health, friendship ... others for the sake of friendship, such as marriage or intercourse, for from this comes the propagation of the human race in which friendly association is a great good.'[33] 'In these passages,' Mackin judges, 'Augustine has enriched the source whence Catholic canonists and theologians will later draw one of their 'secondary ends' of marriage ... the *mutuum adiutorium* of the spouses, their mutual help, or support.'[34] We believe Augustine has done more. He has falsified in advance the claim of those modern commentators who say that only in modern times have sexual intercourse and marriage been seen in the context of the relationship of spouses. But the source of what appears problematic in Augustine's teaching about marriage seems always to derive from what he says against the Pelagians. To this, therefore, we now turn.

The basic position can be stated unequivocally, and there can be no doubt about it: sexual intercourse between a husband and a wife is created good by God. It can, as can any good, be used sinfully but, when it is used sinfully, it is not the good itself which is sinful but its disordered use. It is a balanced principle to which Augustine will return at the end of his life in his *Retractiones*. Evil and sin are never substantial; they are only in the will. Nevertheless, he believes there is in men and women a concupiscence that causes sin, a disordered pursuit by any appetite of its proper good, a pursuit which since the Fall is difficult to keep within proper limits. With this belief in mind, it is not difficult to understand all that Augustine says about sexuality and marriage. Against the Pelagian, Julian, he explains carefully: 'Evil does not follow because marriages are good, but because in the good things of marriage there is also a use that is evil. Sexual intercourse was not created because of the concupiscence of the flesh, but because of good. That good would have remained without that evil if no one had sinned.'[35] His judgement appears beyond doubt: there is one thing that is good, namely, sexual intercourse in marriage, and another thing that is evil, namely, concupiscence, that can mutate the good into evil. His position is much more nuanced than many notice or admit: sexual intercourse is good in itself, but there are uses which can render it evil.

The condition under which intercourse is good is the classic Stoic condition we have already seen in the Alexandrians, namely, when it is for the begetting of a child. After the Fall, any other use, even between the spouses in marriage, is at least venially sinful. 'Conjugal sexual intercourse for the sake of offspring is not sinful. But sexual intercourse, even with one's spouse, to satisfy concupiscence [disordered desire] is a venial sin.'[36] It is not sexual intercourse *per se*

AN IRISH READER IN MORAL THEOLOGY

between spouses that is sinful, but intercourse vitiated by concupiscence. Sexual intercourse for the stoically natural reason, the procreation of children, is good; intercourse that results from concupiscence is sinful. In effect, since the Fall of humankind and the rise of concupiscence, the sexual appetite is always threatened by disorder and, therefore, by sinfulness. It is not, however, the sexual appetite that is sinful; it is good. The Fathers of the Old Testament, Augustine argues, took a 'natural delight' in sexual intercourse and it was not sinful because it 'was in no way given rein up to the point of unreasoning and wicked desire.'[37] It is clear that it is disordered and unreasonable sexual intercourse fired by concupiscence that is sinful, not sexual intercourse *per se*. 'Whatever, therefore, spouses do together that is immodest, shameful, filthy, is the vice of men, not the fault of marriage.'[38] And what is 'immodest, shameful, and filthy' is the concupiscent desire for sexual pleasure.

Pope Gregory the Great shared Augustine's judgement that, because of the presence of concupiscence, even genital pleasure between spouses in the act of procreation is sinful. He went further and banned from access to the church those who had just had pleasurable intercourse. 'The custom of the Romans from antiquity,' he explained, 'has always been, after sexual intercourse with one's spouse, both to cleanse oneself by washing and to abstain reverently from entering the church for a time. In saying this we do not intend to say that sexual intercourse is sinful. But because every lawful sexual intercourse between spouses cannot take place without bodily pleasure, they are to refrain from entering the holy place. For such pleasure cannot be without sin.'[39] Again, it is clear that it is sexual pleasure that is sinful, and it is not difficult to see how such a doctrine could produce a strong ambivalence towards sexuality and marriage. That ambivalence weighed heavily in subsequent history on the theory and practice of Christian marriage.

In summary of this section on the Fathers of the Church, we can say that, though the relational and procreational meanings of sexual activity found in Genesis remain, they have been seriously prioritised. Though the judgement remains that sexuality and sexual activity are good because they were created good by the good God, their goodness is threatened by the pleasure associated with sexual intercourse and by the concupiscence engendered by sin. This position is much in evidence in Augustine who taught that sexual activity in marriage is good when it is for the purpose of procreation and venially sinful when, 'even with one's spouse, [it is] to satisfy concupiscence.'[40] The Catholic aversion to sexual pleasure reached its high point when Pope Gregory Great banned from access to church anyone who had just had *pleasurable* intercourse. We accept as accurate Brundage's judgement of the effect of that patristic history. 'The Christian horror of sex has for centuries placed enormous strain on individual consciences and self-esteem in the Western world.'[41] This might be the place, however, to introduce a linguistic caveat. Medieval Latin had no words for the modern concepts of 'sex' and 'sexuality.' Payer, therefore, correctly points out that 'In the strictest sense there are no discussions of sex in the Middle Ages.' He goes on to point out that Foucault's claim that 'The relatively late date for the invention of sex and sexuality is, I believe, of paramount significance. The concept of sex and sexuality as an integral dimension of human persons, as an object of concern, discourse, truth, and knowledge, did not emerge until well after the Middle Ages.'[42] This caveat has significance for all that has gone before and all that comes after in this book.

Notes

1. Clement, *Stromatum* 3, 5, PG 8, 1143-47.
2. Ibid. 3, 13, PG 8, 1191.
3. For Greek society, see Paige duBois, *Sowing the Body: Psychoanalysis and Ancient Representations of Women* (Chicago: University of Chicago Press, 1988), 39-85. For Jewish Society, see Sirach 26:19; *Mishna*, Ketuboth, 1, 6. For Muslim society, see Carol Delaney, *The Seed and the Soil: Gender and Cosmology in Turkish Village Society* (University of California Press, 1991).
4. Ibid. 3, 12, PG 8, 1186.
5. *Adv. Haer*. 1, 28, 1, PG 7, 690.
6. Ibid. 2, 23, PG 8, 1086 and 1090. See also *Paed*. 2, 10, PG 8, 498.
7. Ibid. 3, 12, PG 8, 1184 and 2, 23, PG 8, 1090-91.
8. Ibid. 4, 19, PG 8, 1333.
9. Lactantius, *Divinarum Institutionum* 6, 23, PL 6, 718.
10. Justin, *Apologia Prima* 1, 29, PG 6, 374.
11. Clement, *Stromatum* 3, 7, PG 8, 1162. In his *Paed*. II, 10, Clement utilises the argument of the Stoic, Musonius Rufus, to establish procreation as the major purpose of marriage.
12. Origen, *In Gen. Hom*. 3, 6, PG 12, 180.
13. Ibid. 5, 4, PG 12, 192.
14. See Eusebius, *Ecclesiastical History*, II, VI, VIII, trs J. E. L. Oulton (Cambridge, MA: Harvard University Press, 1980), 29.
15. Tertullian, *Ad Uxorem* I, PL 1, 1278.
16. Ibid., 1287.
17. See Jean-Claude Guy and Francois Refoulé, *Chrétiennes des Premiers Temps* (Paris: Cerf, 1965).
18. Tertullian, *Ad Uxorem* I, PL 1, 1278-1279.
19. Athanasius, *Epistola ad Amunem Monachum*, PG 26, 1174.
20. John Chrysostom, *De Virginitate* 9, PG 48, 539.
21. Ibid. 10, 540.
22. Basil, *Liber de Virginitate*, 38, PG 30, 746. See also Gregory of Nyssa, *De Virginitate* 7, PG 46, 354.
23. John Paul II, *FC*, 14.
24. *Ad Uxorem* I, 2-3, PL 1, 1277-79. Emphasis added.
25. *Ad Uxorem* II, 9, PL 1, 1302-1303.
26. Tertullian, *De Pudicitia* 16, PL 2, 2, 1012.
27. *GS*, 48.
28. See Augustine, *De Bono Coniugali*, 6-7. See also Aquinas, *ST*, III (Suppl), 41, 4.

29. Augustine, *De Nupt. et Concup.* 2, 32, 54, PL 44, 468-9. See also *De Bono Coniugali* passim, PL 40, 374-396.

30. *De Gen. ad Litt.* 9, 7, 12, PL 34, 397; also *De Bono Coniugali*, 24, 32, PL 40, 394.

31. *De Bono Coniugali*, 9, 9, PL 40, 380.

32. PL 40, 375.

33. 'The good of marriage, which even the Lord in the gospel confirmed ... seems to me to be not only about the procreation of children but also about the natural companionship/friendship [*societas*] between the sexes. Otherwise we would not be able to speak of marriage among the old' (*De Bono Coniugali*, PL 40, 380). Aquinas also had an incipient insight into the relationship of friendship between men and women and into the fact that sexual intercourse in marriage intensified that friendship. 'From the point of view of the union between the spouses, a wife is to be loved more [than parents], because the wife is joined to the husband in one flesh, according to Mt 19:6 ... To the extent of their marital and sexual unions, a man clings to his wife rather than to his parents.' S. Th. II-II, 26, 11.

34. Mackin, *What Is Marriage?* 141.

35. *Contra Julianum* 3, 23, 53, PL 44, 729-30.

36. *De Bono Coniugali*, 6, 6, PL 40, 377-378; 10, 11, PL 40, 381.

37. Ibid. 16, 18, PL 40, 386.

38. Ibid. 6, 5, PL 40, 377.

39. Gregory the Great, *Epistolarum Liber IX Epist.* 64, PL 77, 1196.

40. Augustine, *De Bono Coniugali*, 6, 6, PL 40, 377-78.

41. James A. Brundage, *Law, Sex, and Christian Society in Medieval Europe* (Chicago: University of Chicago Press, 1987), 9.

42. Pierre J. Payer, *The Bridling of Desire: Views of Sex in the Later Middle Ages* (Toronto: University of Toronto Press, 1993), 14.

6 The Sacrament of Marriage: History The Medieval Period

Michael G. Lawler

(Michael G. Lawler, *Marriage and Sacrament: A Theology of Christian Marriage*, Minnesota: Liturgical Press, 1993, pp 54-61 [extract])

Many of the attitudes and teachings of the Fathers with respect to sexuality and marriage can be found in the manuals known as Penitentials, which flourished in ecclesiastical use from about the sixth to the twelfth century CE. The Penitentials were designed to help confessors in their pastoral dealings with penitents in confession, providing lists of sins and corresponding penances. They were, however, more than just lists of sins and penances. They were also manuals of moral education for the confessor, and what the confessor learned, of course, his penitents also learned. Penitentials took the abstract teachings of the church and concretised them at the level of practice, in this case the practice of the new penance introduced by the Celtic monks in the sixth century. They are sure guides for us as we explore the moral teaching of the church at the time of their publication with respect to sexuality and marriage.

McNeill's opinion is impossible to gainsay. 'It is doubtful whether any part of the source literature of medieval social history comparable in importance to the Penitentials has been so generally neglected by translators. The difficulty of the texts and an unjust contempt on the part of some historians for the materials have probably contributed to this neglect.'[1] Luckily, that neglect has been somewhat rectified since McNeill wrote, and we have plenty of material to choose from. Both the sins and the accompanying penances in the Penitentials are frequently curious and extreme, but for the purposes of this book we will concentrate only on those sexual sins inside and outside of marriage, what was sexually prescribed and proscribed in and out of marriage and how seriously offences were punished.

The general rule for sexual behavior in the Penitentials is the ancient Stoic one and the one we have found in the Christian tradition from Clement onwards: sexual intercourse is permitted only between a man and a woman who are married and, even then, only for procreation. Every other sexual act is proscribed and, therefore, non-procreative intercourse is prohibited. The sixth-century Irish Penitential of Finnian of Clonard prescribes that 'If anyone has a barren wife, he shall not put away his wife because of her barrenness, but they shall both dwell in continence and be blessed if they persevere in chastity of body until God pronounces a true and just judgement upon them.'[2] There is, however, no mention of any sin or penance if they do not remain continent. Both oral and anal sex are also prohibited, most frequently between male homosexuals but also between heterosexuals. The Anglo-Saxon canons of Theodore (c. 690) prescribe that 'Whoever emits semen into the mouth shall do penance for seven years; this is the worst of evils,'[3] and 'If a man should practice anal intercourse he must do penance as one who offends with animals,' that is, for ten years.[4] Masturbation falls into the category of non-procreative sexual behavior and is, therefore, prohibited.[5] The Celtic Penitential of Columban (c. 600), closely related to that of Finnian, prescribes that 'If anyone practices masturbation or sins with a beast, he shall do penance for two years if he is not in [clerical] orders; but if he is in orders or has a monastic vow, he shall do penance for three years unless his [tender] age protects him.'[6] This is an interesting exception for those of tender age, though whether age protects from the sin or from the penance is not clear from the text.

Theodore also proscribes male homosexuality with severe penances: 'A male who commits fornication with a male shall do penance for ten years;' 'Sodomites shall do penance for seven years;' 'He who commits this sexual offence once shall do penance for four years; if he has been in the habit of it, as Basil says, fifteen years.'[7] There is some mitigation, however, for what may be seen as experimentation: if a boy engages in homosexual intercourse, the penance is two years for the first offence and four years if he repeats it. Payer notes that 'for the writers of the Penitentials *adulterium* seems not to have been a univocal term but to have had a wider extension than the word adultery does today.'[8] It can be understood in its modern meaning of sexual intercourse between two people, one of whom, at least, is married; it can also be understood in the modern meaning of fornication. It is prohibited but the penances, except for higher ecclesiastics, are relatively short. Finnian decrees that 'If any layman defile his neighbour's wife or virgin daughter, he shall do penance for an entire year on an allowance of bread and water and he shall not have intercourse with his own wife.'[9]

Besides the sexual sins enumerated, there are also concerns for ritual purity, the most widespread being concern for seminal emission other than masturbation, usually named pollution. The early sixth century *Excerpts from a Book of David* prescribes that 'He who intentionally becomes polluted in sleep shall get up and sing seven psalms and live on bread and water for that day; but if he does not do this he shall sing thirty psalms.'[10] The Celtic Penitential of Cummean (c. 650) has a similar canon: 'He who is willingly polluted during sleep shall arise and sing nine psalms in order, kneeling. On the following day he shall live on bread and water or he shall sing thirty psalms.' It adds a second canon: 'He who desires to sin during sleep, or is unintentionally polluted, fifteen psalms; he who sins and is not polluted twenty four.'[11] How one could sin during sleep is a question, but it need not detain us here. What concerns us is the idea of seminal pollution needing the remedy of penance. Sexual intercourse between a husband and a wife is not always a good thing. Cummean prescribes that he who is in a state of matrimony ought to be continent during the three forty-day periods [prior to Christmas, prior to Easter, and after Pentecost] and on Saturday and Sunday, night and day, and in the two appointed week days [Wednesday and Friday], and after conception, and during the entire menstrual period.'[12] A quick calculation reveals that few days remain available for intercourse.[13]

Women's sexual purity also figures in the Penitentials. Theodore prescribes that 'Women shall not in the time of impurity enter into a church, or communicate, neither nuns nor laywomen; if they presume [to do this], they shall fast for three weeks.' He further prescribes that 'In the same way shall they do penance who enter a church before purification after childbirth, that is, forty days,' and 'he who has intercourse at these seasons shall do penance for twenty days.'[14] Recall here Gregory the Great (d. 604), contemporaneous with the early Penitentials, who agreed with Augustine's judgement, that because of concupiscence, genital pleasure between spouses even in the act of procreation is sinful. He banned from access to the church those who had just had pleasurable intercourse and required them to cleanse themselves by washing.

An obvious summary and conclusion emerges from this medieval analysis: a strong Catholic negativity toward sexuality, even between a husband and a wife in marriage. Gula's judgement is accurate. The Penitentials helped shape 'a moral perspective which focused on individual acts, on regarding the moral life as a matter of avoiding sin, and on turning moral reflection into an analysis of sin in its many forms.'[15] They also helped shape, in Catholic moral teaching, an immature focus on genitalia. That focus and the act-centred morality it generated was perpetuated in the numerous manuals published in the wake of the reforms of clerical education mandated by the Council of Trent. These manuals controlled seminary education well into the twentieth century and continued to propagate both an act-centred morality and a Catholic ambivalence toward both sexuality and marriage.[16]

Notes:

1. John T. McNeill and Helena M. Gamer, *Medieval Handbooks of Penance: A Translation of the Principal Libri Poenitentiales* (New York: Columbia University Press, 1990), vii.
2. Ibid 95. Compare the same canon in the Penitential of Cummean, ibid 105.
3. Pierre J. Payer, *Sex and the Penitentials: The Development of a Sexual Code 550-1150* (Toronto: University of Toronto Press, 1984), 165.
4. Ibid 29.
5. Another reason for the sinfulness of every male pollution derived from an ignorance of sexual biology. The ancient Hebrew, Greek, and Roman understanding was that the male seed contained all that was necessary for a new human life; the woman merely provided a suitable 'ground' or 'field' for the male seed, a true *homunculus* or little man, to develop into a fully-fledged human being. To spill the seed anywhere it could not develop properly, on the ground, in a mouth, or in an anal orifice, for instance, was regarded as murder, and murder was always judged to be a serious evil. For detail, see above, note 56.

AN IRISH READER IN MORAL THEOLOGY

6. McNeill and Gamer, *Medieval Handbooks*, 253.

7. Ibid 185. Columban imposes a more severe penance. 'If one commits fornication as the Sodomites did, he shall do penance for ten years, the first three on bread and water; but in the other seven years he shall abstain from wine and meat, and [he shall] not be housed with another person forever' (Ibid 252).

8. Payer, *Sex and the Penitentials*, 20.

9. McNeill and Gamer, *Medieval Handbooks*, 94. For adultery Theodore prescribes a penance of 'fast for three years, two days a week, and in the three forty-day periods' and no intercourse with one's own wife (see ibid 196). Payer explains that the three forty-day periods are the forty days before Christmas, before Easter, and after Pentecost (*Sex and the Penitentials*, 24).

10. Ibid 173. Emphasis added.

11. Ibid 104. Emphasis added

12. Ibid. See also the canons in the Penitential of Theodore. 'Those who are married shall abstain from intercourse for three nights before they communicate,' and 'A man shall abstain from his wife for forty days before Easter until the week of Easter' (Ibid 208).

13. See the figure on the sexual decision-making process according to the Penitentials in James A. Brundage, *Law, Sex, and Christian Society in Medieval Europe* (Chicago: University of Chicago Press, 1987), 162.

14. McNeil and Gamer, 197. See similar restrictions in Theodore (Ibid 208).

15. Richard M. Gula, *Reason Informed by Faith: Foundations of Catholic Morality* (New York: Paulist, 1989), 26.

16. See, for example, the negative and act-avoiding definition of chastity offered by Henry Davis in his influential *Moral and Pastoral Theology* (London: Sheed and Ward, 1936), Vol 2, 172; H. Noldin, *Theologiae Moralis* (Vienna: 1922), especially the treatment of 'De Sexto Praecepto et de Usu Matrimonii;' Arturus Vermeersch, *Theologiae Moralis* (Roma: Pontificia Universitas Gregoriana, 1933), Vol IV, 'De Castitate et Vitiis Oppositis;' Gerald Kelly, *Modern Youth and Chastity* (St Louis: Queen's Work, 1941).

7   Theological Reflection on 'the good of the spouses' (Can 1055 #1)[1]

Patrick Hannon

(*Irish Theological Quarterly*, Vol 66, No 4, 2001, pp 351-364, a lightly revised version of a paper read to a meeting of the Canon Law Society of Great Britain and Ireland))

An invitation from a group of canonists to offer some theological reflections on the *bonum conjugum* cannot be entirely innocent. As an interested outsider, I am aware of the role which the concept of the good of the spouses has come to play in canonical jurisprudence, and of some of the difficulties to which the concept gives rise. And it was with relief that I learned that I am not expected to deal with jurisprudential questions, for the time is past when a moral theologian was *ipso facto* skilled in Canon Law. Theological reflection is something which might be performed at a safe distance from the problems which perplex the judge or advocate or defender of the bond. One thinks of the man who said he'd rather have a moral problem than a real one.

But of course the matter isn't as simple as that, and my task is none the less daunting for being in the realm of theology rather than that of law. For the canonist works with concepts which are ultimately fashioned from theological doctrine. And though it was the canonists themselves who for centuries shaped the doctrine concerning marriage, that time too is past; and theology is being called to account for its absence from the place in which Christian marriage theology has been in the making since the middle ages. Absent it was, and with consequences which have been unfortunate for theology and for law. But it has been summoned to resume its place and its task by the Second Vatican Council, and not least in the Council's affirmation of a *bonum conjugum*.

Canonists will, of course, be aware of the way in which the term *bonum conjugum* came to find a place in canon 1055. Jurisprudence had for some time been straining the capacity of the *tria bona* to express a doctrine of marriage which was in an accelerated process of change. There was impetus to change from inside of jurisprudence itself, as it contended with an evolving understanding of some of the traditional *capita nullitatis*. But this was both reflective of and influenced by developments in the theology of marriage. And both the jurisprudence and the theology were being challenged to change by contemporary experience of marriage, as well as by findings of the human and social sciences.

For the contemporary experience of marriage – though it might be more accurate to speak of the Western experience of marriage – was finding the categories of the canonists and the theologians wanting. That is the import of the introduction of *Gaudium et Spes* to its treatment of marriage and the family in the modern world, and the rationale of its intention 'to present certain key points of the church's teaching in a clearer light ... to guide and encourage Christians and all who are trying to preserve and to foster the dignity and supremely sacred value of married life.'2

An amount of theological thought and debate was brought to a point in the words with which the Council opened its treatment: 'The intimate partnership of life and the love which constitutes the married state has been established by the creator and endowed by him with its own proper laws: it is rooted in the covenant of the partners, that is, in their irrevocable personal consent.'3 The paragraph which follows is a blend of the traditional and the new, but there is an unmistakable break with the past. Marriage is spoken of as *foedus*, not *contractus*. The 'ends' of marriage are not enumerated in the familiar hierarchy. And, in addition to the ancient formulation of the *tria bona matrimonialia*, there is mention of a *bonum conjugum*.

The debate about the hierarchy of ends went back to the 1930s, when authors such as Doms, Krempel, and von Hildebrand began to propose alternative ways of expressing the meaning of marriage. The 1917 Code had canonised prevailing doctrine in declaring that the primary purpose of the contract of marriage is the generation and education of offspring; its secondary purpose, mutual help and the alleviation of concupiscence. It was making use of a concept of 'end' which lay deep in the tradition, and of a naming of ends which was familiar since the middle ages; though it has been remarked that the ordering of the ends in that fashion in official teaching was a recent development.4 The Code's view became that of standard moral theology, but of course moral theology was in any case long shaped by the canon law.5

So, for example, Henry Davis opened his treatise on marriage with the words: 'Marriage is the lawful contract between man and women by which is given and accepted the exclusive and perpetual right to those bodily functions which are naturally apt to generate offspring. The primary purpose of the contract is the generation and education of offspring; its secondary purpose is mutual help and the allaying of concupiscence.'6 H. Noldin's treatise begins: 'Matrimonium ... si consideratur tamquam institutio naturalis et socialis, est viri et mulier is conjunctio ad prolem generandam atque educandam legitime inita.'7

But it was not merely the ordering of ends, or the specification of procreation as the primary end, which attracted the attention of critics, for the theology of marriage in general had come to be treated in terms which were almost exclusively those of law. Noldin's tract will serve as an example. Of the ten *Quaestiones* which comprised the treatise, only the first concerned the nature of marriage, and we have just seen what its starting-point was. There are five Articles in the *Quaestio*, of which only one deals with marriage as a sacrament.8 *Quaestio* 2 is entitled *De proprietatibus matrimonii*: its account of the unity and indissolubility of marriage amounts to a commentary on canon 1013, par 2, to which reference is made in the opening sentence. The remaining eight *Quaestiones* are a summary of the canon law.

True, the 1960 edition – the thirty-second of *de Sacramentis* – gave hints of wider horizons. Among the sources cited in the footnotes were Leo XlII's *Arcanum* and Piuś XII's *Casti Connubii*, and the text adverts to passages from these documents which intimate a richer conception of marriage than might be gleaned from the canonists' treatment, and to which we shall later return. But these passages are simply set beside the canonically derived material, and do not inform the general treatment. It is salutary to recall that a mere five years before the appearance of *Gaudium et Spes* a Catholic moralist could feel obliged to write: *Hac conjunctione diversi sexus personae quadantenus se mutuo complent atque perficiunt, quatenus mas et femina constituunt adaequatum atque camp Ie tum principium generationis, educationis et vitae domesticae; nulla tenus autem affirmari potest, marem et feminam per matrimonium se mutua complere in ratione personalitatis, quasi homo non conjugatus esset imperfectus et indigerent complemento ut sit homo perfectus.*[9]

The theological critique of the concept of marriage which featured in the manuals was, in its inspiration and its general lines, that of the critique of manual moral theology generally. There was a recognition that moral theology had become detached from its context in the great doctrinal affirmations of the faith, that it had lost touch with the sources of Christian theology, and in particular that it had ceased to be nourished by the scriptures, later to be called the soul of all theology by the Second Vatican Council.[10] But there were more particular reasons for paying attention to a renewal of the theology of marriage.

These are summarised in the Preface to Dietrich von Hildebrand's *Marriage*, a key text in the advocacy of what came to be called a 'personalist' approach.

Our epoch is characterised by a terrible anti-personalism, a progressive blindness towards the nature and dignity of the spiritual person. This anti-personalism expresses itself mainly in a radical collectivism and in the different kinds of materialism. Of these, biological materialism is perhaps the most dangerous, for it considers man as a more highly developed animal, his whole personality determined by mere physiological elements. Human life is considered exclusively from a biological point of view and biological principles are the measures by which all human activities are judged.[11]

Against this background, von Hildebrand said, 'It seems very important to stress again the spiritual significance of marriage – and to explain not only its primary end (procreation), but also its primary meaning as the intimate union of two persons in mutual love.'[12] The distinction between meaning and end was taken up some six years later by Herbert Doms, whose *Vom Sinn und Zweck der Ehe* appeared in English in 1939 under the title *The Meaning of Marriage*. In the introduction he offers his reasons for attempting a deeper understanding of

AN IRISH READER IN MORAL THEOLOGY

what marriage means: ' ... modern individualism, the onslaught of pagan theories of marriage and, by no means the least important, the knowledge acquired through the new psychology, have compelled even Catholic writers to look at the matrimonial problems of their fellow Catholics from a point of view very different to that of St Thomas. They have been compelled to pay more attention to the actual relationship of husband and wife than did the "Common Doctor", who was in this closely dependent on Aristotle.'[13]

Doms was careful to point out that a view of marriage as a community of persons rather than merely as an institution to reproduce and rear children was already part of the teaching of many thinkers inside the Catholic Church. 'There have been, as it were, two streams of thought. The one regarding the child as the principle purpose of marriage. The other putting more emphasis on the unity of husband and wife and the help they give one another, especially towards perfection.'[14] He quotes extensively from the Roman Catechism, which gave as the first reason why man and woman should come together in marriage 'precisely this same community of the sexes ... which nature demands and the need of rendering mutual help makes it advisable, in the hope that the man and the woman, sustained by each other, should be better able to bear the harshness of life and the weakness of old age.'[15]

The Catechism had been cited in *Casti Connubii*, where Pius XI introduced a distinction which was to puzzle commentators: 'This mutual interior formation of the partners, this earnest desire of perfecting one another, can be said in a certain very true sense, as the Roman Catechism teaches, to be the primary cause and reason of marriage – if only marriage is taken not strictly as an institution for the proper procreation and rearing of children, but in a broader sense as sharing, a community, a union of their whole life.'[16]

In invoking the Catechism and *Casti Connubii*, as well as older and more modern authors, Doms was anxious to ensure – in vain, as it turned out – that his thesis would not appear to be at variance with Catholic tradition. In a footnote he points out that even Aquinas, whose treatment of the ends of marriage is the principal target of his criticism, had written some fine pages about marital love, and he cites as an example a sentence from the *Summa contra Gentiles*: 'Inter virum ... et uxorem maxima amicitia esse videtur.'[17] He might have added that Augustine, originator of the concept of the *tria bona*, in contending against Jovinian and the Manichees that marriage was good, and beginning his reply to the question 'cur sit bonum', wrote: 'Quod mihi non videtur propter solam filiorum procreationem sed propter ipsam etiam naturalem in diverso sexu societatem.'[18]

It would of course have been odd indeed if Augustine or Aquinas, or any other of the major theologians of marriage, had ignored the personal and relational aspects, for from Genesis to Ephesians these aspects belong to the theology of the Scriptures. I can do no more here than recall a few key texts.

The second creation account in Genesis is the earlier of the two, and its emphasis is primarily relational: it is not good for the man to be alone, and the woman is to be a partner suited to him (2: 18). She is bone of his bones, flesh of his flesh, she is the *ishah* for she is taken from the *ish*; and 'that is why a man leaves his father and mother and attaches himself to his wife, and the two become one flesh' (2:24).[19] In the first creation account the accent is on the procreative significance of sexual difference, yet a relational motif is intimated. Translations concerned to avoid sexist language[20] miss an important nuance, for the Hebrew is more instructively rendered 'God created man in his own image, in the image of God he created him; male and female he created them' (1:27).[21] The human species is created as a sexed couple; man and woman together are 'man'; and man is made in the image of God.[22]

The celebrated opening chapters of Hosea depict the Covenant between Yahweh and Israel as a love-relation or a marriage. In a way the comparison is an obvious one, for both God's covenant and marriage are examples of a *b'rith*, in Jewish thought a special species of agreement or pact. But it is all the more interesting that what Hosea explores is the love-aspect of his and Gomer's relationship, rather than what might be called the legal. That is, from his own intense personal experience with Gomer he comes to glimpse the nature and quality of Yahweh's love for his people. Indirectly, therefore, these chapters are a powerful affirmation of the goodness of marriage and human love; and in due course Malachi will make use of the obverse of the comparison in calling on the married to imitate the love of God.[23] So will Paul, in a passage in the letter to the Ephesians which is at the heart of the Christian understanding of marriage.

A final Old Testament reference is the Song of Songs. Whether this is understood as an allegory of God's love for Israel or, as seems more generally accepted nowadays, as a lyrical celebration of human love, it is certainly 'an affirmation of the creaturely goodness of the relationship between man and woman.'[24] Grelot has summarised its import: 'Without the name of God once being mentioned, everything in human love appertaining to the order of creation is hallowed by implicit reference to a divine norm, part of the Israelite tradition: the monogamous love of two beings called to become *one flesh* as were the prototype couple. The book is clearly not a theological thesis, but it gives us an insight into the psychology of love in the way in which it develops in a biblical climate.'[25]

At first sight, the New Testament data might appear both skimpy and jejune. Little is recorded of any teaching of Jesus concerning marriage, apart from what he had to say about adultery and divorce in Matthew 5 and Mark 10; though of course a new note is struck when he affirms the value of virginity for the sake of the kingdom as recounted in Matthew 19. This theme was to prove problematic in Christian thought, not least as a result of Paul's treatment of it in 1 Corinthians 7. Yet mainline Christian theology persisted in refusing to downgrade marriage and married love, for all that individual authors displayed some ambivalence; and the touchstone of 'orthodoxy' in this regard was another Pauline passage, Ephesians 5:21-33.

The exhortation to wives to be faithful to their husbands is to the modern ear an unpromising opening to a passage which must remain pivotal in any Christian theology of marriage. It is possible to say, of course, that the 'subjection' is a loving subjection, without pejorative overtones of servility or inferiority; and that the injunction to husbands to love their wives as Christ loved the church sets the context and perspective of the earlier injunction in a way that precludes disparagement of women. But perhaps it is better simply to acknowledge that Paul is here as elsewhere taking for granted the existing contemporary social pattern, and that insofar as what is here propounded is an ethic of behaviour, it bears the marks of its time and place of origin, and is not to be transposed to a different place and time.

But what is here propounded is not just a behavioural ethic; for the kernel of the passage is a theological, not an ethical assertion. 'This is a great mystery', says Paul of the Genesis ideal of two in one flesh, 'and I am saying that it refers to Christ and the church' (33).[26] At first sight this is again the obverse of Hosea's comparison, and indeed Paul goes on to propose the love of Christ for his church as a pattern for the love of husband and wife. But the comparison between marriage and the love of Christ and his church is a theological insight of the utmost profundity and it has resonated throughout the Christian tradition; and it remains, I shall suggest later, the key to a faithful understanding of what the gospel means for marriage today.[27]

Von Hildebrand, Krempel, and Doms, and others who wrote in similar vein, in seeking for a wider and deeper 'meaning' of marriage than was available in the manual accounts, were in essence doing no more than recalling the full riches of the Judeo-Christian tradition. But the manner in which some of these authors propounded their case provoked authoritative censure, notably in a Holy Office decree dated 1 April 1944. The question formulated in the decree was: 'Whether the opinion of certain modern writers can be admitted, who either deny that the primary end of marriage is the generation and education of children, or teach that the secondary ends are not essentially subordinate to the primary end, but are equally principal and independent.' The reply was: 'In the negative.'[28]

One may surmise that part of the difficulty which the Roman authorities had with the questioning of the hierarchy of ends arose from the possibility that it might have implications for the traditional teaching on contraception.[29] But perhaps a more pervasive underlying obstacle to a wholehearted welcome for the new 'personalism' was a continuing subordination of moral theology to the categories and concepts of canon law. By that I mean that, as far as the theology of marriage was concerned, the formative principles remained those of the canonists, and the authors of the theological treatises were unwilling to venture far from the familiar landmarks represented by the *tria bona*, the *jus in corpus* and the hierarchy of primary and secondary ends.

Even writers sympathetic to the personalists, for example John C. Ford and Gerard Kelly, were preoccupied – albeit not uncritically – with the jurisprudence of the Rota as well as by the text of the canons. In attempting to develop a view of the secondary ends which envisaged them as 'essential' if subordinate, Ford and Kelly find it necessary to engage closely with the reasoning in a decision *coram* Wynen, the distinguished Rota judge. More tellingly, perhaps, in countering Doms' contention that marriage 'is' before it 'is for' (i.e. procreation, mutual help etc), they say: 'The ontological reality which is marriage, i.e. the juridical bond, has meaning only when one knows what the purposes are for which God created it, and towards which it is by nature objectively ordered.'[30] The essence of marriage is a juridical bond: 'the living realities of marriage' – the living conjugal acts of the partners – are of supreme importance to the *bene esse* of marriage, but they do not make the marriage, they are not its *esse*.

Ford and Kelly's book appeared in 1963, and almost half of the book was occupied with a painstaking attempt to marry personalist insights with canonical doctrine concerning the ends of marriage. The attempt was praiseworthy, and these authors were distinguished practitioners of the art of the moral theologian as this was understood in their time. But it is possible to say now that the undertaking was flawed, for precisely to the extent that it was in the end constrained by a canonical view of marriage, it was theologically misconceived.

The canonist sees marriage as a contract, a matter of rights and obligations, as Denis O'Callaghan observed,[31] and in this he is within his competence. 'What blame there is [for the marriage theology of the period leading up to Vatican II] attaches to the theologian, who took over this legal systematisation and accepted it as a satisfactory structure for a theology of marriage. The closed system of contract with its primary and secondary purposes gained self-sufficiency down through the generations. If a new insight was to win acceptance it had to find a niche in the system. If it did not bed in comfortably it was ignored as irrelevant or rejected as erroneous. Not only did the first tentative attempts at a theology of marriage in the decade 1930-40 founder here, but even Pius XI's encyclical *Casti Connubii* encountered the impasse.[32]

One can therefore glimpse the dimensions of the 'revolution' marked by the publication in December 1965 of *Gaudium et Spes*. In a paragraph the Council put paid to decades of writing and debate – indeed, it might be said, to a way of looking at marriage which was centuries old. True, the text was the fruit of compromise, and some of the elements of its presentation sit uneasily with each other. But the description of marriage as an intimate partnership of life and love, the abandonment of the classification of ends, the replacement of the term contract with covenant, and the introduction of the term *bonum conjugum*: all of these signal and inaugurate, at the level of official teaching, a new theology of marriage.

Magisterial teaching has maintained the direction taken in the teaching of *Gaudium et Spes*. It is regrettable, if inevitable, that the controversy about the teaching of *Humanae Vitae* on artificial contraception has distracted attention from the theological vision for marriage which the encyclical proposes. The lineaments are sketched in paragraph 8:

> Married love particularly reveals its true nature and nobility when we realise that it derives from God and finds its supreme origin in him who 'is Love', the Father 'from whom every family in heaven and on earth is named' ... It is in reality the wise and provident institution of God the Creator, whose purpose was to establish in man his loving design. As a consequence, husband and wife, through their mutual gift of themselves, which is specific and exclusive to them alone, develop that union of two persons in which they perfect one another, in order to co-operate with God in the generation and education of new lives. Furthermore, the marriage of those who have been baptised is invested with the dignity of a sacramental sign of grace, for it represents the union of Christ and his church.[33]

The elements of theological doctrine sketched here are reproduced and more fully developed in *Familiaris Consortio*.[34]

But of course the apparent simplicity of this account is deceptive, for under the surface there lurk questions which are still in the process of address. What is the essence of marriage? asked Robert Sanson in a wellknown article, and one can only agree when he writes: 'No theologian or canonist will ever be able to give a definite answer. The mystery of marriage is bound up with the mystery of God's covenant-relationship with us, and with the mystery of God's own trinitarian relationship.'[35]

The theology of marriage is a theme of sacramental theology, but it touches also on the theology of grace, on christology, on the theology of the Trinity and on ecclesiology, to name but the most obvious related themes. The need to root it in scripture means that it calls for the art and skill of the hermeneute and exegete, and if it is to be nourished by the patristic and medieval theological inheritance, it bespeaks the most careful work in these fields. And of course it must be in touch with – perhaps one ought to say emerge from – the experience of the married, for it is within the marriages of the faithful that the sacramentality of marriage is lived.'[36]

A complicating factor is that each of the areas of theology which bear upon the theology of marriage is itself in the process of development, and a plurality of approaches to each is to be found. Sacramental theology, for example, is no longer solely bound to the concepts and perspectives of neo-scholasticism: the pioneering work of the nineteenth-century Germans Johann Adam Moehler and Matthias Scheeben and, in the first part of this century, of thinkers such as

Odo Casel and Anscar Vonier, made way for the now classic contributions of Karl Rahner and Edward Schillebeeckx; and more recently the enterprise has been joined by feminist and liberation theologians.[37]

Or take the theology of grace. I have a sharp personal memory from student days of the impact of Piet Fransen's *Divine Grace and Man*[38] on an understanding formed for the most part by a study of Van Noort's *De Gratia*. James P. Mackey's *Life and Grace* also offered new horizons.[39] There was an excitement in discovering that de Lubac's *Surnaturel* was becoming part of standard theology. And Rahner again, and of course Lonergan, opened up ways of thinking about the mystery of grace which in more than one way were a revelation. Although Vatican II did not directly address the subject of grace in any one of its documents, its articulation of the church's self-understanding was permeated by the theme, and the work of theologians such as these bore obvious fruit. And again the work is ongoing.[40]

But despite the complexity of the background, as well as of the issues at stake in marriage theology itself, there has been steady and valuable work in the field since the Council. One thinks, for example, of Gustave Martelet, whose *Amour conjugal et renouveau conciliare* represents an early reflection on conciliar doctrine.[41] Karl Rahner's *Marriage as a Sacrament* is still a classic piece.[42] There is useful material in the propositions and papers from the International Theological Commission edited by Richard Malone and John Connery under the title *Contemporary Perspectives on Christian Marriage*.[43] Theodore Mackin's *What is Marriage?* is both instructive and provocative, not least in his interrogation of the canonical tradition from the vantage point of sacramental theology.[44] In *Theology of Christian Marriage* Walter Kasper's calm reflections offer insights into fundamental theological issues and themes.[45]

What is the state of the theology of marriage now? Words of Kasper, though written more than twenty years ago, provide a description which is still apt.

> Although the church has so far not succeeded in satisfactorily reintegrating the different aspects of marriage within a personal perspective, a beginning has certainly been made. It is at least already clear in which direction theologians ought to be thinking with regards to marriage. It is not so much a question of personalising marriage to the extent of stripping it of all its essential institutional elements or freeing it from its existing structures. It is rather a question of preserving, as in the past, the inner unity of the three traditional values emphasised by Augustine and St Thomas: in other words, in continuing to envisage marriage in its natural, social, personal and sacramental aspects, but of no longer taking the begetting of descendants as the only basis for marriage. The point of departure for Christian thinking about marriage today should be the aspect of mutual love and faithfulness.[46]

I indicated at the beginning that I am aware of the fact that the jurisprudents are divided as to the juridical significance of the concept of *bonum conjugum*, as they are to that of related concepts such as *consortium vitae, communio amoris et vitae*, and the like. I hope it won't be taken as an evasion if I say that it is the jurisprudents who in the end must settle the question. But neither, I hope, will it be taken amiss if I suggest that the theological significance of the concept of the *bonum conjugum* cannot be irrelevant to the lawyers' task. And I should like to conclude this presentation with a few remarks in this regard.

It is clear that the introduction of the concept of a *bonum conjugum* was wholly intentional; you have only to read an account of the debates on the text which became paragraphs 48-50 of *Gaudium et Spes*.[47] And when its introduction is taken together with the omission of the ordering of ends as primary and secondary, it is clear also that there is here a deliberate break with a theology which was shaped in great part by the canonical tradition. *Humanae Vitae* goes a step further and abandons the language of ends, as indeed in due course did the 1983 Code. What was hinted at in *Arcanum* and canvassed hesitantly and ambivalently in *Casti Connubii*, and what was contended for by the writers of the 'personalist' school, is now unambiguously a part of the official doctrine of the church.

But there is a deeper reason for heeding the presence in theology and in the law now of a concept of *bonum conjugum*. One of the leading themes in post-conciliar theological writing has been the nature of the sacramentality of marriage; and a crucial emphasis may be expressed by saying that it is in the human reality of couples' loving relationship that the sacramentality of marriage lies. *Ubi caritas et amor, Deus ibi est*; in the unique type of mutual giving of self which is institutionalised in marriage, God's love – grace – is present and active and tangible. The *bonum conjugum*, the mutual enrichment and fulfilment of the partners in their *consortium*, in their *intima communio vitae et amoris*, is at the core of the sacramentality of their union.[48] This is the 'great mystery' of which Paul spoke, and is the heart of Catholic Christian theology of marriage.

One can therefore see the force of Kasper's assertion that the point of departure for Christian thinking about marriage today should be the aspect of love and faithfulness.[49] Doubtless he was speaking in the first place of theology; but it seems obvious that his remarks apply also, albeit *mutatis mutandis*, to the jurisprudence of the marriage tribunals. I say *mutatis mutandis* because of course a juridical perspective is not the same as that of the theologian. The law has its proper purposes and its own inner logic, and it cannot be expected to capture in its formulae the amplitude of a philosophical or theological account.

But neither should jurisprudence be preoccupied with maintaining an inherited conceptual framework for its own sake, or out of loyalty to a narrow-minded view of its own tradition. And from a theological standpoint it must be regarded as going awry if, from such a preoccupation or out of misplaced loyalty, it fails to do justice to the vision for marriage which the Second Vatican Council has retrieved and developed, and upon which it set its seal.

Notes:

1. This is a lightly revised version of a paper read to a meeting of the Canon Law Society of Great Britain and Ireland.

2. Gaudium et Spes, par. 46.

3. Ibid., par. 48.

4. U. Navarrete, 'Structura juridica matrimonii secundum Concilium Vaticanum II' in *Periodica*, 56 (1967), 368.

5. J. Mahoney has referred to 'the casting of moral theology for centuries as the hand-maid of canon law'; *The Making of Moral Theology* (Oxford: Oxford University Press, 1987), 35.

6. H. Davis, *Moral and Pastoral Theology* (3rd edition) (New York: 1941), vol IV, 53. Davis refers to canon 1013, par 1.

7. Noldin-Schmitt, *Summa Theologiae Moralis* (32nd edition) (Innsbruck: 1960), 426.

8. This is Article 2, following an article *de ipsa eius natura*. The others are entitled *De matrimonii divisionibus* (Art 3), *De potestate Ecclesiae in matrimonium* (Art 4), and *De potestate auctoritatis civilis in matrimonium* (Art 5).

9. Op. cit., 426.

10. *Optatam Totius*, Decree on the Training of Priests, par 1S.

11. *Marriage* was originally published in German in 1929 as *Die Ehe*, the first English translation appearing in 1942 (London: Longmans, Green and Co). (It appears that the translation was made by von Hildebrand with the help of Emmanuel Chapman and Daniel Sullivan.) A soft-cover edition entitled *Marriage: The Mystery of Faithful Love* was published by Sophia Institute Press (Manchester, New Hampshire) in 1984, and was reissued in hardcover by the same publisher in 1991. The quotation is from the 1991 edition, xxv.

12. Ibid.

13. Herbert Doms, *The Meaning of Marriage*, trs George Sayer (London: Sheed and Ward, 1939), xv.

14. Op. cit., xvi.

15. Op. cit., xvii, translating the Catechism, lla Pars, cap 8, q 13.

16. *AAS* (1930), 539-592, at 548. The translation here is as in Ford and Kelly, *Contemporary Moral Theology, Vol 2, Marriage Questions* (Cork: Mercier Press, 1963), 138. The authors note that this passage was omitted from the English and from some other vernacular translations when they first appeared, and they add: 'How this accident happened nobody seems to know' (loc cit., n 13).

17. *SCG* III, 123, quoted in nn 7 and 11, op. cit., 217.

18. *De Bono Conjugali* III, 3. Text as in *Bibliotheque Augustinienne, Oeuvres de Saint Augustine, 1er serie, opuscules, II. Problemes Moraux* (Paris 1948). Augustine's intent in speaking of the *bonum* or *bona* of marriage is frequently misunderstood, for want of attention to the context in which he wrote. *De Bono Conjugali* was composed with the Manichees in mind, whose dualist metaphysic led them to regard procreation as ontologically evil. Augustine wishes to establish that marriage is something good in the order of being, in the context a much more radical enterprise than that of justifying it morally. For him the *tria bona* are not mere *bona excusantia*; this is a medieval conception. The confusion is doubtless caused by the fact that Augustine also thought that sexuality was a particularly troublesome locus of the *concupiscentia* or propensity of the human heart to seek fulfilment in created things, by contrast with *caritas* whose origin and fulfilment was in God.

In canonical – or for that matter theological – commentary one of the few authors who represents the position accurately is Cyril Murtagh. In an article on the jurisprudential approach to the *consortium vitae* he writes: 'It is interesting to note that Augustine in writing *De bono conjugali* was attempting to refute Jovinian, while redressing the balance against Jerome's disparagement of marriage in favour of virginity. Thus Augustine discusses in what way marriage is 'good' rather than listing the necessary 'good things" of marriage, and says: 'Quod mihi non videtur propter solam filiorum procreationem, sed propter ipsam etiarn naturalern in diverso sexu societatern.' It is later, in *De Genesi*, that he lists the three *bona*, but he refers back to his fuller treatment in *De bono conjugali*. Treating the three *bona* in a minimal contractual sense led jurisprudence up a blind alley from which Vatican II has extracted it, and led back to a fuller view of marriage. This fuller view is realised in the formulations of the new Code and, as such, is to be a guiding principle of future jurisprudence'. *Studia Canonica*, 9 (1975),309-323, at 323.

19. The Hebrew word rendered flesh, *bashar,* had a primarily physical connotation, and so refers in the first place to the physical act of fusion. But for the Hebrew, *bashar* implied a *nefesh* or *ruah,* either of which we might translate as 'spirit'; there is no body-soul dichotomy, so there is question of what we would call a 'person', represented and manifested in the external physical appearance. Schillebeeckx has used the expression 'the ego in physical form', *Marriage: Secular Reality and Saving Mystery* (London: Sheed and Ward, 1965), vol 1, 43. On this generally, see P. Grelot, *Man and Wife in Scripture* (New York: 1964).

20. e.g. the *Revised English Bible* (a revision of the *New English Bible*), Oxford and Cambridge 1989.

21. RSV translation.

22. There is scope here for a relational interpretation of the concept of *imago dei*, and the possibility of exploring the bearing of the doctrine of the Trinity on the theology of marriage.

23. Mal 2:13-16.

24. Schillebeeckx, op. cit., 81.

25. Grelot, op. cit., 81, emphasis in the text.

26. *To mysterion touto mega estin, ego de ego eis Christon kai eis ten ekklesian.* RSV translation.

27. The exegesis of this passage proffered by H. Schlier in *Der Brief an die Epheser* (Düsseldorf, Patmos-Verlag, 1962) appears to command general acceptance: 'Sofern das Gen 2:24 gemeinte Geschehen, das Mysterium der Ehe zwischen Christus und der Kirche, in der irdischen Ehe von Mann und Frau jeweils nachvollzogen wird, nimmt diese an jenem Mysterium teil und ist in solchem Sinn dann selbst Mysterium' (262).

28. *AAS* 36 (1944), 103, as translated in Bouscaren, *Canon Law Digest*, III, 401-402. Pius XII, in an address to the Judges of the Rota in 1941, had already warned against 'two extremes': 'on the one hand, practically to deny or esteem too little the secondary end of marriage and of the act of generation; on the other hand, to dissociate or separate unduly the conjugal act from the primary end, to which according to its entire internal structure it is primarily and principally ordained.' *AAS* 33 (1941),421-426, at 423; as translated in Ford and Kelly, op. cit., 37. In 1951, in an Address to Midwives, Pius condemned the exaltation of personal values over the procreative end: *AAS* 43 (1951), 848-849.

29. Though none of the authors concerned in fact questioned that teaching.

30. Ford and Kelly, op. cit. 55.

31. 'Christian Marriage: The Evolving Situation', in John Marshall (ed), *The Future of Christian Marriage* (London: Geoffrey Chapman, 1969), 13.

32. Ibid.

33. Tr. CTS London 1968.

34. Tr. CTS London 1981; d. esp. 19-31.

35. R. Sanson, 'Jurisprudence for Marriage: Based on Doctrine', *Studia Canonica*, 10 (1976),5-36, at 29.

36. In the opening article in a review published twice yearly by the International Academy for Marital Spirituality, Klaus Demmer has written: ' ... committed Christians do not recognise themselves in today's theological pronouncements; they get the uncomfortable feeling of being passive subjects of a purely theoretical pastoral ministry, in which the ideas they contribute, be they ever so modest, do not count at all. And yet they, too, are theologians, responsible and capable partners of the teaching authority within the 'communio' of the church. Their life experience is – at least in embryo – already the beginning of a theory which possesses the undeniable advantage of being able to claim for itself practical clarity, and consequently a wealth of facets. The professional theologian takes it up, reflects on it with the help of his professional criteria, and hands it back to his contemporaries. Looked at in this way, theology is a partnership of contemporaries on the level of responsible thinking, and it needs the contribution of the committed Christian.' *Intams Review*, 1, (Autumn, 1995), 18.

37. A good summary account of the history and of recent trends is in *The New Dictionary of Theology*, eds Komonchak, Collins, and Lane (Dublin: Gill and Macmillan, 1990), art. 'Sacrament' (910-922). Cf also *Sacramentum Mundi*, vol 5, art. 'Sacraments' (378-384).

38. Later incorporated in Fransen's *The New Life of Grace* (London: Geoffrey Chapman, 1969), a more extensive and scholarly work.

39. Dublin: Gill, 1966.

40. See Komonchak, Collins, Lane, op. cit., art. 'Grace'.

41. Lyon: X. Mappus, 1967. Already during the Council, Martelet had ventured a sketch of a new theology of marriage in 'Mariage, amour et sacrement', *Nouvelle Revue Theologique*, 85 (1963), 577-597.

42. *Theological Investigations*, Vol 10, (London: Darton, Longman and Todd, 1973), 199-221. See also a brief treatment in 'The Church and the Sacraments', in *Studies in Modern Theology* (Freiburg and London: Herder, 1965), 289-294.

43. Chicago: Loyola University Press, 1984.

44. New York: Paulist Press, 1982.

45. London: Burns and Oates, 1980. This is a translation of a text first published in German in 1977. In the periodical literature (including that of Canon Law), there is valuable writing on some key questions: see, for example, William LaDue, 'Conjugal Love and the Juridical Structure of Christian Marriage', *The Jurist*, 34 (1974), 36-67; Paul Palmer, 'Christian Marriage: Contract or Covenant?', *Theological Studies*, 33 (1972),617-665; E. Kilmartin, 'When is Marriage a Sacrament?', *Theological Studies*, 34 (1973), 275-86. The article by Sanson referred to above (n. 33) points to the questions raised for theology out of jurisprudence and suggests some promising directions.

As regards the theology of marriage in general, Joyce's *Christian Marriage* (London: 1933) remains authoritative, as does H. Rondet, *Introduction à l'étude de la theologie du mariage* (Paris, 1966), and P. Adnès, *Le mariage*, 2nd ed (Tournai: Desclee, 1961), even if these works are the product of their time.

46. Kasper, op. cit., 14.

47. See, for example, H. Vorgrimler (ed), *Commentary on the Documents of Vatican II* (New York: Herder and Herder, 1969), Vol 5.

48. See especially K. Rahner, 'Marriage as a Sacrament', op. cit.; also G. Martelet, *Amour conjugale et renouveau conciliare* (Lyons: X. Mappus, 1967), and Kasper, op. cit. Kasper summarises: 'Marriage, then, is in its own way a form by means of which God's eternal love and faithfulness, revealed in Jesus Christ, are made historically present. The love and faithfulness existing between Christ and his church is therefore not simply an image or example of marriage, nor is the self-giving of man and wife in marriage [merely] an image and likeness of Christ's giving of himself to the church. The love that exists between man and wife is rather a sign that makes the reality present, in other words, an epiphany of the love and faithfulness of God that was given once and for all time in Jesus Christ and is made present in the church' (30).
49. Kasper, loc. cit.

8   Source of Life

Enda McDonagh

(Enda McDonagh (ed), *The Meaning of Christian Marriage: Papers of Maynooth Union Summer School, 1962*, Dublin: Gill & Son in assoc. with The Furrow Trust, 1963, pp 75-91)

Whatever temptation there may have been in the past to see marriage exclusively as the instrument of procreation and so a source of life, the tendency in the modern world is quite the other way. The emphasis is on the personal values and community aspects of marriage, with procreation frequently regarded as an unfortunate side-effect. The purpose of this paper is to outline the church's teaching on the life-giving function of marriage and to integrate it with the no less necessary and no less divine aspect which Father Häring has outlined.[1] To do this it seems best to begin with the divine institution of the human sexes and of marriage.

A Divine Institution
In the first Genesis account of creation we read:

So God created man in his own image, in the image of God he created him: male and female he created them. And God blessed them and said to them: Be fruitful and multiply, and fill the earth and subdue it.[2]

In the second account we read:

Then the Lord God said: It is not good that man should be alone: I will make a helper fit for him … Therefore a man leaves his father and his mother and cleaves to his wife and they become one flesh.[3]

To enable the human race to propagate itself, God created it male and female. It was as male and female that God blessed man and commissioned him to increase and multiply and fill the earth. But the procreational aspect of the divine institution of marriage is balanced in the second account by God's solicitude to provide man with a helpmate like himself whom he called woman, and for whom a man shall leave his own father and mother to form with her such an intimate community in mind and body that they are said to form one flesh. In God's plan, the marriage community is a way of growth and perfection not only for the race through provision of new members, but also for the partners through their mutual love and help.

As for the love-community of one man and one woman forming one flesh, marriage is specifically distinguished by its sexual character. Human reason and observation, apart from revelation, give a sufficiently clear outline of the nature and purpose of man's sexuality in the following terms:[4]

(i)   The organic differences between man and woman are mutually complementary and necessary to each other in providing for the continuance of the race. It is through the conjunction of the male and female sexual organs in the complete sexual act that the necessary prerequisites for forming a new member of the species are completed. This organic 'complementarity' man shares with the animals *in genere*.

(ii) The sexual duality, as manifested in this organic way, forms the basis of an attractive force between male and female which draws them ultimately to that organic union to which the life-giving function and intense pleasure have been attached.

(iii) The duality is not merely bodily or organic, but in man at least applies to higher differences of a sensitive, emotional and even intellectual nature. Although man and woman belong to the same species, they are clearly two different types.

(iv) In man the built-in 'complementarity' of body, emotion and mind is integrated into a rational nature. By this he knows that the instinctive sexuality which suffices for the lower animals does not suffice for the worthy continuance of the race. Neither is it an adequate expression of the relation of the two persons drawn by this attraction. Reason also tells him that the new life to which sexual duality and union are ordained, and the mutual development of man and woman which they make possible, can be achieved only in a stable union of one man and one woman based on the personal love into which their attraction ripens.

Love and Life in Community

The marriage community then may be rightly described as a source of life. As a prelude, however, to fuller understanding of this, it is helpful to consider some of the other communities that we know. For every community in so far as it is based on love is a source of life. And this applies to the supernatural and natural planes.

In the Old Testament the alliance between God and his people was frequently described in terms of the love-relationship of marriage.[5] The life, the spiritual life of the people of Israel, depended on their faithfulness in returning love for love to God.

In the appointed time God in his great love for the world sent his only Son that whoever believes in him, whoever unites himself to him in faith and love, might have eternal life. By his death on the Cross Christ's love ensured the fruitfulness of his bride, the church. From that intimate union between Christ and his church comes the spiritual regeneration of the world. And the regeneration, the new life, is in proportion to the love. The love of Christ is total; the love of the bride, of the whole church and of each individual is conditioned by man's response. For the community of the faithful, life, Christian life, depends on love.

The smaller groups of societies within the church also bear witness to this relation between love and life. The life-giving capacity of a particular diocese or parish or religious house stems from the love which animates it. Even natural (as distinct from supernatural) societies, the State and its various subsidiaries, while they must be governed by the rule of law, draw their life from the love which infuses them and which they inspire. Laws and regulations are necessary for every human society, supernatural and natural, but they do not reflect or inspire its life. The major achievements of society, religious or profane, may be traced to self-sacrifice based on love. Fruitfulness is the characteristic of true unselfish love.

The fruitfulness of married love has a distinctive quality. The life to which it tends of its nature is not simply the cultural or spiritual enrichment of the members of that community, although it includes that, but the creation of a new being, a new person, a new centre of such cultural and spiritual life. The child which is the fruit of their union is the natural term of married love. And the generation of this new living being may be described as the specific end or purpose of marriage and married love.

The Ends of Marriage
This leads inevitably to some discussion of the church's teaching on the ends of marriage and of the controversy which has centred on it in recent times.[6]

The Code of Canon Law describes *procreation et education prolis* as the *finis primaries matrimonii; mutuum adiutorium et remedium concupiscentiae* as the *finis secundarius*.[7] And this mode of expression has long been used in moral theology manuals as well as in writings on canon law.

It has not, however, gone unchallenged. Criticisms of it have taken different forms.[8] To make the procreation and education of children the *finis primaries* seemed inconsistent with the church's insistence on the validity of marriage between sterile people, according to one line of criticism. How could such a marriage be described as a true marriage where the possibility of procreation was excluded from the beginning? Even where the parties are not sterile, the marriage act does not lead automatically to procreation, for this depends on a great many other factors which are not subject to the control of the parties. Procreation then, which is beyond the control of the parties and at times beyond their capacity, should not be described as the *finis primaries* or primary end of their human act in contracting marriage. Its description as such must be attributed to the mistaken biological beliefs of an earlier generation.

A different line of criticism considered the indignity of subordinating two human beings, two persons and their love-relationship – the highest possible relationship between human beings – to the good of the species. The two-in-oneness (*Zweieinigkeit*) of the love-community which the partners formed should be described as at least an equal and independent, if not a superior, end

AN IRISH READER IN MORAL THEOLOGY

to that of procreation. In this way the difficulties caused by sterile marriages or by acts of intercourse which did not lead to generation, or the difficulty of subordinating two persons and their love to some abstract good like that of the species, would be avoided.

Although such criticisms are to be found in the writings of earlier moral theologians such as Linsenmann and Koch, they have been associated in recent times with the name of the now retired Professor of Moral Theology at Münster, Herbert Doms. His celebrated book *Der Sinn und Zweck der Ehe*, first published in 1935 and translated into English as *The Meaning of Marriage*, sparked off a very live controversy. This led eventually to the 1944 Decree of the Holy Office which I now quote in translation:

> Can we entertain the opinion of some modern authorities who deny that the primary end of marriage is procreation and education, or teach that the secondary ends are not necessarily subordinate to the primary end but are equally important and independent? The members of the Sacred Congregation of the Holy Office have decided to reply in the negative.[9]

This reply was approved by Pope Pius XII on 30 March 1944.

The Holy Office decree settled the matter. But the discussion which has gone on in the meantime, and which seems to have gained momentum in the last few years, has been trying to define precisely, if respectfully, the exact sense of this settlement.

It may be conceded that some of the earlier expressions of the church's teaching were lacking in subtlety both in their biological presuppositions, for which the theologians could not always be blamed, and in their ignoring of the personal values of which a full theology of marriage must take account. However, it is important to distinguish the faulty biological presuppositions from the theological principles and the teaching of the theologians and of the church from inadequate expression of this teaching.

The Teaching of St Thomas
For the teaching of St Thomas this task has been accomplished to a large extent by the Professor of Moral Theology at the Gregorian University, Rome, Joseph Fuchs SJ.[10]

St Thomas regarded procreation as the *finis primaries* of sexual duality and of the marriage union,[11] because at the generic or more general level where man is considered as an animal[12] this in fact is clearly nature's purpose. Love and friendship do not of their nature demand sexual union. Procreation does. And because of the distinctive characteristics of the newly-born human being, because of his need of support in his gradual development or education, this sexual union should take place only within the stable institution of marriage.[13]

The medieval misconceptions about biology which St Thomas shared do not preclude the correct understanding of copula as an act of itself necessary and apt for the generation of the human being which, to ensure the due preservation and education of that human being, should take place only in marriage. The union to which man and woman were drawn by their sexual difference and 'complementarity' had this ultimate purpose – new life.

Marriage was also a union of love and the marriage act itself was for St Thomas a meritorious act in the proper conditions.[14] So he was not unaware of the personal values involved. However, his attitude to woman was largely coloured by the outlook of the period in which he lived, and for any activity other than the procreation and education of children he regarded man as a more fitting companion for man.[15] This did not encourage development of the personal values of marriage for man and wife.

In the period after scholasticism, when personal and individual values began to receive due recognition, moral theology was beginning to lose contact with the real stuff of Christian theology.[16] Its separation from dogma in a manner unknown to St Thomas and the scholastics, and its development as an independent science aimed almost exclusively at the training of confessors, had many unfortunate consequences. The predominance of positive law, the emergence of the casuistry manuals and the probabilist controversies left it in a weakened condition. It found itself increasingly isolated from the great theological, psychological and other scientific movements of the time. And marriage, supremely important to the law as a social institution with a definite hierarchy of ends, was treated by the moralist also in purely legal fashion.

The development of the sciences of biology and psychology has not weakened that basic intuition of earlier writers and theologians who saw sexual duality and the union of the sexes as directed of their nature to the generation of new life.[17] Not every complete sexual act generates life, but the penetration and semination of the vagina of the woman by the male organ is an act of itself apt (*per se apta*) for generation. It may be an incomplete cause which must be supplemented by the work of nature, but it is that portion of the complete cause which is placed under man's control. In using his sexual powers then man must take account of this inscription of the divine will in his nature.

The recognition of his moral obligation to co-operate freely with the powers of his nature and direct them towards their God-given ends, emphasises man's personal worth and dignity. The lower animals act by instinct, determined by the rutting season and other instinctual movements. Man can control and direct his sexual activity freely and humanly after the fashion and for the purpose intended by his Creator.

But this involves much more than the correct mechanical application of natural forces. A mechanical concept of nature and natural law has done much to distort the true teaching on marriage, within and without the church. The penetration and insemination by the man of the woman within the marriage union is not all that God requires of man as a human being. The sexual difference is not only clearly directed towards procreation, it is also the source of a powerful attractive force which, issuing in human love, completes and perfects the marriage partners. And the love which develops between man and woman so that they ultimately seek to share life and home, is not less natural or human than the procreation which normally results.

It is misleading then to separate the love-community which two people of opposite sexes tend to set up from the procreative aspect of their sexual duality and union. The love-community with its personal values and procreation do not result as two independent ends or *fines*. And the theory that they do was rightly condemned as an error. The love-union finds its most intimate expression in the procreational act. The procreation and education are accomplished in a manner worthy of human beings when they are the fruit and expression of love. A love which excludes the openness to life which the complete sexual act involves, and a complete sexual act which is not an expression of love, are both repugnant to the nature and dignity of man.

The work of Doms and others gave a much needed revitalisation to the love and community aspects of marriage, which had tended to be overshadowed by the institutional aspect. It was with marriage regarded as an institution designed to supply new members of the race and of the church that the law was primarily concerned. Moral theology in its dependent state could do little more than echo the statements of the law. Some reaction was necessary but like most reactions this one tended to go too far. Father Häring sees, with some justification, a kind of narrow self-perfectionism in the emphasis placed on the mutual love and perfection aspects of marriage at the expense of the procreational elements.[18] It was the tendency to do it at the expense of the procreational element and to introduce an artificial separation between the two (a favourite device of some Protestants in justifying birth-control) that prompted the Holy Office reply. The reply itself is a fresh invitation to understand more fully the purposes of marriage and the relations between them.

This had been expressed briefly already in the observation that the only true married love, the only love on which the marriage-community can be built is that which is open to life, which, in the complete self-giving which it expresses in the partners' community of goods and life, and most intimately in the unity of the marriage acts, tends of its nature to the generation and development of new life. And the only true procreative act is that which furthers and expresses this love.

Duality, Union, New Life

Here it may be worth recounting again the source and genesis of this love. It is based on man's sexual duality. And this sexual character distinguishes it from all other human loves. At the biological level it tends to the union of the sexual organs so clearly designed for each other and so to the placing by the man of the male seed in the vagina, where impelled by its natural power, it seeks union with the female ovum, whence a new being is formed. The final biological term is the new being.

Biologically speaking, the joining of the sexual organs is natural and complete when the semen has been placed by the penis in the vagina, thus permitting the final term, and the human partners have fulfilled their biological function in the furtherance of life. The biological pattern then is sexual duality leading to a union designed to issue in life.

But man is not a biological specimen. He is a self-conscious person, capable of knowing and conforming freely to the demands of his nature. The eventual union which his sexual nature makes possible derives or should derive from a free and reasonable development of the mutual knowledge and attraction of man and woman into personal love. As two intellectual and free beings they know and love each other. Man is drawn to give himself completely to his beloved. At the psychological level, love's self-giving which is expressed in sexual union, proclaims its openness to life.

An enclosed two-in-one selfishness does not allow the love which they share to expand and develop as it should. Unless their love is fruitful, as all true love at whatever level should be, unless it retains that natural impetus which seeks to find expression and to perpetuate itself in a third term, it degenerates. The partners who fear life soon render their love sterile. Seeking to enjoy themselves in a closed circle, they find that their mutual giving becomes rather mutual possession. The husband who in the most intimate expression of love restrains the completeness of his giving by refusing his substance to his wife, and the wife who refuses to receive that substance and yet seeks complete satisfaction, may find at the psychological level, that each is using the other simply for that satisfaction. Selfishness has replaced self-giving. The personal development and perfection which marriage should give, emotionally and psychologically, is thwarted. The person is reduced to the level of an instrument – an instrument of bodily pleasure. To possess in this way, says Simone Weil, is to defile. So far then from promoting the personal values which are so important in marriage, a love which is divorced from life and life-giving retards rather than develops. And this applies to maturity at the sexual level as well as at the other levels of personality. The oft-quoted words of Sigmund Freud underline this:

> The common characteristic of all perversions, on the other hand, is that they have abandoned reproduction as their aim. We term sexual activity perverse when it has renounced the aim of reproduction and follows the pursuit of pleasure as an independent goal. And so you realise that the turning point in the development of sexual life lies in its subjugation to the purpose of reproduction. Everything this side of the turning point, everything that has given up this purpose and serves the pursuit of pleasure alone, must carry the term 'perverse' and as such be regarded with contempt.[19]

Freud's clinical experience and sharp insight confirmed the age-old observation that sexual pleasure and sexual union are by man's natural design directed to the generation of life, and that an attempt to divorce them from that aim is perverse. It is only man who can attempt that perversion, as a free and knowing being. And it is only human love which suffers in its refusal to recognise the divine plan in nature which at the biological and psychological level draws together the diverse organs and persons in a union which issues in new life.

The human and the natural are made in the image of God. This is true in particular of the human tendency to love. For God is love. And when God made man in his own image, male and female he made them. The union of God and his people which was constantly described in terms of the love of man and wife and which has reached a new perfection in the union of Christ and his church is the most fruitful union that we know on earth. Here love is inextricably bound up with life. The pattern of duality of person, unity in love and new life is continually repeated. So much so that St Paul appealed to husband and wife to model themselves on this unity of which they would be a symbol.

And there is a still more exalted and daring divine model of human love and marriage. At the very heart of the divinity lies the Trinity. God is love and that love, as expressed in the Trinity, forms the basis and pattern of married love. For the Father is not the Son and from this duality or otherness in the one divine nature issues as the fruit of their love, the Holy Spirit.

Beyond the Trinity no man can go. This is the centre and source of the universe and of all love in the universe. The love and fruitfulness of the Trinity provide the ultimate basis and model in any analysis of human love and fruitfulness.

To be true to itself at the different levels of animal, person and member of Christ, man's love must follow the pattern of union through self-giving which is destined for new life. It is impossible to speak of married love without reference to its life-giving aspect. And this has led many authorities to describe the procreational purpose of marriage and the marriage act as *la fin la plus spécifique*.[20] In this sense, as the ultimately specifying end which distinguishes the married community from all other communities (the predominant interest of the Code) and married love from all other loves (also in the mind of the Holy Office), procreation and education are described as the primary end of marriage. And what is last in the order of execution, in this case procreation and education, is first in the order of intention. Yet to divorce this end from the community and the love which it specifies, so that the marriage act is regarded simply as an instrument of procreation and one partner *uses* the other for this purpose, is a serious distortion of the church's teaching and an insult to human dignity.

It is as an expression of love that the procreative union of husband and wife is worthily performed. The new life must be the fruit of their love. And in co-operating with the Creator in the formation of a human being, lovable in himself, they act conscious of their dignity and vocation as persons and sons of God.

The two ends are not separable. They are not even completely distinct. Married love tends to fruition in new life. New life should be the fruit of love. And in this mutual love and self-surrender which finds eventual expression in the love and service of their gift to each other – the child – the marriage partners attain their perfection. The immediate end and the one that is frequently predominant psychologically, is their love for each other, its expression and development. But that love and its expression in their union seeks fresh life – the ultimately specifying end of the institution of marriage. This does not subject or enslave the partners to any abstract good such as the continuation of the species. There is no enslavement when man takes account of his nature. That way lies freedom. And it is not a question simply of preserving the life of a species, even the human species, but of helping in the creation and call of new persons who will be members of Christ and eventually the elect of God.

Different kinds of life – Education
To describe marriage as a source of life demands some fuller discussion of the nature of that life. The transmission of physical life to new members of the race, important and necessary as it is, does not by any means exhaust the life-giving capacity and duty of the married couple. Not only must new beings be brought into the world, they must be fed and nurtured and educated to the stage where they themselves can go out into the world as mature persons capable of achieving their own perfection and of handing on in their turn the physical and spiritual goods of mankind to the next generation. The life for which the marriage partners are responsible is not merely the physical life of the children but their emotional, intellectual and religious lives as well.

Life at all these levels which is transmitted by education must, like the physical life of the child, be born in love. Much has been written in recent times about the extent to which the child's first experiences influence his emotional and mental development. The most striking if rather obvious conclusion of all this study is the necessity of an atmosphere of unselfish love between parents for the development of a child free from emotional and neurotic stress. Too many emotional and mental disorders may be traced to unhappy childhood in a divided, loveless home, to the selfishness of a tyrannical father or over-possessive mother. Without the parents' self-sacrifice for each other and for their children which is the hallmark of true love, the genuine education of the children will not be achieved.

This life transmitted by education must also be religious. Generation must be followed by regeneration at baptism. The whole physical, emotional and in-

AN IRISH READER IN MORAL THEOLOGY

tellectual growth of the child must be set in its proper supernatural context in the following of Christ. Religious education includes some knowledge of the teaching of Christ, the practice of prayer and moral training. And it must be based on and issue from love. Too many religious lapses, as well as too many emotional and mental failures, trace their origin to a loveless religion in childhood. 'No life without love' applies above all to the highest form of life, the supernatural and religious.

Education then forms part of what is called the primary end of marriage, the transmission of new life. The love which issues in the physical generation of the new being must serve the new life by providing adequately for its education. Neglect of this aspect of the specific or primary end of marriage has frequently led to a misunderstanding of Catholic teaching.

Responsible Parenthood

The Catholic Church does not maintain that a couple must have as many children as they physically can. Parenthood and child-bearing may not be reduced to the satisfaction of instinctual desire. There is no merit because there is no humanity in the attitude that places all the stress on the physical integrity of the act without any thought for the consequences. Procreation and education form a unit – to take responsibility for one involves taking responsibility for the other. Marriage is designed to serve both.

Responsible parenthood involves providing effectively for the educational needs of the children. For many couples today this means some prior consideration of the frequency and perhaps the number of children. As rational beings, not creatures of instinct, the couple must consider how the children who are to be born of their love may be best cared for. Their own circumstances, physical, economic and psychological, may compel them to consider spacing their children and perhaps occasionally placing an upper limit to the number. This is sometimes imperatively demanded by dangers to the life of woman or child or by their extreme poverty. Other times the reasons are less urgent, but no less real.

Such family-regulation does not contradict the law of love and life on which marriage is based.[21] It cannot detract from the completeness of married love and its openness to life, to guide its expression by reason. The true spontaneity of human love must be preserved, but it should not be confused with submission to instinctual movements. Human love and the spontaneity which so often adorns its expression are deepened and enriched by this control of reason. It does not reveal any lack of confidence in God to consider how one's vocation to co-operate in forming new members of the race and of Christ's Body may be best fulfilled. Trust in God's providence implies no irresponsible abandonment to fate and fortune.

Yet, if family regulation is to safeguard the human and divine values on which marriage is based, it must spring from love's openness to live and not deform the expression of that love in the marriage act. It is meant to enrich the family, not to extinguish it. It aims at the fuller attainment of the procreational, educational and love-ends of marriage, not at the relapse into selfishness through self-indulgence and the avoidance of life. Only in so far as it derives from love and serves life, has it a place in marriage. To achieve that, it must observe the God-given laws of our nature. Family regulation, however desirable, may not be attempted through the deformation of the sexual act by contraception.

The observance of continence on the other hand, absolute or periodic, does not distort the sexual act. And where it is inspired by love and combined with the desire to serve life through adequate education, the protection of the health of the mother or children and so on, it is clearly in harmony with the demands of the married state. The discipline which continence involves gives the parties an opportunity to mature in their love of each other and in its expression as well as in their sexual attitudes. As a mode of family regulation, the avoidance of the fertile period through periodic continence differs essentially from the use of contraceptives.[22] The life-directed tendency of the physical act is preserved intact and the complete self-giving in love which the act expresses is in no way frustrated. And where the restriction is practised from love to promote life, the total value of the marriage commitment is recognised and strengthened. So Pius XII on more than one occasion recommended this mode of family regulation.[23]

Family and Society

In treating of marriage as a source of life, it would be a mistake to focus attention exclusively on the family in itself. From the life within it, physical, cultural and religious, passes the boundaries of the family into the wider communities in church and State. The life of these greater societies depends to a large extent on that life and openness to life of the family.

The religious life of the parish is relative to the vigour of the religious life of the individual families. A vital Christian family is not an isolated unit but a great source of life for the local community and the universal church. The grace it diffuses by its very presence, the example it gives and the active role it plays in parish organisations are commonplaces of experience. At the supremely life-giving level in the church – the sacramental – the family by its united participation at the table of the Lord, by its nurturing of vocations to the sacramental ministry of the priesthood and by its preparation of its members for the sacrament of matrimony, plays a major role.

The life-giving function of the family in secular society is no less obvious and important. The enrichment of human society at all levels owes much to the encouragement and development given to individual talent in the family.

AN IRISH READER IN MORAL THEOLOGY

Apart from the more specialised goods of society, the spirit of love and regard for the human person which should inspire it, depend on the richness of its family life.

Childless Marriages

In this general scheme of marriage as source of life, childless couples have their due place.[24] Although God has not blessed them with the normal fruit of married love, their marriage and their acts of love within that marriage are not cut off from life or fruitless. Their own growth in love and their perfection as persons, in other words, the expansion and development of life in them, comes from their marriage and marriage acts. They should not regard the sexual act as merely a way of pleasure without any responsibility towards life, but as an expression of their complete giving to each other and so serving and enlarging their own lives. The very disappointment at having no children can be a source of maturity at the natural and supernatural levels.

And if they do not undertake some of the joys and responsibilities of parenthood by adopting children (and they should carefully consider this) they may contribute in more abundant fashion to the life of the society in which they live. With increased time and freedom they have the opportunity and obligation to take a more direct part in the religious and secular life of their community. Such couples can and should be important sources of vital activity in church and State.

Conclusion

As a community of love, marriage is distinguished from all other such communities by the sexual character of its love specifically directed towards life. New life through the procreation (and education) of children is the specifying or primary end of the marriage union and of the marriage act. But that union and that act must, if they are to be human and be achieved in a way worthy of human persons, be the expression and result of love. If procreation (and education) and mutual love are to be regarded as the purposes (*fines*) of marriage, they are not only inseparable but, in the full concept of marriage as a community of love designed for life, hardly adequately distinct.

Update

'Source of Life', a companion piece to Bernard Häring's 'Community of Love' was presented to the Maynooth Union Summer School in July 1962 before Vatican II had begun. In the light of the Council (1962-1965) and of the later *Humanae Vitae* (1968) and of the reactions of Bishops' Conferences, theologians and married faithful to these events, I came to the conclusion that, while the married relationship and its sexual expression should always be open to life at diverse levels, the individual act of intercourse may not always be open to new biological life. *E. McD.*

Notes:

1. Cf 'Community of Love', *The Meaning of Christian Marriage*, pp 62-74 .
2. Gen 1:27-28.
3. Gen 2:18, 24.
4. An excellent account of the relationship between the biological data and morality in marriage is given by J Fuchs SJ, 'Biologie und Ehemoral', *Gregorianum*, XLIII (1962), 225-253.
5. Cf Hos 1-3, etc. v supra 'Marriage in Scripture'.
6. Cf Rondet, *Introduction à l'étude de la théologie du marriage*, Paris 1960, 130 ff.
7. Can. 1013, par 1.
8. Cf Fuchs, loc. cit.
9. *AAS* 36 (1944), 103 (1 April 1944). English translation taken from de Fabrègues, *Christian Marriage*, London 1959, 42.
10. Fuchs, *Die Sexualethik des heiligen Thomas von Aquin*, Cologne, 1948; id, 'Die Ehezwechlehre des hl. Thomas von Aquin', *Theol. Quartalschrift*, 128 (1948), 398-426; id, 'Von Sinn der Ehe', *Trier. Zwitschrift*, 58 (1949), 65-75.
11. *Suppl.*, 41, 1c; 49, 2 ad 1; 111, 29, 2c, etc.
12. *Suppl.* 65, 1c.
13. *S. theol.*, II-II, 154, 2.
14. *Suppl.*, 41, 4c; I-II, 24 ad 1; II-II, 153, 2.
15. *S. Theol*, I, 92, 1c.
16. Cf Häring, *The Law of Christ*, I (E. tr.) Cork 1961 14 ff.
17. Fuchs, art. cit., *Gregorianum*, XLIII, 1962.
18. Häring, *Das Gesetz Christi*, III, Freiburg im B. 1961, 335-6.
19. Freud, *General Introduction to Psycho-analysis*, New York 1920, 273.
20. L. J. Suenens, *Un problème crucial: amour et maîtrise de soi*, Bruges 1960, 106 (E. tr., *Love and Control*, London 1961, 94); P. Anciaux, *Le Sacrement du marriage*, Louvain-Paris 1961, 113; B Häring, *Ehe in dieser Zeit*, Salzburg 1960, 351; id, *Das Gesetz Christi*, Freiburg im B. 1961, 321; J Fuchs, 'Biologie und Ehe', *Gregorianum*, XLIII (1962), 246.
21. For a full discussion of this problem, cf de Lestapis, *Family Planning and Modern Problems, A Catholic Analysis*, London 1961.
22. Cf de Lestapis, op. cit., 180 ff.
23. Cf *Address to Fronte della Famiglia*, 26 November 1951.
24. Cf Guitton, *Essay on Human Love*, London 1960, 95-97.

9   The Call to Communion

Cathy Molloy

(*The Furrow*, Vol 55, No 5, May 2004, pp 273-280)

In her article, 'Expanding the Language of Love' (*The Furrow*, December 2003), Anne Thurston raises some important points which are significant for our understanding of human relationships in all their diversity, and of beings as called 'into relationship or communion with one another and ultimately, and essentially with God, who is Love.'[1]

Prompting this article is specifically her reference to the call to love, to *communion*, (my italics), which I believe is more fundamental than any of the labels we put on any of our relationships.

I come to this discussion primarily from the perspective of the theology of marriage and specifically from what many people now consider the impasse that is operative in relation to marriage, divorce, and the Catholic Church, whereby second unions are tolerated but, to participate fully in the Eucharist, couples must exclude sexual intercourse from their shared life. In considering these matters it becomes more obvious that much of what is at issue here is at issue also in other relationships.

The major shift in Roman Catholic theology of marriage at Vatican II which now understands marriage as a covenant, an interpersonal relationship, continues to have far reaching effects. The centrality of love in this relationship is expressed in *Gaudium et spes* with terms such as 'a community of love' (47) used to describe marriage.

Several factors are reflected in the developing theology: the fruits of the return to biblical sources characteristic of Vatican II, for example the notion of covenant and the retrieval of the Song of Songs; developments in the human sciences; insights from the experience of married people. In theology, therefore, there is new awareness of what marriage is, and what it could and should be. Consequently there must be also new awareness of what marriage is not, and what it could not and should not be.

Karl Rahner on Personal Love

In this year of the centenary of his birth, I draw on the writing of Karl Rahner to look more closely at the question of what he calls the 'personal love at the heart of the marriage relationship' in an attempt to be more specific about what is the nature of this love. Just two years after *Gaudium et spes,* in his essay *Marriage As Sacrament* (1967) Rahner treats this topic at some length.

Rahner sees marriage as a sign of personal love at the physical and social level before it is a sacrament. He understands this love of husband and wife for one another (in all its aspects) as from, of, and oriented to God, as acquiring fresh roots through grace and uniting the whole of humanity. In describing personal love thus, I believe Rahner overcomes the spiritual/physical divide that has been so characteristic of talk of love in the Christian tradition. For Rahner love of God and love of neighbour mutually condition one another. Creation is God's self-communication, and he believes God is primarily recognisable in personal interrelationships. Because it is God's love that sustains creation, gives humans life and love, and draws all to God through this love, the love between two people can lead them to reach each other at the deepest level of their being. The personal love which manifests itself in marriage is salvific through its source in the love of God, and intends God not only in the transcendent but in the nearness in which God's self is revealed – the innermost mystery and life of the human person.[2] In short Rahner is saying what we hear so often – where love is, there is God. At some fundamental level people know this. Many couples know this, at least sometimes and to some degree, through the experience of their life together, and perhaps especially through their experience of sexual love as the expression of their desire for unity. Those who wrote of the love described in the Song of Songs as the 'flame of Yahweh'[3] knew this.

I think that the wide significance of Rahner's contribution is based in his belief that all of creation is graced, animated by God's own self-communication. All human love therefore, in so far as it is a going out of self and reaching towards another, is a reaching for God, and even a making present of God's love in our world. Implicit here is that sexual love also belongs in God's love and is of itself sacramental. Although he assumes children to be the natural fruit of this love, Rahner does not suggest that its purpose is other than to draw humans to their Creator and to one another. A most welcome aspect of this understanding is that love need not be split into categories, that God is present in all love. It may be that theologians and other searchers will turn again to Rahner in trying to come to the truth of love in the many human relationships that are not marriage and are yet waiting to be included in the human view of God's saving love.

Rahner's work in this area can be considered a bridge between Vatican II teaching and the subsequent development of theological reflection on the explicitly sexual aspects of marital love in that the way was opened to consider sexual desire, sexual passion and pleasure as sacramental and place of God's encounter with men and women, as means to holiness. The articulation of these has given theology access to new ways of including what was so often excluded from Christian teaching on marriage, with even John Paul II following the trend with his *Theology of the Body* (1997).[4] The almost exclusive, centuries old, appropriation of the Song of Songs by the mystics and those who allegorised it, is redressed by its retrieval for those whose story it primarily and properly is – ordinary men and women whose love for one another is also particularly graced by God, and no less special for being bodily expressed.

The other side of the coin

Awareness of the issue of violence and abuse within marriage and other relationships has been significantly raised in recent years, but there is a lacuna in relation to it in much contemporary theology. Rosemary Haughton's (1987) unforgettable reference to 'a theology of marriage shattered by experience', and the work of some few other theologians, men and women, have been showing the way but still seem not to have been taken seriously in official church teaching and writing on marriage and family. Could clear teaching on what marriage is be accompanied by equally clear teaching on what marriage *is not*? Could the enunciating of the kind of relationship and the behaviours that exemplify Christian marriage sometimes be accompanied by enunciation of some of the more common behaviours that are a travesty of Christian relationship? The reluctance to spell things out regarding violent and abusive marital relationships is striking.

There is growing awareness now of the extent of the problems of marriage breakdown and the consequences suffered by particular women and men and children. As church, in spite of the great work of Accord and other groups, for the most part, we have stood by and failed to show even a minimum level of concern that might be expected of a Christian community. With some few notable exceptions, lay members of the church together with clergy and religious share the responsibility for this. I am referring to the sense of alienation and isolation reported by many in the church whose experience within the church is primarily one of rejection. For many, reintegration of their lives takes place apart from the church which is experienced as unsympathetic. Because of exclusion from the sacraments, due to being in a new relationship, many people see themselves in a 'limbo' situation. They carry the rejection of a failed marriage and they experience rejection by the church. Individual stories about how people have experienced the annulment tribunal make pathetic listening as they recount long years of waiting for their case to be heard, and their very real sense of injustice at the hands of our church, which is otherwise ready to preach to the world about justice. Justice within the church should be as important as the seeking of justice for whatever group. These people feel they are the forgotten ones, the marginalised. And we do well to remember that these are the voices of those who have begun to speak. This injustice within our church is compounded by the fact that too many people have no voice. They have neither the possibility nor the capacity to become involved in lengthy, and costly, and complex procedures, due to lack of money or education, or emotional or psychological strength or stamina or, most often, a combination of all these factors.[5]

In *Familiaris consortio*, (1981), his apostolic exhortation on 'The Community of the Family', Pope John Paul II calls for the church community to support such people, to give them much respect, solidarity, understanding and practical help. For far too many of them the experience is as already described. It has been noted (Parent, 1987) that priests, bishops, and the Pope may well utilise a vocabulary of service, at the same time accompanied by behaviour patterns of power and exclusion. Alongside this is the genuine difficulty of many people in accepting current church discipline that tolerates the common life of a union after divorce but requires that sexual intercourse be excluded in order to participate fully in the Eucharist.

When Communion becomes a burden

In other words, people in this situation are excluded from communion. A heavy burden is placed on them as they are asked, or expected, to make a choice between two kinds of communion. There is the communion that is vital to Christian life, participation in the union of love between Christ and the church, which is signified and effected by the Eucharist, and which their state and condition of life is said objectively to contradict.[6] And there is the communion that is participation in the union of love between the partners, which is signified and effected by sexual intercourse. Both kinds of communion can be occasions of graced experience. Perhaps in so far as the call to communion is to a way of being present with one another and with God who is love, communion is indivisible. If God's love is present in all love, is it right that we seek to split that love, to divide and subdivide it? Could it be that in some instances, rather than contradicting the union of love between Christ and the church, couples who have divorced and remarried might rather be contributing to the sign of that love in the church and in the world?

The special pastoral reason for not admitting the divorced and remarried to the Eucharist, that the faithful would be led into error and confusion regarding the church's teaching about the indissolubility of marriage, may not be so obviously applicable today. With wider education, and the many new means of providing it, might not the faithful be capable of discerning some of the subtler points of the teaching? Might they not be able to distinguish, as the faithful in the Orthodox Church are considered capable of doing, between a first marriage and a subsequent blessing of a marriage, after divorce and the requirements of the church have been met? It may be that this is already happening and that, more than twenty years later, the question of scandal is seen more in terms of the scandal of exclusion than of a lax approach to marriage. Many faithful people find it difficult, even impossible, to understand and accept what they see as excessively rigid and harsh treatment of people in second unions alongside the acceptance and welcome afforded sometimes to people who may be involved in serious exploitation of their fellow human beings. Education for this scandal is needed too.

Impasse

To refer to the current situation regarding marriage, divorce and the Catholic

Church as one of impasse, is not thereby to oppose the ideal of marriage as indissoluble. It is, however, to name the reality that now exists, and to recognise the growing credibility gap within and outside the church. The negative public image attributed to the annulment procedure may not be wholly justified. However, until there is an end to much of the secrecy surrounding it, and a more obvious transparency in terms of how judgements are arrived at, it will remain an unsatisfactory, and in some cases even an unjust way to deal with marriage breakdown.

Impasse and signs of Saving Grace

Naming the present situation as one of impasse is not to imply that remarriage in the church is necessarily the answer. The absolute ban on remarriage in the church would not have to be compromised by offering some welcome, or asking God's blessing on couples in second unions who sincerely desire to belong fully and actively to their church community. In many cases it is obvious that God's blessing is already there, and some formal recognition of this could be a basis for the strengthening of their family bonds. One can only imagine the new life it would bring to the church as a whole. The fact that the exclusion of so many from the Eucharist is a *de facto* exclusion of their children also is another reason for seriously reconsidering the discipline. Assurances that they are part of the church ring hollow when accompanied by the ongoing exclusion from the Eucharist which many experience as rejection, however it is expressed.

I think there are untapped saving graces in theology too which can help. One such might be to look closely at the relationship between liberation and salvation which is central to the discussion on communion in both senses at issue in this article. *Gaudium et spes* speaks about the relationship between temporal, earthly progress and the growth of the kingdom. The one is said to be of 'vital concern' to the other, in so far as it can contribute to the better ordering of human society. Gustavo Gutierrez (1974) affirms the 'global character of the gratuitous gift of God's love'.[7] This affects all areas of human life. We can and should distinguish between the natural and supernatural, but they are ultimately unified. There is only one actual order of salvation, not one of the history of grace and a separate history of nature. Christ brings us liberation from sin, the ultimate root of all disruption of friendship and of all injustice and oppression, to a sharing in the life of God. Salvation is the completion of liberation, communion with God and communion with one another. Gutierrez points out that the kingdom of God is not reducible to human history or human progress, but without historical liberative events there would be no growth in the kingdom. God's saving power is revealed through saving actions in history and through human events. Liberation includes every dimension of humanity, and salvation embraces all human reality, transforming it, leading it to its fullness in Christ. It is the presence of grace in everyone, accepted or rejected, that is important.

Where is grace in the perspective of the many people who find themselves in the impasse described above? Simple questions direct the answer. Where is God to be encountered by human beings today? Where is God to be encountered among the groups who are marginalised by their churches because of what is termed their 'irregular situations'? Does salvation begin now in our liberating graced experiences?

For some, perhaps many, their salvation begins through their re-finding of their self-esteem, of their capacity to go beyond self in loving a new partner, in loving and caring for the children of that union. This is not to imply that salvation can ever be complete in this life. But a question remains. Do we co-operate with grace or do we block it? Of course we block grace by our personal sin, but it may be true also that, as church, we block grace by some of our structures or laws for dealing with internal problems, or particular applications of those laws or structures. It may be that in some instances it is a refusal of grace, rather than a recognising and working with it, that is pushing people to the margins and leading to the kinds of experiences described above.

Communion calls all of us
Returning to Ann Thurston's reminder that we are all called out of ourselves and into relationship or communion with one another and ultimately with God, who is Love, I am heartened by the opening out of the discussion on love and communion in its varied expressions. I am hopeful that we are being led to a way of dealing with the impasse which would more closely approach the truth of who we are as a community of followers of Jesus today. I believe there is struggling to emerge a way which respects our understanding of marriage as an indissoluble relationship, and yet recognises, at the same time, that absolute certainty in all cases is beyond us. Ultimately only God knows all. I am encouraged by the sense that what will emerge will be a more accurate representation of the love God has shown us in Jesus Christ, reflective of the justice, compassion, mercy, and forgiveness we believe in and hope for, in our understanding of salvation.

There is need to reiterate our aspirations towards the Christian ideal of marriage and of other relationships and to accompany this with ongoing education and much greater support for people in difficulties. There is need at the same time to acknowledge what is unsaid, unacknowledged, in the present situation. As far as marriage is concerned the present situation of widespread exclusion, far from strengthening marriage, may be contributing, not insignificantly, to its weakening. Undoubtedly it is weakening the church and we are deprived of many good people, resulting in what may be a refusal of the Spirit as it is within the whole people of God. Change of course involves risk. We can only imagine what might be the positive outcome, for the whole church, and indeed society, of including the divorced and remarried who sincerely want to participate fully. Given what we know from other disciplines of the benefits of reasonable family life, with support and welcome from the church community, it could prove transformative.

Notes:

1. 'Expanding the Language of Love', *The Furrow* (December 2003) p 650.
2. Karl Rahner, 'Marriage as Sacrament', in *Theological Investigations*, (New York: Herder &Herder, 1973) vol X, pp 199-121.
3. Song of Songs, 8:7, *Jerusalem Bible*, Popular Edition (London: Darton Longman &Todd, 1974), p 874.
4. C. Molloy, *Marriage: Theology and Reality*, (Dublin: Columba, 1996), chapter 3.
5. These comments are based on the experience of listening and working with individuals and groups dealing with the issue of marriage breakdown and the church.
6. John Paul II, *Familiaris consortio*, n 84.
7. Gustavo Gutierrez, *A Theology of Liberation*, (London: SCM, 1974), p 177.

10   Autonomy, commitment and marriage

William Binchy

(William Binchy and Oran Doyle (eds), *Committed Relationships and the Law*, Dublin: Four Courts Press, 2007, pp 159-180)

In Ireland today, as in the western world generally, a great debate is taking place about the nature of marriage. I welcome this debate because of its radical character. In contrast to the past three decades or so, in which the rhetoric of no-fault divorce predictably, but to some degree insidiously, transformed the meaning of marriage, without exposing the philosophical core of the issue for public discussion, today we are grappling openly with the crucial issues. What does marriage mean? Is a procreative dimension essential? Does marriage necessarily involve a commitment that is, 'in principle',[1] lifelong? Must spouses be of differing sexes?

Broader questions relate to identifying the best models of interpersonal relationship for rearing children and to how society can most effectively encourage these models to be chosen and to flourish. Debate on these questions involves a complex conjunction of empirical and normative considerations. The empirical issues range over such matters as whether divorce impoverishes women and children, whether a liberal law weakens marital stability and whether married or unmarried cohabitation is a preferable environment in which to rear children. The normative considerations relate to the extent to which society is entitled to encourage people to choose particular models of relationship (by tax breaks or by the denial of legal recognition to particular relationships, for example) and the extent to which the common good should trump the values of privacy and autonomy and the principle of pluralism. I shall not seek to address the empirical issues although they are, of course, crucial in the determination of future social policy on marriage and on committed relationships generally. Instead I shall restrict myself to considering a narrower question. In the light of the values of dignity, privacy, autonomy and pluralism, which have gained a certain ascendancy in contemporary culture, can a case be made out for the legal recognition of irrevocable lifelong commitment? I shall not here be arguing for the abolition of Article 41.3.2 of the Constitution, which prescribes a divorce jurisdiction.[2] Rather shall I be offering for consideration the argument that the law should respect the option of lifelong commitment as an alternative to the option of marriage subject to access to divorce.

It has to be acknowledged that, in the years before the constitutional amendment of 1995 providing for divorce, some people felt that our law was unnecessarily restrictive in recognising[3] only one model of interpersonal relationship – irrevocable lifelong commitment. This single model, while seeking to accomplish important social goals relating to encouraging a secure environment for the rearing of children, scarcely reflected a high degree of respect to the value of pluralism. Yet, what was done in 1995 was the replacement of one model by another model: marriage subject to divorce. The only way in which people can receive legal recognition for their interpersonal relationship in this state is by entering into a commitment which the law insists must be revocable in character. Even as spouses commit to marry until death do them part, the law hears their commitment differently and treats them as having made a commitment of a quite different character. Whatever force the arguments in favour of divorce may have, the values of privacy, autonomy and pluralism are sacrificed by the adoption of a single model of relationship which contradicts the free choice of those who seek legal support for an irrevocable commitment.

HUMAN DIGNITY, PRIVACY, AUTONOMY AND PLURALISM

As a first element in my argument, I wish to consider briefly the four norms of human dignity, privacy, autonomy and pluralism. Each of these norms celebrates the unique value of every human person. Together, they seek to cherish the inherent worth of the individual and the moral power of free human choice.

Human dignity

Human dignity[4] is the core value of international human rights instruments.[5] The Preamble to the Charter of the United Nations in 1945 and the Preamble to the Universal Declaration on Human Rights in 1948 both refer to 'the dignity and worth of the human person'. Both the International Covenant on Civil and Political Rights and the International Covenant on Economic, Social and Cultural Rights recognise 'the inherent dignity and … the equal and inalienable rights of all members of the human family' as the foundation of freedom, justice and peace in the world. Dignity is a value underlying the Irish Constitution.

The concept of human dignity is of an ancient pedigree.[6] Its philosophical origins may be found in Greek philosophy and in Judeo-Christian insight into the unique value and equal worth of every human being.[7]

This insight sadly is not a constant feature of human understanding. Every generation loses its capacity to appreciate the value and worth of some human beings, white or black, men or women, heterosexual, gay or bisexual.

The Preamble to the UN Charter speaks of reaffirming 'faith in human rights, in the dignity and worth of the human person …'[8] The use of such a term with its religious connotations is important in reminding us that our journey from empirical to normative insight does require some internal decision of commitment to the moral significance of human existence.[9]

The Irish Constitution refers to the subject in the Preamble where the 'people of Éire', 'seeking to promote the common good, with due observance of Prudence, Justice and Charity, so that the dignity and freedom of the individual may be assured ...', adopt the Constitution. The Preamble does not enlarge on the nature of 'the dignity and freedom of the individual'.

In *Molyneux v. Ireland*[10] the plaintiff, who was charged with assault under section 28 of the Dublin Police Act 1842, argued that the Act was inconsistent with the Constitution on the basis that it violated the guarantee of equal treatment given by Article 40.1 since that Act gave a power of arrest which had no counterpart outside the Dublin area. Costello P rejected this argument, stating:

The preamble to the Constitution declares that by enacting it the people of Ireland were, *inter alia*, seeking to promote the common good so that the 'dignity and freedom' of the individual might be assured, and it required by Article 40.1 that all citizens 'as human persons' should be held equal before the law. The concepts thereby enshrined are ones which, quite literally, are universally recognised. The 1948 UN Declaration of Human Rights refers in its preamble to 'the inherent dignity of all members of the human family' and declares in Article 1 that 'all human beings are born free and equal in dignity and rights'. Innumerable laws are enacted in every state which treat differently one group or category of persons from other groups or categories of persons by imposing detriments or conferring benefits on one group or category and not on others. Every law which so provides does not of course breach the concept contained in Article 40.1 of the Constitution or Article 1 of the Universal Declaration ... The Supreme Court has explained why. The guarantee in the Constitution is not a guarantee of absolute equality for all citizens in all circumstances, but is a guarantee of equality as human persons relating to their dignity as human beings and a guarantee against inequalities based on the assumption that some individuals because of their human attributes, ethnic, racial, social or religious background are to be treated as inferior or the superior of other individuals in the community.[11]

This perception of dignity as inhering in the human person rather than being contingent on particular external realities is undoubtedly in harmony with the natural law philosophy grounding the Constitution.

In the *In re Ward of Court (No. 2)*,[12] dignity was treated in a radically new way by Denham J. For the first time she identified a right to dignity, in contrast to the perception of dignity as a quality inhering in the human person. She stated:

An unspecified right under the Constitution to (*sic*) all persons as human persons is dignity – to be treated with dignity. Such right is not lost by illness or accident. As long as a person is alive they have this right. Thus, the ward in this case has a right to dignity. Decisionmaking in relation to medical treatment is an aspect of the right to privacy; however, a component in the decision may relate to personal dignity. Is the ward, as described by Brennan J in his dissenting judgement in *Cruzan v. Director, Missouri Department of Health*,[13] 'a passive prisoner of medical technology'? If that be so, is it in keeping with her right as a human person to dignity? Just as 'the individual's right to privacy grows as the degree of bodily invasion increases'[14], so too the dignity of a person is progressively diminished by increasingly invasive medicine.[15]

Denham J considered that a range of factors had to be taken into account by the court in determining where the best interests of the ward lay. These included the wards 'constitutional right to ... (e) Dignity in life. (f) Dignity in death.'[16]

Denham J did not seek to analyse the constitutional 'right to dignity' further. So far as one can see from her brief description of the right, she appeared to regard a person's dignity as being capable of being diminished by invasive medicine; the greater the degree of invasiveness, the greater the consequent diminution of the person's dignity. Dignity would appear thus to be determined by reference to the extent to which the values of autonomy and privacy are compromised by external factors. Dignity, on this view, is not the inherent and equal worth of every person but rather a more fragile and contingent phenomenon, dependent on how others, or even fate, may treat us.[16a]

In the same sense O'Flaherty J described the ward's life as 'technically ... life, but life without purpose, meaning or dignity.' Like Denham J, O'Flaherty J did not appear to regard dignity as a value inhering in the person but rather as a quality that can depart from the person by virtue of external circumstances.

It seems that these strands of judicial perception of dignity as not inhering in every human being are inconsistent with the understanding of dignity that underlies the international human rights instruments, in which dignity has such a prominent positon, as well as being hard to harmonise with the Preamble to the Constitution, which seems clearly premised on the inherent character of dignity.

An aspect of human dignity on which I seek to place emphasis is the freedom of the will. It is part of our essence as human beings[17] that we can exercise moral choice, not based on mere emotional preference but rather by reference to a normative system which we acknowledge as having binding force. We have the freedom to adhere to the norms of this system or to act inconsistently with them: in short, to act well or badly. Respect for human dignity does not seek to relieve us of this freedom or to deny the reality that we are moral agents. If society denies its citizens the opportunity to exercise moral freedom or pretends that people are incapable of making such choices, it contradicts our human dignity in a profound way.

Privacy
The right to privacy is recognised under our Constitution as a personal right

of the citizen. The manner of its recognition is curious. In *Norris v. Attorney General*,[18] the majority of the Supreme Court held that any putative right to privacy was trumped by a range of contervailing factors which rendered consistent with the Constitution the nineteenth-century criminal prohibitions on private male homosexual conduct. It is the minority judgements, however,which have provided the philosophical grounding of the right to privacy.

Henchy J stated:

That a right of privacy inheres in each citizen by virtue of his human personality, and that such right is constitutionally guaranteed as one of the unspecified personal rights comprehended by Article 40, s. 3, are propositions that are well attested by previous decisions of this Court. What requires to be decided – and this seems to me to be the essence of this case – is whether that right of privacy, construed in the context of the Constitution as a whole and given its true evaluation or standing in the hierarchy of constitutional priorities, excludes as constitutionally inconsistent the impugned statutory provisions.

Having regard to the purposive Christian ethos of the Constitution, particularly as set out in the preamble ('to promote the common good, with due observance of Prudence, Justice and Charity, so that the dignity and freedom of the individual may be assured, true social order attained, the unity of our country restored, and concord established with other nations'), to the denomination of the State as 'sovereign, independent, democratic' in Article 5, and to the recognition, expressly or by necessary implication, of particular personal rights, such recognition being frequently hedged in by overriding requirements such as 'public order and morality' or 'the authority of the State' or 'the exigencies of the common good', there is necessarily given to the citizen, within the required social, political and moral framework, such a range of personal freedoms or immunities as are necessary to ensure his dignity and freedom as an individual in the type of society envisaged. The essence of those rights is that they inhere in the individual personality of the citizen in his capacity as a vital human component of the social, political and moral order posited by the Constitution.

Amongst those basic personal rights is a complex of rights which vary in nature, purpose and range (each necessarily being a facet of the citizen's core of individuality within the constitutional order) and which may be compendiously referred to as the right of privacy. An express recognition of such a right is the guarantee in Article 16, s. 1, sub-s. 4, that voting in elections for Dáil Éireann shall be by secret ballot. A constitutional right to marital privacy was recognised and implemented by this Court in *McGee v. The Attorney General*,[19] the right there claimed and recognised being, in effect, the right of a married woman to use contraceptives, which is something which at present is declared to be morally wrong according to the official teaching of the church to which about 95% of the citizens belong. There are many other aspects of the right of privacy, some yet to be given judicial recognition. It is unnecessary for the purpose of this case to explore them. It is sufficient to say that they would all appear to fall within a secluded area of activity or non-activity which may be claimed as necessary for the expression of an individual personality, for purposes not always necessarily moral or commendable, but meriting recognition in circumstances which do not engender considerations such as State security, public order or morality, or other essential components of the common good.'

The last sentence captures the essence of the right. The 'secluded area of activity or non-activity' is not limited to physical seclusion: it clearly has metaphorical force. At the heart of the concept of the right to privacy is the expression of an individual personality: thus the rights of autonomy and dignity are inevitably engaged. Henchy J openly acknowledges – as Walsh J did in relation to the right to marital privacy – that the purposes for which the right is exercised need not necessarily be moral or commendable. The limiting factors are 'considerations such as State security, public order or *morality*, or other essential components of the common good.'[20] Formally, it could be argued that Henchy J's limiting factors are no less extensive than those proferred by O'Higgins CJ, but the right of privacy recognised by Henchy J has a reality and power which contrasts with the ghostly lack of substance of that right in the perception of the Chief Justice.

An argument that might at first appear attractive is that the right to privacy should confer on parties in intimate relationships the entitlement to conduct those relationships completely beyond the scrutiny of the law. The implication is that the right to privacy would be advanced by the dejuridification of marriage and the withdrawal of the law from its role in policing family relationships. Further reflection makes it clear that the concept of the right of privacy does not necessarily imply the absence of legal engagement. On the contrary, parties wishing to exercise their right to privacy are entitled to call on society through its laws to facilitate those choices that are integral to this right.

What does this mean for marriage and divorce? I would suggest that the following important implication is of direct relevance to the thesis that I am seeking to advance. Spouses who wish to marry for life should be let do so by our legal system. This does not mean that the law should be indifferent to that irrevocable commitment: still less does it mean that the law should positively interpret that commitment as being revocable (which is precisely what it is not). The spouses, in the exercise of their right to privacy, are entitled to have the law respect their choice fully by giving it legal effect.

One question that arises from the language of Walsh J in *McGee* and Henchy J in *Norris* has to be confronted. Both judges are strongly of the view that conduct judged by society to be immoral should nonetheless not be criminalised if it falls within the range of the exercise of the right to privacy. Does this mean that the right to privacy includes the right to act contrary to *one's own* value system? If it does, then it might be argued that, whereas respect for human dignity and autonomy entitles (or perhaps requires) the state to hold a person to his or her promise, the right to privacy requires the state to let the person break the promise without sanction. On that basis, the state would not be entitled to deny access to divorce to a promise-breaking person who had committed to a lifelong marriage. Apart from the inherent constitutional inconsistency that this argument involves, two points can be made in reply. First, neither Walsh J nor Henchy J gave a clear blessing to conduct inconsistent with the actor's value system. Secondly, both were speaking in the context of the imposition of a criminal sanction. This is quite different from that of marriage where the only 'sanction' that lifelong marital commitment involves is integral to the promise undertaken and not imposed by an external agency.

Autonomy

Autonomy is a value that has been recognised in Irish constitutional jurisprudence. It is clearly relevant to the question of committed relationships. At the heart of the notion of autonomy is the entitlement of the human person to fashion his or her own future destiny in accordance with that individual's values and existential vision rather than simply complying with a normative system imposed from on high by the state. The value of autonomy is closely linked to the values of dignity, liberty and privacy. All of these emphasise the unique worth and identity of every person and the need to preserve that identity from oppressive intrusions by the state.

Of course, autonomy cannot be permitted to trump other values, notably the protection of others and the common good. I have already indicated that in this paper I do not intend to engage in any process of assessing where the common good lies in the context of marriage. That important question is for another day.

The idea that society should interpret the expression of lifelong commitment as an expression of revocable commitment is surely at odds with respect for the value of autonomy. If the spouses on marrying make it plain beyond argument that they are committing themselves to exclude the option of future resort to divorce, society would not be truthfully responding to that exercise of autonomy by purporting to hear the commitment as less than lifelong in character. Society may, of course, choose to provide a model of marriage based on revocable commitment with a facility for divorce but this does not mean, in respect of those who have autonomously elected for lifelong commitment, that society should override their autonomy. The entitlement to act freely in accordance with one's value system is a clear instance of the exercise of autonomy, not its contradiction.

Pluralism

Pluralism is a value that seeks to accommodate diversity to the greatest extent-possible, consistent with the common good. Our courts[21] have recognised the-pluralist character of our Constitution, which is not based on any single religious perspective. Our society is composed of people with different traditions, philosophies, religious and worldviews. This diversity should be a source of celebration rather than concern.

SOME OBSERVATIONS ON THE NATURE OF COMMITMENT

It may be useful at this point of the argument to make some brief observation-son the nature of the commitment. The title of this book refers to the legal recognition of *committed* relationships: when, we may ask, is a relationship a committed one?

It may be suggested that commitment relates to the moral order. It is not reducible to emotions or to a particular psychological condition. It involves a positive disposition of the will, a free choice by a morally free being. On a determinist hypothesis, in which freedom of the will is an illusion, commitment here would be sucked dry of its moral component and measured exclusively in terms of the presence and intensity of particular psychological and emotional states, judged by empirical criteria relating to their continuity, actual and predicted. What a person said about his or her commitment would be but one (albeit important) piece of the data rather than presumptively representing the external aspect of an act of will.

Let us consider the question of the levels of commitment that a committed relationship can involve. It could be an unqualified and irrevocable one: I take you as my partner, in sickness or in health, no matter how wonderful or disappointing you – or the experience of being with you – may turn out, for as long as we both shall live. This is, of course, the essence of matrimonial commitment where marriage is lifelong in character.

The commitment could, however, be qualified to a limited or substantial extent: I take you as my partner for as long as you are kind to me, or for as long as I find the relationship fulfilling.[22]

Depending on the nature of the qualification, a question arises as to whether the commitment can truly be so described at all. Where, for example, the person making the commitment considers himself or herself free to walk away from the relationship if he or she no longer finds it fulfilling, one can enquire what the true content of commitment is in such a case. Commitment involves applying oneself to a particular goal, restricting or excluding present and future choices and acts that would otherwise have been entirely legitimate. In the delicate area of a personal relationship, where people are called on to exercise testing moral qualities – including patience, generosity, kindness and forgiveness – it seems questionable whether one can speak meaningfully of commitment when the proviso or qualification to the commitment made does not in fact restrict the person's range of choice in the future.

THE CENTRAL THESIS RECONSIDERED

Let me now attempt to reconsider the central thesis of the paper, in the light of the values of human dignity, autonomy, privacy and pluralism which I have adumbrated. What I am trying to encourage is a new beginning, in which the historical accretions of our culture are for the moment ignored and which does not seek to make a prudential assessment of where the common good may direct socio-legal policy on committed relationships. Of course, we are not deracinated individuals with no concern for what is good for our society, but the time has surely come for removing the clutter of old debates from our minds and openly assessing the issue in the light of values that have gained a particular prominence in contemporary society but have not, perhaps, yet been fully analysed. When subjected to that analysis, they show themselves to be the friends, not the enemies, of the deepest moral choices for good that human beings are capable of making.

Whilst many of the most potent emotive arguments in favour of divorce appeal ostensibly to facts – notably the fact of the dead marriage relationship – they contain premises rooted in distinct and identifiable values. These values derive principally from one of two competing sources. The first is that of determinism, which regards human decisions as resulting from a complex combination of social, economic, physical and psychological stimuli rather than as involving free choice. If human beings have no freedom of the will, then it would be cruelty to inflict on them the consequences of decisions that they may have believed at the time were freely made but which were not in fact so. The second, opposing, value does acknowledge freedom of the will but elevates the exercise of choice to a supreme position. On this approach, the exercise of autonomy takes priority over the constraints of moral claims by others for solidarity or support or to the constraints of an earlier exercise of autonomy by the same autonomous being. According to this approach, if I choose to commit myself in one way today, I should be free to commit myself in the opposite way tomorrow. I should be no more the slave of my own past choices than I should be the slave of another person.[23]

The introduction of divorce in 1995 has replaced a single definition of marriage by another single definition of marriage. There are several difficulties with this approach.

First, the new definition of marriage as not involving a lifelong mutual commitment contradicts the actual commitment made by many couples when they marry. Of course, some couples may marry in the new sense of giving a qualified commitment intended to be capable of being contradicted at some time in the future but others will marry on the basis of making an unqualified life-

AN IRISH READER IN MORAL THEOLOGY

long commitment. The new law purports to mishear the public expression of their commitment and treats it as exactly what it is not, namely a commitment with a qualification denying its lifelong character.

The new single definition of marriage created in 1995 clearly conflicts with the principle of pluralism. Whether one approaches the issue from the standpoint of religious or secular values it is plain that the denial of a model of lifelong marriage to those who would wish to commit themselves in that way is anti-pluralist in its intent and effect.

The new single definition of marriage also offends against the value of autonomy. Even if it were considered that this definition is the one that best serves most citizens, individual citizens should be free to make up their own mind on the question and act in accordance with what they perceive to be appropriate to their needs and values. The whole point of respect for autonomy is that society steps back and lets the individual fashion her or his future without being told by the state what is the best (and, in this context, only) legally recognised course of action to follow.

In *In re a Ward of Court (withholding medical treatment) (No. 2)*,[24] the Supreme Court accepted that respect for individual autonomy means that society must stand by and not intervene in cases where an autonomous individual chooses to die by refusing necessary medication. In *North Western Health Board v. H.W. and N.W.*,[25] the Supreme Court held that respect for family autonomy requires society to stand by in many cases where parents make medically unjustifiable decisions which risk causing some injury to their child. If autonomy means that one can make the awesome choice to die when society might regard this as being a grievously mistaken one, it is hard to see why respect for autonomy should not permit a couple legally to commit themselves to each other for life. It is surely a matter for reflection that a decision to end one's life can be a constitutionally protected choice but a decision to marry for life should be treated as contrary to public policy so far as it would call for the support of the law.

We should test the new definition of marriage against a further constitutional value: that of marital privacy. The right to marital privacy was recognised by the Supreme Court in *McGee v. Attorney General*.[26] In this decision – arguably the most important in Irish constitutional jurisprudence[27] – the Supreme Court held that a married couple had the entitlement to have access to contraception which could not be denied them by the law. Walsh J. stated:

> It is outside the authority of the State to endeavour to intrude into the privacy of the husband and wife relationship for the sake of imposing a code of private morality upon that husband and wife which they do not desire.
>
> In my view, Article 41 of the Constitution guarantees the husband and wife against any such invasion of their privacy by the State.[28]

The import of this statement is that married couples should be permitted to prescribe the terms of their relationship in accordance with their own particular values without state intrusion. If the spouses mutually prescribe a marital relationship based on lifelong commitment, that should be their prerogative.

Let us now consider the concept of marriage as an exercise of the constitutionally protected freedom of expression.[29] The whole purpose of protecting freedom of expression is that the state is not concerned with prescribing the content, philosophy or values forming the basis of that expression. The richness of the right consists of the fact that the expression constitutes the outward communication – to other individuals or society in general – of something to which the communicator attaches value.

There is surely truth in the observation that:

[c]ivil marriage is a unique symbolic or expressive resource, usable to communicate a variety of messages to one's spouse and others, and thereby to facilitate people's constitution of personal identity …

First and foremost, civil marriage is nearly always an act and expression of commitment. Marital commitment is expressed not simply by ceremonies, rings and gifts. It is also expressed by the act of undertaking and continuing to live under the responsibilities of civil marriage, and by letting it be known that one is living as a part of a civil marriage. One's statements of marital commitment gain additional credibility for the civil status. A proposition of (civil) marriage is an invitation to a partner to join a publicly valued institution, not simply to maintain a relationship in the realm of the private.[30]

This relationship between private acts and public expression is crucial to an understanding of marriage in society. It is important that the relationship be based on truth. Society is entitled to require that those who seek to engage with society and its laws by making a public commitment to each other for life should mean what they say and not mislead society as to the true nature of their mutual intent. Thus, in *H.H. (otherwise H.C.) v. J.F.F.D.S.*[31], where a spouse sought a declaration of nullity of marriage on the basis that the spouses when entering the marriage had secretly intended to divorce, Carroll J. of the High Court refused to grant the decree and this judgement was affirmed by the Supreme Court.

Part of the necessary cement of society is the general principle that public commitments should not be subverted by freely chosen private reservations. Whereas it is entirely proper that apparently freely made public commitments should be capable of being revealed as having been vitiated by duress, mistake or mental illness, for example, a freely made public commitment, intended to be understood and treated as such by other members of society, should arguably be held binding, even in the face of a later revelation that it was contradicted by a private reservation. The basis of this approach is that society must be able to rely on a presumed consistency between public and private commitment. Indeed that is one of the reasons why marriage is adorned with such ceremonial and unambiguous social markers. The converse of this, of course, is

AN IRISH READER IN MORAL THEOLOGY

that spouses who make a lifelong commitment should be entitled to have society respect their choice. If, in a society with a divorce jurisdiction, the spouses make it perfectly clear that the nature of their commitment excludes the option of divorce, society should not insist on defining marriage inconsistently with their choice.

A further reason why the new single model of revocable marriage may be considered to fail to protect the constitutional and human rights of citizens is its interference with the constitutionally protected right to marry. Such a right has long been recognised in Irish constitutional jurisprudence.[32] When its existence was first acknowledged, and re-affirmed subsequently in several decisions, divorce was prohibited under Article 41.3.2. That is, of course, no longer the case. But does this mean that the right to marry in the sense of making a mutual lifelong commitment has, as a result of the change to Article 41.3.2, ceased to exist? Is the constitutionally protected right to marry now only the right to marry without a legally recognised lifelong commitment?

To answer yes, one would have to repudiate the human rights basis for recognition of the right to marry and adopt an unashamedly positivist philosophy whereby rights are traced not to inherent human dignity and capacity but to the external, contingent state of positive law. It would mean that, if the law abolished the right to marry, the human right to marry would thereby cease to exist. One would need to be a very doctrinaire proponent of legal positivism to make such a claim.

What is the solution to this conflict? In order to give due respect to these values it may be considered necessary that people should be permitted to make legally recognised mutual lifelong commitments if they so choose as an aspect of their human dignity, and in the autonomous exercise of their free will. This does not mean that others, who wish to marry on the basis of retaining the option of divorce, would be prevented from doing so under the existing constitutional dispensation.

LIBERTY AND SERVITUDE

Let us now consider two arguments that could be marshalled against the idea that irrevocable lifelong committed is entitled to legal support. One speaks the language of liberty; the other, of servitude.

Liberty

It may be argued that the essential characteristic of liberty is the right to change one's mind: having chosen one course of action, to choose another; having committed, to resile from that commitment. To foreclose future options is to deny one's essential freedom of choice. Thus, to commit oneself never to act contrary to one's present desires is to engage in a process of thought and action which must always be open to the possiblity of future, inconsistent, thought and deed.

How sound is this argument? Does it survive an analysis of the nature of commitment as a free human choice? If one can meaningfully speak of commitment as being within the range of human moral capacity, then the libertarian argument is in some difficulty, since the inhibition on the entitlement to act in the future inconsistently with the commitment one has made springs from the nature of the commitment itself. To commit is, in essence, to foreclose present and future options. If I commit irrevocably to do X, the denial of my liberty now and at some future time to act inconsistently with that commitment is integral to the commitment rather than something separate from it. To argue that the value of liberty trumps irrevocable commitment is to make a normative argument – that liberty should trump it – rather than to demonstrate that irrevocable commitment is defeated by liberty. The contours of liberty are not necessarily shaped in such a way as to defeat irrevocable commitment. On the contrary, since liberty is an aspect of human choice, it may be argued that liberty is at its most profound and free when a human being knowingly and freely chooses to restrict the scope of his or her range of future choice.

Servitude

The argument against irrevocable commitment based on the notion of servitude is that people should not be entitled to turn themselves into slaves by denying their own liberty. Just as one should not be entitled to place oneself in actual bondage to a slave-owner, similarly one should not be permitted to foreclose one's future options to such an extent as to deny oneself essential liberty of action. This argument is somewhat less ambitious than the liberty-based argument just considered: it does not reject the foreclosure of any future option as being inconsistent with one's freedom but instead contends that at some point the restriction of future choice becomes so oppressive as to constitute servitude.

Let me readily acknowledge that concern for avoiding servitude does indeed justify placing some limits on the exercise of personal automony. No one would seek to defend a law that permitted people to place themselves – even for some initial financial consideration – into slavery. But is the promise, traditionally made when marrying, to commit to one's spouse 'for better, for worse, for richer, for poorer, in sickness and in old age' truly so oppressive as to constitute servitude? Undoubtedly some people think so and would not wish to make a commitment of this character; others, who take a different view, should be denied legal support for that choice only where it is clear that the commitment in question is truly oppressive. That may involve consideration of empirical data, which I have sought to avoid in the present paper, but I would suggest that there is much evidence that human beings can make this commitment without becoming slaves in the process.[33]

One should retain a sense of realism. The sanction for breach of a lifelong commitment is simply the denial to one who makes the commitment of the en-

AN IRISH READER IN MORAL THEOLOGY

titlement to obtain from the law a divorce decree with the consequent possibility of having the name of marriage attributed to a subsequent relationship during the lifetime of one's spouse. People are free to leave their partners, even partners to whom a lifelong commitment has been made.

NO NEED FOR LEGAL RECOGNITION OF LIFELONG COMMITMENT?

Could it be argued that there is simply no need for special legal recognition to be afforded to lifelong commitment? After all, nothing in the present constitutional dispensation prevents any spouse from making such a commitment and keeping it. Providing access to divorce does not make it compulsory. Forcing the other spouse to keep his or her promise may be considered to interfere with his or her autonomy.

I acknowledge the truth of the first part of this argument but I would suggest that it is not the whole truth. The distinctive character of marriage as a legal concept is that it represents an engagement by the spouses with society. Marriage is not simply a private phenomenon: society is implicated. The spouses when marrying communicate with society and call on society to pay attention to what they are doing. Under our present constitutional regime, marriage as a legal concept links the spouses to society by rendering their mutual promises eligible for respect by society, subject only to the entitlement to divorce on the conditions set out in Article 41.3.2 of the Constitution and the Family Law (Divorce) Act 1996. It would, of course, be possible to remove any connection between marriage and society by abolishing the legal concept of marriage; but, as long as marriage remains a legal concept, society has an interest in what the spouses actually promise. If the particular promise by both spouses is to exclude their future resort to divorce, each of the spouses has a legitimate entitlement to expect that society, having been engaged, will heed the nature of the spouses' promises and not actively frustrate their fulfilment. As to the suggestion that the exclusion of the other spouse from access to divorce represents an interference with that other spouse's autonomy by the first spouse, it may be pointed out that the inhibition is inherent in that other spouse's exercise of autonomy when making the irrevocable commitment.

LIFELONG MARRIAGE AND THE PRESENT
CONSTITUTIONAL DISPENSATION

Let me now consider briefly the important question whether it is possible under the present constitutional dispensation to make an irrevocable lifelong commitment that has legal recognition and support. I should point out that, whatever the answer to this question may be, it does not affect the strength or weakness of the central thesis of this paper which is that the commitment of this type *should* have such recognition and support.

I suspect that the initial response of a court to the argument that lifelong commitment has legal recognition and support at present would be that this simply cannot be the position. The whole purpose of the divorce referendum of 1995 was to change the nature of marriage by removing the lifelong element from its definition. If people could sidestep this fundamental change, they might be considered to be violating the policy underlying the amendment to the Constitution.

It is perhaps worth reflecting on what is at stake here: could it be that lifelong marriage has become contrary to public policy? That stark consequence was not prominent in the advocacy in favour of the constitutional change.

What arguments would those seeking legal protection for the option of lifelong marriage be likely to advance? The most obvious is that they have a constitutional right to waive their right of access to the courts for divorce.

Irish jurisprudence on waiver of constitutional rights is at an early stage of development.[34] All we have are relatively unconsidered judicial statements, often lacking the cautious qualifications[35] or depth of analysis which the seriousness of the issue demands.

It seems that one may waive one's parental rights in respect of one's children.[36] If one can do this – with its stark and irrevocable consequences – the case against waiver of one's constitutional rights to divorce may not seem particularly radical.

A decision that is of some interest in this context is *Egan v. Minister for Defence*.[37] Here a commandant in the Air Corps sought to retire prematurely from it in order to take up a financially more attractive position. The Minister, exercising his functions under section 47(b) of the Defence Act 1954, refused him permission. Barr J rejected an attack on the constitutional validity of the statutory provision as violating the commandant's asserted right, under Article 40.3 of the Constitution, to use his labour as he saw fit and to transfer his service, subject to contract, from one employer to another. Barr J observed:

> If a constitutional right in the form postulated by the applicant exists (and I make no finding in that regard) it could not apply in his circumstances because ... he had entered into a voluntary contract to serve in the permanent defence force until the retirement age applicable to his ultimate rank and he was bound to remain in the army for that period. Accordingly, the right to transfer his labour to a civilian employer does not arise until the period of his service comes to an end by effect of time or otherwise, or he is given permission by the Minister to retire early.[38]

It seems, therefore, that one may waive one's constitutional right to transfer one's employment. The analogy with marriage is not perhaps a very romantic one but the point is nonetheless important. A person can choose to exclude a constitutional entitlement and to foreclose constitutionality supported choices over an extended period into the future. Of course, the commitment made by

AN IRISH READER IN MORAL THEOLOGY

Commandant Egan had not the intimate character of marriage and was not for life, but these differences do not render the case irrelevant to the general question of waiver.

The courts could take the attitude that access to divorce is not simply a constitutional right, which may possibly be waived, but rather is part of the fundamental machinery of the social structure relating to personal status. In another context it has been observed that:

> [p]erhaps the best solution is to regard the right to jury trial not merely as a right which is simply personal to the accused, but rather as a mandatory constitutional rule ('a constitutional imperative') which is not susceptible of waiver by the accused.[39]

It may be that the courts would similarly regard the institution of divorce, which is associated strongly with the question of legal status. Our courts have already shown themselves opposed to the idea that the estoppel principle should deny recognition to a foreign divorce otherwise capable of recogntion under the rules of private international law. Estoppel differs from waiver in that estoppel results in the denial of recognition to a factually true situation whereas waiver involves an act of choice which does not contradict reality in any way. Nevertheless there is a common denominator between the two in that both raise an issue as to whether facts relating to the parties' conduct *inter se* should trump public reality. This suggests that the estoppel cases could have some influence in the context of our discussion.

It seems, therefore, that, while it is possible that courts would apply the waiver principle in respect of the right to divorce, they are by no means certain to do so. If they were impressed by strong arguments based on dignity, privacy and autonomy, in conjunction with the philsophy of moral freedom on which the edifice of our legal system is constructed, the courts would – and, I suggest, should – look with favour on the entitlement of spouses to make legally enforceable lifelong commitments to each other.

SAFEGUARDS FOR ENTERING LIFELONG MARRIAGE

If lifelong irrevocable marriage were to be recognised as a lawfully supported option, it would seem sensible for the law to have very stringent safeguards to encourage the parties to reflect in depth and at length on the awesome nature of the commitment that they are contemplating, to ensure that they have been fully informed of the consequences – personal and legal – of this choice. There is evidence that spouses entering marriage overestimate the prospects of its success. This depressing reality must be conveyed clearly to the spouses. The couple must not only be completely informed on all of these implciations; it is essential that they should have the mental capacity and maturity to enter into this kind of commitment.

Translating these desiderata into practice suggests that there should be a prescribed period of some considerable duration in which the parties, before marrying, would be informed and counselled and engage in the appropriate professional consultations to seek to ensure that they have the maturity that this challenge requires. Parties could not reasonably complain that these state-imposed inhibitions interfered with their autonomy: the whole point about these inhibitions would be to respect the free exercise of autonomy.

CONCLUDING OBSERVATIONS

The purpose of this paper has been provocative: to encourage engagement, contradiction and further progress in the debate on marriage. Few people are likely to have a strong prejudice in favour of the argument I have presented. Those who associate the benefits of marriage with the common good will be cautious about the emphasis on individualist norms, which in much discourse are regarded as competing with common good considerations; those who favour autonomy and privacy may regard the emphasis on free choice to act in accordance with one's normative system as a species of closet moralism. To the first of these groups, I would point out again that this paper has purposely excluded from its scope all consideration of the common good, not because it is not of importance – it is in fact crucial – but simply in order to purify the analytic focus of the thesis. To the second group, the challenge is to address the nature of human dignity and freedom of the will and to rejoice in the repertoire of choice to which we, as human beings, can aspire.

Notes:
1. *D.T. v. C.T.* (Divorce: Ample Resources) [2002] 3 IR 334, at 405 (Supreme Ct, per Murray J). See further Byrne & Binchy, *Annual Review of Irish Law 2002*, pp 263-82, especially p 267.
2. Article 41.3.2 provides as follows:
A Court designated by law may grant a dissolution of marriage where, but only where, it is satisfied that
i. at the date of the institution of the proceedings, the spouses have lived apart from one another for a period of, or periods amounting to, at least four years during the previous five years,
ii. there is no reasonable prospect of a reconciliation between the spouses,
iii. such provision as the Court considers proper having regard to the circumstances exists or will be made for the spouses, any children of either or both of them and any other person prescribed by law, and
iv. any further conditions prescribed by law are complied with.
3. The concept of legal recognition of a particular relationship is complex. It can refer to the ascription of a name ('marriage' for example) or the conferral by the State of legal benefits on a particular category of relationship or the ascription of a range of mutal rights and obligations – a legal status, in effect – to that relationship. Names are important. They carry a clear message of social approval (or disapproval) – and legitimisation (or delegitimisation). As to the ascription of legal benefits in the context of marriage, it

is worth noting that the Irish Constitution has been interpreted as requiring the State only to desist from discriminating against marriage (*Murphy v. Attorney General* [1982] IR 241, *Muckley v. Ireland* [1985] IR 472, *Hyland v. Minister for Social Welfare* [1989] IR 624, *Greene v. Minister for Agriculture* [1990] 2 IR 17), while entitling the State to discriminate in favour of marriage (*O'B v. S*, [1984] IR 316).

See further, Hogan & Whyte eds, J. M. Kelly, *The Irish Constitution* (4th ed, 2003), paras 7.6.14–7.6.27. The question whether marriage should involve a State-prescribed range of rights and obligations raises major issues for debate in the context of autonomy, gender equality and paternalism. I shall merely note here that Irish law, which formerly contained significant gender inequalities at a formal level, failed until 1976 to provide effective protection to wives living with husbands who did not support them, to wives whose husbands beat them or to wives whose husbands sold the family home over their head. Even today, wives have no automatic entitlement to a share in the family home, the Supreme Court having invoked natural law principles, quite unconvincingly, to strike down as unconstitutional a fairly modest legislative initiative: see *In re Article 26 and the Matrimonial Home Bill 1993* [1994] 1 IR 305, analysed by Hogan, 16 *DULJ* 175 (1994).

4. See D. Kretzmer & E. Klein (eds), *The concept of human dignity in human rights discourse* (2002); Feldman, 'Human dignity as a legal value' [1999] *Public L* 682 [2000] *Public L* 61.

5. See Dicke, 'The founding function of human dignity in the Universal Declaration of Human Rights', in D. Kretzmer & E. Klein (eds), op. cit., 111.

6. See Canick, 'Dignity of man' and '*Persona*' in Stoic anthropology: some remarks on Cicero, *De Officiis* I, 105-107, in D. Kretzmer & E. Klein (eds), op. cit., 19.

7. Cf Starck, 'The religious and philosophical background of human dignity and its place in modern constitutions', in D. Kretzmer & E. Klein (eds), op. cit., 179, at 180-1 (footnote references omitted):

> The recent affirmation of human dignity in constitutions and international declarations is a product of a relatively secular age. Yet the development of the underlying idea – the concept of what a human being is – closely parallels the development of Christian thought. Both the Old and New Testaments state that the basis of human dignity is the fact that humans were created in the image of God (Gen 1:27; Eph 4:24). If follows that every human being has inalienable value in his or her own right, which is why no human being may be treated as a mere object or as a means to an end.
>
> A second strand of the concept of human dignity finds its origins in classical antiquity. Philosophers in this period recognised characteristics of human beings that distinguish them from animals, namely their capacity for rational thought and free will, and from this starting point, began to recognise human dignity in citizens. Later, their theory was extended in a more cosmopolitan context to all human beings.
>
> A strong social component characterises the classical and Christian concepts of freedom which the notion of human dignity underpins: human beings were always seen as interdependent, social creatures. This is evident from the concepts of the *polis*, of the community of believers, of general fraternity and of solidarity. Human freedom was anchored in divine law, in natural law and in moral law.
>
> Christian life and belief, in which human beings depend (*religio*) on God, on Jesus Christ as intercessor and saviour and on the Christian community, led by the Holy

Spirit, transcend the physical world. In this context, it is usual to speak of metaphysics. Thus, human beings have a metaphysical anchor, which provides the basis for their freedom, and for their equality and fraternity: all human beings are, in equal measure, the image of God. Human dignity does not mean unlimited self-determination, but self-determination which is exercised on the basis that everyone – not simply the person claiming the right to self determination – is of value in his or her own right.

8. Emphasis added.

9. Just as the Charter uses the word faith in its non-doctrinal connotation, so do I. There is need for our society to acknowledge the entitlement of religious language and concepts to be heard, and heeded, in philosophical, ethical and political debate; that entitlement should not rest on any necessary acceptance of the empirical validity of any doctrinal proposition of any particular religion but rather on the philosophical depth and ethical force of the language and concepts. Cf Byrne & Binchy, Annual Review of Irish Law 1995, 174-7; R. Dworkin, *Life's dominion* (1993).

10. High Ct, 25 February 1997.

11. Pages 3 to 5 of Costello P's judgment.

12. [1996] 2 IR 79.

13. 497 US 261 (1990).

14. *In re Quinlan*, 355 A. 2d 647 (1976).

15. [1996] 2 IR, at 163.

16. Id., at 167.

16a. One should here acknowledge that the word 'dignity' can be used to describe the characteristic of human valour and self-composure in adverse or hostile circumstances. Denham J is clearly correct in noting that people have a right to be treated with dignity in the sense that others – even society – should not subvert their self-respect. These usages of the term 'dignity' are, however, separate from the dignity to which the Irish Constitution and the several international human rights instruments refer.

17. Of course not every human being has the capacity to exercise free choice: mental incapacity can be of such a character as to render a marriage invalid. The jurisprudence on this area of the law of nullity of marriage is less than fully satisfactory: see Byrne & Binchy, *Annual Review of Irish Law 2002*, pp 293-303.

18. [1984] IR36 (Supreme Ct, 1983), critically analysed by Gearty, (1983) 5 *DULJ* 3 (ns) 264, Quinn, 'The lost language of the Irish gay male: textualization in Ireland's law and literature (or the most hidden Ireland)', (1995) 26 *Columbia Human Rts L Rev* 553.

19. [1975] IR 284.

20. Emphasis added. It is worth noting that elsewhere in his judgement in Norris, Henchy J invoked the values of dignity and pluralism in support of the principle of legal deference to variations among individuals' moral codes. The fact that homosexual conduct was contrary to the standards of morality advocated by the Christian Churches in the State should not, in Henchy J's view, be treated as a guiding consideration: 'What are known as the seven deadly sins are authorised as immoral by all the Christian Churches, and it would have to be conceded that they are capable, in different degrees and in certain contexts, of undermining vital aspects of the common good. Yet it would be neither constitutionally permissible nor otherwise desirable to seek by criminal sanctions to legislate their commission out of existence in all possible circumstances. To do so would upset the necessary balance which the Constitution posits between the com-

mon good and the dignity and freedom of the individual. What is deemed necessary to his dignity and freedom by one man may be abhorred by another as an exercise in immorality. The pluralism necessary for the preservation of constitutional requirements in the Christian democratic State envisaged by the Constitution means that the sanctions of the criminal law may be attached to immoral acts only when the common good requires their proscription as crimes.'

21. Cf *McGee v. Attorney General* [1974] IR 284, at 318; *The State (Keegan) v. Stardust Tribunal* [1986] IR 642, at 658; *Coughlan v. Broadcasting Complaints Commission* [2000], 3 IR 1.

22. Cf Stanton Collett, 'Recognizing same-sex marriage: asking for the impossible', 47 *Catholic U.L. Rev.* 1245, at 1255 (198).

23. I have already argued that this is an impoverished understanding of autonomy, in failing to recognise the human capacity to exercise autonomy to choose to act in accordance with one's normative system.

24. [1996] 2 IR 79. For analysis, see Byrne & Binchy, *Annual Review of Irish Law 1995*, 156-81; Whyte, 'The right to die under the Irish Constitution' [1997] *European Public Law*; O'-Carroll, 'The right to die: a critique of Supreme Court judgment in "the Ward case" (1995) 84 Studies 375; Feenan, 'Death, dying and the law' (1996) 14 *ILT* (ns) 90; Hanafin, 'Last rites or rights at last: the development of a right to die in Irish constitutional law', (1996) 18 *J of Social Welfare & Family L* 429; Tomkin & McAuley, '*Re a Ward of Court:* legal analysis', (1995) 2 *Medico-Legal J of Ireland* 45; Iglesias, 'Ethics, brain-death and the medical concept of the human being', id, 51, especially at 56-7; Kearon, '*Re a Ward of Court*: ethical comment', id, 58; Mason & Laurie, 'The management of the persistent vegetative state in the British Isles' [1996] Juridical Rev 263, especially at 270-2. Much of the commentary, even by some of those sympathetic to the outcome in the case, is critical of the court's analysis. Dr John Keown, writing in the *Cambridge Law Journal*, observed that, '[i]f this is the sort of reasoning a written Constitution produces, long may we remain without one': 'Life and death in Dublin', [1996] *Camb. L. J.* 6, at 8.

25. [2001] 3 IR 622.

26. [1974] IR 284.

27. The decision explores the relationship between the law and private morality, the impact of fundamental values of justice and charity on constitutional analysis and the potential for constitutional analysis to change in the light of changes in dominant values in society. The latter issue was an important element in the Supreme Court decision of *Attorney General v. X* [1992] 1 IR 1, critically analysed by Byrne & Binchy, *Annual Review of Irish Law 1992*, 154-208.

28. [1974] IR, at 313.

29. Article 40.6.1.1 of the Constitution.

30. Cruz, '"Just don't call it marriage": the First Amendment and marriage as an expressive resource', 74 *S. Calif. L. Rev.* 925, at 928, 932 (1999).

31. High Ct., Carroll J, 19 December 1990, affirmed *sub nom. H.S. v. J.S.*, Supreme Ct., 3 April 1992. For analysis, see Byrne & Binchy, *Annual Review of Irish Law 1990*, 301-6; *Annual Review of Irish Law 1992*, 347-9.

32. Cf Kelly, op. cit., paras 7.6.12–7.6.13; J. Casey, *Constitutional law in Ireland*, 425-7 (3rd ed., 2000); *Ryan v. Attorney General* [1965] IR 294; *Murray v. Ireland* [1985] IR 532. An important question of characterisation arises here. If the right to marry is rooted exclusively in Article 41 it may be more difficult to convince a court that such right is not contingent on, and determined by, the contours of the legal institution of marriage prescribed by

Article 41, namely (since 1995) one that does not involve a legally supported lifelong commitment. If, however, the right to marry is based (either exclusively or in addition to Article 41) on Article 40.3, it may be easier to argue that the right extends to one involving permanent commitment. In *Murray*, Costello J considered that the right to marry fell under Article 40.3. In *Foy v. An t-Árd Chláraitheoir*, High Ct., Mc Kechnie J, 9 July 2002, counsel for the respondents conceded that the right to marry was founded on Article 40.3. There is no right to divorce under the European Convention on Human Rights: *Johnston v. Ireland* 9 EHRR 203 (1986). Under the same Convention, the right of transsexuals to marry persons of their former sex was recognised in *Goodwin v. United Kingdom*, [2022] 2 FLR 487, analysed by Probert, 'The right to marry and the impact on the Human Rights Act 198', [2003] *Internat'l Fam. L.* 29; Bessant, 'Transsexuals and marriage after *Goodwin v. United Kingdom*', [2003] *Fam. L.* 111. In *Foy v. An t-Árd Chláraitheoir, supra*, decided very shortly before Goodwin, McKechnie J rejected the argument that transsexuals had the constitutional right to marry.

33. It is worth noting that Article 4 of the European Convention on Human Rights, which prohibits holding anyone in slavery or servitude, has not been invoked to strike down lifelong marriage. The potential dissonance between *F. v. Switzerland*, 10 EHRR 411 (1988) and *Johnston v. Ireland* 9 EHRR 203 (1986), on the scope of the right to marry under Article 12, and the relationship between Articles 8 and 12, should be noted.

34. See Kelly, op. cit., paras. 7.1.16-7.1.78.

35. Thus in the Supreme court decision of *The State (Nicolaou) v. An Bórd Uchtála* [1966] IR 567, at 644, Walsh J (for the court) observed that there is no provision in Article 40 which prohibits or restricts the surrender, abdication, or transfer of any of the rights guaranteed in that Article by the person entitled to them. It

scarcely is the case that waiver of one's right to bodily integrity against torture or, more radically, that waiver of one's right to life is unproblematic.

36. This subject raises large jurisprudential issues. I will limit myself to noting that it is possible, consensually, to lose one's parental rights through adoption and that the process of adoption prescribed by the Adoption Act 1988 contains a concept of 'abandonment' of parental rights that appears to extend to consciously chosen waiver.

37. High Ct., 24 November 1988.

38. Page 16 of Barr J's judgement.

39. Kelly, op. cit., para 7.1.76.

AN IRISH READER IN MORAL THEOLOGY

11   Love in Marriage: How New was Vatican II?

Denis O'Callaghan

(*Irish Theological Quarterly*, Vol 46, No 4, 1979, pp 221-239)

'The intimate partnership of life and love which constitutes the married life has been established by the Creator ... Christ our Lord has abundantly blessed this love ... Married love is an eminently human love, an affection between two persons ... It can enrich the sentiments of the spirit and their physical expression with a unique dignity ... Married love is uniquely expressed and perfected by the exercise of the acts proper to marriage ... The acts in marriage by which the intimate and chaste union of the spouses takes place are noble and honourable; the truly human performance of these acts fosters the self-giving they signify and enriches the spouses in joy and gratitude ... Marriage and married love are by nature ordered to the procreation and education of children. Indeed, children are the supreme gift of marriage' (*Gaudium et Spes*, par 48-50).

This celebration of married love links eros and agape, situating the sexual life of the couple within a human and Christian context where parenthood and partnership combine into one cycle of love, with the sex act as meeting point of that love and the child as arrival point. Here the Constitution *On the Church in the Modern World* shows Vatican II as pastoral council, confronting the needs of people not just the problems of theologians. While it borrows from psychology a language to analyse and describe human experience, it uses the timeless insights of scripture to speak to heart and spirit – the Book of Genesis, the Song of Songs, the Letter to the Ephesians.

Inevitably there is a contrast with the treatment of marriage familiar to us in legal code and moral textbook. Canon law identified the bare bones of the marriage contract establishing the family unit as essential human and Christian institution. This basic exercise was and is surely necessary. The textbook concerned itself with the definition of precise moral norms. It incorporated an amount of pastoral experience when it came to fleshing out the concepts and to applying the norms, but the concepts themselves and the statements of norm tended to live more in the world of the theologian.

Any tradition, theological or otherwise, builds up a weight and a logic which reject as unorthodox whatever does not belong, unless this latter has undeniable authority on its side. This is where Vatican II comes in. The pattern of Christian marriage and family life set out there with all authority has already profoundly affected the course of systematic and moral theology.

The contemporary sexual ethic follows through the line taken at Vatican II when it emphasises the intrinsic meaning of genuine love as moral imperative healing, protecting and sustaining the partners, giving human quality to their sexual lives, motivating them to meet the call of new life generously as command and blessing of God Creator, controlling self-indulgence and acting as antidote to those forces which would turn sexuality into sexology. Cardinal Hume, shortly after his appointment to the See of Westminster, numbered among the church's most urgent tasks that of finding a more compelling language for our sexual ethic. The context of that language will be the human person and the mysteries of life and love which sex serves.

The fact that mainstream theology had so little to say about love in marriage requires some explanation. We shall address ourselves to this presently. However, theology should not be confined to its technical phenotype. We must ask whether, over to the side of the main channel along which formal teaching had built up so strong a current, there were quieter and deeper waters of Christian living with few marker buoys and few chart entries. Every now and again they may have eddied into the main current as prayer from the liturgy of marriage, as marginal phrase in some official document, as passing comment in some established author, or as the random witness of some relatively eccentric and unorthodox writer. It will be difficult to trace these extravagantia because they do not figure in the *loci communes*, those catalogues of textual references which mark the beaten path. What one discovers will be haphazard, scattered bits and pieces of evidence which may seem slight enough counterweight to the formal tradition, but which may indicate a *Sitz im Leben* for marriage richer in human and Christian terms. It seems reasonable to suggest that Vatican II did not invent a theology. Rather did it present and give structure and authority to an authentic Christian experience, to a theology which was lived rather than written.

Looking back over the centuries where men of the calibre of Augustine, Aquinas and Sanchez set the pattern of thought, one observes general acceptance of the basic fact that marriage made man and wife one in mind and in heart. In effect this should classify marriage as a relationship of love, but the word love was not in favour as a theological expression for this truth. When we set out some of the relevant strands in the tradition we shall see why. Love was questionable on a number of counts. In the context of marriage it carried not only a very definite sexual connotation but it was seen as close kin to infatuation, an *ignis fatuus* precarious and little amenable to reason. Behind convictions such as these lurked the dark shadow of the Fall which had introduced unruly concupiscence into man's being and had above all affected his sexual life. It is true to say that the classical authors read the effects of the Fall through eyes already jaundiced on sex. It was not the theology of the Fall in itself which brought them to so pessimistic a view of man's sexual nature.

Across the spectrum the state of marriage was seen essentially as a *coniunctio animorum*. Roman law supported this viewpoint when it defined marriage in the hallowed phrase *'viri et mulieris coniunctio individuam vitae consuetudinem retinens'*, and stated *'non coitus matrimonium facit sed maritalis affectio'*. It was

AN IRISH READER IN MORAL THEOLOGY

from this viewpoint that Augustine considered the marriage of Mary and Joseph a true marriage.[1]

Aquinas could not have been more positive: 'The essence of marriage consists in a certain inseparable bond between two minds which pledges husband and wife to unbreakable faith with each other.'[2] While this statement owes its inspiration to scripture, Aquinas had before him also Aristotle's *Ethics*, bk 8. Here Aristotle sets out the value, nature and pattern of human friendship and proposes marriage as one type of friendship. Marital friendship is based on the natural attraction between man and woman. Its purpose is not just the propagation of the species but a common life of partnership where one complements the other and where children act as bond of union between the parents. When Aquinas came to treat formally of the emotional life[3] he could invoke Aristotle's authority on the basic goodness of the emotions and on the relevance of the golden mean to emotional feelings and expressions. On love he could say: 'There is this much of union in love that as a result of the joy felt at the thought of the object, a person feels towards that object as if it were himself or part of himself.' In answer to the question as to whether love harms the lover, a question prompted by the *amore langueo* of the Song of Songs, he replied that on the contrary love makes one a better person provided it attaches one to a good which is right and proper.

For Aquinas and his predecessors there was little problem with married love in *actu primo*, at an ontological and ethereal level. The problem was married love in *actu secundo*, as it was actually lived. Here love was sexual and on the pronouncement of this fateful word spectres came crowding in. Here love was also passionate, unpredictable, ungovernable and, in a word, irrational. Venus and Eros were perennial problems.

Married love and Venus

Any effort to integrate married love with its sexual expression, and above all with sexual pleasure, was fraught with almost insurmountable difficulties for the theological tradition reaching back to Patristic times. That tradition said a ready enough yes to marriage – while emphasising that for the Christian consecrated celibacy was the better way, a more conditioned yes to marital intercourse, and a very hesitant yes to sexual enjoyment. This ambiguous attitude owes its origin not to any specifically Christian conviction but to various cultural influences which are usefully classed under the portmanteau term dualism. New-Platonism with its idiom of distrust of the flesh is typical, but the general atmosphere is much older and far more universal. The view of woman as bewitching and of sex as contaminating or fascinating can be charted not just in Mediterranean culture but in Celtic mythology and in Hindu lore.[4] In the Bible itself the Book of Leviticus is clear evidence of this attitude. Still, it is fair to ask why Western Christian culture took the Book of Leviticus approach to sex so much to heart and closed its eyes to Genesis, and to Song of Songs. The contrast between the Mediterranean authors and that strange collection of texts known as the *Pseudo-Clementine Letters* is striking. These texts issuing from a Christian community in Asia Minor (refugees from the destruction of Jerusalem in 70 AD?) are Jewish rather than Hellenist in outlook. Their attitude to sex has that saner balance which is evident over most of the Old Testament. This is not true of the West. The Neo-Platonists were certainly a powerful force but there were other factors also. When Christian authors and preachers like Tertullian and Jerome read books such as Ovid's *Ars Amatoria* or surveyed the lascivious life of the Imperial City, was it any wonder that they turned if not to out and out rejection of sex at least to the rigidly strict discipline to be found in a Stoic like Seneca? Tertullian's views on sex and marriage showed such a *saeva indignatio* that he had few followers. Jerome gave a more human face to a pessimism which was in itself quite extreme.[5] He was certainly a powerful influence and in his letters provided a quarry for the cynics and satirists of later centuries. In *The Canterbury Tales* Chaucer puts his words on the lips of the Wife of Bath. Still, putting men like Tertullian and Jerome in the stocks would not be fair to the main tradition. Therefore to speak for this, we shall choose Augustine as central figure.

In his *Soliloquy* he makes his personal position quite clear: 'I am convinced that above all other things I must keep free of sexual intercourse. I know nothing can cast down the manly soul from its citadel so effectively as feminine blandishments and those sensual contacts without which one cannot live married life. Therefore, in all justice and expediency, I am quite satisfied that for my freedom of soul I should debar myself from desiring, seeking or marrying a wife.'[6]

It is difficult to assess how much Augustine's experience before conversion affected his views on the sexual life which married people live. But given these views, it is little wonder that in his early writings he looked back with nostalgia on marriage as he pictured it in Paradise where the species would be propagated asexually. Subsequent debates with the over-pessimistic Manicheans and the over-optimistic Pelagians brought him to a somewhat middle ground: 'Carnal libido, through which ejaculation of the male semen takes place, was either absent altogether from Adam's experience before the Fall, or else it was his sin which introduced de-ordination into it. If libido were absent then he could have moved his genital organs and put seed in the womb without its help. If libido did exist then he could have activated it by a simple act of will.'[7] It was along the lines of this final position that later tradition formed its consensus, accepting not only sexual propagation, but also libido and well-ordered sexual enjoyment as connatural to man. So Aquinas: 'The existence of sexual organs and sexual differentiation clearly prove that in the state of innocence mankind would have been propagated not by direct divine intervention in some angelic fashion but

AN IRISH READER IN MORAL THEOLOGY

by sexual copulation, an act which would in that state have been free from all taint of lust, even though enjoyment would have been greater because nature would have been more refined and the body more sensitive.'[8]

Concupiscentia, the term which we translated 'libido' in the above text, is there employed by Augustine in a neutral and descriptive sense connoting sex desire and enjoyment. But in his writings and in the literature generally it has the evaluative nuance of passion, inordinate desire and pleasure, lust as in Aquinas' text above. This deordination, the disturbance of the dominion of man's reason, was traced to the Fall. While admitting that the Fall affected the whole of man's nature, bodily and spiritual, tradition saw it as particularly operative in man's sentient nature, especially in the sexual sphere. When Augustine writes in this vein there is very little relief in the dark picture he draws. Rebellious and unruly concupiscence overpowers the will, and suffocates reason, thereby depriving man of his most noble faculty.[9] This rebelliousness is both consequence and cause of sin. It occasioned the shame that moved Adam and Eve to cover their nakedness, and it is through the carnal expression of it that their sin is still transmitted from parent to child.[10]

Augustine admitted that the evil of concupiscence was offset when libido was used for its properly ordered function of procreating: 'One who uses sexual intercourse and its attendant shameful libido in a lawful manner employs an evil object in a right way: one who uses it in an unlawful manner employs an evil object in a wrong way.'[11] He knew right well that according to his norms very few married people used sex legitimately: 'In day-to-day conversation with those who are married or were married have we ever heard anyone admit that he never slept sexually with his wife except when he wanted a child?'[12] He concluded not that his view was unrealistic but that in moral terms celibacy was more viable than marriage.

We have given Augustine's position at some length because it was so important for subsequent tradition. Admittedly, that tradition often tended to take hold of the darker side of Augustine. This is so in the case of Gregory the Great, a man whose pastoral and moral writings had very wide influence. His *Responsum* to Bishop Augustine of Canterbury was constantly invoked: 'A man who has slept with his wife should not enter the church without first washing himself with water, nor should he enter the church immediately even though he has washed ... Until the fire of concupiscence has been doused in his soul, he should not regard himself as a worthy member of the brotherly community ... In saying this we do not say that marriage is blameworthy, but since lawful conjugal intercourse cannot take place without pleasure, one should abstain from entering a sacred place, because pleasure always necessarily implies guilt.'[13]

Ascribing these views to Pope Gregory, with their echo of taboo and prohibition already familiar from the Book of Leviticus, guaranteed them widespread acceptance. Bede quoted the *Responsum* extensively in his *History of the English*

Church and People[14] and Gratian incorporated it as the decretal *Vir cum propria*.[15] Its authority was now beyond question. Huguccio, the most influential commentator on the *Decretum* of Gratian, spelt out the implication clearly: 'Conjugal intercourse can never take place without venial sin at least, because there is always some heat, some itch, some pleasure in it, and that is venial sin.' The Penitentials took up the theme – three days' fast from bread and water for intercourse on Sunday, sexual abstinence for a week before and after the Eucharist, sexual abstinence for the *Quadragesimae* of Easter, Christmas and Pentecost. It is obvious that the nuances of Augustine have been long forgotten, though his name was used to endorse all this because the *Decretum* side by side with *Vir cum propria* attributes to him the recommendation: 'On the approach of Christmas Day and other church feasts, one should abstain not only from concubinage but from lawful sexual intercourse.'

This close link forged between sex and sin was a constant problem for a pastoral tradition which had to make sense of marriage for the ordinary Christian. Aquinas' commentary on 1 Corinthians 7 is a unique insight into how he came to straighten out some of the strands from the tangled skein.[16] His analysis ends with a principle which, later accepted word for word by Sanchez,[17] became classical for the textbook: 'The marriage act is without sin in two cases only, namely when motivated by the wish for offspring or by the duty of conceding the marriage right. Otherwise it always implies sin, at least venial.' But in the two cases where it is allowed the marriage act is meritorious as act of the virtue of religion and as act of the virtue of justice respectively.

No doubt, the modern reader will express disappointment that these great thinkers were unable to relate married love to its sexual expression, in spite of the possibilities contained in the 'two-in-one-flesh' of Genesis. The cultural barriers were simply too great, and we shall see that these cultural barriers stood not just in the way of Venus but in the way of Eros as well.

Married love and eros
We have already mentioned that for Augustine the union of Mary and Joseph was a true marriage, and indeed *the* true marriage. This chaste *fraterna societas*, brother-sister union, was the paradigm of Christian wedlock. Augustine admitted that in experience it rarely occurred even among the elderly whose marriages in theory it justified.[18] Aquinas followed quite similar lines. The marriage of Mary and Joseph was 'all the more perfect and holy in that it was immune from all carnality'.[19] The ideal marriage is virginal, sealed by a pact of mutual continence, 'in which husband and wife are made one not by the lust of joined bodies but by the affection of united wills'.[20] The idealisation of married love as *amor amicitiae*, love of friendship, without any admixture of *amor concupiscentiae* showed up typical romantic love in poor light. Aquinas' mentors, Lombard and Aristotle, gave little encouragement to any more optimistic view.

     AN IRISH READER IN MORAL THEOLOGY

For Lombard the principal reasons for marriage were the biblical ones – procreation of children (Genesis 1) and the avoidance of fornication (1 Cor 7). Other worthy reasons were the reconciliation of warring families and the restoring of peace. Less worthy motives were worldly gain and 'the beauty of man or woman which often drives spirits inflamed with love to seek marriage so that they may satisfy their desires'. Lombard comments that, in spite of opinions to the contrary, the consensus is that this last kind of marriage is still valid 'even though love was the motivating cause'.[21]

Aristotle appreciated the fickle quality of much that passed as love: 'Young people are amorous; they love for passion and pleasure, and this gives intensity to their love. For this very reason their love quickly evaporates; often they fall in and out of love the same day. While love lasts they want to remain constantly in one another's company … But when beauty fades the friendship often ends.'[22] One should not be surprised if what Aquinas has to say about love in marriage is in this tradition. Even Genesis and Ephesians are read in its light. Gen 2:18 raised the question of the man-wife relationship. For Aquinas woman is called man's helpmate in terms of her contribution to the generative process. 'In all other activities man finds a better companion in man than in woman.' Woman is man manqué, conceived when the male seed is either defective in itself or weakened by some fortuitous circumstance like the Sirocco (the *plumbeus Auster* of Horace). The fact that woman is produced from man's rib (not head nor foot) indicates that he should treat her as partner who is subject to his better judgement but still not to be despised.[23] Gen 2:24 raised the question of comparative duties to wife and parents. In any dilemma here Aquinas comes down on the side of the priority of love for parents once the husband has dispensed his bounden duties of affording his wife sexual rights and a home.[24]

All this may jar modern sensibilities but, in the tradition, Aquinas following Aristotle is quite a positive voice. The really pessimistic attitude to eros in marriage goes back to other sources which were embodied in Christian literature at a very early date. Lucretius, *De rerum natura*, lib 4, was a classical text, all the more influential in that it came from a background so soberly philosophical. Much quoted was the Pythagorean tract, *Sententiae Sexti*, which contained the striking maxim: '*Omnis ardentior amator propriae uxoris adulter est.*' Jerome combined both authors very effectively: 'The Sapiens should love his wife with discretion not affection … Nothing is more degrading than to love one's wife as if she were a mistress … To marriage is granted the sober task of producing children, the ecstasy found in a prostitute is to be condemned in a wife.'[25]

A late sixteenth century physician, Paul Zacchia, whose *Quaestiones Medico-Legales* was quoted as authority in the Roman courts for more than a century, says about lovers: 'They are to be numbered among the demented and melancholic.' His straightforward verdict is '*amor devastat, depravat, confundit*'. The seat of love is the liver. Its bilious nature is a vagrant force which disturbs reason's equilibrium by stirring the fantasies of the imagination. He lists statement after statement from poet, dramatist and philosopher indicating the symptoms and implications of the malady.[26]

Zacchia is a very useful witness for the ambivalent attitude to love. Side by side with the above he will carry a paragraph strikingly poetic on a love which is reasoned, which sharpens the mind, refines the senses and adds sweetness to life. Similarly in regard to sex we read the following contrasting statements in the one chapter: 'Nor is there any other better way than (marital intercourse) for fostering mutual love, for as Plutarch says: Venus is the primary safeguard against betrayal of the marriage bed': 'Whatever about the other animals man must not seek pleasure from his wife; the name of wife is a name expressing dignity not pleasure.'[27]

Majority report and minority views

The short sketch above on Venus and Eros simply gives us the flavour of that theological world which brought forth our classical textbooks. It was a *science de cabinet* all the more firmly closed on the one side by the discipline of canon law and on the other by reaction against profane culture. On the first count, the canon law of marriage centred attention on justice rather than on love. Starting from 1 Cor 7:3-4 on marriage as contract, the medieval schools defined its object as the 'exchange of rights to sexual acts in order to procreate'. Love and personal relationship were irrelevant to an extent that we find hard to credit. On the question of the right of the husband to extort sex from his bride by force or threat, it is instructive to compare Sanchez, *De Matrimonio* and Pope Paul, *Humanae Vitae*.[28] On the other count, there were the Courts of Love. We find no mention of these Courts nor of the Troubadour mystique of love in classical medieval authors. One suspects that what the theologians knew of this other side confirmed them even more strongly in their tradition. Christian reaction could not but be negative to a philosophy which either celebrated adulterous passion – the *domna* is typically another man's wife – or which made sex into an elaborate art bearing no relation to family responsibility. It comes as no surprise to learn that a twelfth-century Paris divine, Andreas Capellanus, who took to sponsoring the *amour courtois* was degraded for his pains.

Looking back over the centuries it seems fair to say that classical theology encountered insurmountable obstacles in coming to terms with sexuality as a human and Christian phenomenon. Because libido was cast under the rubric of concupiscence, it surrounded itself with a negative resonance which made very difficult any positive assessment of marriage as sexual union or of married love embodying sex as its natural expression. Love as the basis of solid domestic virtue posed no problem. Neither did love as ideal virginal union of heart and mind. The problem was the love of the Song of Songs, a love which would integrate Venus and Eros in marriage into a valid generous human and Christ-

AN IRISH READER IN MORAL THEOLOGY

ian experience. I trust that the reader will accept that the ambiguity endemic in the literary sources, which were invoked and in the culture generally, made synthesis very difficult. It certainly would be quite anachronistic to expect some such synthesis as is found in Vatican II's Constitution *On the Church in the Modern World*. Perhaps though there were some strands even in the theological tradition which blazed a trail and pioneered the line which had its terminus in that Constitution. We shall now address ourselves to that question.

Peter Abelard (+ 1142)

Abelard's *Sic et Non* analysis of traditional positions was well suited to tease out some of the ambiguities in the area with which we are dealing. He maintained that pleasure in food and in sex was part of the Creator's intention and that one could not judge this pleasure wrong when properly used, otherwise the Creator himself would be guilty of occasioning sin. Employing a typical method of logical analysis, he asked whether it was consistent to hold that God made food and sex pleasurable but intended that these activities should never be used with pleasure. If there was a duty to propagate the race in accordance with Genesis 1, and if there was a marriage duty in accordance with 1 Cor 7, how could there be sin in doing what was commanded? Those who concluded from Psalm 50:7, 'Behold I am conceived in wickedness', and from 1 Cor 7:5, 'I say this in terms of a concession', that lawful sex pleasure implies guilt were led more by adherence to a beaten path than by respect for reason. In his view the judgement of the psalmist referred not to pleasure but to the state of sin which all men inherited at conception, and Paul was simply admitting that if married partners did not decide to live a life of sexual abstinence, they were permitted to use sex.[29]

These may not appear very striking statements today. In their time they were. Abelard's use of parallel scripture texts was a corrective to previous selective exegesis. Unfortunately, his own personal history did not put him in a strong position to influence the tradition.

Hugh of St Victor (+ 1141)

In his tract *On the Virginity of Mary*[30] Hugh developed a deeply scriptural appreciation of married love. For him marriage is primarily a community of love in which husband and wife take each other as companions or soul-mates for life. In this union of love the heart finds a partner whom it binds to itself permanently in an exclusive and unique fashion. For Hugo, the normative emphasis in the Creation narratives was that of Genesis 2 (partnership) rather than that of Genesis 1 (parenthood). He sees the task of propagating the race as a purpose enjoined by God on a state of life which already had meaning in itself. While this family task brings a new fruitfulness and selflessness to a marriage, marital consent is still essentially consent to a community of life and love. The mutual consent to sexual intercourse is an extension of this.

His analysis of Genesis 2:24 is most interesting. In any conflict between the love for one's parents and the love for one's partner, the gratuitous love of choice takes precedence over the natural love of state. 'In this unique community in which a man owes himself to another he does not set aside his love of parents so that he may give exclusive attention to his wife, but he prefers wife to parents and puts affection for her before affection for them.' In passing he comments that the phrase 'cleave to a wife' in this same verse has reference not to sexual intercourse but to that union of mutual love which is marriage, whereas the phrase 'they shall be two in one flesh' refers to the purpose for which marriage exists. We can see here perhaps a suggestion of the difference which Herbert Doms would later see between essence and purpose in marriage.

For Hugh there is a marked distinction in marriage between love and sex, a distinction dictated by his concern to substantiate the marriage of Mary and Joseph. In the phrase of Ephesians 5, the sexual consummation of marriage is described as a 'great sacrament', the symbol of the unity of nature between Christ and the church, but the union of hearts in marriage is the 'greater sacrament' the symbol of the unity of grace between God and human soul. The priorities are very clear here. The quite common teaching on the marriage act as symbol of the unity of Christ and the church[31] should have effectively exorcised the ghost of dualism. But the symbol tended to remain at a theoretical level and so did not really affect moral attitudes. Hugh himself could still say 'Marriage is all the more true and holy when it is covenanted in the bond of charity rather than in the concupiscence of the flesh and in the flames of lust'. No matter how exalted the symbolic meaning, sex at the level of actual experience still had concupiscence as its cross reference.

Peter de Palude (+ 1342)

One of the strangest developments of all occurred when Peter de Palude maintained that what was later known as *coitus reservatus* was lawful between married partners. The age old principles which he undoubtedly accepted should have marked as libidinous a sexual act where ejaculation of seed was withheld so that procreation could be avoided. The inconsistency remains in his pages. His central text reads: 'It does not appear that a husband sins mortally if before the act is completed he withdraws to avoid producing more children than he can rear, unless in the course of it has provoked orgasm in his wife. Similarly if in this way he avoids having (full) intercourse with his wife, the common opinion would hold that he did not deny her the marriage due. It does not appear that he even sins venially, because it is lawful to seek not to have more children than one can rear, and he is not bound to seek the marriage due nor to consummate an act already begun unless his wife requests this.'[32]

Even though authors pointed out that in this Peter was quite eccentric, his

AN IRISH READER IN MORAL THEOLOGY

view gained the support of theologians like Antonius of Florence[33] and of canonists like Sanchez.[34] In our own times came that idealisation of *étreinte reservée* as expression of married love celebrated by Paul Chanson in his *Art d'aimer et continence coniugale*.[35] A few months after this book appeared the Holy Office demanded that it be withdrawn from circulation and two years later (30 June 1952) issued a monitum to all writers and confessors that they should not speak of *coitus reservatus* 'in terms which suggested that there was no objection to it from the point of view of the Christian moral law'.

Whatever about the ethical pros and cons of *coitus reservatus*, Peter de Palude is important because his theory could have opened up the whole question of the place of sex in marriage and its relationship to married love. In effect it did not succeed in doing this. The ensuing discussion stayed very much within traditional lines.[36]

Nicholas of Oresme (+ 1382)

The polymath Nicholas, astronomer, physicist, theologian, Master of the College of Navarre in the University of Paris, and Bishop of Lisieux, produced a French translation and commentary on the *Pseudo-Economics* of Aristotle.[37] His work blends scripture and commonsense into a handbook for the day-to-day living of marriage. Here we find a real effort to integrate love and sexuality.

> It often happens that two young people, a man and a woman, love each other in a special way by choice and with heart-felt joy, with a love that is reasoned, though at times not correctly reasoned … Sometimes this is a chaste love and prepared for marriage. And if sin should enter in it is a human fault. But to approach anyone indifferently with no other love than the desire to satisfy one's concupiscence, this is a bestial sin.
>
> Nature granted carnal pleasure to the animals only for the purpose of reproduction; but it accorded the human species this pleasure not only for reproduction of its kind but also to enhance and maintain friendship between man and woman. This is implied in Pliny's statement that no female, after she has become pregnant, seeks sexual union, except woman only (*Nat. Hist.* VII, 5). This explains the statement in (Aristotle's) *Politics* 11, 1, that two friends desire to become a single being. Thus we may say that husband and wife are more nearly a unit than the male and female of other species because the first woman was formed from a rib of her husband and this was not the case of the other animals. For this reason, scripture says that a married couple is two persons in a single skin (Gen 2:24). Thus we may now perceive how this life of husband and wife together is based upon friendship.

Nicholas teaches the need for an act of love on the part of the husband. His lovemaking should be marked by a general refinement and sensitivity to his wife's feelings and disposition. His general attitude to her in day-to-day domestic life is the *mise en scène* of their sexual life. He must perform the sexual act reverently and decently as befits its quality and meaning. The husband must satisfy his wife's desires so that she will not be tempted to look for love elsewhere, but he must not over-awake or overengage her sexually, lest she become dangerously restive in his absence.

All in all this is a striking synthesis of sex, love and marriage. These three are accepted as quite natural and as belonging together. Here is something quite other than an apology for sex and grudging excusation of sexual pleasure. But Nicholas does not seem to have had any influence whatever on the theological tradition.

Denis the Carthusian (+1471)

The catechism for married Christians of Denis the Carthusian, *De laudabili vita coniugatorum*,[38] was first given general circulation in 1530. It is strange that married people should have had to look for guidance to a Carthusian mystic. His treatise provides fifteen reasons for the goodness of marriage and sets out the blessed nature of married love. This love is spiritual, natural, social and carnal. The marriage act is good as an expression of charity or spiritual love but also as an expression of carnal love, a love based on 'sensual delights'. He says that 'The married can mutually love each other through the mutual pleasure they find in the marital act.' Admittedly, he concludes with a strong warning against uxoriousness and with the reminder that according to the *Revelations* of St Bridget of Sweden a man was damned for loving his wife too carnally. In fact, he had quoted earlier Jerome's comment that 'a too ardent husband is an adulterer'. All that he is saying here is that if pleasure becomes an end in itself it is no longer serving married love. It was these terms that later pastoral theology condemned sexual intercourse practised *ob solam voluptatem*.

Martin le Maistre (+1481)

Le Maistre was convinced that the prevailing teaching on the use of sex in marriage was quite unrealistic and subversive of genuine morality. He set out to reach a balance by using Aristotle's concept of the golden mean to site marital chastity as virtue between the opposing vices of profligacy and insensibility. Having stated that sex is good when it serves the purposes of procreation, of rendering the debt, and of avoiding adultery, he adds: 'It sometimes happens that libido is so vehement, and so disturbs the mind that a man is scarcely master of himself ... Calming of the mind through marital intercourse is not serving lust but placing lust under the yoke of reason.'[39]

This statement may not strike us as very *Bahnbrechend* but in its time it marked progress to a more rounded human picture of the place of sex in the overall life of the married person. It contrasted with the general theory that a request for intercourse for the purpose of allaying sexual tension (*in remedium concupiscentiae*) was morally reprehensible.

John Maior (+1550)

On the question 'When is it lawful to know one's wife?' this Scotsman remarked, 'Here I find great variety among the doctors, men in my opinion far too rigid.' Having given the usual reasons justifying sex in marriage he continues, 'Whatever men say, it is difficult to prove that a man sins in knowing his own wife for the sake of pleasure.' This is no more wrong, he says, than to eat a sweet apple for the pleasure of it. Indeed to say otherwise is to convict the majority of married people of living in sin.[40]

This doctrine was nothing more than drawing to its logical conclusion the philosophy of act and pleasure which Aquinas had taken from Aristotle, the view that the goodness or badness of the pleasure essentially depends on the goodness or badness of the act which it accompanies.[41] Unfortunately, the phrase *sex for the sake of pleasure* suggests that pleasure is made an end in itself, that one party uses the other as a means to his own sexual gratification. Here Nicholas of Oresme and Denis the Carthusian were on more solid ground when they invoked love rather than pleasure as term of moral reference.

Francis de Sales

It is evident that little of the experience of the lay person in the world, and in particular of the married person, was so far channelled into the theological tradition proper. Francis de Sales, Bishop of Geneva, preacher of missions, director of souls and saint, was well placed to do this. When we read his *Introduction to the Devout Life* we should note how he reads the scriptural emphases, and applies them to day-to-day life, keeping in mind that he published his book in the very year 1608 that Sanchez was putting the finishing touches to his *De Matrimonio*. We make no apology for the following long quotation. It has a unique quality and breathes the spirit which made de Sales the pastor *par excellence*.

> Above all, I exhort married persons to have that mutual love which is so earnestly enjoined by the Holy Ghost in the scriptures. It is little to have natural love, for a pair of turtle doves has the same; or mere human love, for in that the heathens were not lacking; but I say with St Paul (Eph 5:22, 25): 'Husbands, love your wives, as Christ also loved the church ... Let women be subject to their husbands, as the Lord.'
>
> It was God who brought Eve to Adam and gave her to him as his wife, and it is God, my friends, who with his invisible hand bound the knot which unites you and gave you to another; therefore give good heed that you cherish a love which is holy, sacred and divine.
>
> The first result of such love is the indissoluble union of your hearts. If two pieces of wood are carefully glued together, their union will be so close that it is easier to break them in some fresh place than where they are joined; and God so united man and wife, that it is easier to sever soul and body

than those two. And this union is less that of the body, than of the heart, its affections and love.

The second result of this love is inviolable fidelity. Of old a man's seal was always engraved on a ring which he wore on his finger, as is frequently testified in holy scripture; and this is the meaning of the marriage ceremony. The church, through her priest, blesses a ring, that it may never be given to any other woman as long as this one lives. Then the bridegroom places the ring on the hand of his bride, that she in like manner may know that her heart must never be given to any other man but to him whom Christ has given her.

The third end of marriage is the birth and bringing up of children. And surely it is a great honour to be permitted to increase the number of souls whom God will save, and who will serve him through all eternity; your part being to bring forth those bodies, into which he will infuse an immortal soul. Therefore do you, husbands, preserve a tender, constant and heartfelt love for your wives; the woman was taken from that side which was nearest Adam's heart, that she might be the more heartily and tenderly loved.

Love and fidelity always engender confidence; and for this reason saints in the married state have used mutual caresses – caresses truly loving but chaste, tender but sincere. So Isaac and Rebecca, the most chaste married couple of the olden time, by their mutual conduct, at once edified Abimelach and made him to know that they were man and wife. The great St Louis, equally rigorous towards himself and tender in his love for his wife, was almost blamed for his softness in caressing her, although in truth he merited rather praise for knowing how to adapt his brave and martial spirit to those endearments which tend to keep up and nourish the mutual love and affection of husband and wife.[42]

Francis de Sales was a man of unusual understanding. The married Christians who had him as spiritual guide were indeed favoured, and down the years his writings published in the vernacular were fortunately more accessible to a lay audience than were the professional volumes of men such as his contemporary Sanchez. One wonders what effect, if any, he had on these professional authors. One cannot recall any worthwhile mention of him in the classical manuals on sexuality and marriage.

But he was certainly well placed to influence the pastoral scene of his time, belonging as he did to that elite group known as *L'Ecole Française* which did so much for Catholic reform in the France of the seventeenth century, not least through inspiring missionaries like Vincent de Paul, John Eudes, and Jean-Jacques Olier. But in comparison even with these De Sales stands apart for his broader vision, for his greater belief in the goodness of God's creation, and indeed for his closer contact with the day-to-day reality of the Christian life of the layman. His more generous humanism offset to a degree that Augustinianism which supplied his contemporaries with an endless source of moralising. Francis may not have reached a final synthesis of a theology of secular realities, but he was definitely a pioneer, and his writings were a source of inspiration to many saintly married men and women who recognised God's creating and redeeming hand in the lives they were leading in the world.

Conclusion

Without question the synthesis of love, sexuality, partnership and parenthood in the context of Christian marriage set out by Vatican II is unprecedented. The Council read the signs of the times, crystallised the *sensus fidelium* and showed close contact with Christian family life lived in the Spirit. If classical theology had not reached that synthesis, we have seen that at least there were some straws in the wind. There were also some indications in earlier official teaching of a wider perspective than that of the textbook. That pastoral handbook *The Roman Catechism* or *The Catechism of the Council of Trent* contained some perceptive remarks on the meaning of love in Christian marriage which should have merited more reflection from theologians. Then there was that extraordinary paragraph in Pius XI's *Casti Connubii*, 'This mutual interior formation of husband and wife, this persevering endeavour to bring each other to the state of perfection, may in a true sense be called, as the Roman Catechism calls it, the primary cause and reason of marriage, so long as marriage is considered not in its stricter sense as the institution destined for the procreation and education of children, but in the wider sense as a complete and intimate life-partnership and association.' It is said that some early translations simply omitted this paragraph, seeing in it a possible source of confusion in the context of the traditional parenthood-partnership hierarchy of purposes in marriage, and that in spite of the final saving clause or apologia in the paragraph itself.

That whole debate on the comparative importance of the twin purposes of marriage had generally unhappy effects. It siphoned off a great deal of theological energy that would have been better expended on more productive subjects. It also hindered the first steps towards the synthesis reached by Vatican II. In 1944 the Holy Office replied in the negative to the question: 'Whether the opinion of certain modern writers can be admitted, who either deny that the primary end of marriage is the generation and education of children, or teach that the secondary ends are not subordinate to the primary end, but are equally principal and independent.' It is accepted that a book by Herbert Doms, *Vom Sinn und Zweck der Ehe*, was one of the principal targets of this intervention. One wonders whether the censors were fair to Doms. He distinguished what marriage *is* from what marriage *is for*, the meaning of marriage as two-in-oneness from its essential purposes. The *is* of marriage is a community of love, and this love embraces the couple in the roles both as partners and parents.[43] When Vatican II spoke of love in marriage it was moving along the same lines.

It deliberately avoided any reference to primary-secondary purposes in order to get away from what had become a sterile theological debate.

Following on Vatican II, theologians now speak of love as the soul of marriage. It links man and woman in life-long faithful partnership where 'I love you' means 'I love you alone', 'I love you always'. The marriage act expressing that love is a symbol deeper than any words. Through it love crowns wedlock with the gift of new life and *inspires* to the joint task of bringing new life to adulthood. The couple become partners in parenthood: in the child their love lives. And they become parents in partnership: their first duty to their child is that they love each other.

In this article I confined my interest to theological writing. I was aware that I was leaving aside a whole corpus of sermons and nuptial liturgies which may well provide a wider human and Christian *Weltanschauung* for marriage. These are far more difficult to control and a great deal of primary research still remains to be done in unpublished sources.

Charles Paris, in *Marriage in XVII Century Catholicism*[44] has sifted through the published sermon collections and catechisms of an important century in the French church. Doctrinally these faithfully reflect the theology of Augustine and Aquinas. They speak of married love from two angles – that of the agape of Eph 5, the celestial symbol of the faithful love of Christ for his church, and, secondly, that domestic understanding, mutual support and co-operation embodied in the distinctive roles evidenced by the family ethic of the time. There is no synthesis of agape and eros, and certainly no relating of love to its sexual expression. In his final summing-up Fr Paris writes, 'Love has often been spoken of in these pages but it was for the most part identified with the intimate relationship of man and divinity. The intimate union of man and woman, better known as sexual intimacy, did not come within the scope of true love. Sex was spoken of as duty, obligation of justice, not as an expression of love … The need for union and intimacy between husband and wife was often expressed in both sermon and catechism but it could not be sexual intimacy since the latter, even in its most legitimate expression, was branded with sinfulness, or, at the very least moral weakness.' Here again is that aura of concupiscence and the need always to 'excuse' the use of sex long current in medieval theology.

In two articles titled 'Love and Marriage in the Middle Ages'[45] Fr Fabian Parmisano has given us a foretaste of his Cambridge dissertation on love and marriage in the poetry, liturgy and pastoral theology of the fourteenth century. This promises to be a very worthwhile study and should show that in the liturgy at any rate there seems to be some vindication of the place of The Song of Songs in an orthodox Christian context – *Lex orandi lex credendi*.

In *Gaudium et Spes* Vatican II forged links between Creation and Redemption. Love and sexuality are redeemed and redeeming realities. Teilhard de Chardin said: 'Passion itself is placed at the service of Christ'. The understanding reached here by Vatican II is, if you will pardon the jargon, self-authenticating. 'Truth can impose itself on the mind of man only in virtue of its own truth, which wins over the mind with both gentleness and power.'[46] It has proved itself also by results on the evangelical principle: 'By their fruits you will know them.' Movements such as the Catholic Marriage Advisory Council, the Christian Family Movement, or Marriage Encounter show the Spirit in action, inspiring married Christians to recognise in their family lives a way of salvation.

This is one area where theology must listen to and not quench the Spirit. Still, even when surrounded by the carnival of the heart, theology must not lose its head. It should plead long experience as its title to hold a watching brief in case eros, having evaded the Scylla of the Manicheans, pile up on the Charybdis of the Pelagians. The task of systematising and building up a balanced picture is a sober and sobering enterprise. Here in the words of St Paul theology is called on to 'Prove all things, hold fast that which is good' (1 Thess 5:21). In that final picture the thought of Augustine and Aquinas will surely be represented and shown to better effect in that the cultural modes which trammelled them will be set aside. Love, now as then, will need to be anchored firmly in an institutional context which in the last analysis will best safeguard its promise of personal fulfilment and permanence. The wisdom of the Christian ages will speak for this givenness of the family unit where man and woman surrender themselves one to the other irrevocably in the cause of love and life. That same wisdom will keep before the eyes of a more optimistic theology the ambiguity of the human condition where pride, avarice, lust, anger, gluttony, envy and sloth constantly hinder the Spirit. Exorcising the dualist presupposition, which made for an ontological split between a higher spiritual nature and a lower bodily nature, will leave the person still divided against himself in his decisions for good, still unable to integrate his whole being towards love of God and neighbour. The term concupiscence favoured by the patristic and scholastic traditions reflected not just a dualist philosophy but an intrinsic factor of the human condition, a factor which means that the mode of human being which man experiences as normal now is not the mode intended by God in the beginning.'[47] A Christian ethic of sexuality and marriage must take account of a truth which is so closely knit through the many strands of the mystery of redemption as defined by the church. Augustine and Aquinas, admittedly speaking with very human voices and in very historically conditioned terms, are perennial witnesses to a mystery known only by revelation.

Notes:

1. *Contra Julianum* 5, 12, 46-7. PL 44, 810-11.
2. S.T. III, q. 29, c.4.
3. S.T. I, II, qq. 26-29.
4. On cultic purity in the Graeco-Roman tradition see A. D. Nock, *Essays on Religion and*

the Ancient World, Oxford 1972, Vol 1, pp 63 ff for a very useful selection of temple inscriptions dealing with sexual taboo. He comments: 'Out of such beliefs which are in essence magical, ethical consideration can grow: in a large measure it is from the notion of the avoidance of ritual defilement and a loss of magical force that the idea of chastity develops.' Still it is fair to say, and Nock would be the first to admit it, that in the philosophical tradition of Aristotle in particular there is an ethical appreciation of the virtue of chastity on a level with other moral values which is independent of the ritual factor.

5. A high reputation as a biblical scholar gave wide currency to Jerome's views. His paraphrase of Paul's 'It is good for a man not to touch a woman' as 'It is evil for a man to touch a woman' shows his temper. There is strong suspicion that in translating the Book of Tobias, which he regarded as deutero-canonical, he interpolated some of his own views on sex. His Vulgate version alone carries the well-known section 6:16-22.

6. *Soliloquium* l, 10. PL 32, 878.

7. *Contra Julianum Opus Imperf.* 6.22.PL 45, 1553. This was Augustine's last theological writing.

8. *I, q. 98, art 2. Already in In Sent.* IV, 26, 1 ad 3 Aquinas had stated that sex was connatural to man and created as such by God.

9. The moral privation implied by the fact that reason is absorbed by libido is a theme reaching back to Aristotle through Jerome. On this see Aquinas, 1, 11, q. 34 art. 1; *Suppl.* Q. 42 art. 3, q. 49 art. 1, q. 64 art. 7-9, and Ligouri, *Theol, Mor.* Lib. 3, n. 432.

10. *De peccato originali* 34, 39. CSEL 42, 197; *Contra Julianum Opus Imperf.* 2, 218. PL 45, 1237. Some special influence of the devil over man's sexual nature became a commonplace for later theology. Aquinas said: 'Since the corruption of original sin through which man is enslaved is transmitted to us by the act of generation, God has permitted the devil to have a malevolent control over this act more than over others', *Suppl.* Q. 58, art. 2 ad 1. The title *De frigidis et male ficiatis* in the Decretals of Gregory IX gathered around itself a large amount of arcane and occult lore on this topic.

11. *De nupt. Et concup.* 2, 21, 36. CSEL 42, 209.

12. *De bono coniug.* 13, 15. CSEL 41, 208.

13. *Epist.* XI, 4, 64. PL 77, 1196. There is some doubt about authenticity – see M. Deansley and P. Grosjean, 'The Canterbury Edition of the Answers of Pope Gregory I to St Augustine', *Jour. Eccl. Hist.* 10 (1959), pp 1-49. Apocryphal or not, many of Gregory's parables and tales became the stock in trade of the medieval preacher, such as his story about the woman carried off by the devil on the feast of San Sebastiano because she had sexual relations with her husband on the previous night – see Aquinas, *Suppl.* q.64, art. 8 ad. 1.

14. Bk 1, ch 27.

15. *Decretum Gratiani* C.7, c. 33, q. 4.

16. *In s. Pauli Epistolas,* 1 Cor. 7 *lectio prima.*

17. *De matrimonio,* lib, 9, disp. 1.

18. *De nupt. et concup.* 1, 11, 12. PL 44, 421-1.

19. *In Sent.* IV, dist. 26.

20. Ibid. dist. 30.

21. *Sent.* IV, dist. 30.

22. *Ethics* bk 8, lect 3, n 1173; lect 4, n 1587.

23. On all this see I, q. 92, artt. 1-4.

24. II, II, q. 26, art. 11.

25. The texts of Sextus and Jerome were readily available in Gratian's *Decretum* C. 32, q.

26. Lib. 1, tit. 5, q. 10, nn. 1-54.

27. Lib. 7, tit. 3, q. 1.

28. *De Matrimonio*, lib. 2, dist. 22, nn. 1-4; Humanae Vitae n. 13.

29. *Ethica* c. 3. PL 178, 640-2. See also his reply to the forty-second question submitted by Heloise. *Heloissae Problemata* PL 178, 723-730.

30. PL 176, 859-864.

31. It is found in Hincmar of Rheims, *Epistola* 22, PL 126, 137, in Yves of Chartres *Epistola* 242, PL 162, 250, in Peter Lombard, *Sent.* IV, dist. 26, c. 7, in Aquinas *Suppl.* Q. 62, art. 2 ad 1.

32. *In IV Sent.*, dist. 31, q. 3, a. 2.

33. *Summa Theol.* Pars. 3, tit. 1, c. 20, par. 1.

34. *De Matrimonio* liv. 9, disp. 19, nn. 3.

35. Editions Familiales de France: Paris 1950.

36. On the whole question one should read Adam Exner, *The Amplexus Reservatus seen in the History of Catholic Doctrine on the Use of Marriage*, University Press: Ottawa 1963.

37. *Le liver de Yconomique d'Aristote*, edited by A. D. Menut in *Transactions of the American Philosophical Society* (New Series), vol. 47, part. 5.

38. *Opera Carthusianorum* (Tournai 1896-1913), vol 38.

39. *Quaestiones Morales* vol 2, c. *de temperantia*. Interestingly, Le Maistre taught in the same College of Navarre in the University of Paris as Nicole d'Oresme had done a century earlier.

40. *In IV Sent.* dist. 31.

41. *Ethics* bk 10, lect 8, n 2050.

42. *Introduction to the Devout Life*, ch 38. See also ch 39 for his advice on the use of marriage, something which is 'holy, just and commendable in itself and so profitable to the commonwealth.'

43. Doms wrote: 'Perhaps it would be best if in future we gave up using such terms as primary and secondary in speaking of the purposes of marriage. It would be best if we just spoke of the procreative and personal purposes immanent in marriage, and distinguished them from its meaning. It is not our business to say exactly which of these purposes is the more important; for while one is more important from one point of view, from another point of view it is less so' – English version, *The Meaning of Marriage*, London 1939, p 88.

44. This was a doctoral dissertation at the Institut Catholique de Paris, published by Desclée: Tournai, 1975.

45. *New Blackfriars*, August and September 1969.

46. Vatican II, *Dignitatis Humanae*, pr. 1.

47. The analysis of the concept presented by Karl Rahner thirty years ago is still very well worth reading – 'Theological Concept of Concupiscentia' in *Theological Investigations* – I, Darton Longman Todd, 1961.

Part Three
Family

12   Marriage, Friendship and Community

Bernadette Kimmerling

(*The Furrow*, Vol 31, No 6, June 1980, pp 366-373)

Lay people can contribute to a renewed theology of marriage by reflecting on, and articulating their experience. To do this they must try to identify the trends which seem to be universal or at least general in their own marriage. This is what I shall be trying to do here, although I acknowledge that in an article of this length many points will have to remain undeveloped.

One of the most significant facts about marriage today is that people live longer. Hence a marriage can be expected to last, not twenty years, as when life expectancy was forty, but perhaps for half a century. I am not sure that existing theory of marriage (psychological, sociological and theological) takes this seriously.

Marriage involves (i) the loving relationship of the couple and (ii) the loving relationship of parenthood. Perhaps we now need to advert to a third dimension which is equally important. This third dimension is the loving relationship of the couple with the wider community. This is an aspect which was not entirely ignored in the past but which now needs to be given fuller recognition. All three dimensions usually co-exist in a marriage but each in turn comes to the fore, if the marriage lasts a sufficiently long time. In previous generations, because of the brevity of most marriages, the first two dimensions most frequently occupied the foreground. In modern marriage, the third dimension may be expected to assume greater importance than hitherto. By the time a couple who have a loving relationship come to the midpoint of their lives they hopefully will have achieved a certain degree of maturity, autonomy and separateness. Parenthood may no longer demand all their energies (they may even be geographically separated from their children) yet they still have half their lives to live. What then is to be their role and function as a Christian couple for the rest of their lives? I believe that it is at this point that the third dimension, the loving relationship with the wider community, comes to the fore.

Marriage: The Primary Commitment
Before moving on to discuss more fully the third dimension, I'd like to look first at the loving married relationship and its development up to this point. I want to try to identify two forces which are at work in preparing the couple for, and in precipitating them into, their community role.

I believe there are two powerful agents which influence the evolution of a marriage. They are: (i) Love and an awareness of its transforming power; (ii) The psychological pressure from within the individual to undertake the inter-relational task of creative friendship, appropriate to the mid-life stage of adult development.

I will deal with love and its transforming power first. I see the marriage of the couple as their response to deep urges within themselves. These urges are normal and universal and are associated with the developmental task appropriate to this stage of young adult development, i.e. the establishing of a loving intersexual relationship. While some of this may be understood consciously, many of the needs and desires are inchoate or unconscious. They are not merely sexual in nature although they are linked with the need to acquire a sexual identity. Their origins lie deep in the personality, and their nature will not be fully recognised or articulated until they have been fulfilled in the relationship. One of the most powerful of these desires is the (unrealisable) desire to merge or unite with the person who is loved. During the first years of marriage the partners, in seeking this immature type of unity and in failing to achieve it, confront for the first time in their lives the reality of their own separateness and isolation. This growth towards separateness passes through various recognisable stages. First there is a sense of loss or mourning for a unity which was thought to have existed and which now is seen never to have existed at all. Then there is a lonely resignation to this loss, followed by a mobilisation of the will in an attempt to accept it constructively. Finally there comes a time when a reaching out of this separateness to the other occurs. This reaching out is not just an event which occurs as a result of a decision made by the person concerned – it is much more than that. There is always an element of letting go, of being forced to let go, of no longer being able to hold back. It is a gesture which seems to be forced out of one by the circumstances of one's life rather than something one deliberately decides to do. It is experienced as submission to some force which is greater than oneself. It is an experience of total vulnerability. I believe that this point can be described as the breakthrough of the spirit. Love is now perceived as surrender – a giving up of oneself. It permeates the entire personality and is recognised as the most important power in life. The experience is one of *metanoia*. New insight occurs. Life is lived from then on, on a new level of awareness. Separateness, which was at first a cause of mourning, then resignation, followed by acceptance, finally becomes a fact to be celebrated and rejoiced in. The experience is that of redemption, redemption by love, of being set free or of discovering that one is free. It is a deeply spiritual experience. The interpersonal processes which contribute to and lead up to this redemption are the loving sharing of emotions, activities, ideas and insights. Interpersonal conflict will be experienced by each partner as the various stages leading up to the breakthrough are negotiated. This conflict gives rise to suffering and a sense of alienation. Trust in one another is necessary to carry the intriguing element in the whole matrix because it underpins the entire process and new levels of it are continually being created through these interactions.

The growth of trust is synonymous with the growth of love. Insight is gained into the notion that the growth of trust and love is accompanied by an increased capacity for suffering. What a strange and apparently arrogant choice one makes when one decides to love another and, knowing the twofold consequence of love, what test of one's belief in love itself is involved! Trust for this reason is to me the most difficult of all the choices to be made in marriage. Permanence (which is a condition of Christian marriage) provides the time and security for the working out of this dimension of marriage. In the final 'letting go' which is the culminating element in the redemptive process, trust is at last seen to be the entrusting of oneself to another.

The force which has been at work in a hidden way during this first phase of marriage surfaces at this point of breakthrough and is now fully recognised as the force of love. Its power to transform is appreciated properly for the first time. The presence of this new type of love in the marriage, and the awareness of its transforming power, seem to compel the couple to use this new power. But there may be no clear insight or indication as to where or how it is to be used apart from the family situation. And so a feeling of power without direction exists.

I believe that it is at this point that the second force comes into play and it is this which determines the direction in which the marriage moves.

The second force is, as I have already said, the psychological pressure from within the individual to undertake the inter-relational task of creative friendship which is appropriate to the midlife stage of adult development.

To explain my point and illustrate how the second force works in the thrust towards community building in marriage, it is necessary to remember that psychological development does not stop in early adulthood but continues right through life (although the later stages are not as well researched or documented in psychological literature). I believe that spiritual development goes hand in hand with, and is nudged forward by, physical and psychological factors. I would see positive spiritual growth as that which takes into account and is in harmony with the other two. The movements which occur in both these areas are the sources of the challenges which initiate spiritual growth. They are the material through which salvation is worked out. They provide constant challenge and conflict. The individual's response to the challenges and his resolution of the conflicts are the stuff of moral choice and hence of spiritual life. Therefore, to aid spiritual development we must constantly deepen our understanding of the natural processes at work in our lives. For this purpose, I'd like to focus on what I believe to be a much neglected aspect of the psychological development of the person in mid-life – namely, the task of developing creative friendship, because I see that this task, if properly carried out, will be the cornerstone on which Christian communities will be built.

The growth of the personality from childhood through adolescence up to

AN IRISH READER IN MORAL THEOLOGY

the point where marriage and parenthood occur has been fairly adequately explored by psychologists. Each stage of life up to this point is seen to have interpersonal tasks which are appropriate to it; and the successful resolution of these tasks contributes to the growing maturity and spirituality of the personality. These interpersonal tasks are all associated with the creation of relationships of love, with different categories of people – with parents and family in early life, with peers during the latency period, with the opposite sex during the teen years. Then follows the selection of a mate, courtship, marriage. It sometimes incorrectly appears that the circle is complete when the individual in turn becomes a parent; but this is not so – the line is a curve, not a circle. The formation of these relationships roughly spans the first half of life. It will be seen from this that up to this point at no time has friendship been the primary task or the particular psychological phase (with the possible exception of the latency period when rudimentary friendships were formed). It has been secondary to the main relationship in each phase. I believe that at the mid-point of life, friendship becomes more significant than it ever has been before and might even be regarded as the primary task of mid-life adult development. (This fact I think has particular significance in the lives of celibate and single persons. Friendship has to be used by them to achieve a positive sexual identity – a task more usually worked out within the married relationship.) The readiness of the couple to undertake the task of creative friendship appears to me to coincide with the completion of the redemptive phase in the couple's relationship. In doing so, it makes their inclination towards community more effective. The conscious recognition of the power of love as an agent of growth and transformation gives greater impetus and urgency to the desire to form meaningful and loving friendships. This call to friendship has an element of insistence which cannot be ignored. The call to love is probably felt more consciously and urgently than during any of the previous developmental phases. It is not seen as a call away from the loving relationship with the spouse but as a logical extension of the primary relationship. This urgency I'm sure is explained by the fact that there is a greater awareness than ever before of the spiritual dimensions of the call and the responsibility therefore to answer it.

These friendships are obviously different in kind, quality and depth from premarried ones. Their quality will be determined by the quality of the marriage relationship. When the marriage relationship is fundamentally loving, the shallow and more casual type of friendship which characterised the less mature premarried person, will no longer satisfy – particularly when compared with the deep level of loving established between the couple. It becomes increasingly difficult to live at a shallow level outside the marriage and a deep level within it; hence the need to seek something better and deeper in friendship. The successful resolution of this task of forging creative friendships can, as in the preceding phases, lead to greater maturity and richness of life.

So these two – (i) love and an awareness of its transforming power and (ii) the psychological pressure from within the individual to undertake the inter-relational task of creative friendship which is appropriate to the mid-life stage of adult development – these are the forces which combine to propel the couple into the third dimension of marriage, i.e. community building through relationship. Each partner then feels free and even urgently obliged to turn outwards with redemptive love towards others. Not necessarily others of their own choosing, but those whom God in one way or another brings into sharp focus. This focusing on another can have an emotional or a sexual element as the presenting symptom. As a result many people are afraid to probe deeper and run away. For others the question arises whether the trust and love established between the couple is sufficient to carry the partners through this emotional desert which exists while one or other partner is 'about his father's business'. These redemptive sorties out of the basic relationship can only be carried through if the commitment to the marriage is total. As a criterion of their wholesomeness, the effect they have on the primary relationship within the marriage has to be honestly evaluated and found beneficial. The risk is great and very real and the passive partner lives through this period of risk with great suffering, pushing his faith and trust in his spouse beyond its existing boundaries, forging for the future a new trust of greater beauty and depth.

There is a giving and a receiving in these friendships (and they can be with people of both sexes). Growth occurs. Permanent bonds of sustaining love can be created by the mutual sharing which occurs. The privacy and dignity of the person must be respected. A community of love is formed. The quality of love created will be dictated by the honesty, openness, authenticity and maturity of the people involved. The relationship, while very different in kind and in depth from the marriage relationship, is nevertheless no less important when viewed from the perspective of eternity. That which is received in such a relationship is brought back to the marriage to enrich it so that stasis or arrest does not occur. That which is given is carried further out into the community by the beneficiary in his or her other relationships. And so the couple become a base or source from which love is mediated to the community.

This view of marriage would question the current use of the word 'exclusive' and make us rethink what we mean by it. As it is understood at present it militates against the discovery of the third dimension. It would enlarge our understanding of the word 'total' when used in the context of marriage. The totality of one's commitment is an ever-increasing thing according as one's capacity increases and one's potentiality is realised. If contributed to only by a partner it would be limited by virtue of the limitations of the couple themselves, but by receiving from outside sources and by acknowledging that no one person can complete us, the totality of commitment within marriage reaches greater depth.

I believe that the redemption of the couple by one another and entry into the third dimension of marriage is only achieved by suffering and a necessary period of moral confusion. The call to love others in this new way can seem for a while irreconcilable with one's commitment to one's partner. The working through of this conflict can be a deep source of pain, tension, anxiety, emotional guilt and confusion for the couple; and much time may be needed for them to live their way through to the answer. But there is an answer – a positive and Christian one. When it is finally discovered it is then clearly realised that the two types of love do not clash with one another. The new love can gradually be integrated into the lives of the partners. In this way the first significant step towards community is taken.

Infidelity: an inauthentic response
The outline which I have given of the evolution of a marriage in the direction of the wider community may appear to be an idealised version; but it does reflect a trend to be seen operating in many Christian marriages. I believe it could be encouraged to operate in many more, if the church could be more specific in her identification of the challenges posed at each new stage of adult psychological development, particularly from mid-life on. The challenges of each new phase present themselves regardless of whether the ones posed in the previous stage were properly resolved or not. But the likelihood of any one stage being successfully completed is increased if the preceding one has been dealt with effectively. Hence, in a good Christian life, one is likely to see a sequence of good parent-child relationships leading to normal teenage relationships, satisfactory marriage, responsible parenting and finally deep creative friendship. Meanwhile, in less privileged lives, one can see a progression from impoverished childhood to troubled teens, unhappy marriage, inadequate parenting and infidelity, the latter being the inappropriate and inauthentic response to the normal psychological task of friendship at this time of life. In infidelity, people may be seeking not just to work out the task of friendship but may also be seeking to complete the unfinished tasks of earlier stages.

I believe that for the average Christian couple the call to community, or the challenge to form community through creative friendship (I wonder is this the only way of forming community?), could be made simpler and the danger of this challenge being inappropriately responded to by infidelity lessened, if the church in her pastoral capacity could provide some sort of education, information and support for couples in mid-life, the sort of support which is now available to engaged couples and young married people. The tasks in life become more difficult as the couple age because they become more specifically spiritual. These spiritual demands are in sharp contrast with the values of the materialistic world; a dichotomy exists. The ethos of the modern world is heavily weighted in favour of young adulthood and its intersexual development task.

There is little stress or value placed on middle life or old age. The tasks of these ages, when portrayed at all, are depicted in their negative aspects, e.g. infidelity and exploitation of the human person. Is it any wonder then, in the absence of the portrayal of the ideal or positive goals to be striven for in mid-life, that couples sink into apathy? It is a pity, when their lives could be so filled with joy in the pursuit of Christian ideals.

The church could help in this respect by researching and sign-posting the stages of life and spiritual development for middle life and old age. This information would need to be available in a form and a language which could be understood by all. In this way, the whole question of the temptation to be unfaithful could be approached in a positive and constructive way. It could be seen as a conflict to which there is a positive solution, a Christian solution. Instead of viewing it in an entirely negative way as temptation, it could be presented positively as a challenge to love. Instead of being regarded as something which might arise in some marriages, this conflict could be acknowledged to be part of the normal marriage packet, particularly in a loving relationship. It could be recognised that it will probably occur as the outcome of normal adult development. We need to stress more fully that the call to love is inherent in the temptation to infidelity. Are we not all, married and celibate alike, called to love? How often, I wonder, is that call to love not recognised because it is hidden in a situation which at first appears to threaten or be irreconcilable with our primary commitment.

We need to hear more about the theology of risk as an essential requirement for love. The grey areas, which are present so often in human relationships, should be given wider recognition as the soil in which the individual works out his salvation. Finally it should be made clear that the call to love is the call to enter into community, first the community of the couple, then of the family and finally the wider community. This final call should be recognised for what it really is, a normal phase of mid-life development, the logical and inevitable outcome of a loving married relationship and the life task of all Christians.

Update
The last section is judgemental. For a more nuanced development of this idea see my 'A Spirituality of Sexuality', Parts 1, 2, 3 in *Doctrine and Life*, Aug, Sept, Nov 1986. *B.K.*

13 Children's Rights and the Family: Myth and Reality

Ursula Kilkelly

(*Studies: An Irish Quarterly Review*, Vol 97, No 385, Spring 2008, pp 7-18)

Introduction

Although Ireland has perhaps come late to children's rights, they are not a new concept. The international community, in the form of the League of Nations, recognised children's rights as early as 1924 when it adopted the first Declaration on the Rights of the Child. The United Nations also adopted a Declaration on the Rights of the Child in 1959, and in 1989 children's rights were recognised as part of binding international law in the unanimous adoption by the General Assembly of the Convention on the Rights of the Child. The adoption of the Convention was endorsed around the world and it was quickly established as the most widely accepted instrument in international law. Ireland added its voice to the chorus in 1992, when it made a formal legal commitment accepting the Convention's obligations and undertaking to implement its provisions.

Ireland has made some progress in this area in recent years, adopting the National Children's Strategy,[1] establishing the Ombudsman for Children and appointing a Minister for Children. But, according to the Committee on the Rights of the Child, the expert international body that monitors implementation of the Convention, Ireland continues to lag behind in many areas, notably in the prevalence of paternalistic attitudes to children and the failure to recognise the position of the child as an independent rights-holder.[2] This has been recognised by Irish experts also[3] who have noted that Ireland's progress in realising children's rights is hampered by the terms of the Constitution whose strong provision for the family (and silence on independent rights for children) has dictated the direction and nature of law, policy and practice in many areas. Although the influence of the constitutional framework can be witnessed in the daily decisions of teachers, health care professionals and others who work with and for children,[4] it is most clearly illustrated by the handful of cases decided by the Supreme Court in this area. The purpose of this short article is to consider the relationship between children's rights and the family in the context of both the Convention on the Rights of the Child and the Irish Constitution. It does so by introducing children's rights generally and with reference to the family, before considering the implications of the current constitutional position, and proposals to bring it further into line with Ireland's children's rights obligations.

The Convention on the Rights of the Child: An Introduction

The Convention is a blueprint for the treatment of children in all areas of their lives and, accepted by 193 states worldwide, it reflects universal acceptance of best practice in relation to children. It is a comprehensive and detailed instrument that recognises children have rights in school, in the family and in society. The Convention makes provision for particularly vulnerable children, like refugee children, children without parental care, children in conflict with the law and those who have suffered abuse or exploitation, and it provides a minimum standard below which the treatment of all children must not fall. In this regard, it provides for the right to an adequate standard of living (art 27), the right to health and health care (art 24) and the right of equal access to education (art 28).

The Convention's General Principles

The Convention has four key provisions as fundamental guiding principles. These are the child's right to life, survival and development (art 6), the child's right to enjoy all rights without discrimination (art 2), the requirement that the best interests must be a primary consideration in all actions concerning the child, known as the 'best interests principle' (art 3), and the child's right to express his/her views and have them given due weight in all matters affecting the child in accordance with the child's age and maturity (art 12). These general principles inform all of the Convention's provisions[5] and taken together, they embody the ethos of the Convention, which aims to affirm the status of children as rights-holders, as individuals worthy of respect for the children they are rather than the adults they will become, and as active rather than passive participants in decisions made about their lives. The importance of treating children as equals, taking a child-centred approach and listening to children, thus capture what the Convention as a whole is trying to achieve in bringing about a sea-change in attitudes towards children.

Protection, Provision and Participation

A useful way to summarise the Convention's other provisions is to categorise them according to the three Ps of Protection, Provision and Participation.[6] 'Protection' rights include the child's right to protection from all forms of harm and abuse (Art 19) and to protection from sexual and commercial exploitation (Arts 32-36). This group also includes provisions that highlight the state's duty to respond effectively to children who have suffered harm, including by ensuring they receive the necessary support and follow-up (Art 19, 39). These provisions require strong protection for children at risk and attempt to ensure that all children have the opportunity to enjoy a childhood without violence. In the view of the Committee on the Rights of the Child, the Convention also requires the abolition of the physical punishment of children.[7] 'Provision' refers to the child's rights to have his/her basic needs fulfilled including the right to identity (Art 8), education (Arts 28 and 29), play (Art 31), health care (Art 24) and social security (Art 26). It also includes those provisions which make special provision for the rights of children with disabilities (Art 23), migrant children and those from minority groups (Arts 22, 30) and children without parental care (Art 20, 40). The final category of 'Participation' rights includes the child's right to be heard (Art 12), to access information (Art 17), including about his/her rights (Art 42), as well as the rights to freedom of expression (Art 13), religion (Art 14) and association (Art 15). These provisions recognise children's capacity to participate in decision-making that concerns them and aim to empower children, to give them a voice and to promote their constructive involvement in decision-making that affects them. 'Participation' rights also aim to prepare children for full active citizenship and their exercise is thus an essential part of preparing for the move from childhood to adulthood where these rights are taken for granted.

The Convention and the Family

As the consensus around these issues demonstrates, these rights are not especially controversial and few would dispute the importance of ensuring that they are fully vindicated against the State. Where some might have difficulty is with respect to the exercise of children's rights in the family. Talk of children's rights in this context is sometimes seen as a threat to the rights of parents, an attempt to undermine their authority or to seek to interfere on a greater scale with the integrity of the family. Visions emerge of children 'divorcing' their parents and being emancipated to live independently of those who seek to control them, or of the state regularly substituting its authority for that of parents. However, these positions misunderstand the meaning of children's rights and their role and importance in the family context. In particular, the Convention occasionally suffers from the misconception that it is anti-family, and that children's rights *per se* involve the zero sum game of taking rights from adults.[8] However, nothing in the text of its provisions supports these conclusions. In fact, the importance of the family to the child and of the child to the family is emphasised throughout the Convention. From the outset, the family is recognised as the fundamental unit of society and the child's need to grow up in a safe family environment is recognised. The importance of the family to children is also expressed with a strong emphasis on the important role that parents play in guiding and influencing their children in the exercise of their rights and generally. Frequent references are made to parents, legal guardians and extended family with a role in the child's life and the rights of parents are given explicit recognition. Specific provision is made for the child's right to know and be reared by his/her parents (Art 7), the right to enjoy regular and direct contact with parents following family separation (Article 9) and the right to be provided with alternative, family-based care, including adoption, where children are deprived of their family environment (Arts 20, 21). Special provision is made for children who find themselves living in different countries to their parents, and applications for family reunification must be handled in a humane, positive and expeditious manner (Art 10).

The balance between parents' and children's rights is delicately struck in Article 5 which contains the principle of evolving capacity. Here, the Convention recognises the rights and duties of parents to provide appropriate direction to their children in the exercise of their rights. However, this is to be done in a manner consistent with the child's evolving capacities, neatly demonstrating the gradual way in which parents' role in the protection of their children's rights transfers to the children themselves as they mature and develop to take on this role for themselves. This principle not only recognises the importance of parents providing support and guidance to young people in the exercise of their rights but also deals with the reality that very young children are not in a position to exercise their rights for themselves. In this way, Article 5 creates a bridge for children to cross with the help of their parents to bring them from early childhood, where parents can be expected to take all the decisions about their life and wellbeing, to adolescence where young people on the verge of adulthood can expect to take the majority of those decisions themselves. The role of the parents is explicitly recognised throughout this process as an important one of guide, adviser and supporter, and the position of the child is one of moving ever closer to full capacity.

The Convention is also clear that the State has a duty to support the family and parents in their child-rearing role. Article 18 is unequivocal that parents have the primary responsibility for the upbringing and development of their child, but it is explicit that the state has a duty to support parents through the provision of financial and other supports, and the development of children's facilities and services. Overall, the Convention is unequivocal about the importance of the family to the child, about the important role that parents play in the child's family life, and that the state has a duty to act in a positive manner to support, maintain and if necessary reinstate the family relationship.

It is clear, therefore, that the Convention and children's rights are entirely consistent with respect for the family and the role of parents in their children's lives. There is consistency too between the Convention and the Irish Constitution in relation to the importance of the family to society and to the child. Where difficulties appear in the constitutional framework, however, is with regard to the near absolute autonomy that parents enjoy as against the State, and the impact that this can have on the lives of their children, particularly in the absence of express constitutional rights for children. This will now be explored.

The Irish Constitutional Position
It is perhaps well known that the Irish Constitution (notably Articles 41 and 42) contains strong protection for the family, meaning the family based on mar-

riage, recognising it as an institution with inalienable and imprescriptible rights. In addition, the courts have recognised, through case-law, that children have the right to belong to a family, to have that family protected, to be educated by the family and to be provided by its parents with religious, moral, intellectual, physical and social education.[9] While these rights are clearly important, two concerns arise here: the first is the failure on the part of the State to fully vindicate these rights for children and their families. For instance, full implementation of a child's right to a family would require that adequate family support be available to help families in difficulty, would ensure family-based care for children who find themselves without parental care and would provide that any measures designed to help vulnerable children would focus on the family rather than on the individual (child or parent) in need. Similarly, vindication of the child's right to a family, and indeed the family's rights more generally, would ensure that unmarried fathers be supported to have a meaningful social as well as legal relationship with their children, would actively promote and support the involvement of all parents and extended family in their children's lives and would ensure that non-discriminatory legal provision was in place to protect and promote the child's relationship with his/her parents, regardless of their marital status. None of these propositions are anti-family or interfere in any way with its authority, yet they are also central to fulfilling the rights of children to, and in the family.[10] The second problem with the current constitutional provision is the balance, or rather the lack of balance that it strikes between the rights of parents and the rights of children.[11] In particular, the constitutional position of the family works to emphasise the rights of parents and gives them a higher value than the rights of children. This is compounded by the inadequate provision for children's rights in the Constitution and the fact that existing provision is linked inextricably to the family, meaning that children are not recognised to have rights of their own. Parents' rights, commensurate with the rights of the family, have been interpreted in almost absolute form and in a manner that has excluded giving due weight to the rights of the child where conflict exists. This position has its origins in Article 42.5 of the Constitution, which provides that the State must endeavour to supply the place of parents who have failed in their physical and moral duty towards their child but only 'in exceptional circumstances'. According to the Supreme Court, this operates as a presumption that the welfare of the child is to be found within the family (based on marriage) unless there are compelling reasons to the contrary.[12] This is a high threshold for state intervention in the family, which has made it difficult to ensure that children at risk are adequately protected. More importantly, this has prevented decisions being made on the merits of the case with the interests of the children being the primary factor.[13] Together, then, the constitutional emphasis on the family has led to the rights of children being ignored or underplayed in favour of the rights of parents.

Two examples illustrate the problem here: the first, known as the PKU case, was a Supreme Court case from 2001 concerning a dispute between the Health Board and the parents of a new-born who refused to give their consent to have the heel-prick test carried out.[14] The Health Board believed the test was strongly in the child's interests but the parents disagreed believing it caused harm to the child. The Supreme Court held that no matter how unreasonable the decision of the child's parents, it was one which they were entitled to make under the Constitution. The overwhelming benefits to the child of having the test done were thus a secondary consideration to the State's duty to respect the integrity of the family in the circumstances of the case. A key issue in this case was that the Oireachtas had not made the PKU test mandatory and the Court was reluctant to do this by case-law. This notwithstanding, one of the judgement's notable features was the absence of any real consideration for the rights of the child. While the Court might have reached the same conclusion were it required to give weight to the child's right to health and development, such a judgement would have resulted in clear recognition that the rights of the person at the centre of the case, who incidentally enjoyed no independent representation of his interests before the court, were also worthy of respect. It is also arguable that such a decision would have been child-centred and based on the merits of the case, rather than a deferral to a default position of respect for the rights of the parents, whose views in this case were described by the Court as 'irrational'.

A second case of note is that known as 'Baby Ann'[15] which involved the placement of a child for adoption and her parents' efforts to have their daughter returned following a change of heart. In September 2006, the High Court found there to be compelling reasons why Ann's welfare was not best served by returning her to her natural parents – she had become highly attached to her adoptive parents with whom she had lived for almost two years and other factors suggested that transfer of custody could not successfully be undertaken without causing her emotional and psychological harm. However, in November 2006, the Supreme Court reversed this decision holding that the correct test was whether the parents had failed in their duty to their child. As they had not – placing her for adoption did not constitute such failure – the Court found no basis for displacing the presumption that Ann was best raised in their care. It was clear, overall, that the constitutional position of the family based on marriage made it virtually impossible for baby Ann to be adopted regardless of the benefits of that decision for baby Ann herself. While it is difficult to say with certainty whether the Supreme Court would have reached the same conclusion were it required to give due consideration to the rights of baby Ann as part of its decision-making process, it would nonetheless have resulted in a judgement that at least recognised that the child involved also had rights that are worthy of consideration. Of note here, of course, are the child's right to know and be raised by her natural parents, but also relevant is the child's right to have decisions taken that are consistent with her best interests. In this way, the Baby Ann case makes clear that the current constitutional provision involves the operation of a strong presumption in favour of respect for the integrity of the marital family as opposed to any decision based on the merits of what is in the individual child's interests. Accordingly, these cases illustrate that children are silent in the Constitution, and especially where their parents' rights are involved, their rights are largely ignored.

The Way Forward?

These problems are not new and the need for reform has been recognised for some time. Their complexity means that there is no quick fix and any change must be very carefully thought-out and considered. The government appears finally to have some interest in amending the Constitution in this area and proposals are currently before an All-Party Oireachtas Committee. Without pre-empting this process, it is inescapable that the current proposals for constitutional amendment are *ad hoc* and offer little hope that the root and branch reform required is going to be undertaken at this time.[16] The decision to place the new provision into Article 42, which deals with the family and education, rather than Article 40, which deals with personal rights, will ensure that it is limited to these areas of the child's life and will not have broader influence. In terms of substance, the proposal to inset a statement 'acknowledging' the rights of the child is similarly unlikely to add any real value to the current position given that the courts have already made similar statements to this effect. Other proposals, like that to enable children born to married parents to be adopted, are worthwhile, but they are not statements of principle and as a result will affect only a small number of children. Overall, the proposals will not ensure that all decisions made concerning children will be determined by their best interests; nor will they promote the necessary change in attitudes towards children required to ensure the development of genuinely child-focused law and policy in all areas that affect children, including the family.

As to what ought to happen, it was highlighted above that in 1992 Ireland signed up to the Convention on the Rights of the Child and undertook to realise Convention rights for all children. The Committee on the Rights of the Child has urged Ireland to give further effect to the Convention in Irish law and to incorporate its general principles into the Constitution. Accordingly, we should look to the Convention when seeking to identify a set of core principles and values that should inform law, policy and practice in relation to the treatment of our children. In this regard, an important starting point would be to insert into the Constitution an unequivocal statement of children's rights in the form of a general commitment – like the general one in Article 40.3 – that the State has a duty to respect and vindicate the rights of the child. This would highlight our commitment to ensuring that the rights of children be promoted and protected thereby drawing a line under the past where this clearly was not the case. In addition, consideration should be given to establishing as a constitutional principle that all actions concerning children should regard the best interests of the child as a primary consideration. These provisions taken together would provide the courts with a way of taking the interests and rights of the child into account in individual cases and would have the added value of promoting a more child-centred approach among decision-makers – from government to local practitioners – having a clear knock-on effect on the way children are treated. Of course, a more far-reaching proposition would be to follow those countries that have given constitutional expression to the right of the child to be heard in decisions made about them. This would serve to ensure not only that children's voices are heard and taken into account in line with their age and maturity, but it would also, more generally, raise the profile of children and ensure that they are treated as individuals in their own right. It would provide strong support for a child-focused approach to decision-making, and minimise further the risk of children's rights being ignored or underplayed. Finally, to ensure that all children enjoy the equal benefit of their rights, it is important to assert in the Constitution the principle that children should not suffer any discrimination in the enjoyment of their rights. This would not only promote equal access to services, including education, it would also prevent the adoption of policies and measures that discriminate against children including on the grounds of disadvantage, disability, illness, family status, religion or nationality.

Conclusion

This short article set out to discuss children's rights in the context of the family with reference both to possible myths about the Convention on the Rights of the Child and the reality of current constitutional provision. While the cases highlighted may be rare, there should be no misunderstanding about the relevance of the Constitution to children's daily lives in the family and outside. Similarly, it is important to recognise the depth of the relationship between children's rights and the family and the fact these are mutually dependent, rather than mutually exclusive, concepts. In this way, the view that children's rights are in themselves anti-family is to misunderstand the role that rights can play in protecting the child within the family and promoting the role the family must play in both supporting children to exercise their rights and as a children's right in itself. At the same time, the rejection of children's rights in the family is to take an idyllic view of childhood where the interests of parents and children always coincide. While this is normally the case, Ireland has seen more than its share of cases where the presumption that children were safe in their families had catastrophic effects on the children involved. That is not to argue for the diminution of the importance of family integrity or an increase in the level of state interference in the family. Rather it is to consider a rebalanced model of constitutional provision which adds children's rights into the mix and recognises that a children's rights approach to children's issues has greater potential to unlock better treatment for children, greater access to services and better support for families, than one that seeks purely to protect the family from the interference of the State.

Bibliography

Marshall and Parvis, *Honouring Children. The human rights of the child in Christian perspective* (Edinburgh: Saint Andrew Press, 2004).

Carolan, 'The Constitutional Consequences of Reform: Best Interests after the Amendment' 3 (2007) *Irish Journal of Family Law* 9.

Fortin, *Children's Rights and the Developing Law*, 2nd Ed (London: LexisNexis Butterworths, 2003).

Kilkelly and O'Mahony, 'The Proposed Children's Rights Amendment: Running to Stand Still?' 2 (2007) *Irish Journal of Family* Law 19.

Notes:

1. National Children's Office, *Our Children Their Lives: A National Children's Strategy*, Department of Health and Children, 2000.

2. Committee on the Rights of the Child, *Concluding Observations: Ireland* CRC/C/15/Add.85 (1998) and Committee on the Rights of the Child, *Concluding Observations: Ireland* CRC/C/IRL/CO/2 (2006).

3. See, for example, *Eastern Health Board, Kilkenny Incest Investigation: Report presented to Mr Brendan Howlin, TD, Minister for Health* (Dublin: Stationery Office, 1993) and *Report of the Constitution Review Group* (Dublin: Stationery Office, 1996).

4. See generally Kilkelly, *Obstacles to the Exercise of Children's Rights in Ireland* (Dublin: Ombudsman for Children, 2007).

5. Committee on the Rights of the Child, *Reporting Guidelines*, CRC/C/5 at para 13.

6. Hammarberg, 'The UN Convention on the Rights of the Child – and How to Make it Work' (1990) 12 *Human Rights Quarterly* 97.

7. Committee on the Rights of the Child, General Comment No 8 *The right of the child to protection from corporal punishment and other cruel or degrading forms of punishment* CRC/C/GC/8 (2006). See also the United Nations Secretary General's Study on Violence against Children at www.violencestudy.org, paras 26 and 30-37.

8. See Kilbourne, 'The Wayward Americans – why the USA has not ratified the United Nations Convention on the Rights of the Child' (1998) 10 *Child and Family Law Quarterly* 243.

9. In *Re JH* [1985] IR 375.

10. See further Kilkelly, *Obstacles to the Exercise of Children's Rights in Ireland* (Dublin: Ombudsman for Children, 2007).

11. O'Mahony, 'Children, Parents and Education Rights: A Constitutional Imbalance' (2004) 3 *Irish Journal of Family Law* 3.

12. In *Re JH* [1985] 375.

13. See Carolan, 'The Constitutional Consequences of Reform: Best Interests after the Amendment' (2007) 3 *Irish Journal of Family Law* 9.

14. *North Western Heath Board v HW and CW* [2001] 3 IR 622.

15. *N and Others v Health Services Executive* [2006] IESC 60.

16. See Carolan, above, and Kilkelly and O'Mahony, 'The Proposed Children's Rights Amendment: Running to Stand Still?' (2007) 2 *Irish Journal of Family Law* 19.

14   The Church, Society and Family in Ireland

Garret FitzGerald

(Linda Hogan and Barbara FitzGerald (eds), *Between Poetry and Politics: Essays in Honour of Enda McDonagh*, Dublin: Columba Press, 2003, pp 105-116)

I start with the fact that tensions between the individual and society lie at the root of the human condition. For the human being derives from a particularly social species of mammal, the ape, but by virtue of the development of a self-conscious intelligence has become a highly individualistic species.

The reconciliation of these two conflicting aspects of humanity poses a permanent ethical problem. On the one hand, the individual human being expects and is entitled to the respect due to a self-conscious being; on the other hand, individual human beings have to find a way of controlling their individualism to a sufficient degree to be able to live together in amity.

It has always seemed to me that a particular strength of the Christian church has been the balance it has struck between the individual and society. The individual, seen as made in the image of God, is accorded huge respect, but the need for a social ethic to optimise relations between these individuals has been given equal recognition.

Of course Christianity derived from Judaism, to which much of the credit for this harmonisation of the individual and the social must be given. But building on this inheritance, Christianity produced a philosophically sophisticated ethical structure that in the broadest sense has stood the test of two millennia.

True, there have from time to time been aberrations. Some at least of the strictures of the Christian moral code as it has reached us after such a long period of time reflect *ad hoc* responses to specific past situations. Examples of this include the Council of Trent's over-reaction to the problem of clandestine marriages, which it declared to be invalid rather than illicit, or the continuing claim by the Roman Catholic Church, inspired by over-enthusiastic missionary zeal, to have the power to dissolve marriages with or between non-Christians where this might facilitate conversions to Christianity. And, more generally, a church with a celibate clergy clearly went over the top on the subject of some aspects of sexual behaviour.

But, overall, the balance maintained by Christianity between the individual and the social was well-judged – and in terms of optimising the human condition in society, its ethic compares favourably with the extremes of both socialism and economic as well as social liberalism, as these developed in the nineteenth and twentieth centuries. Both of these 'isms' were challenged at different times and in different ways by the Roman Catholic Church in particular.

Only for a relatively short period in the mid-twentieth century did the church allow itself to become concerned primarily with extreme socialism which, for all the moral attraction of its appeal to justice and equity, ensured by its dismissal of the market system its own eventual failure.

From the start, the church's instincts were right in identifying the extremes of liberalism, in both their economic and social manifestations, as posing by far the most enduring threat to an ordered and just society. Economic liberalism's threat to the social order derives from its insidious appeal to human self-interest, often at the expense of social solidarity, while for its part extreme social liberalism appeals to human impatience at restraints on individual behaviour required for the good of society.

Both forms of liberalism involve much more powerful self-interested motivations than the concern for justice and equity that lies behind socialism, and the relative proportions of time and effort that the Catholic Church devoted in the nineteenth and twentieth centuries to what it identified as two rival secular heresies was well-judged. For a few decades in the mid-twentieth century, it did focus its criticisms principally upon extreme socialism, but for most of the nineteenth and the remainder of the twentieth century it directed its strictures primarily at the threats emanating from extreme liberalism.

The fact that the Catholic Church seems to have judged wisely the relative magnitude of what it saw as two rival threats to a balanced social order does not, of course, mean that its specific critiques of either socialism or liberalism were always well-judged. In the nineteenth century, and especially during the papacy of Pius IX after his early shift to the right, it went totally overboard, even going as far as to denounce democracy – although that curious throw-back to attitudes close to those of the *ancien regime* was firmly and quickly corrected by his successor Leo XIII.

The radical changes in society that have taken place since the end of the nineteenth century have posed an exceptional challenge to human beings in society, and to societal norms we have inherited from the past. Some of these norms are firmly founded in human nature itself; others may derive from the way people can best live together in a particular culture, e.g. in a tribal extended family culture effectively independent from and unaffected by the kind of organised state system to which we are accustomed.

The Roman Catholic Church has sometimes been tempted to over-generalise from its experience of the particular culture within which it developed in the Middle East/Europe area – proclaiming norms that may be historically or geographically specific to this area as applicable to human nature itself and thus to be part of a natural law. But, by and large, its ethical norms are well-rooted in the character of the human condition itself.

Where it seems to me that the Roman Catholic Church in particular has recently lost much of its former power to influence social behaviour has been in

AN IRISH READER IN MORAL THEOLOGY

its overuse of authority rather than reason in promulgating its views on social morality. It had always been shy of pointing to the rational basis of so much of its moral teaching – perhaps because it feared that this might expose occasional irrational elements that had been allowed to creep into its teaching in response to particular challenges it had faced at various points in the past.

There can be no doubt about the significance of the 1960s worldwide, although the form that its impact on society took varied from country to country. In the United States, and in much of Europe, it involved an actual sexual revolution. In Ireland its immediate impact was, perhaps, less drastic, but an interaction between the global liberal mood and the debates of the Second Vatican Council made many Irish people for the first time think seriously and for themselves about the moral teachings of their religion.

Amongst many thinking Catholics, the early impact of this process was positive. The Catholic Church, instead of being passively accepted as part of the national wallpaper, so to speak, came to be seen in a new and generally more challenging light. For the first time a genuine interest in theology emerged amongst sections of the laity. The concept of the church as the people of God, rather than just the episcopacy and clergy, gripped the imagination of many Catholics.

But into this new situation was thrown in mid-1968 the bombshell of *Humanae Vitae*. For many married people, this created, at least for a period, agonising problems of conscience. They were torn between traditional, instinctive loyalty to church teaching and what they saw as their marital responsibilities. For some the strain on their adherence to their church proved too great. Others, often aided by sympathetic confessors, many of whom found the theology of this document unconvincing, survived this test and, despite their rejection of this particular teaching, remained practising Catholics.

In this connection it is worth remarking that the problem with this document did not lie with its basic insight into the potential impact of widespread availability of contraceptives upon extra-marital sexual behaviour – an insight that has been fully justified by events – but rather in the conclusions it drew from this insight with regard to the use of such methods by couples seeking to regulate the spacing of their families.

On the one hand, given the Catholic Church's earlier acceptance of the use of women's ovulatory cycle for this purpose, its objection to other means being employed towards the end of spacing and limiting pregnancies could not be justified on grounds of intent. At the same time, whilst there was a difference between the ease and effectiveness of these two methods, this was a matter of degree that could not, rationally or theologically, carry the weight of permitting one and flatly rejecting the other for family planning purposes.

Moreover, at quite another level, *Humanae Vitae* can be argued to have taken inadequate account of the change that had by then taken place in the global population situation. Insofar as the church's earlier negative approach to family size limitation may have been influenced by the appropriateness at the time it was written of the biblical injunction to 'increase and multiply', by 1968 there was clearly a strong ecological case for reversing this injunction by seeking instead to slow down population growth in order to avoid overcrowding the planet. That would appear to have been more in line with what the church describes as a 'natural law', designed to optimise the conditions for human existence.

As had been the case with some other earlier aspects of its teaching on sexual matters, the Catholic Church's disciplinary insistence on clerical celibacy – designed in an earlier period both to secure the undivided attention of clergy to their duties and to prevent the alienation of church property by their families – deprived it of the insights that a married clergy (and above all a married episcopacy!) might have had into issues of this kind.

The impact of all this upon hitherto unthinking acceptance of the church's authority, already under question as a result of the changed mood of the 1960s and perhaps also as a result of the well-reported debates in the Council, proved quite profound. Thereafter, to an ever-increasing extent, many Irish Catholics began to do their own theology, so to speak, testing the Catholic Church's teaching against their own rational morality. In many, probably most, cases, the test was passed – for, except where some aberration had distorted the church's teaching at some point in the past, Christian morality was of course firmly based on natural morality – viz. the ordering of social relationships in a manner conducive to the optimisation of the human condition.

But authority had lost its power to compel. Indeed to some degree 'authority' had become a bad word – as 'authoritarian' had already become, at least from the period of fascism earlier in the century.

Given the manner in which, over the centuries, the church had identified, in many cases correctly, the kind of criteria for behaviour that would secure optimal relationships between individuals in society, a visionary and prophetic church might perhaps have chosen to grasp this opportunity to demonstrate the extent to which its inspiration in the past had in fact led it to develop a wise balance between individualism and social needs – wiser than that of various discredited rationalist attempts in the nineteenth and twentieth centuries. Such a demonstration of the value of its insights and of their broad compatibility with natural reason might have strengthened its moral authority and reduced its increasingly counter-productive dependence on deploying its hierarchical authority, with a view to attracting rather than seeking to compel adherence to its views.

Instead, the central authorities of the church preferred to command the absolute allegiance of its clergy to its teaching on the contraception issue by intensifying disciplinary measures *vis-à-vis* theologians whose views it disapproved of, and by appointing as bishops only members of the clergy who agreed in all respects with the views of Rome on this matter.

Over the past thirty-five years these authoritarian measures proved hugely counter-productive. In order to avoid censure by higher authority, perhaps even loss of their clerical status and thus of their livelihood, very many of the clergy have been forced to dissimulate their views on an issue which, to say the least, was not central to the faith. This has, of course, hugely weakened the moral authority that they exercise as individuals, which derives from their giving witness to the truth as they see and believe it.

This uncomfortable situation, continuing over several decades, left the laity ill-prepared for the revelation in the 1990s of an unresolved back-log of clerical child abuse cases in at least the English-speaking world. These crimes had been carefully hidden from view by church authorities more concerned about institutional 'scandal' than about the protection of children – which for many of the laity is the most crucial moral issue of all, and one to which, unhappily, many bishops, perhaps trapped by their celibacy, proved disastrously insensitive.

The fact that decades of past abuse came to light and were investigated and prosecuted within a relatively short period of time has given an exaggerated, indeed false, impression of the scale of this problem and this, together with the insensitive attitude of the church authorities to the clerical paedophile problem, shattered the confidence of many lay people in their church.

Meanwhile, the younger generation of Irish society had for long been protected by both church and state from changes in *mores* in the world outside Ireland. With the advent of television this dangerously over-protective screen disappeared almost overnight and, within the short space of thirty years, Irish society faced changes that elsewhere in the developed world had taken place over a whole century.

To give but one example, between the mid-1960s and the end of the century the proportion of births outside marriage rose from 1.5% to 33%. Of course the former figure may have under-stated the scale of extra-marital intercourse in the pre-contraception 1960s, when some non-marital pregnancies were converted into marital births through shotgun marriages and a small number were also aborted in Britain. But the current 30% non-marital birth proportion equally under-states the extent to which today's first pregnancies are extra-marital for, when account is taken of the fact that three out every eight first non-marital births are now aborted in Britain, it emerges that over half of all first pregnancies in our state are now non-marital.

In the even shorter period of twenty years since 1980, the proportion of women married by the age of 25 has fallen from 53% to 8%. And whereas in 1980 over two-thirds of first marital births were to women under 27, only one-sixth of first marital births are now to women in that age group.

Today only a small minority of non-marital births are to teenagers: one-sixth, as against two-fifths in 1981. By contrast, the proportion of non-marital births to women aged 25 and over is rising towards half of the total. Many of these non-marital births now are to couples in a stable non-marital relationship: one-sixth of couples with children under 5 are co-habiting rather than married.

How has all this impacted upon Irish family life? To date little has been written about the effect of these huge, and extraordinarily rapid, changes in *mores* upon our society, and in particular upon inter-generational family relationships. So, for the moment, pending overdue sociological research in this area, for an impression of this aspect of Irish family life we must depend upon anecdotal evidence.

What can, I think, be said is that in contrast to the starkly negative and defensive character of the church's reaction to these changes in Irish social *mores*, Irish parents and grandparents seem generally to have chosen to protect the integrity of their family relationships by accepting co-habitation by their children, even where this continues after the birth of a child. They tend to keep to themselves any qualms they may have about this practice.

I believe that there has always been a marked difference between the approaches of urban working-class families and that of other social groups to non-marital pregnancies. In contrast to middle class urban, and almost all rural families, urban working-class families, at any rate in the larger conurbations, have long tended to incorporate into the nuclear family the non-marital child of a daughter living at home, treating it as if it were a late-arriving sibling.

We know all too well what happened in the past in many other families, however. A birth would be handled with secrecy, the child adopted, often outside Ireland, and its mother sometimes even incarcerated thereafter in a convent asylum.

Although today there certainly remain girls who greatly fear parental disapproval, parental attitudes seem now to have generally changed. I suspect that today an abortion in Britain is more often the choice of a mother unwilling to become a single parent rather than a choice determined by fear of parental disapproval of single motherhood.

In general it seems to me that most parents have a more relaxed relationship with their children than formerly and, however much they may privately regret their children's different approach to sexual matters, they seem to forbear from overt criticism or disapproval of co-habitation. It may even be that the sense of family solidarity has been strengthened rather that weakened by the need of the parents to accommodate to a rapidly evolving society.

There is also clear evidence that this more relaxed parental approach is reciprocated by their children. Precisely because so many Irish parents, and grandparents, have adapted successfully to a rapidly changing social situation, many young people in Ireland today have more open, and thus often stronger, relationships with their parents and grandparents. Just as they benefit from tolerance on the part of the older generation, so also, I observe, do they respect that generation's uncensorious commitment to their traditional views on these matters.

In the absence of research into these issues, some concrete evidence of the continuing strength of Irish family relationships can be found in the quite disparate approaches of Irish and English students to the choice of third-level institutions to attend. In England there has traditionally been a positive preference amongst third-level students for a university distant from their home – although for economic reasons the proportion of English students choosing a university near their homes is estimated to have doubled in the past few years. English school-leavers appear to have seen their entrance to third-level education as an opportunity to get away from their families. And there is anecdotal evidence that, in many English families, parents and children have lost contact at that point.

By contrast in our state, students have always shown a marked preference for a university or Institute of Technology near their home, unless of course, they intended to pursue a course not locally available. This partly reflects the fact that, in contrast to Britain, standards in Irish universities are fairly uniform: there is no strong academic reason to choose one rather than another and a dominant consideration for a majority of third-level students appears to be the nearness of their chosen third-level institution to their homes. And where students' homes are too remote from their third-level institutions to permit daily commuting, they very often return home each weekend. Thus, in contrast to England, third-level education in the Irish State has not sundered the relationship between the generations.

The situation in Northern Ireland is somewhat different, for Protestants in particular. For obvious reasons, there has been always a greater tendency by Protestant than Catholic third-level students in the North to see themselves as part of a wider United Kingdom educational system. In recent times this factor, combined with the stronger educational motivation of Catholics, has led both of the Northern Ireland universities to have a majority of Roman Catholic students, which seems to have further accelerated the flow of Protestant third-level students to Britain. The fact that there are only two universities in Northern Ireland may also have encouraged this outward flow to Britain which, even amongst Catholic students, is many times greater than in the case of the Republic.

But a higher proportion of Catholic than Protestant students seem to return to Northern Ireland and, of course, in both parts of the island, (in marked contrast to what was the case in the nineteenth century and the first half of the twentieth, when emigration in most cases involved a final breach with home), many young emigrants, whether or not they have been third-level students, now take advantage of much cheaper travel to return frequently to their homes in Ireland.

Despite the gap in social attitudes that has sprung up between the generations in the past thirty years, the strength of Irish family ties has been well maintained. This aspect of Irish society is little recognised and is, I believe, greatly underestimated by commentators on the Irish scene. It is an important stabilising factor in a rapidly changing society, and is something that should be cherished and built upon.

It should be recognised that it is precisely because the older generation has not sought to impose on its teenage and adult children the minutiae of the moral code in which they were raised in earlier decades that Irish family life has survived the immense strains of this recent period of ultra-rapid social change.

Of course, in all this we must distinguish between the hedonism of sexual promiscuity, on the one hand, and what seems, on the other, to be an altered approach by a new generation to family formation, involving in the case of very many young people what are, in effect, trial marriages in the form of a period of co-habitation before commitment through a marriage ceremony to a permanent relationship.

It is clear that for whatever reason many young people today are hesitant about entering into a life-long commitment to a partner and, insofar as they are willing to contemplate this possibility, feel it unwise to do so without a preliminary experimental relationship. The sources of their hesitation about a commitment for life are unclear, especially as these doubts seem to be shared by many young people who are themselves products of successful marriages as well as by those less fortunate in their upbringing. The longer span of human life under modern conditions does not seem, as has sometimes been suggested, an adequate explanation, because the lengthening of young people's expectation of life has evolved over a longer period than that within which this decline in commitment has taken place.

The traditional argument against trial unions have behind them the experience of many centuries. But we live in a different world today. And the decision of many young people to approach a life commitment to a partner by this different route cannot reasonably be described as irresponsible. Indeed, as they see it, they are acting more responsibly than those who make a life commitment without first testing their compatibility by means of a prior period of cohabitation.

Although my own experiences and instincts have favoured entering early into the kind of permanent commitment that we sanctify as marriage, I have to accept that early marriages often carry a risk of breakdown because of lack of maturity on the part of one or both partners. I am forced to recognise that the recent practice of postponing a permanent commitment and the initiation of the procreation of offspring until the late 20s or early 30s may have a good deal to say for it, even if earlier child-bearing is more attuned to female biology.

AN IRISH READER IN MORAL THEOLOGY

The latest data on marriage breakdown, from the 2002 Census, does actually suggest that marriage postponement in the 1980s and 1990s may have had a favourable impact on marriage breakdown – for the proportion of early marriages breaking down is lower now than formerly, although this may be because some at least of the early marriages in the 1970s may have been shotgun affairs.

Of course, the fact that parents and grandparents have been wise in not challenging this generational shift in the sexual mores of their progeny is not of itself an argument for the church to modify its teaching on the subject. Nevertheless, it is certain that, in the long run, the interest of church and society lies in maximising the number of stable unions within which children are brought up in happy surroundings, and perhaps the church should not be too dogmatic about how best to secure such an outcome under modern conditions – for which past experience may not provide an infallible guide.

Part Four
Divorce and Remarriage

15   Jesus' Attitude to Divorce

Wilfrid Harrington OP

(*Irish Theological Quarterly*, Vol 37, No 3, July 1970, pp 199-209)

The teaching of Jesus on divorce seeks to restore marriage to the pure form the creator God intended it to have. God had seen that it is not good for man to be alone (Gen 2:18); so he had given him a wife, 'his best possession, a helper fit for him and a pillar of support' – one without whom 'a man will wander about and sigh (Sir 36:24f). As helpers in marriage, man and woman could depend upon and trust each other in the same way that they could call God their helper.[1] Theirs was to be a covenant between persons; theirs was to be a relationship keeping the one commandment of total self-giving, of love which lays down life.[2] But, human helpers could seem to betray trust, and such perfect love would not be easy to find or keep. Divorce, and all it stands for of human imperfection, came to cast a shadow upon the relationship of marriage.

Nowhere in the law is the permission of divorce explicitly spelled out; rather it seems to have been a custom taken for granted and seen as Israel's privilege, an unrestricted right given only to the husband to repudiate his wife without her having any redress. Moreover, nowhere in the Law are the grounds for divorce precisely stated.[3] In the primary text of divorce legislation which we do have, Deut 24:1-4, it is said that a husband could repudiate his wife for 'something indecent', a 'disgraceful' or 'scandalous' thing – some fault which he had found to impute to her. However, he was required to produce a 'writ of divorce' for her, a document setting her free from further obligation to him and allowing her to remarry (cf Is 50:1; Jer 3:8). Thus, by demanding at least certain legal formalities, the law was really designed to protect the woman in some small way by limiting the capriciousness of the husband; it also forbade divorced couples to remarry each other (Deut 24:4). Because the phrase 'something indecent' was so perturbingly, perhaps invitingly, vague, there arose in rabbinic circles frequent casuistic discussions as to what grounds for divorce this referred to. The school of Shammai taught that this 'something indecent' meant unchastity alone, that adultery and immorality were the only valid reasons for divorce.[4] Hillel and his followers, by contrast, taught that the phrase referred to anything displeasing which a man might find in his wife – from a meal she had burned to her untidiness, or to his finding another woman more attractive. Contemporary evidence shows that the Hillelian viewpoint prevailed at the time of Jesus. As we shall see, the statements of Jesus on divorce have, to some extent, been framed in the light of the Shammai-Hillel controversy.[5]

Divorce: The demands of Jesus

Mark 10:2-12. Jesus' teaching on divorce occurs directly in five places in the New Testament: 1 Cor 7-10 f; Mk 10:2-12; Lk 16:18; Mt 19:3-9; 5:31f. Although Paul's text was probably the first to be written down, Mark's account is the first synoptic record of the historical circumstances in which the teaching was given at the beginning of the Judaean ministry (Mk 10:1; cf Mt 19:1). In Mark's formulation, the question is not related to the Shammai-Hillel controversy. It concerns simply divorce as such and originated either within the Marcan material or within a group of early Christians among whom the question of divorce was a problem;[6] in fact, several manuscripts of Mark omit 'the Pharisees' so that the questioners fade into the background. In any case, the question is but the opening of this pronouncement-story in which Jesus recalls the ideal of marriage as instituted by God in the beginning and reiterates it in a new and binding law (Mk 10:2-9).

Jesus declares that Moses had written this 'commandment' on divorce through his failure to truly understand God's moral demands and to obey the higher law contained in Genesis. The Deuteronomic legislation was not really a law but a dispensation in view of Israel's stubbornness (cf Deut.10:16, Ezek 3:17); Jesus had come to put a new heart and a new spirit within them and to take away their heart of stone (cf Ezek 36:26). In the beginning, God had no divorce in mind: by creating male and female God intended marriage to be for one man and one woman bound together in the indissoluble union of persons implied by 'one flesh'. This monogamous union, moreover, was indeed indissoluble and unbreakable not only by reason of the two being one, but also because God himself brings the partners together and is the author of the marriage bond: 'What, therefore, God has joined together, let not man put asunder' (Mk 10:9). The Law itself, with its permissive clause of Deut 24:1, could have no lasting, binding obligation in the face of the finality of God's intentions; Jesus dared to nullify this concession – to set himself against legal casuistry and stipulations, as well as against current rabbinic interpretations – because he recognised that divorce itself had never been a law of God.

Mark 10:10-12 is an addition to the pronouncement-story: v 10 is an editorial link and vv.11f are isolated *logia* (cf Lk 16:18; Mt 19:9; Mt 5:32). This appendix is presented as an exposition which Jesus gives his disciples in private (cf Mk 4:10ff; 7:17ff; 9:28f); it transcends Jewish law in v 11 and contradicts it in v 12. Jesus declares that not only is divorce forbidden, but also remarriage following divorce constitutes adultery because the first marriage bond has never been broken: 'Whoever divorces his wife and marries another commits adultery against her' (v 11). The words 'against her', referring to a man's first wife, go beyond Jewish law which did not consider that a man could commit adultery against his own wife. The following saying, extending the same principle to the wife and peculiar to Mark, is best considered to be a secondary addition made by Mark (or his source) to expand the teaching of Jesus so as to meet the needs of Gentile Christians living under Graeco-Roman law.[7] For, under Jewish law, and thus in a discussion with the Pharisees, the situation would not have arisen since a woman was not allowed to divorce her husband. The appendix as a whole confirms Jesus' teaching on the indissolubility of marriage and sets husband and wife in a relationship of perfect equality. This teaching is unequivocal; it is a decisive, positive attitude which has influenced the teaching of the whole New Testament on marriage.[8]

Paul. The primary divorce text in Paul is essentially a repetition of Jesus' prohibition of divorce and his teaching that any divorce which might occur had no effect whatever on the bond of marriage. 'To the married I give charge, not I but the Lord, that the wife should not separate from her husband (but if she does, let her remain single or else be reconciled to her husband) – and that the husband should not divorce his wife' (1 Cor 7:10f). This declaration of indissolubility is amplified by two other texts which, taken together, state that a wife is bound to her husband as long as he lives, but that after his death she is free to remarry without committing adultery (1 Cor 7:39; Rom 7:2-4). Thus, in a marriage in which both parties are Christian, Paul recognises the possibility of separation if the couple finds cohabitation impossible; but, speaking on the Lord's authority, he definitely does not permit remarriage in such a case because the bond between the spouses is not dissolved.

Paul's position is not so clear in his treatment of mixed marriages (i.e. for him, a marriage between a Christian and a pagan). 'If (in a mixed marriage) the unbelieving partner agrees to separate, let him or her do so; in such a case the believing brother or sister is not slavishly bound (*ou dedoulotai*),' that is, he or she is not obliged to strive to maintain or re-establish the marriage bond at any price (1 Cor 7:15). Paul does not seem to envisage the possibility of another marriage; that is made possible only by death (7:39; Rom 7:1-3). Generally in the past, and to some extent today, exegesis has seen the 'Pauline privilege' expressed in this text, and the phrase 'not slavishly bound' is taken to refer to the marriage bond. Against this interpretation it may be observed that the apostle in 1 Cor 7:39 and Rom 7:2, where he does undoubtedly refer to the marriage bond, uses the verb *deo*, 'to bind'.[9]

Luke 16:18. The isolated *logion* on divorce and adultery which we found in Mark 10:11f occurs in its Lucan form in a group of three sayings loosely connected by the catchword, or idea, of 'law' and preparatory to the parable of the Rich Man and Lazarus (Lk 16:19-31). Speaking to the Pharisees, Jesus condemns outward punctiliousness in observing the Law without the true religion of the heart known only to God (16:15); he tells them that the new age has dawned in which the good news of the kingdom of God would replace their legalism (16:15), although every 'dot' of the spirit of the old law would reach fulfilment in himself (16:17). As an example of this (although the sequence is hard to follow), Luke then cites Jesus' saying on divorce – thus condemning all specious reasons for divorce and restoring marriage to its original purity. In the Lucan version of the saying, only the man is spoken of as taking the initiative in divorce and re-marriage – but with the further observation (in contrast to Jewish law) that a free man who marries a divorced woman also commits adultery.

Mt 19:3-9 and 5:31f. A *logion* on divorce appears in two places in Matthew's gospel: in an historical setting parallel to that of Mark (Mt 19:3-9) and in one of the antitheses of the Sermon on the Mount (5:31f). For the most part, the differences between Matthew and Mark in the historical context containing Jesus' teaching on divorce are not significant, although they are interesting. In Matthew, the reference to Moses is first made by the Pharisees and at a later point in the story (Mt 19:7); and here included in the story itself without any transition to a new setting (19:9). But there are two distinctive points within Matthew's version which have a real importance and seem to be related to each other. The first of these occurs in the Pharisees' question: 'Is it lawful to divorce one's wife for any cause?' (19:3). Since the phrase 'for any cause' (*kata pasan aitian*) can be related to the Hillel-Shammai controversy, it might be thought that the question as it stands in Matthew is original, that here indeed is its *Sitz im Leben Jesu*. However, we shall see that the phrase may, with greater justice, be taken as Matthew's own scribal addition designed to bring Jesus' teaching into line with the issue that concerned the Jews. The second main point of difference with Mark, one related perhaps to the addition of *kata pasan aitian*, is Matthew's famous exceptive clause, which occurs in 5:32 also and seems to suggest an exception to Jesus' absolute prohibition against divorce. 'Whoever divorces his wife, except for unchastity (*me epi porneia*) [in 5:32, *parek tos logou porneias*, 'except on grounds of unchastity'] and marries another commits adultery' (Mt 19:9).[10] If we take the view that the clauses do indeed constitute an exception, we must try to understand their place as secondary interpolations in a categorical *logion* of Jesus. We have noted how in 1 Cor 7:10f, Paul makes allowance for the possibility of separation without remarriage; we have seen how both Paul and Mark have adapted their teaching to Gentile-Christian circumstances. Thus, we may be prepared to see Matthew's exceptive clauses in the same light. In short, the teaching of Jesus on divorce, like so much of his teaching, underwent modification in the living, everyday circumstances of the early church; we can understand this process now by looking more closely at the context of his saying on divorce in the Sermon on the Mount (Mt 5-7).

Divorce: Modifications of Jesus' demands

The early church began to experience the fulfilment of their Lord's promise (Jn 16:13) when they looked back upon his life and teaching and, guided by the Spirit, sought ways to make the truths they found there applicable to their lives. They began to understand what he meant by calling for that which sets the tone for the Sermon on the Mount – a 'righteousness exceeding that of the Scribes and Pharisees' (Mt 5:20). Precisely because his demands were so absolute, his teaching such an 'impossible ethic', the first Christians came to realise that this unqualified righteousness had to find flesh and bone within a changing community. The 'sermon' in Mt 5-7 helps us to see how the early church faced up to this task.

Two basic sources stand behind the material in the Sermon on the Mount.[11] The first source, commonly designated Q, consists of material common to Matthew and Luke and presents Jesus' words, in all their uncompromising nakedness, as he first taught them to his disciples. Q reflects the crisis ushered in by the coming of Jesus, and his ethical teaching is presented as absolute demands which are part of this crisis; it resounds with the Baptist's words, 'Even now the axe is laid to the root of the trees' (Mt 3:10; Lk 3:9). The material in this source is not so much catechetical and exhortatory as radical. It reflects the enthusiasm of the earliest Christians, an enthusiasm engendered by the initial impact Jesus had made upon them in the immediate post-Easter period of the church. This led them to dare the impossible, to attempt to carry out the absolute nature of his demands, such as in the experiment in voluntary communal living recorded in Acts. But just as this experiment was short-lived because the community was forced to face the reality of other circumstances, so too the reality had to be faced that enthusiasm was not enough: although Jesus had inaugurated a crisis, this had not resulted visibly in a completely new order of life. The 'impossible ethic', the teaching of Q, had to be applied to everyday affairs. It was not enough to wait in idleness for the Parousia: 'If any one will not work, let him not eat' (2 Thess 3:10).

This process of applying the teaching of Jesus in the early church can be discerned in the second source of material behind the Sermon on the Mount, a source designated M. The key characteristic of this block of Jesus' teaching is regulatory rather than radical (although the intensity of his demands is preserved), and these regulatory or explanatory words became used as guides in daily living; the glorious light of Easter had to become filtered, as it were, into the light of common day as time went on. In considering what the validity of Jesus' teaching meant, the church came to recognise what was possible and what was impossible, what absolute and what relative. In this process – which was concerned not only to reproduce the words of Jesus but to apply them to problems of personal conduct – his words changed to make them practicable. Moreover, often this regulatory material in M is ascribed *in toto* to Jesus in cases where we cannot always be sure that the words originated with him at all.[12]

Thus, Matthew modifies the total prohibition of divorce as both Mark and Luke record it. The hard radicalism of the saying is made softer, and in Matthew the church is seen to have interpreted the traditions it received with a view towards presenting Jesus as a practical legislator. The evangelist has

AN IRISH READER IN MORAL THEOLOGY

recognised the spirit of M and, like a scribe trained for the kingdom of heaven (Mt 13:52), has plied his own skill. Paul, too, had recognised that the ongoing processes of daily living in the church would call for modification of his Lord's teaching: 'If possible, so far as it depends on you, live peaceably with all' (Rom 12:18).

The modification of Jesus' teaching expressed in the exceptive clauses of Matthew is by no means unique. Perhaps the most striking example of the way in which the most radical commands of Jesus are not fulfilled here and now is his teaching on swearing (Mt 5:33-37). In the new kingdom which he ushered in there can be no place for oaths because there can be no place for dishonesty or untruthfulness. Jesus rejects oaths altogether – 'I say to you, do not swear at all (*me omosai holos*)' (5:34) – as well as certain Jewish casuistic practices in which a man swore by the name of God but without explicitly mentioning it, for oaths are but a concession to an imperfect older order. Moreover, he goes on to say that, in a Christian brotherhood, all that should be necessary between persons is a simple statement of 'Yes' or 'No' – thus implying that not only oaths, but also promises and vows, are forbidden because they are unnecessary (Mt 5:37; cf Jas 5:12). Anything more than a simple 'Yes' or 'No' is a consequence of the evil in this present world.[13] Thus, here we have an absolute prohibition of Jesus; but to what extent has it actually been observed? We may think of the instances in which oaths are called for today within the church.[14] Thus, considering that Christians continue to live in 'this present world' in which the fullness of the kingdom has not yet arrived, may we not ask if, in certain cases, we could see Jesus' absolute prohibition of divorce in the same light as his absolute prohibition of swearing?

Another clear example of a modification in Jesus' teaching is the practical interpretation of his prohibition of violence: 'Do not resist any one who is evil. But if anyone strikes you on the right cheek, turn to him the other also' (Mt 5:39). Jesus taught that evil, even violence, should never be opposed;[15] but the adaptation of his words in a practically contrary sense has not, as a rule, caused any particular difficulties or qualms of conscience. Perhaps the absolute quality and lofty expectation, virtually impossible to fulfil, of the 'crisis teaching' of Jesus can be best summed up in the demand he makes: 'You therefore must be perfect, as your heavenly Father is perfect' (Mt 5:48; cf Lk 6:36). This can only offer an ideal after which to strive; it offers man a vision of what he can be capable of because Jesus has liberated him and made possible the seemingly impossible by his coming. Moreover, although it remains a vision and an object of hope, the ideal is realisable in a practical way in the midst of society in a real world precisely because the very meaning of the person of Jesus is the opposite of all legalism, and his absolute demands, paradoxically, do not lay down absolute rules to govern Christian behaviour in every situation. Practical realisation of his demands is the achievement of his Spirit, of his love, which can discern the moment and replace a dead formula with the needs of living persons.

Jesus' prohibition in the context of Christian marriage

If we are to see Jesus' prohibition of divorce in true perspective, we must understand the biblical, and specifically the New Testament, view of marriage.[16] In this view, marriage emerges as something far more than a valid contract, than a consent vowed at one, finalising moment. In this view the 'consummation' of marriage must consist of more than the initial act of sexual intercourse – even as the scriptural idea of being 'two in one flesh' implies a covenant relationship between persons far beyond physical union. The consent of marriage is rather an ongoing commitment of man and woman united to live a real life under many changing circumstances; and it is in the process of *living* this reality that the 'evil of the world', human weakness, material difficulties, or whatever one wishes to term the problems which do arise, can often break in and destroy a true marriage, so that it is no longer alive but dead. Sometimes it would seem that the church has fixed upon the New Testament's requirements *against divorce* while at the same time neglecting its requirements *for marriage*: can a marriage be called a true marriage if these demands too are not also met?

If we turn to the summit of New Testament teaching on marriage, Eph 5: 21-33, we learn that the love of a husband for his wife should be a reflection and a fruit of the self-giving love of Christ for his bride, the church – the union which is the archetype of all Christian marriage even as the union of the first couple is its prototype. Yes, 'as Christ loved the church and gave himself up for her' (Eph 5:25), so too should man and woman love each other and lay down their lives for each other in marriage (cf Jn 15:13). This is the ideal. But, the Christian life is a practical life, and marriage must be lived by men and women who are not angels; thus, after Paul has developed the mystery of the ideal marriage between Christ and the church, he repeats the practical necessity for mutual love and reverence and respect between husbands and wives (Eph 5:33). And so, it could be argued that when these basic conditions for a true marriage are not fulfilled, the church's rigid interpretation of Jesus' prohibition of divorce results in the very thing of which he himself accused the Pharisees: the practice of laying heavy burdens, impossible to bear, upon men's shoulders, without lifting a finger to bring relief (cf Mt 23:3f).

Conclusion

'Love your wife (and, it must follow, your husband).' Here is a command ringing out clearly from the pages of the New Testament – but has it truly been given as much attention as Jesus' command prohibiting divorce? Yes, this commandment, about loving one's wife or husband, should not be passed over lightly or taken for granted. For, even if it does not seem to have been over-

AN IRISH READER IN MORAL THEOLOGY

cases where a person is psychologically incapable of committing himself or herself to another in close permanent relationship? Admittedly, the traditional concepts of consummation and impotence are more legally manageable, but legal manageability can hardly be the final index.[5]

To examine here the ecclesiastical tradition in the matter of divorce discipline would take us much too far afield. In this tradition there certainly is plenty of evidence of the church's emphasis on indissolubility of marriage and her opposition to divorce and remarriage. But evolution of the tradition is constantly marred by controversy and by efforts of compromise which seem questionable to us. I will indicate a few of the problems:

a) The confusion between prohibition and invalidation. Many of the Fathers regarded the remarriage of divorcees as sinful. Therefore, they were subject to a period of penance before they were admitted to church Communion, but they were then allowed to live with their second marriage.

b) The implication that the innocent husband of the adulterous wife could remarry whereas the wife in like case could not. This implication is contained in the writings of many of the Fathers and in Synodal Decrees of the first ten centuries. This inequality of the sexes was rejected by some Fathers – they allowed innocent wives to remarry (Origen, Basil).

c) Before one can speak about divorce at all one must have decided when a marriage comes into being. Tradition varied on this point between the moment of consent and the moment of intercourse. The theological tradition, based on the School of Paris, through its chief spokesman Peter Lombard, emphasised exchange of consent as the moment of marriage. The Canonical tradition, based on the School of Bologna, emphasised the act of intercourse as the factor which finalised the marriage contract. In the twelfth century, Alexander III accepted the thesis of the Parisian School, but gave some force also to the act of consummation – consent rendered a marriage valid, consummation rendered it indissoluble, a symbol of the union between Christ and the church. This is fundamentally the position on Christian marriage today.

In this article I wish to leave aside the intricacies of church discipline and practice, and ask the more basic question: 'Is divorce admissible?' 'How does one argue for or against divorce?'

Speaking about the indissolubility of marriage in natural law, one fact strikes one immediately – marriage cannot be completely indissoluble in the nature of things because the church claims to have power to dissolve marriages and in fact does so. These are real dissolutions of the bond and admit the parties to remarriage. Explain this how one will, one must admit that divorce is sometimes right and lawful. It is certainly not intrinsically evil. Therefore, when the church grants these dissolutions she does not do violence to man's nature or human society; she acts within the natural framework of marriage. This fact of church dissolution will and must qualify any statement of Catholic theology to the effect that marriage is absolutely indissoluble in natural law.

The nature of marriage as a human institution is established from the manner in which it serves the person in community. It is not as if there were a pre-existing structure of marriage into which man's attitudes and behaviour must be forced; man comes before his institutions and so one fills out one's concept of marriage by observing man's needs as child, parent and partner in the family unit and as person in society.

The analysis of the family unit is the classical approach to the moral structure of marriage. The Scholastics read the qualities of marriage, its unity and indissolubility, in its two essential purposes, parenthood and partnership. These they called respectively the primary and secondary purposes of marriage, and these considered as sources of obligation were called primary and secondary precepts of the natural law of marriage. The realisation of these purposes required in their eyes that marriage be monogamous and indissoluble.

No one will question the statement that from the point of view of the family and of the community, the life-long indissoluble marriage is the ideal.

In such a marriage the children are guaranteed the security of a parental home in which they can achieve maturity and adulthood. After all, when one says marriage is directed to parenthood one does not mean just the biological production of children but the whole process of personal formation and rearing to adult independence. This is a long-term task for parents, and the children need not only the presence of their parents here and now but the confidence that they will always be there.

In such a marriage the partners also find that security and trust which are necessary for their happiness. It banishes fear of desertion in adversity or old age, a consideration important above all for the wife. The knowledge that no matter what happens they will always have each other is happiness itself. In fact, the mere possibility or suggestion, of divorce would destroy that security in their possession of one another, and throw a shadow over their love. Love develops in and through fidelity. It indicates a life-long union. In marriage 'I love you' means 'I love you forever.' Anything else would make love not a gift of self but a mere loan and calculation. In marriage the partner gives to the other everything that he is and shall be. Leaving the way open for an eventual separation would undermine love at source.

Obviously, the existence or continuation of a structure does not guarantee the character of the people involved – their frankness and patience in dealing with each other, the generosity and warmth of their love, their consideration and thoughtfulness, their industry and providence, their sensibility and sympathy. A marriage structure can provide the basic background pattern for achievement of personal quality in the marriage relationship; it cannot supply it or supply for it. I think that traditionally moral theologians and canonists have been guilty of a serious oversight here. They have placed emphasis on the external pattern rather than on the very meaning of marriage, on its permanence and stability rather than on its quality. Their attitude suggested that it did not matter how a marriage was lived provided that it continued to exist.

This brings one back to a point made earlier. The structure of marriage is really derived from rational analysis of the over-all human values which it serves in the family unit and in society. It is not as if there were some pre-existing blueprint written in human nature in a kind of invisible ink which the trained mind can read. Man does not discover by following hidden clues what the pattern of marriage is. He concludes what it should be by examining the values which it serves in the person, in the family and in the community. Natural values come before structures; they determine what the structures must be. Analysis of the whole complex of personal relationships in the family community and in the social community indicate the pattern of marriage as institution.

This analysis is not a purely pragmatic undertaking; it is also critically philosophical. One does not just analyse what these relationships are, one also analyses what they should be. The pattern of marriage to which one concludes is to some extent an ideal; it is larger than life. The ideal begins by taking for granted the everyday factors of human experience and then goes on to point out what our structures must be if they are to fulfil man's responsibility to the person-in-community, to history and to civilisation. Actual life will usually be a compromise with the ideal; imperfect human situations may make the ideal unattainable in the here and now. Compromise is an unfortunate coincident of the human ethic.

Moral responsibility means taking account of all the factors of moral significance in a given situation. This will mean identifying and giving due importance in the scale of value to all human circumstances and foreseeing the possible consequences of what one does or omits. Responsible moral decisions will sometimes be unable to safeguard all the values – one value may have to be subordinated to another. In some provinces of action the only way to safeguard a fundamental moral value may be by refusing for all practical purposes to permit any compromise in regard to it, because the very possibility of compromise may erode that value beyond recall (e.g. the right of life). If such a value is of crucial importance in the community at large, there may be a duty to protect it by a principle so general that it admits no exception.

It is against this background one seeks to make a judgement on the admissibility or otherwise of divorce in a natural law context. The values to be taken into account are: the welfare of children (their maintenance, education, happiness and security); the welfare of the partners (support in prosperity and adversity, security into old age, the living out of the life-long surrender which their love demands); the welfare of the community (certainty of parenthood or legitimacy where children are concerned, harmony in personal and sexual re-lationships which a stable institution of marriage secures, the guarantee of equality to all citizens, and concern that the old and the weak are not exploited). In making a judgement on the pattern of marriage, one is not confining oneself to the situation of any individual family unit; one is dealing with an institution in society and so the repercussions of decisions go far beyond the individual case.

I also think that if one is honest in affirming that personal values precede and determine human structures, one must admit that the structure may vary with civilisation, with the vastly differing circumstance of man's life across space and time. The criterion which will decide whether a given marriage structure is valid in natural law will be the extent to which it safeguards and promotes the relevant human values to the greatest extent that this is possible in a given civilisation or historical situation of mankind. By civilisation we mean a way of life, the complex pattern of structure and attitude which mark a particular culture. In a primitive or inadequately developed civilisation, for example, polygamy may happen to be the marriage structure which best safe-guards the basic values in human sexual relationships. Where the man's role is that of patriarch, *pater familias*, father-leader of an extended family, where he tends to marry late in life, where the woman is in need of protection from an early age and where the only available protection is marriage into a plural fam-ily unit, then, at that stage of their civilisation, it is difficult to say that polygamy is contrary to natural law.

Only as society develops and the emancipation of women proceeds and wider possibilities come into being in their way of life, will the monogamous structure become of proximate obligation as the structure which achieves the human values now realisable for them. A change in the human situation comes before and conditions a change in structure.

The same could hold in regard to divorce, though it is more difficult to en-visage situations where this would be admissible in a primitive society. It is more difficult because such divorce would seem of sheer necessity to result in cutting wives and children adrift without any provision or protection, an action which could not but be irresponsible in a totally unorganised society.

In primitive tribes one might see polygamy as a more acceptable way of avoiding the hardships which would be caused by divorce. At least the wife and her children are guaranteed security and, where the plural household is an accepted pattern, discord and jealousy are not as great as one would expect.

It is obvious that this suggests a certain variability in the pattern or structure of marriage to meet the greatly differing situations in which man may find him-self. This is not a novel and untraditional position, but the cruder weapons necessitated by political controversy have pushed it into the background.

Even the quite rigid *a-priori* Scholastic teaching on natural law allowed for some variation in its principles, depending on circumstances of time and place.[6]

This variation was not just a difference in application due to man's ignorance of the full extent of his obligations. It was a difference in applicability, the historical human situation determining the natural law precept. Even though St Thomas did use on a number of occasions the axiom *natura humana mutabilis est*, this did not mean that he had worked out very explicitly the notion of variability. In fact, for him the central emphasis was the essential immutability of natural law, since this was fundamentally based on man's metaphysical nature, which is the same for all men. The principles based on metaphysical nature are the primary principles of natural law; they never vary and can never be dispensed. The principles which take into account man's historical nature, which depends on how man realises himself in space and time, are the secondary principles of natural law; these hold true in the majority of cases but they may cease to bind or they may be dispensed.

I am aware that St Thomas is not consistent in his use of the terms primary and secondary; they are sometimes epistemological, sometimes ontological. When he applies these terms to allow for variability there is some hint of a circular argument: if precepts can vary (above all if they have varied in biblical history) then they are classed as secondary. Otherwise they qualify as primary. All I wish to state here is that Thomistic tradition does allow for actual variability in some natural law precepts, and that this is applied to the precepts of monogamy and indissolubility. Naturally, the incidence of polygamy and divorce in the Old Testament made this question very real for St Thomas. Here of course, he had the *deus ex machina* of divine dispensation, the plea that God had dispensed the Patriarchs from the laws of monogamy and indissolubility. But he does seem to use dispensation in a wide sense, not just of an explicit inspiration but of a legitimate interpretation of the facts of the case. If his *Commentary on 1 Corinthians* chapter 7, written late in life, were available to us it would very likely have put his teaching on the variability of marriage structure beyond doubt, because here he would have had to explain whether the Pauline Privilege was an exception to the general law. By ill-fortune or by design these few chapters have been lost from the *Opera Omnia* of St Thomas.

Whatever about St Thomas' position, it is certain that theologians of the calibre of Suarez, Sanches, Bellarmine did not feel free to say that absolute indissolubility was imposed by natural law.[7] An Instruction of the Holy Office in 1817 refers to this dispute among theologians and admits its force.[8]

In all this tradition the important point was that the scriptures permitted divorce in pre-Christian times and that the church grants it in Christian times. Therefore divorce does not contradict man's nature. This point is certainly worthy of notice but it is not a satisfactory explanation to say that this is a divine dispensation. One might draw a different conclusion from it – not that the original law of indissolubility is sometimes dispensed but that it has meaning only in that it safeguards and promotes the fundamental human values of the person in the family unit and in the community at large.

It has been already mentioned that indissolubility is the ideal in marriage – this is the ultimate in security for the parent-child husband-wife relationship; this is what love means at its deepest and finest. Divorce always spells a failure in marriage and a failure in love. Unfortunately, in human life as we know it, failure is endemic. If one refuses to contemplate it or to admit it one is simply closing one's eyes to the facts of life. This is why one has to contemplate divorce at all; and it is contemplated only as a compromise which may salvage something from a situation of failure. Our natural law is not the law of some Utopian existence but the law of imperfect human life; *nemo tenetur ad impossibile.*

From the natural law viewpoint marriage must certainly be a stable institution. A transient mating arrangement would contradict every human value that marriage stands for. One would also outlaw without question arbitrary divorce at the whim of either party. Even when both parties agreed on divorce, there is no guarantee that this would be a responsible decision which takes account not just of their own interests but of the interests of the children and of the community at large.

The positive side of this is that the natural law does not outlaw *responsible* divorce, a divorce which takes account of all the human values, personal, familial and social in the situation. Since prejudice, emotion and personal interest will tend to distort the objective facts of the case, divorce should be classed as responsible only on the intervention of an outside authority. Theological tradition takes account of this in its distinction between intrinsic indissolubility and extrinsic dissolubility. It is on this title that it justifies the dissolutions given by church authority.

What about State divorce? Does the State qualify as a responsible authority? *In principle* it seems impossible to exclude it, at least where non-Christian marriages are concerned. In regard to these marriages it is understood that the State can exercise a very wide control. It can establish impediments and a solemn form which touch the validity of the marriage. It is also by definition in a position to take a comprehensive view of all the factors in the situation which a responsible decision requires.

But State divorce as it works out in practice does not meet the requirements of responsible intervention. Sociology teaches that where it is introduced it tends to get more and more out of hand and to undermine radically the whole meaning of marriage as a stable institution. The real objection to State divorce as we know it is not that it contradicts an inviolable law of indissolubility but that it places the whole institution of marriage in jeopardy, and in trying to remedy situations of human failure introduces further insecurity into marriage which sparks off far more human problems than it sought to correct in the first place.

This wider form of moral argumentation against State divorce seems quite valid. In fact, it seems to be the only form of argument which is open to one from the viewpoint of natural law. At this stage, an obvious objection comes up: What about the cases in which a marriage has finally broken down, when two people cannot bear the sight of one another, when children are being neglected, ill-treated and torn apart by divided loyalty? In practice separation may be the remedy in this case; no one has the right to force people to live in inhuman circumstances. One says separation, not divorce, because the possibility of separation does not undermine the stability of marriage as does the possibility of divorce and remarriage. In fact, the last resort of separation without the opportunity of a new marriage may urge people to make an effort to get along together and get their marriage to work.

In suggesting separation as a last resort one is not putting it forward as a desirable alternative to divorce. Both these are funeral services for a dead marriage. If the community intervenes only in this way it too has failed. Its more positive contribution should be in preparing people better for marriage so that they use more foresight in entering it and appreciate better what it means, and in providing counselling services for marriages which are showing signs of strain.

Any discussion of divorce in a Christian context must take account of Christ's teaching on this subject. It has been suggested above that natural law does not in principle outlaw divorce, in particular divorce on the intervention of responsible authority. Is it possible that the divine positive law of the Bible outlaws it? A very strong church tradition claims that here divine positive law either clarifies or confirms natural law or supplements it with a more stringent obligation of indissolubility. The 1817 Instruction of the Holy Office, already mentioned, says: 'All divorce among Christian partners ... is nothing else but an enormous attack, if not against natural law (this point is disputed among Scholastics), certainly against divine written positive law as is especially clear from the Council of Trent.' In many church documents, for example *Casti Connubii*, divorce is said to be contrary to divine law, without stating whether this is natural law or divine positive law.

There is no need here to examine in detail the teaching of scripture on divorce. This has been done so well by other writers.[9] Whatever position a Catholic may hold on the textual interpretations involved he cannot read them as imperative of absolute indissolubility. The church practice of dissolving marriage must be a factor in his explanation. From the context of the so-called Pauline Privilege (1 Cor 7:12-13) it is not certain that Paul envisages the possibility of re-marriage for the convert who separates, but this is certainly the significance which church doctrine and discipline have read into his words. Any explanation which ignores this or the wider dispensing power which the Pope exercises on the basis of the so-called Petrine Privilege is not acceptable. The typical canonical interpretation holds that in her practice of dissolution the church employs a divine dispensing power and that this was allowed for in

Christ's promulgation in Matthew 19:6: 'What God has joined let no man disjoin.' Canonists interpret man here as any human power, leaving a field of competence for the church using divine power. This fundamentalist approach to the scripture text is not convincing. Even less convincing is its theological attitude which makes God out to be the voluntarist God of the Nominalists.

Christ's teaching is to be seen in a different light. He was a prophet bringing a new spirit, a set of attitudes and values which were a challenge to human nature and exceeded the righteousness of the Scribes and Pharisees (Mt 5:20). Everywhere he preaches radical demands for entry into his kingdom, 'Be you perfect as your Father in Heaven is perfect', 'Love one another as I have loved you', demands which can never be satisfied in the literal or legal sense, but which are obligatory for the Christian as the ideals which he must have before him, the vision of that which he must strive to be. Christ reacted against methods of the Scribes and Pharisees which made void the substance of God's commands by facile wordplay. Unlike John the Baptist, he steered well clear of questions concerning legal limits and minimal obligations, because this would tend to identify him with the casuist tradition of the Rabbis. It is in this light that we must interpret his gruff retort to the brothers who approached him for a decision in their dispute about land title: 'Man, who made me a judge and divider over you?' (Lk 12:14). His teaching was a clarion call for radical change of life, and he did not weaken it by exceptive clauses or qualifications or confuse it with casuistry, which is the language of compromise.

When the Christian community came to live these radical demands in their everyday life they found that the reality of human limitation and circumstance forced on them compromise and modification in various measures. To meet Christ's words in their full force in all situations was found to be impracticable, seeing that they had still to live in the present world where the fullness of his kingdom was not yet realised. The first experiments in communal living where the community would have everything in common failed to continue once the first enthusiasm ceased, once the expectation of an early *Parousia* declined and once the imperfection of human nature came to be appreciated. The necessity for an oath as a guarantee of honesty and fidelity and the need for self-defence as protection against unjust aggression came to be recognised in the same way.

Why should we exclude divorce from this interpretation? Why should we read Christ's words here and only here as an absolute prohibition? The fact that Christ appealed to man's ideal state, 'in the beginning it was not so', is an indication of how we are to read his words. The 'hardness of heart' which required the compromise of the Mosaic legislation in Deuteronomy still persists. If one interprets Christ's words in their full rigour as promulgating an absolute law against divorce, how did the church come to develop her practice and how can she justify her policy of dissolution? Perhaps Paul in his admission of the convert's privilege and Matthew in his 'except for adultery' clause are already

AN IRISH READER IN MORAL THEOLOGY

adapting Christ's radical teaching to the limitations imposed by man's actual circumstances? The real danger is that the compromise will not remain a compromise and will not be seen as a compromise, that the Christian will accept it as of right and as something which has merit in itself, and will use it to give rein to selfishness and lust. In this case Christ's teaching has been betrayed and the attitude which he condemned has triumphed.

It may be necessary to say that this article is not making a case for divorce nor is it making the case against divorce as explicitly and as trenchantly as it might be made. It is making a case for honesty in discussing divorce. Personally, I am convinced that the case against State divorce is extremely strong when one contemplates the effects which the practice has had on marriage and the family wherever it has been introduced. The sociologist can make the case for this side of the matter far better than the theologian. Far too often the official churchman's intervention is resented as dictation and the prejudice he engenders may spoil what is a good case on its own merits. Asseverations that the position is not debatable nor discussable may simply inspire suspicion that the position cannot stand up to investigation or criticism. The form of argument which the man in the street finds convincing is that which leads to some such conclusion as that stated by Sir Jocelyn Simon, President of the Probate, Divorce and Admiralty Division of the High Court in London: 'It is a great mistake to think that divorce is or ever can be a process generally devoid of pain for the parties (at least one of them) and their children. If it can be avoided, human happiness will generally be advanced.'[10]

Does this mean that the Christian as Christian and, in particular, the Catholic as Catholic has nothing to say on the subject of civil divorce legislation? The *Declaration on Religious Freedom* of Vatican II certainly states that he may not impose his religious convictions on those who do not share them: 'In all his activity a man is bound to follow his conscience faithfully, in order that he may come to God, for whom he was created. It follows that he is not to be forced to act in a manner contrary to his conscience. Nor on the other hand is he to be restrained from acting in accordance with his conscience, especially in matters religious … Government is to see to it that the equality of citizens before the law, which is itself an element of the common welfare, is never violated for religious reasons, whether openly or covertly.'[11]

One must not draw from this the conclusion that the Christian or Catholic should remain neutral on questions of public morality. His convictions about right and wrong are as relevant here as his convictions about expediency and inexpediency in purely political matters. He has an interest and duty to see that the law does not depreciate community values which are important in his eyes. He may very reasonably oppose a movement to introduce civil divorce legislation on the grounds that inexorably and progressively it undermines the stability of marriage and family life. If there were a compromise solution which avoided this consequence and met the wishes of those citizens who had different moral convictions then he should accept this. But this compromise has not yet been discovered in the matter of divorce law. Such legislation tends to become even more extensive through subsequent acts of legal reform. The very possibility of divorce, particularly when it takes the form of a threat to apply for a divorce, often spells the end of a marriage where reconciliation would otherwise be possible.

It is evident that this question presents a real dilemma for the person who is committed to the Christian ideal of marriage. He must recall Christ's judgement on the Mosaic divorce legislation. Christ did not question the good intentions of Moses, who was forced to make a compromise which would introduce some order into a situation occasioned by his people's insensitive conscience, 'hardness of heart'. He certainly blamed those who erected this compromise into a universal right and used it in arbitrary fashion: 'Is it lawful to divorce one's wife for any cause?' This is the question to which State divorce inevitably leads and Christ's answer to it must be relevant for the Christian. In a pluralist society he may not impose his viewpoint as a purely Christian or denominational conviction, but he surely may do so as the conclusion of rational observation and social experience.[12]

Notes:

1. CTS trans. Nn 34-35
2. *La Civiltá Cattolica* 24 (1965), 603.
3. Burns and Oates/Herder and Herder, 1967.
4. See the article on the Petrine Privilege in *Seminarium* 18 (1966) 715-741 by Arthur Jorio, a judge in the Roman Rota. A disappointing aspect of this article is that the author avoids discussion of the point made by Archbishop Zoghbi, even though it was precisely this which moved the editors to commission the article.
5. On this question see Dr J. Dominian, 'The Christian response to Marital Breakdown', *The Ampleforth Journal* 73/1 (1968), 3-13.
6. See M. B. Crowe, 'Human Nature: Immutable or Mutable', *The Irish Theological Quarterly*, 30 (1963), 204-231.
7. See L. Ryan, 'The Indissolubility of Marriage in Natural Law', *The Irish Theological Quarterly*, 30 (1963), 293-310; 31 (1964), 62-70.
8. *Collectanea S. Sedis,* Hong Kong 1898, n.1406.
9. See Donald W. Shaner, *A Christian View of Divorce* (Brill: Leiden 1969), and his comprehensive bibliography. Cf Wilfrid Harrington, 'Jesus' Attitude towards Divorce.'
10. *The Times,* 20 February 1970.
11. nn 3-6.
12. The attitude of Anglican divines in the face of civil divorce legislation is informative here. See *Putting Asunder: Report of a Group Appointed by the Archbishop of Canterbury* (SPCK 1966) for the views of F. D. Maurice, John Keble and T. A. Lacey.

19   Rethinking the Indissolubility of Marriage

William Cosgrave

(*The Furrow*, Vol 31, No 1, January 1980, pp 8-23)

Introduction

Marriage in the contemporary world is beset by many major problems, one of the most serious and complex of which has to do with its permanence or indissolubility. Modern secular man takes it for granted that, even if marriage is ideally permanent, it can in fact be terminated by civil divorce. In the Christian church this issue is widely discussed and is the subject of a debate that engages the attention and the talents of many of the church's best scholars. Much progress has been made in recent times but a great deal remains to be done before a general consensus emerges in this whole area. No one has all the answers and no proposal or position is without its difficulties.

Perhaps one of the most promising approaches to this question of the permanence or indissolubility of marriage is the one that seeks to rethink the basic ideas in which the debate is conducted and thus to present a renewed and hopefully more adequate understanding of indissolubility as an essential aspect of marriage. This article is an attempt to outline this approach which, as might be expected, is as yet rather exploratory and tentative. It remains open to further insights and development but at the same time one is convinced that it is only along these general lines that any real and lasting progress will be made.

The present teaching of the church and its difficulties

What the Catholic Church teaches and has taught for many centuries on the indissolubility of marriage may be summed up in two basic statements:

(a) A consummated marriage between two baptised people is absolutely indissoluble and the church has no power to dissolve it. The reason for this is usually stated to be that such a marriage symbolises the union of Christ and his church in the fullest way and since the Christ-church union cannot be broken or dissolved, neither can the consummated marriage of two baptised persons, i.e. a sacramental or Christian marriage. Consummation in this understanding means physical consummation which is effected by the performance of a single act of sexual intercourse between the spouses after their marriage. However, such consummation only renders the marriage absolutely indissoluble if both spouses are baptised Christians. If neither or only one is baptised, the marriage is not a sacrament and so could still be dissolved by the Pope for some sufficient reason, e.g. 'in favour of the faith', etc. Hence, neither consummation alone nor sacramentality alone is sufficient to make a marriage absolutely indissoluble. It requires a combination of both to do so.

(b) Any other marriage between baptised or unbaptised persons, is potentially dissoluble by the Pope in virtue of his ministerial or vicarious power as Vicar of Christ on earth. For example, a non-consummated marriage of two Catholics can be dissolved by the Pope for the sake of the spiritual welfare of one or both of the partners. A similar marriage of two non-Catholic Christians can be dissolved for the same reason, and one between two non-Christians is open to papal dissolution 'in favour of the faith', i.e. so that one of them or even a person to whom one of them is married, may marry a Christian. This means that the great majority of marriages in the world are potentially open to papal dissolution, and it seems that the Pope has more power over non-Christian than over Christian marriages, since there is no kind of non-Christian marriage that the Pope is unable to dissolve, whereas he cannot dissolve a consummated Christian marriage.

It is a well-known fact that this teaching of the Catholic Church in regard to the permanence of marriage has been and is the subject of considerable discussion and controversy. This debate has raised several significant questions or problems, which may be summarised as follows:

(i) In the church's present teaching, what has become of the traditional Catholic principle that marriage is by its nature indissoluble? It seems that this natural law principle is in practice abandoned by the church and is no longer the basis of papal action.

(ii) How is the church's practice compatible with the New Testament? It seems it is impossible to reconcile it with the teaching of Jesus and the rest of the New Testament: either it goes too far, if Jesus proclaimed the absolute indissolubility of all marriages, or it does not go far enough, if the New Testament teaches indissolubility merely as an ideal or even as a moral obligation. However one approaches the teaching of Jesus, there seems to be no way of interpreting it which does not render it incompatible with the church's teaching on the indissolubility of marriage. The church's position is, in other words, either too weak or too strong.

(iii) The claim that the Pope's power over marriage is based on Christ's grant of power and that he, therefore, acts in the name of God and not as a human authority seems to some to be questionable on scriptural grounds and, in addition, to reduce God to the stature and style of a medieval sovereign granting privileges to his favourites.

(iv) Another commonly-used argument supporting the papal power over marriage states that, since the church does in fact dissolve marriages, therefore she can do so. Theologians today treat this with considerable caution and point out that it involves a very legal and juridical approach to the whole question.

(v) Finally, a significant criticism of the present position on indissolubility is that it fails to take the reality of marriage and, especially, the reality of permanence in marriage sufficiently seriously. The church's teaching that a consummated Christian marriage is completely indissoluble is maintained, irrespective of whether a particular marriage relationship has proved to be actually permanent or not. In other words, the fact of consummation is held to guarantee and indeed to achieve the actual permanence of a Christian marriage, no matter what the facts of the case may be or how 'dead' the marriage in question is.

This position, which is possible only in a highly legal and, hence, extrinsic understanding of marriage and its permanence, clearly ignores important facts about the state of the individual marriage relationship, and this inevitably raises serious questions about its realism and, hence, its adequacy.

In the light of these questions and of other data, especially from the New Testament, many theologians are tending to think that the church has gone too far in her practice of dissolving marriages and should restrict herself more in the future. There is even the distinct possibility, some say, that she should dissolve no marriages at all. This certainly seems to be the direction in which the New Testament points.

On the other hand, some suggest that the church has more power to dissolve marriage than she uses or even claims. They say that the reasons given for saying she cannot dissolve a consummated sacramental marriage are unconvincing and that, in fact, the church has power to dissolve any marriage.

It can be seen from these diverse views that the problem of indissolubility is very complex and controversial. Some elements of a consensus do, nevertheless, seem to be emerging slowly and hesitantly, e.g. that Jesus taught the absolute indissolubility of marriage, and that some unions never reach the level of truly Christian marriage and so could be dissolved. There seems little likelihood, however, of any general agreement or end to the debate in the near future.

This position of uncertainty and division has inspired some theologians to look elsewhere for a way out of the dilemma. They believe they found it in the attempt to give a radical reinterpretation to the basic categories in which the discussion is conducted, and to work on from there. We believe that this is a worthwhile and significant endeavour and so we will devote the rest of this article to an exposition and explanation of its main lines.

Renewed understanding of permanence in marriage
To begin we may reflect briefly on the word indissolubility itself. It is a technical legal term, which is seldom used outside the context of marriage and its permanence. It belongs in the area of law and contract and it is quite appropriate and necessary there. It does not, however, fit very well into a renewed theology of marriage precisely because it is a legal term. The reality it refers to is better expressed by using the word permanence of marriage and, consequently, that is the word we shall prefer. At the same time, because the word indissolubility has such a long history in the context of marriage, we will use it occasionally as synonym for our primary word permanence, inaccurate though that may be.

(a) Marriage in the light of Vatican II

Before Vatican II the usual understanding of marriage was very juridical and physical. It was viewed as a contract in which rights were exchanged to acts suitable for procreation (cf *Code of Canon Law*, c. 1012-1081). Vatican II (in *Gaudium et Spes*, nn 47-52) and subsequent theology have, however, provided us with a much more personal and hence more adequate understanding of marriage. We now see it as a personal sexual relationship or community of love between a man and a woman, an intimate partnership of love and life which is permanent and exclusive as well as being procreative and open to growth. Marriage has a social dimension too and, because of this, it has been structured by society and has thus become the institution of marriage, surrounded and protected by law, custom and ritual. Thus, marriage is primarily a personal relationship which is at the same time an institution with a legal aspect and from this latter viewpoint it is seen as a contract that is guaranteed by law. Note that it is the *relationship* that is institutionalised and given the legal status of a contract, because it is the relationship that is the first and fundamental reality.

This change in our understanding of marriage has already shown itself at the legal level in the recognition by the church of the fact that one who lacks the capacity to establish and maintain a truly marital relationship or community of life is considered incapable of marrying validly. On this ground the church now declares marriages null and void and the draft of the revised *Code of Canon Law* accepts this idea.

Similarly, one can argue, the church is logically bound to use this Vatican II understanding of marriage, when it comes to dealing, not now with the beginning of marriage as in annulment, but with its ending, which is what is in question when permanence or indissolubility is under discussion. We will now attempt to explain and apply this.

(b) Marriage as permanent

The traditional understanding of the permanence or indissolubility of marriage is very legal, as is to be expected, given the juridical and legal view of marriage itself that then prevailed. Since, however, this view of marriage is clearly inadequate, as the Council showed, so too is the understanding of permanence which is based on it. In the light of Vatican II, then, we understand permanence in marriage in the following way.

Marriage as a personal sexual relationship is ideally and in the intention of the couple a permanent relationship, that is, one that should last till the death of one of the partners. But it is more. This ideal of permanence involves and gives rise to a moral obligation on the couple to work to the best of their abilities to ensure that their marriage does in fact become permanent. In other words, inherent in the marriage union itself there is an unconditional and very serious moral demand or duty to strive for permanence and to do all possible to build up one's marriage relationship so as to achieve it. The couple's response to this obligation or call will, or at least should, be the whole long-term process by which, throughout the course of their marriage, they deepen their love for each other, grow ever closer to each other and become so much two-in-one that their union will in fact last and be actually permanent.

This actual or realised permanence will be achieved and assured if the couple continue to love one another and develop their relationship. But at no point in their married life does permanence become an accomplished fact, so that one can say their marriage is now actually permanent. Such permanence can only be realised and known with certainty after the marriage has in fact lasted to and ended with the death of one of the spouses. Thus, when it is achieved, actual permanence (as distinct from the ideal and the obligation) is an effect of the couple's commitment and relationship, an after-the-fact description of a relationship which has been worked on and developed, and to which they have both been faithful till death.

Such a position can, of course, be reached only with time; it is not the work of a day or a week, much less of an individual action, but of months and years, and, of course, in some cases it will never be reached at all. When it is reached, however, we are in the presence of a truly permanent marriage.

In this conception of permanence in marriage, then, we are concerned with an inter-personal, moral and hence also in a real sense ontological bond between the partners, which is given legal support and standing. But there is no question of a legal bond, which seems to be quite independent of the marriage relationship and what happens to it. Such a bond is difficult to conceive of and does not seem to correspond to any reality in our experience.

To speak of the permanence of marriage in these terms gives us a very different concept from that of the tradition. This does not, however, invalidate it, since it seems to be the logical consequence or extension of the church's present understanding of marriage as expressed in Vatican II and much of contemporary moral experience, and hence is closer to the way we should speak of permanence in marriage in the future.

(c) The consummation of marriage

In this context it will be useful and important to discuss a question that is traditionally very closely related to the permanence or indissolubility of marriage, namely, the consummation of marriage.

The traditional understanding of consummation, deriving from the teaching of Alexander III (d. 1181) who was the first to incorporate it into the official teaching of the church, is a very physical one: consummation is brought about by the first act of sexual intercourse after marriage, and when the marriage is sacramental, it is made absolutely indissoluble by this single act. It is irrelevant whether the act is loving or performed in an atmosphere of unconcern or even hatred, or whether it was mutually desired or almost forced. If it takes place, its human, personal quality or lack of it does not matter as far as consummation is concerned. From the viewpoint of the canonist this was a very clear, easily recognisable and legally provable criterion of indissolubility and was consequently welcomed. Today, however, its inadequacies are being pointed out by many theologians, who are anxious to develop a more human and personal understanding of consummation in line with the understanding of marriage in Vatican II. They are insisting that it is impossible for an act of physical intercourse to consummate or complete marriage in any human, personal sense. Rather, consummation or completion of marriage as a human, personal relationship is and must be a quite different reality, which will very likely include physical intercourse, but is in no way to be identified with it. It is the whole profound process by which two people build and deepen their love relationship at all levels, so that they are truly and fully committed to each other in a union which, though not perfect, has, nevertheless, a real completeness or fullness. Such a marriage is truly consummated in personal terms and as such is a clear and full symbol of the union and love between Christ and his church.

Now clearly, when a marriage is consummated in this sense, it will have acquired an added depth and strength, which will go a long way towards ensuring that it will in fact be a permanent marriage. Indeed, it is true to say, that, as a matter of fact, in the great majority of cases, a marriage consummated in this personal sense will actually be permanent, i.e. will last till the death of one of the partners. Consequently, it will be highly unlikely that such a consummated marriage will break down.

Failure to achieve permanence and the dissolution of marriage
In the light of the understanding of permanence presented above, we may go on to spell out what a non-permanent and hence dissoluble marriage is and how it might come about.

When a couple, for whatever reason, do not respond to their obligation to make their marriage permanent or indissoluble, then we are in the presence of a serious failure. In addition, the marriage may be in the process of disintegration or even be completely shattered and dead. In such a case the couple's failure is complete and their marriage as a personal relationship no longer exists. Clearly, there are degrees of failure here, ranging from total to very insignificant, and each individual marriage must be treated on its own merits. But there is no doubt that such failures do occur in marriage and indeed today they are very frequent.

In this context the question arises: what is to be the response to this phenomenon of failure to make the marriage permanent and indissoluble? First of all, such failure, in whatever degree, is a disvalue or evil and frequently a serious one, both from the viewpoint of the spouses and also that of society and the church, when Christians are involved. Something now exists that should not exist, what ought not to be has come to be. This failure is a (serious) non-moral evil and at times there will be moral evil or immorality involved on the part of the couple, or at least one of them. Secondly, the simple fact of failure does not remove the couple's serious moral duty to do all possible to make their marriage permanent. Hence they are still bound, especially if they are Christian, to take measures to overcome their failure, however complete it may appear to be. They are called to do all possible to restore their relationship to its previous depth and even to build it up to the highest level they are capable of. This may include the call to sincere repentance for their own share and forgiveness for their partner's share in the failure; at the very least it will require them to do all they can to eliminate the evil of failure from their lives and so revive their marriage. Sometimes this will succeed and the marriage will be revived, to some extent at least. In other cases, however, the marriage may be found to be beyond saving and to be truly dead. Here the failure to make the marriage permanent is complete and the marital union has proved dissoluble and not permanent; it has, as a matter of fact, broken down totally and irretrievably.

What is the proper response to such a situation? Obviously there is the task of declaring that the marriage is in fact dead. This is primarily the responsibility of the couple, since they are in the best position to know the full story about their marriage from the inside. They ought not to take this step lightly and this is particularly true for Christians. When they do so, they are bound to exercise a responsibility in keeping with the seriousness of the matter in question. This is not such a novel idea, since it is the couple's decision to enter marriage in the first place, to apply for an annulment, or to seek a dissolution, thereby implying in the latter two cases that the marriage is already broken down and dead.

In this context the role of the church for Christians and for Catholics in particular would be to confirm (or perhaps not to confirm) this decision of the couple by submitting the case to a procedure or process specifically designed for this purpose. At the completion of this procedure, the official church would declare publicly and ecclesially that the marriage in question was (or was not) broken down and dissolved. It is clear in this conception of the matter that the church does not in fact dissolve the marriage but merely recognises that it is already dissolved. Dissolution is a declaration that the marriage relationship is at an end; it does not, however, actually terminate it. In this it is like an annulment, which is only a declaration of nullity, not something that actually makes the marriage null and void there and then. This understanding of dissolution differs from the present position where a dissolution of marriage, as for instance in a case of non-consummation, does in fact terminate the marriage, as distinct from merely stating that it is already terminated. The change seems justified, however, given our renewed understanding of permanence in marriage, and our rejection of the highly legal approach to it in the present theology of indissolubility.

In all this discussion of the breakdown of marriage and the response to be made to it, there has been no mention of the possibility of remarrying after the dissolution has been declared by the couple and the church. This possibility does of course exist in such cases and we must now consider it.

Remarriage after marital dissolution

We have just seen that dissolution of a marriage is possible, as it is in the present discipline of the church, and divorce is merely another name for this. We now confront the issue of whether the spouses of the dissolved marriage may remarry. Like dissolution, this is a crucial question and, as we have mentioned, is very controversial in both church and State today.

The first response to the question of remarriage after marital breakdown is 'no'. We have said that the failure to make the marriage permanent and indissoluble is a non-moral evil or disvalue. Remarriage, far from removing this evil, would only perpetuate it, weaken the force of the moral call to permanence and tend to undermine the stability of marriage itself. These are serious evils and cannot easily be allowed to happen, much less be caused by one's deliberate action. Hence, because of these facts, one is morally obliged not to marry again after his first marriage has been dissolved. To do so would be morally wrong, because it would be causing, without proportionate reasons, the non-moral evils just mentioned.

This reference to proportionate reasons raises the next question here. May one never remarry after the failure of his first marriage? Can there not sometimes be proportionate reasons for doing so, as there can be proportionate reasons in certain circumstances for allowing or even causing other non-moral evils, e.g. taking another's property, telling a falsehood, even taking human life, etc.? This is really the crunch question here and it seems there is no way of avoiding the answer 'yes'. Remarriage can and will be morally right, when one has proportionate reasons for it, or, in other words, when it is the lesser of two (or more) non-moral evils in a particular case. As we have said, remarriage after marital breakdown is in itself a non-moral evil or disvalue but not a moral evil, i.e. it is not in itself immoral. Hence, it may be morally justified in a situation where the evils it involves are outweighed or at least equalled by the evils it prevents, i.e. by the good it does. This good will be that of the personal and spiritual welfare of the individual persons whose first marriage has failed. We conclude, then, that remarriage after marital breakdown will be morally right when the individual spouse's welfare requires it. Once again it will be the individual who will make the judgement about the presence of proportionate reasons in his own case, and of course only he can make it.

This is, naturally, a very important decision or judgement that may not be lightly made but should be approached with a seriousness corresponding to the seriousness of the matter in question. The church will respect this judgement, just as she respects a person's decision to enter marriage for the first time and his judgement that his marriage has failed irrevocably. But in deciding what are proportionate reasons in this area, perhaps the church through her official teaching authority, her moral theologians and others, could provide some guidelines for the individual, as she does in other moral dilemmas. She could also decide that such a second marriage should not be officially and ecclesially celebrated or witnessed to in and by the church, or at least not in the same way as a first marriage, since such a celebration might obscure the church's commitment to the basic New Testament doctrine of the permanence or indissolubility of marriage and might make it more difficult to teach it effectively to her members. In the present practice of the church, no distinction is made between first marriages and those taking place after the official dissolution of a previous marriage. This, however, is only what one would expect, given the deeply legal understanding of the whole question. In a renewed view of the matter some distinction would need to be made, but its precise nature is to some extent a matter for discussion.

The sacramentality of marriage and its permanence

The fact that marriage is a sacrament is not in question here; rather it is assumed. Some questions do arise, however, especially in regard to what some call 'automatic sacramentality'. These are real and significant problems but we cannot go into them in this context. We are focusing, rather, on the effects of the sacramentality of marriage on its permanence. In other words, we are looking at how the fact that marriage is a sacrament affects or can affect its indissolubility.

We have stated the church's present position that a sacramental marriage, if it is consummated, is absolutely indissoluble and the church has no power to dissolve it, because it is a perfect symbol of the union of Christ and his church, which is itself completely unbreakable.

Now, there is no doubt that the marriage of two Christians is a symbol of the union of Christ and his church. If we understand consummation in the personal sense mentioned above, we can add that such a consummated marriage between Christians is a fuller and more complete symbol of that union than a marriage that is not (yet) consummated. However, it is the consummation, not the sacramentality, that gives it this added strength and depth, though it can be granted that its sacramentality confirms and supports this by giving a deeper meaning and significance to the marriage and adding a deeper motivation for seeking to make it permanent. This understanding of the effect of sacramentality on the permanence of marriage is in line with what theologians are saying today about the relation of Christianity to morality in general, and the influence it has on marriage in particular. To claim that sacramentality adds a special permanence of indissolubility to a consummated marriage would be seen today as contrary to the traditional and generally held principle that Christianity adds no new content, in terms of material norms, to morality or the moral life. In short, sacramentality, important though it is, is not really significant as far as the permanence of marriage is concerned. Hence what is true for Christian marriages, in regard to permanence, holds for non-Christian ones too.

Some practical implications

(a) In the church today there are many thousands of Catholics whose marriages have broken down irretrievably and who are now living in second 'marriages', which in the eyes of the church are invalid. Such people are officially barred from the sacraments because of their irregular marital status, and for many of them it seems that they will remain excluded from confession and Eucharist for the duration of the 'marriage', which in some cases may be for life. Some attempts are being made today by theologians and others to solve this problem and some put forward what are called 'pastoral solutions' to deal with it.

Now, given the present teachings and practice of the church on indissolubility, this is the only kind of approach to this pressing problem that is possible. However, if one were to adopt the understanding of indissolubility outlined above, the matter would take on a quite different appearance and significant steps could be taken to overcome it.

Many of the first marriages in question, which are long since dead, could be declared dissolved, as already explained, and the partners would then be free to marry again. Those of them who had already entered a second union could then decide with the aid of officially proposed guidelines, whether they were morally right to enter such a union and the official church would declare whether or not she would celebrate them by some kind of liturgical service. In this way the huge and urgent problem of Catholics remarried after a previous valid marriage would be well on the way to being solved.

(b) Our view of indissolubility has implications also for the annulment tribunals at work in the church today. In practice at present, a marriage is never accepted for submission to an annulment tribunal unless and until it is certainly dead and irretrievably broken down. If there were any hope of reconciliation it would be sent back, so that that possibility could be explored.

Now, granted that the complete breakdown of a marriage is a necessary precondition for annulment proceedings to begin, it would seem that the simpler, quicker, more humane and more Christian thing to do would be to have the marriage in question declared dissolved – which it obviously is. This would spare the partners the unpleasant task of going through the long, slow and often difficult and upsetting process of annulment, which in the end might fail anyway, not just because there was no case but quite often because it could not be proved or the evidence could not be obtained. Given the nature of the annulment, this absence of proof or evidence is not surprising, since it concerns an event of the sometimes quite distant past.

If this approach were taken, as it would seem it should logically be, then the annulment tribunals would to a large extent be emptied, and most of their work would be done in another and better way. This is no doubt a radical approach to the matter but it seems justified on the principles proposed and explained earlier in this article.

Difficulties in this view

A first difficulty seems to arise from the church's constant teaching that a couple cannot dissolve their own marriage, i.e. that every marriage is intrinsically indissoluble in an absolute sense. Does our position not seem to go contrary to this principle?

To answer this we must recall that the church's position just mentioned is based on the assumption that marriage is a contract over which the church has certain powers, including that of dissolution in certain cases. However, as Vatican II says and as we have seen, marriage is not simply a contract; it is rather a personal relationship of a particular kind, whose legal standing is expressed in contractual terms.

Now, experience teaches that human personal relationships usually break down (or develop) from within, i.e. by means of and because of the personalities and activities of the partners in relation to one another, and marriage is no exception. Hence it is to be expected – and experience confirms this – that a marriage which breaks down completely will generally do so because of factors intrinsic to it, i.e. because of the partners and what they are and do in relation to each other. In such a case one may say that the marriage in question is or has proved to be intrinsically dissoluble or non-permanent, and the church can declare this to be the case.

We believe that this position is commendable for the additional reason that it ensures that the evil is avoided, which the church was guarding against in the principle mentioned above, viz the termination of a marriage by the mutual consent of the partners. Without the church's official declaration of the dissolution of the marriage, the couple's decision to terminate their union has no force at the ecclesial level.

Another difficulty, in our view, may be expressed by saying that what we have said seems to imply that a marriage is permanent and indissoluble if it 'works'; it is dissoluble if it does not.

This statement contains a truth which we may express as follows. If an individual marriage does 'work', so that it grows and deepens to the level where it has acquired a real stability and strength, then it will have achieved a true and, perhaps, definitive permanence. If, however, it does not 'work' to the extent of breaking down completely, then it will have dissolved itself and proved not to be permanent and indissoluble.

A further difficulty now presents itself. Experience suggests that some marriages are not consummated and yet are not totally broken down. Now, the question is: can these simply be declared dissolved at the request of the couple, given that they are not (yet) actually dissolved and dead?

This is largely a theoretical problem, since in most such cases the couples will not want to terminate their marriage. If, however, in a rare case they do, then the church will first of all seek to induce them to revive their marriage and begin working towards realising the ideal of permanence. If this proves a failure, then the church will have no option but to refuse to declare such a marriage dissolved, since to do so would be contrary to the facts: it is not, as a matter of fact, dissolved.

A final difficulty remains to be faced. The view proposed in this article could be said to provide a system of easy divorce and remarriage which might well give rise to the same kind of harmful consequences that result from many of the systems of civil divorce to be found in the contemporary secular world.

Our answer to this would be simply to deny it. Such is not our intention nor, we believe, would what we have put forward lead to that. It would seem likely, however, that our proposal would result in an increase in the number of declarations of dissolution by the church, but this would only be a facing of the facts about marital breakdown and dissolution, just as the ever-increasing number of annulments being given in the church today represents a facing of the facts in that area too.

Statistics show that the number of marriages breaking down in the church today, especially among teenage couples, is very high and is continually rising. This very disturbing situation constitutes the really big problem and challenge facing the church at the present time in the area of marriage and it calls for urgent and effective measures.

In the long run the only really effective way to deal with marital breakdown is to prevent it, prevention being better than cure, as the old saying has it. Consequently, the church must do all possible to ensure marriages do not break down. In effect, this means that she must take the facts about marriage itself, as well as about its permanence, more seriously. One of these facts is that marriage today demands much more of the spouses than it did in the past. Hence, both partners must be and be seen to be capable of taking on these additional responsibilities. To ensure this, measures such as the following would seem helpful and indeed necessary: raising the age at which one may marry validly in the eyes of the church, demanding a higher level of instruction and formation in all that concerns marriage, providing more adequate pastoral care for married couples, etc.

If these steps were taken, the number of marriages breaking down would be reduced significantly, and the proposal we have put forward would be available, not as an easy way out of marriage, but as a last resort for those who had, unfortunately, failed to make their marriage permanent.

Summary and Conclusion

The understanding of the permanence or indissolubility of marriage put forward in this article commends itself for negative and positive reasons. Negatively, the present theology and canonical practice of the church is open to serious theoretical and practical objections. Positively, and more importantly, our approach to the whole matter seems a logical extension of Vatican II's understanding of marriage and, hence, is more in line with the New Testament teaching on and the contemporary reality of marriage and its permanence. It applies the personal, non-legal, categories of the Council to the question of the permanence of the marriage relationship. In consequence, we arrive at a more adequate idea of what a truly permanent marriage is: an interpersonal union which has grown and developed to such an extent that it lasts till the death of one of the partners, and thus is, in fact and in law, undissolved. In the light of this we considered the failure to make a marriage permanent, the dissolution of marriage and the possibility of remarriage, arriving at the conclusion that such a remarriage after the dissolution of a previous marriage can sometimes be morally acceptable, though the official church might or might not celebrate it formally, or might do so in a way different from a first marriage.

Our discussion of the sacramental dimension of marriage indicated that this is not a decisive aspect of the matter as far as the permanence of marriage is concerned. We, then, discussed two significant practical consequences of our understanding of permanence (or indissolubility) and, finally, we looked at some difficulties involved in our position.

It will no doubt be difficult to translate the theological understanding of indissolubility that we have presented into legal categories. But, as has been stated, this does not excuse the church from the task of doing so. It will be the business of canonists to undertake this important work in consultation with theologians and other experts.

Pope John Paul II, in his address to the College of Cardinals on the day after his election as Pope, said that 'our minds must first be in accord with the Council if what is implicit in it is to be made explicit'. This article is, I believe, in accord with the Council and is an effort to make explicit what is implicit in its teaching on marriage and, in particular, on the permanence or indissolubility of marriage. What has been said is far from being presented as certain and fully worked out in all its aspects and implications. Rather it is put forward tentatively and in the knowledge that it is open to improvement and perhaps even correction, while being in general along the right lines.

Bibliography:

Anglican Commission, *Marriage, Divorce and the Church.*

Baggott, P. A., *Doctrine and Life*, Sept 1975, p 647ff.

Brown, R., *Marriage Annulment in the Catholic Church*, p 50ff.

Cunningham, T., *The Meaning of Christian Marriage* (edited by E. McDonagh), ch 6.

Curran, C., *New Perspectives in Moral Theology*, ch 7.

Curran, C., *Ongoing Revision*, ch 3.

Dedek, J., *Contemporary Sexual Morality*, ch 7.

Doherty, D., *Divorce and Remarriage.*

Fagan, S., *Doctrine and Life*, Dec 1972, p 625ff.

Harrington, W., *Irish Theological Quarterly*, July 1970, p 199 ff; April 1972, p 178 ff.

Haughey, J. C., *Should anyone say forever?*, ch 3.

Keane, P., *Sexual Morality*, p 140ff.

Kelleher S. J., *Divorce and Remarriage for Catholics?*

Kelly, K., *Divorce and Second Marriage: Facing the Challenge.*

Macquarrie, J., *Christian Unity and Christian Diversity*, ch 9.

McCormick, R., *Theological Studies*, March 1971, p 107 ff; March 1972, p 91 ff; March 1975, p 100 ff.

McGrath, P.J., *The Maynooth Review*, Nov 1975, p 45ff.

O'Callaghan, D., *Irish Theological Quarterly*, July 1970, p 210 ff; April 1973, p 162 ff.

Paul VI, *The Regulation of Birth*, nn 7-9.

Pius XI, *Christian Marriage*, nn 31-36.

Ryan, S., *The Furrow*, March, April and May, 1973.

Schillebeeckx, E., *Marriage (Secular Reality and Saving Mystery)*, vol I, ch 5, vol 2, p 63ff.

Vatican II, *The Church in the World Today*, nn 47-49.

Wrenn, L. (ed), *Divorce and Remarriage in the Catholic Church.*

Part Five
Inter-Church Marriage

20   Inter-Church Marriages

Michael Hurley

(*One in Christ*, Vol 9, 1973, pp 35-42)

Present ideals

Interchurch marriages are to be encouraged in so far as they promote the cause of Christian unity. This of their nature they are calculated to do because they are Christian marriages. It is the very meaning of a Christian marriage that it deepens the love and unity of the partners and constitutes for others a sign and cause of loving unity. In deepening the love and unity of partners who belong to different church traditions (and in helping to bring together the friends and acquaintances of each) an interchurch marriage deepens the love and unity of the separated Christian Churches. It is a foretaste of church union. To manifest this, an interchurch marriage should be celebrated jointly: the appropriate clergy of both partners should officiate together in one and the same ceremony.

Interchurch families can and ought to have a double church loyalty.[1] The home as 'the domestic church'[2] should be not only a believing and witnessing community but also a worshipping community. Family worship, family prayers are an important if not an essential expression of this ecclesial character of the home. 'It certainly need not be presumed that all Marian devotion and remembrance of the dead should be excluded.'[3]

> It is important that from an early stage before marriage the couple attend each other's church services, at least occasionally, not simply as an educative exercise but in order to share as far as possible and permissible in the act of worship. Such sharing may become physically difficult where there are young children, and it is important that before that time, so far as possible, the parents feel at home in one another's churches. Couples will naturally tend to make equal financial contributions to each church and also try to make mutual visits to each other's churches. Strict equality may become difficult and, provided mutual trust has been established, may become unnecessary. It is, however, important that at no time of their lives should either parent lose all contact with the other's church.[4]

In general the couple can and ought to participate in the life and work of both their churches and in that of other churches (in the whole ecumenical movement) at local and higher levels, 'doing everything together as far as conscience permits'.

Joint Religious Education: 'Both husband and wife are bound by that responsibility [for the children's religious education] and may by no means ignore it or any of the obligations connected with it.'[5]

The general rearing of the children into the Christian life … is very far from exclusively concerned with denominationally ecclesiastical matters. It has to do with manners, relationships in the family, the priorities for available money and so forth, where the parents will above all be anxious to set a genuinely Christian example and provide a Christian atmosphere in the home. What worries us is never any denominational difference but very often the question whether our inclinations and habits are indeed of Christ or are enslaved to the powers of this world. In so far as Christian teaching comes in, it will be the teaching of the one, catholic faith, to the extent that we are able to grasp and expound that … How much better to have to fill out a child's understanding later on with specific differences and relationships between the various churches than to have to wean him or her from the long-assumed view that only one of them matters and that the others are but pale imitations, even fakes.[6]

Interchurch families may consider themselves as belonging to both churches, as having 'dual membership': A growing number of Christians, through participation in the ecumenical movement, in the life and work of other churches, come to know and feel themselves as belonging to these other churches, as constituting with them a believing and witnessing community. Hence, they do not hesitate to become a Eucharistic community, to share occasionally in each other's Eucharists on appropriate occasions. Present Roman Catholic discipline does not permit this latter practice but the state of theology on the subject of admission to communion and intercommunion makes it impossible to condemn it outright.

The church 'subsists', is incarnate, more or less, in all the Christian traditions. The Spirit of Jesus dwells in each and uses its institutions to communicate himself and his gifts. By baptism, therefore, which begins our initiation into the church, we belong radically and potentially to all the incarnations, embodiments of the church, to all Christian churches. If we grow up and are nurtured in one particular church or communion we come to belong to this exclusively. We can, however, grow up and be educated in more than one; in that case our upbringing will make us belong to more than one.

The children of an interchurch marriage, in so far as it is intended that they be brought up with a special allegiance to the two churches of their parents, ought to be baptised jointly by the appropriate clergy of both churches. Such a joint ceremony would manifest the particular meaning of the baptism: incorporation into the church in both denominations with right of access to the sacraments and other ministrations of both.

Joint religious instruction of the children of an interchurch marriage, at least up to their early teens, has become a real, but as yet unexplored, possibility because of the developments in the field of catechetics (which are all the more remarkable – at least in the case of Roman Catholic catechetical experts – in view of the fact that the explicit, direct aim has not been ecumenical) and also because Christians of all traditions now accept that what unites them is far more extensive and far more important than what divides them. Christians of all traditions have now come so far in their thinking that they can agree on the basic meaning of the Eucharist.

Ordering the sacramental life, the liturgical life of an interchurch family does raise problems, but the major ones in this area come from the present unsettled state of the theology of initiation in all denominations: lack of clarity and agreement (within each denomination) as to the proper relationship between baptism, confirmation and Eucharist, as to the meaning of confirmation and the universal appropriateness of infant baptism. At least in the case of an interchurch marriage which does not involve a Roman Catholic (e.g. a Methodist and an Anglican) what reasons are there why the children should not be confirmed (received into full membership) and be admitted to first communion in both churches at the appropriate times? Experimentation (with all due prudence) in this area should be less difficult for non-Roman Catholic Western Christians. Some Roman Catholic theologians would consider such experimentation as already possible even in the case of an interchurch marriage involving a Catholic. Ideally the ceremony of 'first communion' ought to take place in the context of a 'joint Eucharistic celebration'.

Present problems

A Roman Catholic at present must seek permission to enter into marriage with a non-Roman Catholic Christian. To receive this permission he must promise to do all in his power to have the children baptised and brought up as Roman Catholics.

The immediate concern is not, I think, to see whether this condition is justifiable and (if not) how to proceed in order to have it altered or removed. My concern certainly is short-term: granting that this condition does exist, I wish to examine it more closely, to establish its precise meaning with a view to seeing whether it might not, for the moment at least, be tolerable. In this regard the following considerations seem relevant.

This promise is not only compatible with, but demands for its due and proper fulfilment, the ecumenical upbringing of the children (at least to the extent envisaged in JPC i.e. 'double loyalty' if not 'dual membership'). This follows not only from the Roman Catholic Church's official commitment to ecumenism but also, in particular, from the very Vatican document cited above which states that both husband and wife are responsible for the children's religious education and may not ignore any of the obligations connected with it. Taken in context, therefore, this promise, so far from excluding the non-Catholic parent from the religious upbringing of the children, ensures that this can be undertaken jointly. The whole religious education and the major part, certainly, of the religious instruction of the children of an interchurch marriage can be undertaken jointly by the parents. The Roman Catholic or Anglican or Protestant upbringing of children cannot, in these days, be anything but ecumenical.

The promise is, in any case, conditional and in no way pre-empts the future. The Roman Catholic promises to have the children brought up as Catholics if the marriage is blessed, in fact, with children and if the Catholic upbringing of the children proves to be a real possibility.

Hence (a) a Roman Catholic, who sees that his Presbyterian partner's position (and with it the family's livelihood) depends on the family being brought up as Presbyterians, can make this promise here and now with sincerity because he knows that, if a child arrives and if this situation still obtains, he is at full liberty (to say the least) to have the child brought up as a Presbyterian. Doing all in his power to have the child brought up as a Catholic cannot mean seriously endangering the livelihood and consequently the happiness and unity of the family. He will still, of course, be able and obliged to play a full part in the religious education of the child and to play a major part in its religious instruction.

(b) A Roman Catholic who has not been practising his Christianity for some time can make this promise here and now with sincerity because he knows that, if a child arrives when the most he could do would be to give the child a very inadequate Catholic upbringing, he is at full liberty (to say the least) to have the child brought up in the Christian tradition of his partner. Doing all in his power to have the child brought up as a Catholic cannot mean endangering the due adequate religious upbringing of his family.

(c) The same would hold for a Catholic father who sees that his profession, while it lasts (he is, for instance, a seaman) will keep him away from home five months or more of the year.

The papal *Motu Proprio* which enjoins this promise makes no explicit provision for granting or obtaining a special dispensation from this condition. (Cf by contrast Infra 11B). This fact confirms the conditional nature of the 'promise'. It is difficult to envisage a case in which such a dispensation would be necessary in order to obtain the desired results.

Partners to an interchurch marriage who cannot now (on the threshold of their marriage) envisage themselves bringing their children up either in loyalty to or in membership of both churches, who can only envisage themselves as bringing the children up either as Roman Catholics or as (for example) Methodists in the 'traditional' way they themselves were brought up, ought not now to pre-empt the future by entering into an agreement to have the children brought up one way or the other, because they know not what they shall be as the grace and experience of married life draw them ever closer together. The Catholic may indeed make his promise, and similarly the other partner if he so wishes, but only because such a promise is conditional with inbuilt limitations and thus does not pre-empt the future.

The promise required now of a Roman Catholic does not seem so objectionable that a Christian of another tradition, or the Catholic himself, cannot tolerate it in order to succeed in getting married. It is to be duly noted that no promise of any kind is expected from the non-Catholic and that, if he is asked or invited to declare his attitude, he is being asked or invited to declare simply and precisely his attitude to his Catholic partner making the promise as explained.

Anyone actually engaged in counselling couples contemplating an interchurch marriage can have no doubt that the really urgent matter is how, on the occasion of this problem, (a) to educate both parties out of their moral fundamentalism and enable them to see this and other moral issues for what they really are; (b) to educate both parties out of their ecumenical ignorance and indifferentism and enable them to take an informed active interest in promoting Christian unity. The prospect of an interchurch marriage is one of the best opportunities available for promoting ecumenical concern and education among many clergy and laity.

A Roman Catholic marrying a Christian of another western tradition must, for validity, have his marriage witnessed by the catholic parish priest of the place. Provision is made for a special dispensation from this obligation (the so-called 'canonical form'). Since 1970 the local Catholic bishop may grant the dispensation 'if serious difficulties stand in the way of observing the canonical form'. Our problem in Ireland is how to encourage our bishops to grant these special dispensations. The dispensation ought to be granted when it will improve relations between the churches concerned (and this it will inevitably do at present and in the near future as long as a sense of grievance about Catholic interchurch marriage legislation, rightly or wrongly, persists) and when the partners request the dispensation for their own good or for the good of their relatives. It is often forgotten that this is a special dispensation (to marry a non-Catholic) and is not granted i.e. unless and until the Roman Catholic has indicated his or her willingness to make the promise discussed earlier. If the problem of the 'promise' has been solved and if both partners wish for good reasons to be married in the non-Catholic church, they should be encouraged to persist and persevere (like the man in the gospels) in their request for the dispensation from the 'canonical form'.

With regard to the celebration of an interchurch marriage the following points are worthy of mention:

It is not permitted to have another religious marriage ceremony before or after the Catholic ceremony, for the purpose of giving or renewing matrimonial consent.

Permissible is a wedding ceremony in the church of one partner, followed by a service of blessing or thanksgiving in the church of the other, so long as the second service does not include a second exchange of marriage vows.[7]

Though permissible, this practice is not to be recommended. Ecumenism

AN IRISH READER IN MORAL THEOLOGY

means doing everything together as far as conscience permits and not doing everything one after the other. Besides, any form of double ceremony is in danger of giving the false impression that something or other was lacking in the first. Much to be preferred is participation in the service by the clergy of both partners.

Where the couple desire it and their respective clergy or ministers are willing, it is possible for both clergy to take part in the wedding ceremony. The minister or priest of the church in which the wedding takes place will normally preside [and receive the exchange of consent] but the other may assist in the ceremony.[8]

A celebration of the Eucharist is not to be recommended in so far as both partners cannot be admitted to communion.

Joint Pastoral Care
Local Ordinaries and parish priests ... are to aid the married couple to foster the unity of their conjugal and family life, a unity which, in the case of Christians, is based on their baptism too. To these ends it is to be desired that those pastors should establish relationships of sincere openness and enlightened confidence with ministers of other religious communities.[9]

The British Joint Working Group states:
Joint pastoral care by the priest and minister of both bride and bridegroom is obviously the ideal when the partners themselves wish it ... They are not likely to be willing to work together in this difficult field unless they are already co-operating more generally ... Joint pastoral care presupposes mutual trust and respect between the clergy of the partners and a clear understanding that neither wishes to proselytise.[10]

The absence of joint pastoral care for interchurch marriages in Ireland is nothing more or less than a reflection of the general absence of ecumenical co-operation. Regular meetings of clergy at local level to discuss matters of common interest are an absolute necessity.

Notes:
1. *Joint Pastoral Care of Interchurch Marriages in Wales and Scotland: Recommendations by the Joint Working Group of the British Council of Churches and the Roman Catholic Church in England, Wales and Scotland,* par 27-32.
2. Vatican II, *Constitution on the Church,* par 11, Abbott, 29.
3. JPC, par 29.
4. JPC, par 30.
5. *Motu Proprio* of March 1970 in *One in Christ,* 1971, p 212.
6. Martin Conway, Anglican parent, *One in Christ,* 1969, p 73.
7. JPC par 24.
8. Idem.
9. *Motu Proprio* 1970.
10. JPC, pars 8, 9, 11.

21   Inter-Church Marriage: An Anglican View

David Woodworth

(*The Furrow*, Vol 22, No 10, October 1971, pp 603-614)

In a sermon preached on 24 January 1971 in Canterbury Cathedral, during the Week of Prayer for Christian Unity, the Archbishop of Canterbury said:

> I believe that the new papal *Motu Proprio* on mixed marriages brings a good deal of help to a vexed problem, so long as it is acted upon to the full.[1]

The Archbishop's proviso is relevant to the Irish situation, in which the terms of Norm 7 of the *Motu Proprio*, 'Matrimonia Mixta', may well allow the free spirit of this document to be suppressed at a local level by an attitude of scrupulous legalism. This tension between spirit and letter has to be contained and understood in any discussion of the joint pastoral care of mixed marriages.

The tension is there, long before a marriage is contemplated. This much is evident from the current debate on education. Both the Roman Catholic Church and the Church of Ireland discourage the social contacts which may ultimately lead to a mixed marriage. Both recognise that such a union raises practical problems injecting, as it may, a divisive element into the marriage. Both recognise that doctrinal differences raise specifically religious questions about such a marriage. Consideration of these problems has led to the ghetto mentality which prevails in parts of the Protestant community.

Eoin de Bhaldraithe has treated of the ghetto with insight and charity.[2] Members of the Church of Ireland have seen – and still see – the Roman Catholic attitude to mixed marriages as a way of snuffing out their church. Although this may be a prejudice, it is none the less real, and is reflected in the words, 'To wish for the death of another church is something akin to murder.'[3]

In passing he mentions that bulwark of the ghetto, exclusive dances: 'As usual the minority runs its own dances.'[4] So the minority is a club, as it were, with the right to restrict admission to its halls. It is good to know that this is considered 'usual'. Personally, I find it both artificial and embarrassing. The confrontation at the door may well be the first contact which a Roman Catholic has with a Church of Ireland priest: the two parties may understand the issues, or they may not. Either way, potential future relations with a Church of Ireland cleric will be soured by the memory: 'He's one of the crowd who refused me admission to St Mary's Hall.' Of course this is an attitude springing from ignorance. But ignorance is a notable factor in many cases which are pastorally 'difficult'.

It is as well to state clearly that this is a problem. The 'minority' views its 'own dances' as places where the relationships which lead to marriage may well begin. Therefore, it is because of Roman Catholic law on mixed marriages, and not because they are Roman Catholics, that individual Roman Catholics are, generally, excluded. Eoin de Bhaldraithe has shown great insight into this initial problem in the words, 'Because of our laws this friendship [i.e. between Protestants and Roman Catholics] cannot go beyond a certain point.'[5] This stumbling block is, in the words of the same writer, 'one of the big inhibiting factors not only in ecumenical relations but also in community relations in general'.[6]

As one who is firmly committed to the ecumenical ideal, I can only hope that the Church of Ireland will have the requisite courage to adapt its viewpoint to any implementation of the full spirit of the *Motu Proprio, 'Matrimonia Mixta'*.

Joint pastoral care begins, however, at some point quite distant in time from such discomfiting encounters. It should commence at that moment when it is apparent that an engagement will be announced. At this point, the respective clergy should make contact, and should together see the couple. Both clergy will, naturally, try to defend the spiritual integrity and conscience of those within their care.

This meeting, if it takes place at all, has too often been seen as a skirmish. Such a view completely overlooks the spirit of the *Motu Proprio*, as expressed in Norm 14, which states, inter alia: 'It is to be desired that those [Catholic] pastors should establish relationships of sincere openness and enlightened confidence with ministers of other religious communities'.[7] If, in this sentence, 'should' carries the same moral weight as 'ought', then the *Motu Proprio* demands that there be joint pastoral care of the couple. It is careful to point out that relations must be ones of 'sincere openness and enlightened confidence'.

Here, surely, there is recognition of the initially opposed stances of the two clergy concerned. The Roman Catholic will seek to support his position by appeal to legal arguments. The Anglican will smell out what he sees to be the weak points in the documents behind such arguments. To me the 'serious difficulties' which allow of dispensation from the canonical form (Norm 9)[8] offer a fairly obvious line to follow. Another may be found in the words of Norm 11: 'If it [the celebration of the mixed marriage] is to be taken from the Roman Ritual'.[9] Now 'if' is a small word, but it can imply that other circumstances may obtain. Hence, it can be argued, Norm 11 takes into account an occasion when a Roman Catholic may be married before a Roman priest, who is assisting a Church of Ireland cleric conducting a wedding according to the rites and ceremonies of that church.

Indeed, there will be a need for 'sincere openness and enlightened confidence' at this delicate stage. Without such qualities, any future joint pastoral care will be jeopardised by an inevitable souring of relations, if not mutual distrust.

This stage of the problem was set out by Michael Hurley five years ago.[10] It may be summarised thus: the Roman Catholic position – church unity will solve the problem of mixed marriages; the Anglican position – the present difficulty over mixed marriages will have to be solved before any church union. These two positions are irreconcilable. In the face of this problem, the author put in a plea for 'gradualism'. I believe that this gradualism may be workable in the spirit of the *Motu Proprio*.

It is most necessary, in the shadow of these difficulties, that the clergy concerned have a sound personal relationship. They must be able to be candid with each other, to maintain a point without aggression. There must be mutual respect for the integrity of the other, and no suspicion of ulterior motives. Perhaps the only conclusion, in some cases, will be an agreement to differ. If this relationship cannot be established, or is fractured, at this stage, then joint pastoral care, after the marriage, is an unattainable ideal.

The pattern of co-operation varies enormously throughout the country. Generally speaking, parochial contact, or its absence, reflects the attitudes of the respective bishops. By keeping this point in mind, over-optimistic interpretations of this essay will be avoided.

Personal relationships between pastors of differing confessions should have begun long before there is any occasion to discuss a specific couple. Joint work in the community is a sound basis for contact, but contact should develop into the kind of friendship were neither feels strange when asked to say grace at the other's table. In the country, in small towns and villages, it is easier to form such relationships than in the larger urban areas. The Church of Ireland man in these rural places has a smaller flock, and sees his ministry as part of a wider pattern, so he becomes involved in the life of the whole community. There is paradox here. Where the Church of Ireland is most in danger of absorption by intermarriage, it is often most radical in its search for Christian understanding.

On 18 June 1969 the House of Bishops of the Church of Ireland issued a directive to the clergy. Its central statement was as follows:

> Where a document in writing has been received by the local Church of Ireland Bishop from the relevant Roman Catholic authority saying specifically that no written or verbal *Ne temere* promise has been or will be demanded of the Church of Ireland party, it will be in order for a Church of Ireland clergyman to attend, and if requested, to robe and assist at a mixed marriage in a Roman Catholic church.
>
> Conversely, where no official written assurance of this kind is given by the officiating Roman Catholic clergyman, and where the *Ne temere* promise has been or is being made, it is desired that no Church of Ireland clergyman should attend such a wedding in a Roman Catholic church. He should not be present either as an officiant or as a guest in the body of the church.

This was quite a strong directive. It should be noted that the major objection was to promises made by the Church of Ireland party. But the *Motu Proprio* elicited a brief set of 'Comments'[11] circularised to the clergy for their guidance in July 1970. It is another forcefully worded document; it lays stress on the 'equality and freedom' necessary for pastoral care, and acknowledges that 'certain new features give some hope for an ultimate solution in that they appear to imply greater flexibility'. These 'comments' conclude with the words, 'We must hope that this is but an interim document' and call for a re-thinking of the subject by 'both churches together', as quoted by Eoin de Bhaldraithe in his article.[12]

I refer to these documents at some length to show to what extent the Roman Catholic stand on mixed marriages generates a counter-reaction which, if not understood as such, may hinder the close relations necessary for joint pastoral care.

The innovation in the *Motu Proprio* is to be found in Norm 7, which gives great power to the local bishop. Where he is progressive, the spirit of the *Motu Proprio* lives; where he is conservative, it may be suppressed. Ireland is notorious for its resistance to change, and I fear that, in many parts of this land, the optimism of the Archbishop of Canterbury will not be realised. The journal *Theology* in an editorial said, of Norm 7: 'The unlimited discretionary restrictive power contained in the last dozen words will be noticed.'[13] The fear of a restrictive attitude, in Ireland, is borne out by the enormous variations in the Episcopal directories which accompany the *Motu Proprio*. In Switzerland and Germany, for instance, parish priests may grant dispensations for mixed marriages. So far, only three directories, Irish, Scottish and Italian, make no mention of interchurch co-operation. This should sound a note of warning, that the spirit may be suppressed, at least in parts of Ireland.[14]

A point made by the recent report, 'The Joint Pastoral Care of Interchurch Marriages in England, Wales and Scotland'[15] is that the care of the families of those who are affianced must not be overlooked. Too often, there is a temptation to centre one's pastoral activities on the couple, without due regard for the delicate relationships which have to be built between their respective families.[16]

For the most part, mixed marriages in Ireland belong to the third category given by Eoin de Bhaldraithe, namely, those where 'both [parties] wish to remain faithful to their own churches'.[17] Hence, I should like to adopt the convention of other writers, and term such unions 'interchurch marriages'.

The whole question centres upon the children: on their frequency, on their education and on their faith.

The conception control issue, over-exposed in other contexts, is not given the prominence it deserves in this context. A gross simplification would be the case of a husband (Church of Ireland), who knows that further additions to the family could be economically unsound, and also knows that the use of oral or mechanical contraceptives will be seen as sinful by his wife. The Church of Ireland has accepted the Lambeth Conference Resolutions 112, 113 and 115 of

1958, which may be summed up by saying that 'marriage is a vocation to holiness' (113) in which 'the responsibility for deciding the number and frequency of children has been laid by God upon the consciences of parents' (115); and 'Christians need always to remember that sexual love is not an end in itself' (113).[18]

Pastorally, this is a delicate problem at any time. It is far more so in an interchurch marriage. Norm 6 requires that both parties should be 'clearly instructed on the ends and essential properties of marriage'.[19] This difficulty can only be resolved in accordance with each particular case. Certain points of interpretation in the matter of education and faith will also be relevant, as are the words (interpreting the French document of 1968) 'The good of the marriage and of the family is primary'.[20]

With regard to the education of the children, there appears to be a very large assumption that Norm 4 refers to this matter. The relevant words are as follows: 'The Catholic party ... is gravely bound to make a sincere promise to do all in his power to have the children baptised and brought up in the Catholic Church.'[21] Now, it is a parent who brings up his children, delegating to the teacher certain magisterial and disciplinary functions. The home, not the school, is the place in which the living faith is passed on. Formal religion may be instilled at school. The child is imbued with the faith at home.

Further, there is an internal inconsistency in the *Motu Proprio* at this point. In its introductory section, education is recognised as a particularly difficult problem, 'in view of the fact that both husband and wife are bound by that responsibility and may by no means ignore it or any of the obligations connected with it'.[22] Clearly, this implies a joint decision by husband and wife. Such a decision, if truly 'joint', will have to be reached by the civilised process of give and take. But the Roman Catholic party has no room to manoeuvre, since, in accordance with Norm 4, he has promised to do 'all in his power' to have the children 'brought up in the Catholic Church'. Either, then, there is genuine freedom to make a joint decision, or there is not. The *Motu Proprio* cannot have it both ways.

The Latin of the document may provide the clue. The older, and more rigorous, *omnia pro posse* (all in his power) has become the slightly less austere *omnia pro viribus*, in Norm 4. This is but a light straw in the wind, yet, taken with what has already been said, it would seem to indicate that the spirit of the *Motu Proprio* is behind a freely taken joint decision, rather than a legally enforced requirement. Always provided, of course, that such a free decision is taken in the full knowledge of all the teaching involved.[23] The Belgian Episcopal Directory takes this broader view, referring to 'a truly fruitful Christian education'.[24]

The faith of the children, and of the parents, provides a more cheering field of opportunity for joint pastoral care, since it is less hedged in by legal formalism.

Here there is much in common. The primacy of scripture, as the ultimate source of all teaching, is agreed. Tradition, too, takes its place, in as much as the Church of Ireland accepts the rulings of the first four General Councils, that is to say, Nicaea, Constantinople, Ephesus, Chalcedon. It follows that the two major Creeds (Apostles' and Nicene) are accepted as giving the kernel of Christian dogma. There is the three-tiered pattern of ministry, with bishops, priests and deacons: a form of church polity which members of the Church of Ireland deem to be Catholic. As regards the papacy, both churches should keep an eye on the working documents issuing from the Anglican-Roman Catholic conversations. For instance: 'Anglicans ... are divided from it [the Roman Catholic Church] principally by the problem of papal authority ... with the attendant problems of doctrines ... which have been declared binding by papal declaration.'[25] But compare: 'The original text of the statement on the papacy by Lambeth 1968 contained these words. "Within the whole College of Bishops and in ecumenical council it is evident that there must be a president of the whole church. This president might most fittingly be the occupant of the historic See of Rome".'[26] Neither statement is definitive. Each represents a genuine aspect of Anglican thought.

What unites is of far more importance than that which divides. Both churches centre their worship on the Eucharist. In this context, above all, I welcome Eoin de Bhaldraithe's sentiments about joint Eucharistic prayer,[27] which means that the whole family will occasionally attend (but not all will receive Communion) each other's Eucharist. With the rapid liturgical changes at present taking place, there is no reason why either party would feel in the least strange in the context of the other's worship.

Such an exercise can only meaningfully take place within the framework of joint pastoral care. Otherwise, a corporate act of worship will be construed as a potential defection by one party, and so exacerbate any latent tension between the two communities.

A family should be bound together in its praying at home. Roman Catholicism has a strong and simple devotional discipline in the Rosary. In the Church of Ireland, the habit of regular private prayer is still present, as is regular reading of the Bible. Regrettably, with that church, family prayers seem to have died out. Within the context of the interchurch marriage, there is considerable room for movement, in that the two traditions overlap to a great extent. This common ground should be used as much as possible. Clergy should do all in their power to emphasise that this area of agreement exists.

The English report on interchurch marriages stresses the need for joint family prayers: 'If such prayers are important to any Christian family, they are particularly so to an interchurch family'.[28] It goes on to make the point that prayers for the dead and Marian devotion present some difficulty. There is undoubtedly a divergence here, as on the question of the invocation of saints.

On the one hand, the Roman Catholic priest has an opportunity to indicate, to the Church of Ireland party, that there is a great difference between the expressions of popular piety and the theological judgements which lie behind them.

On the other hand, the Church of Ireland priest can point out that, among other things, his church keeps the major New Testament feasts of the church, together with twenty-five saints' days (two of which are dedicated to the Blessed Virgin Mary) in the course of the year; these are commemorations. *Magnificat* – the song of the Virgin – is an integral part of regular worship. In addition, many Anglicans feel that, while they may express their wonder for the incarnation in the words of the Angelic Greeting to the Blessed Virgin Mary, they must stop before the words *ora pro nobis* in the Ave.

I have said this much to dispel the illusion that saints and angels are disregarded in the Church of Ireland.

With reference to this particular region of pastoral care, these words from the Lambeth Conference 1968 Report, from the section 'Renewal in Unity', provide a particularly relevant guideline: 'We should do together everything which conscience does not compel us to do separately.'[29] Of course, this is a guide for Anglicans only, yet its spirit is echoed in some words from the Belgian Episcopal Directory on the *Motu Proprio*. This Directory says, of the partners in an interchurch marriage, that, 'in the little church of their family they can also be a prefiguration of the Christian unity which is yet to come'.[30] The very nature of an interchurch marriage demands that we lay stress on its unifying potential, rather than on the divisiveness which it may engender, hence the emphasis given to ecumenical attitudes in much of what I have written.

There must be a genuine desire to further the good of the whole family, entailing compassion and humility on the part of both pastors. There are obvious dangers implicit in playing semantic games with 'good' in this context, to say nothing of the unholy trio of legalism, triumphalism, and a shallow irenicism.

Most of what I have said so far has been about the care of marriages where both partners are active supporters of their own Christian tradition.

In Ireland there are some non-practising Roman Catholics and some non-practising Anglicans. Generally, the clergy become proprietorial about these people if they enter into an interchurch marriage. Since we are a nation of churchgoers, it is difficult to admit that there are lapsed Christians amongst us. Neither church is likely to allow a lapsed Christian to adopt the confession of his spouse, without trying to persuade him otherwise. Nevertheless, this type of mixed marriage is beginning to take place. Are our relationships with each other good enough for discreet clerical contact on these problems as they occur? Not everywhere. Yet there is recognition of this problem, and its solution, in these words of Eoin de Bhaldraithe: 'We too, must have many mixed marriages which are material for evangelisation – whose first need is to have the gospel preached to them'.[31] The realisation that the gospel is prior to confessional instruction is the foundation of pastoral concern in these difficult cases.

Until this point, my tone has been, in the main, optimistic. But we know that such situations can be a bed of nettles. I must redress the balance.

There is the difficulty arising from the relationship of the inter-church family to either community. The whole family never belongs, one member at least feeling that he – or she – is odd. A massive re-education of the parish is necessary to overcome this. But people will still be suspicious, because the children of interchurch marriages tend to contract such marriages themselves. This can be an unhappy circle in human relationships. It is also detrimental to growth in the Christian faith. The parish must be taught to avoid the overreactions of tolerant superiority and enthusiastic chumminess. Instead, it must learn to accept the interchurch family as a unit towards whom the parish is responsible, and whom the parish recognises as having a right to participate in its fellowship.

I have already mentioned the importance of reciprocal trust between clergy in this matter of joint pastoral care. This is a delicate relationship, and easily prevented from even beginning. Personalities may not be in tune. The time of training is a major factor here. If either man has been tutored within the rigid framework prior to Vatican II, he will find it hard to conceive of joint pastoral care. Both have been trained to the idea that Rome never changes, though with differing interpretations of this conviction.

Local events and local history have a significant influence on this matter. A present full of violence, or a past brimming over with inter-communal bitterness, is not conducive to a calm discussion of interchurch marriages. Nor, for that matter, is the failure of a bishop to find the pastorally liberating spirit of the *Motu Proprio* a positive contribution to sound relationships with this sphere.

It is trite but true to say that time will solve these problems. But time is not on the side of minorities and a final solution by absorption is not acceptable.

Consideration of the relationship between law and love, and of that supreme divine law (referred to by Eoin de Bhaldraithe)[32] is enough to show that one may question the premises upon which the *Motu Proprio* rests: so runs the Church of Ireland view. The *Motu Proprio* reaches back to the days when an Anglican was a heretic. Now, as we all know, he is a separated brother. There is quite a difference. The contrast is heightened by the following passage from the allocution of Pope Paul VI at the canonisation of the Forty Martyrs on 25 October 1970:

There will be no seeking to lessen the legitimate prestige and worthy patrimony of piety and usage proper to the Anglican Church when the Roman Catholic Church – this humble 'Servant of the Servants of God' – is able to embrace her ever beloved sister in the one authentic community of the family of Christ.[33]

So, from heretical to brotherly (although separated) to 'ever beloved sister', all in the space of about ten years. In the face of such softening in terminology, it is scarcely surprising that Church of Ireland clergy are taking a strong line in a liberal interpretation of the *Motu Proprio*.

In conclusion, the key to this joint ministry lies in the personality and vision of the pastors themselves. There is a great challenge and a greater need. The challenge is the candid promotion of unity. The need is the removal of the scandal of disunion within a particular family. Together, the two churches can find a solution. To refuse such co-operation is to violate the spirit of the *Motu Proprio*.

Notes:
1. Quoted in *One in Christ*, 1971, vol 7, nos 2-3, p 255.
2. *The Furrow*, March 1971, vol 22, no 3, p 130, 'The Joint Pastoral Care of Mixed Marriages' by Eoin de Bhaldraithe.
3. Ibid.
4. Ibid.
5. Ibid.
6. E. de Bhaldraithe, art. cit., p 131.
7. *Motu Proprio, 'Matrimonia Mixta', The Furrow*, December 1970, pp 793-798.
8. Ibid.
9. Ibid.
10. Michael Hurley, 'Mixed Marriages', *The Furrow*, May 1966.
11. 'Comments on the *Motu Proprio* on Mixed Marriages', unsigned.
12. *The Furrow*, March 1971, p 133.
13. *Theology*, July 1970, p 289.
14. For the general survey, see *One in Christ*, 1971, vol 7, nos 2-3, pp 217, 218 *et seq.*
15. Published by BCC and *One in Christ*.
16. Op. cit., p 3, section 7.
17. E. de Bhaldraithe, art. cit., p 127.
18. *The Lambeth Conference 1958*, SPCK, pp 157, 158.
19. *The Furrow*, December 1970, p 796.
20. E. de Bhaldraithe, art. cit., p 121.
21. *The Furrow*, December 1970, p 796.
22. *The Furrow*, December 1970, p 795.
23. See Kevin T. Kelly, 'A New Deal for Inter-church Marriages', *The Clergy Review*, August 1970, for a fuller treatment.
24. *One in Christ*, 1971, 2-3, p 233.
25. 'The Venice Conversations', *Theology*, February 1971, p 55.
26. Ibid., p 56.
27. E. de Bhaldraithe, art. cit., p 129.
28. Op. cit., p 11.
29. From Resolution 44(1), *Lambeth Conference 1968*, SPCK, p 41.
30. *One in Christ*, 1971, 2-3, p 223.
31. E. de Bhaldraithe, art, cit., p 129.
32. Art. cit., p 132.
33. As quoted in *Theology*, February 1971, p 49.

22   The Centenary of *Ne Temere*

Eoin De Bhaldraithe

(*Doctrine and Life*, Vol 58, No 10, December 2008, pp 34-41)

The decree *Ne Temere* came into force on Easter Sunday 1908. Perhaps it is a little late to commemorate it now, but the original also worked by delayed action. It was not until 1911 that the effect of the decree became apparent and Protestant fury exploded in Ireland.

Background

We begin with some description of the situation before 1908.[1] The Council of Trent had made witness by a priest a necessary condition for the validity of marriage. Church law like this would immediately become state law but now much of Europe was Protestant, so it was decided that it would not come into force there till it was promulgated in each parish. Thus it became law in Catholic countries but not in Protestant areas. This reflects the fact that *cuius regio eius religio* (everyone in the region must follow the religion of the ruler) was strictly implemented. Sometimes it was promulgated in 'mixed' countries like Ireland but when it was, mixed marriages were always regarded as exempt, so marriage of a Catholic in a Protestant church was always valid.

There was also a medieval law against marrying heretics. This held sway in the Catholic areas but it was not implemented in mixed countries; indeed it was the general view that the law was not in force there. So in those countries a Catholic could validly and lawfully marry a Protestant. This was the situation in Ireland and England.

In the Catholic countries it was generally impossible to marry a Protestant but in 1748 it was allowed in Poland provided both parties promised that all the children would be Catholic. This then applied to all Catholic areas. It was still understood that it did not apply to other places.

The evidence of James Doyle, Bishop of Kildare and Leighlin, before a committee of the House of Lords (1825) is often quoted: 'There is no such prohibition (of Catholics intermarrying with Protestants) arising from the Council of Trent and I do not know of any such prohibition ...'. Catholic clergy do advise, he said, that the children of mixed marriages be Catholic because ministers of religion 'seek to make all the proselytes they can'. An article in the official *Irish Ecclesiastical Record* in 1915 explained how it was 'all right' to be married before non-Catholic ministers in England.

Ne Temere

When *Ne Temere* was issued it contained a clause that mixed marriages would be included 'unless it has been decided otherwise for some areas'. Almost all agreed that it would not then apply to Ireland as such an exemption has been given. But as it was being implemented, the Pope made a personal decision that it would apply to Ireland.

Henceforth mixed marriages in Ireland in a non-Catholic church would be invalid in Catholic eyes. To the legislators in Rome this seemed to be a neat little bit of legal tidying-up but it was a huge change that was bound to lead to trouble in the charged sectarian atmosphere of Ireland. Anyone who married in a non-Catholic church could later claim that the marriage was not valid and desert the spouse. Or put it the other way, if a Catholic decided to desert his Protestant spouse, the clergy could justify it by saying that the marriage was not valid anyhow. This was what happened in Belfast.

What about the promises? Apparently Pius X had some thought that they would not be required. It is interesting that they were not an issue in the McCann case. However, the new *Code of Canon Law*, introduced in 1918, insisted on the promises.

Mrs Agnes McCann

Alexander McCann had married Agnes in her Presbyterian church some time after Easter 1908. Later Alexander deserted her, taking their two children and, she claimed, all her belongings. The local priest claimed that he urged him strongly to have the marriage validated in a Catholic ceremony but Agnes refused to comply.

A Unionist member for Trinity College raised the issue in Parliament in London and so the McCann case became a national issue, hotly debated in Parliament, at public meetings and in the press. Joseph Devlin, Nationalist MP for West Belfast, produced a letter from Alexander in the house claiming that the marriage was unhappy and that he did not desert her on the advice of the priest. It was claimed that she was a sectarian shrew who 'sang hymns and cursed the Pope all day long'.

Peter Finlay SJ of Milltown Park, claimed in a pamphlet that the Catholic 'was conscientiously bound to separate from the Presbyterian woman unless she consented to a revalidation of the marriage'.

At a mass meeting in Belfast, Dr Crozier, Anglican Bishop of Connor, delivered a very hardline speech. Even *The Church Times* chided him for it. A sense of outrage characterised the whole Protestant discussion of the affair. The veto of the House of Lords had just been abolished so it was presumed that it was only a matter of time till a Home Rule Bill was passed. John Gregg was Anglican Dean of Cork at the time, later to become, successively, Archbishop of Dublin and Armagh. He asked, 'How can you expect us to trust ourselves to you? This decree is a wanton attack on Irish unity and can only make Protestants more irreconcilable to the idea of Home Rule than ever.'

The Presbyterian historian, John Barkley, tells us that the General Assembly switched to almost total opposition to Home Rule, 'a very different situation from that of twenty years earlier'. He believes that the reason for the switch was 'the prominence of the *Ne Temere* decree and the McCann case in the speeches of the period'.

Official Catholic reaction

At first there was very little Catholic reaction. After the 1916 rebellion, however, the British Government convened The Irish Convention to decide on a constitution for Ireland. It failed mainly because Sinn Féin decided to boycott it. Four Catholic bishops sat on it. Colonel Wallace, Grand Master of the Orange Order denounced *Ne Temere* as 'the final proof that Home Rule is Rome Rule'. Bishop O'Donnell (later to be Cardinal) gave a conciliatory reply saying that the decree could be withdrawn or modified. H. T. Barrie, leader of the Northern Unionists, said that if the bishops were to recommend the Pope to withdraw it, 'they would make a settlement much easier'.

Future historians will be able to tell us what negotiations went on with the Vatican, but about this time the Irish bishops did receive a special faculty to fix up marriages that were invalid because they were performed before a Protestant minister. The priest had to remind the Catholic of the obligation to ensure as far as possible that the children would be Catholic. This faculty seems to be intended for cases like that of the McCanns. If it were available in 1911 the extreme advice of Finlay would not be possible.

The faculty was only for existing marriages, probably with children, and got no publicity, so it did little or nothing to help Catholic-Protestant relations. The terms of the faculty are very interesting as this is what is now proposed for all mixed marriages by the Anglican-Roman Catholic Commission. Instead of the Catholic having to promise to do all in his power, it would be sufficient to remind him of that obligation.

The discipline of the promises now became standard in Ireland if mixed marriages were to be valid in Roman Catholic eyes. Garret Fitzgerald claims that the situation caused the Protestant population in Southern Ireland to fall by one per cent a year between 1946 and 1961.

In 1949 a Protestant woman married a Catholic farmer near Fethard-on-Sea and had given the promises to rear the children as Catholics. In 1957 she left her husband taking the two children. She would only return if the children could be reared as Protestants. Local Catholics boycotted the Protestant shops. A music teacher lost all her Catholic students. A Catholic teacher withdrew from a Protestant school. The boycott received strong support from the hierarchy, especially from Bishop Michael Browne of Galway, but was widely condemned by lay Catholics including the Taoiseach, Éamon de Valera.[2]

Change

It was only the contemporary ecumenical movement that brought a change. *Matrimonia Mixta* (*MM*) of 1970 removed the promises for the Protestant party. The Catholic party still had to promise to do all in his or her power to raise the children as Catholics. The Northern European bishops took the view that when one took the rights of the non-Catholic party into account a decision could be arrived at whereby the children could be reared as non-Catholic. This led to an immediate easing of the situation there.

There was no such will to change in Ireland or England. At a meeting of the Canon Law Society of Great Britain and Ireland in 1985 an English bishop said that when *MM* was issued in 1970 the bishops did not realise that the law was changed. It was strange indeed that with a room full of canon lawyers to advise they did not realise this. After Cardinal Heenan's death in 1977 a new approach was introduced. The bishops now accepted that some, at least, of the children could be reared as non-Catholics.

A miniature McCann case broke out again. In 1978 Prince Michael decided to marry an Austrian Catholic. Dispensation was refused because she was considered not to be doing 'all in her power'. Prince Charles criticised church institutions for their intransigence. The Archbishop of Glasgow replied in traditional polemical terms. In Northern Ireland several speeches were made opposing the possibility of a Catholic heir to the throne, while apparently being somewhat tolerant of a Catholic Queen Consort. A few years later when all the fuss had died down the Catholic authorities decided that Princess Michael was now doing 'all in her power' and allowed the marriage in a Catholic ceremony. The same issue was still there but at least now there was a possibility of progress.

It was about this time in Ireland that the bishops introduced a pre-marriage course for mixed couples with the participation of the Protestant or Anglican clergy. This was apparently due to the leadership of Cardinal Ó Fiaich and Bishop Cassidy. In 1984 the bishops were invited to speak at the New Ireland Forum. When asked about mixed marriages, Cassidy said that the bishops had considered asking for a special concession for Ireland but decided there was no hope of getting it. It was very like Bishop O'Donnell. Both men were speaking in an all-Ireland body called to devise ways of co-existence for Catholics and Protestants. The same issue was still a problem. Both indicated a willingness to go further than church law would allow, and in both cases it was Vatican policy that created the obstacle.

The Irish Directory of 1983 stated that:

The religious upbringing of the children is the joint responsibility of both parents. The obligations of the Catholic do not, and cannot, cancel out, or in any way call into question the conscientious duties of the other party.

This is a principle to build on for the future. It is based on the teaching on religious liberty of the Vatican Council, which was in turn an effort by the church to catch up with the liberty included in the Declaration on Human Rights as adopted by the United Nations.

For the millennium year, Pope John Paul organised a liturgical service of repentance for the past sins of the Catholic church. The denial of religious liberty would certainly be one of those sins. So it would be appropriate for some church authorities to apologise for the imposition of *Ne Temere* in Ireland, for the polarising effect it had and for the lack of appreciation of the Christian status of other churches.

Present situation
At present the best pastoral option is to raise the children with double belonging.[3] It is not double membership, but the children should be reared with a knowledge and love of both churches. The Catholic bishops recommend that holy communion be given to both parents on occasions such as first communion. If children are baptised in the Church of Ireland, for example, they could be given communion in the Catholic church under the new rules.

What of taking communion in the Anglican or Protestant church? A meeting of interchurch families stated the following:

It is not excluded that Catholic spouses in an interchurch marriage, following their own consciences, and recognising the fruitfulness of the ministry and sacraments of their spouse's church, could find in their own particular situations reasons that make such sharing of eucharistic communion spiritually necessary.[4]

This enables a very desirable reprocity, for the mixed couples are ahead of the churches in their ecumenical position. Pope John Paul II said to them in England:

You live in your marriages the hopes and difficulties of the path to Christian unity. Express that hope in prayer together, in the unity of love. Together invite the Holy Spirit of love into your hearts and into your homes. He will help you to grow in trust and understanding.

One suspects that Cardinal Basil Hume has a strong input into this statement. Official documents emphasise the difficulties of mixed marriages but now the Pope tells them that they also live out the very hopes of Christian unity. The near enthusiastic language used is that of communion, and who would deny that this is anything less than perfect in the family that has the Spirit in heart and home? It is an acknowledgement that some couples are ahead of the churches in the quest for unity. It is also a reminder that canon law will always lag behind, especially in ecumenical questions.

We have come a long way from *Ne Temere* and all the conflict it engendered in Belfast and elsewhere. Referring to the coalition of Sinn Féin and the Democratic Unionist Party, Pope Benedict said that it was a powerful Christian witness. To foster and sustain this development is therefore the Christian way forward. Ecumenism with 'nice' Protestants like the high church Anglicans may be easy enough, but now we are asked to deal with the most extreme group. Not only that, but we need to bring our own extremists along with us.

In our situation today we must encourage cordial relationships between the two communities. To do this we need to move beyond sectarianism.[5] To live together in peace with our Protestant neighbours is surely a high priority with the Catholic Church; indeed this is not enough. Our ultimate aim must be full reconciliation of all Christians. A century ago the discouragement of mixed marriages served to create a greater gap than ever between the two communities. Now those who intermarry and retain the practice of their faith become an icon of what the whole of Irish society should strive for.

Notes:
1. We depend mainly on our former articles, 'Mixed Marriages and Irish Politics', *Studies* 77 (1988) 284-99 and 'Mixed Marriages in the New Code: Can we now implement the Anglican-Roman Catholic Recommendations?', *The Jurist* 46 (1986) 419-51.
2. J. H. Whyte, *Church and State in Modern Ireland 1923-1970* (Dublin: Gill & Macmillan 1971) 322-25.
3. G. Kilcourse, *Double Belonging: Interchurch Families and Christian Unity* (New York: Paulist 1992). Kilcourse was secretary to the National Conference of Catholic Bishops in USA.
4. *Interchurch Families and Christian Unity: a paper adopted by the Second World Gathering of interchurch families from eleven countries, held in Rome in July 2003.*
5. Joseph Liechty (American Mennonite) and Cecelia Clegg (Scots Catholic religious) offer a programme based on five years of research in *Moving beyond Sectarianism* (Dublin: Columba 1999).

Part Six
Admission to the Sacraments
of those in unofficial unions

23 Indissolubility of Marriage and Admission of Remarried Divorcees to the Sacraments

Séamus Ryan

(*The Furrow*, Vol 24, No 6, June 1973, pp 365-374)

This rethinking of the ideas of sacrament and consummation clearly presents problems for the church's canonical discipline which has operated with a considerably less nuanced concept of sacrament and a rather different idea of consummation. The mind leaps immediately to the possibility of reassessing the indissolubility of many marriages which hitherto qualified as *ratum et consummatum*, but which might now qualify as unconsummated and thus be subject to dissolution by the power of the keys. We also saw, however, that a number of theologians were not at all happy with power too readily claimed in the past by papal authority in this respect; indeed, some would go so far as to suggest that the church should really dissolve no marriages at all, and may well have erred pastorally in the past at least in the extent to which she made use of this power (according to John Noonan several thousand marriages were dissolved in this way each year).

We must never forget that the church's first obligation is to be faithful in her preaching and practice to the moral imperative laid on her by the Lord to protect and safeguard the sacred bond of marriage. The German theologian Joseph Ratzinger is quite right in saying that a church can never tolerate what he calls a 'two-sided state of affairs', i.e. preaching indissolubility of marriage on the one hand and yet seeming to follow a practice of dissolution or divorce on the other hand.[1] From this point of view the church's insistence on the dogma of indissolubility and the simultaneous mushrooming in recent times of papal dissolutions in favour of the faith presented a strange anomaly. We find the church at the Council of Trent defending its admittedly stern practice on the grounds that it was simply acting in fidelity to the teaching of the gospel. As Ratzinger says, this is the only thing the church can do; yet he goes on to concede that the church in her pastoral practice is allowed room for manoeuvre in certain 'marginal cases where in order to avoid worse things, she has to remain below what she really ought to be'.

To what extent can the church remain below what she ought to be and not cease to be the true church of Christ? This is the fundamental question. It may well be that the church *could* dissolve marriages not truly consummated in the sense explained above, but at which point would such dissolution of marriage be truly incompatible with the moral imperative of the gospel? Because the church *can* do something it does not always follow that she *should* do it. Richard McCormick SJ puts the case rather well:

Would use of her dissolving power in sacramental consummated marriage cases (i.e. consummated according to the old discipline) threaten the integrity of the teaching of Christ? If it would – in our time and culture – it seems clear that it is not a possible form of Christ's paschal ministry of forgiveness, for it would undermine the common spiritual good.[2]

Clearly a great deal will depend on whether such concessions on the part of the church are truly limited to rare and marginal cases, and do not become an every-day practice. If the latter be the case, the church would be untrue to her own calling in allowing what ought not to be to become a regular occurrence. Yet there is evidence from the very early days that the church, though uncompromising in dogma, at times chose to be flexible in her pastoral concern. Sometimes she acts contrary to what she should be, but not without reason, usually to avoid greater evils.

Today the church is faced with a new situation where civil divorce is widespread. Vance Packard in his study *The Sexual Wilderness* (New York 1968) cites the statistic that in Los Angeles county in 1966 there were four divorces or annulments for every five marriages. In the United States as a whole each year there is about one divorce for every four marriages. America is moving towards a situation in which only 50 per cent of the marriages remain even normally intact. Amid such a world it will require from the church profound theological and pastoral discernment to decide how best to confront man with Christ's imperative without at the same time failing to be the minister of his merciful love.

It may be, as John Noonan says, that the 'great conscious endeavour of the past was the preservation of the ideal of indissolubility, whatever the pain to individuals' (*The Power to Dissolve*, Introduction, p xvii). If this was so, and Noonan's own historical investigation offers a good deal of evidence in favour of his thesis, it has been the contribution of more recent studies to stress the obligation of the church not only to preserve the ideal, but also to stress her equally important mission to mediate God's mercy to all, including the victims of broken marriages.

The exercise of this mercy, many theologians believe, may best be shown not in a greater readiness to dissolve the bond of marriage, and not even through the present alarming escalation of grounds for annulment in certain matrimonial tribunals, but rather in a reassessment of the present discipline governing the admission of divorced and remarried to the sacraments. Should those who are involved in a second marriage after a valid sacramental first marriage be admitted to the sacraments? Ten years ago a theologian advocating a change in the church's discipline in this matter would have been a lone voice indeed; today many have re-approached the whole question and are advocating a very different conclusion.

For the sake of clarity it seems best to divide the treatment of this question into a number of stages: (1) The present teaching and practice of the church;

(2) The arguments in favour of retaining present discipline; (3) The 'internal forum' solution; (4) The arguments in favour of admitting the divorced and re-married to the sacraments under certain conditions.

The present discipline

When a marriage breaks up, the sole concession which the Code allows to human frailty is the possibility of 'separation of bed and board' (*CIC* c. 1128-32). Catholics who enter a second marriage are considered bigamists and public sinners in the eyes of the law (*infamia juris*). If they continue in this union despite the warning of ecclesiastical authority, and if the measure of their guilt warrants it, they should be excommunicated (c. 2356). They are not, therefore, automatically excommunicated as is often popularly believed; in practice, however, they are excluded from the Eucharist since in the eyes of the church they are living in a sinful union which is not a valid marriage. They may be admitted to the sacraments only if two conditions are fulfilled: (a) there must be cogent reasons for not breaking up the present union (e.g. the good of the children), and (b) they are prepared to refrain from the use of marriage and live a 'brother and sister' relationship. Even this arrangement is possible only when their situation is not publicly known and therefore not the cause of any scandal.

Arguments in favour of maintaining the present discipline

One of the most significant contributions to the debate has appeared in the *Clergy Review* in recent years under the feature 'Moral Theology Forum'.[3] Two of the three contributors to the forum argue strongly in favour of the church's discipline, but the third, Father Kevin O'Kelly, is more cautious. He states the case for the present discipline in the following manner:

> It is probably a fact that some priests would be prepared to give the sacraments in such cases but I would suspect that a superficial pastoral practice in this matter could easily lead to liturgical schizophrenia. The sacraments cannot be separated from life. If someone whose first marriage was certainly valid is now living in a well-established second marriage, this second marriage is now an important part of his or her life. Simply to offer to give the sacraments without facing the problem of the Christian significance of this part of life would seem to be evading the issue. And it is precisely about the status of this second union that there is so much discussion these days. The more traditional view would hold that this second union is 'living in the state of sin' and hence must be given up. This view is slightly modernised by stressing the notion of growth in the moral life and so it would allow for the fact that the abandonment of this second marriage might take time. It would also cater for the 'impossible situation' by offering the brother-sister alternative.[4]

In a lengthy article in the German *Herder Korrespondenz*, W. Löser SJ assembles the arguments for and against a change in the church's discipline. He cites at length a noted Swiss canonist, R. Gall, who spells out the reasons for the present law and practice:

According to the Catholic understanding of indissolubility they now live in an invalid marriage and consequently in a sinful situation. Their marriage relationship contradicts the clear demand of Christ and the moral law of God, and is sinful and adulterous like all sexual relationships outside marriage. It must be presumed that they are aware of the serious sinfulness of their conduct. From the fact of their objectively invalid marriage one can and must conclude to a personally sinful will in the partners. To admit them to the Eucharist would imply an evident and impossible inconsistency: officially they have set themselves in opposition to Christ and his will, whereas reception of the Eucharist would seem to imply the very opposite in an equally official way.[5]

The most passionate and eloquent defender of the church's present discipline is the noted German Catholic writer Ida F. Görres. In a recent book she puts her argument well:

The church offers a striking alternative to the man who finds himself in such a situation of conflict – conflict between the promise of a new life and love and the bond of his broken marriage: either the heroic renunciation of the former because of his belief in the sacrament, the deep mystery of marriage, and the moral law of God – or openly violate that law and accept the responsibilities, consequences and suffering which follow on that step. There can be something in life which is even worse than sin – the utterly despicable deceit which wants at one and the same time to enjoy the fruits of sin and the advantages of virtue, the intoxication of anarchy and the blessings of law. This case of mind is calculated to destroy whatever vestiges of nobility and self-esteem are still left in the winner ... I believe this with all my heart. The move to admit married divorcees to the sacraments is simply a delusion and contrary to ordinary common sense. You can't have your cake and eat it. As an Indian proverb puts it, you can't grill half your chicken, and still expect the other half to lay eggs for you.[6]

Authors like Ida Görres are perfectly aware of the painful burden which this discipline imposes on divorced and remarried Catholics. In order to strike a consoling note they sometimes appeal to the idea of *sacramentum in voto* – sacrament by desire, an idea which is well known in sacramental discipline, for example, baptism by desire, spiritual communion. The real desire which is often present in such cases for a true and holy marriage may well make their union a 'source of grace' for both partners, and therefore, 'sacramental'. This is naturally something we have to leave trustfully in the hands of God whose ways are not our ways. He has bound us to his commandments and to the sacred signs of his church, but in the dispensing of his grace and help he himself is not bound to, or limited by these means. He can give the grace of the sacrament (*res sacramenti*) even without the external sign (*sacramentum*).

The internal forum solution

There are two instances where the problem of an invalid marriage can be handled in the internal forum and where reception of the sacraments may be reasonably justified.

(a) The first of these is the situation where there is good reason to believe that the first marriage was not a valid Christian marriage, though this cannot be easily established by canonical procedures. Father Kelly mentions three possible cases:[7]

(i) Where the first marriage seems certainly invalid for reasons recognised by Canon Law, but unfortunately there is not sufficient proof available.

Father Kelly agrees with Father Häring that in such a case (where a partner may be morally or even absolutely certain of the invalidity of the first marriage), a priest should normally be able to arrange for the reception of the sacraments without much difficulty, provided, of course, that scandal is avoided:

The penitent is a sincere person; he knows for certain the facts that prove the invalidity of the first marriage; but in view of the complicated canonical procedure, he is not able to give the kind of proofs that are required by many ecclesiastical tribunals. If the confessor or pastor or ecclesiastical official feels sure that this is the situation, there should be no delay for an internal forum solution. If the persons involved live in a stable marriage, they should be assured that in conscience they can consider their marriage as valid before God.[8]

(ii) Where the first marriage seems to be entirely invalid for reasons recognised by Canon Law, but legal procedures have only just begun, and a final verdict may not be expected for some time.

In such a case the second marriage cannot be simply viewed as a sinful union, and Father Kelly and others have no doubt but that to refuse the sacraments would be a failure in Christian love:

If a couple in this situation sincerely ask for forgiveness and request to receive Holy Communion, they ought not to be refused.

This was a much more urgent problem prior to the speeding up of canonical procedures in recent times. However, it is still not unknown for marriage cases in some tribunals to be drawn out over a number of years, and this in spite of the recent *Motu Proprio* (March 1971) from Rome expediting such canonical procedures.

(iii) Where the first marriage is regarded as certainly invalid by the person impugning it, but the reason adduced, although acknowledged as probably sufficient by many theologians and canonists, is not yet accepted in tribunal jurisprudence.

AN IRISH READER IN MORAL THEOLOGY

We have already noted (in Section II above) the marked shift of emphasis in Vatican II from the pre-conciliar concentration on marriage as contract to the broader and richer idea of 'covenant' or 'partnership of life and love'. This development in the church's thinking – so evident in *Gaudium et Spes* – has inevitably led the canonists to rethink and reformulate the properties of true matrimonial consent. It is not enough that the consent be free; there is also a question of having the real ability – physical, psychological, emotional – to assume the responsibilities which are taken on in this partnership of life and love. Ecclesiastical tribunals in recent years have had to explore very thoroughly a whole further area as a possible source of nullity – the area of psychological impotence.

Thus a fair number of marriages have been annulled in recent years on the score of what the canonists call 'lack of due discretion', viz lack of a certain basic maturity, at least the minimum required for a person to bind himself effectively in a marriage contract. Many canonists would agree with Ralph Brown, the celebrated *officialis* of the Westminster Tribunal, that lack of due discretion should be made a diriment impediment to marriage.[9] In this situation where the grounds for annulment are obviously undergoing a serious evaluation by canonists, it is only to be expected that certain unions, whose validity was hitherto unquestionable on strict canonical grounds, might no longer be considered by the experts to be a true Christian marriage. It is this present situation that category (iii) is meant to cover.

We had occasion to point out in another context (Section II above) that Canon Law – just as any general law – can never be sufficiently precise and nuanced to do justice to every situation. It would be impossible to devise a matrimonial jurisprudence which could infallibly establish the nullity of all invalid marriages. Father Kelly quotes the *officialis* of the Liverpool Tribunal:

Theology and law will never run along parallel lines, and there will always be an area of living beyond the competence of the law and which must be left to the concern of the theologian.[10]

Father Kelly concludes with a note of caution against the danger of promoting sheer subjectivism by failing to distinguish clearly between an unfounded vague conviction about the status of the marriage and a solidly-based theological argument demonstrating clearly that some element essential to Christian marriage was lacking – an argument which would receive solid backing from many theologians and canonists, even though not officially approved as a norm for ecclesiastical tribunals.

In the three cases mentioned – with due provision made for avoiding possible scandal – the author believes that a priest would be justified – at least temporarily – to give absolution and administer Holy Communion.

(b) We began by considering the situation (a) where there is good reason to doubt that the past marriage was a valid Christian marriage. The second situation which is open to being dealt with in the internal forum also is the case where the first marriage was a true *ratum et consummatum* marriage but where the parties are nevertheless *in good faith* about their second marriage. They believe that this is now their true marriage, a genuine marriage before God. Häring allows for the reception of the sacraments when a person in such a situation is in genuine good faith. His analysis of a possible case is worth citing:

> In many cases there might well have existed a disturbed conscience and a feeling of guilt when the person entered a canonically impossible marriage ... It may be that the person gradually came to the conviction that he was not so wrong when he remarried. If the couple live a good life and are blessed with good children, and so on, often the people convince themselves that God has his own way of manifesting his saving will. I think there can be full sincerity in this kind of thinking. It does not necessarily manifest a general lack of repentance. The pastor should not try to convince the couple of the opposite when this is psychologically impossible. If the people are in good faith about their marriage, while repenting humbly all their sins which they recognise as sins, we should leave them in their good faith even if, as representatives of the church, we cannot positively approve their remarriage.[11]

Arguments in favour of admitting divorced and remarried to the sacraments

There remains the case which really comes under category 4 mentioned above, because it is in connection with it that a number of theologians and canonists call for a change in the church's discipline and pastoral practice. It is the case of the couple who believe that the first marriage was a true Christian marriage, and know that all is not well and cannot be well with their present union. Yet they sincerely desire to live a full Christian life. Father McCormick SJ catches rather well the dilemma of their situation:

> The couple believe that the first marriage was a genuine Christian marriage. They know it failed and they know about indissolubility. They know something is wrong with their present marriage. This is an extremely touchy matter, because it cannot be approached in terms of the standard understanding of good faith. Sincerity, repentance, marital mentality – all these, yes; but not total good faith about the present marriage. No one with a sense of realism, compassion, and his own limitations will feel complacent and secure in his reflections on this type of situation. It fairly bristles with problems.[12]

The bulk of recent literature on the pastoral care of the remarried divorcee is devoted to a consideration of this thorny problem.

concerned with this aspect of marriage, the church must admit that this command, united with the one commandment that Jesus left us that we love one another, is the one most flagrantly and consistently unfulfilled simply because it is the most difficult one; and Jesus, who understands human nature far better than we do, knows that man can be no less hard-hearted and in need of provision for his weak humanness in this most intimate realm of marriage nowadays than when he first spoke. Love, seeking only the good of the beloved, is the true marriage bond; love is, or should be, the call impelling a man to leave his father and mother and to cleave in life-long union to his wife. Jesus prohibited divorce, and that prohibition is absolute. But he prohibited divorce, under the assumption that the marriage involved is a true marriage; and if love, and all that flows from it, is a measure of what true marriage means, so should love – the love of Jesus himself – be the guiding norm by which the church, his spouse on earth and always subject to him, dares to pronounce on divorce. The early Christians had the courage to take seriously the human understanding and sympathy of their Lord.

The church in our day has summoned married couples to live in affection, faithful love and respect for each other as persons – that thus they might 'follow Christ who is the principle of life'.[17] Indeed, he did come to give life, he who *is* Life, and one way he revealed this was through the gentleness and mercy he always showed towards any kind of human weakness, to weakness also in the realm of married life and sexuality. He was filled with compassion on the multitude because they were like sheep without a shepherd (Mk 6:34); he came to give liberty to those who are oppressed (cf Lk 4:18; 7:22); he gave first place in the kingdom to tax-collectors and harlots (Mk 21:31f). He welcomed the ministrations of a branded woman (Lk 7:36-50), chose to give his sublime teaching on the Living Water to one whose marriage record was not exactly untarnished (Jn 4:7-30, 39-42), and refused to condemn a woman taken in adultery (Jn 8:3-11). Surely Jesus would want this same spirit of gentle mercy and compassion to prevail when the church begins to apply his teaching on divorce. To grant a divorce and the right to remarry in cases where a marriage is not truly lived as such (and so is not truly a marriage) may open up whole new opportunities of life and love for persons, may give individual Christians the comfort of knowing a Shepherd again.

Notes
1. It is significant that the word used in Gen 2:18, 20, *ezer* (helper, standby) is frequently applied to God himself – as in many of the psalms.
2. Like the story of God's forming woman from man's rib, Adam's gladness over having been given 'bone of his bones and flesh of his flesh' (Gen 2:23) conveys an intimate connection between persons, the closest possible of blood relationships (cf 29:14). Together with the idea of a man 'cleaving' to his wife (2:14), it expressed the truth of being 'one flesh', and this implies a bond of unswerving devotion far transcending sexual union.

3. Deut 22:12-19, 28f give two instances when divorce was forbidden: when a man had wrongly accused his wife of not being a virgin at the time of her marriage to him, and when a man had been forced to marry an unbetrothed virgin after having had sexual intercourse with her.

4. In Jewish law 'adultery' always signified sexual intercourse between a married woman and a man other than her husband. Thus, whereas a woman could commit adultery against her husband, a man could not commit adultery against his wife but only against another married man.

5. The controversy can be traced more explicitly to the precise meaning of the Hebrew words for 'something indecent' in the text of Deut 24:1. The phrase is *erwath dabhar* which literally means 'shame of a thing', and thus 'something shameful'. The school of Shammai took both words together (the correct procedure) and interpreted them as 'adultery'. The school of Hillel explained the phrase by taking the two words separately, so that grounds for divorce could be: a) *erwah*, or shameful immorality on the part of the wife; b) *dabhar* or 'anything' at all the husband found displeasing. We shall see how the precise phrase can be related to the interpolation of the divorce text in Mt 5:32 on account of man's *sklerokardia*, 'hardness of heart' – his unteachableness.

6. Cf V. Taylor, *The Gospel According to St Mark,* London, 1953, 415; D. E. Nineham, *Saint Mark,* London, 1963, 259-260.

7. This interpretation is based on the textual reading which is followed in the RSV and has good claim to be the original. However, there are two other well-attested readings of which the more important, for our purpose, is that in which the woman is referred to as 'leaving' (*exelthe*) her husband rather than 'divorcing' him. Many critics see this reading as the later one, an attempt to bring the *logion* into agreement with Jewish custom. V. Taylor, however (op. cit., 420-421) puts forward this *exelthe* as the most likely original reading. He points out that the other readings, both speaking of 'divorce', seem on the contrary to be attempts to bring the *logion* into line with Gentile practice. He says that Jesus more likely had in mind a Jewish situation, and that this reading agrees with 1 Cor 7:10 in which Paul gives a 'word of the Lord' that a wife should not 'depart' (*choresthenai*) from her husband.

8. V. Taylor, speaking of how Jesus raised marriage to its highest dignity, writes, 'This positive emphasis is his gift to the church and to the world.' But he goes on to say that it is more difficult to apply the teaching of Jesus to divorce in the modern world: 'For Christians, his words are regulative, but in particular cases they need to be interpreted under the guidance of the Spirit' (op. cit., 421).

9. Cf J. B. Baur, *Bibeltheologishes Worterbuch,* Gray/Wien/Koln, 1962, 210; R. Schnackenburg, *The Moral Teaching of the New Testament,* 1965, 249-150.

10. As in the case of the phrase 'something indecent' in Deut 24:1, the real difficulty in interpreting Matthew's clause arises from its brevity and vagueness. Traditionally, the Greek Orthodox and Protestant position has been to see the 'exception' as giving permission, in the case of adultery, for the dissolution of a marriage and the freedom to remarry. Objections against this viewpoint are that the usual Greek word for adultery is *moicheia* and that Matthew would seem to be contradicting himself outrightly if adultery itself were admitted as an exception (besides the fact, of course, that this clause is not found in either Mark, Luke, or 1 Cor 7). The classical Roman Catholic interpretation has held unchastity to mean some marital infidelity justifying 'separation from bed and board', but without the freedom to remarry, since the marriage bond cannot be broken.

Recent interpretations have launched out into new directions. One of the more interesting of these is the suggestion that *porneia* is a rendering of the Hebrew word *zenuth*, 'fornication' – a technical term used in Jewish law for invalid or irregular marriages, such as those forbidden within certain degrees of kinship (cf Lev 18:6-18). In a Jewish world where so many Gentile elements were beginning to prevail, such marriages would have been frequent during the time of Jesus and the early church; and in forbidding 'unchastity' (*porneia*) to Gentile Christians it is to this type of marriage that the apostles were referring in the Council of Jerusalem (cf Acts 15:20, 29; 21; 25). Thus, according to this viewpoint, Jesus is saying in Matthew that anyone who divorces and remarries commits adultery – except in the case of these invalid marriages (*porneia*) which had never been marriages at all. There has also been an attempt to see *parektos logou porneias* of *erwath dabhar*, 'something shameful, indecent'; but this leaves the *me epi porneia* of Mt 19:9 unexplained. We may mention also the 'preteritive' interpretation, where the clauses are seen as exceptions to the whole proposition. Thus we could read 5:32: But I say to you that everyone who divorces his wife – setting aside the matter of *porneia* becaue it is not involved – makes her an adulteress'. One cannot help feeling that all such explanations are primarily concerned to justify Roman Catholic practice. If we look to the text of Matthew it is certainly more natural to see the clauses as an exception. For a comprehensive treatment cf J. Bonsirven, *Le Divorce dans le Nouveau Testament*, Tournai 1948; J. Dupont, *Mariage et Divorce dans l'Evangile*, Bruges 1959; B. Vawter, 'The Divorce Clauses in Mt 5:32 and 19:9', *Cath. Bibl. Quart.* 16 (1954), 155-167; A. Mahoney, 'A New Look at the Divorce Clauses in Mt 5:32 and 19:9', *Cath. Bibl. Quart.* 30 (1968), 29-38; O. Rousseau, 'Divorce and Remarriage: East and West', *Concilium* vol 4, no 3, 1967, 57-69.

11. Cf W. D. Davies, *The Setting of the Sermon on the Mount*, Cambridge 1964, 366-401.

12. Indication of this can be seen, for example, in a comparison between 1 Cor 7:10-13 and Mk 10:12. Paul has taken care to indicate that his words are not those of the Lord; Mark in a similar extension of Jesus' words to a Gentile environment gives no indication of this process. He, or his source, simply freely ascribe the words to Jesus.

13. Cf Schneider, Omnuo, in *Theol. Wört. z. N.T.*, V, 177-185.

14. A glaring example has been the positively neurotic preoccupation with the anti-modernist oath. Its multiplication not only entirely ignored the words of the Lord but betrayed a lamentable lack of theological acumen.

15. G. B. Caird's comment on Apoc 13:9f opens up the perspective of Jesus' demand: 'When one man wrongs another, the other may retaliate, bear a grudge, or take his injury out on a third person. Whichever he does, there are now two evils where before there was one; and a chain reaction is started, like the spreading of a contagion. Only if the victim absorbs the wrong and so puts it out of currency, can it be prevented from going any further.' *The Revelation of St John the Divine*, London 1966, 170.

16. Cf the author's treatment of the subject in *The Promise of Love: A Scriptural View of Marriage*, London and New York, 1968.

17. Cf *Gaudium et Spes*, Part II, ch 1, par 52.

16   Survey of Periodicals: Indissolubility of Marriage

Séamus Ryan

(*The Furrow*, Vol 24, No 4, April 1973, pp 214-224)

This article is devoted to a review of recent writing on two important stages of development which are clearly discernible in the history of the question of the indissolubility of marriage: (1) the teaching of the Fathers; and (2) the diverging canonical traditions of the Eastern and Western Churches. This can be done only on very broad lines.

The teaching of the Fathers

Some readers will be already acquainted with the recent controversy between Victor Pospishil, an American canonist, and Henri Crouzel, a noted French patristic scholar.[1] The debate centres on the interpretation of a number of patristic texts bearing on the question of the legitimacy of re-marriage after divorce or separation. In 1967 Pospishil published a book entitled *Divorce and Re-marriage: Towards a new Catholic Teaching*. The main contention of the book is that 'a distinct majority of the Fathers and ancient ecclesiastical authorities permitted the re-marriage of husbands of adulterous wives' – a thesis based on the examination of a great number of patristic texts. Father Crouzel, a recognised scholar in this particular field, analysed the same texts, and came to quite a different conclusion. In reply to this criticism Pospishil has not been very convincing in the defence of his original thesis; he admits that most of the texts cited are ambiguous, and eventually has to take refuge in an appeal to the marriage legislation, prevailing under the Christian emperors, which admitted divorce and re-marriage. This, he claims, is a clearer indication of the mind and practice of the church than even the writings of the Fathers.

A number of further studies tend very definitely to confirm the findings of Father Crouzel.[2] He has since published a widely-acclaimed book which ranges exhaustively over the whole history of the church's attitude to divorce in the first five centuries.[3]

Contrary to what has often been suggested about the Fathers of the early church, his researches have shown a remarkable uniformity in the church's tradition of these early centuries. In this whole period he finds in the West only one author who expressly defends the legitimacy of re-marriage after separation from one's partner. The Eastern world furnishes none at all in the first five centuries. The single example in the West is Ambrosiaster, an obscure author probably writing in Rome in the second half of the fourth century. His text reflects the legal inferiority of women which found expression in so many of the customs and laws of the time:

It is not permissible for a wife to leave her husband because of fornication or apostasy … for the inferior cannot at all use the same law as the superior … But it is permissible for a husband to take another wife when he has put away his sinful wife, because the man is not bound by the law in the same manner as the woman.

This passage from Ambrosiaster is in direct reference to the controversial clause 'except for unchastity' in St Matthew's gospel (5:32 and 19:9), but the remarkable thing is that he is the only author in all these early centuries (east or west) who interprets the verse of Matthew in the sense of conceding a right to re-marry in the case of the adultery of one's spouse.[4] This text of the unknown Ambrosiaster was accorded an unwarranted significance in the middle ages when it was handed down under the name of Ambrose of Milan, and thus the sentiment which it expressed was linked to the authority which this great Father of the western church enjoyed.

It is above all St Augustine who emerges as the genuine spokesman of the Fathers and acknowledged defender of the indissolubility of marriage. He reflects the unanimous teaching of the early church when he rules out the possibility of re-marriage for either party of a Christian marriage during the lifetime of their spouses.[5]

All this, however, does not mean that divorce was completely unknown in Christian antiquity. Here a careful distinction – not without importance for the church of our own time – must be made between what was accepted as being in accordance with the Christian ethic and what was merely tolerated. A few instances have been recorded in the early church which show a certain tolerance towards divorcees who have re-married. The Council of Arles in 314 is a good example of how the church manages – not without a certain tension – to maintain a combination of strict principle with a certain amount of pastoral compromise. Canon 10 affirms the doctrinal position forbidding re-marriage to husbands who had left adulterous wives, but then goes on without any consciousness of self-contradiction to adopt a more flexible pastoral attitude and advises bishops not to be too intransigent in difficult cases.[6]

Along the same lines we find Augustine – undoubtedly the champion of indissolubility in the early church – asking whether baptism should be refused to a divorced man who has remarried, and cannot now leave his second wife. Augustine's own view is that his error is 'pardonable', particularly if he is the innocent party to the breakdown of the first marriage.[7]

Very similar to this is the well-known text of Basil. Though he refuses to recognise a re-marriage as a true marriage, in certain cases he is willing to tolerate it provided the partners accept a severe penance imposed on them by the church.[8] Again there is question of a certain tolerant attitude here. Basil makes it clear that the second marriage is clearly in violation of the church's teaching, yet he does not seem willing to press home all the consequences of that teaching in each particular case.[9]

The classical example of such tolerance in the early church, and one which is often cited, is a passage from Origen's *Commentary on St Matthew*:

Moreover it has happened that even some leaders of the church – despite what we find written – have permitted a woman to marry even while her husband is still living. They have done so in contradiction to the word of scripture … (1 Cor 7:39 and Rom 7:3 are cited) … However, they have not acted entirely without reason. Indeed it would seem that they tolerated this weakness to avoid greater evils, despite what has been commanded from the beginning and written in the scriptures.[10]

Here we have an example of the early church as she tries to cope with the problem of divorce and re-marriage in a world whose laws and standards often reflected a very different mentality from that of the gospel. East and West show themselves at one in the acceptance of the basic principle of the indissolubility of Christian marriage. Separation is permitted and in certain cases strongly counselled, but marriage during the lifetime of one's partner is excluded. The early church presented this teaching faithfully, but yet in her concrete pastoral concern she sometimes chose to tolerate a situation or a practice which did not entirely conform to this teaching, but yet was not such as could be simply excluded or condemned. Origen has given us the classical formulation of this procedure in telling us that the church sometimes tolerates a practice which conflicts with 'the scriptures and what was handed down from the beginning' and does this not without reason but to avoid greater evils. It is a good example of the church's awareness that she must be uncompromising in dogma and yet sometimes flexible in her pastoral concern, tempering the force of the law to man's weakness, careful not to crush the bruised reed or quench the smoking flax. This is not without its significance for contemporary theologians and canonists who are legitimately enquiring what dogmatic and pastoral stand the church must take today in the face of the serious situation represented by the spread of divorce in the world.[11]

The divergence of East and West
The Western Tradition
After the patristic era there is evidence of a rather varied discipline in the Western Church in some regions, particularly Germany and England.[12] We find local synods and some penitential books which seem to permit divorce and re-marriage in a number of cases. There seems to have been a considerable amount of fluctuation in the canonical discipline of the church up to the twelfth century. It was around 1150 that Gratian composed his monumental work – *Concordantia discordantium canonum* – in which he attempted to bring into some kind of unity the conflicting laws which up to then existed only in smaller collections and had not been forged into a single corpus. Gratian's influence on canonists and theologians in the centuries which followed can scarcely be exaggerated. The

true Christian tradition concerning divorce Gratian finds in the teaching of St Augustine; of this he has no doubt. Even when he finds indication of a different viewpoint in some *acta* of Pope Gregory II, he does not hesitate to say that Gregory is wrong and that he acted contrary to 'the true canonical tradition and the teaching of the gospel and St Paul'.

Evidence of a conflicting discipline elsewhere, for example in Germany, is simply interpreted by Gratian as an interim concession of the church to an uncivilised people whose conversion from paganism to Christianity was a very gradual process. Here again we are still very much in the line of the ancient tradition: the church's teaching excludes divorce and remarriage, but in the pastoral practice of the church certain limited measures are tolerated particularly in a situation where a rigorous imposition of the full demands of the Christian law would require a moral heroism which must not be lightly presumed. It was precisely on these grounds that Gregory II in 726 allowed certain conditions in the matter of re-marriage to Boniface on the German mission – *contrary to what had been handed down but not entirely without reason* – to borrow Origen's classic formulation from more than four centuries previously.

The same concern to do justice to both the truth and the mercy of the gospel is evident in a number of penitential books from this same medieval period. This explains the early canonical tradition which in some places admitted divorcees (men who had re-married after the adultery of their wives) to the sacraments after a period of penance. It must be remembered too that the distinction between the lawfulness and the validity of marriage was not as clearly established as it became in later times.

The Eastern Tradition

We have seen how much at one the Fathers of East and West were in their exclusion of divorce in the early centuries. How is one to explain the marked divergence in canonical practice which became such a contrasting feature of church life in East and West in the middle ages? The teaching of Gratian, securely established throughout the Western Church by the beginning of the thirteenth century, and the contrasting canonical practice of the Eastern Church which shows itself increasingly tolerant of divorce.[13]

Joseph Ratzinger rightly indicates that we too readily make the mistake of overlooking how much both traditions have actually in common. It may be true that a second marriage is allowed in the Eastern Church for various reasons, yet it must be remembered that it is not recognised as a full sacramental marriage. It remains in the thinking of the church very much a 'second-class' marriage, a 'tolerated' marriage. Even admission to the sacraments is granted only on this same grounds of tolerance or *economia*, as it is generally called today. There are plausible grounds for thinking that, in according full sacramental status only to the first marriage, the church wishes to indicate that the bond of marriage, once sacramentally solemnised, is in some sense basically indissoluble. In a recent lengthy article, Father Adnes SJ believes that this way of thinking would represent the mind of a number of theologians in the Orthodox Church, though he admits they would be a minority group.

We have already seen that in the early church both Origen and Basil testify to a practice according to which the church tolerated a second marriage in certain borderline circumstances. There is, however, an important difference between this and the discipline which gradually evolved in the Eastern Church in the early middle ages: now the rare borderline cases of the patristic age have become more in the nature of daily occurrences; in their number and frequency they have led to the establishment of a canonical practice which has obscured the church's own basic position on indissolubility.

Thus we have the West and the East going their different paths – in the West an insistence on the principle of indissolubility to the point of intransigence so that even the toleration of marginal cases almost entirely disappears (to reappear – or so it would seem to some – under a new guise in the Pauline Privilege under Innocent III and later the Petrine Privilege, and in the extension of causes of nullity which is still somewhat fluid today). In the East, on the other hand, the pastoral tolerance of the church is extended far beyond marginal cases, so that inevitably Christ's unequivocal commandment is gradually watered down to the extent of no longer forming and shaping the basic pattern of Christian life as it should and must do if the church is to truly remain the church of Christ.

If one were to seek a basic reason for this extraordinary development, it is to be found in the considerable influence which the imperial civil law of the Roman Empire exercised on the canonical tradition of the Eastern Church. This was not true to the same extent in the West once the Emperor transferred to Constantinople in the fourth century. This is the verdict of Dauviller and De Clercq, the co-authors of an extensive study of marriage in oriental Canon Law:

It was through civil law that divorce entered the Byzantine Church. This is explained by the dependence which the Bishop of Constantinople – who owed the independence of his See to the proximity of the Emperor – manifested towards the secular power.[14]

The distinction between the laws of God and the laws of men of which the Fathers were so acutely aware becomes blurred, and the church leaves it more and more to the Christian State to elaborate a Christian law. This meant that the civil law did become progressively 'christianised', but unfortunately there was also a movement in the other direction with the laws of the church becoming secularised. In the context of marriage it meant that the church's range of tolerance (*economia*, *epikeia* or condescension, as it is variously called) was gradually extended to cover such cases of divorce and remarriage as had hitherto been accepted in Roman imperial law. Eventually in 883 we find officially accepted into the Canon Law of the Byzantine Church the *Corpus Juris* of the

AN IRISH READER IN MORAL THEOLOGY

Emperor Justinian. This meant that from the ninth century on it became official procedure on the part of the church to grant divorce and this for an ever-increasing variety of reasons.

Significantly enough the Eastern Church – unlike the Roman – does not have its own separate ecclesiastical tribunal to deal with matters touching on marriage and divorce. Such questions are decided by the secular authority in its court of law. Thus if a divorce decision is pronounced it is not by any ecclesiastical tribunal but by a civil tribunal; the bishop is notified of this decision and he declares if the marriage is truly dissolved.[15] As might be expected, therefore, the Eastern Church has tended to go step by step with the multiplication of divorce laws in civil legislation, and more particularly since the nineteenth century. A recent article by J. Kuntz mentions ten cases in which the Orthodox Church permits divorce with a right to remarry:[16]

1. Evidence of force or coercion to marry.
2. Adultery or sexual perversion.
3. Psychotic tendencies or concealment of a contagious disease prior to marriage.
4. Acts or threats against the physical well-being or life of the spouse.
5. Life-time sentence or incarceration of the spouse for more than seven years.
6. Leaving the domicile for more than three years without the consent of the spouse.
7. Desertion or abandonment of the domicile by the spouse for more than three years.
8. Coercing the wife to commit immoral acts or adultery.
9. Denial of conjugal rights, or impotence.
10. Alcoholism, gambling, or generally squandering one's material resources at the expense of the family's well-being.

Another author admits that the most generally-accepted reason for divorce in practice is the somewhat vaguely expressed 'incompatibility of disposition' or the simple fact of not being able to get along together.[17]

It is easy then to see the different road the East has travelled in this matter. In the absence of any imperial power in the West it fell to the Pope to determine the law and practice of the church. The difference in canonical practice is ultimately to be traced to the fact that in the East it was imperial law, in the West the papal authority which decided the question.

Needless to say not all theologians in the Orthodox Church are entirely happy with the present discipline of their church in this matter. Some of them recognise its origin and like the following Orthodox theologian express their discomfiture:

For my part I would say that it is a heritage which has come to us from outside, from Roman law codified by the emperors Theodosius and Justinian, and which the church had to accept when she was closely linked with the empire from the time of Constantine onwards.[18]

Yet despite the widespread availability of divorce, there is some evidence in the Orthodox tradition of the indissolubility of marriage. We have already seen some indication of this. Already from the earliest times the tradition of the Eastern Church has always looked upon a second marriage even after the death of a spouse as not being quite on the same level as the first marriage. A third marriage is barely tolerated (only under certain conditions), and a fourth marriage is absolutely excluded as null and void.

Part of the difficulty is one of terminology. The Orthodox theologian does not apparently share the conviction we take for granted, viz that the church is empowered to break the bond of marriage or dispense from it. They understand divorce much more in Origen's terms as a merciful tolerance in a situation where the church decided not to insist on the full rigour of the law, but to 'temper the wind to the shorn sheep'. To be intransigent may only lead to greater evils. Undoubtedly this concept of *economia* has a lot to recommend it, and has a long history in the church. If used with discretion and prudence, it could be a useful complement to our canonical tradition of dispensation and annulment which have been coming under severe fire in recent years. It could provide a merciful pastoral solution in particularly complex situations which the general law is inadequate to meet. This would be no reflection on the truth of the general law, but rather a recognition that few laws are sufficiently precise and nuanced to do justice to every situation. Many would argue that we have always recognised this in our moral theology, though we have usually called it by some other name. Thus we have the principle that lying is always wrong, but we find it necessary to leave ourselves a way out on occasion by recourse to various subterfuges which go under the fancy names of mental restriction or reservation. Murder is always wrong, yet we need to make use of some subtle appeal to the act of two effects or some other *deus ex machina* to let us off the hook on occasion. It has been suggested that the Eastern Church concept of *economia* is deserving of study by Catholic theologians and canonists. Recently Father Denis O'Callaghan had this to say about it:

The Eastern Church concept of *economia* should be looked at again ... Maximus IV Saigh, the Melkite Patriarch, explained this doctrine as follows: 'It confers on the church all the power which it needs to find a pastoral solution for those particular cases which the general law is unable to solve. Man is not made for the law. The law is made for man; the supreme law is the salvation of men.' We need not accept the actual way in which the Eastern Church has applied this concept to marriage, but in itself the concept has a lot to recommend it. For one thing, it avoids the sense of self-righteousness which our Western tradition of dispensation tends to foster in the fortunate ones who have succeeded in squeezing an annulment through some chink in the law – and it may bring some order into a tangled pastoral situation.[19]

Father O'Callaghan is careful to emphasise that it is an expedient proposed for discussion – not something put forward which has already been worked out in all its implications.

Finally, the Eastern theology of marriage conceives the breaking of the marriage bond in a different way from our usual understanding of it. As the Orthodox theologian sees it, it is not the church that dissolves the marriage, but the marriage which dissolves itself. The church confirms that the marriage has ceased to exist, and that therefore the parties are free to marry again. This raises a serious question: What is the marriage bond? Is it something *ontological* – something really distinct from the commitment which the parties make to each other so that it can be thought of as continuing to exist even when this commitment has died?

We may not agree with the great Orthodox theologian A. Schmemann but he does raise a question about the nature of the marriage bond which the theologian has to face squarely:

The marriage *is* indissoluble, yet it is being dissolved all the time by sin and ignorance, passion and selfishness, lack of faith and lack of love. Yes, the church acknowledges the divorce, but she does not divorce! She only acknowledges that here, in this concrete situation, this marriage has been broken, has come to an end, and in her compassion she gives permission to the innocent party to marry again.[20]

This clearly raises again the host of questions with which we began this survey: What is the marriage bond? Does the breakdown of a marriage affect the indissolubility of the bond? Is the consummated marriage of two Christians always indissoluble? What is consummation – a single act, or a continuous process of growing together in all areas of married life? Should those who are remarried after divorce be permitted to receive the sacraments? Theologians are facing these questions anew today.

Notes:

1. The debate between the two has been documented by a number of articles in the *ITQ*: H. Crouzel, 'Remarriage after Divorce in the Primitive Church: a propos of a Recent Book', *ITQ* 38 (1971), p 1; V. Pospishil, 'Divorce and Remarriage in the Early Church', *ITQ* 38 (1971), pp 338-47.

2. P. Adnes SJ, 'De indissolubilitate matrimonii apud Pares', *Periodica* 61 (1972), pp 195-223; P. Stockmeier, 'Scheidung und Wiederverheiratung in der alten Kirche', *Tubinger Quartalschrift* 151 (1971), pp 39-51.

3. *L'Eglise primitive face au divorce. Du premier au cinquième siècle* (Paris, 1971).

4. When we consider the controversy which this Matthaean text occasioned in later centuries, it is very surprising that only two of the Fathers advert to it as raising a problem, Hilary of Poitiers and Augustine, neither of whom draws the conclusion that in the case of adultery the innocent party may remarry.

5. In this respect he likens Matrimony to Baptism and Orders. In spite of the breakdown

of a marriage the partners are still bound by the sacrament, just as baptism is not lost by loss of faith, nor ordination by suspension or defection.

6. H. Crouzel, art. cit., p 28. In these first five centuries what came to be later known as the 'Pauline Privilege' is simply unknown. Augustine and some others show themselves absolutely opposed to any such concession. The early Fathers did not regard the text of St Paul (1 Cor 7:15) as according permission to marry, but only permission to separate. This would be the interpretation generally favoured by biblical scholars today.

7. Augustine, *De fide et operibus* (413 AD), ch 19, n 35.

8. The penance in question was very severe: seven years. One year among the 'Mourners' (i.e. standing in the porch of the church); two years with the 'Listeners' (i.e. allowed to be present only for the Liturgy of the Word); three years with the 'Kneelers' (i.e. kneeling while the rest of the faithful stood), and finally the seventh and final year with the 'Bystanders' (i.e. taking their place with the faithful but excluded from the Offertory Procession and the Communion).

9. H. Crouzel, art. cit., p 27.

10. Origen, *Patrol Gr.* 13, col. 1245.

11. A survey made in the US in the fifties estimated that about 20 per cent of all marriages involving Catholics were invalid. More recent surveys would seem to indicate an even higher percentage.

12. For material in this section I am largely dependent on the following: O. Rousseau, 'Divorce and Remarriage: East and West', *Concilium* (April 1967), pp 57-69; R. Weigand, 'Das Scheidungsproblem in der mittelalterlichen Kanonistik', *Tub. Quartal.* 151 (1971), pp 52-60; P. Adnes, art. cit., pp 218-19; J. Ratzinger 'Zur Frage nach der Unauflöslichkeit der Ehe' in Heinrich/Eid (ed), *Ehe und Ehescheidung* (Munich 1972), pp 11-34.

13. No extensive research has been done in this area, but a few recent articles have discussed this question: O. Rousseau, art. cit.; N. van der Waal, 'Secular Law and the Eastern Church's Concept of Marriage', *Concilium* (May 1970), pp 76-82; P. Adnes, op. cit., pp.218-23.

14. J. Dauviller and C. De Clercq, *Le mariage au Droit canonique oriental*, p 85.

15. Cf N. Chatzimichalis, 'Pratique pastoral de l'Eglise de Grèce à l'endroit du mariage et du divorce', *Revue de Droit Canonique* 17 (1967) p 339.

16. J. M. Kuntz, 'Is Marriage Indissoluble?', *Journ. of Ecum. Studies* 7 (1970), p. 337.

17. N. Chatzimichalis, art. cit., p 342.

18. E. Melia, 'La pastorale du mariage dams l'Eglise Orthodoxe', *La vie spirituelle* 121 (1969), p 591.

19. From a lecture delivered to the Irish Theological Association, January 1973. An expanded version will shortly be published in the *ITQ*.

20. A. Schmemann, 'The Indissolubility of Marriage: the Theological Tradition of the East', in W. Bassett (ed), *The Bond of Marriage* (Indiana, 1968), p 104.

17   The Myths of Divorce:
A Survey of Some Recent Literature

Séamus Murphy

(*Milltown Studies*, No 35, Spring 1995, pp 69-88 [extract]. This is part of an article written in the period leading up to the divorce referendum of 1995.)

Since other western countries have had liberal divorce regimes for a quarter of a century, their experience should be informative for the Irish electorate as the divorce referendum approaches. This paper is a discussion of some of the literature and recent trends in marital patterns.

Despite across-the-board party political support for (or acquiescence in) divorce, inquiry to party press offices at the time of writing (October 1994) revealed that no major party had a formal policy on divorce. Although the 1992 Government White Paper on marital breakdown deals comprehensively with most matters relating to marital breakdown and divorce, at no point does it attempt to justify the claim that divorce is the appropriate response to breakdown. It offers detailed proposals regarding the grounds for divorce; but the legal grounds on which individuals might obtain divorces have little to do with the reasons why public policy might introduce divorce.

The coming of 'no-fault' divorce
In England, adultery was the only legal basis for divorce until 1937, when further fault grounds such as cruelty and desertion were added. However, it became clear that many couples were manufacturing 'fault' in order to get divorced. In the 60s, a Church of England committee (known as 'the Archbishop's Group') and the Law Commission both recommended allowing divorce on the basis of 'irretrievable breakdown', i.e. non-fault grounds. The laudable goal was to eliminate the hurtful recrimination and legal charade that fault grounds seemed to involve, recognising that such wrongdoing as adultery, desertion, or cruelty might be more symptomatic than causal with respect to a marriage in trouble. From legal, procedural and therapeutic points of view, the change had much to recommend it; the Law Commission, however, was sceptical about the idea of the Archbishop's Group that judges would have the time or the ability to determine whether and how particular marriages had irretrievably broken down (Stone, p 406). At any rate, the outcome was the Divorce Reform Act (1969). In the USA, California led the way to a like conclusion in the Family Law Act (1969), introducing 'no-fault divorce' as it was later dubbed. Similar liberalisations followed in other western countries in the 1970s.

(From here on, I use the term 'divorce' to mean divorce on the basis of irretrievable breakdown, i.e. no-fault divorce.)

The change was revolutionary, although it did not seem so at the time. In most states, fault grounds were not entirely abolished, being allowed as alternative grounds; see Glendon (1987, 1989). The liberalisation fundamentally altered the law's view of divorce: from a remedy available to the injured party, to an option exercisable by either partner at will, regardless of the other's wishes, for more or less any reason. This in turn implied a change in the understanding of marriage: from a lifetime commitment whose failure could only arise from avoidable human fault, to a limited-liability joint venture terminable for a variety of reasons. On the earlier view, marriage was in the control of the two partners, and they were expected to stick to their commitments; the latter view implied either that it was not in the control of the partners, or that it was not reasonable to expect life-time commitment. The clearest presentation of this revolution is Weitzman (1985).

Overall, it was expected that the new law would raise divorce-levels in the short run, but lower them in the long run. As we now know, the first part of the prophecy came true and the second part was decisively falsified; see Stone (1990) and Goode (1993). Divorce-levels rose following the introduction of no-fault divorce and have remained high ever since. The US rate rose from 8.3 (per 1,000 marriages) in 1960 to 21.0 in 1988, the rate in England and Wales from 2.0 (1960) to 12.7 (1989), and Nordic countries had roughly similar increases. The rate in France held steady at 2.6 (1960) and 2.9 (1970), then rose to 8.5 (1986); West Germany stood at 3.7 (1960), 4.9 (1977) and then rose to 8.8 (1987).

The current rate of marital breakdown in the Republic of Ireland is about 3.0: this is an inflated figure relative to the figures given for other countries, since the number of breakdowns is usually higher than the number of divorces. Not all breakdowns end in divorce, even where divorce is easily obtained.

Twenty years after ...
Recent literature on divorce is noticeably different from that of the 60s and early 70s. Max Rheinstein (1972) is sceptical that there is any real evidence to show that liberal divorce laws encourage higher divorce rates, whereas William Goode (1993) is struck by the overall increase in the level of human suffering arising from divorce and considers that 'current high divorce rates represent a fundamental change in family patterns as more people move away from commitments to family obligations' (p 318). Around 1970, the idea that liberal divorce would lead to the breakdown of the family was considered a fringe view, with little hard evidence to back it. Today, Goode (1993) and Stone (1990) are sombre with respect to the chances of the traditional family based on lifelong monogamy surviving. A vivid illustration of the shift is provided by the contrast between the first (1981) and second (1988) editions of Levitan *et al*; in the

former they pooh-poohed the doomsayers, emphasising the family's resilience, but some half-dozen years later they too felt that 'widespread family breakdown is bound to have a pervasive and debilitating impact not only on the quality of life but on the vitality of the body politic as well' (p viii).

In part, the change is due to the fact that there are now so many people affected by divorce that the consequences and aftermath of divorces have drawn much more study and research from sociologists and psychologists; see Goode (1993).

Personal and psychological survival

The most interesting material available in recent years comes from three women: Judith Wallerstein on the social/psychological effects on children, Lenore Weitzman on the economic impact of no-fault divorce on women and children, and Mary Ann Glendon on the transformation of marital law.

Wallerstein works with divorcing families, and her (1980, 1990) are among the best known pieces of research on the effects of divorce on children and ex-spouses: the first is a five-years-after report, the second is the ten-year report. Her project was to follow some 60 families, including 131 children, through the process of coping with divorce. She targeted white middle-class families where other problems such as racism and poverty would be largely absent.

Her findings overturn the idea that children are hurt, not by the divorce *per se*, but only by the preceding marital fighting dissension. In her (1990), she describes how she initially received funding for a one-year study of divorcing families, thinking that one year would be enough time for the vast majority of people to adjust. She goes on:

But when we conducted follow-up interviews one year to eighteen months later, we found most families still in crisis. Their wounds were wide open. Turmoil and distress had not noticeably subsided. Many adults still felt angry, humiliated and rejected, and most had not gotten their lives back together. An unexpectedly large number of children were on a downward course ... Our findings were absolutely contrary to our expectations.

This was unwelcome news to a lot of people ... They said children are really much better off being released from an unhappy marriage. Divorce, they said, is a liberating experience.

But that is not what we were hearing from our families. There was a whole group of youngsters who did not believe the divorce was really happening until a year or so later (pp xv-xvi).

The five-year follow-up found about a third of the children doing well, some of these better than they had during the failing marriage. Well over a third were doing much worse. Even five years later, the majority of children still hoped their parents would reconcile. As regards the adults, half the men and two-thirds of the women were 'more content with the quality of their lives'. The rest were worse off. Ten years on, approximately half reported themselves happy, the divorce apparently put behind them; the rest were still intensely angry, hurt, and unhappy.

Wallerstein's work makes it clear that divorce causes much pain and trauma, and (to my mind) her findings cast serious doubt on the claim that the availability of divorce reduces the net level of pain and suffering. Much of the evidence she found would seem to indicate that it does the opposite. A case can be made that there is likely to be just as much pain going the divorce route, and for as long, as would going the route of marriage counselling and the slow struggle to make one's marriage work.

In her conclusion, Wallerstein disclaims any intention of arguing against divorce. She is clear, however, that divorce is not a quick solution to marital breakdown, and is pessimistic about the future of marriage and about people coping with divorce, finding that, overall, children are doing worse than ever before.

Economic consequences of divorce
The classic work in this area is Lenore Weitzman (1985). It demonstrated that no-fault divorce had unforeseen negative economic consequences for wives and children; on average, divorced women and minors in their custody had a 73% drop in income, while divorced husbands had an average rise in income of 42%. As the divorce rate soared, American children became poorer: the percentage living in poverty went from 15% in 1970 to 21.3% in 1982. In the case of the UK, Eekelaar and Maclean (1986) found that the vast majority of divorced women with children are forced into poverty. Recent legislation in the USA at federal level has pushed the states towards improving the support given to ex-wives and children, but it has yet to be seen if it will be successful; see Garfinkel *et al* (1991). At the time of writing, it was estimated that in the state of Maryland alone, with a population comparable to that of the Republic of Ireland, unpaid child support amounted to some $700 million (*Washington Post*, 5 Nov 1994).

Other studies from the USA found that women divorced in no-fault divorce states received less alimony and child support than did those in fault divorce states. Parkman (1992) takes this line of thinking further, noting that there are a variety of assets, other than the actual material property and current incomes of the divorcing spouses, that need to be taken into account in reaching an equitable settlement. Where once the family farm or business would be the major economic asset, higher education and professional training are now more likely to be the important economic assets; and these can not be divided or sold.

The older fault model typically envisaged the wife suing for divorce, charging the husband with adultery/cruelty: found guilty, he was punished by having to pay hefty alimony. A number of men and certain feminist groups argued for equality, the men because they thought the courts were biased in favour of women, the feminists because they objected to the older model of the family where the woman's central (and sole) role was as housewife and mother. The issue was no longer what the wife deserved by way of compensating alimony but whether there was any reason why she could not get a job and support herself; see Weitzman, pp 148, 360-363. No-fault divorce was predicated on the assumption that men and women could be so treated at the time of divorce that they would emerge equally well-off. Weitzman's work is compelling testimony to the claim that this is not possible, and that the family with children cannot, no matter how elaborate the legislative provision, be 'divided' equally.

As well as divorce leading to impoverishment, poverty increases the probability of marital breakdown: the causal connection runs both ways. Divorce is more common among people in low-skill jobs, people with low levels of education, and the unemployed; see Martin and Bumpass (1989) and Voydanoff (1990). If part of the pressure on remarriage comes from trying to support the children of a previous marriage, what hope is there for the second marriage of those from low-income groups? Poverty and poverty-making factors such as unemployment tend to raise the probability of divorce, at least as much for remarriages as for first marriages.

In the light of the fiscal constraints under which Irish governments must operate for the foreseeable future, it is not credible that the Irish state will be able to ensure that the requisite child-support and financial entitlements of dependent spouses will be forthcoming, no matter how much legislation there is. In principle, the economic ill-effects of divorce should be remediable; in practice, they are never fully made up even in such countries as Sweden.

The introduction of divorce is likely to compel women to enter the labour-force in far greater numbers. Since Ireland already suffers from high unemployment, the end-result will be more unemployment, the impoverishment of women and children, and the imposition of a crippling welfare burden on the state.

The evolution of family law
Glendon (1981, 1987, 1989) offers an illuminating description of and a wide legal perspective on the dramatic changes in family law which took place in most western countries during the 1969-85 period. Glendon (1987) examines the variation between different western countries as regards provision for divorce and abortion, and finds that the USA is most permissive on abortion and divorce, and most niggardly when it comes to child support and alimony. She suggests that the roots of this lie in an exaggerated emphasis on individual rights, together with the common law's traditional disinclination (unlike the European civil law) to set ideals for society to reach. Her work should be of particular interest to us in Ireland since, having a common law tradition, a written constitution, a Supreme Court, and the English language, we are far more likely to be

influenced by American jurisprudence than by the civil law tradition of France and Germany or the social welfare ethos of the Nordic countries.

Developments since 1970 have revealed as unrealistic the notion that judges could seriously investigate 'irretrievable breakdown'. Busy judges have neither the time nor the expertise to determine whether the marriage is beyond retrieval, so it is no accident that judicial denial of divorce is extremely rare. Not surprisingly, Sweden, Finland and some 19 US states have abolished judicial discretion to deny divorce. In practice, the marriage is treated as irretrievably broken down if one of the partners tells the court that it is so: there is no point in further judicial inquiry.

As Glendon shows, family law has changed drastically and almost beyond recognition since 1970 in most western countries, changing our notion of marriage to an arrangement terminable at will. Weitzman (1985) remarked: 'When we change the rules for divorce – that is, when we change the rules about what is expected of husbands and wives upon divorce – we also change the rules for legal marriage: we implicitly create and "institutionalize" new norms for marriage' (p xv). In her words, the introduction of no-fault divorce leads to a revolutionary shift: from state protection of marriage to facilitation of divorce, from a lifetime contract to an optional time-limited commitment, from protection for housewives and mothers to gender-neutral rules, and from partnership to individualism (pp 366-377).

Divorce on the basis of irretrievable breakdown will have long-term radical effects on our marital and familial eco-system. The idea that introducing divorce is a limited change, affecting only those who suffer because they cannot remarry, is untenable. The literature of twenty years ago gave some support to that idea; recent literature, noting that one in every two US marriages fails and that over half the children born in the USA today experience disruption of their parents' marriage before they are eighteen, would regard it as naive. Even researchers in favour of divorce, and arguing that the effect of the law on divorce-rates cannot be measured, e.g. Eekelaar (1991), would still admit that '[i]t would now be difficult to maintain that there is no connection between increased availability of divorce and increased marriage breakdown' (p 56). Ruth Deech (1994) is a *mea culpa* from a barrister who was involved in formulating Britain's 1969 Divorce Reform Act, and who is appalled at the outcome a quarter of a century later.

Myths of divorce

The Ur-myth is that divorce is a necessary evil, giving the benefits of regular marriage as we know it to those unreasonably deprived of it. The following myths are based upon it.

Myth no 1: Absence of divorce forces people to live together even though they're not married, thereby increasing the levels of cohabitation and illegitimacy.

If this were true, countries with divorce should have little cohabitation or illegitimacy. But, in fact, the sharp rise in the divorce-rate has been accompanied by a marked rise in cohabitation and illegitimacy rates. While the rate of extra-marital births in Ireland is currently about 20%, the proportion in Britain is comparable, having held steady at 5%-7% from 1800 to 1965, and then soaring to over 20% by 1986; see Stone (1990). Divorce does not solve that problem.

Throughout the western world, cohabitation levels have risen dramatically since the late 60s. In the USA, unmarried cohabitation rose from about 50,000 (1950) to 2.2 million (1986), the latter equivalent to about 6% of all unmarried adults; among divorced people in their late twenties, the rate is about 16%; see Glick (1988). In France, 17% of the marriage cohort of 1968-69 cohabited pre-maritally, while for 1976-77, the figure was 44%; in West Germany, the number cohabiting rose in the 1972-82 period by 277%; see Goode (1993), pp 50-51. Nor does cohabitation amount to an equally good form of consensual union. A number of North American studies, including Bumpass and Sweet (1989), found that 40% of cohabitations break down before marriage, and where marriage occurs, the probability of breakdown is 50% higher than it is for those who don't cohabit before marriage. Axinn and Thornton (1992) found that, while the premarital cohabitors tended to be people who were more tolerant of divorce, the actual experience of premarital cohabitation made them significantly more likely to divorce. Bumpass, Sweet and Cherlin (1991) observed that previously-married cohabitors are much less likely to remarry than the never-married. Blanc (1987) found that the majority of Scandinavians whose marriages broke down resorted to cohabitation rather than remarriage.

These are remarkable findings, undermining the received liberal wisdom. One would have thought that the easy availability of divorce would have made marriage more attractive. Yet easy divorce may actually be discouraging people from getting married and encouraging cohabitation; see Goode (1993), p 324; Stone (1990), pp 413-414; Wright (1994), p 133.

Myth no 2: Legalising divorce doesn't cause marital breakdown.

The kernel of the myth is the idea that each couple or family live in a world of their own, unaffected by what's going around on them, and not at all influenced by the state's policy. It assumes that the forces at work on a couple to keep them married or push them apart are (or should be) largely internal to the marriage. It is judged, rightly, that people should be as free as possible of pressure with respect to questions of marrying and staying married; and it is then judged, wrongly, that the only external pressure on married people is the law preventing them from divorcing. But the existence of other pressures leading to breakdown (factors such as unemployment, alternative partners, the nature and conditions of social benefits for married persons and for single persons, etc.) are ignored; and the idea that the legal prohibition of divorce may actually function as a counter-pressure, equalising the pressures to divorce, is never considered. It is an assumption that the freedom of the marital partners is best served by allowing easy divorce.

It is also wrong, as Deech (1994) notes, to assume that marriages separate neatly into two camps: the happy who would never want divorce, and the unhappy for whom nothing but divorce would do. All marriages are both happy and unhappy, sometimes more happy, sometimes less so, and they tend to change over the years, influenced by a range of social factors, including ideas and values; see Fine and Fine (1994).

Myth no 3: Divorce is not 'an attack on marriage or the family'.
Traditional monogamous marriage has been greatly weakened in most western societies, and divorce is one of the complex of social factors which has helped bring that about. The possibility of having a lifelong marriage is not something that couples create by and for themselves alone: it is a social and cultural creation. The law does not simply recognise or register changes in social mores: it cannot but promote them or block them; see Glendon (1989) and White (1990).

No-fault divorce attacks marriage at particular points. First, it makes the position of the non-consenting spouse untenable, since obtaining a divorce on the basis of irretrievable breakdown does not require the agreement of both parties. No-fault divorce shifts the law's weight to the side of the partner who wants divorce, regardless of whether that partner has been heartless or irresponsible.

Second, divorce undermines those marriages where one spouse is not active in the labour-force and is devoting her time and energy to home-making and child-rearing. It makes full-time home-making a high-risk option since, in the event of divorce, the home-maker will be at a severe economic disadvantage with respect to employment and income. Since marketable skills quickly become obsolete, married people will have to take stock of this, and act accordingly. This may lead to a trend already evident in marriages in the USA, viz what Goode (1984) called 'disinvestment' in the marriage; see also Popenoe (1993). It is bad enough that in many cases economic pressure compels both parents to work; it is worse that the state's introduction of divorce should oblige each to keep his/her career going. As Lenore Weitzman remarked so perceptively, the rules for divorce tell you what the rules for marriage are; and no-fault divorce will change the rules for marriage so that it will be very risky for either partner to invest such long-term trust in the other as is involved by withdrawing from the labour-market in order to make a home and raise the children. As no-fault divorce has operated, 'the law's implicit message is that one's own career is the only safe investment' (Weitzman, p 376).

Third, divorce will render vulnerable the middle-aged woman who has devoted herself to home-making and child-rearing. Her investment in the marriage was her work for home and children, and her husband benefited by it. No-fault divorce will enable him to cheat her on the return she deserves. Here too, the government proposal is an attack on marriage, on heavy investment in it, and on wives particularly.

Fourth, Eekelaar (1991) pp 42ff draws attention to the fact that almost no attention was given to the needs of children during the gradual liberalisation of divorce law. The battle for divorce was won elsewhere with relatively little attention paid to children's needs.

Myth no 4: Keeping the ban on divorce shows a lack of compassion for those who suffer because they can't remarry and who would be made happy by remarriage.
It is an assumption that unhappiness is the sole or even the most important cause of marital breakdown. Goode (1993), pp 319-320, rejects the claim that there is a straightforward correlation between the number of people unhappy in marriage and the divorce-rate. Stone (1990) argues that the rise in cohabitation, accompanying the arrival of no-fault divorce and the rise in divorce levels, casts serious doubt on the natural assumption that divorce arises from unhappiness. He wonders if it may not in fact be due to a 'reduced respect for marriage ... If this is so, the level of happiness does not enter into the picture'. Referring to the motivating force of 'ideologies of individualism, the pursuit of personal happiness, and the expectation of relatively speedy gratification', he commits himself to the view that the demand for 'instant gratification of individual desires tends to erode the sense of obligation and responsibility both within family and in society at large, and in consequence leads to a rise in the divorce rate' (pp 413-414).

The first part of the myth is that unhappiness and divorce are tightly linked; the second part is that remarriage will produce happiness. For the latter, the evidence indicates otherwise: Wallerstein (1990), p 30 found that 'the dominant pattern is for one to find a lasting second marriage while the other has a second or perhaps third divorce or never remarries at all'. It is possible that up to half the divorcing partners will be more unhappy as a result of divorce and remarriage.

If the claim that divorce and remarriage tended to raise the overall levels of personal happiness were true, then the sociologists should be finding higher levels of marital satisfaction being reported in high-divorce societies. No evidence is available to back this supposition. There is some evidence to suggest that the levels of marital satisfaction may even be dropping in such societies; see Glenn (1991), and Lee, Seccombe and Skehan (1991). Popenoe (1993) notes the decline in the number of joint checking accounts and the rise in the number of pre-nuptial agreements. These are signs of reduced investment and lowered expectations.

Part of the myth is that when a divorce is sought both partners want it. Often one partner is deeply opposed, and her happiness may be ruined by divorce; and is it not an injustice to place, as a matter of law, the happiness of the person who wants out before the happiness of the one who is willing to try to make the marriage work?

Examining how people explain their divorce-process, Hopper (1993) found that while both partners were aware of marital difficulties, 'no one described divorce as a mutual decision even though in most cases noninitiating partners, as well as initiators, had been considering divorce' (p 804). He cites a large number of studies showing that most divorces are non-mutual. (This is not undermined by the fact that when couples reach the court they may have agreed: beyond a certain point, it is irrational for the noninitiating partner to go on fighting an unwinnable battle, when she should be concentrating on getting the best possible settlement.)

Hopper (1993) and other researchers have found evidence indicating that people are by no means at their most rational when deciding to get divorced; see also Bugaigis *et al* (1985) and Donovan and Jackson (1990). Booth and White (1980) reported that there were factors which prevented unhappily married people from thinking about divorce and factors which encouraged the happily married to consider divorcing. Hopper noted that, while divorcing persons would each be clear as to who was the initiator and who the noninitiator, there was no corresponding pattern in the events and feelings prior to the announcement by the initiator of intent to divorce. Another liberal assumption is in trouble, viz that the decision to divorce by an adult individual is typically a rational decision.

The partner reluctant to divorce is probably the one who would be more likely to make a success of a later marriage; while the run-away partner will inevitably bring the same problem behaviour to the next marriage. Common sense should tell us that the bit about compassion is a myth: as though, somewhere, there were pain-free marriages to be had for all.

Finally: the greatest dishonesty in the myth is its ignoring of children. As will be seen, children's happiness is damaged, not helped, by divorce. Since the children's happiness and that of one spouse is lessened by divorce, the probability is that divorce reduces net happiness.

Myth no 5: People have higher expectations in marriage, which is good; more breakdowns are an inevitable by-product.
Higher expectations of marriage lead to divorces only in conjunction with less willingness to work at marriage and make sacrifices for the sake of the marriage, or in conjunction with human resources inadequate to the expectations. Stone (1990) suggests that, at the same time as the willingness to commit and endure has declined, 'the expectation of sexual and emotional fulfilment from marriage has recently risen to quite unrealistic levels' (pp 413-414). Is it not

AN IRISH READER IN MORAL THEOLOGY

reasonable to give some credence to the hypothesis that western trends could be summed up as: higher expectations plus disinvestment equals greater marital dissatisfaction?

It may also be worth questioning the idea that the natural (as distinct from the ideal or the possible) state of marriage is happiness, and not just contentment. It seems unwarranted to believe that, if a marriage is less than fully happy, it is radically flawed.

Myth no 6: Children are hurt, not by the divorce itself, but by the breakdown that preceded it.

Wallerstein (1990) noted that children 'can be quite content even when their parents' marriage is profoundly unhappy for one or both partners' and added that only one in ten were relieved when divorce occurred. She found that children simply hoped that the fighting would stop: 'They do not prepare themselves for divorce, and when they are told that a divorce is imminent, many refuse to believe it' (p 11). Five years later, the majority of children in her study still wanted a parental reconciliation; not merely would they clutch at straws suggesting it might happen, they would even hope that subsequent marriages would end in divorce so that the original family would be put together again. She adds: 'After the first five years, they were also intensely angry at their parents for giving priority to adult needs rather than to their needs. Few children were truly sympathetic or really understood why their parents divorced, even when the parents thought it was obvious' (p xvii).

The myth also assumes that divorce is a brief event, like a mercy-killing. Wallerstein (1990) shows that divorce is a lengthy process, whose effects last for years. Nor can children 'bounce back' from a sharp drop in living standard. Glick (1988) cites US studies showing that children of divorced parents had a 50% greater probability of being divorced themselves than had other children; see also Kitson *et al* (1985), Mott and Moore (1979), and Eekelaar (1991), p 46. Elliott and Richards (1991) found that the remarriage of the custodial parent appeared to make children more disturbed.

The easy availability of divorce is undermining those cultural mindsets which led people to think that children should come first. Thornton (1989) found that the proportion of people who disagreed with the statement 'parents should stay together for the sake of the children' jumped from 51% in 1962 to 82% by 1985: by the mid-80s, less than 1 in 5 American parents felt that children's interests should come first. Citing Thornton, Popenoe (1993) remarks: '... divorce feeds upon itself. With more divorce occurring, the more normal it becomes, with fewer negative sanctions to oppose it and more potential partners available ... Divorces in which children are involved used to be in the category of the unthinkable. Today, children are only a minor inhibitor of divorce' (p 532). Preston (1984) suggested that the nuclear family is divesting itself of care for children. Social acceptance of a right to divorce (*de facto* or *de jure*) means that children count for less.

Several years ago, researchers found, to their surprise, that the presence of pre-school children is a factor leading to thoughts of divorce; see Booth and White (1980). There has been a shift in the view of marriage, towards seeing it as essentially an arrangement for the personal happiness and self-fulfilment for the marrying parties; see Davis (1985). But it fits badly with the rights of children.

All this is part of what is meant when Catholics speak of the 'culture of divorce' and view it as anti-child. A culture in which the right to divorce, based on the right to autonomy (or privacy), is enshrined, is one in which the rights of children to two parents, a stable home and some self-sacrifice by adults have been overridden. The Catholic view is clear: children's rights are such that there can be, in practice, no adult right to autonomy allowing withdrawal from commitments and duties to spouse and children. Legal provision of divorce undermines that, since it gives a *de facto* right to withdraw to adults.

The evolution of the welfare state means that the state can (to some extent) provide financial support for children and single parents. With the disappearance of the extended family, the nuclear family is the indispensable provider of love, emotional security, and appropriate gender role-modelling for children: precisely what the state cannot provide, in principle or in practice. Social welfare cannot provide what children most need: that is sufficient reason to rule out as an injustice the divorce of parents with children.

Myth no 7: The absence of divorce oppresses women.

Do women benefit from divorce? South and Trent (1988) noted a significant correlation between the sex ratio and the divorce rate for a wide range of countries: where there was a high sex ratio (i.e. a relative undersupply of women) divorce rates tended to be low, and a low sex ratio was accompanied by high divorce rates. This is usually explained by hypothesising that, with a scarcity of women, men are more likely to value their wives; see also Trent and South (1989). It also suggests that women are more inclined to commit themselves to working at the marriage, and in general to be less inclined to think of changing marital partners. Easy divorce appears to be a tool for gender exploitation of women by men. Weitzman (1985) and numerous other studies detail the impoverishment of women and children arising from no-fault divorce. With age, men benefit far more from divorce than women do. Past their best years for good looks and reproduction, women are more vulnerable than men whose later years may be years of higher earnings; see Wright (1994) and Goode (1993). Older women find it harder to remarry than do older men. The primary beneficiaries of easy divorce are rich, powerful men who trade in their wives for younger models. As the billionaire Paul Getty remarked, 'You have to be a business failure to stay married to the same woman all your life.' Wright (1994) takes the view that economic inequality is monogamy's big enemy, that divorce favours powerful wealthy men at the expense of poorer men, and that easy divorce facilitates class and gender exploitation.

Myth no 8: Divorce frees people for better relationships.
It frees them, yes: but at the cost of making other good marital relationships less likely. The Divorce Action Group wants second marriages to have the same high status as the first marriage; it does not see that making divorce easily available undermines the high status of all marriages. As Weitzman and many other analysts have shown, the introduction of no-fault, no-consent divorce has changed the shared social understanding of marriage elsewhere to something indistinguishable from legalised cohabitation. The DAG and co. have forgotten the Prisoner's Dilemma and the Free-rider Problem, which illustrate the frequent clash between the rational course of action for the self-interested individual, and the rational course of action for the community in seeking the common good: one can be a successful free rider only if others are not doing so. Freedom to divorce benefits me only if others (prospective replacement spouses) still believe in total commitment. Myth no 8 holds true only if very few others divorce, which is not the case any more in most western countries. It is easy to see how being able to divorce and remarry might benefit an individual; but once many people claim this benefit, the benefit tends to be lost, and perhaps turn into a net loss. Marital (as distinct from divorce) trends elsewhere (described above) indicate that the pursuit of individual interest in this matter ultimately undermines that very good to which divorce was meant to be a shortcut.

Easy divorce makes everybody less likely to invest deeply in marital relationships, since they never know when the other party might pull the rug out from under them, with the full connivance of the law. The US's National Center for Health Statistics reported in 1980 that while two-thirds of first marriages continue for ten years, only about half of remarriages continue as long. On the divorce-proneness of second marriages, see Booth and Edwards (1992), Martin and Bumpass (1989), McCarthy (1978). As noted earlier, there is also an intergenerational transmission of divorce: children of divorced parents are more likely to get divorced themselves and to see it as the appropriate response to marital difficulties. Divorce can become a way of life passed on along with the other social *mores*. Divorce frees people for shallower relationships and for loneliness.

Modern marriage is increasingly limited to two functions: child-rearing and provision of mutual affection and friendship between spouses. But as Kitson *et al* (1985) remark: 'Ironically, of the ties that bind people together, emotional support and gratification are the most fragile and easily disrupted aspects of a relationship. This is particularly true with the growing emphasis ... on individualism, self-fulfilment, and personal satisfaction.' Assuming that the rationale behind the move to introduce divorce is (in part) the reasonable goal of facilitating marital happiness and well-being, the assumption that facilitating the dissolution of marriage is the way to attain those ends is unfounded. Unless the government thinks that stability and commitment have little to do with happiness and well-being, it is hard to see why it would think that divorce will promote those goals.

Myth no 9: Marital breakdown happens, whether we like it or not: refusing to legalise divorce is refusing to face reality.
If one party deserts or moves out and stays out, that will count as 'irretrievable breakdown' on the proposals for divorce offered in the Government White Paper, sections 11.8 -11.11. This means irresponsibility or incompetence should be facilitated. It means that such adult traits can't be changed, and that a marriage is out of the control of the couple.

With respect to public policy, it is fatalistic. It echoes the old idea of historical inevitability: Social Change or History is marching inexorably in a certain direction, and we are impotent to stop or divert it.

Myth no 10: There's no such thing as a 'divorce culture'.
A divorce culture is any system of values and attitudes expressed and reinforced behaviourally which:
(a) holds that, grounded in the right to autonomy, there is a right to divorce overriding marital or parental commitments and a right to remarry at will, and that there need be no reason, other than one's will, to justify exercising them; or
(b) views marriage as a project aimed essentially at the mutual fulfilment (emotional, sexual, etc.) of the partners, continuation of which is irrational when it no longer achieves it in the subjective judgement of either partner; or
(c) rejects as irrational or repressive the view of marriage as a state in which the individuals give up their autonomy with respect to backing out of marriage, so that there is no right to divorce; or
(d) rejects in principle the view that parents should be prepared, even when they are not getting on, to stay together for the sake of the children.

The dominant secular culture of the western world is increasingly characterised by (a)-(d). A divorce culture will typically generate (i) increased cohabitation, (ii) higher rates of illegitimacy, (iii) a rising number of female-headed families, with increasing numbers of young males growing up with no appropriate gender role-models, (iv) impoverishment of children.

Much recent scholarly work (Davis, Glendon, Goode, Roussel, Stone,

Wright) acknowledges that in the western world the understanding of marriage has changed greatly since 1970 in the direction of the understanding of marriage found in what I have called 'divorce culture'.

Myth no 11: In any case, Ireland has a strong Catholic ethos and so legalising divorce would affect only a few people, and not become widespread.
On this one, the available evidence backs the Catholic bishops: in the USA, Catholics are just as likely to get divorced as anybody else.

Conclusion
Overall, the evidence indicates that divorce solves no problems, but rather adds further problems. The best presentation of the case against divorce is still the 1986 pastoral of the Irish bishops; the literature surveyed in this article provides much backing for the positions it adopted. On balance, it seems that we would be worse off with divorce in the form that is currently on offer than being without it. At the same time, it is not practical to opt for a restrictive fault-based system of divorce.

It is not possible to have it both ways: to have a little divorce only, restrictive and/or based on fault, the exception rather than the rule. The law/morality distinction may have very little relevance to the issues at stake in the referendum; it would be relevant only if the issue facing us was solely a matter of law, and not a matter of cultural ethos. But the evidence from abroad is such that we can no longer doubt that introducing divorce will set us, probably irrevocably, on the same road of fundamental change of marriage and family life that other countries have travelled. Those who see divorce as a right have (whether they realise it or not) a very different understanding of marriage from the Catholic one; as Weitzman (1985) rightly noted, the rules for divorce tell you what the rules for marriage are. The great issue facing us is not primarily what should be done about marital breakdown but which of the conceptions of marriage shall be the dominant one in Irish society: the liberal, *laissez-faire* marriage, terminable by either party at will, or the Christian lifelong commitment. It is that issue of culture and ethos, rather than the legalities of divorce, which is at stake in the forthcoming referendum.

References:
W. Axinn and A. Thornton (1992), 'The relationship between cohabitation and divorce: selectivity or causal influence?' *Demography* 29: 357-374.
Irish Bishops (1986), *Marriage, the Family and Divorce* (Dublin: Veritas).
A. Blanc (1987), 'The formation and dissolution of second unions: marriage and cohabitation in Sweden and Norway', *Journal of Marriage and the Family* 49: 391-400.
A. Booth and L. White (1980), 'Thinking about divorce', *Journal of Marriage and the Family* 42: 605-616.

A. Booth and J. Edwards (1992), 'Starting over: why remarriages are more unstable', *Journal of Family Issues* 13: 179-194.

M. Bugaigis, W. Schumm, A. Jurich, and S. Bollman (1985), 'Factors associated with thoughts of marital separation', *Journal of Divorce* 9: 49ff.

L. Bumpass and J. Sweet (1989), 'National estimates of cohabitation: cohort levels and union stability', *Demography* 25: 615-625.

L. Bumpass, J. Sweet, and A. Cherlin (1991), 'The role of cohabitation in declining marriage rates', *Journal of Marriage and the Family* 53: 913-927.

K. Davis, ed (1985), *Contemporary marriage: comparative perspectives on a changing institution* (New York: Russell Sage Foundation).

R. Deech (1994), 'How we helped destroy marriage', *The Daily Mail*, 23 Sept 1994.

R. Dixon and L. Weitzman (1982), 'When husbands file for divorce', *Journal of Marriage and the Family* 44: 103-115.

R. Donovan and B. Jackson, 'Deciding to divorce: a process guided by social exchange, attachment and cognitive dissonance theories', *Journal of Divorce* 13:4.

J. Eekelaar (1991), *Regulating Divorce* (Oxford: Clarendon Press).

J. Eekelaar and M. Maclean (1986), *Maintenance after Divorce* (Oxford: Clarendon Press).

J. Elliott and M. Richards (1991), 'Children and divorce: educational performance and behaviour before and after parental separation', *International Journal of Law and the Family* 5.

M. Fine and D. Fine (1994), 'An examination and evaluation of recent changes in divorce laws in five Western countries: the critical role of values', *Journal of Marriage and the Family* 56: 249-263.

I. Garfinkel, D. Oellerich, and P. Robins (1991), 'Child support guidelines: will they make a difference?', *Journal of Family Issues* 12: 404-429.

M. Glendon (1981), *The New Family and the New Property* (Toronto: Butterworths).

M. Glendon (1987), *Abortion and Divorce in Western Law: American Failures, European Challenges* (Cambridge: Harvard University Press).

M. Glendon (1989), *The Transformation of Family Law* (Chicago: University of Chicago Press).

N. Glenn (1991), 'The recent trend in marital success in the US', *Journal of Marriage and the Family* 53: 261-270.

P. Glick (1988), 'Fifty years of family demography: a record of social change', *Journal of Marriage and the Family* 50: 861-873.

W. Goode (1984), 'Individual investments in family relationships over the coming decades', *Tocqueville Review* 6: 51-83.

W. Goode (1993), *World Changes in Divorce Patterns* (Yale University Press).

Government White Paper (1992), *Marital Breakdown: a review and proposed changes* (Dublin: Government publications).

B. Gunter (1977), 'Notes on divorce filing as role behavior', *Journal of Marriage and the Family* 39: 95-98.

J. Hopper (1993), 'The rhetoric of motives in divorce', *Journal of Marriage and the Family* 55: 801-813.

G. Kitson, K. Babri, and M. Roach (1985), 'Who divorces and why: a review', *Journal of Family Issues* 6: 255-293.

G. Lee, K. Seccombe and C. Skehan (1991), 'Marital status and personal happiness: an analysis of trend data', *Journal of Marriage and the Family* 53: 839-844.

220

- S. Levitan *et al* (1981, rev ed 1988), *What's happening to the American family?* (Baltimore: Johns Hopkins Press).

J. McCarthy (1978), 'A comparison of the probability of the dissolution of first and second marriages', *Demography* 15: 345-360.

T. Martin and L. Bumpass (1989), 'Recent trends in marital disruption', *Demography* 26: 37-51.

F. Mott and S. Moore (1979), 'The causes of marital disruption among young American women: an interdisciplinary perspective', *Journal of Marriage and the Family* 44: 335-366.

A. Parkman (1992), *No-Fault Divorce: What went wrong?* (Boulder: Westview Press).

D. Popenoe (1993), 'American family decline, 1960-1990', *Journal of Marriage and the Family* 55: 527-555.

S. Preston (1984), 'Children and the elderly: divergent paths for America's dependents', *Demography* 21: 435-457.

M. Rheinstein (1972), *Marriage Stability, Divorce, and the Law* (University of Chicago).

L. Roussel (1989), *La Famille incertaine* (Paris: Editions Odile Jacob).

S. South and G. Spitze (1986), 'Determinants of divorce over the marital life course', *American Sociological Review* 51: 583-590.

S. South and K. Trent (1988), 'Sex ratios and women's roles: a cross-national analysis', *American Journal of Sociology* 93: 1096-1115.

L. Stone (1990), *Road to Divorce: England 1530-1987* (Oxford University Press).

A. Thornton (1989), 'Changing attitudes toward family issues in the United States', *Journal of Marriage and the Family* 51: 873-893.

K. Trent and S. South (1989), 'Structural determinants of the divorce rate: a cross-societal analysis', *Journal of Marriage and the Family* 51: 391-404.

P. Voydanoff (1990), 'Economic distress and family relations: a review of the eighties', *Journal of Marriage and the Family* 52: 1099-1115.

J. Wallerstein (with J. Kelly) (1980), *Surviving the Breakup: How Children and Parents Cope with Divorce* (New York: Basic Books 1980).

J. Wallerstein (with S. Blakeslee) (1990), *Second Chances: Men, Women and Children a Decade after Divorce* (New York: Ticknor and Fields).

L. Weitzman (1985), *The Divorce Revolution: the unexpected social and economic consequences for women and children in America* (New York: Free Press).

L. White (1990), 'Determinants of divorce: a review of research in the eighties', *Journal of Marriage and the Family* 52: 904-912.

R. Wright (1994), *The Moral Animal: Evolutionary Psychology and Everyday Life* (New York: Pantheon Books).

18   Theology and Divorce

Denis O'Callaghan

(*Irish Theological Quarterly*, Vol 37, No 3, July 1970, pp 210-222)

Divorce is one of those unlucky subjects on which a writer is expected to be partisan and a reader prejudiced. For most Catholics it is a matter which inspires loyalty rather than enquiry. The fact that other Christian Churches have taken a different line on this question and that States have claimed the right to grant divorce in the face of strong Catholic opposition has made this matter a touchstone of Catholic orthodoxy in public morals.

In recent years the history and doctrine of the church's internal divorce discipline, canonically termed dissolution of the marriage bond 'in favour of the faith' (i.e. for spiritual reasons), has come up for a good deal of discussion. The prevailing discipline was summed up by Pius XI in *Casti Connubii*:

> If the stability of marriage appears in some rare cases to be subject to exception – as in certain natural marriages contracted between pagans, or between Christians, in the category of marriages ratified but not consummated – such exception does not depend upon the will of man or of any merely human power, but upon the divine law, of which the church of Christ is the sole guardian and interpreter. But no such dissolving power can ever, or for any cause, be exercised upon a Christian marriage ratified and consummated. In such a marriage the matrimonial contract has attained its final perfection, and therefore by God's will exhibits the highest degree of stability and indissolubility, which no human authority can put asunder.[1]

At the fourth session of Vatican II the Melchite Archbishop Elias Zoghbi suggested that the church might extend her practice of dissolution beyond this limit: 'There is here an exegetical, canonical and pastoral problem which cannot be ignored. It is a matter for the church to decide on the opportuneness of admitting a new cause for dispensation analogous to those which she has introduced in virtue of the Petrine Privilege.'[2] Fr Victor J. Pospishil in his book *Divorce and Remarriage: Towards a New Catholic teaching*[3] followed out this lead and proposed that the Catholic Church should adopt the Eastern Orthodox tradition in which consummated Christian Marriages are dissolved in certain circumstances, particularly for adultery. This pressure is difficult to stem within the terms of the traditional debate, since the evolution of the present discipline has been haphazard to a degree.[4] The contemporary discussion has raised by the way some fundamental questions: When is a marriage a marriage? Is consummation a matter of personal relationship or of physical sex? Should the diriment impediment of sexual impotence be extended by analogy to cover

Notes:

1. J. Ratzinger, 'Zur Frage nach der Unauflöslichkeit der Ehe', *Ehe und Ehescheidung* (ed Heinrich-Eid, Munich 1972), pp 50-51.

2. R. A. McCormick SJ, 'Notes on Moral Theology', *Theological Studies* 33 (1972), 1, p 100.

3. The main participants to the forum are: J. McManus CSSR, H. Allard, K. T. O'Kelly. The contributions in question appeared in the following issues of the *Clergy Review*: February 1970, pp 123-141; June 1970, pp 440-460; January 1971, pp 34-41.

4. Art. cit. (note 3 above), *Clergy Review* (February 1970), p 136.

5. W. Löser SJ, 'Für und wieder die Zulassung Geschiedener zu den Sakramenten', *Herd. Korr.* 26 (1972), 5, p 244.

6. I. F. Görres, *Was Ehe auf immer bindet* (Berlin 1971), p 82.

7. Art. cit., p 137.

8. B. Häring, 'Internal Forum Solutions to Insoluble Marriage Cases', *Jurist* 39 (1970), 1, p 25.

9. R. Brown, 'Immaturity as an impediment to Marriage', *Theology Digest* 18 (1970), l, p 60.

10. Art. cit., p 140.

11. B. Häring, art. cit., p 25.

12. R. A. McCormick SJ, 'Notes on Moral Theology', *Theological Studies* 32 (1971), 1, p 119.

24   Living with Ambiguity

Anne Thurston

(*Doctrine and Life*, Vol 44, No 9, November 1994, pp 537-542; Kevin Kelly (ed), *Divorce and Second Marriage: Facing the Challenge*, Kansas City: Sheed & Ward, 1997, pp 206-211)

The pastoral approach of the German bishops is very welcome and signals the right direction for the debate. The letter shows sensitivity and realism, it recognises the complex and different situations within which people find themselves and emphasises the process of discernment alongside due respect for conscience.

I would like to respond from a different perspective. I should start by declaring my personal interest: seventeen years ago I married my husband, a divorced Anglican with one daughter, in a civil ceremony. Like many other couples in these situations the process of church annulment was neither appropriate nor desirable. What follows is not a personal history but some comments and questions derived from my experience. It would, however, be dishonest not to admit that the analysis which follows conceals a great deal of pain, tension and struggle. All human relationships are immensely complex, all human experience is marked by ambiguity; in certain situations the complexities and ambiguities are intensified; this is one such example.

The official position of the Roman Catholic Church is that divorced and remarried people cannot be admitted to the Eucharist because 'their state and position in life objectively contradict that union of love between Christ and the church which is signified and effected by the Eucharist.' There follows the requirement for careful discernment to distinguish between different situations in order to determine what persons may be readmitted to the Eucharist.

The problem with this approach is that it remains, in principle at least, very much a single issue approach to a moral problem. Behind it lies the good to be protected – the indissolubility of the marriage union. The question which needs to be asked here is whether this is the greatest good? There is a much wider context within which the process of discernment could take place.

Bernard Häring, in his very useful book on this subject[1] takes as his first principle the primacy of grace over the law and then looks at the practice of the Eastern Church with its vision of 'the economy of salvation'. Explaining what this means with reference to marriage, Häring describes the 'moral death' of a marriage. 'Briefly, moral death is accepted as having taken place when there is no longer within this marriage any potential of salvation, indeed when living together in fact works against the salvation and integrity of the other partner.' (p 45). As Häring points out, the concept of sacramentality is integrated into 'an all-embracing vision of the total sacramentality of the Christian economy of salvation'. After such a 'death' has occurred, there follows a period of mourning and healing, before a second union is contemplated. This process remains very close to what people actually experience.

Covenantal process

One of the problems in the practice of the Roman Catholic Church is that the move towards a description of marriage as covenant rather than contract has not sufficiently penetrated pastoral practice when it comes to the breakdown of marriages. The important question is not whether a marriage is validly contracted – and most marriages are – but whether it has developed into a 'human relationship with potential for salvation'; in other words, whether the contract has become a covenant. This is a process; it happens over time, or not at all.

If we allow for the concept of marriage as process and not 'state', then we can accept that some marriages do not/cannot realise their potential. There are relationships which become destructive for all involved and where, without stretching language far beyond what words can bear, it is not possible to talk of such marriages as 'symbolising the union between Christ and the church'. Paradoxically, the second union, which is regarded as the sign of contradiction, may in fact be the means of restoring faith, of renewing hope and of embodying love. Indissolubility is misunderstood if it is seen as an externally imposed law. It is rather a law written in the human heart: human relationships reach for permanence, long for communion.

There is, or need be, no contradiction between support for this deep human need – life-long commitment to one partner – and the recognition that people fail, that relationships fail. The attempts to extend the concept of nullity seem to me inappropriate here. The fragile nature of all human relationships is not sufficiently recognised in a process which requires ultimately that the failed marriage is negated rather than taken up in the human experience of the gap between what we desire and what we realise. What we long for, what we most deeply desire, shapes our lives. This is the framework within which we can speak of the ideal of indissolubility.

We need rituals

Compassionate and graced pastoral care for those whose marriages have broken down and a discerning and sensitive approach to all involved in second relationships will enhance and not detract from marriage as a sign of grace, as a sign of God's covenant.

Again the Eastern Church offers us a model. The liturgical celebration of a second marriage includes an expression of sorrow for the failure of the first relationship. In every case of marital breakdown it is possible and desirable to express sorrow without appropriating blame. The plea for forgiveness, for mercy, acknowledges our dependence on God's grace. The second union can then be celebrated without denial and with a fuller understanding of ambiguity, of failure, of sin and of grace.

We need such rituals here. Without them the pastoral solutions as suggested by the German bishops remain too much in the private sphere and fail to recognise the full ecclesial dimensions of separation and divorce, except in negative terms – no official liturgical acts are considered appropriate. A ritual which allowed both lament and celebration would speak very deeply to the human experience and would allow it to become a source of grace for the whole Christian community. Those who have suffered the pain and trauma of divorce are not just in need of the compassionate understanding of the Christian community but may themselves be bearers of wisdom for that community. The present procedures see the pastoral work as a one-way process; but those who have experienced failure are also those who have had the opportunity to grow in faith. Many involved in second relationships bring a deepened sense of commitment to those relationships. They may bring a richer understanding of the process of marriage. They may also be involved in caring for children of the first union and through that may gain insights which need to be shared.

What is required is a nuanced discussion which takes account of all the complexities involved. But such a discussion is not possible if there is an insistence on divorce in terms of an absolute evil and if indissolubility becomes an absolute good. The indissolubility of the marriage union should be seen as a good which flows from the grace of marriage, and cannot be imposed legally upon it. A marriage which becomes a sacrament carries within it the seeds of its own indissolubility; separation from one's partner becomes unimaginable. The Christian tradition provides both a vision and a story which help to protect that fidelity. Following from that it should be possible to argue that divorce is never a good in itself and is always tragic, but in a broader context of the whole economy of salvation it may become a 'necessary evil' and in that limited sense a 'good', relative to a greater good.

Like all moral issues this is extremely complex, and the context into which I want to place this debate is far wider than any notion of personal self-fulfilment. There is a whole web of relationships here and so there are no purely individual decisions of conscience. The Christian Churches have a valuable contribution to make towards a renewed understanding of the place of marriage in contemporary society but they can make such a contribution only if they recognise that some marriages do fail and if they approach the question of divorce and remarriage with realism and thus with credibility.

I suggest that the way forward is not to extend the remit of the marriage tribunals but to continue to develop the pastoral approach, learning from the experiences of the married and of the divorced. The language of nullity does not do justice to the complexities and ambiguities of lived experience. If we listen

AN IRISH READER IN MORAL THEOLOGY

to those whose marriages have failed, for whatever reason, the language used always refers to the existence of a marriage, in however fragile a condition. Particularly when children are involved it is essential to affirm the union, even while lamenting its failure. For all of us, it is possible to move forward only if we are able to accommodate past experiences and not deny them.

It is possible, as evidenced in the Eastern Church, to continue to support lifelong commitment and to help to heal marriages and finally to recognise failed marriages without searching for the 'fatal flaw' which might prove that there was in fact no marriage. Marriage can be supported in a context which recognises that we are all flawed and limited and that this is the human condition. The sayings of Jesus in relation to divorce cannot be isolated from the total thrust of his message and above all of his practice which demonstrated the primacy of grace over the law. Bernard Treacy talks about holding two truths together, with church bodies giving a strong support for marriage and also providing a healing and helping community for those whose marriages have broken down. Laws are necessary but clumsy and limited ways of organising human affairs; they never absolve us from the exercise of discernment or from the exercise of making responsible and conscientious decisions.

The table of healing love

So far, I have not referred to the question of exclusion from the sacraments. If we reject the nullity approach and operate instead with the concept of affirmation of the ideal of lifelong fidelity alongside a recognition of human fragility and failure, then exclusion from the table of healing love makes no sense. It is particularly ironic when one observes the table-practice of Jesus: 'He has gone in to be the guest of a man who is a sinner …'; 'Now if this man were a prophet, he would have known …' The Pharisees who are astonished that Jesus has not washed before the meal have their notions of purity overturned and the lawyers are admonished for loading people with burdens hard to bear. It seems clear that those who cannot take the radical inclusiveness of the practice of Jesus are the only ones excluded from his fellowship; in fact, they exclude themselves. These are the texts which need to be read alongside the words of prohibition on divorce.

The exclusion of this particular group also raises the deeper question about our theology of church and of Eucharist. What does it mean to insist that the divorced and remarried are to share in the life of the church, in its liturgy, its prayer and its works while remaining excluded from the sacraments? This proposal appears to be a contradiction in terms and implies a reduced and impoverished understanding of sacrament. It is difficult to see how one can be welcomed as a member of the church and excluded from the symbolic celebration of that membership. Francis Moloney, addressing this topic, speaks of a problem with the church's understanding of itself as 'the perfect society rather than a pilgrimage of sinners'.[2]

On a different level, the exclusion of the divorced and remarried from the sacraments creates a situation of enormous tension for those who experience their 'irregular unions' as a sign of grace, as a source of life, and are denied the possibility of publicly acknowledging that grace.

Perhaps it is in this context that we might speak of scandal – for many who have lived through these situations, or who have observed others struggling with the contradiction between their interpretation of their own experience and official church pronouncements, it is truly a scandal that they are not admitted to the sacraments. It is important also to acknowledge that the current teaching of the church causes much anguish and pain, not alone to those caught up in these situations but also to those who are ministering to them. For this reason it is necessary to hear all the voices in any debate on the issues.

I have attempted to argue here without the support of emotional factors which are bubbling just below the surface. My main thesis is that the context in which we discuss these issues must be broadened and that the perspective within which we view this and other moral issues is that God has created us in love and for freedom, and desires our good. What structures can we put in place to make it most likely that we can live this good? Finally, I quote Häring again:

> What is primarily and ultimately involved is whether the church in its entire existence, in its dealing with the law of Christ and in its turning to those who have been hurt or who have failed, can ever more strongly be experienced as the sacrament of Christ's reconciling mercy.

Update

It is somewhat strange to observe one's earlier self and know how much has changed. I am now married almost 35 years and have seen one of our children marry and I remain committed to the idea and the reality of marriage, its profound gifts and its dynamic nature. I continue to see the understanding of 'indissolubility' as a stumbling block. The ideal and value of committed faithful love is not necessarily compromised by the recognition of human frailty and failure. Paradoxically the experience of a failed marriage on one side may in fact deepen the desire and commitment in the second union. Marriages, or rather married persons, grow into and become 'one' and sometimes fail to do so for a very wide variety of reasons. Becoming one flesh – until the pair cannot imagine their lives apart from one another – doesn't happen with the first (or twenty-first!) sexual consummation of the marriage and to suggest this seems to imply a kind of physicalism that seems inappropriate. Until the teaching church attends to the lived experiences of married couples, its pronouncements will have little resonance.

And in regard to the Eucharist, my own sense is that pastoral wisdom and careful discernment of the particular situations will do, and already are creating norms in practice. *A.T.*

Notes:

1. Bernard Häring CSsR, *No Way Out: Pastoral Care of the Divorced and Remarried*, St Paul Publications, 1989.
2. Francis Moloney, *A Body Broken for a Broken People: Eucharist in the New Testament*, Collins Dove 1990, p 136.

25 Divorce, Remarriage and the Eucharist: A Further View

John McAreavy

(*Doctrine and Life*, Vol 45, No 2, February 1995, pp 171-177)

I read with interest Anne Thurston's article 'Living with Ambiguity' in *Doctrine and Life*, November 1994 (pp 537-542). I appreciate her honesty and courage in making her own personal situation clear. Indeed it must be difficult to write calmly about the issue of the divorced and remarried when it comes so close to the bone. She writes that her analysis 'conceals a great deal of pain, tension and struggle' (p 537). In taking up my pen in response to what she has written I do so because, as she says, 'it is necessary to hear all the voices in the debate on the issues' (p 542) and not out of any desire to add to her pain; even less do I want to be accused, like the lawyers in the gospel, of loading people with burdens hard to bear.

I should perhaps also declare an interest, though one not as personal as Ms Thurston's: for a good many years I was a full-time official of the Armagh Regional Marriage Tribunal and I still assist in the ministry of that tribunal. In that office, I met many women and men who were in second unions and who yearned to be in full communion with the church and be able to receive Holy Communion. There were also many who had found a second partner with whom they wished to live in the sacrament of matrimony and for whom a first marriage often appeared only as an obstacle to the happiness they sought in life. I do not claim that the pain of those who minister to those in broken marriages is comparable to the pain of the people directly involved, but to share their journey, even for a while, was to share some of that pain with them. This pain was all the greater when one was unable to bring men and women the complete relief they sought. There were, thankfully, also situations where it was possible to bring the result that people sought, but these were, in the nature of things, rarer.

Anyone who addresses the situation of the divorced and remarried in the church must keep in mind the pain of those who are directly affected by it. This however should not prevent the church from remaining faithful to its own faith. The pastoral response of the church must always be based on revealed truth. The sacrament of marriage is of divine institution; it is not a purely human institution and the church is not free to change God's arrangement in order to solve the dilemma of those who live in situations of painful ambiguity.

Formation of the bond of marriage

Vatican II taught that the married state 'is rooted in the covenant of the parties, that is, in their irrevocable personal consent' (*Gaudium et Spes*, n 48). Marriage receives its stability from the human act 'by which the partners mutually surrender themselves to each other.' The Council then added: 'For the good of the partners, of the children, and of society this sacred bond no longer depends on human decision alone' (*Gaudium et Spes*, n 48). The Code of Canon Law followed this perspective when it states in its foundation canon on marriage:

> The marriage covenant by which a man and a woman establish between themselves a partnership of their whole life, and which of its own very nature is ordered to the well-being of the spouses and to the procreation and upbringing of children, has, between the baptised been raised by Christ the Lord to the dignity of a sacrament (1055, par 1).

It is the clear tradition of the church that marriage between the baptised, once brought into being by the consent of the parties and consummated, is indissoluble. It no longer depends 'on human decision alone'.

The fact that the bond of marriage comes into existence at a specific point gives a married couple the firm parameters within which they can develop their relationship. The use of covenant language in Vatican II was not intended to blur the edges of the process of forming the bond of marriage; it was intended to highlight the sacramentality of marriage. This is clear in the statement that 'just as of old God encountered his people with a covenant of love and fidelity so our Saviour, the spouse of the church, now encounters Christian spouses through the sacrament of marriage' (*Gaudium et Spes*, n 48). To state that 'the important question is not whether a marriage is validly contracted ... but whether it has developed into "a human relationship with potential for salvation", in other words, whether the contract has become a covenant' (p 538) creates a false antithesis. The 'validity' of a marriage is not an abstract concept; it refers to the support that the church community gives to a marriage by recognising it and expressing its willingness to 'stand by it'.

Marriage does not become a covenant as a process over a period of time. In the commitment of a baptised couple – expressed in their consent – 'to love each other truly, for better, for worse, for richer, for poorer, in sickness and in health, till death do [them] part' the covenantal love of Christ for his spouse, the church, is already imaged and present. As Fr Denis O'Callaghan wrote, 'The marriage relationship of baptised husband and wife becomes by that very fact a redeeming force, a situation which makes present God's saving love in Christ here and now in the family unit.'[1]

It is of course true that for the marriage to become a fruitful sacrament for the parties, they need to deepen their love for each other, their trust in each other, and the other aspects of married life that make it a source of joy for themselves and for all who experience it. This is a process; this is something that happens over time; but we should not confuse this 'working at' the marriage relationship with the existence of the marriage itself.

As I intimated above, the purpose of giving marriage a juridical firmness from the beginning is not to render the process of working at the marriage relationship unnecessary; rather it is to provide the solid context within which a man and woman, knowing that they are both seriously committed to each other, can take the risk of total honesty. To say that 'a marriage which becomes a sacrament carries with it the seeds of its own indissolubility' (p 540) overlooks the fact that indissolubility is already a quality of the marriage from the outset. The indissolubility and fidelity of the baptised married couple is based on the unconditional fidelity of the new covenant between Christ and the church.

The suggestion that the juridical existence of a marriage relationship in some way depends on the existential quality of the marriage at any point is entirely contrary to the tradition of the church. What, for example, is one to say about the quality of married life of an old couple when the husband or wife is suffering from senile dementia or Alzheimer's disease? When love has worn thin and all that remains is the grim determination to be faithful to a partner who once was charming and generous, but who now, for all practical purposes, is gone? Should the weak have to wonder, in the lines of the Beatles song: 'Will you still feed me, will you still need me when I'm sixty-four'? Who is to judge when and how effectively a marriage relationship reflects the love of Christ for the church? The call to fidelity never ends, just as the marriage never ends.

It is the clear tradition of the church that once a marriage has come into existence it can be dissolved only by the death of one of the spouses. To speak of the 'moral death' of a marriage as Häring does, is entirely misleading if it means that a marriage ceases to exist due to the failure of the parties to realise in their relationship what they had hoped. The refusal of the church to concede that the parties can bring a valid marriage to an end is not a refusal to face the reality of marriage breakdown. This has always been a fact of church life. It is evidence of human weakness and of the effects of sin. However, the church must be faithful to the teaching of Christ. As the International Theological Commission stated:

> Faithful to the radicalism of the gospel, the church cannot refrain from stating with St Paul the apostle: 'To those now married, however, I give this command (though it is not mine; it is the Lord's): a wife must not separate from her husband. If she does separate, she must either remain single or become reconciled to him again. Similarly, a husband must not divorce his wife' (1 Cor 7:10-11). It follows from this that new unions following divorce cannot be considered regular or legitimate.[2]

Fr Wilfrid Harrington explained the radical nature of marriage in the teaching of Christ. Refuting the idea that Matthew 19:9 is an exceptive clause, he wrote:

Jesus is not abrogating the Mosaic legislation, nor is he (or a secondary editor) reducing his radical demand to something more palatable. On the contrary, he is emphasising the risks which mankind as a whole must face when the sexuality in [human] nature is confronted with the indissolubility of marriage ... Marriage is a call to a life of total sacrifice and self-giving ... if one's spouse is unfaithful, a life dedicated to him or her may have to be totally thrown away, laid down in love (since there is no possibility of enjoying another such partnership) ... Christian love must continue faithful, even if rejected, loyal even if deserted, and abiding even if unrequited. Why? – *for the sake of God's love shown in the very union of man and woman* [my emphasis].[3]

Since it is the new covenant, the love of Christ for his Bride, the church, which is sacramentally present in the commitment of baptised husband and wife, the radical break that occurs when someone, who was validly united in marriage to their spouse, subsequently remarries is objectively very serious. The words of the church's magisterium on divorce are not just rhetoric; as the *Catechism of the Catholic Church* states:

> Divorce does injury to the covenant of salvation, of which sacramental marriage is the sign. Contracting a new union, even if it is recognised by civil law, adds to the gravity of the rupture (n 2384, p 511).

Marriage is not something that the church somehow 'got involved in'. It is crucial to God's revelation of himself as the faithful Spouse to his Bride, the church. Indeed one theologian has written that 'the relationship of Christ to the church can only be understood if one understands marriage.'[4]

Eucharistic Communion a sign of Ecclesial Communion
The reception of Holy Communion by those who are divorced and remarried is a problem because 'their state of life *objectively* [italics mine] contradicts that union of love between Christ and the church which is signified and effected by the Eucharist' (*Familiaris Consortio*, n 84d).

The word 'objectively' is important because the church makes no judgements concerning the motives of those concerned. Moreover there is no judgement of the human quality of the second relationship. However, this second relationship makes it inconsistent for those concerned to participate to the fullest extent in the celebration of the Eucharist. It does so because it creates an obstacle between those involved and the church.

Those who do not share the faith of the church are unable to receive Holy Communion in the Catholic Church because they are not in full ecclesial communion with the Catholic Church; those who are in second unions or irregular unions are unable to receive Holy Communion because their state and condition of life 'objectively contradict that union of love between Christ and the church which is signified and effected by the Eucharist' (*Familiaris Consortio*, n 84).

Anne Thurston writes that 'it is difficult to see how one can be welcomed as a member of the church and excluded from the symbolic celebration of that membership' (p 542). The experience of the catechumenate in the early church, the experience of canonical penance at the same period, and the concept of 'degrees of communion' which underpins the church's approach to ecumenism provide a theological model for the situation of those who are – and remain – members of the church but who, because 'their state and condition of life objectively contradict that union of love between Christ and the church which is signified and effected by the Eucharist' cannot receive Holy Communion. It is not true to say that this practice is only consistent with a view of the church as a 'perfect society'. The present practice is based both on the scriptures and on the teaching of the early church.

This is not to suggest that such a theological solution will be easy for those concerned. It will often be 'a situation of great tension' (p 542). Many Catholics, however, realise instinctively that their second relationship creates an obstacle for their communion with the church. The discipline of the Catholic Church in this matter is by no means 'a single issue approach to a moral problem' (p 537). It takes account of the covenantal nature of marriage and also of the implications of the celebration of that new covenant in the Eucharist.

Anne Thurston writes that 'compassionate and graced pastoral care for those whose marriages have broken down and a discerning and sensitive approach to all involved in second relationships will enhance and not detract from marriage as a sign of grace, as a sign of God's covenant' (p 539). I agree. There is an onus on the church to do all in its power to ensure that those in second unions experience the tender care of the Good Shepherd in the pastoral charity of priests. They should also experience a welcome and acceptance from the faithful in their parishes. The emphasis in church documents on what the divorced and remarried cannot do should not obscure the fact that they remain our brothers and sisters who bring their own gifts to the ecclesial community and who are entitled to encouragement and support. They should be encouraged to investigate the possibility of the annulment of their first marriage. The ministry of the marriage tribunals is a ministry of truth and justice: truth, because its purpose is to discover the truth about the circumstances of the first marriage; justice, because the rights of other parties are involved, the first spouse, the children of the marriage, and the church community which is affected by the fate of every marriage. An individual might judge that the process of annulment is not appropriate or desirable for them. The church, however, in coming to a decision as to the validity of a marriage, will not give this decision on the basis of what is appropriate or desirable. Those charged with making such decisions must make them on the basis of the church's law and having God alone as their guide.

The debate provoked by the German Bishops' document and the instruction of the Holy See has served to highlight an area of the church's life which needs continuing theological and pastoral reflection. It is vitally important that the theological and pastoral options followed do justice to the church's understanding of marriage and the Eucharist and, not least, its compassion for those in difficulty.

Notes:

1. 'Theology Forum: No Sacrament, No Marriage', in *The Furrow* 26 (1975), p 232.
2. 'Propositions on the Doctrine of Christian Marriage', in *Origins*, 8 (1978), p 239.
3. 'Jesus' Attitude towards Divorce', in *Irish Theological Quarterly* (ITQ), 39 (1972), pp 183-185. This interpretation is confirmed in Raymond Collins' *Divorce in the New Testament* (Collins, 1992).
4. M Schmaus, *Dogma 5: The Church as Sacrament*, p 271.
5. *A Body Broken for a Broken People*, p 136.
6. See H Crouzel, *L'Eglise primitive face au divorce*.

26   Irregular Marriage: A New Deal

Brendan Hoban

(*The Furrow*, Vol 50, No 4, April 1999, pp 195-203)

One of the few certainties in the Maastricht debate some years ago was that, while more than a million explanatory leaflets were sent to the citizens of Ireland, only a tiny percentage of those debating the proposed treaty read the actual document. For those who persisted with the turgid euro-speak and the often impenetrable meaning, one of the few surprises it surfaced was that hoary old theological chestnut we call the principle of subsidiarity. Imagine. Once you fought your way through the contorted sentences and the plethora of subjunctive clauses, there it stood glistening in the clearance. Pius XI would have been proud. Since his day it has been a prominent part of Catholic teaching.

In essence, the principle of subsidiarity states that what individuals can do, societies should not assume and what smaller societies can do, larger societies should not take over. And this principle has been applied to civil society by every Pope since Pius XI. Pius XII gave it an added impetus and importance when he suggested that it should also apply to the church and Paul VI accepted it as a principle for the reform of canon law. So far so good. But what happened to it since? Now it only surfaces occasionally when the church, with a certain sleight of hand, lectures civil society on what true democracy means but it doesn't sit very comfortably with the restoration policies of the present time.

A church that once inched its way towards a suggestion of democracy is now trying to come to terms with the fact that, in church terms, democratisation – the key impulse of our age – is something of an aberration. Cardinal Ratzinger of the Congregation for the Doctrine of the Faith seems uncomfortable with the growing authority of national episcopal conferences. Episcopal conferences in turn are becoming tetchy with the occasional bishop who prefers to take an individual approach. The paper trail from diocesan offices in the general direction of parish priests is consuming ever greater swaths of the rain forests in the Amazon basin as efforts are made to set down in more and more detail the rubrics of pastoral practice. All of this in a society that almost universally acknowledges the primacy of accountability and partnership. All of this in a culture that stresses the freedom (of the individual) and the need for the individual to make decisions, albeit in the context of greater order.

The only exception to the present centralising policy is at local level where parish priests (or at least some of them), anxious to acknowledge the tenor of the age as well as preserve a modicum of sanity, are learning the pastoral wisdom of applying Pius XI's principle to interested laity and even to recalcitrant curates. Despite the prevailing winds from Rome, subsidiarity is a concept whose time has come.

Intercommunion

The debacle of the publication of *One Bread, One Body* makes the point. The most important contribution the bishops of England, Ireland, Scotland and Wales could have made to the delicate issue of intercommunion was to say nothing. Sometimes silence is the best option. Intercommunion has already happened. What is needed now is the delicate implementation of norms flexible enough to meet the complex needs of individual interchurch families at parish level. It needs to be acknowledged that decisions made on the ground by foot-soldiers are infinitely more pertinent and ultimately more useful than grand statements sent out from base-camp.

An example. The daughter of a Church of Ireland father and a Roman Catholic mother prepared for her first communion in the Catholic Church. Her father, who is a sincere and committed member of his church, took an active interest in his daughter's preparation to the extent that he attended presacramental preparation meetings for parents. Before First Communion day, he approached the Roman Catholic curate and asked to be allowed to receive Communion with his daughter. After some discussion, the curate agreed and the man quietly accompanied his daughter, his wife and their other children as they all received together. A few comments were made afterwards but the circumstances were such that the decision fitted easily into the faith pattern of the people. The man's commitment to his own faith and the respect he had shown to his daughter's faith were sufficient to glean widespread, though not universal, approval in the parish. A parishioner who didn't agree with the priest's decision contacted the bishop, a wise man, who decided to say and do nothing.

Some years later, the same young girl prepared for her Confirmation with the same support and commitment of her father. Again her father went to the local curate, this time a different curate. The priest was appalled; it was out of the question, there was the matter of transubstantiation and all that sort of thing and he informed the father that he would be reporting him forthwith to the bishop. Word spread in the parish and the bishop found himself having to adjudicate on the issue. He asked the father of the child not to approach the altar for Communion. In the event, the only member of the family to receive Communion was the girl who was confirmed. It was her last Communion in the church of her baptism. She – and the rest of her family who are Catholics – no longer attend church though they occasionally accompany their father to his church.

To continue the metaphor, foot-soldiers often have a certain freedom to operate at ground level while generals cannot be seen to deflect from the official line. No is always the easier word to say. Bishops, because of their official teaching role, often feel they have to say the hard word in public while accepting that in pastoral practice the complexities of a particular situation demand a more user-friendly mode. This can sometimes be presented as an unacceptable swerve around the truth. Saying one thing at official level, turning a blind eye at a pastoral level – hard on the sin, soft on the sinner.

External and internal fora

Not so. The distinction between external and internal fora is fundamental to Catholic theology. For instance, in the pastoral care of those in irregular marriage situations (which I'll be discussing in more detail later on) the marriage tribunal system constitutes the external forum. The internal forum at parish and at individual conscience level has, in practice, a freedom that the external forum hasn't got. So those in marriages whose nullity cannot be adequately demonstrated are sometimes at parish level admitted to the sacrament.

So analogously, while the clear statement of *One Bread One Body* is that Roman Catholics must not receive Communion in a Reformation Church and Protestants – apart from a few limited exceptions – cannot receive Communion in a Catholic Church, the internal forum option comes into play. The limited official exceptions allowed for in the document – more limited and less generous than other similar documents around the world – in effect give the green light in specific cases. The internal forum mechanism will help to solve individual problems at parish level. So that even though the official document gives the impression of a large door slamming shut, the detail provides the internal forum with some room to operate effectively and sensitively at parish level. The fact that some bishops have disempowered their priests by withholding decisions appropriate to the internal forum demonstrates at best a lack of trust, at worst a failure to understand a fundamental of pastoral practice. Bishops are not super PPs.

In dealing with people in irregular marriage situations, the distinction between the external forum (the marriage tribunal) and the internal forum (pastoral practice) is an accepted and widespread pastoral strategy. There is an effective and necessary gap between what bishops teach at national or diocesan level and what individuals and families can achieve. And in terms of the care of those in irregular marriage situations, the marriage tribunal is often an ineffective forum.

Marriage tribunals today are ineffective for two main reasons. One is that despite the refinement of the canon law of marriage through the burgeoning level of applications for decrees of nullity (particularly on the grounds of lack of due discretion and inability to fulfil), church law is still a very blunt instrument in terms of dealing with many individual situations. While the official guidelines tend to lump together all those in irregular marriage situations, as *Familiaris consortio* points out, pastors are obliged 'to exercise careful discernment of situations between those, for example, who have sincerely tried to save their first marriage and have been unjustly abandoned, and those who through their own fault have destroyed a canonically valid marriage.' Pastors operating at individual and family level recognise how unhelpful it is to speak in general terms about those in irregular marriage situations. Every case is different.

For example, there is all the difference in the world between those who decide to live together without much thought and less commitment, and those whose marriages may well be invalid but there simply isn't moral certainty in legal terms to justify the granting of a decree of nullity. There is all the difference in the world between those whose relationship is clearly transitory and insubstantial, and those who have six children and are living exemplary lives. There is all the difference in the world between, in the words of *Familiaris consortio*, 'those who are sometimes subjectively certain in conscience that their previous and irreparably destroyed marriage had never been valid' and those who, through the convenient inability of a first partner to fulfil the obligations of marriage, can walk away from a union to which they never made any real commitment.

Tribunal personnel accept that it is extremely difficult to prove non-consummation, for example, but it can be quite obvious to the particular individual involved that what presented as a marriage was clearly not a Christian marriage and yet that individual, because the law is not sophisticated enough to deliver a just verdict in the circumstances, is expected to abstain for life from sexual relations with someone who is, for all intents and purposes, a life-long partner and the father or mother of his or her children. Clearly in justice these are areas where the internal forum comes into play. And the tradition has been that special allowance is made at individual level. (More about that later.)

Justice issue
The other reason why marriage tribunals are ineffective is that the resources available to them are inadequate to meet the needs of the task in hand. It is surely a first principle that baptised Christians have the right in justice to have their church adjudicate on the status of their relationship. Two factors conspire to lessen the ability of the church to respond. One is that in some societies the level of breakdown is such that it is quite impossible to deal with every case. An American priest, who spent most of his life working in a marriage tribunal and is now a parish priest in the United States, estimates that almost 30% of his parishioners are in irregular unions. It is simply impossible to deal with that phenomenon through a tribunal system. The only other alternative is dealing with it through the internal forum, the parish. He believes that the time has come to develop some structure at parish level to adjudicate on the hundreds of unions involved and to place that structure at the heart of parish life.

The other factor is the level of putative invalidity in unions where one or both partners are oblivious to the problem. 'There's a lot of invalidity out there.'

I heard a canon lawyer say some years ago, 'The only marriages we know are valid are those that have failed to get a decree of nullity.' I think he meant it to be funny but when pressed on the subject he conceded that while, according to his criteria, 'there must be thousands and thousands of invalid unions out there, don't send them to us.' Such levity, while unusual in canonists, disguises a real truth. In some situations tribunals achieve little more than help to convince us that as a church we are dealing credibly with the question that every baptised Christian has a right to ask his or her church: am I married? The conclusion is that the external forum is not equal to its task. The internal forum needs to become more active and more structured at local level if justice is to be done.

There are real difficulties here. One is that accepting the reality of, and the need for, the internal forum in terms of ministering to those in irregular marriage situations at parish level, often carries with it the charge of redefining what Christian marriage is or adopting situation ethics or existentialist morality or whatever you are having yourself. We need to be clear at the outset that the external-internal axis is an accepted concept in Catholic theology and acceptable in pastoral practice. Finding a formula to cut a track through the detail of an individual life or a 'marriage' relationship is not about finding a way to sideline our understanding of 'covenanted relationship' that Christian marriage is. It is rather, as Pope John Paul said in York, reaching out in love 'to those who know the pain of failure in marriage … by showing them Christ's compassion'.

Way forward

The internal forum is already operative at a pastoral level and there is no reason why it cannot be developed further. A possibility would be the formation of a small group, comprising a priest and a woman spiritual director, to work directly with couples in irregular unions. For example, a divorced or remarried person may believe in conscience that his/her previous union was invalid. The reason for this view can be explored as the details emerge. At a certain stage the priest and spiritual director, in conjunction with the couple, will be able to form a judgement concerning the validity or invalidity of the marriage, with consultative backup from a marriage tribunal. It may be that the person deliberately withheld consent to the marriage, or may have entered the marriage with the intention of never having children, or with a divorce mentality ('If this doesn't work, I'll walk away'). The individual may have already presented his case to a marriage tribunal but it may not have been possible to substantiate his claim in the external forum due to lack of evidence. If the priest or spiritual director feels he or she is morally certain that the first marriage is invalid, in view of the fact that the person has a natural right to marriage and further that he is unable to exercise that right in the church, a decision to receive Communion will follow.

The standard official response of the church is that the reception of Communion by a person in an irregular union contradicts the union of love between Christ and the church as signified in the Eucharist, and that such reception would be a cause of scandal as it would indicate that the church does not believe in the indissolubility of marriage. The official solution for the couple is either separation or living together 'as brother and sister', that is, without sexual intimacy. Both are an example of a clerical solution to a canonical problem, at once perfectly logical within accepted legal frameworks but not making much sense in the wider world.

For instance, the meaning and substance of the phrase 'giving scandal' has shifted so significantly in recent years as to render it practically meaningless. If a responsible and committed couple in a stable and permanent relationship – faithful to the practice of their faith and respected in their local faith community for the manner in which they bring up their children in the faith – receive Communion with their children at Mass on Sunday, is it giving scandal today? Surely we know enough about structural injustice and social sin and moral failure at all levels of the church to moderate our traditional certainty about scandal and scandalgivers. There is also the consideration that blanket denial of the sacraments to those in irregular unions may give scandal at a different level, by weakening our witness to the compassion of Christ to those in need. The gospel injunction to remove heavy burdens and all that. The furtive reception of Communion a few parishes away or several miles down the road is, for a variety of personal, social and pastoral reasons, inadequate and unhelpful.

There are obvious difficulties too with the other solution for a couple in an irregular union, 'living together as brother and sister'. While this may seem a logical and serious suggestion among those who live in the clinical world of Canon Law, it bears little relationship with the lived experience of couples. It is not just impractical, even incredible, but it postulates an embarrassing lack of understanding of the implications of such a solution. It might be unkindly said that only celibate lawyers could have come up with that one. There is too the further matter that it predicates a very limited view of Christian marriage, with an undue focus on sexual intimacy and without the wider sense of a relationship that gives it substance.

So the standard official response can be unhelpful and needs to be moderated by a sensitive and knowledgeable response at a personal level, based on the rights of the individual baptised and the pastoral needs of a given situation. The crucial point is that Catholic teaching launched from Rome or the diocesan office is not susceptible to the pastoral nuances of irregular situations. Cardinal Ratzinger himself recognised that individual pastoral solutions were not just necessary but 'in harmony with our ecclesiastical traditions':

> Whenever in a second marriage moral obligations have arisen toward the children, toward the family and toward the woman, and no similar obliga-

tions from the first marriage exist; whenever also the giving up of the second marriage is not fitting on moral rounds, and continence does not appear as a real possibility in the practical order; it seems that the granting of full Communion, after a time of probation, is nothing less than just, and is fully in harmony with our ecclesiastical traditions (see Ladislas Orsy, *Marriage and Canon Law*, Delaware: Michael Glazier 1986).

The only forum where the compassion of Christ can be brought to bear on the pain often involved in such human dilemmas is the personal, internal forum. In comparison the external forum is ineffective and marriage tribunals in the main recognise this truth. My fear is that bishops, in the present climate of recentralisation, may be tempted to abrogate an effective and pastoral function. This may be particularly true at a time when bishops regularly receive reams of unsolicited advice by way of phone calls and letters from a wide spectrum of 'traditional' Catholics, ranging from those who don't understand to those who are permanently, so to speak, out to lunch. What is needed now is an encouragement of, and a more realistic assessment of, the possibilities that the internal forum offers. Priests working in parishes need to feel trusted, empowered and facilitated in helping to remove burdens impossible to bear. The possibilities for extending the remit of the internal forum are not just obvious or necessary but already becoming part of accepted norms of pastoral practice in our progressively uncertain times. Informal blessing ceremonies and the blessing of rings are not a feature of the pastoral care of those in irregular unions. The local parish is quietly beginning to find its own hymn sheet, and a function of the marriage tribunals in the future will be to resource whatever local structure emerges as the *de facto* forum for dealing with those in irregular marriage situations.

Some time ago the religious correspondent of *The Independent* (London), Andrew Brown, took exception to the way in which the English Conference of Roman Catholic Bishops dealt with an edict from the Congregation of the Doctrine of the Faith. The statement, a response to a request from three German bishops that the traditional ban on divorced and remarried people receiving Communion be re-examined, reaffirmed the general teaching that Communion was available only if they agreed to 'abstinence from the acts proper to marriage'. Brown took exception to the bishops' spokesperson asserting that the document was not discussed because it contained nothing new. It would have been more truthful, Brown said, 'to say that they had not discussed it because they had no intention of acting on it ... the ban on remarried divorced people receiving Communion is broken almost everywhere, and with the tacit but clearly understood support of the bishops involved.'

In an ideal world, the journalist's penchant for unmasking hypocrisies in unpopular institutions, the church lawyer's confidence in the canons at his disposal to make sense of life, and the bishops' responsibility to reaffirm the

AN IRISH READER IN MORAL THEOLOGY

indissolubility of marriage would all knit conveniently together in a seamless garment of commitment and compassion. But there is no ideal world, just the limited mess of unreason and inconvenience, through which we struggle to find a human and a moral path. Those dealing with difficult situations at an individual and personal level haven't the luxury of having it all worked out beforehand. Life is awkward and messy and the loose ends cannot always be tidied up to everyone's satisfaction. That's why the internal forum – a theologically based traditional pastoral strategy – can be an effective and sensitive mechanism for the pastoral care of those in irregular unions. What we need to do now is to develop its remit in a changing world.

Part Seven
Homosexuality

27   Understanding the Homosexual

Raphael Gallagher

(*The Furrow*, Vol 30, No 9, September 1979, pp 71-81)

Whatever occasional doubts the manual tradition of moral theology allowed itself, none of these doubts emerged in its treatment of homosexuality. It was a sin *contra naturam*. This technical term acquired in time the full moral indignation implied in calling the practice 'unnatural'. The manual treatment of homosexuality was usually short, precise and confidently presented as the only possible one, given the unanimity of the biblical data, theological tradition and the attitudes of the believing community.

The question is, nonetheless, undergoing serious review. Many pressures have combined to force moral theologians to reflect in a scholarly and sensitive way on the factors involved in making a judgement on homosexuality; the ongoing revision of the methodology of moral theology itself, new exegetical interpretations of the relevant biblical data and increasing evidence from the scientific community on the causes and development of homosexual orientation and actions in particular persons. These pressures have become public and have been harnessed by politically conscious homosexuals.[1]

Like other arguments where the political rights of a minority and ethical analysis in a wider sense cross lines, the debate on homosexuality is now very confused and confusing. One's ethical statements are weighed for their political bias pro and con. Many debates on homosexuality reveal prejudice, fear and unsupported statements rather than the elements of reason and freedom which, theoretically, are the basis of ethical analysis.

Because of this prejudice and confusion of terms, the central issue for the theologian (priest, counsellor) at this stage is to meet the homosexual with a factual understanding of the situation. I am seeking to present this factual understanding from a double standpoint: a review and assessment of the relevant literature and, perhaps more importantly, what I have learned from homosexuals themselves and from those who have been working with homosexuals over a considerable period of time. In general my remarks are based on an analysis of male homosexuality; female homosexuality has not as yet received a comparable amount of clinical study. From this factual understanding, I shall be trying to build up a framework for a moral evaluation of homosexuality and, at a third stage, guidelines for a pastoral approach.

For the sake of an authentic presentation, I leave this account to the writer's own words and expressions:

The most important thing that happened to me was the realisation that homosexuality was natural for me and from God. How that came about is too complex, and painful, to relate fully. The long years away from the sacraments, believing that homosexuality was unnatural and that any 'thought, word or deed' which centred on it was grave sin, had been traumatic. Drink and depression were one result. Increasing isolation and inability to communicate were another. But through it all I never turned away from God (as I see it now) and I never stopped praying. More especially I never missed Mass on Sunday except inadvertently. Gradually prayer (which was never very large in quantity or regularity and often informal, though I believe its intensity made up for that) led me to read the psalms with increasing regularity, the New Testament, classics of spirituality (especially the *Imitation of Christ*, which always had a special place) and finally the Old Testament, followed by a rag-bag of stuff. By now I had somehow vaguely begun to realise that if God loved me and (what was a shattering thought) had even made me in his own way his son, then my orientation towards homosexuality must be meaningful. It must be my road to salvation, to him. I could not develop this line of thought too well, since to me it bordered on the blasphemous. Then I fell in love. That was certainly the most important single fact in my life. It is hard to describe; all I will say is that well into my forties my whole life became centred on one man. It had the effect of heightening my consciousness of the goodness of my kind of love, and of making more urgent the need to relate it to my belief in God's goodness. Prayer and reading led me on to the ever firmer conviction that now that I loved one person its consummation could not be bad. Then I found Norman Pittenger's *Time for Consent*. Here was a divine, even if not a Catholic one, urging powerfully for what I now believed. I knew that in God's providence I was a homosexual, and that he had given me a love for one man. I thanked him for that love, however painful it might be in the circumstances of my life. For whatever I may have believed, the Catholic Church still said that what I was experiencing was grave sin. Then I started a rosary novena. I should explain that I have always had a firm belief in this form of prayer and that on the few occasions on which I had completed such an exercise, my request had been granted. When I started this one it was with the vague wish that somehow my terrible dilemma would be solved. Gradually I felt the urge to go to confession and even before I had finished the novena I had done just that. It would take too long to relate how I met the local curate, though I have no doubt at all that the hand of God led me there along a seemingly devious path. Communion followed. From then on I got all the help I needed and learnt to accept what was clearly God's will. It is hard, and sometimes still depressing, since the life I live does not permit my kind of love to become manifest. And if anything my feelings are even stronger now than they were when I first fell in love. But now I have the certainty of God's love, of the rightness of what I feel and of the goodness of this life. I have regular and frequent communion where I can tell God in the most intimate way of my fears and my joys. The occasional doubts and fears are stilled by prayer (and by the good advice which is always available to me). The pain is eased by association with Jesus. The fact is that by accepting what I am and what I have been given (including all the material gifts which have come in abundance), trusting in God, thanking him for my love and even the pain which it brings, I am able to make life meaningful as it never could have otherwise been. The alternative had been drink and self-destruction. Now I feel safe, secure in God's love and unafraid.

This man has reached a mature acceptance of his homosexuality. He has self-respect, and is a respected member of his profession, his neighbourhood and his church. Most homosexual autobiographies will not be as happy in their final resolution. One of the reasons for this is the ignorance and prejudice of professed Christians. There is a grave lack of factual information; the homosexual question is bedevilled by a facile use of terms which owes more to prejudice than dispassionate knowledge so that a fundamental authority in all moral argumentation – the authority of the facts – is obscured.

Questions of terminology

The word homosexual means, literally, same-sex; it could therefore be used to cover any relationship with members of one's own sex. In practice its use is narrower. A working definition of this view of homosexuality would be: a predominant, continual and exclusive psychosexual attraction towards members of the same sex.[2]

It is precisely on the level of definition that we encounter our first difficulties in assessing homosexuality. The attempt to categorise human beings into two mutually exclusive categories – a sort of majority and minority – of heterosexuals and homosexuals is an oversimplification and leads in the long term to dubious attitudes.

The perplexing nature of human sexual experience defies any such neat division. Homosexual tendencies are a stage in most people's development; many heterosexuals have homosexual leanings; sexual preference and sexual behaviour are not always the same. Between the extremes of exclusive heterosexuality and exclusive homosexuality there is a range of sexual attitudes and conditions which cannot be accurately covered by the use of the univocal term 'homo' (same) or 'hetero' (other) sexual behaviour.

Because the term homosexual is not the neat self-contained definition it is sometimes presumed to be, certain uses of the term should be avoided. It has multiple connotations, so any facile labelling of a person as homosexual should be avoided. 'Homosexual' is often used as if it automatically conjured up a whole personality and way of life. For example, the statement that Shakespeare

AN IRISH READER IN MORAL THEOLOGY

was a heterosexual elicits no special response from people, but merely imply that he was a homosexual and many people will believe they have unlocked the final mysteries of *Hamlet* or *Macbeth*.

There is, further, a distinction between the homosexual *condition* (exclusive sexual attraction to persons of the same sex) and homosexual *acts* (sexual acts between persons of the same sex). This is important because it clarifies the nature of true homosexuality from that of those who perform homosexual acts occasionally but not because they are incapable of heterosexual love.[3] Many people are capable of homosexual activity; even if they engage in such activity they should not be automatically labelled homosexual in the true sense. They could, for instance, be bisexual. Many who react too strongly to occasional homosexual acts may achieve the very opposite to what they intend and force a person to consider permanent homosexual activity.

The sexual spectrum is a wide one. The division of sexual preference into homosexual and heterosexual is too facile. A person should not be known as a 'homosexual' but as a person who, among other factors, happens to have as one element in his make-up a sexual and emotional preference for persons of his own sex. This mistake of ignoring the primary focus on persons for the narrower focus on sexual preference is a form of sexism. It is a mistake that is, paradoxically, found both among those who oppose all forms of homosexuality and those who militantly campaign for homosexual rights.

Empirical evidence suggests that only in a few individuals is sexual orientation totally exclusive; there is no rigid polarity between heterosexual and homosexual orientations. A facile classification of a person as a homosexual or heterosexual is not fully accurate or in accordance with the developmental possibilities inherent in each person.

Dispelling some myths
One of the major obstacles which prevent a proper understanding of homosexuality is the number of popular myths which surround the subject.

How many homosexuals are there? It seems safe to assume that the number is the same in Ireland as in most other countries, i.e. from 2.5% to 5% of the total population. On this basis there are between 100,000 and 200,000 homosexuals in Ireland.

Who are they? One popular myth associates homosexuals with particular professions. This is unfounded; homosexuals are to be found in every profession, social class and background. Some are married, often because of family pressure; some are not. It is usually not possible to tell from a person's appearance that he is homosexual, contrary to the widespread image of male homosexuals as effeminate and female homosexuals as aggressively masculine. Most homosexuals are not recognisable by appearance or mannerisms in social and professional life.

Are they child-molesters? The incidence of homosexual offenders in this regard has not been proven to be greater than among other members of the population. Seduction by an older person is rarely the sole cause of homosexual practice. Where this happens the younger person is often not an unwilling partner.

Are homosexuals promiscuous and unable to form enduring relationships? Given the current negative attitudes of society, the homosexual has great difficulty in forming open relationships confidently, but lasting relationships are formed in spite of these strong social pressures.

The persistence of myths about homosexuality is a sign of prejudice and intolerance; because many people never give themselves the chance to understand homosexuals the stereotyped images remain. We must learn to accept that somehow, in God's providence, some people are homosexual. They may be a deviant group in the statistical sense, but it is an unfair conclusion to *automatically* infer from this that a particular person is morally unnatural. Homosexual emotions are real for these people; the social climate for all of us would improve if we could accept the fact that among our friends and neighbours, relatives and colleagues there are some people who happen, among other aspects of their personality, to be homosexual.[4]

Origins and causes

A survey of the scientific findings on the origins of homosexuality reveals a bewildering complex of technical facts.* New data are continually coming to light about the human body – it is only in the last five years that a new set of hormones has been clearly identified.

Firstly, the physical determinants of sexual behaviour. Human sexual behaviour depends on the individual's reproductive equipment and bodily responses. Though the outline stages of sexual development are relatively clear (chromosomes, gonads, hormones, physical, psychosocial) the relations between the stages, and possible combinations, are not. Studies of how and when the brain becomes functionally differentiated into male and female patterns, and the effects of these differences upon adult behaviour, are in progress. Although few scientists would seem to advance a narrowly physiological cause for human sexuality, these physiological variables cannot any longer be ignored. Some areas of the brain are linked to sexual behaviour and the brains of males and females develop differently as a result of endocrine influences. A full discussion of this would lead us into the highly technical world of androgens and oestrogens, hormones and gender identity. This is not necessary in the context of this article, except insofar as it points to the growing scientific awareness of how people reach a sexual identity. The exact influence of hormone factors on the development of human sexuality remains uncertain, but in the light of recent research there is a clear possibility that such factors have practical importance for our understanding of homosexual behaviour.

AN IRISH READER IN MORAL THEOLOGY

Moral theologians and those working in a more directly pastoral context must adjust to the possibility that an element of one's sexual orientation is established prenatally. Since the brain's receptivity to sex-hormone activity is established prenatally, the individual may have no real choice in the matter. Sexual orientation could be as inevitably set in the prenatal period as is the colour of one's eyes or hair. As yet medical analysis of this situation is at an early stage of development, but there is enough evidence to suggest a strong possibility of such prenatal sexual orientation. A person cannot be classified as 'immoral' if this orientation is contrary to accepted mores, just as a blind person cannot be judged immoral if, prenatally, the visual tracts are not complete. Science is not suggesting this as the sole cause of homosexuality, but as one possible factor which must be reckoned with. Such evidence should make us careful in making moral categories for homosexuals before we know all the facts.[5]

Secondly, there are the environmental determinants of sexual behaviour. Just as the physiological explanations of the origins of gender identity and human sexual behaviour are under review, there is also study of the complex psychological and sociological data which are part of the environment within which sexual behaviour is determined. The theories of Freud, Adler and Jung are, in general, received with a certain scepticism because the generalised assumptions on which their conclusions are based have been shown to be in many cases inadequate. This points to the overall difficulty of research in this area. Psychoanalysts should, however, be given credit for calling attention to many interesting features of homosexual behaviour, in particular the influence of parents, family structure and early educational background. But their sometimes complicated theories are likely to apply to only a minority of cases.[6]

Both these areas of research point to the possible factor of sex-role inversion. In the past, homosexuality was simply regarded as a *perversion* of the natural order. We must now accept the possibility that homosexuality is a true *inversion*, that is, due to a variation in the statistically normal patterns of physical and environmental growth, a person's ultimate psychosexual identity can be irreversibly determined in certain circumstances. At the moment of birth the new-born child's anatomical sex will determine the style of upbringing considered suitable for a male or female. A further stage develops in infancy when the child's psychological gender identity is stabilised. Further stages will reveal the growing person's erotic preferences and capacity to enjoy love-relationship. All four stages may be in harmony. But in the case of the homosexual, anatomical sex and gender identity may not be in accord with erotic preferences and love relationships. In the face of scientific evidence, we must be careful in apportioning moral blame for this development.

The final outcome of a person's sexual orientation depends on the interaction between environmental circumstances and physiological make-up. Which is the more important and how they interact on each other remain matters for further enquiry. The unfinished research should make us hesitate in giving simple judgemental answers. Most homosexuals are within the accepted human range of social ability, intelligence and competence at work. A homosexual orientation is the fact for some people but they should not be morally classified on this fact alone, just as a heterosexual orientation is not in itself a sufficient basis for a full moral evaluation of a person.[7]

Social and ecclesial attitudes

The alienation and loneliness of many homosexuals have been contributed to in no small way by the attitude of society and of the churches. Homosexuals are a minority group and they feel they are the victims of discrimination. The complication that this 'being different' is considered morally wrong leads to a profound sense of alienation. Our immediate concern here is a review of ecclesial attitudes to homosexuals. These attitudes have been fostered in the main by scripture and reinforced by theological tradition.

The use of scripture in moral theology is notoriously difficult and the particular case of homosexuality bears this out. Certain scripture passages which were usually taken as a comment on homosexuality alone, can now be seen to be concerned with other matters also. The classic reference to Sodom (Gen 19:1-19) as being exclusively concerned with the sin of homosexuality (sodomy) is now seen by exegetes as being too narrow an interpretation. The biblical author is also concerned with the lack of hospitality and the idolatrous practices of the people of Sodom – these violated basic values of Jewish life. The context of the condemnation of homosexuality is a cultic one – it was seen as part of the Canaanite cult and therefore to be excluded by people who accepted the sole Lordship of Yahweh. A further nuancing of the biblical data concerning homosexuality is necessary when one realises that these passages were written in relation to particular problems and situations. The concern of Paul in other classic references to homosexuality (Rom 1/18ff, 1 Cor 6:9-10) is, thus, primarily with the problem of idolatry and the punishment of God which follows on this. In neither of these passages is Paul attempting to offer a judgement on homosexuality as a human condition. His wrath is directed at the general level of dissolute sexual behaviour (lust, in the sense of total absence of a personal element) which he regarded as the inevitable consequence of idolatry. Homosexuality is an incidental, though important, illustration of his main theme.[8]

We should be cautious in using scriptural texts in moral analysis because a lack of appreciation of the full context might lead us into fundamentalism. It would be equally simplistic, at the other extreme, to ignore either the biblical concern with homosexuality as one manifestation of idolatry or the overall heterosexual emphasis of the scriptures. Perhaps our main difficulty with the use of scripture in this area is that the phenomenon of inversion seems to be un-

AN IRISH READER IN MORAL THEOLOGY

known to them – that is, the case of the true homosexual for whom heterosexual sex would be impossible.

When the Bible classifies homosexuality as a sin, it is condemning lustful activity towards members of one's own sex. The scientific data available to the biblical authors did not allow them comment on another facet of homosexuality, that is, when it is a true inverted condition for an individual.[9]

The moral evaluation of homosexuality

For the manual tradition of moral theology homosexuality was a perversion of the order of nature; the moral response was, therefore, a total condemnation. In line with the then accepted biblical data it has nothing to say about the perplexing problem of homosexuality as an inversion.

In judging the morality of homosexual acts, the criterion will be: is this an instance of human love that is at its deepest a fruit of the love of God? It is the task of moral theology to develop a methodology which will help in the assessment of whether homosexual acts are in an authentic line with other acknowledged instances of human loving, e.g. friendship, married love.

The morality of homosexual acts, like that of all human acts, must be determined according to the general principles of moral theology. The most important implication of this statement is that the morality of homosexuality is to be determined according to the criteria of all moral judgements – the human nature of the act itself, the motivation of the person involved in the action, the full circumstances of the act, and the likely foreseeable consequences. Only when we have taken account of all these factors (the *fontes moralitatis*) can we begin to offer a moral judgement. This statement would be generally accepted by moral theologians today; it implies a rejection of the simplistic moral judgement based on any of the elements taken in isolation – for instance on the 'nature of the act' alone or 'consequences' alone, and implies that, in particular moral cases, it is the proportion between the above elements that will be decisive. The statement of the theoretical context for the moral judgement of homosexual acts provides a framework for the evaluation of the different views which are offered in current literature:

(a) Homosexual acts are intrinsically evil: this is the traditional view, and is strongly based on the evaluation of homosexuality as an inordinate use of the sexual faculty, because it excludes all possibility of procreation. The only moral advice which this view allows is one of sublimation and abstinence; the sublimation of sexual desire to the heterosexual level and abstinence sustained by the avoidance of the occasions of sin. A celibate friendship was allowed in rare and isolated cases.

(b) Homosexual acts are essentially imperfect: this is a modification of the above view. It accepts the presupposition that the ideal norm of human sexuality is within the context of the love-union of male and female. But it accepts, too, the reality that some cannot reach this ideal and that it is at times necessary to accept homosexual expressions as the lesser of two evils and as the only way in which some people are able to reach an acceptable level of human dignity in their lives. It acknowledges that human sexuality has a meaningful purpose beyond marriage and procreation alone, even though this remains the ideal.[10]

(c) Homosexual acts are evaluated in terms of their relational significance: this is a further, and more liberal, modification of the traditional view. The essential criterion offered is the quality of the relationship and this view would regard homosexuality in itself as morally neutral; it becomes moral or immoral according to the absence or presence of expressions of a loving relationship. Mutual love, fidelity and human caring are equally important considerations in discussing sexuality.[11]

(d) Homosexual acts are legitimate in themselves. For those espousing this view homosexuality is not really a problem at all, though society and the church have made it so. Homosexuality is accepted as a normal condition for a considerable number of people though they are statistically a minority and hence, for them, the full physical expression of a stable homosexual relationship is correct and moral.[12]

These views reflect the spectrum of tensions within moral theology today. They represent, at the one end, the essentialist view of a strictly interpreted natural law and, at the other, the committed existential option to particular ways of living. Before stating my own view, I would like to put it into the context of an overall understanding of the moral issues involved.

The problem of homosexuality cannot be morally assessed outside the proper understanding of sexuality taken in its wider sense. And here we must take cognisance of the changed emphasis on procreation in a theological understanding of sex. It can no longer be regarded as the single dominant norm by which all sexual behaviour is judged. The reality of personal sexual encounters is too wide to be compressed into the univocal notion of procreation. The majority of sexual activities even in a heterosexual context, are no longer seen to involve procreation at every level of expression. If we are to face the undoubted problems of sexuality in our time, we must move away from a procreational view of sexuality to a more personalised and relational one. It is the trivialisation of human personal encounter that is the central problem. Many have adopted a consumer attitude to sex – the encouragement of cheap and disposable sex to the detriment of deep personal encounter and growth. This is the heart of the problem.[13]

It is easy to outline the ideal of sexuality. It is something that is totally personal, formative of true love, life-giving and a harmonious element in society. We know that all sexuality falls short of this ideal. The aim of the moral life is to come as near as possible in our behaviour to this ideal.

For that reason I think a good moral guide for homosexual actions is: *the principle of the practical ideal*. It stresses that we aim at the ideal and is practical at the same time. I see this as a better formulation than currently proposed principles (e.g. the principle of compromise, the principle of the lesser of two evils, the theology of exceptions) on account of its more positive tone. Because the Christian view of morality must always be a morality of conversion, we can never lose sight of the ideal of sexuality towards which our constant conversion turns us; and because we are conscious of our human limits we aim at the ideal that is practical in the actual circumstances and conditions. It is important in discussing homosexuality that we do not fall victim to the sexist mistake of reducing a person to the level of sexual acts; equally important is the continual effort to relate the ideal to what a person can achieve now.

The limitation of the traditional approach to homosexuality is the lack of practicality; for instance, how can we presume that the charism of celibacy, a free gift, has been bestowed on this particular person of homosexual orientation? The mistake of the extreme modern view is to reduce the elements of the ideal of conversion to unacceptable levels. The principle of the practical ideal allows for a positive mediation between these extremes. In particular it allows for an understanding of the irreversible homosexual condition which is a reality in some people's lives.

Within the spectrum of current views which I outlined above, I would see this principle as a more positive formulation of (b). Because of the human condition there is an element of incompleteness in all our sexual activity. The critical question for the moral theologian is: when is the expression of this incompleteness in our actions a moral fault? In my view of homosexuality, it becomes immoral when, after an analysis of the significance of the action itself, the motivation, the circumstances and the consequences, a person has not made a serious effort to live the ideal that is practical in the circumstances of his life. Placing the emphasis on a balance between the Christian ideals of sexuality and an understanding sensitivity for the individual person is in line with the best traditions of moral theology. The words of St Alphonsus are worth recalling: 'Some assert that it is sufficient to know the principles; they are altogether mistaken. The principles are few and known to all, even to those who have only an elementary moral knowledge. The greatest difficulty in the science of moral theology is the correct application of the principles to particular cases, applying them in different ways according to the different circumstances' (*Dissertatio*, 1755, c 4, n 122).

Morality and the medical treatment of homosexuals

A further ethical issue is the treatment of homosexuals. Because homosexuality was regarded as totally undesirable in any circumstances, it was presumed to be medically correct to root it out by all possible means.

A more enlightened approach gained impetus from the decision of the American Psychiatric Association (15 December 1973) to delete homosexuality from its official lists of mental disorders. The burden of their statement is that homosexuality is not properly classified as a psychiatric illness, and that until it (homosexuality) is properly classified it will not be understood correctly. The problem is an acute one for those homosexuals who are in our mental homes; are they there just because they are homosexuals or has society put them under the type of unbearable pressure that necessitated psychiatric treatment?

Methods of treatment have varied from the crude (e.g. castration) to the sophisticated (e.g. hypnosis, sex-suppressant drugs, electroplexy, sex-change operations, aversion therapy). Apart from the fact that these treatments do not, it seems, have a high success rate, I think the main moral issue centres on the critical area of the free human response.

Our moral awareness should make us eye very carefully any effort to manipulate people, especially manipulation through behaviour control. By behaviour control I mean the modification of other people's behaviour by methods other than a freely elicited response based on a person's own conscious choice. Any use of behaviour management, which has little regard for freedom and dignity, is more in keeping with a utilitarian approach to ethics rather than with a Christian view of the radical freedom and inviolability of the person. No person should be subjected to an attempted behaviour modification or aversion therapy that is not based on a person's own free, conscious and convinced decision.[14]

Because of the doubtful moral practice involved, and further a lack of evidence that the methods succeed anyhow, many of the medical profession now avoid aversion therapies and behaviour modification techniques for homosexuals. Since these methods are available, a particular homosexual might wish to try them, and this willingness to co-operate could increase the likelihood of change in orientation. But any undue coercion to induce reluctant individuals to undergo such treatment can not be condoned in a Christian view of morality.

Therapy, in which doctor and patient are partners, may have a role in the context of a person coming to terms with his homosexuality. Better personal and social adjustment is a more likely outcome than a changed sexual orientation. The homosexual's first need is self-acceptance and a reasonable adjustment to society and sexual matters generally. I find myself, on this question, in general agreement with the opinion of D. J. West:[15] 'This policy will inevitably be criticised by some as a capitulation to the patient's neurosis, and by others as a medical licence for immorality, but in many cases it is no more than an honest admission of the realities of the situation. At least it involves no irrevocable steps. If the patient finds gay life not to his liking he is free to revert to a celibate existence. The therapist's aim is to alleviate irrational fears, to widen the patient's horizon, but not to dictate the choices he must make.'

Pastoral reflections

The Catholic Church in Ireland has been slow to accept the need for special pastoral care for homosexuals. An exception has been a Legion of Mary group which, for over twenty years, has done extraordinary work among the homosexual community in a quiet and discerning way. My own awareness of the extent of the pastoral problem of homosexuality in Ireland has come through contact with this group of dedicated Catholic workers. These concluding remarks reflect, I hope, the spirit which these people have brought to this neglected apostolate. They will serve, too, as a way of articulating a pastoral approach implicit in the general observations offered above.

(1) The homosexual should not be rejected by the Christian community because he is a homosexual. Neither should he be met with mere pity and sympathy because of his 'unfortunate' position. The first pastoral need is to create a moral community which is better informed on the origins and results of homosexuality.[16]

(2) The Christian community should re-examine whether some of its attitudes towards homosexuals owe more to prejudice than real concern with the facts. Unconscious prejudices, the fruit of biased educational attitudes, can make an effective dialogue with the homosexual impossible. It is the responsibility of each Christian community to become a true eucharistic fellowship where people of every temperament and tendency – all of us sinners – can find a place in the accepting community of Christ.[17]

(3) While urging a tolerant attitude to homosexual persons, the homosexual way of life should not be glamourised. It is not homosexuality which is the basis of one's claims to acceptance and human rights; it is the fact that we are all brothers and sisters under the Fatherhood of God. Homosexuals should avoid an identification of their claim for justice with their homosexuality; on the other side, and as a way of ameliorating the social climate, our legislators could consider the possibility of decriminalising homosexual acts between consenting adults.

(4) Homosexuals who are Catholics have the same sacramental needs and rights as other members of the church. *Ubi dubium, ibi libertas*: in the light of the uncertain scientific and theological understanding of homosexuality there is a sufficient basis for admitting the individual homosexual in good conscience to the sacraments.[18]

(5) The most crucial area of difficulty for the homosexual is the achieving of satisfactory inter-personal relationships. In a predominantly heterosexual world many homosexuals are lonely, lack self-esteem and are driven to seek superficial encounters as the only available means of acceptance, even though a temporary one. The Legion of Mary group which I mentioned above organises a weekly meeting where homosexuals discuss their problems and make friends. This has been of great benefit; such meetings should be encouraged as

an interim step until it is possible to have a more open acceptance of homosexuals within the community.

(6) On the question of urging treatment for homosexuals, we should act with caution. Psychiatric therapy and psychological counselling should never be imposed; they have value when freely chosen by the homosexual himself. Instead of trying to 'change' people, the realities of a particular situation are often best met by helping a person adjust to the orientation which they already have.

My main concern in this article has been to urge a consideration of the facts of homosexuality before we come to a moral judgement. Sensitive discernment of all the facts is the soil in which a mature moral attitude grows. The primary fact to be considered is that the homosexual is a person, made in God's image, capable of loving and being loved. How this love can be expressed is a moral dilemma, both for the homosexual and for the community.

Notes:

1. Cf Curran, C, 'Catholic moral theology in dialogue', *Fides* 1972, ch 6.
2. *Encyclopedia of Bioethics* (Reich, W, ed), Collier, Macmillan 1978, vol 2, pp 667 ff.
3. The Vatican *Declaration on Certain Questions concerning Sexual Ethics* (January 1976) accepts this general distinction, but in its short paragraph on the subject does not draw out all the logical implications of this acceptance in pastoral practice. Fr Visser, one of the authors of the *Declaration*, expanded some of the positive pastoral implications in a subsequent interview (*L'Europa*, 30 January 1976).
4. Cf Moss, R, *Christians and Homosexuals*, Paternoster Press 1977, pp. 16 ff.
* For the technical medical evidence in this article the writer would like to thank Dr Austin Darragh, Director of the Clinical Pharmacology Unit, Biological and Medical Research Institute for contributing to and correcting the section on endocrine influences, and to two psychiatrists for their corrections on the sections on environmental influences and medical treatment. The views in the article are the writer's own.
5. Much clinical research in this area is being carried out at the Endocrine Unit, St James's Hospital, Dublin. The direction of the tentative conclusions so far is in the general line of the pioneering work of Money and Erhardt.
6. *Encyclopedia of Bioethics*, loc. cit.
7. A comprehensive and scholarly study of the determinants of sexual behaviour in West, D. J., *Homosexuality Re-examined*, Duckworth 1977, pp 59ff.
8. Cf *Jerome Biblical Commentary* (Chapman 1978), on the passages quoted above.
9. Kimball Jones, H, *Towards a Christian Understanding of the Homosexual*, SCM 1967, pp 65ff.
10. This would seem to represent the views of Curran (op. cit.), and McCormick, R, *Theological Studies*, 1972, pp 112 ff.
11. For an expanded version of this view, see Baum, G, 'Catholic Homosexuals', *Commonweal*, 1974, pp 479ff.
12. Cf McNeil, J, *The Church and the Homosexual*, Sheed, Anderson and McMeel, 1976.
13. A balanced discussion of these issues can be found in Keane, P, *Sexual Morality*, Paulist Press 1977, chs 1 and 5.
14. Häring, B, *Manipulation*, St Paul Publications 1975, ch 3.

15. West, op. cit., p 271.

16. This factual information is in continual research; cf *The Lancet*, 'Sexual Behaviour and Sex Hormones', 7 July 1979.

17. Cf the pastoral letter of the Bishop of Brooklyn, *Sexuality – God's gift*, 11 February 1976.

18. This is the approach implicit in Capone, D, 'Riflessione sui punti circa l'omosessualitá', *Osservatore Romano*, 29 January 1976.

28   Homosexual Relationships

Áil n Doyle

(*Doctrine and Life*, Vol 59, No 3, March 2009, pp 24-34)

On 23 December 2008 Pope Benedict gave his traditional Christmas speech to Curia officials. The speech was widely misquoted even in reputable newspapers and journals. In dealing with the major thrust of the Pope's speech I am drawing exclusively on an item by the American Catholic News Service.

Speaking of the Holy Spirit's presence in the church events of 2008, the Pope warned that the church's teaching on ecology needs to be understood as arising from God the 'creator Spirit' – who made the earth and its creatures with an 'intelligent structure' that demands respect. Because of faith, the church has a responsibility for protecting the created world and for proclaiming publicly this environmental responsibility.

The Pope went on to explain why the human being must be at the centre of the church's ecological concern. Not only must the church protect the environment as a gift of creation that belongs to everyone, it must also protect man against self-destruction. Man, he said, as a creature, no less than the tropical rain forests, deserves our protection. By 'self destruction' the Pope said he meant 'contempt for the Creator', examples of which could be found in so-called 'gender issues'. He offered marriage as a case in point. Marriage as a permanent union between a man and a woman was something instituted by God as 'the sacrament of creation'.[1]

The Pope did not mention homosexuality and it is regrettable that there was such widespread misquotation. Nonetheless, I believe that the speech can be legitimately interpreted as saying that homosexuality is not in accord with the order of nature.

The Pope's remarks have provoked strong reactions on each side of the homosexuality debate. Some have rejoiced in what they see as the 'tough line' he has taken against homosexuality, others accuse him of promoting bigotry and hatred against gay people.

The Pope is not alone in his condemnation of homosexuality. Some of the evangelical wings of the Protestant Churches are more vehement in their opposition. It will become a big issue in this country in the near future, as the debate on proposed legislation permitting civil partnership of homosexual people gets under way.

The Irish Government's Proposal on Civil Partnership
The Irish Government has published the General Scheme (Heads) of the Civil Partnership Bill 2008. It is a long and complex document but highlighting even

AN IRISH READER IN MORAL THEOLOGY

a few Heads gives an idea of its general thrust. Head 123 of the Bill provides that cohabitants mean two adults, including those of the same sex, who live together as a couple in an intimate relationship. If they have registered their partnership in the required way, they will be entitled to many of the same rights as married couples including rights under the Succession Act and the Family Home protection Act, recognition of foreign partners and pension entitlements. The Bill specifically provides that civil partnerships will not be the same as civil marriage and that homosexual partners will not be eligible to be considered as adoptive parents. There is much more in the proposed Bill that requires further elaboration and discussion. There will be opportunities for further discussion when the Bill is published and the debate gets fully under way.

Like the Pope's statement, the Bill has provoked considerable reaction, both positive and negative from individuals, from groups, from politicians and from bishops. The Primate of all Ireland recently spoke out against the bill. (No opinion has been expressed by the Episcopal Conference of Irish bishops.) While the Bill deals with both heterosexual and homosexual civil partnerships the stronger negative reaction is in respect of homosexual partnerships. Those who oppose the proposed legislation see it as a threat to the constitutional protection of the family articulated in article 41 of the Constitution.

In this article, my focus is homosexuality from a Christian faith perspective and particularly from the perspective of the Catholic tradition. I believe that knowledge of the issues will lead to greater understanding and may lead to a fresh look at the traditional teaching.

My Journey

Twenty years ago, as a mature student of theology, I believed that homosexual relationships were objectively morally wrong but that, depending on the circumstances, individuals engaging in homosexual contact might not be subjectively culpable. While I rejected the ugly comments made about homosexual men by many of my acquaintances and occasionally by my friends, I believed that homosexual people were different from heterosexual people and were probably suffering from arrested development. I thought all homosexual men were like the camp individuals who appeared in many BBC sit-coms.

Despite this I was shocked by the insensitivity to the difficulties of homosexual people contained in the *Letter* to *The Bishops of the Catholic Church on the Pastoral Care of Homosexual Persons* published in 1986 by the Congregation for the Doctrine of the Faith, under the Prefectship of Cardinal Ratzinger. I decided to look more closely at the topic.

Because I was influenced both by the teaching of my church and also by the culture in which I lived, I knew that I would have to engage with a number of different aspects. I knew that an in depth study of the biblical material was required, together with a study of the particular natural law theory espoused by the Roman Catholic tradition, but I also recognised that I had to engage with what secular experience had to say – both the codified experience of the empirical sciences and the individual experiences of homosexual people. I knew that, in addressing any moral issue, one has to listen carefully to those most affected.

The Bible and homosexuality

I am a Catholic but my engagement with the biblical material took me to both Catholic and Protestant biblical scholars. I knew the dangers inherent in biblical interpretation. I knew that the way in which the texts are approached is fundamental to authentic interpretation. Literal translations must be ruled out, as must proof-texting, i.e. seeking proof from the texts for conclusions already arrived at through other methods. Also to be ruled out is plucking a text from its context and attempting to build on it a concrete behavioural moral norm.

Despite this awareness I, like those who appeal to the Bible to endorse their condemnation of homosexuality, believed it was an open and shut case – the Bible condemned homosexual activity – end of story. On reflection, I realised that the Bible condemned much that would not be seen today as morally wrong and endorsed much we today would consider morally reprehensible. I concluded that, influenced by the culture in which I was reared and lived, I was bringing my existing negativity to the documents. A fairly in-depth engagement with the material raised many questions for me and left me querying my hitherto unquestioning assumptions.

The major texts, which traditionally have been quoted as condemning homosexuality, are: Gen 19, Lev 18:22 and 20:13, 1 Cor 6:9-10 and Rom 1:24-28.

It was perhaps the story of Sodom and Gomorrah in Gen 19 which most challenged my biblical understanding of homosexuality. Initially I rejected, almost as amusing, the theory that the main focus of the story was not homosexuality but rather the inhospitality shown to the visitors by the people of Sodom. After considerable reading and reflection I came to the conclusion that lack of hospitality was indeed the focus.

A number of arguments convinced me. First, there is a definite link between the preceding chapter where Abraham is sitting in his tent by the oaks of Mamre but, on the arrival of three visitors, he and Sarah offered hospitality by preparing food for them and urging them to refresh themselves. We know that Sarah was rewarded by conceiving a son. Second, the similarity of the Sodom story to stories circulating at the time in the Ancient Near East is persuasive. The focus of these stories is lack of hospitality to the stranger leading to destruction of a city, and in at least one story, the one person who extends hospitality being saved, only to be turned into a pillar of stone, because she looked back contrary to instruction.

Even more persuasive is that in the 12 subsequent biblical texts which refer to the sin of Sodom, not once is homosexuality referred to as that sin. Some do not specify the sin, some see it as idolatry, some as pride and Ezek 16:49 sees it as denying food to the poor and needy. Of further significance is Luke's reference to any inhospitality which might be shown to the disciples: 'I tell you, it shall be more tolerable on that day for Sodom than for that town.' (Lk 10:10-13.)

Situating these facts within the context of the necessity in ancient times of extending hospitality to travellers as their safety could be assured only within the city walls, together with the constant reference in both Testaments to that obligation, led me to query the traditional interpretation with which I was familiar.[2]

I query also how the Leviticus texts are so readily appealed to in order to denounce homosexual contact and no mention is ever made of the proscription of having sexual relations with a menstruating woman. Much is made, also, of homosexual contact being described in Leviticus as an *abomination*. That the author refers to all sins that he condemns in the chapter as *abominations* is overlooked. Further, to focus on one word shows no awareness of the way in which language develops and changes. Today to call something an *abomination* does conjure up something horrendous but even this is evolving as, for example, we frequently hear road conditions or the weather referred to as abominable. Also worth noting is that up to the 14th century the word was seen to derive either from the Latin *abominabilis* (deserving imprecation or abhorrence) or the French *abominari* (to deprecate as an ill omen). From the 14th to the 17th centuries the word was spelt *abhominable* and explained as *ab homine*, away from man, meaning beastly or inhuman. (OED) This introduced the notion of a new degree of heinousness to homosexual contact and of it being of a different order to any other sin, which still endures.

In the vice list in 1 Cor 6:9-10 sexual perverts are condemned together with those who engage in eight other vices including idolators, robbers and the greedy. I query how the emphasis is so fixed on those engaging in homosexual activity not inheriting the kingdom of heaven that it appears to be forgotten that the other sinners referred to in the vice list will also be denied entry into the kingdom. More fundamentally, the major point made at some length by Paul, just a few verses earlier, that going to law against each other was a defeat for members of the faith community, is ignored.

The reference to both male and female homosexuality in St Paul's letter to the Romans 1:26-28 is unequivocal in its condemnation of homosexual practices of both men and women (the only biblical reference to women). I believe it is legitimate, however, to interpret this and other biblical condemnations of homosexuality as of their time and that new insights must be allowed to lead to a reappraisal of the biblical material.

I am not suggesting that the Bible is not negative in its attitude to homosexuality. What I am saying is that the homosexuality the Bible is condemning is not the reality that I, and many Christians are now espousing, namely mutual, loving, exclusive lifelong relationships by those whose orientation is homosexual. I concur with Bruce Vawter in his *Commentary on Genesis* that 'while the Bible knew homosexuality only as selfish perversion and lust, we today have knowledge which the biblical writers did not have and knowledge carries with it the duty to understand'.

Natural Law theory and homosexuality
The Catholic Church appeals to scripture in its condemnation of homosexuality but over the centuries the main thrust of its condemnation was the natural law theory of sexuality proposed by St Thomas Aquinas. St Thomas proposed that from observing the animals we know that the function of the sexual organs is procreation. As homosexual relations cannot be procreative it therefore follows that such relations are immoral. This position has been attacked on many fronts. Josef Fuchs makes the point that what is given to us in nature can communicate to us what it is and how it functions, i.e. the reality that the Creator intended it to be. One cannot move from that to investing such reality with moral instruction of how we are to use it. I would make two further suggestions. First, to equate loving human sexual intimacy with animal copulation is to demean the human person, and second, it has now been established beyond doubt that a significant number of animals of a variety of species engage in homosexual copulation.

In more recent years the church's natural law theory on homosexuality emphasises the complementarity of the sexes as set forth in the Creation texts. No one would deny the concept of the complementarity of the sexes suggested by these texts, but appealing to them as condemnation of loving homosexual relationships is simply forcing them to say too much.

Natural law theory cannot provide once and for all moral proscriptions derived from a primary natural law principle because, as Aquinas himself acknowledged, secondary principles derived from the primary principles will of necessity be more detailed; they will be influenced by particular circumstances and counter qualifications which will affect the conclusions drawn.

There was a dynamic quality in much of Aquinas's moral teaching that got lost somewhere along the way. Josef Fuchs engages with the question of the evolving nature of morality: he argues that the natural moral law cannot be regarded as a static quantity and reality. Man is a historical being, it follows therefore that the natural law must be understood in the dynamic sense 'as the ever new and still to be resolved problem of being a person in this world'.[4]

Homosexuality and experience
Turning from biblical strictures and natural law theories to the empirical sciences, anthropology tells us that homosexuality was one of the most ancient

AN IRISH READER IN MORAL THEOLOGY

forms of sexual relationship known to humankind. In some societies it was frowned on, in others it was seen as neutral and in yet others it was seen as the highest form of sexual relationship. In none, however, was it seen as the dominant form of sexual relationship. (This should allay fears that if homosexual relationships are recognised by the state there is a danger for society at large due to falling birth rates. Falling birth rates may have been a pertinent issue in early Christian times when the world population numbered 200 million. It now numbers 6.5 billion and is set to rise to 9.2 billion by 2050.)

Medical research as to why some people's orientation is homosexual while the majority orientation is heterosexual is inconclusive, but there is considerable evidence to suggest that while chromosomal sex is determined at fertilisation it is copper-fastened at a later stage of foetal development. In the second trimester of the pregnancy the foetus's sexual organs produce both male and female hormones. These hormones imprint the sex of the individual on the developing brain. Cells in some areas of the brain receive only female hormones and cells in other areas of the brain receive only male hormones. It is on the basis of the proportion of each of these hormones in the brain that 'a male or female neuronal circuitry is established in the brain independently of the genetic sex'.[5] Twenty years ago this was regarded as random and not attributable to genetic factors. Increasingly, as more people are open about their orientation, many families are discovering that there is a genetic dimension to sexual orientation.

The greatest arguments concerning sexual orientation arise in the mental sciences. Frequently very firm views are held as to whether orientation is decided by nature or nurture. Together with what is set down above, and having read a significant body of writing advocating each position, I find the nature argument more convincing. Whether nature or nurture is the determining factor is of major importance. If orientation is determined by nurture then it is believed it can be 'cured', changed. Efforts by evangelical religious groups and by psychologists to change a person's sexual orientation have done great damage to a gay person's sense of self and self-esteem. The debate continues and recently we heard Iris Robinson, a Northern Ireland MP at Westminster, advocating therapy to 'cure' people of a homosexual orientation 'to enable them to live in accordance with God's law'.

Personal stories of homosexual people
The personal stories of gay men and women must be listened to. In my early teaching years in the 1990s, some gay students wrote in their essays of their suffering at being homosexual in a predominantly heterosexual world and their distress at being alienated from their church. The literature confirms what was in those essays. I give two examples, each severely edited for brevity. The first is the story of a man living in Dublin in the 1980s who suffered because of estrangement from his church due to his sexual orientation:

The long years away from the sacraments, believing that homosexuality was unnatural and that any thought, word or deed which centred on it was grave sin, had been traumatic. Drink and depression were one result. Increasing isolation and inability to communicate were another.

This man subsequently got help and his whole life changed.

... The most important thing that happened to me was the realisation that homosexuality was natural for me and from God ... I had somehow vaguely begun to realise that if God loved me and (that was a shattering thought) had even made me in his own way his son, then my orientation towards homosexuality must be meaningful.[6]

The second concerns Claude, who as a young man consulted all the literature on homosexuality available to him. Many years later he wrote:

You can't name a book that I didn't consult. And in each of them the message rang out loud and clear: you're a criminal and your crime is against God, nature, society and yourself.[7]

These are old accounts. Undoubtedly some gay people still suffer in this way, but today many Catholic and mainstream Protestant gay people have either abandoned their faith altogether or have come to terms with their orientation and rely on their own consciences rather than the teaching of their church. This is not the case for many evangelical Christians in a variety of countries including Northern Ireland. A few stories of gay men as recently as 2007 (included in a Report of the Presbyterian Church Board) illustrate their pain. One writes:

People in church would crack jokes about 'Gays' and I just wanted to crawl into a hole ... I respect my minister and his teaching, but when homosexuality was mentioned in church the biblical position of calling practising homosexuality sin was outlined without ever a word of compassion or understanding for people like me who were struggling so hard and hadn't chosen to feel the way I did.

Another writes that, as a member of a church group, he had participated in an award scheme that was established to help others. He continues:

When they discovered my sexuality they asked me to leave as they didn't feel it was appropriate to have someone like me working in such an environment, i.e. in a religious setting with an influence on children.

Another contributor to the Report writes:

We drive them away from our churches, especially evangelical churches, where they assume they will be condemned. We distort their view of God by implying that he shares our hate of gay people. Our passing remarks and sweeping generalisations in favour of a hard line against gays force many silent sufferers into the misery of secret loneliness … Fear, disgust, hostility and self-righteousness are not Christian reactions.[8]

Learning from Tradition

The personal stories of gay men and women cannot be ignored. Together with a new look at the biblical material, at the natural law teaching and at evidence from the empirical sciences many may come to the conclusion that mutual, exclusive lifelong relationships should not be condemned. Rather they should be supported.

There should not be anxiety about the church reviewing its position. The Christian Church is located in history. It is a dynamic church. Throughout the centuries it has changed in response to new experiences and new contexts. How easily we gloss over the story in Acts 15, which is read in our Catholic Churches every third year. Circumcision was central to faith in the early church. It was a sign of the covenant between God and Moses. From their experience in their mission to the Gentiles, Paul and Barnabas believed it should no longer be a requirement for entry to the Christian community. They brought their concerns to James and the elders in Jerusalem who reflected on the matter and concluded that circumcision should no longer be a requirement for the admission of Gentiles to the community of faith. While circumcision is not an issue for us today the account is of relevance. We should heed its underlying thrust that the experience of those most closely engaged with an issue must be listened to and subject to reflection and prayer allowed to promote change. Without change, the church would long ago have withered away and died. Tradition is important but it is not static. It evolves in response to the lived experiences of members of the faith community reflected on in the light of the gospel.

Notes:

1. http://www.catholicnews.com/data/stories/cns/0806399.htm
2. I have drawn on the Genesis Commentaries of a number of scripture scholars, notably Claus Westermann, Walter Brueggmann and Bruce Vawter.
3. Josef Fuchs, *The Word Becomes Flesh*, Gill & Macmillan, Dublin, 1981, p 17.
4. Josef Fuchs, *Human Values and Christian Morality*, 1970, 188ff.
5. Church of England Board for Social Responsibility, *Homosexual Relationships: A Contribution to Discussion*, Church Information Office 1979, 46-48.
6. Quoted in Raphael Gallagher, *Understanding the Homosexual*, Veritas Publications 1985.
7. Peter Coleman, *Gay Christians: A Moral Dilemma*, SCM press London, 1989.
8. Presbyterian Church, Northern Ireland Board of Social Witness, *Social Issues and Resources Panel Pastoral Guidelines – Homosexuality*, March 2007.

29 Dissecting the Discourse: Homosexuality and Same-Sex Unions

Barry McMillan

(Bernard Hoose, Gerard Mannion and Julie Clague (eds), *Moral Theology for the 21st Century: Essays in Celebration of Kevin Kelly*, Edinburgh: T and T Clark, 2008, pp 133-142)

Introduction

One of the distinguishing characteristics of Kevin Kelly's published theological work is its combination of, on the one hand, theological rigour and, on the other, particular sensitivity to the concerns arising in the real, lived lives of people. His is, then, not a theology that addresses the pastoral, so much as one that emanates from the pastoral. In works such as *New Directions In Moral Theology*,[1] *New Directions In Sexual Ethics*,[2] and *Divorce and Second Marriage*,[3] amongst others, what can be seen is the result of his having looked unflinchingly at the real pain of people he has encountered in his ministry, and of his interrogation of, and challenge to, the theologies which cause, contribute to, or sustain that pain. For Kevin Kelly, the pastoral is the political, (and the political the theological). As a consequence, he is more likely to ask, as a starting point in any given instance, if it is the theology that is flawed, rather than assume that it is the people who are flawed and the theology unassailable.

This paper seeks to follow his example – by having as its focus a source of pain in the real, lived lives of people, and by interrogating and challenging the theology which causes, contributes to, and sustains that pain. The pivot around which the paper rotates is the Catholic Church's condemnation of same-sex unions. This is for two reasons. Firstly, because condemnation is the totality of what the hierarchical church offers on the matter, and such a singularly barren position constitutes a theological and pastoral privation of such degree as to demand having attention focused on it; and secondly, the theology which underpins and drives the condemnation is based on such a series of long-held, unreflected-upon stereotypes and jaundiced perceptions as to warrant the highlighting of the extent of their inadequacy.

A Moral Taxonomy of Abstraction

Magisterial and hierarchical discourse on homosexuality is characteristically conducted in terms of 'condition', 'acts', 'disorder', and 'depravity'. The abstractionism which powers such rhetoric serves an important function in that it enables the discourse to operate in a clinical, dis-interested fashion, where the attribution of descriptions such as 'objective disorder'[4] and 'strong tendency ordered toward an intrinsic moral evil'[5] can be carried out as the efficient exercise of a moral taxonomy of abstraction. Conducting discourse about 'homosexuals' or 'homosexual persons' in terms of organs and orifices and presumed sexual behaviours maintains decontextualisation and dehumanisation, and allows the discourse to continue – indeed, enables it to replicate itself and its ill-informed presuppositions and stereotypes – at a safe, self-sustaining, distance from the real, lived lives of the gay men and lesbians who are its object. Characteristically, in magisterial and hierarchical discourse on homosexuality, if there is one thing notable by the starkness of its absence, it is advertence to gay men and lesbians simply as people:[6] people – with hopes, aspirations, needs, failings, and feelings; people – who are fathers, mothers, sons and daughters, brothers, sisters, and friends; people – who seek, amidst the ordinariness of daily life, to live, love and, importantly, experience the fulfilment that committed loving relationship can bring. It seems unnecessary to point out that, in these regards, homosexuals are just the same as heterosexuals, yet this is not a conclusion one would draw were one's perspective and experience to be confined to magisterial and hierarchical Catholic teaching and writing on homosexuality and same-sex unions.

That the idea of relationship, and its correlates such as love, commitment, fidelity, trust, and devotion, are fundamentally threatening to the maintenance of the nature and content of traditional Catholic discourse on homosexuality is illustrated by the push to clarification and correction which follows upon the perception of any senior hierarch's having ceded such qualities to homosexual relating. In February 1995, in his *Note on the Teaching of the Catholic Church Concerning Homosexual People*,[7] Cardinal Basil Hume of Westminster stated:

> Love between two persons, whether of the same sex or of a different sex, is to be treasured and respected ... When two persons love, they experience in a limited manner in this world what will be their unending delight when one with God in the next. To love another is in fact to reach out to God, who shares his lovableness with the one we love. To be loved is to receive a sign or share of God's unconditional love ... To love another, whether of the same sex or of a different sex, is to have entered the area of the richest human experience.[8]

Cardinal Hume's reflection, rich and beautiful, also apparently treated manifestations of love, *qua* love, on equal terms. However, subsequent to the publishing of the *Note*, it was deemed necessary that a clarification be issued – a clarification which emphasised that, despite what had been stated here, it was to be reiterated that physical expression of homosexuality remained contrary to the teaching of the church.[9]

In a not dissimilar fashion, in November 2004, in an interview with the *Irish Independent*, Archbishop Diarmuid Martin of Dublin commented:

I recognise that there are many different kinds of caring relationships and these often create dependencies for those involved. The State may feel in justice that the rights of people in these relationships need to be protected … I have a wide range of relationships in mind. I do not exclude gay relationships but my main concern is with all caring relationships where dependencies have come into being.[10]

Some days later, a press release from the Dublin Diocese Communication Office was deemed necessary in order to offer clarification:

Nothing in Archbishop Martin's actual comments … supports the claims that he was advocating 'spousal rights' for gay persons, much less marriage or civil unions.[11]

The point to which attention is drawn here is that the notion of loving, stable relationship (and its correlates), employed in the context of homosexuality, threatens and subverts the standard dehumanising and decontextualising discourse of traditional Catholic moral theology in this area, and the stereotypes that it evokes and sustains. Traditional Catholic discourse on homosexuality trades both explicitly and implicitly on the stereotype of the promiscuous homosexual man, indulging in multiple, narcissistic, self-gratifying, hedonistically motivated, random sex acts. It is a stereotype readily conjured up by a discourse of 'tendency,'[12] 'disorder,'[13] 'lack,'[14] 'depravity,'[15] etc, but it is a stereotype which is simply exploded if the terms of the discussion should become commitment, compassion, care, loyalty, monogamy, and fidelity.

In discussing the film *Brokeback Mountain*, in 2006, *Sunday Times* columnist Andrew Sullivan observed:

Where once they were identified entirely by sex, now more and more [people] recognise that the central homosexual experience is the central heterosexual experience: love – maddening, humiliating, sustaining love.[16]

Gareth Moore, in similar vein, observes that:

[I]t is becoming clear to more and more people that homosexuals are capable of loving devotion and self-giving in their personal relationships, including their sexual relationships, and that they, as well as everybody else, should have the chance to taste the fulfilment that such relationships can bring ...[17]

In magisterial and hierarchical discourse the nature of the discussion of homosexuality as yet, however, shows no signs of such evolution. Discussion of homosexuality is almost always (explicitly or implicitly) taken to infer a discussion about, and the presumed sexual activities of, gay men. Lesbians – in a manner reminiscent of Queen Victoria's mystification regarding them and her incapacity to acknowledge them – might as well not exist. Thus, the characterisation of, and the reduction of, 'homosexuality' as referring to gay men and to

AN IRISH READER IN MORAL THEOLOGY

a focus in particular on the act of anal penetration – designated the homosexual act – remain to the fore. This combined disregard of female experience and typical presentation of gay men as so fixated upon, and so engaged in, the act of anal penetration such that it is their defining characteristic, is revealed therefore as, rather, the defining characteristic of the discourse about homosexuality. In such light, the emphases in the discourse would seem to reveal more about the concerns of those authoring the discussions than about those about whom the discussions are authored. On the evidence, and given the extent of the emphases, there seems little way of understanding the skewed nature of the discourse other than that it is primarily informed and driven by some foregrounded melding of phallocentrism, penetratocentrism, and coprophobia in the perceptions and sensibilities of those dictating the terms of the discussion. It also, moreover, declares a startling lack of awareness about, or acknowledgement of, the range of sex acts in which heterosexuals engage. As it stands, therefore, magisterial and hierarchical discourse on homosexuality declares little more than its own impoverishment and the degree of its inadequacy for addressing its subject.

Drawing attention to the foregoing is important because the unreflected-upon stereotypes and jaundiced perceptions highlighted, and the conceptual legacy they sustain, constitute the stultifying parameters of traditional Catholic discussion of homosexuality and related matters. Clearly, hedonistic and narcissistic gay men exist, but the reification of such individuals into the defining archetype of an entire diverse subsection of humanity is simply as indefensible, as unethical, and as misleading as predicating a discussion of heterosexuality on the basis that it is typified by the behaviour of hedonistic and narcissistic heterosexual men. The purpose of drawing attention to the functioning of the archetypes and stereotypes and the conceptual legacy they bequeath is to acknowledge them, and in that acknowledging to set them aside. In the purview of this paper, gay men and lesbians are not reduced to abstracted organs, orifices, or orgasms, but are considered people – three-dimensional, sexual, spiritual, relational, embodied persons, with three-dimensional, sexual, spiritual, relational, embodied lives and loves.

The Condemnation of Same-Sex Unions

There are, at this point in time, numerous and continuing examples and occurrences of magisterial and hierarchical condemnation of same-sex unions. The Congregation for the Doctrine of the Faith's June 2003 *Considerations Regarding Proposals to Give Legal Recognition to Unions Between Homosexual Persons* (issued during the prefecture of the then Cardinal Ratzinger), states:

> Legal recognition of homosexual unions or placing them on the same level as marriage would mean not only the approval of deviant behaviour, with the consequence of making it a model in present-day society, but would

also obscure basic values which belong to the common inheritance of humanity.[18]

It also instructs Catholic politicians that they have, under pain of grave sin, 'a moral duty ... to vote against it', elaborating:

When legislation in favour of the recognition of homosexual unions is proposed for the first time in a legislative assembly, the Catholic law-maker has a moral duty to express his opposition clearly and publicly and to vote against it. To vote in favour of a law so harmful to the common good is gravely immoral.

When legislation in favour of the recognition of homosexual unions is already in force, the Catholic politician must oppose it in the ways that are possible for him and make his opposition known ...[19]

In June 2005, the by-then Pope Benedict XVI, at an address in the Basilica of St John Lateran in Rome stated:

The various forms of the dissolution of matrimony today, like free unions, trial marriages and going up to pseudo-matrimonies by people of the same sex, are rather expressions of an anarchic freedom ...[20]

In January 2006, in a speech to political leaders from the Rome area, the Pope spoke against government recognition of same-sex unions, calling it a grave mistake:

It is a serious error to obscure the value and function of the legitimate family founded on matrimony, attributing to other forms of unions improper legal recognition, for which there really is no social need.[21]

Other hierarchs, in other territories, have been still harsher in their condemnation. In March 2004, Bishop Nicholas DiMarzio of Brooklyn, New York, discussed the church's position in an interview on radio station WROW-AM, condemning same-sex marriage as something that might, by extension, be compared to a legal union of people with their pets:

I will give you an example, O.K.? You want to reduce something to the absurd, which is basically rhetorical use of an image: Why can't we have marriages between people and pets? I mean, pets really love their masters and why can't we have a marriage so they could inherit their money?...There is no end to it ...[22]

In February 2006, in the Spanish diocese of Ciudad Real, Bishop Antonio Algora, in light of Spain's move to recognise same-sex unions, likened the Spanish Prime Minister Jose Luis Rodriguez Zapatero to the notoriously depraved Roman Emperor, Gaius Caligula:

If Zapatero wants to become Caligula, it's up to him, but without doubt peo-

AN IRISH READER IN MORAL THEOLOGY

ple will have to learn who Caligula was and what customs he imposed on Rome, it's as simple as that.[23]

Conspicuously, none of these statements, and most obviously the latter two, was deemed to warrant additional subsequent clarification or correction. The magisterial and hierarchical condemnation of same-sex unions is, plainly, complete and total. Regrettably, it is also tainted with wholly unnecessary disparagement and ignorance and, as is illustrated, in some instances a particularly invidious strain of splenetic hyperbole.

Such collective and forceful condemnation, however, raises key questions. In the face of such resistance to state-endorsed same-sex relationships, and in light of such intractable condemnation, what option or alternative does the hierarchical church offer to gay men and lesbians? The weight of pastoral responsibility comes to the fore at such a juncture. Condemnation, in and of itself, is insufficient. What 'good news' is to be offered to gay and lesbian people in place of the legally sanctioned and societally supported same-sex unions that they seek?

The Imperative to 'Chastity'
With all homosexual sexual activity condemned, and formal recognition of same-sex relationships actively resisted and condemned, the *Catechism of the Catholic Church* states the course of action thereby decreed for gay men and lesbians:

> Homosexual persons are called to chastity. By the virtues of self-mastery that teach them inner freedom, at times by the support of disinterested friendship, by prayer and sacramental grace, they can and should gradually and resolutely approach Christian perfection.[24]

Patently this is an uncompromising assertion that demands interrogation and evaluation. To return to an earlier consideration – might it possibly be the case that it is the theology which is flawed, rather than the people?

In the Christian tradition, chastity is traditionally understood as being manifest in a number of ways. Given that heterosexuality is presumed normative for sexual relationship, it is heterosexual experience which is traditionally cited to illustrate and illuminate these ways. The first expression of chastity is that way in which it is embraced as a vow or evangelical counsel – as a radical form of sexual continence or virginity performed as an act of Christian witness. The aspect of note for our purposes is that such chastity is personally chosen by individuals as a vocational expression of religious conviction or of their relationship with God witnessed to by the church. A second expression of chastity is as the virtue by which the married conduct their sexual lives, described by Vincent Genovesi (citing Donald Goergen) as that way which, 'moderates one's sexuality and enables a person to place genitality's intense physical pleasure at the service of love.'[25] As with the first expression, such chastity is freely embraced by those with whom it resonates as the appropriate mode of their sexual be-ing. In the third expression, traditionally delineated as the chastity of the single person, living chastely is (for the vast majority of those who embrace it) that choice to live in a non-genital fashion until such time as, a change in relational situation arising, acting genitally becomes appropriate and, in the new context, chaste in its own way.[26] Again here, a key element of the character of chastity is that it is entered into freely as the individual's chosen and elected appropriate mode of sexual be-ing.

Such outline then leads to consideration of the injunction that 'homosexual persons,' as a class of person, should 'lead a chaste life'.[27] For many, or even most, gay men and lesbians,[28] it is not the case that living without physical sexual expression is what resonates with them as the appropriate God-given living out of their relational lives. The choice of chastity, as outlined in the first and third expressions above, does not accord with their sense of who they are, and are called to be, as persons. In the core of their being they have no sense that God will find any joy in their living lives of reluctant loneliness and isolation. However, given that their sexual expression is condemned, and their relationships and unions condemned and opposed, these gay men and lesbians are denied by church teaching any principle or mode by which they might live and manifest loving, committed, faithful relationship. They seek to live sexual relationship chastely but are told that this is simply not possible for them to do.

In light of the content of church teaching on homosexuality and same-sex unions, the chastity demanded of gay men and lesbians is, consequently, categorically different from that of the assumptively heterosexual categories of the tradition, and different, especially, from the category of the chastity of the single heterosexual person – the category into which they are conventionally directed and consigned. The reasons why are threefold. Firstly, the gay and lesbian people here described are either not single, or not drawn to singleness as their mode of living and sexual be-ing. Secondly, for the vast majority of single heterosexuals who choose to live chastely, their lack of genital expression is elected, comprehended, and adopted, as a temporary mode of living, a transitional mode on the way to another, namely marriage, where physical sexual expression is both foundational and central. In contrast, given church teaching, the chastity advocated for homosexual people is not, and cannot be, a stage on the way to a sexually active chastity, but is, in contrast, a fixed, life-long state without transitional character. Fundamentally, therefore, the state being entered into by both groups cannot be said to be the same. Thirdly, and most significantly, key to the character and nature of all three of the expressions of chastity found in the tradition is the element of election. Choice, as it must be, is a fundamental element of the pursuit of virtue. Without the element of choice, what would be enacted would not be virtue but merely behaviour.

328   AN IRISH READER IN MORAL THEOLOGY

Action demanded and undertaken without freedom or without election is simply coercion. In the matter under discussion, therefore, what is being prescribed as chastity for homosexuals is not in fact chastity – this is a misnomer. What is being prescribed is, more correctly, an impelled and imposed celibacy. In real terms, gay men and lesbians are, rather, being instructed by the church to be life-long celibates. In light of the combined condemnations of homosexual sexual expression and same-sex unions, the only possibility the church presents to gay men and lesbians is an imperative to life-long imposed celibacy.

To have arrived at this point is to have arrived at the heart of the matter. Is an imposed life-long celibacy a viable concept, either theologically or pastorally? The sources best suited for enquiry into the characteristics and qualities of celibacy are the church decrees, exhortations, and encyclicals concerning or addressing Catholic priesthood.[29]

Presbyterorum Ordinis,[30] *Sacerdotalis Caelibatus*,[31] *Pastores Dabo Vobis*,[32] and *Veritatis Splendor*[33] all go to some lengths to emphasise and reiterate that celibacy is a charism gifted by God, but a charism not given to everyone, and unsustainable by purely human endeavour.

Sacerdotalis Caelibatus, §5 describes celibacy as 'a special spiritual gift,' while *Presbyterorum Ordinis*, §16 describes it as freely received 'as a grace of God'. Illustrating that the charism of celibacy is not given to everyone, not even to those who have very good reason to desire it, *Sacerdotalis Caelibatus*, §7 highlights the question of 'whether it is right to exclude from the priesthood those who, it is claimed, have been called to the ministry without having been called to lead a celibate life,' and goes on to answer in the affirmative.

According to *Sacerdotalis Caelibatus*, §62, in the embracing of celibacy, a free choice must arise within the individual, 'In virtue of such a gift … the individual is called to respond with free judgement and total dedication, adapting his own mind and outlook to the will of God who calls him.'

Veritatis Splendor, §22 highlights the unsustainability of celibacy by purely human endeavour:

> And Jesus, referring specifically to the charism of celibacy 'for the kingdom of heaven' (Mt 19:12), but stating a general rule, indicates the new and surprising possibility opened up to man by God's grace … To imitate and live out the love of Christ is not possible for man by his own strength alone. He *becomes capable of this love only by virtue of a gift received* …[34]

To sum up, Donald Cozzens, who has written extensively on the subject of celibacy, draws an unequivocal conclusion, illuminating to the argument herein. If we accept, he says:

> … that healthy, life-giving celibacy is a charism given by God to relatively few individuals, mandatory celibacy emerges as an oxymoron. Gifts that are grounded in the grace of God simply cannot be legislated.[35]

It is clear then that the charism of celibacy is described in church teaching as something which cannot be implemented by warrant of authority alone, nor just adopted at will – even by those strongly motivated to do so. In other words, gritting one's teeth and being determined to be celibate because one has been told to, not only cannot work, but is never going to work. Nevertheless, and despite its own teaching on celibacy, the magisterial and hierarchical church continues to pursue its insistence that gay men and lesbians must be denied the flourishing of long-term, committed relationship and live by a celibacy not of their choosing but which is demanded from, and imposed upon, them. It is a desiccated logic, with tragically painful consequences for countless people.

Such then, is the paradox with which the magisterial and hierarchical teaching presents gay men and lesbians: physical sexual expressiveness is denied them as deviant and disordered; the fulfilment of committed relationship is denied them as anarchic and false; the imposed celibacy as a life-long vocation demanded of them is unsustainable. In the light of such contradiction, one is left with thoughts of experts in the law who load people down with burdens and do nothing to assist them,[36] and of bread being sought but stones being offered.[37]

Conclusion

Others, elsewhere, have dealt sufficiently with the finer points of whether the fact of something's being considered sinful by the Catholic Church should warrant its not being made legal in democratic, multicultural civil societies, such that it is not here necessary for me to rehash those arguments. My own point is a simpler, and more strictly theological, one. In its proscription of same-sex sexual expression and same-sex unions, on the one hand, and its prescription of an imposed life-long celibacy, on the other, what the teaching of the church has to offer gay men and lesbians is a rock and a hard place, and, moreover, a rock and a hard place that make no apparent sense, even on the church's own theological terms. The magisterium and hierarchy are actively, determinedly working to restrict and undermine the flourishing of the committed, loving relationships of homosexual people that already exist and for which they seek social recognition and support. Such interference in, and imposition upon, the flourishing of human relationships in such a dogged and determined manner, of necessity, must require the provision of a profoundly meaningful and utterly persuasive case. Certainly, it requires a great deal more than theological contradictions and inconsistencies, and the blank inarticulacy of blanket condemnation. One is left with the conclusion that, as part of an operative theology of sexuality, the teaching of the church on same-sex sexual expression and unions is ultimately contradictory theologically and untenable pastorally.

AN IRISH READER IN MORAL THEOLOGY

Notes:

1. Kevin T. Kelly, *New Directions In Moral Theology: The Challenge Of Being Human*, London: Geoffrey Chapman, 1992.

2. Kevin T. Kelly, *New Directions In Sexual Ethics: Moral Theology and the Challenge of AIDS*, London: Geoffrey Chapman, 1998.

3. Kevin T. Kelly, *Divorce and Second Marriage: Facing The Challenge* (New and Expanded Edition), London: Geoffrey Chapman, 1997.

4. Congregation for the Doctrine of the Faith, *Homosexualitatis Problema*, October 1986, §3.

5. Ibid.

6. Even a document entitled in the manner of the New Zealand Catholic Bishops' Conference's *People In Homosexual Relationships* (2000), by its halfway point descends into the rhetoric of 'condition' and of being 'resigned' to an 'inclination'. Though not beyond criticism either, the United States Conference of Catholic Bishops' pastoral message *Always Our Children: A Pastoral Message To Parents Of Homosexual Children And Suggestions For Pastoral Ministers* (1997), in its distinctive approach, represents something of an exception that proves the general rule outlined here.

7. This document was an expansion of an earlier document, published in 1993, entitled, *Some Observations on the Teaching of the Catholic Church Concerning Homosexual People*.

8. Basil Hume, *Note on the Teaching of the Catholic Church Concerning Homosexual People*, February 1995, §§9/10, in *Origins*, April 27 1995, Vol 24, No 45, pp 765-769.

9. The amended text of the 1995 document, dated April 1997, is available on the website of the Catholic Bishops' Conference of England and Wales at: http://www.catholic-church.org.uk/citizenship/mfl/homosexuality/hs970400.htm. Accessed February 8th 2007.

10. David Quinn, 'Archbishop Backs Legal Rights for Gay Couples', *Irish Independent*, 16 November 2004.

11. Dublin Diocese Communication Office, 'Press Release: Archbishop Martin's Comment on Gay Marriage', 22 November 2004.

12. Congregation for the Doctrine of the Faith, *Persona Humana*, December 1975, §8.

13. *Homosexualitatis Problema*, §3.

14. *Persona Humana*, §8.

15. *Catechism of the Catholic Church*, Dublin: Veritas, 1994, §2357.

16. Andrew Sullivan, 'Gay Cowboys Embraced by Redneck Country', *The Sunday Times*, 26 February 2006.

17. Gareth Moore, 'Sex, Sexuality and Relationships', In Bernard Hoose, (ed), *Christian Ethics: An Introduction*, London: Cassell, 1998, p 224.

18. Congregation for the Doctrine of the Faith, *Considerations Regarding Proposals to Give Legal Recognition to Unions Between Homosexual Persons*, July 2003, §11.

19. Ibid, §10.

20. Benedict XVI, *Address of His Holiness Benedict XVI to the Participants in the Ecclesial Diocesan Convention Of Rome*, 6 June 2005.

21. Benedict XVI, *Address of His Holiness Benedict XVI to Members Of The Regional Board Of Lazio, the Municipal Corporation Of Rome and the Province of Rome*, 12 January 2006.

22. Thomas J. Lueck, 'Bishops Assail Gay Marriages as a Threat', *The New York Times*, 10 March 2004.

23. 'El Obispo de Ciudad Real Compara a Zapatero con Cal gula por Impulsar el Mat-

rimonio Gay', *El Pais*, 14 February 2006. 'Si Zapatero vuelve a ser el Cal gula de la época del siglo II, allá él. Sin duda alguna, la gente tendrá que aprender quién era Cal gula y las costumbres que impuso en Roma, as de sencillo.'

24. *Catechism of the Catholic Church*, §2359.

25. Vincent J. Genovesi, 'Sexuality', in Joseph A. Komonchak, Mary Collins, Dermot A. Lane, (eds), *The New Dictionary of Theology*, Dublin: Gill and Macmillan, 1990, p 953. Genovesi is citing Donald Goergen, *The Sexual Celibate*, New York: Seabury Press, 1974.

26. There will, of course, be those heterosexuals for whom subsequent committed sexual relationship simply does not occur, but the point remains that the choice to be, or remain, chaste is a free one, with an ongoing potential openness to transitioning to the sexually active chastity of the second expression outlined.

27. *Homosexualitatis Problema*, §13.

28. It is acknowledged that it might be the case that any individual gay man or lesbian might, of course, choose to pursue vowed or consecrated chastity, or to live singly and non-genitally.

29. The content of the summary that follows is reiterated and underpinned in canons 247 and 277 of the *Code of Canon Law*.

30. Second Vatican Council, *Presbyterorum Ordinis*, December 1965.

31. Paul VI, *Sacerdotalis Caelibatus*, June 1967.

32. John Paul II, *Pastores Dabo Vobis*, March 1992.

33. John Paul II, *Veritatis Splendor*, August 1993.

34. Emphasis in the original.

35. Donald Cozzens, *Freeing Celibacy*, Collegeville, MN: Liturgical Press, 2006, p 33.

36. Luke 11:46

37. Matthew 7:9.

30   Moral Argument and the Recognition of Same-Sex Partnerships

Oran Doyle

(William Binchy and Oran Doyle (eds), *Committed Relationships and the Law*, Dublin: Four Courts Press, 2007, pp 124-140, 151-158 [extracts])

Introduction

Writing in the US context, Carlos Ball attempts to justify the use of moral argument by a gay rights advocate. He begins by noting how such arguments have traditionally been eschewed by gay rights advocates:

> For most of the history of the gay rights movement in the United States, it has been possible and even advisable for its supporters to avoid engaging questions of morality directly. Arguments based on notions of morality have been used primarily by opponents of gay rights to justify the differential treatment by society of lesbians and gay men. It is the purported immorality of a gay and lesbian sexuality, for example, that justifies in the minds of some denying same-gender couples the right to marry ... In response to these and other familiar arguments raised by opponents of gay rights about the immorality of gay and lesbian sexuality and relationships, most supporters of gay rights (including political activists and academics) prefer to sidestep moral arguments altogether and instead rely on what are taken to be morally neutral (and largely liberal) arguments based on considerations of privacy, equality and tolerance.[1]

Ball refers to this avoidance of moral arguments as 'moral bracketing' – a 'strict separation of moral, philosophical, and religious views ... from considerations of justice'.[2] This moral bracketing, sometimes phrased as a right to privacy in matters of sexual intimacy, well served the political objective of the decriminalisation of homosexual activity.[3] Ball argues, however, that most of the controversies over homosexuality are moral controversies. Correctly, in my view, he argues that 'even the paradigmatic right to privacy in matters of sexual intimacy ... is most convincingly grounded on a moral conception of the potential for human flourishing that inheres in the exercise of self-determination or autonomy'.[4] Claims that the State should provide recognition for same-sex partnerships necessarily require some argument as to why such recognition should be provided: these are moral arguments.[5] Intellectual honesty and political expediency combine: gay rights advocates must rely on moral arguments.

Now I do not conceive of myself as a gay rights advocate, although perhaps that is (part of) what I am. More particularly, my purpose in this paper is not to construct the most convincing moral argument in support of the recognition

333

of same-sex partnerships. Rather my purpose is to examine a number of moral arguments advanced in support of and against such recognition. My selection of arguments is, as will quickly become apparent, far from exhaustive. I focus on natural law arguments against partnership recognition and egalitarian arguments in favour of recognition. My basis for focusing on natural law arguments is my intuition that arguments against the recognition of same-sex partnerships are at root moral arguments that rely on some natural law type account of human sexuality. My basis for focusing on egalitarian arguments is my intuition that equality provides the most compelling basis on which to argue for partnership recognition. Clearly my argument is incomplete, but my hope is to make some contribution to those aspects of this debate that I have chosen, somewhat arbitrarily, to focus on. Within these limits, the purpose of this paper is ultimately two-fold: first, to assess whether some recognition of same-sex partnerships is morally permissible or required; secondly and if so, to assess which form of recognition best reflects the moral argument that justified recognition in the first instance.

Two points that generally cause difficulty must be clarified. First, as noted above, I agree with Ball's contention that rights to privacy, whereby the state allows to the individual a zone of personal autonomy within which to make her own choices, are themselves moral propositions. Notwithstanding that the substance of the right is the non-imposition of the state's moral code within that zone of autonomy, the belief that the state should not impose its moral code is itself a moral belief. It is a moral belief about the importance of individual autonomy in certain areas. Some advocates of such a right might agree with this characterisation; others might not. For the purposes of this paper, whether one agrees with the characterisation or not is irrelevant. Privacy rights rest on moral beliefs about the appropriate limits on the actions of the state.

Secondly, the word 'moral' is itself, in a very literal way, ambiguous. This becomes clear if one considers how the word 'moral' is the opposite of two other words: 'amoral' and 'immoral'. 'Amoral' is essentially a descriptive word, connoting (although this meaning may have been hijacked) 'having nothing to do with issues of right or wrong'. 'Immoral' is an evaluative word, connoting 'against a code of what constitutes right or wrong'. Thus the word 'moral' itself must have two meanings: one descriptive, one evaluative. Used in the descriptive sense, a 'moral' proposition is one that purports to provide a reason for behaving or not behaving in a particular way. Used in the evaluative sense, a 'moral' proposition is one that truly does provide a reason for behaving or not behaving in a particular way. The purpose of this essay is to assess moral (in the descriptive sense) arguments in order to identify the moral (in the evaluative sense) position on the recognition of same-sex partnerships.

I shall begin with an examination of Finnis's natural law theory and his particular application of that to the question of partnership recognition. Although there are many variants of natural law theory, I focus on Finnis for the reason that he advances a natural law argument that unequivocally rejects the civil recognition of same-sex partnerships. If I can show Finnis's argument to be unfounded, my case is stronger than if I had undermined a natural law theory that was more moderate in its approach. Having considered Finnis's argument, I shall consider egalitarian arguments in favour of partnership recognition. In doing so, my primary concern (in this paper) is to defend egalitarian arguments against the general claim that there are no valid egalitarian arguments. I shall conclude with an assessment, in the light of egalitarian arguments, of various forms of partnership recognition currently under discussion.

THE NATURAL LAW ARGUMENT

Outline of the natural law argument against partnership recognition
Finnis articulates a natural law argument against the recognition of same-sex partnerships.[6] In outline, this argument is as follows: marriage (ie the presumptively procreative union of a man and a woman) is a basic good; it is impermissible to intend to destroy, damage, impede or violate any basic human good or to prefer an illusory instantiation of a basic human good to a real instantiation of that or some other human good; accordingly, the state should not recognise and thus legitimise same-sex partnerships, as these partnerships are illusory representations of the basic good of marriage and thus inimical to that basic good. In order to understand and evaluate this argument, it is necessary to understand the broad outlines of Finnis's natural law argumentation.

Finnis's theory of natural law
Finnis asserts that there are seven basic values or goods: life, knowledge, play, aesthetic experience, sociability (friendship), practical reasonableness and religion. These goods are not themselves moral propositions, but are rather basic facts about human nature on which moral argument is based. In establishing that something is a basic good or value, Finnis seems to place most importance on two discrete observations. The first is the observation of an inclination; the second is the observation of the grasp of value. Finnis considers these in the context of knowledge. He notes that 'curiosity' is a name for the inclination that we have when, just for the sake of knowing, we want to find out about something.[7] However, there is more to this than just inclination for, on reflection, one can perceive that there is a good in this inclination:

> Commonly one's interest in knowledge, in getting to the truth of the matter, is not bounded by the particular questions that first aroused one's desire to find out. So readily that one notices the transition only by an effort of reflection, it becomes clear that knowledge is a good thing to have (and not merely for its utility), without restriction to the subject-matters that up to now have aroused one's curiosity.[8]

Thus, basic goods are identified by both inclination and grasp of value. It is not sufficient that there be a common urge to do a particular thing, there must also be a sense of the worthwhileness of doing that thing. Finnis undertakes a similar, although abbreviated exercise, in respect of the other basic goods.

Three points must, in particular, be noted about the basic goods. First, they are self-evident. Finnis asserts, for instance, that the good of knowledge is 'self-evident, obvious'; it cannot be demonstrated, but equally it needs no demonstration. This does not mean, however, that it is self-evident to everyone:

> On the contrary, the value of truth becomes obvious only to one who has experienced the urge to question, who has grasped the connection between question and answer, who understands that knowledge is constituted by correct answers to particular questions, and who is aware of the possibility of further questions and of other questioners who like himself could enjoy the advantage of attaining correct answers.[9]

This self-evidence is a proposition of rationality, not psychology. The soundness of the assertion that knowledge is a self-evident good is not addressed by any inquiry into the physical, biological or psychological conditions under which a person might make such an assertion. The issue of value is not addressed by such factual inquiries. Conversely, one should not commit the naturalistic fallacy and attempt to derive value from purely factual observations:

> [I]f one is to go beyond the felt urge of curiosity to an understanding grasp of the value of knowledge, one certainly must know at least the fact that questions can be answered. Moreover, one certainly will be assisted if one also knows such facts as that answers tend to hang together in systems that tend to be illuminating over as wide a range as the data which simulate one's questions. But one who, thus knowing the possibility of attaining truth, is enable thereby to grasp the value of that possible object and attainment is not inferring the value from the possibility. No such inference is possible. No value can be deduced or otherwise inferred from a fact or set of facts.[10]

Similarly one cannot infer the value of knowledge from the mere fact that all people desire to know, nor from the mere fact that all people not only desire to know but also affirm the value of knowledge. Conversely, the mere fact that not all people desire to know or that not all people affirm the value of knowledge is not sufficient ground for denying the self-evident good of knowledge. The self-evidence of the goodness of knowledge boils down to the following: it can be denied, for it is not a principle of logic conformity to which is essential if one is to mean anything, but to deny it is 'to disqualify oneself from the pursuit of knowledge'; it is as 'straightforwardly unreasonable as anything can be'.[11]

The second point to be noted about basic goods is that they are basic. That is, they are not instrumental to other goods; they are irreducible. Thus, when

AN IRISH READER IN MORAL THEOLOGY

Finnis speaks of knowledge, he is more precisely speaking about speculative knowledge. That is, he speaks of knowledge for its own sake rather than knowledge as instrumental to some other end, such as money-saving, personal advancement or, indeed, other goods such as environmental protection or the preservation of life. This is not to say that knowledge for other ends is not a good, but simply that it is not an instantiation of knowledge as a basic good.

The third point to be noted about basic goods is that they are not moral propositions. They do not of themselves and in the abstract possess moral force; they do not of themselves and in the abstract direct that certain things should be done or not done, allowed or disallowed. It is through the good of practical reasonableness that the basic goods are brought to bear on particular situations. This represents the (moral) natural law method of working out the natural law from the first (pre-moral) principles of natural law.

In working out such a stance, Finnis identifies a number of basic requirements of practical reasonableness. I propose only to outline these here in order to provide a rough sense of the character of moral reasoning, as envisaged by Finnis. First, one should adopt a rational and coherent plan of life: this requires one to view one's life as a whole.[12] Secondly, one should adopt no arbitrary preference amongst the basic values. Although any coherent plan of life requires one to concentrate on one or some of the basic goods, such a commitment is rational only if it is made on the basis of one's assessment of one's capacities, circumstances and tastes. It would be unreasonable to concentrate one's efforts in this way as a result of a devaluation of one of the basic goods.[13] Thirdly, one should not have arbitrary preferences among persons. Fourthly and fifthly, one must maintain a certain detachment from one's projects (such that one would not consider one's life as devoid of meaning if one project were to fail) and yet, at the same time, one should be committed to one's projects, having undertaken them. Sixthly, the consequences of particular courses of actions have a certain, though limited, relevance for the morality of choosing one course of action over another; efficiency can be taken into account to a limited extent.

Seventhly – and of particular importance for Finnis's later arguments in relation to the recognition of same-sex partnerships – 'One should not choose to do any act which *of itself does nothing but* damage or impede a realisation or participation of any one or more of the basic forms of human good.'[14] This injunction applies, Finnis argues, because the only reason for doing such an act would be that its good consequences outweighed the damage done in and through the act itself. Such reasoning involves a necessarily arbitrary and delusive, and hence inappropriate, consequentialist weighing. As the goods are equally basic and do not share any common essence, they are incommensurable: they cannot be weighed against each other in the manner required by consequentialist logic.

There is a distinction, Finnis argues, between acts which promote one basic good but indirectly damage another basic good and acts which do nothing but damage basic goods.[15] The latter are prohibited; the former may be permitted:

> [T]o indirectly damage any basic good (by choosing an act that directly and immediately promotes either that basic good in some other aspect or participation, or some other basic good or goods) is obviously quite different, rationally and thus morally, from directly and immediately damaging a basic good in some aspect or participation by choosing an act which in and of itself simply (or, we should now add, primarily) damages that good in some aspect or participation but which indirectly, via the mediation of expected consequences, is to promote either that good in some other aspect or participation, or some other basic good(s).[16]

Clearly, the key problem here is how to differentiate between those acts which indirectly damage a basic good and those acts which directly damage a basic goods. Finnis describes this as a problem of individuating acts. If an act is individuated, it follows that its consequences are also individuated acts. If an act is not individuated, it follows that its consequences can be seen as part of the one act, and hence as indirect effects. We decide whether an act is individuated by reference to 'those factors which we gesture towards with the word "intention"':

> Fundamentally, a human act is a that-which-is-decided-upon (or -chosen) and its primary proper description is as what-is-chosen. A human action, to be humanly regarded, is to be characterised in the way it was characterised in the conclusion to the relevant train of practical reasoning of the man who chose to do it. On the other hand, the world with its material (including our bodily selves) and its structures of physical and psycho-physical causality is not indefinitely malleable by human intention. The man who is deciding what to do cannot reasonably shut his eyes to the causal structure of his project; he cannot characterise his plans *ad lib*.[17]

Eighthly, one must favour and foster the common good of one's community. Ninthly and finally, one must follow one's own conscience: thus if one decides to do what one believes is wrong, one breaches a requirement of practical reasonableness.

For Finnis, morality is the product of these requirements. Each of these requirements provides a reason for acting or not acting in a particular way. Put together, they constitute morality. Therefore, it is not permissible to rely on one of the requirements, say efficiency, to the expense of the others. Morally sound judgements can only be reached if all the requirements of practical reason are taken into account.

Finnis and the criminalisation of same-sex activity
Finnis identifies a particular position on homosexuality (at the time described as the 'modern [European] position',[18] although this description might now

AN IRISH READER IN MORAL THEOLOGY

require change) whereby criminalisation of homosexual activity or conduct is considered wrong, and unreasonable discrimination by public bodies against homosexuals is prohibited. However, the other side of this position is that it does not outlaw discrimination by private persons against homosexuals and it discourages the promotion of forms of life which both encourage homosexual activity and present it as a valid or acceptable alternative to committed hetero-sexual union. Although this position might at first appear contradictory as to the moral character of homosexual activity, it is explicable – in Finnis's view – by reference to the concept of subsidiarity. Thus the position identified by Finnis unequivocally views homosexual activity as morally wrong, but also considers that 'the state's proper responsibility for upholding true worth (morality) is a responsibility *subsidiary* (auxiliary) to the *primary* responsibility of parents and non-political voluntary associations'.[19] Under this account, the state does not assume a directly parental disciplinary role in relation to consenting adults. On the basis of this, a distinction is drawn between supervising the truly private conduct of adults and supervising the public realm. The public realm is particularly important as it is there that the young are educated and assisted in avoiding bad forms of life.[20] The supervision of that public realm is an important "part of the state's justification for claiming legitimately the loyalty of its decent citizens'.[21]

Thus Finnis advances an avowedly moral argument against the recognition of same-sex partnerships that does not extend to the criminalisation of same-sex activity or conduct. This argument, although based on sophisticated moral reasoning, employs as a determining criterion the public/private distinction. As such, it is not far removed from liberal arguments for privacy and individual autonomy, although it adopts a position on what constitutes a morally acceptable exercise of individual autonomy that would probably find little favour with most who classify themselves as liberals. For present purposes, however, it suffices to note that Finnis's argument against the recognition of same-sex partnerships, although based to a certain extent on the immorality of same-sex conduct, does not extend to the criminalisation of such conduct. Although this point is important in itself, it also demonstrates that Finnis's argument cannot plausibly be criticised on the grounds that it represents an unwarranted interference with personal liberty.

Same-sex partnerships, marriages and basic goods
Imagine an unsophisticated political debate about homosexuality and, in particular, about the recognition of same-sex partnerships. An unsophisticated supporter of such recognition might rely on hazy propositions of equality and personal freedom. An unsophisticated opponent of recognition might adopt a position against homosexual activity on the basis of its unnatural (by which is meant non-procreative) characteristics. On the basis of this, she argues, the state

should prohibit such activity or, at the very least, deny recognition to relationships in which such activity (we assume) will take place. Our supporter of such recognition responds by arguing that non-procreation is also a feature of much heterosexual activity (even in the absence of contraception) and of many heterosexual marriages, at least for certain periods, whether through choice or capacity. Accordingly, she concludes, the non-procreative characteristic of same-sex activity does not justify a position criminalising same-sex activity or denying the recognition of same-sex partnerships. Our opponent of recognition, not to be outdone, responds that marriage is not just about procreation, however; it is also about care and companionship. Aha, our supporter concludes, same-sex partners can also demonstrate care and companionship: if that is the basis for recognition of heterosexual marriage, we should also recognise same-sex partnerships.

This is in many ways an unsatisfactory argument. The supporter of recognition fails to specify or justify the appropriate default position for the debate: recognition or non recognition? In particular, the positive arguments in favour of such recognition are not clearly spelt out. The opponent of recognition, on the other hand, probably commits the naturalistic fallacy in deriving moral propositions from observations of biological facts. Finnis, in particular, would make no such claim. As already discussed, his moral argumentation consists of the exercise of practical reason in choosing to act – or not act – in order to promote one of the basic goods. For these reasons, I am not identifying the position of any theorist with the arguments put forward by my imagined supporter and opponent of recognition. However, their discussion does highlight a feature in this debate. A natural law theorist, if she is to justify non-recognition of same-sex partnerships at the same time as recognition, in the form of marriage or otherwise, of heterosexual partnerships, cannot rely simply on the basic good of life (or procreation) as that would seem to preclude recognition of some marriages – it is an under-inclusive rationale. However, if she relies on the basic good of friendship, it would seem to include recognition of same-sex partnerships – it is an over-inclusive rationale. If the recognition of marriage is justified in terms of either of these basic goods (in other words, if marriage is viewed as a secondary good, instrumental to one or more basic goods), the moral position against the recognition of same-sex partnerships and, indeed, against same-sex activity is undermined.

I have set out this argument in some detail because I see Finnis's argument against the recognition of same-sex partnerships as being a response to it, although he does not state it as explicitly as I have done. For Finnis articulates a position against the recognition of same-sex partnerships that is based on none of the basic, self-evident goods identified in *Natural Law and Natural Rights* but rather on the new basic good of marriage:

[I]n sterile and fertile marriages alike, the communion, companionship, *societas* and *amicitia* of the spouses – their being married – *is* the very good of marriage, and is an intrinsic, basic human good, not merely instrumental to any other good. And this communion of married life, this integral amalgamation of the lives of the two persons … has as its intrinsic elements, as essential *parts* of one and the same good, the goods and ends to which the theological tradition, following Augustine, for a long time subordinated that communion … Parenthood and children and family are the intrinsic fulfilment of a communion which, because it is not merely instrumental, can exist and fulfil the spouses even if procreation happens to be impossible for them.[22]

Thus marriage is itself a basic good; it is – contrary to earlier church teaching – neither subordinate nor instrumental to other goods, such as life (procreation) or friendship. Such goods are intrinsic and essential parts of marriage, but marriage is itself a primary good. By this stage, it should be obvious that, marriage being a basic good, other forms of relationship will be deemed morally dubious. Nevertheless, it is worth considering Finnis's argument in some detail as it throws light on a number of other issues.

Procreation and friendship are essential elements of marriage: they make marriage what it is. But marriage itself is a basic good: the sexual union of wife and husband within marriage makes them one reality and allows them experience their real common good, their marriage. Outside of marriage, sexual union does not allow for the experience of such common good, because there is no common good being served by the union. This, for Finnis, is particularly the case in respect of the sexual acts of same-sex partners:

[T]hose acts cannot express or do more than is expressed or done if two strangers engage in such activity to give each other pleasure, or a prostitute pleasures a client to give him pleasure in return for money, or (say) a man masturbates to give himself pleasure and a fantasy of more human relationships after a gruelling day on the assembly line … [T]here is no important distinction in essential moral worthiness between solitary masturbation, being sodimised as a prostitute, and being sodimised for the pleasure of it.[23]

Sexual acts can only be 'unitive' in their significance if they are marital. This is not a licence for non-procreative sexual acts within marriage, however, as owing to the good of marriage having two essential elements (procreation and friendship) sexual acts are not marital unless they are acts both of friendship and of procreative significance. 'Procreative significance' does not mean being capable of generating or intended to generate but rather means being acts of the reproductive kind. Acts of procreative significance would thus, presumably, include unprotected vaginal intercourse between a woman and a man (even if one or both parties is sterile), but not (artificially?) protected vaginal intercourse or any other types of intercourse.

Finnis's assertions here must be understood in their proper context. He relies on no empirical, anecdotal nor, presumably, experiential basis for his comments about the characteristics of same-sex activity. His assertions, I think, do not purport to be factual descriptions in that sense. This is not to say, however, that his assertions are counter-factual. Rather, his assertions are evaluative descriptions of a world in which marriage is a basic good. The described characteristics of homosexual activity cannot be taken as independent support for his moral views, let alone for his assertion that marriage is a self-evident good. If nothing else, this would infringe Finnis's own injunction against reliance on the naturalistic fallacy. Rather, the described characteristics are incidents of a reality in which marriage is a self-evident good. Although both the status of marriage as a self-evident good and the characteristics of homosexual activity are important parts of Finnis's overall moral position, only the former is of argumentative significance, as it is the former that determines the latter. Finnis's argument, that is, turns on the status of marriage as a self-evident good and not (directly at any rate) on his described characteristics of homosexual activity.

Communal self-delusion and false instantiation of basic human goods

The final step in Finnis's argument is that non-marital sexual unions represent illusory instantiations of a basic human good. It is a moral principle, as seen earlier, that one may never intend to destroy, damage, impede, or violate any basic human good, or prefer an illusory instantiation of a basic human good to a real instantiation of that or some other human good. It is this proposition that transforms same-sex partnerships into something specifically and radically immoral, something that no state, attempting to achieve the common good of its citizens, should countenance. Same-sex partnerships are not simply inimical to those who take part in them (as private same-sex activity might arguably be):

> [The deliberate genital coupling of persons of the same sex] treats human sexual capacities in a way which is deeply hostile to the self-understanding of those members of the community who are willing to commit themselves to real marriage in the understanding that its sexual joys are not mere instruments or accompaniments to, or mere compensations for the accomplishment of marriage's responsibilities, but rather enable the spouses to actualise and experience their intelligent commitment to share in those responsibilities, in that genuine self-giving.[24]

In Finnis's view, one can only view homosexual acts as acceptable if one views sexual capacities, organs and acts as instruments for gratifying the individual selves who have them. In his view, such an acceptance is itself inimical to marriages:

> A political community which judges that the stability and protective and educative generosity of family life is of fundamental importance to that community's present and future can rightly judge that it has a compelling

interest in denying that homosexual conduct – a 'gay lifestyle' – is a valid, humanly acceptable choice and form of life, and in doing whatever it properly can, as a community with uniquely wide but still subsidiary functions, to discourage such conduct.[25]

Problem with Finnis's argument: marriage as a self-evident good
As noted above, in 1980 Finnis identified only seven self-evident goods, not including marriage. Although he noted that the list was not exhaustive, he did make a number of important methodological points about any tendency to recognise further self-evident basic goods. These methodological points provide good reasons not to identify marriage as a basic, self-evident good and thus require further consideration.

Finnis recognises that, as well as the seven self-evident basic goods, there are countless objectives and forms of good. But he suggests:

> [T]hese other objectives and forms of good will be found, on analysis, to be ways or combinations of ways of pursuing (not always sensibly) and realising (not always successfully) one of the seven basic forms of good, or *some combination of them*.[26]

He accepts that there might be more than seven self-evident basic goods and that people might reasonably not accept his list, still less his nomenclature – the words 'life', 'knowledge' and so on simply gesture 'towards categories of human purpose that are each, though unified, nevertheless multi-faceted'.[27] But again he makes the point:

> Still, it seems to me that those seven purposes are all of the basic purposes of human action, and that any other purpose which you or I might recognise and pursue will turn out to represent, or be constituted of, some aspect(s) of some or all of them.[28]

Thus Finnis strongly, although not dogmatically, maintains that there are only seven self-evident basic goods. He further suggests that any inclination to identify other forms of good as further self-evident basic goods is probably mistaken for one of two reasons. Either the new form of good is a means to achieving a basic self-evident good. Or the new form of good is a representation or combination of a number of basic self-evident goods. Neither of these propositions means that the new form of good is no longer good nor worth pursuing. Rather, their import is simply that the good should not be perceived as a basic, self-evident good in its own right.

Each of these injunctions seems apposite to Finnis's subsequent identification of marriage as a basic, self-evident good. His reasoning on this, as set out above, is that marriage is a good comprised of both life and friendship. However, applying Finnis's own reasoning from *Natural Law and Natural Rights*, one should probably reject that as a basis for the assertion of marriage as a self-evident good. That assertion is either the mistaken elevation of an instrumental good into a basic good or the mistaken characterisation of a combination of two goods as a unitive basic good. These contentions are born out by Finnis's own comments about marriage in *Natural Law and Natural Rights*.

As noted above, the first requirement of basic reasonableness is to have a coherent life plan. In analysing this requirement, Finnis notes a number of projects which one might adopt in order to achieve particular basic goods:

> Commitment to the practice of medicine (for the sake of human life), or to scholarship (for the sake of truth), or to any profession, or to a marriage (for the sake of friendship and children) ... all require both direction and control of impulses, and the undertaking of specific projects.[29]

I am taking this passage out of context. Nevertheless, it demonstrates Finnis's understanding, in *Natural Law and Natural Rights*, that marriage is in some way instrumental to the goods of friendship and children (life/procreation) in much the same way as the practice of medicine is in some way instrumental to the good of life, and scholarship is instrumental to the good of knowledge. Such an understanding is consistent with Finnis's overall methodology, set out above, but not with his argument as set out in 'Law, Morality and Sexual Orientation'.

Finnis's argument in 'Law, Morality and Sexual Orientation' is also problematic with regard to other aspects of his general theory of natural law. In *Natural Law and Natural Rights*, he makes a number of other general points about the basic goods:

> More important than the precise number and description of these values is the sense in which each is basic. First, each is equally self-evidently a form of good. Secondly, none can be analytically reduced to being merely an aspect of any of the others, or to being merely instrumental in the pursuit of any of the others. Thirdly, each one, when we focus on it, can reasonably be regarded as the most important. Hence there is no objective hierarchy amongst them.[30]

The second point in the above paragraph goes a little further than the point already made: basic goods are not instrumental or derivative in any sense, not even to or of other basic goods. The third point in the above paragraph is that there is no objective hierarchy between the goods. Finnis's argument against the recognition of same-sex partnerships, principally the assertion that there are eight basic goods including life, friendship and marriage, is profoundly problematic in the light of these requirements of natural law theory. The problem with Finnis's argument against the recognition of same-sex partnerships, apart from its treatment of marriage as a basic good comprised of other basic goods, is that it necessarily introduces a ranking of basic goods. In his characterisation of same-sex partnerships as inimical to the good of marriage, notwith-

AN IRISH READER IN MORAL THEOLOGY

standing the ignored extent to which they are instrumental to the basic good of friendship, Finnis effectively ranks the good of marriage above that of friendship. Finnis might respond, however, that this arises not because of a preference for marriage over friendship, as basic goods, but rather because of the fact that marriage is a basic good whereas same-sex partnerships are, at best, only instrumental to a basic good.

This response, however, points up the crux of the problem. It would perhaps be permissible to rank marriage – as an instrument – above same-sex partnerships as the former promotes two basic values (life and friendship), whereas the latter promotes only one (friendship).[31] However, when the instrument of marriage is characterised as a basic good, against all the methodological injunctions set out in *Natural Law and Natural Rights*, any such ranking becomes an implicit ranking of the goods themselves. This becomes clear if one considers something that might be instrumental to marriage, such as tax breaks for married couples. If marriage is a self-evident good, such an instrument could plausibly be seen as a secondary good. However, that which is instrumental to friendship, such as same-sex partnerships, is deemed illegitimate. This implies a ranking of the good of marriage over the good of friendship.

A response to this argument is to maintain that the basic goods are not being ranked. Instead, this response argues, same-sex partnerships are bad not because marriage is more important than friendship but rather because same-sex partnerships harm marriage whereas tax breaks for married couples do not damage any basic good. However, it is not the case that natural law theory prohibits all acts that harm basic goods. As noted earlier, natural law theory prohibits acts that are intended to do nothing but harm to a basic good. When one act, objectively speaking, both serves one basic good and damages another basic good, one determines its legitimacy by focusing on intention. This emerges from Finnis's discussion of the doctrine of indirect effect. As noted above, Finnis argues that it is permissible indirectly to damage a basic good in one's pursuit of another basic good, but it is impermissible directly to damage a basic good. This substantive distinction imposes a methodological need to distinguish between individuated and non-individuated acts. One does this through reference to the intention with which the acts are performed:

> Fundamentally, a human act is a that-which-is-decided-upon (or -chosen) and its primary proper description is as what-is-chosen. A human action, to be humanly regarded, is to be characterised in the way it was characterised in the conclusion to the relevant train of practical reasoning of the man who chose to do it. On the other hand, the world with its material (including our bodily selves) and its structures of physical and psycho-physical causality is not indefinitely malleable by human intention. The man who is deciding what to do cannot reasonably shut his eyes to the causal structure of his project; he cannot characterise his plans *ad lib*.[32]

On this basis, it is difficult to see how choosing a same-sex partnership can be morally unacceptable. Even if marriage is a basic good, and even if that basic good is damaged by same-sex partnerships, such damage is inflicted indirectly. That is, such damage is an incidental side-effect of the person's efforts to pursue the good of friendship. This respects the person's own characterisation of her action, the reason why she has acted in this way. Perhaps Finnis could avoid this problem, and thus maintain his position against the recognition of same-sex partnerships, by characterising marriage as a more important good than friendship, but such a move is wholly incompatible with his basic position that there is no hierarchy as between the basic goods. In short, Finnis has provided no basis on which a position against the recognition of same-sex partnerships can be reconciled with his general natural law theory.

Based on these observations, one can develop two responses to Finnis's overall argument against the recognition of same-sex partnerships. The first, which is of limited use and value, amounts to little more than a personalised attack on Finnis himself. This response would argue that the tension between *Natural Law and Natural Rights* and 'Law, Morality and Sexual Orientation' illustrates that, for Finnis, the category of supposedly basic and self-evident goods is infinitely expandable to meet the demands of whatever moral conclusion is desired in a particular context. This argument is, I think, of limited value as it seeks to draw inferences about Finnis's state of mind from his writings. Although this might be a worthwhile focus of inquiry for a psychologist or a biographer, it is of little assistance to the working out of moral justifications. For even if the argument is sound – and I am unsure as to whether it is – it provides no direct response to the argument actually advanced in 'Law, Morality and Sexual Orientation'. Finnis and, *a fortiori*, anyone else would still be entitled to stand over that argument. For these reasons, this response is argumentatively useless for those concerned to rebut the moral propositions advanced by Finnis in 'Law, Morality and Sexual Orientation'.

The second and, I think, stronger argument is that *Natural Law and Natural Rights* provides compelling reasons, from natural law theory itself, as to why the natural law argument against the recognition of same-sex partnerships is deeply flawed. That argument, at least as advanced by Finnis, fundamentally relies on the characterisation of marriage as a basic, self-evident good. For it is only that characterisation that allows same-sex partnerships to be viewed as an illusory (and therefore damaging) instantiation of a basic good, rather than as an instrument to promote another basic good, that of friendship. This characterisation of marriage as a basic good, however, constitutes unsound natural law theorising in that it either mistakes an instrument for a basic good or it creates a new basic good out of a combination of two other basic goods. The proposition that marriage is a basic good, essential to Finnis's argument, is not a valid proposition of natural law theory. The argument must therefore fail.

. . .

The most important feature that an equality argument must capture in order to be convincing is the way in which inequalities as between some persons or groups is of more concern than inequalities as between other persons or groups. Very broadly speaking, there are two competing accounts of equality on this point: process equality and substantive equality. Under process equality, what is important is the process of differentiation which amounts to unequal treatment. Such a process must rationally take account of only relevant differences between different persons or groups. Provided it does so, equality is observed. Under substantive equality, what is important is the relative position of groups in society. Where one group is unjustly subordinated, it would be wrong to exacerbate that position of relative subordination; further, one should act to remedy the situation.[33]

There is much academic debate as to which of these constitutes the better understanding of equality. This perhaps misses the point: both capture values that we consider important. I have argued in a different context that we should be more concerned to advance substantive equality than process equality because currently substantive inequality is much more entrenched than process inequality. For present purposes, however, I wish to make a different point. If one accepts that partnership recognition is a good and that the relevance of a strictly egalitarian principle is that it provides an independent basis for arguments as to how that good should be distributed, it seems that one's conception of equality should be more sensitive to the actual distribution of goods than to the process through which such goods are distributed. That is, one should favour a substantive conception of equality over a process conception. I shall operate on this basis for the purposes of this paper.

I have elsewhere outlined a substantive conception of equality that turns on status groups and the need to avoid the unjust subordination of already unjustly subordinated groups. On this analysis, gay people are a status group in that they, to varying extents, conceive of themselves as a group, are conceived of by others as a group and their status is tied to their membership of that group. They are subordinated within society in a number of ways. Of most relevance to the present issue is the denial of partnership recognition to them. That is, although gay people can have partnerships recognised by the state – i.e. they can get married – they can only do so by denying what they are and opting into heterosexual marriage.[34] In this way, the basic structure of subordination of gay people in current times is much the same as it has always been: acceptance and respect within society is possible, but only to the extent that one pretends to be what one is not. The closet lives on. This focus on status ties this conception of equality quite closely to the context in which, considering Raz's arguments, we considered that egalitarian principles most clearly had force: the distribution of intangible goods. For the reason why people want intangible goods is because of what such goods say about a person's place in society, their status. To deny an intangible good is to deny status. It is to say: although this good costs us nothing to give, we deny it to you simply because you are not worthy – you are inferior to us.

Now it is of crucial importance to this conception of equality that it only prohibits the *unjust* subordination of already unjustly subordinated social groups. This does not mean that one must find an argument, outside of equality, as to why the subordination is unjust, but rather that one may conclude that inequality for some groups or in some circumstances, is justified. For this reason, it must address arguments to the effect that, although the denial of partnership recognition amounts to subordination, it is not unjust either because it is just to subordinate homosexuals generally or because it is just to subordinate homosexuals in this particular way. Although many moral arguments have been put forward to this effect, I propose here to deal with those advanced by Finnis and discussed earlier in this article.

In this regard, the justice arguments for the subordination of homosexuals generally, and for the subordination of homosexuals particularly through the denial of partnership recognition, run in parallel. For the general subordination argument appears to turn on the fact that sex is an act directed to the production of human life (a good) and non-procreative sex is inimical to that good of human life. This is similar in form to the more particular argument that marriage is a basic human good and any form of partnership which purports to be marriage but does not have that unique synthesis of friendship and life-production is inimical to that basic good of marriage. I have already outlined the flaws with the marriage argument: it simply posits marriage as a basic good, in contravention of the general methodology of the natural law. As such, it provides no reason, beyond bald and questionable assertion, as to why same-sex partnership recognition would be wrong. There are similar flaws with the general sex argument for unless one makes life subordinate to the good of marriage (and, quite apart from the problems of recognising marriage as a basic good, natural law methodology again prevents this), non-marital sex would have to be regarded as a legitimate means of advancing a good while non-procreative marital sex would be illegitimate. The position against homosexual acts can only be maintained by introducing other distinctions that are unacceptable for the natural law theorist. In this way, the justice arguments for both the general subordination of homosexuals, and the particular subordination through the denial of partnership rights, both founder on the insuperable difficulties of developing a coherent and justified set of distinctions which endorse marital non-procreative sex, but prohibit non-marital procreative sex. Non-procreative marital sex is of course a good thing: it is instrumental to the good of friendship (and, indeed, play). By the same token, homosexual sex is instrumental to the good of friendship, a good that is also served by the recognition of same-sex partnerships. For all these reasons, I suggest that there is no basis in justice for the denial of partnership recognition to gay couples.

THE FORMS OF PARTNERSHIP RECOGNITION

In the light of these various moral arguments about partnership recognition, it is appropriate to consider the various forms of partnership recognition that are currently proposed. This is not intended as a detailed discussion of current proposals, but rather an attempt to clarify the moral implications of various forms of partnership recognition.

Retrospective partnership recognition (the presumptive scheme)

In many ways, this is not partnership recognition at all. Under this approach, the state retrospectively recognises non-marital partnerships when the partnership comes to an end, either through death or through dissolution. When the partnership comes to an end, the state makes such property adjustment orders as appear just and could provide tax breaks equivalent to those afforded to married couples in relation to their property. This could be done either on a generic or a case-by-case basis.

Typically, the trigger for such retrospective partnership recognition is a certain amount of time lived together. For instance, if two persons have lived together for three years (leave aside for present purposes the character of that relationship) and one dies without having made a will, the intestacy rules might be amended to be more favourable to the other party. The advantage of such an approach is that even people who do not formally enter into a relationship receive some protection. Others, however, construe this as a disadvantage in that people may become subject to obligations that they have not voluntarily undertaken. More seriously, people who have consciously decided not to seek recognition from the state may find themselves unwillingly saddled with such recognition. This objection could be overcome, however, by making the scheme presumptive only, i.e. by allowing people to opt out of it.

Of more relevance to the current concerns, however, are the egalitarian implications of such a stance. As suggested above, one can divide partnership recognition into two aspects: symbolic and practical. The practical impact of retrospective recognition is important: persons are protected from unfortunate events and, depending on the extent of legal measures possible upon retrospective recognition, could be put into effectively the same situation as heterosexual, married couples where a marriage comes to an end, either through death or separation. The symbolic impact of retrospective recognition is, however, much less. For the state is effectively saying that non-marital partnerships are only deserving of recognition once they are over. Most people who want their partnership recognised would, I suggest, want it recognised while still in existence. This lack of symbolic impact is of particular concern for egalitarian principles which turn on comparative recognition. Retrospective recognition of partnerships effectively denies non-marital partnerships the intangible elements of recognition for as long as there is anything there that can be meaningfully recognised.

General partnership recognition (contractual)
Under this approach, any two people could, upon application, have their partnership recognised by the state. One can imagine various procedures and substantive requirements that would have to be met, but these are unimportant for present purposes. This recognition would thus be available to heterosexual and homosexual partnerships, but also to non-sexual partnerships, such as that between two sisters who have lived their lives together in one house. It is difficult to deny the justice of the claims of that latter group of people. For why should the state, in its formal recognition of people's personal relationships, confine itself to sexual relationships? There are other types of relationships, very important for those involved in them. Any reconfiguration of partnership recognition laws should make some provision for people in long-term personal but non-sexual relationships who would like such relationships recognised by the state.

However, one wonders how many people in non-sexual relationships would want their relationship recognised in this way. Such an approach would cause difficulties if one person were to meet someone else and wish to marry that person. Presumably one could not be married and in a civil partnership at the same time. Would one have to divorce your sister, for example, in order to get married? This points up the issue that the relationships between elderly sisters, although raising mutual moral rights and duties and although they should be protected and recognised in some way by the state, are not really the same as sexual relationships. Most importantly, I suggest, people in such relationships do not aspire to the same exclusivity that is generally accepted as the ideal in sexual relationships. Thus, although non-sexual long-term relationships deserve protection, it is doubtful whether a contractual civil partnership scheme, broadly analogous to marriage, is the best method of providing that protection.

From the perspective of egalitarian principles, one would also have reservations about the limits of this approach. For, although not as blatant as blanket non-recognition for same-sex relationships, it could be seen as a form of the closet in that it would allow the state (or society) to pretend that homosexual relationships have more in common with asexual relationships than with heterosexual relationships. The ultimate in state recognition – marriage – would be reserved for heterosexual relationships. In this way, the state would again provide practical benefits for same-sex couples while still denying status to such couples. For these reasons, while there are merits to a general partnership recognition scheme of this type, if it leaves marriage as an option for heterosexuals and implicitly equates homosexual relationships with asexual relationships, it would be objectionable on egalitarian grounds. The primary objection here is not to non-sexual relationships being equated with homosexual relationships, but rather to heterosexual relationships being elevated above homosexual relationships. That said, the combination of the two amounts to a powerful statement against homosexual relationships: such relationships will only be recognised by the state because the state can pretend that they are not really sexual relationships. The sexual relationships of homosexuals are not recognised for what they are; homosexuals themselves remain invisible to the law.

Civil recognition scheme for same-sex partnerships
Such an approach would address some of the egalitarian concerns with retrospective recognition and general partnership recognition. However, it would still implicitly elevate marriage (and by extension heterosexual relationships) over homosexual partnerships. Even if precisely the same benefits were afforded to each type of relationship, the implicit statement of the state, given the generally positive cultural associations with the word 'marriage', would again be that homosexual relationships are inferior to heterosexual relationships. This would be an inequality for which no justification has been shown.

Civil recognition scheme for all partnerships, in addition to opposite-sex marriage
This form of recognition poses the same egalitarian concerns, although considerably diluted, as civil recognition only for same-sex partnerships. Again, the implicit statement of the state is that homosexuals are less worthy than heterosexuals as only the latter are entitled to the ultimate good of partnership recognition in the form of marriage. However, the force of this statement is in this case mitigated as it is provided that heterosexuals may also choose civil recognition as an alternative to marriage. Thus, heterosexuals are still held up as being more worthy than homosexuals, but the sting of this statement is lessened by the fact that civil recognition is not deemed to be an option beneath heterosexuals.

Gay marriage
It might follow from the discussion thus far that the most egalitarian solution to the partnership recognition issue is to allow gay people to get married. However, the institution of marriage raises egalitarian concerns of its own. This is because of the extent to which it is gendered, i.e. the extent to which it ascribes presumptive gender roles to the partners. Those who choose to marry choose an institution in which the following roles are presumptively assigned according to gender: child-rearing, wage-earning, meal-cooking, lawn-mowing, light-

bulb-changing, blocked-drain-cleaning, clothes-washing, rodent-killing, etc. These roles are not rigid; many married couples can and do negotiate (in a loving way) the roles that each partner will play. However, such negotiation takes place against a background of what is assumed appropriate for each partner, given their sex.

It would be wrong to single out the institution of marriage as being responsible for these gender roles. To a certain extent, marriage probably reflects general societal ideas of what is appropriate work for men and women. To that extent, presumptive gender roles might persist in heterosexual civil partnerships. However, marriage remains more marked in this respect, for marriage explicitly and unashamedly celebrates ascribed gender roles in its very essence: marriage is a union of 'husband' and 'wife'. For this reason, the presumptive gender roles in marriage are stronger than the presumptive gender roles in a heterosexual civil partnership.

Why should this matter? What is wrong with ascribed gender roles? The problem is that ascribed gender roles form the basic structure of the subordination of women. Whereas the structure of subordination of gay people turns on self-denial and public denial, the structure of the subordination of women turns on role differentiation as between men and women. Women as a subordinated group in society have traditionally lost out through the division of labour as between men and women. The relative emancipation of women has largely consisted of challenges to that division of labour.

As an institution, marriage reinforces that role differentiation and – in so doing – reinforces the subordination of women. Same-sex relationships challenge role differentiation as between men and women because it is necessary (and not just possible) that at least one partner adopt a role that is traditionally ascribed to the opposite sex. In this way, same-sex relationships can be a wider egalitarian force in society, helping to dismantle generally accepted ideas of appropriate gender roles. This egalitarian potential could be undermined, however, if same-sex partnerships were to be recognised through the form of marriage. For by labelling one member of a same-sex partnership 'husband' and the other 'wife', the partners would not only indicate their willingness to conceive of their relationship in terms of wholly inappropriate gender roles but also undermine the challenge that same-sex relationships in general pose to ascribed gender roles. For these reasons, it can be argued that gay marriage is an appropriate, egalitarian response to the question of same-sex partnership recognition.[35]

Against this, however, it could be argued that nothing would undermine gender roles within marriage more than opening it up to same-sex couples. Although in the short-term there might be a tendency to 'gender-ise' the same-sex partners, in the long-term the more likely impact would be to 'de-gender-ise' the opposite sex partners within marriage. Given this potential, and given the unique and generally positive cultural resonance of marriage, the only truly egalitarian approach is to allow gay people to marry.

Civil partnership recognition for all!

If one continues to have egalitarian reservations about marriage, however, a scheme of civil partnership open to all, combined with the abolition of state marriage, would be the most appropriate egalitarian response to this issue. Given the abolition of state-recognised marriage for heterosexuals, there would be no inegalitarian concerns in making such civil recognition available to non-sexual, personal relationships, as well as to homosexual and heterosexual relationships. On the other hand, one could give different names to the recognition of sexual and non-sexual relationships. As each is a new institution, there would be no implicit denigration of the form of relationship recognised by the other.

Such an approach would not prevent individuals or communities (religious or otherwise) adopting their own definitions of marriage. Thus a couple could choose to get married in the Catholic Church, for example, and also have their relationship recognised by the state in the form of a civil partnership. However, the state would not deem this form of relationship to be more worthy than any other committed relationship, whether a heterosexual partnership not sanctified by a church or a homosexual partnership.

Conclusions

In the current political context, it is most unlikely that Ireland will opt for the abolition of state recognition for marriage coupled with a civil partnership scheme of this type. In that context, I suggest a civil recognition scheme open to all sexual relationships and incurring all the rights and obligations of marriage. At the same time, there should be a retrospective, presumptive scheme that would provide minimal, but significant, rights to people who lived together in a relationship of mutual support. The benefits would be provided retrospectively, i.e. after the relationship ends. Such an approach would meet the needs of non-sexual couples without inappropriately preventing them from forming sexual relationships; it would not impose stringent rights or obligations on people without the consent of those people. Conversely, if people in sexual relationships want those rights and obligations, they always have the option of having their partnership recognised.

CONCLUSION

This paper has tried to assess a number of moral arguments concerning the recognition of same-sex partnerships. This was done in the belief that this is an essentially moral issue. My suggestion is that natural law arguments, traditionally most opposed to the very idea of homosexuality, do not provide a coherent basis for opposing same-sex partnerships. I accept that there are other arguments, apart from natural law arguments, against same-sex partnerships. For this reason, the conclusions I draw are open to critique on other grounds. That is work for another day. Nevertheless, I have argued that egalitarian principles provide a compelling basis for arguments in favour of same-sex partnership recognition. When one considers the precise form that such recognition should take, one encounters competing egalitarian concerns. Nevertheless, an approach that is sensitive to the iniquity of differential recognition provides the most compelling analysis of the issue.

Notes:

1. Carlos A. Ball, *The Morality of Gay Rights* (Routledge, London, 2003), at 1.
2. Carlos A. Ball, *The Morality of Gay Rights* (Routledge, London, 2003), at 1.
3. Ball also argues that moral bracketing, even in the form of neutral equality arguments, provided the basis for obtaining from the state the protection afforded by anti-discrimination legislation. I am not as convinced on this point as, I think, any detailed examination of the 'relevance' criterion that tends to inform such legislation shows that it is not neutral and, indeed, imports moral arguments. Given Ball's later comments on moral argument in general, I suspect that he might agree with this observation.
4. Carlos A. Ball, *The Morality of Gay Rights* (Routledge, London, 2003), at 5.
5. Although it is possible to argue that recognition should be provided to all relationships unless there is a good reason not to, this does not seem a particularly attractive proposition. In any event, it requires moral argument to support the proposition that recognition should presumptively be provided to all relationships. In the context of positive state action (at the very least), moral arguments are unavoidable.
6. John M. Finnis, 'Law, Morality and Sexual Orientation' 69 *Notre Dame Law Review* 1049 (1994).
7. John M. Finnis, *Natural Law and Natural Rights* (Clarendon, Oxford, 1980), at 60.
8. Finnis, *Natural Law and Natural Rights*, at 61.
9. Finnis, *Natural Law and Natural Rights*, at 65. This amounts to little more than a declaration that those who consider knowledge important think knowledge important, thus offering little independent support for the contention that knowledge is a basic good. However, this perhaps misses the point: the whole point of self-evident goods is that they cannot be justified by reference to something else. They are self-evident.
10. Finnis, *Natural Law and Natural Rights*, at 66.
11. Finnis, *Natural Law and Natural Rights*, at 69. Again, however, the circularity is plain: why does it matter if one disqualifies oneself from the pursuit of knowledge unless one first accepts that knowledge is a basic good?
12. *Natural Law and Natural Rights*, at 103-105.
13. *Natural Law and Natural Rights*, at 105-106.
14. *Natural Law and Natural Rights*, at 118. Emphasis original.
15. Such indirect damage is inevitable given that, for example, time expended promoting one basic good (for instance, knowledge) is time taken away from the promotion of another basic good (for instance, life). These moral propositions amount, I think, to what is commonly referred to as the doctrine of indirect effect. Finnis notes that this raises the problem of individuating actions, i.e. if one characterises an action as individual,

one implicitly treats the consequences of that action as individual and as actions in themselves. Accordingly, the consequences cannot be seen as indirect effects of a morally good action. On the other hand, if an action is not individuated, its consequences can be seen as indirect effects and therefore permissible. *Natural Law and Natural Rights*, at 119.

16. *Natural Law and Natural Rights*, at 120.

17. *Natural Law and Natural Rights*, at 122. Internal cross-references omitted.

18. Finnis, 'Law, Morality and Sexual Orientation', at 1051.

19. Finnis, 'Law, Morality and Sexual Orientation', at 1052. Emphasis original.

20. Although Finnis provides other grounds for the different roles afforded to the state in the public and private realms respectively, this ground may prove problematic or at least more complicated and in need of greater explanation. There are families in which for morally unsound reasons (on Finnis's terms), younger members of the family are encouraged to view homosexual activity and same-sex relationships as acceptable and praiseworthy. It is unclear whether the principle of subsidiarity is capable of supporting the public/private distinction in this context.

21. Finnis, 'Law, Morality and Sexual Orientation', at 1053.

22. Finnis, 'Law, Morality and Sexual Orientation', at 1054-1055. Emphasis original.

23. Finnis, 'Law, Morality and Sexual Orientation', at 1067.

24. Finnis, 'Law, Morality and Sexual Orientation', at 1069. Emphasis original.

25. Finnis, 'Law, Morality and Sexual Orientation', at 1070.

26. Finnis, *Natural Law and Natural Rights,* at 90. Emphasis added.

27. Finnis, *Natural Law and Natural Rights,* at 91.

28. Finnis, *Natural Law and Natural Rights,* at 91.

29. Finnis, *Natural Law and Natural Rights,* at 104. Ellipsis original.

30. Finnis, *Natural Law and Natural Rights,* at 92.

31. Even if this argument is sound, it is unclear that it applies to other heterosexual partnerships. At the very least, further arguments would have to be found.

32. *Natural Law and Natural Rights*, at 122. Internal cross-references omitted.

33. For a slightly more detailed consideration of this issue, see Nicholas Bamforth, 'Same-Sex Partnerships and Arguments of Justice' in Robert Wintemute and Mads Andenaes (eds), *Legal Recognition of Same-Sex Partnerships: A Study of National, European and International Law* (Hart, Oxford, 2000).

34. For discussion on the parameters of these conceptions of equality, see Oran Doyle, *Constitutional Equality Law* (Roundhall Thomson, 2004), at 201-231. The account I provide there is mediated somewhat by limits on judicial power. No such limits apply in this context.

35. Indeed, as a matter of Irish law, it is questionable whether gay people have the requisite capacity to form valid heterosexual marriages. See *C v C* [1991] 2 IR 330. As a side issue, this raises the possibility that, in Ireland, it is not simply the case that gay marriage is not allowed but rather that gay people are excluded from all marriage. This changes slightly the contours of the debate.

36. There is a symmetry between this position and that advocated by Finnis. The difference is that Finnis believes that homosexuals would be bad for marriage because marriage is for partners of the opposite sex. I am suggesting that marriage would be bad for homosexuals because marriage is for partners of opposite gender.

Part Eight
Sexual Abuse

31   Child Sexual Abuse: Rules for the Debate

Patrick Hannon

(*The Furrow*, Vol 54, No 2, February 2003, pp 67-74)

'Peter Saunders is a man torn between loyalty to the church and loyalty to victims of clerical abuse'; so begins an article in a recent issue of *The Tablet*. Peter Saunders has good reason to wish to be loyal to victims of sexual abuse by clerics and religious, for he himself is a survivor. And it should go without saying that the sense of being torn must be at its most acute in someone who has been abused and in whom religious faith and church allegiance have yet persisted. But the description of his dilemma will strike a chord even in people who have not been abused but who have entered, so far as this is possible, into the sufferings of the abused, and who wish only both that justice is fully done and that the Catholic Church comes through the current controversy. I mean, of course, people for whom faith and church allegiance are important, those people who have been shocked, angered, thrown into a profound dismay by the ceaseless spate of revelations of harm and of betrayal of trust, but who are nevertheless held by their religious convictions and loyalties and who want, desperately, a truthful and just end to the present distress.

Tension

It's difficult to live with the tension generated by these loyalties, and it's difficult sometimes to avoid reacting: against the church leader who, despite everything, still seems more interested in defending church institutions than in acknowledging fault and making reparation; against the journalist who takes liberties with the facts, spins a story or a headline, questions the *bona fides* of those who are manifestly trying to deal with the situation in the best way they can; sometimes even against a survivor who seems implacable, intent only on a revenge which is blind in its object and in its methods.

There is no comparing, it is rightly said, the sufferings of victims and the pain of those who must now answer for the failures of the 'institutional' church. Probably only someone who has been abused can empathise adequately with the suffering of the abused. And – especially if one is a religious or cleric – one needs to be constantly on guard lest one's responses are merely reactionary. Yet one sometimes feels for the church representative whose honest effort to right past wrongs is met only with incredulity and derision.

Perhaps we are still at a stage in the process of disclosure/reparation when it is impossible to think straight concerning what has been uncovered about the misdoings of Catholic clergy and religious, and about the ineptitude and sometimes dishonesty with which complaints have been met. Some people fear that we shall never emerge from it. But attempts to think straight and to act justly and with compassion, whether in reference to complainants or to those against whom the complaints are being made, are not helped by the kind of polarisation which constantly threatens.

Polarisation

It's depressing to be a party to conversations in which all media people are assumed to be interested only in getting at 'us' and in circulation or audience figures. Some are, some aren't. Of course it's depressing too to meet evidence of suspicion and hostility toward all clergy and religious on the basis of the conduct of some. These are extremes, and probably most people still are somewhere in the middle, pulled now this way, now that – sharing, if they are Catholics, in the kind of dilemma felt by Peter Saunders.

How do attitudes become polarised? There are, I suppose, people who start off polarised, so to speak – people who are determined to hold to their side of the story regardless of what is said by those on the other side. This can only beget an equal and opposite reaction, and positions on both sides are hardened, perhaps irremediably. But there is another way in which polarisation may occur: that is, when someone or some group come to believe that they are not being heard, when they feel that whatever they say, whatever the truth, falsehood and injustice are what will prevail.

Polarisation precludes reconciliation – one should perhaps say, precludes truth, the only sure basis for healing and for a prospectful resolution of all of the problems which attend child sexual abuse. There are people who, wholly understandably, will never be reconciled to the horrific contradictions involved in the abuse of children by men and women in whom, in virtue of their religious authority, absolute trust was placed. It's impossible to guess how many Catholics, themselves victims/survivors or not, will walk no more in the faith in which they were raised.

That, obviously, is a problem for the Catholic Church and its leadership, and just now it's not at all obvious how it might be met. But it's only part of the problem facing the wider Irish community, for even were the 'Catholic' problem to achieve some sort of resolution, there is still the fact that abuse by religious personnel accounts for only 3.2% of the extent of the problem in Ireland. Polarisation always threatens resolution, but a polarisation which is untrue to the facts must make resolution impossible.

I said earlier that it may be that we are still at a stage in the process of disclosure/reparation when it is impossible to think straight; if that is so, the hope for a constructive public debate upon the issues is for the moment remote. It may also be that for various reasons a public working-through of the specifically Catholic Church dimension of the problematic is necessary before the wider problem can even be addressed. And in terms of the purging of the church, it's imperative that no short-circuiting of this process is attempted. But it is well to keep in mind that the wider problem will not be addressed so long as we are locked into the church context. And even the church dimension cannot adequately be addressed if a polarisation of viewpoint is allowed to set the terms of debate.

Resolution? – 'Rules for the Debate'

More than a quarter of a century ago, at an especially low moment in the abortion debate in the US, the late Richard McCormick SJ commented upon the destructive polarisation which had come to mark that debate. He acknowledged the difficulty in breaking through to a space in which disciplined and constructive argument might take place, but he ventured a suggestion. 'Many of us have become bone weary of this discussion. But to yield to such fatigue would be to run from a problem, not wrestle with it. If stay we ought and must, then it may be of help to propose a set of 'rules for conversation', the observance of which could nudge us toward more communicative conversation.'[1] He formulated a set of nine such 'rules', and some of them might be instructive for us.

Discussion about child sexual abuse is not of course a debate in the sense that one might have a debate about abortion legislation. No-one, for example, wants to say that child sexual abuse is defensible, no-one doubts that those who perpetrate it must be brought to book, and no-one (I hope) seriously doubts that those who have or have had a position of responsibility in relation either to abusers or to the abused must be called to account. What is and will be in debate is the detail, or some of it: the procedures for dealing with complaints, the remedies available to complainants, the best way to deal with the convicted, the nature and degree of accountability of those in authority, the adequacy of responses to date – above all, the measures to be taken to ensure that children are protected for the future.

So there is need for debate, and even if calm debate is not yet possible or at present even foreseeable, some of McCormick's 'rules', *mutatis mutandis*, could help in an Irish public debate about child sexual abuse. For example he calls on protagonists to attempt to identify areas of agreement, to represent the opposing position accurately and fairly, and to try to identify the core issues at stake. These seem obvious, bland even, and yet only with difficulty are they implemented in practice. McCormick explains why the first can be troublesome: 'Where issues are urgent and disputants have enormous personal stakes and investments, there is a tendency to draw sharp lines very quickly and begin the shootout.'[2] The same dynamic will militate against the implementation of the second and third.

Two other rules, adapted, could improve our debate and the prospects of a good outcome; as expressed by McCormick they are: *Avoid the use of slogans* and *Distinguish the pairs right-wrong, good-bad*. Elaborating on the first he writes: 'Slogans are the weapons of the crusader, one who sees his role as warfare, gen-

AN IRISH READER IN MORAL THEOLOGY

erally against those sharply defined as "the enemy". Fighting for good causes clearly has its place, as do slogans … But slogans are not very enlightening conversational tools, simply because they bypass and effectively subvert the process of communication.'[3] Sloganising, or something like it, occurs when for example media coverage of child sexual abuse in the Catholic Church is said to be motivated by anticlericalism, or hostility to religion, or concern for sales. It occurs also when all church authorities are portrayed as interested solely in the preservation of the institution. It occurs when – one hopes now rarely – complainants are dismissed as cranks, neurotics, trouble-makers. And it occurs when abusers are scapegoated or demonised.

Right and Wrong; Good and Bad

The meaning of the second rule, *Distinguish the pairs right-wrong, good-bad*, may not be immediately clear from this formulation. It refers to the fact that one might perform a wrong action without being to blame, or fully to blame; and so one ought not, on that basis, be judged a bad person. By the same token, one might perform a good action without, by that fact, establishing oneself as 'good'. The reason for this is that a moral evaluation takes into account not only *what I do*, but *what I understand and mean* by what I do, as well as the *circumstances* which may, as the saying goes, alter cases.

I could do something that's on the face of it 'right' (helping someone in need) for the wrong reason or with a wrong attitude (out of a desire to impress, patronisingly, motivated solely by guilt); and the moral value of what I've done is accordingly impaired. It's also the case that someone who has done evil things, who was perhaps an evil person, may repent their wrong-doing and try to live a good life again. So from the fact that someone has *acted wrongly*, it doesn't follow that she or he is a *bad person*; and since the outsider normally doesn't know what goes on in the heart of another, or what the full circumstances are, it behoves us not to judge.[4] This doesn't detract a whit from our entitlement to be appalled at wrong-doing and to condemn it in the strongest terms. It does affect the question of how we ought to deal with the wrong-doer.

When a particularly horrific evil is perpetrated it's difficult to keep the distinction here in question in mind. We saw this not long ago in public reaction to the death of Myra Hindley; there were people who could not be persuaded that someone who caused so much evil might have repented, let alone that a psychopathology might have diminished her culpability in the first place. Similar reactions follow disclosure of the more shocking instances of child sexual abuse. Some people are impatient with suggestions that those who abuse children often do so because they themselves have been abused; and they are dismissive of suggestions that the convicted should be given an opportunity for rehabilitation. And some are unable to accept that a child abuser might repent and change his or her ways.

The distinction alluded to by McCormick can't be dismissed as yet another instance of verbal gymnastics of a sort sometimes ascribed by their critics to ethicians. It's recognised by the law, which takes an accused's 'mind' or inner psychological state into account before giving judgement as to guilt, and in deciding on an appropriate penalty. And in any case it's familiar in everyday less dramatic experience, for we find ourselves recognising that someone who does something wrong 'couldn't be blamed', for he or she 'couldn't help it', either because of ignorance or mistake or because driven by fear, or by some compulsion outside of conscious control. Neither is it right to dismiss the possibility of someone's repenting their wrong-doing, and starting again on the path of good living. This too is a matter of common human experience, the experience of each one of us in our own case. And to deny the possibility is at odds directly with the Judeo-Christian religious tradition, which affirms the constancy of God's forgiving love and the permanence of God's invitation to repentance.

It's understandable when those who have suffered abuse, whose suffering has perhaps been aggravated by attempts to evade responsibility and to cover up, are unable to acknowledge such distinctions and possibilities – which makes it all the more moving and humbling when individuals display the kind of understanding and compassion which recognition of them calls for. It's a different matter when outsiders – and I'm thinking here especially of some (repeat, some) media commentary – depict attempts to draw attention to these dimensions as attempts at institutional self-exculpation or, worse, as seeking to minimise the enormity of abusers' crimes.

Three More Rules

The foregoing was suggested by McCormick's 'rules for conversation', adapted to fit the subject-matter and the circumstances in which the Irish debate on child sexual abuse is taking place and will develop. To the selection from Mc Cormick's list here presented I think we might add three further proposals.

The first is that all parties should respect each other's *bona fides*. I grant that this is difficult if not impossible in some cases. How can you accept the *bona fides* of a church or other official if you even suspect that that official's concern is not with your problem but with protecting the institutions of which he or she is representative and custodian? One fears lest there are such still. How can church people respect the *bona fides* of a media person or other commentator who is determined to have the last ounce of the last pound of flesh, regardless of accuracy, regardless of the claims of fairness. One fears that there are such still. The *bona fides* of complainants must always be respected, but that cannot mean ignoring the fact that some accusations are false.

The second rule is that there must be 'patient attention to the facts' – the phrase, I think, is Iris Murdoch's. What are the facts about the incidence of child abuse among the clergy? Do we know any facts about the putative connection between the present discipline of celibacy and child sexual abuse? (It cannot be right to refuse to explore the possibility.) Are there different kinds of offenders, and what are the facts about the possibilities for rehabilitating some kinds? What is the incidence of re-offending? What are the facts about this or that particular person who has been convicted and who has paid the penalty laid down by law? Discussion so far has not always been marked by patient attention to the facts.

The third rule is one specific to the debate about child abuse by Catholic clerics and religious. It might at first sight look like the kind of nicety that could trouble only someone who had nothing pressing to think about. Yet I believe that, from the church's point of view, it is of profound importance in this as in so many other matters. It is that the word 'church' should not be used when what is meant is church leaders or members of the clergy or religious communities. The Second Vatican Council went to pains to repudiate the notion that 'church' is identified with office-holders and those ordained or consecrated to special roles or states. That hasn't put an end to the practice – including among church leaders and officials themselves – of speaking as though it is.

This is not, I'm afraid, a piece of harmless carelessness. For a start it may distort the perception of the dilemma expressed by Peter Saunders. Loyalty to 'the church' is loyalty to the whole community called church. Normally this calls for loyalty to the leadership, but of course victims who are Catholic are also of the church, as are their families and friends, and as are the people envisaged here as sharing, even if differently, in the kind of dilemma in which Peter Saunders finds himself. Loyalty to the church may require stringent criticism of leadership, and it will certainly require resistance to any attempt to evade responsibility in the matter of child sexual abuse.

A second unfortunate consequence of the identification of the church with its leaders or officials is that these latter may well come to make the identification, even if only unconsciously. And any propensity to envisage the situation as one of 'them' and 'us' risks being intensified accordingly. This appears to have happened in some dioceses in the United States where, astonishingly, some priests were reported as regarding the laity who became involved in the controversy as engaged in some sort of power bid. It can only be hoped that such a bizarre misjudgement is not made here.

Thirdly – again as with other matters – when the church is conceived only in terms of hierarchical leaders and officials, it is all too easy for other members to ignore their own responsibilities. Those in official positions have of course first responsibility both as to what went wrong and as to how it may be righted. But – especially as to how wrong may now be righted – we all share responsibility, however in any given situation this responsibility is to be exercised.

It's not, I hope, unrealistic to look forward to a time when the problem of child sexual abuse in Ireland can be addressed calmly but with maximum effectiveness. As far as the Catholic Church is concerned, in Ireland as elsewhere, it has generated a massive problem of credibility, and yet, amazingly, there is a store of good will which may sustain those charged with the task of trying to bring some healing. One hopes of course that no-one in authority in the church is in any doubt now as to the gravity of the problem, in itself and as, literally, a scandal; and one hopes that the good will is not misinterpreted or squandered. And for the church debate and for the wider debate that is still to come, perhaps some 'rules' such as those here suggested might not come amiss.

Notes:

1. McCormick, R. A., *How Brave a New World?*, London: SCM, 1981, chapter 9, 'Rules for Abortion Debate', 176-187. This first appeared in *America* 139 (1978), 26-30.
2. *How Brave a New World?*, 177.
3. Op. cit., 178.
4. The case is different with the law, for a court must judge guilt or innocence before the law, and it will have rules of evidence and other procedures which try to ensure that this is done as fairly as possible.

32   In Service of a Different Kingdom: Child Sexual Abuse and the Response of the Church

Eamonn Conway

(E. Conway, E. Duffy and A. Shields (eds), *Child Sexual Abuse and the Catholic Church – Towards a Pastoral Response*, Dublin: The Columba Press, 1999, pp 76-90)

Introduction

This article sets out to explore theologically some aspects of the recent Irish experience of child sexual abuse by priests and religious and to assess the implications for the life and ministry of the church.

The insights of psychologists, of lawyers and of other professionals are indispensable to the church at this time. But the church is not like any other body in society. The church has a unique mandate to proclaim God's unconditional love, to embody it and to model this love for all of humankind. When church personnel abuse children, something has gone drastically wrong, and it strikes at the very nature of the church. It is the contention of this article that only a theological reflection, in dialogue with the work of psychologists and the experience of counsellors, can unpack fully the significance of recent events for the mission of the church.

This article attempts such a theological reflection. The first part will take up comments by people who have worked with victims and offenders and suggest some implications for the church's self-understanding and for society as a whole. The second part will re-visit the core message of Christianity and in that light suggest that the experience both of victims of sexual abuse and sexual offenders needs to be listened to by the church if it is to fulfil its mission at this challenging time.

Sexual abuse and dominative power

Olive Travers, in her book *Behind the Silhouettes*, argues that sexual abuse is often as much about control and power as it is about sex; that the control which sex offenders exercise over their victims serves as a compensation for the powerlessness they feel in relationships with other adults.[1] Non-fixated offenders, and most priests and religious who abuse belong in this category, usually perceive themselves as powerless. At the same time they can hold rigid views about the traditional roles of men and women in society.[2]

Marie Keenan, a psychotherapist with the Granada Institute, Dublin, believes that power imbalances in society are part of the culture that allows sexual abuse to thrive.[3] Specifically with regard to clergy who have offended, she has commented that few of them are sexual deviants as such. However, they have

365

had great difficulty in dealing with their sexuality and with holding positions of power:

> Where they (clergy) come off the page in assessment is in terms of sexual conflict and uncontrolled hostility … a tiny minority of abusive priests had a psychologically deviant profile but many had great difficulty in dealing with their sexuality or dealing with having positions of power and yet a feeling of no power over their own lives.[4]

The English Benedictine, Sebastian Moore, also discusses the relationship between clergy sexual misconduct and the exercise of power. In a recent collection of essays published to honour his eightieth birthday, Moore writes:

> Celibate priesthood is extraordinarily symptomatic of the arrested condition of the Western male. We are the sons of Mother Church, our phallic energy exiled in obedience to her command. Our history shows, especially in the higher echelons of the priesthood, the resultant transformation of phallic energy into dominative power. And now our order is manifesting, to an embarrassing degree, the symptoms of denial, of resistance to the change which is being demanded of man generally … as dioceses are bankrupting themselves with lawsuits over our sexual irregularities …[5]

Moore situates the relatively small number of sexual misconduct cases by clergy, within the wider context of the abuse of power in the church. Western culture, according to Moore, has been characterised by this need among men to dominate, and the church, far from challenging this tendency, is in danger of being the last bastion of it in Western society.[6]

The psychological evidence referred to earlier would seem to suggest that few clerical sexual offenders are technically sexual deviants. It would seem, however, that frequently their abuse of children has to do with power and control, and their inability to resolve such issues in a mature way. There are many instances of the abuse of power and control by priests and religious other than sexual abuse. For the most part, these abuses are not illegal and therefore do not lead to criminal charges. However, in terms of the church's self-understanding these are no less wrong and sinful. In terms of the church's unique mission to the world they are no less dimming of the light the church is called to be in the darkness of everyday exploitation, injustice, and violation of human dignity.

It is remarkable that the revelation of abuse, both physical and sexual, by priests and religious has been like music to the ears of so many people, including practising Catholics. The sad reality is that while few experienced this kind of abuse themselves, many experienced other kinds of abuse of power by authorities in the church. When many Catholics hear about cases of abuse, I believe that in their own minds, perhaps unconsciously, they connect these stories with their own memories of abuse and hurt by clerics. These memories have never found expression until now. The cases of child sexual abuse may have become a vehicle for the expression of a wider experience of the abuse of church power.

The reaction so far: scapegoating

There is a tendency in the media to make sexual offenders seem as unlike the ordinary person as possible. But as Travers notes, 'sex offenders are just like us. We all have the potential within us to abuse … All of us are abusive in our relationships to some degree. We lose our tempers with children, we use our power over them, we let our moods determine their treatment.'[7] The response has been to distance us as far as possible from sexual offenders. Cameras in slow motion and graphic headlines attempt to portray abusers as a subhuman species. Society demands lengthy prison sentences as punishment. Within prison, sexual offenders must be segregated from 'ordinary decent criminals'. On release, no community wants them. There are calls for the registration and/or the tagging of sex offenders, the twenty-first century equivalent of 'branding', a practice most societies would now consider barbaric.

It is superficial to see these responses as motivated only by a concern for the sensibilities of victims or the protection of children.[8] The truth is that sexual offenders are a painful reminder to all of us of our own potential to abuse and hurt others, especially in areas of sexuality and relationships. By distancing ourselves from sexual offenders, we can distance ourselves from that part of us which we do not even wish to acknowledge. Travers refers to this as scapegoating. Scapegoating, according to the cultural theorist René Girard, is the most primitive means of restoring order and harmony in a community.[9]

Since the beginning of time, communities have been establishing themselves 'over against' individuals whom they have identified as a threat. Community is formed or re-formed in working together to defeat a common enemy; unlikely alliances are forged and potentially divisive squabbles are resolved or left aside. When the perceived enemy has been defeated and expelled, and when harmony is restored to the community, the community finds it is in a better state than before. It is then presumed that all the ills which beset the community were in fact the fault of the individual now expelled and that it is his/her defeat and expulsion which has brought about the new spirit of co-operation and understanding.

This concept of scapegoating explains some of the reaction to sexual offenders in contemporary Irish society and in the media. First of all, sexual offenders serve as scapegoats for our general discomfort with our sexuality. In Ireland, within a few short years, we have gone from being a society within which even mature discussion of sex was taboo, to one which not only condones but also actively encourages all sexual activity so long as consent is given. Every day of the week, sexuality is violated and exploited in the interests of the market and the media. The images, which titillate us all, whether in tabloids or on television or in films, create an environment which supports sexual violation and exploitation. They lead us to think that all our sexual dreams and fantasies can be satisfied, and that we have a right to satisfy them. They caricature any form of conscience with regard to sexuality.

At some deep place in ourselves we know that sexuality is precious and sacred. Yet we rarely challenge the popular sexual discourse and images. It is reassuring, therefore, to have a clearly labelled class of people called 'sexual offenders' over against whom we can assure ourselves of our own sexual propriety. Sex offenders are those whose sexual lives are out of control. The rest of us are ok.

Sex offenders must take full responsibility for their crimes. They are guilty of horrific violations of human dignity. At the same time, however, they may be innocent of much for which society punishes them. It is no more their fault than it is ours, that we live in a society in which sex is the most marketable of commodities. It is not their fault that we live in a society which is sexually immature, in which many people are frightened of their sexuality, and find it difficult to express it in ways that build relationships and give life in every sense of the term. It is not their fault that we live in a society, which, despite the prosperity of some, leaves many of its citizens disempowered and with a sense of helplessness, which is in turn compensated for by a variety of forms of addiction. It is not their fault that public attitudes make it very difficult for people in trouble with their sexuality to seek help. Lastly, it is not their fault that there is so little help available for the few who have the courage to seek it.

At some level we know all this, and occasionally we feel guilty about it. But the existence of a clearly labelled category of criminals makes it easier for us to run away from the criminal neglect in which we all share as members of society.

The church can scapegoat offenders too
Turning to the reaction within the church, we find that many priests and religious, including those in leadership, have shown great compassion and understanding towards colleagues convicted of sexual abuse. Their capacity to cope with a colleague who has offended has been determined by their own level of self-knowledge and self-acceptance. Many have realised that 'but for the grace of God' it could be them. Some while journeying with imprisoned colleagues, have heard the call to travel a painful road of personal reflection themselves, reviewing their own sexuality and how it finds celibate expression.

Bishops and congregational leaders genuinely have been torn in their efforts to be compassionate and at the same time pastorally responsible to victim and offender. At one level, the protection of children, legal considerations, and the public demand for justice have determined church policy. At a deeper level, however, there are signs of scapegoating within the church as well, signs that it has been considered better 'to have one man die for the people than to have the whole nation destroyed'.[10] As Girard notes, expulsion is always unifying. It restores order and harmony to the community. It enables the flock to believe it is 'pure' again. It encourages the view that while there may have been one or two 'rotten apples', the barrel itself is sound. The permanent exclusion from active ministry of priests and religious who have been convicted of sexual offences allows us to believe that with it, all clerical problems have been resolved and that we can get back to business as usual. The clerical caste, as such, remains intact and deeper questions need not be asked. We need not ask, for example, how much energy and resources we have invested in the on-going care and support of priests. We need not raise questions about the kind of structures of organisation that are in place and whether or not they permit or encourage priests and religious to relate and behave in a mature manner. And we can dismiss as irrelevant questions about the appropriateness of a highly authoritarian, exclusively male celibate style of leadership.

Psychologists and prison officials call repeatedly for society to move beyond the dynamic of scapegoating. They urge us all to reflect on our shared culpability with regard to sexual crime.[11] They actively seek a role for communities in responding to offenders and for a shift from retributive to restorative models of justice. The church needs to put its full weight behind such calls. As we shall now go on to see, such calls are precisely in accord with gospel principles. However, the church is in a weak position to support these worthwhile demands unless it is itself prepared to implement them within its own ranks.

Jesus Christ and Forgiveness of Enemies
A close examination of the significance of the life, death and resurrection of Jesus Christ shows that in principle the church is well placed to call people out of their instinctive reaction to sexual abuse into a response which promotes healing and which upholds the dignity both of victim and offender. In order to appreciate this, we must take a fresh look at Jesus as portrayed in the gospels.[12]

Jesus made it possible for all people to understand that God's unlimited graciousness was the most original and firm basis for human relationships. However, as a race we had 'fallen' into a different, damaging and destructive manner of being in the world. Instead of relying for our identity on the fact that we were creatures of a gracious God, we felt we had status only when others considered us to be important. We sought security not in God's fidelity to us but in the fact that we owned or possessed more than other people did. Our sense of our own goodness depended on us defining others as less good than ourselves. We were united to people not by the realisation that we were all brothers and sisters, but because we found some other people whom we considered our common enemies. We emphasised their otherness and we confirmed our shared identity by defining ourselves over against them. Violence against other people became acceptable as a way of defending our place in the world and of holding on to our sense of dignity and well-being. When someone hurt us, we came to believe that we had to hit back or else we would be seen as weak.

Scapegoating became an acceptable and even necessary way of achieving social order and harmony. Hebrew religion had, for centuries, made use of an actual scapegoat upon whom the sins of the people were periodically unburdened and who was then driven out into the desert. The evil was thus understood to be removed from people's midst. But this ritual practice was only a reflection of what was happening every day: adulteresses were stoned, demoniacs banished, tax collectors ostracised, lepers outcast, and sinners were considered excluded from both God's company and that of decent people.

Jesus stepped right into the middle of this way of being in the world and called for a total halt to it. He said,

> You have heard that it was said, 'An eye for an eye and a tooth for a tooth.' But I say to you, do not resist an evildoer. But if anyone strikes you on the right cheek, turn the other also; and if anyone wants to sue you and take your coat, give your cloak as well; and if anyone forces you to go one mile, go also the second mile. Give to everyone who begs from you, and do not refuse anyone who wants to borrow from you ... You have heard that it was said, 'You shall love your neighbor and hate your enemy.' But I say to you, Love your enemies and pray for those who persecute you, so that you may be children of your Father in heaven; for he makes his sun rise on the evil and on the good, and sends rain on the righteous and on the unrighteous.[13]

When we read this text, our first reaction might be that it requires people to accept violence and abuse as their lot, to 'put up' with it, hoping that somehow in the end God will make it up to them. This and other texts have been so interpreted in the past. But that was not the meaning or the intention of Jesus. On the contrary, Jesus is calling people to take the most radical and powerful stand that is possible against violence by refusing to allow themselves to be drawn into it by those who violate or abuse them.

Jesus called for a new basis for human relationships. In the end he offered his life as that basis. If people needed a victim to be the source of unity with one another, then he was prepared to be that victim. Jesus very deliberately stepped outside the cycle of violence and he showed that people are most fully human, most fully themselves, when they do what he did. God's resurrection of Jesus completes the story. Faced with the gravest provocation of all, the murder of God's own son, God still refuses to be drawn into the reciprocity of violence but responds instead with the ultimate gesture of love, the resurrection of Jesus and the gift of eternal life for all which it signifies.

What Jesus wanted was for all people, whether rich or poor, to be truly free. And the path to true freedom was paved only with God's unconditional love.

As long as we depend on the approval of others for our sense of well-being, we are not free. As long as we need to see others as bad so that we can feel good about ourselves, we are not free. As long as we allow the behaviour of others towards us, whether benevolent or hostile, to determine the extent of our graciousness and self-giving, we are not free.

Our *self-giving* is most clearly tested when it comes to the question of *for-giving*. It is at this point that we come most clearly to recognise the fundamental principles by which we have chosen to live our lives. When somebody wrongs us, it might appear that the natural response is to seek revenge, to retaliate. But what Jesus showed is that *this is not the most natural response*. The most original human response, the response that most accords with true human nature, is to forgive. To forgive is to decide that the person who has offended will not define or limit the extent of my graciousness and self-giving. To forgive is to decide that even in the face of hurt and violation, I will continue to take the risk of giving of myself. To forgive is to decide that I still trust in the power of love to heal and transform, and this despite the horrible violation and hurt that has occurred.

I can only forgive if I do not depend on the 'putting down' of the person who has wronged me in order that I can stand up straight again. I can only forgive if I know that I do not need the wrongdoer's pain in order to feel good about myself. The only thing that can ultimately heal me is the conviction that I am loved exactly as I am and that this love for me is the only thing that matters. If I believe this, then I *must* forgive in order to be true to this love and true to my deepest self. Anything short of forgiveness is allowing the wrongdoer to have the last word regarding the extent of my self-giving.

Sexual abuse is possibly the most difficult of all violations to forgive. Sexuality belongs to that which is most intimate in us. Through our sexuality we can physically express our nature as gracious, self-giving beings. When somebody violates us sexually, they damage this nature. Rape literally means to seize and carry off something. When somebody is raped, it is their capacity to give of themselves, which is seized and plundered. The very aspect of their nature by which people enflesh their desire to give of themselves totally, is sacrileged.

It is a moment of breakthrough in terms of healing when victims of horrendous sexual abuse come to forgive those who have violated them. It is also, according to psychologists, a necessary moment in the healing process:

> Anger and lack of forgiveness can keep the adult victim locked in a destructive relationship with her abuser and allow the abuser to continue to ruin their lives. Forgiving does not mean excusing, but it allows the adult to let go of her own crippling anger and resentment and desire to punish her abuser. A rich spiritual life can give adult victims the strength to bear the pain of what has been done to them and to rebuild their lives.[14]

What Christianity has to offer is precisely that conviction at which victims of sexual abuse most need to arrive. It is the conviction that I am loved exactly as I am, and that my deepest self is held in being by God's love for me. By remembering this love I am able to forgive my enemies by acting towards them in a way that is gratuitous, by breaking out of the cycle of hatred, by refusing to be entrapped within the reciprocity of violence.

Christianity has also something to offer the perpetrators of sexual abuse. To them it says, it is only a superficial part of yourself that you seek to gratify by sexual abuse. You are grasping and seeking after a sense of well-being by over-powering others, by dominating them, by attempting to steal love from them, by forcing them to express bodily an acceptance of you for which you crave. But what you crave in your deepest self, that is unconditional love and acceptance, is already yours as a gift if only you could realise it, and if only you had the courage and the humility to accept it.

It has more to say to the offender. It says, faced with the shame of your sexual abuse of another person, Christianity asks you not to think that this defines you as a person. It is God's love and this alone which defines you, not anything you do, whether good or evil. You cannot shake off this love. It is unconditional. When you realise fully the enormity of what you have done you may be tempted to despair. Your sense of self-worth may have been totally eroded by a sense of self-hatred. It is at this moment that you, just like your victim, must remember God's love.

God's gratuitous love is always there in our lives. It is not as if something new is added in the face of our sin and need of forgiveness. Forgiveness, rather, is the particular form which God's love takes when faced with the reality of our sin. Sin not only sunders our relationships with those against whom we sin. It also sunders our relationship with our deepest selves. When we sin we lose contact with our own goodness. We see only our sin and are tempted to allow ourselves to be defined by it. But God's love offers to restore us to ourselves, to heal us. It as if God says to us, 'I know there is more to you than what you have done. I see that. I want you to see that yourself. I know that there is goodness in you that is deeper and more original than your sinful action. I believe in that goodness. I restore you to it and I want you to live out of it.'

A Mission to *the church*
Victims of sexual abuse who arrive at some level of healing, and abusers who come to acknowledge the full significance of their wrongful actions, realise that violence and hatred, revenge and retribution cannot bring them peace. They have reached a vacuum in their humanity that only gratuitous, self-giving and forgiving love can fill. Difficult as it is to believe, many victims of sexual abuse by priests and religious still turn to Christian faith if not to the church in order to be healed. They do so because they have plumbed the dark and hidden depths of their humanity. And they know in the light of their painful journey

AN IRISH READER IN MORAL THEOLOGY

that only a God who loves as the God of Christ does, who 'loves humanity at its worst' (Moore) can re-fashion their lives.

These people have a mission to the church. They call the church to recover its own hidden depths in Jesus Christ which have been obscured by centuries of conformity to the very kinds of exercise of power and sources of status and security which Christ abhorred. Whether as victims or abusers, these people bear the marks of the worst excesses of the abusive power we are all inclined to wield by virtue of our fallen nature. They more than anyone else know its futility.

According to Pope John Paul II, the church 'needs heralds of the gospel who are experts in humanity, who have penetrated the depths of the human heart'. The church has been sent such heralds from among those who have survived the trauma of sexual abuse, whether as victims or offenders. We are being called to listen to them, to listen to their stories and to listen to what the very occurrence of sexual abuse within the church is saying to us. Disturbed Catholics ask when it all will finish. They long for an end to the revelations and the scandals, the constant undermining in the media. They cannot wait for a bright new chapter in the life of the church. In this article I have been suggesting that we have a long distance to go until we reach that new chapter. We have a long and painful path of conversion to travel first, a path that will lead us to re-discover the foundations of the church and to re-examine our way of being in the world in the light of our discoveries. However, until we go down that path, regardless of how correctly we celebrate ritual and cite formulae, 'the Christian faith is not being taught, and the words have been pressed into service of a different kingdom.'[15]

Notes:

1. Olive Travers, *Behind the Silhouettes*, Belfast: Blackstaff, 1999, 74.
2. By 'non-fixated' is meant offenders who do not have a primary sexual preference for children but who turn to children for sexual satisfaction to compensate for difficulties in (sexual) relationships with other adults. These offenders are not, strictly speaking, paedophiles (Cf Travers, *Behind the Silhouettes*, 47).
3. Address to the NCPI Conference, Athlone, 26 April 1999.
4. Marie Keenan, quoted in the *Irish Independent*, 26 April 1999.
5. Sebastian Moore, 'The Bedded Axle-Tree', *Jesus Crucified and Risen*, William Loewe and Vernon Gregson (eds), Minnesota: Liturgical Press, 1998, 218.
6. Moore offers the explanation that the Western male psyche has not advanced beyond a relationship to women that is shaped by the relationship of the young man to his mother. Men first encounter women in the role of son to mother. In this relationship men sense the overwhelming 'natural' superiority of women as mothers and, though they grow up physically, emotionally they are unable to move beyond this first relationship into a partnership of equality. Thus, men seek to subjugate women in an effort to overcome their feelings of inferiority towards them. To compensate for women's 'natural' supremacy, men have developed a 'cultural' pre-eminence. In a state of emotional

fixation on the mother, there is no place for male sexual energy, which must find other outlets.

7. Olive Travers, interviewed in *The Irish Times*, 15 Feb 1999. Cf her book, p 46.

8. 'Both offenders and victims are members of society and what we have to say about them also applies to us. We have to ask ourselves in what ways we are victims and/or offenders and to what extent we have contributed to the abusive behaviour and twisted thinking which resulted in sexual abuse' (Travers, 90).

9. Cf for example, *Violence and the Sacred*, London: John Hopkins Press, 1977. Girard's work has been taken up by a number of theologians. Most notable are Raymund Schwager, *Must there be Scapegoats? Violence and Redemption in the Bible*, San Francisco: Harper & Row, 1987, and James Alison, *The Joy of Being Wrong, Original Sin through Easter Eyes*, New York: Crossroad, 1998.

10. John 11:50

11. '... we are ourselves either colluding with a society which tolerates abuse or seeking to live in one which discourages abusive relationships at all levels. We need to be less complacent about the media messages which exploit and objectify sexuality' (Travers, 112).

12. Here the author wishes to acknowledge the work of James Alison, *The Joy of Being Wrong, Original Sin through Easter Eyes*, New York: Crossroad, 1998.

13. Matthew 5: 38ff

14. Travers, 105. Speaking at the National Conference of Priests of Ireland Conference on Child Sexual Abuse, May 1998, a law lecturer at NUI Galway, Dr Tom O'Malley, stated that, 'Victims' desire for revenge might not be in the best interest of victims themselves and only prolong their suffering.'

15. Alison, p 2.

33 Journey to Loss: Living the Murphy Report

Marie Collins

(John Littleton and Eamon Maher (eds), *The Dublin/Murphy Report: A Watershed for Irish Catholicism?* Dublin: Columba Press, 2010, pp 55-62)

A few days after the publication of the Murphy Report a lady approached me in the supermarket. She took my hands and said: 'You have been talking about this for years, but it is only now I understand, I understand what you have been telling us.' This lady represents many in the country who for years have heard about clerical sex abuse through the media, by reading the testimony of survivors in the Ferns, Murphy and Ryan Reports. They have heard the Catholic Church leadership's denials, have listened to the shock they expressed at the Reports, as if it was all news to them. Church leaders claiming that they did not understand abuse, they were doing their best, had been on 'a learning curve'. While suggesting through their apologists that the whole issue was a media conspiracy 'by anti-Catholic journalists,' or that many accusations were false, or that victims who spoke out were only looking for revenge or money.

At the same time, those in leadership were constantly making statements about how they always put the safety of children first, that the care for victims and their families was a priority and there had never been any cover up. All the apparent sincerity, shock and reassurances had convinced many Catholics that their church leaders were being unfairly blamed for the bad apples in their ranks; they had been doing their best to help survivors and to handle this crisis, which was no fault of theirs. Who would believe, who could believe that those at the very top in the Catholic Church, those who would see themselves as our moral leaders, would allow known predators, guilty of rape and other horrors against innocent children, to remain free in positions of trust to carry on the same crimes against even more children?

The Murphy Report on the Archdiocese of Dublin has blown all these denials and obfuscation [1.17-1.9]* out of the water. It confirmed that those in Catholic Church leadership in Dublin over decades had known they had predatory paedophiles in their parishes, but instead of reporting their crimes to the Garda [1.32] moved them from parish to parish with no concern for the children they were putting at risk. They had deliberately misled survivors and their parents using a uniquely Catholic Church means of lying with an easy conscience called mental reservation [58.20]. The Murphy report said clearly what survivors had been saying for years, that the men in leadership roles in the church knew what they were doing, but cared more for the institution than for the children [1.15].

The smoke blown in the eyes of the laity had cleared; it was now obvious what had been going on. At last the truth was there for all to see and the church hierarchy had nowhere to hide. The lady in the supermarket now 'got it'. This encounter left me pondering on how long it had taken me to reach that point and then realise that I could no longer be comfortable as a practising member of my church.

I had not lost my faith through my abuse experience. Sexually assaulted as a child by a priest, I had turned all the blame in on myself [58.4]. When I told my abuser what he was doing was wrong, he said he was a priest, that 'he could do no wrong'. I had been taught to respect and look up to my priests; he was revered and deferred to by the adults around me. I was a Catholic child who had just made her confirmation. I believed him – he was a priest and priests didn't lie. If he was not doing wrong then it must be me. I was left full of confusion, misguided guilt and a total loss of self-esteem. This caused enormous damage to my health and my life but I remained a faithful Catholic.

Twenty five years later I revealed my abuse, for the first time, to a doctor. I came to realise through the work of my doctor that I was not responsible for what had happened to me. I decided I must tell the church authorities in case this man was still in a place of trust with children. I believed they would take the action needed to ensure he would never be able to repeat his actions on other children. I spoke with a priest in my parish whom I had known for some years. He would not allow me to tell him the name of the abusing priest. He did not want to know the name – saying if he 'knew it' he would 'have to do something': he clearly did not feel he needed to do anything. His reason? He said what had happened had probably been my fault and then went on to tell me I was 'forgiven'! This response devastated me.

These words pushed me back into a pit of despair. All that guilt which my doctor had worked so hard to erase came rushing back. Did I question for one minute this priest's sincerity? No. Did I believe him when he said he thought it was probably my fault? Yes. He was a priest and I had great respect for him. Did I realise he was following a church policy – confirmed by him to the Garda nineteen years later? [13.12] Of course I didn't. I was thirty-eight years old and a good Catholic all my life. I respected my priests. This priest's words destroyed all the therapeutic work that my doctor had done. I once more closed down and vowed to myself never to talk to anyone again on the subject. I went on suffering the depressions and anxiety states which had been part of my life since the abuse. My abuser was left unfettered in daily contact with the children in his parish, their parents blissfully unaware of the danger their children were in. As the Murphy Report shows [13.14], during this period he was having ten to twelve-year-old children in his house, getting them to change their clothes there before taking them swimming, photographing them and making recordings of them. What else he was doing we can only surmise. But the 'don't ask, don't tell' [1.31] policy was more important to my local priest than any concern about what might be happening to his colleague's young charges.

AN IRISH READER IN MORAL THEOLOGY

It was ten more years before I was well enough to try once more to report my abuse to the church. I wrote to the Archbishop and the day came for me to make a detailed report to the Chancellor of the diocese. I was nervous and emotional. Almost at once he told me he had checked the accused priest's file and there had 'never been a complaint' about him before. Did I believe him? Of course I did. He was a senior priest, a Monsignor. By now I was forty-eight years old and still a respectful, trusting Catholic. He asked if I was sure I wanted to go forward with my report and warned that it could end up in court, even suggesting that it might be 'too much for me'. I felt he was truly concerned for me. I was very vulnerable and this made me wonder if I was doing the right thing.

It was now thirty five years since I'd been abused. Maybe the priest had only done it that once and regretted it all his life, maybe it would not be fair to him now to bring it all up. If no one else had ever complained the old feeling that somehow it might be my fault rose in me again. Did I know the Archdiocese had not only proof on file that he was an abuser from the era of my youth [13.5], but also that there had been concerns raised about his behaviour with children by members of his parish only two years before? [13.14] No I did not.

I had no inkling it was a policy of the diocese [1.35] and of this Chancellor [1.61] to lie to victims reporting abuse by denying previous complaints, when all the while they knew that such complaints existed. Unaware of this, I wrote to the Chancellor the next day to thank him for his kindness and concern for me!

At this time the hospital authorities where the abuse took place, to whom I had also made a report, contacted the Garda and they came to interview me. I also saw my doctor and became firm again in my resolution to carry forward what I had started. I still had no doubts at all about my Catholic faith. I found great consolation during this time in my religion.

I experienced a great deal of anxiety and emotional turmoil in the following months. The abusive experiences of my childhood were constantly on my mind and I needed increased medical assistance. The Chancellor waited five months after the priest had admitted my abuse to tell me. When I asked the Chancellor if he had given this information to the Garda , he assured me that he had. Later the Garda told me this was not true. I had been relieved when the Chancellor told me my abuser had been removed from his parish, but my relief was short-lived. I soon discovered this was also not true. I then discovered the other admitted instances of criminal acts on my abuser's file. I asked if the Garda had been given access to the file, and was told that they had. Again, the Garda informed me this was not true [13.39]. Who was lying to me? Why was a self-confessed abuser being left in a position of trust with children? If what the Garda said was true, why was the church not helping them in every way? Could they be protecting a child abuser? Surely not!

I wrote to the Chancellor to ask my abuser what he had done with an indecent photograph he had taken as part of my assault. He wrote that the priest said he had destroyed the photo. I passed this letter to the Garda . I was soon on the receiving end of the Chancellor's wrath – he threatened to sue me for this action. I consulted a barrister who confirmed that my actions were legal and correct. At the same time the Garda told me the Chancellor was refusing to sign a statement confirming he wrote the letter. When he discovered that I knew this, he made a complaint against the Garda who had told me – he wanted her punished for being honest with me. I was struggling [13.79] to help the Garda investigation and the church was obstructing this process despite knowing the priest was guilty. I could not believe it! Why? I was beyond doubt and confusion. Now I was angry.

My anger and disillusionment grew over the next months. Numerous attempts to get assurance from the church that this admitted abuser was not in a parish and would never again be in a ministry in contact with children met with equivocation. The archbishop found my queries 'difficult questions' [13.49]. How could an archbishop of my church, knowing a man was a paedophile, find it difficult to decide if he should be in a position of trust with young children? The church always found it so easy to have a moral certainty in how I should live my life – what was morally right or wrong was black and white, no grey areas allowed. Did this only apply to little people like me but not to those in higher places?

I discovered the reasons for the archbishop's difficulty when I met with him some months later. This man was 'a priest', the archbishop told me. I could not 'ruin his life'. He was entitled to his 'good name' and his 'reputation'. The archbishop said that he could ignore the procedures set down in the Catholic Church's own child protection document regarding co-operating with Garda and removal from ministry, as they had 'no power in canon or civil law' [13.49] [57]. I asked if in that case it was morally right to tell the people the church was following these guidelines to the letter? He answered that he 'had to follow canon law and his legal advice'. Morality, it seemed, did not matter. Nor did it come into the equation when weighing the abusing priest's 'right to his good name' against the safety of children. I could not reconcile the church I thought I knew all my life with the church I was now seeing up close.

The priest was eventually convicted of my abuse and of assaulting another child almost twenty years after me. That day the archbishop issued a public statement[1] saying how 'deeply' he felt for the victims and asking for prayers for us as we had 'suffered so much' and were 'deserving of our special concern'. This made me despair of his hypocrisy. What care or concern had this man or his officials shown privately to me in the previous two years? I had been considered a difficult troublemaker [13.34]. He went on to state: 'The diocese has been co-operating with the Garda .' This was a lie intended to mislead the faithful people of the Catholic Church and the wider community. This was mental

AN IRISH READER IN MORAL THEOLOGY

reservation [58.19/58.20] in operation. It was not a lie to these moral leaders – because they had not said – 'the Diocese has been co-operating *fully*' – the word 'fully' being mentally reserved. The fact that the wording used was meant to deceive the public was fine by them.

This was the final straw. I saw in a new light those moral leaders of my church who all my life I had looked up to, who preached the gospel and whose rules I had always done my best to follow. They were at ease in ignoring all moral values and behaving in a totally unChristian way to protect an institution that was more important to them than the words of Christ. How had I ever looked up to these men, how could I ever have trusted and respected them, how could I ever believe a word they said again?

I could no longer sit at Mass and listen to a representative of this church telling me how to live my life when those in leadership were quite prepared to believe none of this applied to them. I am sad to lose an important part of my life. My family and I had always been involved in our parish. My son had been an altar boy, my husband a member of the choir and I a member of a number of parish groups. I ask myself if I can ever find my way back. I still have my Christian belief and I pray as I always have. I still believe the Catholic Church is the church which Jesus Christ founded but I believe it has lost touch not only with the people but also with the very basics on which it was founded. The men in leadership, surrounded as they are by like-minded people and living in a world of canon law and arcane tradition, have completely lost touch with the origins of the church and with the people who – they constantly tell us – *are* the church.

While working with the Lynott Group on *Our Children Our Church*2 we were listing personnel in one section when the term 'lay religious' came up. A canon lawyer in the group stated we could under no circumstances use that terminology. We must use 'un-ordained'. 'Lay' was a derogatory term which would be resented by the religious congregations if used, as in times past the lay religious carried out the manual labour in congregations and so were seen as a lower class than the ordained. It was pointed out that this was the twenty-first century! He insisted 'lay' was a derogatory term and could not be used. The most illuminating aspect of this incident was that the majority of the clerical/ religious members of the group could not understand why the lay members found this archaic thinking alarming.

The Vatican to date have not approved mandatory passing to the civil authorities of complaints of child abuse against a priest received by the church authorities in Ireland. Their stated reason: 'The making of a report put the reputation and good name of a priest at risk' [7.13].

This might come as news to many in Ireland who have been constantly reassured by the hierarchy that all complains are immediately reported. If Jesus Christ were among us now would 'good name' and 'reputation' be his priority or the safety of little children?

After the Murphy report, the hierarchy in Ireland must realise that they need to earn back trust and respect. There is only one way to do that. A new era of honesty and humility has to begin, and the laity must be part of the renewal. The Vatican must give its *recognitio* to a policy of mandatory reporting and the state has to be allowed free access to all church records involving the handling of child abuse allegations past and current. There must be an unambiguous commitment from the Vatican and the Irish hierarchy to the Irish people that mental reservation will never be used again in any context.

The Irish Bishops' Conference, in their statement of 9 December 2009, stated: 'We are shamed by the scale of extent to which child sexual abuse was covered up in the Archdiocese of Dublin and recognise this indicates a culture that was widespread in the church. The avoidance of scandal, the preservation of the reputations of individuals and of the church, took precedence over the safety and welfare of children. This should never have happened and must never be allowed to happen again. We humbly ask for forgiveness.'

Within weeks, we had the unedifying sight of former Dublin auxiliary bishops backtracking on this and attacking the current archbishop for actually acting in accordance with it! One bishop (Dermot O'Mahony) even stated that 'the acceptance by media and current diocese policy that a cover-up took place must be challenged.' The leadership must realise that this is the twenty-first century; that they are now dealing with a well-educated population who will listen to the words and compare them with their actions.

The mechanisms to involve the laity as outlined in Vatican II must be put in place. No longer the two worlds – the ordained above, the laity below: we must go forward side by side. Together, let us get back to being the church Jesus Christ founded. Then, maybe in time, I will find my way home.

Notes:
* Note that numbers included in brackets refer to sections in the *Commission of Investigation: Report into the Catholic Archdiocese of Dublin July 2009* (Murphy Report).
1. Press Release, 27 June 1997.
2. Catholic Church Child Protection policy document published in 2005.

AN IRISH READER IN MORAL THEOLOGY

34 'Them and Us':
The Clergy Child Sexual Offender as 'Other'[1]

Marie Keenan

(Tony Flannery (ed), *Responding to the Ryan Report*, Dublin: The Columba Press, 2009, pp 180-220)

Although disclosures of sexual abuse by Catholic clergy have been reported in many countries throughout the world, the relationship between church and state in Ireland has made the Irish experience fairly unique. Inglis (1998, 2005) argues that the Irish take on sexuality and the historical position of the Catholic Church in Ireland has contributed to this situation. My view is that the changing understanding of childhood and the form that professional discourses have taken in relation to abuse perpetrators in the United States and Ireland has also created a background for the manner in which child sexual abuse by Catholic clergy is currently narrated. On this issue, Irish professionals are inclined, regrettably, to follow closely what happens in the United States. There is much to be learned from the Scandinavian countries on how to handle crime in general, and I think we could do well to look to Berlin rather than Boston if we need guidance on sexual abuse in general. We must also situate and understand our own problems within our uniquely Irish context.

This article examines child sexual abuse by Catholic clergy in two jurisdictions, Ireland and the United States, with inevitable limitations in both cases. These jurisdictions are selected because most of the research on this topic emanates from the United States and because my own research with Catholic clergy is situated in Ireland. The article begins by taking a brief but critical look at the dominant discourses of child sexual abuse, as these discourses form part of the context in which sexual abuse by Catholic clergy is currently understood in Ireland. Drawing on sociological and psychological perspectives as well as my own research and clinical experience, the article then examines what is reliably known about Catholic clergy who have sexually abused minors and about the role or otherwise of the institution of the Catholic Church in relation to these abuses. Whilst much of the literature from the United States provides the quantitative data on the nature and scope of the problem, my research provides the qualitative picture of the lived experiences of Catholic clergy who have sexually abused minors. The article concludes by arguing that if we truly want to help children and create a safer society for all men, women and children in Ireland, then we need to get beyond a blaming stance and towards more preventative and rehabilitative/restorative perspectives.

The Power of Language

Many scholars argue that language and its usage are central to the emergence of social problems (Hacking, 1999:27; Jenkins, 1998:7; Best, 1995:2; Berger & Luckmann, 1991:39; Kincaid, 1998:5). How a problem is 'languaged' will influence whether or not it will be privileged over other issues and what 'core features' will become 'taken-for-granted' as central to the problem's depiction. Jenkins (1998:9) argues that none of the words or concepts that are often used in relation to child sexual abuse represents universally accepted or 'objective' realities. Rather, many of the words used in relation to this problem's definition, such as sexual abuse, victim, survivor, paedophile, molester, pervert, sexual deviant are rooted in the attitudes of a particular time and each carries its ideological baggage. Jenkins (1998) warns that it seems impossible to write on the topic of child sexual abuse without using language that appears to accept the ideological interpretations of a particular school of thought. In so doing, it forecloses the exploration of other avenues of interpretation. Interpretation is hugely important when it comes to this issue, especially when it comes to assessing the motivation of individuals who acted or failed to act in relation to children in times gone by. Whilst it is objectively correct that many children are and have been exploited sexually and that many suffer as a result, many other 'taken-for-granted' assumptions in relation to child sexual abuse certainly require further debate and analysis. Different eras have produced different perspectives on child sexual abuse and in each era the prevailing opinion is supported by professional discourses that present what is described as convincing 'objective' 'empirical' research that is said to represent more advanced thinking than what went before (Jenkins, 1998). What appears to be the case is that one 'reality' prevails until another replaces it, and each formulation is presented as progressive, claiming that the contemporary beliefs are 'true' whereas the previous ones were not (Jenkins, 1998). To say that political and ideological agendas are not influencing how the problem of child sexual abuse is construed would be to neglect that which is most obvious.

Several scholars (Jenkins, 1998:2; Hacking, 1999:127; Johnson, 1995:22) observe a tension in the professional and social field in relation to current discourses of child sexual abuse in which the holders of the 'truth' of the situation, those who are seen to have the 'correct' interpretation of events, are juxtaposed against those who are said to be 'in denial'; those individuals whose interpretations are seen as suspect. Protagonists for one side argue that recent realisations of the size and nature of child sexual abuse are made possible by the growing accumulation of 'objective' knowledge and the lifting of taboos that limited research in the past. Those who disagree are seen as 'in denial'. The attempt to silence one's opponents who do not agree with a particular version of events is a central feature of the public discourse of child sexual abuse in Ireland and in the United States.

AN IRISH READER IN MORAL THEOLOGY

Kincaid (1998:13) argues that Western culture has 'enthusiastically sexualised the child while denying just as enthusiastically that it was doing any such thing', such as during child pageants in the United States and in certain spheres of the pop music industry. According to Kincaid (p 20), a society that regards children as erotic, but also regards an erotic response to children as criminally unimaginable, has a problem on its hands. In his opinion, the true nature of the abuse of children is still denied, largely because the complexities involved in the interplay of childhood, sexuality and adulthood are also denied, whilst attention is focused on the 'monster' who is seen as 'other' (Kincaid, 1998:20). Kincaid argues that if a society wants to protect children from sexual abuse and understand how the problem is constituted, then the discourse must change to one in which the problem of child sexual abuse is located within the general adult population and not with a few individuals who are identified as 'monsters'. Ultimately, a better understanding of the complexities of adult and child sexuality will lead to greater protection for children (Kincaid, 1998:22) and less marginalising of men.

Changing Understanding of Childhood

Since the mid 1970s changes have occurred in how childhood is understood, which may have a bearing on current-day perceptions of abuse victims and indeed on abuse perpetrators. In most Western societies, childhood is seen as an age-related phenomenon which prescribes legal rights and responsibilities that take effect at different ages (Corby, 2000:10). Despite these age-related demarcations children grow at different rates both physically and psychologically and there is not uniformity in how the child is seen throughout the world.

The most influential work on childhood in the twentieth century has been that of Philippe Ariès (1962), a French social historian. In *Centuries of Childhood* (1962:125) Ariès argued that it was from the seventeenth century onwards, with the advent of a form of education dominated by religion-based morality, that children became separated from adults in the way known today. Ariès (1962: 126) saw this as a backward step.

Other scholars (De Mause, 1976:1; Pollock, 1983:7; Wilson, 1984:183) criticise the work of Ariès (1962) and argue that he does not have the evidence to back up his wide-ranging claims. Some scholars (De Mause, 1976:1; Stone, 1977:70) see the development of the concept of childhood as highly progressive. They argue that developments in the concept of childhood heralded a time when children were now recognised as a distinct group from adults, with their own particular developmental needs and vulnerabilities that made them deserving of special rights. These scholars argue that developments in the concept of childhood did much to improve the lot of children. De Mause (1976:1) argues that 'The further back in history one goes the lower the level of childcare and the more likely children are to be killed, abandoned, beaten, terrorised and sexually abused.'

It is highly likely that there is no universal experience of childhood, nor has there been in the past, and it is highly possible that children of different classes, genders and races have had, and continue to have, widely differing experiences of childhood (Corby, 2000:15). In the Irish situation, Buckley *et al* (1996:12) observed, if the period up to the 1970s was to be characterised by the era of the 'depraved child' (when child care interventions were viewed as a means of social control and of 'disciplining' the children of the poor) and the 1980s were characterised by the era of the 'deprived' child (when the influences of developmental psychology were being felt, emphasising emotional and psychological dimensions to the welfare of children), the 1990s and 2000s must certainly be considered the era of the 'abused child' and the 'sexually abused child' – and this era shows no signs of abating. However, it is also worth noting that as an Irish public gets rightly upset and angry about the childhood experiences of the children of the Irish industrial and reformatory schools of the 1950s, 1960s and 1970s, countless children live in poverty in Ireland in the year 2009, and services for children with disabilities and those in the care of the state due to family breakdown are grossly neglected and underfunded (O'Brien, 2009a; 2009b; 2009c; 2009d; 2009e). The changing concepts of childhood have had a significant influence on social change in Ireland since the 1980s.

Changing Concepts of Child Sexual Abuse
Jenkins (1998:xi) traced the history of adult/child sexual relations (today known as child sexual abuse) and argues fairly convincingly that although the term child sexual abuse has a long history it was not until the mid 1970s that it acquired its present cultural and ideological significance, 'with all its connotations of betrayal of trust, hidden trauma and denial'. In Jenkins's opinion (1998:234) modern concepts of child sexual abuse are linked to what he sees as irreversible social, political and ideological trends (the vulnerability of children and their need for protection, political and social equality for women, and the power of medico-legal discourses of sexuality) which make it likely that contemporary formulations of the child abuse problem will not diminish in the near future. This is a concept that has changed over time and child-adult sex has not always offered the same meaning and implications for the child or adult as we have come to accept as taken-for-granted truth today.

Whilst Freud wrote of 'damage' to children who had experienced abuse, it is only since the 1970s that this idea has re-emerged as worthy of professional and public interest (Jenkins, 1998:18). For some earlier periods of the twentieth century it was not uncommon for some of the clinical literature to suggest that that in many cases of adult-child-sex the child was the active seducer rather than the one who was innocently seduced and the idea prevailed that children produced such offences for their own psychological reasons (Jenkins, 1998:2). Such thinking certainly influenced aspects of professional practice in the 1970s.

AN IRISH READER IN MORAL THEOLOGY

Child sexual abuse was seen as an infrequent occurrence unlikely to cause significant harm to the vast majority of subjects. Today children who have been experienced sexual abuse are sometimes regarded as 'damaged for life' (Jenkins, 1998:2) – a label I also find myself equally rejecting on their behalf. Just as children are not the active seducers neither are they 'damaged' for life – traumatised, hurt, angry, upset, maybe. For those people who are labelled as 'damaged', often by a well intentioned professional or public discourse, an additional burden to that already endured can be an unintended consequence. My professional involvement with individuals who have experienced all kinds of trauma and abuse has taught me that it is always possible for human beings to turn their tragedy into something that makes even greater human beings in the world, especially when the trauma and the wrongs inflicted are truly acknowledged and lamented. The potential for the human spirit to rise above adversity never ceases to amaze me.

Images of child sexual offenders have also changed dramatically over time. Once seen as benign molesters, 'a species of defective' individuals, known to all and not doing much harm, child sexual offenders are now seen as evil sex 'fiends' who possess the most dangerous and sophisticated criminal intellects. Child sexual offenders are also thought to have access to the latest form of technology and communication (Jenkins, 1998:18) and to operate in 'rings'. The perpetrator of child sexual abuse, who was once seen as a 'harmlessly inadequate', is now referred to as a 'dangerous predator' (Jenkins, 1998:2; Hudson, 2005; Greer, 2003). In much public discourse, child sexual offenders are now seen as posing danger to every child in all situations and their behaviour and personhood is often little removed from the worst multiple killers and torturers (Jenkins, 1998:2; Hudson, 2005:26; Breen, 2004b:9). The resultant public discourse is one of retribution, in which risk management and public notification of the dangers posed by certain individuals are preferred to the more rehabilitative or restorative ideals. Risk management rather than reparation and social inclusion become the focus of social policy and political action. The child abuse victim is portrayed as damaged for life and the child sexual offender is viewed as the most evil of human beings.

The Creation of 'Types'

The primary focus of the psychological literature on the child sexual offender is an individual one, with a strong emphasis on understanding the causes of the crime and the vulnerability factors that might lead an individual down a sexually abusive path. Generally the aim of a psychiatric perspective is to measure and classify, identifying the predictive personality variables that are seen as playing a causative role in creating the phenomenon. The predominant focus of the psychiatric and psychological literature is one of individual limitation; resulting in a professional discourse based largely on ideas of deviance, deficit and individual pathology. Medical definitions have also influenced legal perspectives, leading to medico-legal dominance of the public discourse.

Within medico-legal discourses the child sexual offender is classified as a paedophile or conceptualised as suffering from 'cognitive distortions' or 'deviant sexual attraction'. At any rate he is conceptualised as different from 'normal' men; belonging to a different 'class' or 'type' – a member of a class apart. This construction of the sexual offender has been challenged by some scholars within the discipline of psychology (Marshall, 1996b; Marshall *et al* 2000; Freeman-Longo and Blanchard, 1998). However, despite this challenge, the power that professional disciplines exercise in the creation of knowledge appears to be rarely questioned, and with some notable exceptions it is rare that the social consequences of these particular 'findings' are addressed (Freeman-Longo and Blanchard, 1998; Marshall *et al* 2000; Marshall, 1996b).

Bell (2002:83) offers some observations on the tensions between individualisation and 'types' and the techniques that are used in certain disciplines, such as psychology, medicine, social work and criminology, in order to produce information about individuals, which is then subsequently used to identify and govern others of the same 'type'. O'Malley (1998:1) observes such a process in the Irish legal system, whereby as soon as a person is formally or informally judged to be a 'sex offender' or 'child abuser', he is socially classified under that heading only. What matters is the very sexual nature of the offence and the classification that follows (O'Malley, 1998:1; Hudson, 2005:26; Bell, 2002:83). Such classifications, which are often based on psychiatric categorisations, lead to marginalisation and demonising of individual men.

Bell (2002:84) argues that the processes by which child abuse becomes known within the disciplines of medicine, psychology and social work and the techniques by which 'the population at risk' is constituted and governed, through law, social work or police practices, need to be analysed rather than taken-for-granted as 'objective' truth. The variety of figures that emerge from such professional discourses and labelling practices, such as 'child abuser', 'paedophile' 'child at risk'' abuse victim', give rise for concern (Bell, 2002; Hacking, 1999; Mercer and Simmonds, 2001; Haug, 2001; Cowburn and Dominelli, 2001). Power is at play within such professional disciplines and in effect careers are built on developing new classifications and categorisations systems for human beings. In the United States, psychiatric classifications underpin the whole counselling 'industry', and individuals cannot recoup the cost for counselling from their insurers unless they have been given a DSM diagnosis (a psychiatric classification) (Freeman-Longo and Blanchard, 1998). Classification systems serve interests beyond the people whose lives are subjected to such categorisations. Classification systems also serve as instruments of objectification, measurement and economic gain. Classification systems certainly concern me, mainly because of their potential to contribute to further oppression, marginalisation and abuse, producing the very effects we are attempting to alleviate in the first instance. Such labels are also of little value when treating individuals who have experienced childhood abuse or individuals who have perpetrated sexual offences.

My argument is that attention must be paid to the practices and techniques that help construct child sexual abuse and the child sexual offender in particular ways, such as 'a danger to every child'; otherwise socially sanctioned practices of dehumanisation, oppression and marginalisation are endorsed, in the absence of good data, but based on ideology and power. All of this takes place in the name of child protection. What is important here is that power relations and vested interests are concealed whilst the cast of villains is construed and elaborated.

In arguing for this I am arguing for a safer society for all and for a society in which all abuses of individuals can be abhorred and challenged, and not just the abuses that happen to catch public attention as worthy of intervention at a particular time. If traditional views of power are based on ideas of domination by individuals or groups, such as in feminist understanding of gender hegemony and patriarchal social structures (Herman, 1981:177; Mercer and Simmonds, 2001:171; Cowburn and Dominelli, 2001:401; Kelly, 1997:10), modern power is located in the strategies and techniques employed to bring forth consensus (Lukes, 2005). In producing 'apparent' consensus on a topic, by silencing certain voices and rendering invisible the power forces at play, a cultural narrative emerges that offers a very narrow range to the public discourse. Both traditional and modern practices of power must be kept to the fore in understanding how child sexual abuse comes to be and how it comes to be understood.

The Media and the Child Sexual Offender
Several scholars (Best, 1995a; Jenkins, 1996; Breen, 2004a, 2004b; Greer, 2003) have analysed the role of the print and electronic media in influencing public opinion on sexual offenders and in using shaming techniques and strategies to marginalise and punish. The mass media is said to play a significant role in setting public agendas on a wide variety of issues, and the media coverage of a story can also alter public perception of its central participants (Breen, 2004a:3). The term 'typification' is used to refer to the process by which 'claims-makers characterise a problem's nature', suggesting reasons for the problem, interpreting the motivations of its elements and recommending solutions (Best, 1995a:8). This process is often evident in media representations of certain social problems. In most Western societies it has become common to use a medical model to typify social problems, implying sickness/disease, treatment and cure (Best, 1995:14). Crime is often typified through the medium of a 'melodramatic' model, which sees 'victims' as exploited by 'villains' who must subsequently

be rescued by 'heroes' (Nelson-Rowe, 1995:84). In an extension of the melodramatic model, Johnson (1995:19) argues that 'horror stories' serve a function in typifying the nature of child sexual abuse and many of its characters. Johnson suggests that the media's use of the 'horror' story is also a way of gaining privilege for child sexual abuse over other aspects of child maltreatment, child poverty and child neglect (p 20)

The use of media templates is even more illuminating. According to Kitzinger (2000:62) media templates are routinely used to emphasise only one clear perspective, to serve as rhetorical shorthand/shortcut, and to help audiences and producers place stories in 'a particular' context. These templates have a threefold effect: (a) they shape narratives around specific issues, (b) they guide public opinion and discussion, and (c) they set the frame of reference for the future (Kitzinger, 1999, 2000). Even though the events once reported might have long since passed, they continue to carry powerful associations that have long outlived their potential immediate usefulness (Kitzinger, 1999, 2000). (Examples of media templates are 'The Wall Street Crash of 1929', which serves as a media template for the reporting of financial issues and problems; 'Vietnam' for a failed or mired war; 'Watergate' for political scandals (Breen, 2004a:5). The power of the media template lies in its associative force (Breen, 2004a:5). The same can be said about Ireland.

In Ireland, the coverage of sexual abuse by Catholic clergy led to the emergence of a new media template, 'Brendan Smyth'. Fr Brendan Smyth, a Norbertine priest, had been convicted in June 1994 on seventeen counts of sexual abuse of children stretching over thirty years. An investigative journalist, Chris Moore, reporting for Ulster Television, showed that the clerical authorities had known for years of Smyth's crimes and had dealt with them simply by moving him on, with the suggestion that they covered up his abuses (Moore, 1995). A series of political events concerning the mishandling of the case in the Attorney General's office led to political tensions which eventually brought down the government in the Republic in 1994 (Moore, 1995). While reporting this case, a new category of sexual offender, 'the paedophile priest', was invented by the media (Ferguson, 1995:248; *Boston Globe*, 2002:7). Furthermore, the media also relied heavily on powerful visual images. From the outset, the media had repeatedly used the same photograph of Brendan Smyth's bloated and angry face, staring straight into the camera, so that he became 'the living embodiment of the greatest demon in modern Ireland' (Ferguson, 1995:249). Long after his death, this photograph often accompanied media reports of sexual abuse by other clergy. This is partly the context in which the child sexual abuse by Catholic clergy has gained public attention and in which the changing constructions of the abuse victims of Catholic clergy and the clergy perpetrators have taken hold. The media template has also led to a view of clerical men who have abused children as a homogenised group, whose offending histories are the same, and all of whom represent continuous danger to children, always and in every situation

Sexual Abuse by Catholic Clergy: The Extent and Form of the Problem
It is difficult to estimate the extent of sexual offending in the general population and it is equally difficult to estimate the extent of sexual offending by Roman Catholic clergy. Most estimates of sexual offenders are derived from forensic sources and some studies acknowledge that those arrested or convicted represent only a fraction of all sexual offenders (Abel, Becker, Mittelman, Cunningham-Rathner, Rouleau and Murphy, 1987:89; O'Mahony, 1996:210). Sometimes the extent of sexual offending is gleaned from the extent of victimisation, but that too is difficult to estimate because of variations in the values, customs, definitions and methodologies that are used in international and comparative studies (Finkelhor, 1994:409). Child sexual abuse is also believed to be significantly underreported (McGee, 2002; O'Mahony, 1996; Russell, 1983). These factors make for difficulty in assessing both the extent of the problem of child sexual abuse and the actual number of sexual offenders in a given population. However a meta-analysis of a number of studies on victim prevalence in the United States is currently accepted as offering good baseline international data (Bolen and Scannapieco, 1999:281). This study reported that the overall prevalence of male children who are sexually abused is 13% (one in six to eight boys) and the prevalence of female children who are sexually abused is 30-40% (one in three girls) (Bolen and Scannapieco,1999:281)'

A study aimed at establishing the extent of sexual violence in Ireland, the SAVI study (McGee *et al*, 2002:88) estimated that Roman Catholic clergy abused 3.9% of all adults who had been sexually abused as children in Ireland (5.8% of all male victims and 1.4% of all female victims). Data collated by an Irish journalist (Quinn, 2005:26, 27) from a number of Catholic dioceses in Ireland, estimated that 4% of all priests and religious in Ireland have been accused of abusing minors over a period of fifty years. The comparable figure of men in the general population who are said to sexually abuse children, although difficult to estimate, is put at 6% by one of the leading researchers in the world on this topic (Hanson, 2003).

The available data provides good support for the argument that the extent of the problem of sexual abuse of minors by Roman Catholic clergy is no greater than in the general population. Whilst the population of priests are a highly selected, highly educated, highly formed group of men, there is in fact no evidence that child sexual abuse is less prevalent in the educated or highly educated male population. In fact, some might argue that the highly educated might be more able to hide their abuses and that it may be more prevalent in this group of men, although more hidden. However, I believe that sexual abuse by Catholic clergy is a subject that requires further research and understanding, as Catholic clergy are distinguished from other men in a number of respects and the Catholic Church is one of the largest religious organisations in the world, representing an influential force in many societies and in the lives of its many members. For millions of people, Catholic clergy are, or have been, the spiritual, moral and ethical leaders.

Catholic clergy represent a group of men pledged to celibacy and the occurrence of sexual activity, especially of an abusive kind, contradicts everything that the institution publicly stands for. In addition, the strong emphasis on moral conscience and moral theology in religious and seminary formation, which takes place in an all-male celibate environment, makes the preparation for this professional and vocational life fairly unique. The accusation that church leaders responded in a similar manner to abuse complaints in Ireland and the United States, (as well as from what we know in Canada, Australia and England), a response that is now seen as having compounded the problem, raises questions about the systemic nature of the problem. Whilst the statistics suggest that 92%-96% of the Roman Catholic clergy did not abuse minors there is much to be analysed and understood about what distinguishes abusive from non-abusive clerical men.

'Normal' Catholic clergy

While it is not correct to suggest that in all cases child sexual abuse is about sexuality – as power, anger and attempts at making contact are also said to play a role – however, every sexual offence has a sexual dimension, otherwise, without consideration of sexual motivation it is difficult to explain why an offence is sexual in nature (Finkelhor, 1984:34). My own research suggests that sexuality concerns are highly implicated in child sexual abuse by Catholic clergy, but it must be stressed that this is a problem that has no one single cause. As most of the literature on 'normal' clergy emanates from the United States, the extent to which some of the themes apply to an Irish Catholic clergy population also requires further analysis. However, a number of themes emerge from the literature on 'normal' clergy, which may be relevant to our understanding of Catholic clergy who have sexually abused.

The literature on normal clergy (mainly from the USA) points to the fact that priests live in an environment that is beset with contradictions, such as a promise to celibacy, but inadequate preparation for living a healthy celibate life (Ranson, 2002a; 2002b); a need for intimacy, but inability to negotiate intimacy within the confines of a celibate commitment (Papesh, 2004); problems with sexuality and sexual orientation, but a need to conceal sexuality concerns (McGlone, 2001:119). Considerable skill is required for living the life of the Catholic clergyman and one would imagine that the training for clergy would be hugely important in this regard. It is interesting, therefore, to note that the literature on 'normal' clergy shows consistently that clergy do not feel well prepared in the seminaries and houses of formation for their lives and ministries (Loftus, 2004:92; Sipe, 2003:277; Hoge, 2002:98; Papesh, 2004:70), nor do they feel adequately supported by church hierarchies in living that life (Lane, 1997:62). This is a theme that also arises in the research on clergy men who have abused.

The literature on 'normal' clergy also suggests that the spaces for clergy in which to speak are few, leading some of them towards the protective environments of spiritual direction, personal psychotherapy and the confessional (McGlone, 2001:119; Ranson, 2002b:220). However, overall the picture is one of clergy keeping their personal, sexual and emotional lives private from other clergy. Cozzens (2004) argues that clerical culture supports such non-disclosure of emotion, including emotional distress. In my research, the confessional emerges as the most important site for disclosure of personal distress, including sexual offending, and it emerges as the most important site from which the participants seek emotional support. Few of the men in my study used spiritual direction.

A most striking feature arising from the examination of the literature on 'normal' clergy in the United States is the view that up to 50% of Roman Catholic clergy are sexually active at any one time, despite vows of chastity and a commitment to celibate living. Several studies (McGlone, 2001; Nines, 2006; Sipe, 2003) report this trend. This is an important finding because it indicates that sexual abuse of minors by clergy may be part of a bigger problem of celibate sexuality for the Roman Catholic Church. This is not to say that celibacy singularly 'causes' clergy to sexually abuse minors – but nonetheless celibacy may play some role in leading clerical men down this path. Clergy engaging in 'consensual' sexual relationships is merely a disciplinary matter for the Roman Catholic Church, but an organisation that publicly proclaims the sexual abstinence of its members, whilst at the same time it tolerates or denies their sexual activity, is itself already in trouble.

Clerical men who have sexually offended against minors
Sometimes the question is raised why individuals with a disposition to prey sexually upon minors gain admission to the priesthood and why they are not weaned out before they infiltrate the organisation. Examined closely, this question suggests a number of assumptions: that priests and religious who come to be accused of the sexual abuse of children have a predisposition to do so, that such inclinations can be discerned at the point of entry to the seminary or while they are seminarians, and that some men become priests and religious in order to gain access to children to abuse. By implication the assumption is that the sexual abuse of a child by Catholic clergy is the result of individual pathology or predisposition – a theory that is favoured by some men in leadership in the Catholic Church. The response often suggests the need for better screening for clergy at the point of entry in order to pick up individuals with a disordered psychological state.

Whilst screening the clergy might be important for a lot of reasons, the assumption that it will pick up those men who might come to be accused of the sexual abuse of children is not borne out by available research and clinical experience. My research and that presented by other clinicians and researchers (Kafka, 2004; Marshall, 2004), including the John Jay team (Terry, 2008:567; Smith *et al*, 2008:580) lead to this conclusion. Even those men who initiated sexual abuse soon after ordination, and whose abusive pattern spanned a long duration, did not meet the paedophilia typology, as they would not have waited so long to begin their abusive 'careers' if they were paedophiles. Many so-called paraphilic interests, such as paedophilia, are said to begin in adolescence. If these men did have a diagnosable disorder on which they would act out, it would be expected that they would have done so sooner (Tallon and Terry, 2008:626). In my own study, in which eight of the nine men abused post-pubertal males (and one also abused a female), and one abused younger male children, I reached the same conclusion, based on an analysis of the men's narratives and of their case files. Tallon and Terry (2008:625) also concluded that it is unlikely that clerical and religious men who have sexually abused minors have specifically chosen a profession in the Catholic Church so that they could gain access to children to abuse. I have reached a similar conclusion (Keenan, 2006).

Several other studies have reviewed aspects of the psychological functioning of clerical men who have sexually abused minors, looking for clues to their abusive actions and decisions. Lack of intimacy and emotional loneliness is considered important by a number of clinicians and researchers (Loftus and Camargo, 1993:292; Sipe, 1995; Loftus, 1999; Kennedy, 2001). Depression and difficulty expressing emotional concerns is seen as important by others (Plante, Manuel and Bryant, 1996:135; Robinson, 1994:365). Whilst McGlone (2001:88) found that 59% of non-offending or 'normal' clergy identified themselves as having received some form of psychological treatment or counselling, mainly relating to depression, sexual orientation, sexual identity issues and alcoholism, Flakenhain *et al*, (1999:330) indicated that only 1.8%-2.5% of sexually offending clergy ever sought psychological help prior to treatment for their sexual offending. Clergy who were identified as child sexual offenders simply did not seek help for their sexual and emotional problems. This is also something that emerges in my own research.

Anger and over-controlled hostility was also reported as part of the profile of clerical men who have sexually abused minors (Plante, Manuel and Bryant, 1996:135). A style of relating that tended towards passivity and conformity, and in some instances a tendency towards shyness is also reported in some of these studies (Rossetti, 1994:4; Loftus and Camargo 1993:292). Anger was also implicated in the offending of the men who participated in my own research – anger that came from a lifetime of submission and attempts at living a life that was impossible to live. My research suggests that the practices of obedience and the absence of personal autonomy in clerical and religious life must be considered significant in the sexual offending of Roman Catholic clergy – especially if obedience becomes an instrument of oppression in the hands of church leaders who work in a spirit of power and control rather than a spirit of guiding leadership.

Some studies found that ignorance of sexual matters (Loftus and Camargo, 1993:292), lack of knowledge of the basic physiology of sexuality and of the emotional responses in sexually charged situations (Loftus and Camargo, 1993:300) and what is described as sexual and emotional underdevelopment (Flakenhain et al, 1999:331) were all found in sexually offending Catholic clergy. However, Loftus and Camargo (1993:292) also found that all groups of clergy attending a treatment centre in Canada for a range of issues were ignorant of sexual matters and not just those who had abused minors.

Several studies have reported that clergy who have sexually abused minors have experienced sexual abuse themselves in childhood, sometimes by another priest or religious (Robinson, Montana and Thompson, 1993 (66%); Connors (1994) (30%-35%); Sipe (1995) (70%-80%); Valcour (1990:49) (33%-50%)). This is also the case in my own research in which six of the nine participants reported a history of sexual abuse; five were abused in childhood and one in the seminary. This is an important finding, although sexual abuse in childhood may never be used to justify the later practice.

The implication of the fact that five of the men in my study had experienced sexual abuse in childhood is that they entered priesthood and religious life with feelings of shame, and fear of speaking about their experiences. As in many situations involving child sexual abuse, the men in my study were drawn into secrets by their abusers, leading them to assume responsibility for the sexual 'relationship'. They believed themselves to be complicit in what was happening and therefore equally culpable. Unfortunately for the participants in my research, their experiences of childhood sexual abuse were not discussed during their time in formation for priestly or religious life – neither they nor anybody else mentioned it.

Another issue that is often raised in relation to clerical men who have sexually abused minors relates to the question of homosexuality. Is the sexual abuse of minors by Catholic clergy the result of the ordination of men of a homosexual orientation? On closer examination this question assumes that homosexuality per se is responsible for the sexual abuse of minors by Roman Catholic clergy. However, this is not seen to be the case by much research on the subject. McGlone (2002) suggests that 46%-66% of Roman Catholic clergy who sexually abuse children and young people are of a homosexual or bisexual orientation. However, there is no evidence that sexual identity and sexually abusive behaviour have the same origins. Adult heterosexuality is still reported as the predominant sexual orientation of men who sexually abuse pre-pubertal children, both males and females, whilst adult males who abuse adolescent males are much more likely to be men of a homosexual orientation (Marshall, 1988:383-391; Langevin, 2000:537). However, it is not simply the case of hetero-sexual men abusing pre-pubertal girls and homosexual men abusing boys, as heterosexual men also sexually abuse pre-pubertal boys, and indeed these data may not be relevant anyway for clergy men who represent a distinct group (Marshall, 2004; Kafka, 2004; Terry, 2008).

Seven of the nine men who participated in my own research were men of a homosexual orientation. Their narratives suggest that for all of them their dif-ficulties in coping with celibacy and sexuality were compounded by a denial and fear of their homosexuality. Without institutional support, the project of constructing the 'clergy' man as a 'gay' man was a concealed affair and an in-dividual and isolated journey. The religious and cultural *mores* of their day made acknowledging homosexuality something the men could not contem-plate. Whilst this situation created significant intra-personal conflicts for them, there is no suggestion by the men that their homosexuality 'caused' them to sexually abuse minors, even in situations where they abused adolescent males. The analysis of their narratives suggests that aspects of their concealed sexual-ity and struggles with celibacy and emotional loneliness, and not sexual orient-ation *per se*, must be considered significant for their sexual offending. My research suggests that the challenges of celibacy were no greater or less for men of a homosexual orientation than they were for heterosexual men, and conceal-ment of sexual desire was evident for all men, regardless of sexual orientation. The fear of unmasking was, however, a constant fear for men of a homosexual orientation, and their identity and self-confidence was severely constrained by such fear.

The existing literature on sexual abuse by Catholic clergy does not give enough prominence to the distinctly important issue of what might be referred to as homophobic tendencies within the Catholic Church and how this disables the development of human sexuality and the natural expression of sexual desire and relationship. This is of particular relevance since what could be re-garded as 'homophobia', certainly seeing homosexuality as dysfunction, is in-stitutionalised by the Catholic Church and to some extent supported by social structures. Homophobia is a particular feature of male gender socialisation and sexual identity and is a central aspect of a complex range of internalised and externalised male behaviours. This is ever more so for a group of men who are socialised together into a life of celibate living in an all-male institutional envir-onment.

The relevance of homophobia in the response of the Catholic Church to clergy sexual abuse cannot be over-emphasised. In particular I am concerned about the hegemony of hetero-normative culture and the spiritual and emotional 'violence' experienced by clergy men in their development, largely perpetrated by a homophobic culture that is rigidly articulated – even today – through aspects of the Catholic Church hierarchy. The recent proclamations by the Catholic Church, which essentially links child sexual abuse by clergy to the issue of homosexuality, are fundamentally flawed and have no basis in empirical or respectable research, scientific knowledge, common social *mores* or a theology of justice. Indeed, this misinformation and the frequency of homophobic condemnation by church hierarchy contribute significantly to an obfuscation of the facts about child sexual abuse and human sexuality and *de facto* to opportunities for the recurrence of abusive behaviours.

Something that is not much reported in the literature on clerical men who have sexually abused minors, but that I found in my own research, relates to the role of fear. It is apparent from an analysis of the men's narratives that the participants in my study constructed their priestly or religious vocation on fear – fear of breaking their celibate commitment and fear of displeasing others (particularly those in authority). For these men the resultant way of 'doing' priesthood involved strategies such as adopting a submissive way of relating to others, avoiding relationships with women and avoiding particular friendships with men. In essence, these men avoided intimacy. Such strategies produced poor adult attachments, a fear of emotional and physical intimacy and prolonged emotional loneliness. Although three of the men in my study said that they learned their initial fear of displeasing others and of emotional disclosure in their families of origin, and two of the men believe that they developed these patterns in response to childhood experiences of sexual abuse, all of the men believed that these problems were compounded by their experiences of seminary life and during their time in formation.

Based on an analysis of the literature on 'normal' and offending clergy, and my own research, my conclusion is that individual pathology is insufficient to explain sexual offending by Roman Catholic clergy and that alternative interpretations must be explored. When comparing clergy offenders with non clergy offenders a similar conclusion is reached. The broad consensus in the psychological literature is that Roman Catholic clergy sexual offenders represent an atypical group of child sexual offenders (Kafka, 2004:49; Marshall, 2003) and that situational and contextual factors must be considered significant in their sexual offending (Marshall, 2003; Brenneis, 2001:25; Tallon and Terry, 2008:627).

The individual and the institution

The features of the institutional church that are said to contribute to a climate in which sexual abuse by Catholic clergy becomes possible include the theology of sexuality, the ecclesiastical structure of power relations and hierarchical authority, clerical culture and seminary formation. These aspects of the institution are influenced in turn by its traditions and teachings that are seen by some scholars to have rendered sexual abuse by clergy and the subsequent responses of the Catholic hierarchy almost inevitable (Frawley-O'Dea, 2004; Kung, 2003; Berry, 1992; Sipe, 1995; Cozzens, 2004; Papesh, 2004; Ranson, 2002a, 2002b; Dokecki, 2004; Oakley and Russett, 2004; Doyle, 2003, 2004; Gordon, 2004; Celenza, 2004). Whilst many within the leadership of the Catholic Church think and operate in terms of individual pathology rather than systemic break-down, the evidence seems to point otherwise. This is not to say that individuals are not responsible for the actions they take, but it is to point to the fact that in trying to understand the problem (and presumably seek solutions) an approach that merely focuses on the individuals who have been 'named and shamed' is to fail. As the identity of the clerical male takes its shape from the institution of the Roman Catholic Church, breaching the boundaries of his identity (as in the case of the clergy perpetrators) or working for the best interest of the church (as in the case of church leaders who are said to have failed in the handling of abuse complaints) is, therefore, an institutional issue.

As the question of celibacy is often mentioned in relation to sexual abuse by Catholic clergy, I will make reference to what the men in my research had to say in relation to celibacy and their subsequent sexual offending. All the men believed they took on the celibate commitment willingly and hoped that after ordination or profession they could take it for granted and get on with their lives. They found a similar expectation on the part of their superiors. The absence of open and honest dialogue in the seminaries, combined with the silence from church leaders, mentors and other priests, on the struggle of celibate sexuality, contributed to this perception.

These men had an intellectual understanding of the meaning and purpose of priestly celibacy and chastity at the time that they were ordained or professed. They accepted celibacy freely as a 'gift' or a 'sacrifice', and none of them believed the vow of celibacy was responsible for their sexual abusing. Celibacy as a 'loss' was not considered. In order to live as 'good clergy-men' they tried to become sexless beings and avoid intimate or close relationships with adults. They believed this was the best way to do 'celibacy'. The men did not engage with the emotional aspect of such a loss until they were experiencing significant emotional and social conflicts.

The participants in my research believed that they were not adequately prepared emotionally and sexually for a celibate commitment, and they were unrealistic in thinking they could walk this path alone. Their experience in the seminary neither supported nor challenged them sufficiently to be honest with their emotional and sexual selves. Five of the nine men reflected that they had no way of knowing how difficult life-long abstinence from sexual relations would be when they accepted the vow. Eight of the nine men had no sexual experience in relationships whatsoever before entering the seminary or religious life. It is evident from the men's narratives that many of them had difficulty coping with celibacy and that it created significant intra-personal conflicts for them. However, as much sexual abuse of minors and sexual boundary violations are perpetrated by adults who have adult sexual outlets available to them, one could reasonably suggest that there is no necessary link to be made between the commitment to celibate living (and the lack of sexual outlet) and sexual abuse of minors. The narratives in my study suggest that whilst the discipline of celibacy itself is not the main problem, the lack of preparation for living a celibate life and the lack of support in living the celibate commitment must be considered significant in the men's subsequent sexual offending, especially as the men tried to live without emotional intimacy as a way of protecting their celibate commitment. In such situations the problems of emotional loneliness and isolation were heightened, and with them the risk of sexual boundary violations. Their understanding of the theology of sexuality, that was devoid of the latest research on the biological and psychological aspects of human sexual development, must also be considered significant in the subsequent sexual violations. This view supports other research in this area (Bennett *et al*, 2004).

Recidivism, repeat offending and effectiveness of treatment

Although media accounts of clergy abuse continue to flourish, many of the most publicised accounts portray the clergy offenders as a homogeneous highly predatory group. My research and that presented by the John Jay Study (John Jay College, 2004, 2006) suggests that such constructions of the clerical child sexual offender do not bear a strong relationship with the reality. Current constructions of the clergy child sexual offender are influenced by power relations, vested interests and professional judgements. Rather than representing the 'objective' reality that they purport to be, professional discourses help construct the child sexual offender as fundamentally different from the rest of society, and in doing so they unwittingly contribute to the situation where child sexual offenders are marginalised and demonised. Despite the heterogeneity of clergy men who have sexually abused minors, they are often portrayed singularly as 'monsters', 'beasts', 'predators' in the media, creating a moral panic that inflates the risk of sex offending by misrepresenting the recidivism rates and construing all sex offences as paedophilic in nature (Douard, 2007; Jenkins, 1998). Although there are certainly dangerous clergy offenders who recidivate at high rates, this is only a small minority, and further research is necessary to understand how those clergy who desist and stop their offending come to make such decisions, and what factors distinguish those men who stop their offending from those clergy who continue to recidivate after treatment interventions. The data on recidivism following current sexual offender treatment is very heartening.

By far the most comprehensive review of psychological treatment for sexual offenders is that conducted by the Collaborative Outcome Data Project Committee in the United States (Hanson *et al*, 2002). This committee was formed in 1997 by a group of leading researchers with the goal of organising the existing outcome literature for sexual offenders and encouraging new evaluation projects to be conducted in a manner that will make for more comparable research and lead to cumulative knowledge. The project is ongoing but the first report concluded that current psychological treatments are associated with reductions in both sexual and general recidivism (Hanson *et al*, 2002:169). In what is regarded as a highly robust study, the Committee reported that after an average of four to five years of follow up, 9.9% of the treated men had sexually reoffended compared to 17.4% of the untreated groups (p 187). The study reported conclusively that current treatment is effective in reducing sexual offending and in fact since 2002 even greater treatment effects have been reported by some treatment providers (Serran, 2006). The public misconception that treatment does not work for sexual offenders, which was propagated by earlier works that relied on outdated and unsatisfactory treatment approaches (Furby *et al*, 1989), needs revision in the light of current encouraging research outcomes. This trend is expected to continue as there have been considerable changes in treatment programmes since the 1970s and the studies of the newer forms of treatment are only recently becoming available (Hanson *et al*, 2002:188). In addition, clerical men who have successfully completed treatment are reported to have an even lower recidivism rate than general child sexual offenders (Hanson *et al*, 2004), with some treatment centres reporting recidivism rates for treated Catholic clergy of less than 3% (Rosetti, 1997).

Church leaders have in many ways fallen into a trap of succumbing to the portrayal of clergy offenders as a homogenised and a highly recidivistic group and current regulation and management of clerical men who have sexually abused minors suggest that this is the case. There is also evidence to suggest that the church leadership is fearful of an angry public and an ever vigilant press and that fear is driving some of the decisions made. The church's zero tolerance policy that mandates the permanent removal of clergy with even a single substantiated allegation of historical sexual abuse against a minor, supports this analysis. The one-size-fits-all approach to managing clergy offenders adds further weight to the claim.

Control of abuse – Abuse of control
In many senses control of sexual abuse by Catholic clergy is fast becoming the abuse of control by some parts of the leadership of the Catholic Church. Mistakes are being made in the name of child protection, just as mistakes were made in the past, in the name of church protection. At the very least current policies for the handling of abuse complaints have contributed to endless pain and trauma for several priests against whom false allegations have been made; policies and processes that have without doubt violated their civil and human

rights. Relationships between bishops and clergy are also being damaged by such policies and practices in ways that only the future will fully unfold. In addition the one-size-fits-all approach to the management of clergy who have abused and the policies that govern many of their highly regulated lives suggests that some of the principles of reparation and forgiveness, on which the Catholic Church is built, are seldom to be found.

The handing over of thousands of documents without regard to the rights of countless individuals, gives further testimony to a Catholic Church leadership so besieged by the popular discourse that good decisions are still not being made. Documents pertinent to the relevant inquiries should and could have been handed over to the various Commissions of Inquiry and Commissions of Investigation in a manner that protected the rights of 'innocent' individuals, who did not ever want the details of their experiences put before any court, albeit a quasi one. Their experience is one of betrayal. Many clergy and indeed church leaders might also have a right to feel betrayed at the manner in which the processes were handled. The judgemental tone of many of these final reports suggests that, rather than providing constructive lessons from the past that can help with preventing similar tragedies from happening again in the future, many of these reports seem intent on public humiliation of individuals. Time will undoubtedly bring scholarly and critical analysis of many the procedures employed by, and reports produced by, the Commissions of Inquiry and Commissions of Investigation into sexual abuse by Catholic clergy and the handling of abuse complaints by the Catholic Church hierarchy.

Conclusion
Sipe (1995:134) refers to the sexual abuse of minors by Roman Catholic clergy as 'the tip of the iceberg' when it comes to problems with sexuality for the Roman Catholic Church. Because illicit sexual activity may well be more likely when there is little openness about or value placed on sexual honesty and sexual maturity, the sexual abuse of minors by Catholic clergy may well serve to bring the general state of sexual health and maturity of Roman Catholic clergy into view. It could be argued that the sexual abuse problem by clergy has accelerated a simmering problem and represents a systemic push to bring the sexuality of clergy onto the church's agenda. My research on child sexual abuse by Catholic clergy suggests that child sexual abuse by Catholic clergy must be considered against the background of the literature on 'normal' clergy and clerical sexuality and not as an unrelated sphere of clerical activity. The need for compassionate leadership has never been more urgent.

My conclusion is that child sexual abuse by Catholic clergy represents a complex interplay of individual and systemic factors and no one cause can be seen to determine the problem's nature. Whilst some works on the subject tends to be about deviant or 'perverted' Catholic clergy, my research shows how ordinary men walked their way into abusing children and minors and it points to the small, maybe understandable compromises that ordinary men made on the road to abusing (Keenan, in press). For many of us this can be more confronting than other accounts of sexual abuse by Catholic clergy; mainly because it can no longer just about 'paedophile priests', but maybe about you and me. Much public commentary on the subject tends to be about 'perverted' clergy, psychological dysfunction or criminal danger. The search is for an overall character trait or personality type that explains it all. My conclusion is that this is a meaningless search. New thinking is urgently required. By truly examining its developmental and systemic pathways, we may be able to go some way towards preventing future offending by Catholic clergy and towards healing the myriad of lives ruined by the legacy of child sexual abuse within the Catholic Church – victims, perpetrators and both sets of families as well as the Catholic laity and many Catholic priests and religious, their bishops and leaders, some of whom live lives as frightened and broken men and women.

Notes:
1. This article has been abridged with the approval of the author.

Bibliography:
Abel, G.C., Becker, J. V., Mittelman, M., Cunningham-Rathner, J., Rouleau, J. L. and Murphy, W. D. (1987), 'Self-reported sex crimes of non-incarcerated paraphiliacs', *Journal of Interpersonal Violence*, 2 (1), 3-25.
American Psychiatric Association (APA) (1994), *Diagnostic and Statistical Manual of Mental Disorders*: IV, Washington, DC: American Psychiatric Association.
Ariés, P. (1962), *Centuries of Childhood*, Harmondsworth: Penguin.
Arthurs, H., Ferguson, H., and Grace, E. (1995), 'Celibacy, secrecy and the lives of men', *Doctrine and Life*, 45 (7), 471-480.
Ashenden, S. (2002), 'Policing Perversion: The Contemporary Governance of Paedophilia', *Cultural Values*, 6: 197.
Balboni, S. (1998), *Through the 'Lens' of the Organizational Culture Perspective: A Descriptive Study of American Catholic Bishops' Understanding of Clergy Sexual Molestation and Abuse of Children and Adolescents*, Unpublished PhD, Northeastern University, Boston, Massachusetts. Available at www.BishopsAccountability.org accessed 10/1/07
Bell, V. (2002), 'The vigilant(e) parent and the paedophile: *The News of the World* campaign 2000 and the contemporary governmentality of child sexual abuse', *Feminist Theory*, 3 (1), 83-102.
Bennett R. and the staff of the National Review Board for the Protection of Children and Young People (2004), *A Report on the Crisis in the Catholic Church in the United States*, Washington DC: The United States Conference of Catholic Bishops.
Benyei, C. R. (1998), *Understanding Clergy Misconduct in Religious Systems. Scapegoating, Family Secrets and the Abuse of Power*, New York: The Hayworth Pastoral Press.
Berger, P. and Luckmann, T. (1966), *The Social Construction of Reality. A Treatise in the Sociology of Knowledge*, Harmondsworth: Penguin Books.

Berry, J. (1992), *Lead Us Not into Temptation, Catholic Priests and The Sexual Abuse of Children*, New York: Doubleday.

Best, J. (1995a), 'Typification and social problem construction' in J. Best. (ed) *Images of Issues, Typifying Contemporary Social Problems*, (pp 1-16), New York: Walter de Gruyter.

Best, J. (ed) (1995b), *Images of Issues, Typifying Contemporary Social Problems*, New York: Walter de Gruyter.

Blanchard, G. T. (1991), 'Sexually abusive clergymen: A conceptual framework for intervention and recovery', *Pastoral Psychology*, 39, 237-245.

Bleibtreu-Ehrenberg, G. (1990), 'Pederasty among primitives: Institutional initiation and cultic prostitution', *Journal of Homosexuality*, 20 (1-2), 13-30.

Bolen, R., and Scannapieco, M. (1999), 'Prevalence of child sexual abuse: A corrective meta-analysis', *Social Services Review*, 73, 281-313.

Boston Globe Investigative Staff (2002), *'Betrayal: The Crisis in the Catholic Church'*, Boston: Little Brown.

Boswell, J. (1990), *The Kindness of Strangers: The Abandonment of Children in Western Europe from Late Antiquity to the Renaissance*, New York: Vintage.

Breen, M. (2004a), 'Rethinking Power: An Analysis of Media Coverage of Sexual Abuse in Ireland, the UK and the USA', Paper presented at the Kogakuin University/University of Limerick International Conference of Science and Humanities. Marsh. Unpublished paper.

Breen, M. (2004b), Paedophiles as depraved monsters and other evil beasts: Media portrayals of Irish and UK child sexual abusers. Submitted for consideration.

Brenneis, M. (2001), 'Personality characteristics of clergy and of psychologically impaired clergy: A review of the literature', *American Journal of Pastoral Counselling*, 4 (77), 7-13.

Bryant, C. (1999), 'Psychological treatment of priest sex offenders', in T. G. Plante (ed), *Bless Me Father For I Have Sinned: Perspectives on Sexual Abuse Committed by Roman Catholic Priests* (pp 87-110), Westport, CT: Praeger Publishers.

Buckley, H., Skehill, C. and O'Sullivan, E. (1997), *Child Protection Practices in Ireland. A Case Study*, Dublin: Oak Tree Press.

Camargo, R. J. and Loftus J. A. (1992), 'Child sexual abuse among troubled clergy: A descriptive study.' Paper presented at the 100th Annual Convention of the American Psychological Association, Washington, DC. (unpublished paper).

Camargo, R. J. and Loftus J. A. (1993), 'Clergy sexual involvement with young people.' Paper presented at the 101st Annual Convention of the American Psychological Association, Toronto Canada (unpublished paper).

Catechism of the Catholic Church (1994), Dublin: Veritas Publications.

Celenza, A. (2004), 'Sexual misconduct in the Clergy. The Search for the Father', *Studies in Gender and Sexuality*, 5 (2), 213-232.

Code of Canon Law (1983) (English translation), Great Britain: Collins.

Commission on Child Abuse Report (2009), Dublin: Government Publications (Also referred to as the Ryan Report).

Corby, B. (2000), *Child Abuse: Towards a Knowledge Base*, Milton Keynes: Open University Press.

Cowburn, M. and Dominelli, L. (2001), 'Masking hegemonic masculinity: reconstructing the paedophile as the dangerous stranger', *British Journal of Social Work*, 31, 399-415.

Cozzens, D. (2000), *The Changing Face of Priesthood*, Collegeville, Minnesota: Liturgical Press.

Cozzens, D. (2004), *Sacred Silence. Denial and the Crisis in the Church*, Collegeville, Minnesota: Liturgical Press.

De Young, M. (1982) 'Innocent seducer or innocently seduced? The role of the child incest victim', *Journal of Clinical Psychology*, 11, 56-60.

Dokecki, P. (2004), *The Clergy Sexual Abuse Crisis*, Washington, DC: Georgetown University Press.

Doyle, T. P. (2003), 'Roman Catholic clericalism, religious duress and clergy abuse', *Pastoral Psychology*, 51, 189-231.

Doyle, T. P. (2004), 'Canon Law and the clergy sex abuse crisis: The failure from above', in T. G. Plante (ed), *Sin against the Innocents. Sexual Abuse by Priests and the Role of the Catholic Church* (pp 25-38). Westport, Connecticut, London: Praeger.

Doyle, T. P., Sipe, A. W. R. and Wall, P. J. (2006), *Sex, Priests and Secret Codes. The Catholic Church's 2000-year Paper Trail of Sexual Abuse*, Los Angeles: Volt Press.

Dublin Archdiocese Commission of Investigation. (2006). March

Dunne, J. and Kelly, J. (2002), *Childhood and Its Discontents: The First Seamus Heaney Lectures*, Dublin: Liffey Press.

Flakenhain M.A. (1999), 'Cluster analysis of child sexual offenders: A validation with Roman Catholic priests and brothers', *Sexual Addiction and Compulsivity*, 6, 317-336.

Featherstone, B. and Lancaster, E. (1997), 'Contemplating the unthinkable: Men who sexually abuse children', *Critical Social Policy*, 17 (4), 51- 71.

Ferguson, H. (1995), 'The paedophile priest. A deconstruction', *Studies*, 84 (335), pp 247-256.

The Ferns Report (2005), Delivered to the Minister for Health and Children, Ireland.

Finkelhor, D. (1984), *Child Sexual Abuse: New Theory and Research*, New York: Free Press.

Finkelhor, D. (1994), 'The international epidemiology of child sexual abuse', *Child Abuse and Neglect*, 18, 409-417.

Fones, C. S. L., Levine, S. B., Althof, S. E. and Risen, C. B. (1999), 'The sexual struggles of 23 clergymen: A follow-up study', *Journal of Sex and Marital Therapy*, 25, 183-195.

Fortune, M. (1994), 'Is nothing sacred? The betrayal of the ministerial or teaching relationship', *Journal of Feminist Studies in Religion*, 10 (1), 17-24.

Foucault, M. (1988). 'The Dangerous Individual', in L Kritzman (ed), *Politics, Philosophy, Culture: Interviews and Other Writings 1977-1984*, (pp 125-51). New York: Routledge.

Foucault, M. (1990), *The Care of Self. The History of Sexuality: 3*, trs Robert Hurley, London: Penguin.

Foucault, M. (1992), *The Use of Pleasure. The History of Sexuality: 2*, trs Robert Hurley, London: Penguin.

Foucault, M. (1998), *The Will to Knowledge. The History of Sexuality: 1*, trs Robert Hurley,. London: Penguin.

Foucault, M. (2004), *The Archaeology of Knowledge*, trs A. M. Sheridan Smith. (First published in 1969; first published in English 1972). (Sixth edition). London: Routledge Classics.

Francis, P. C. and Turner, N.R. (1995), 'Sexual misconduct within the Christian Church: Who are the perpetrators and those they victimize?', *Counselling and Values*, 39, 218-228.

Frawley-O'Dea, M. (2004), 'Psychosocial Anatomy of the Catholic Sexual Abuse Scandal', *Studies in Gender and Sexuality*, 5 (2), 121-137.

AN IRISH READER IN MORAL THEOLOGY

Freeman-Longo R. E. and Blanchard, G. T. (1998), *Sexual Abuse in America: Epidemic of the 21st century*, Vermont: The Safer Society Press.

Goldner, V. (2004), 'Introduction – The Sexual-Abuse Crisis and the Catholic Church. Gender, Sexuality, Power and Discourse', *Studies in Gender and Sexuality*, 5 (1), 1-9.

Goodstein, L. (2003), 'Decades of damage: Trail of pain in Church crisis leads to nearly every diocese', *New York Times* (12 January).

Gordon, M. (2004), 'The Priestly Phallus. A Study in Iconography', *Studies in Gender and Sexuality*, 5 (1), 103-111.

Greeley, A. M. (1972a), *Priests in the United States: Reflections on a Survey*, Garden City, New York: Doubleday.

Greeley, A. M. (1972b), *The Catholic Priest in the United States: Sociological Investigations*, United States Catholic Conference, Washington DC: United States Catholic Conference.

Greeley, A. M. (1993), 'How serious is the problem of sexual abuse by clergy?' *America*, 168 (10), 6-10.

Greeley, A. M. (2000), 'How Prevalent is Clerical Sexual Abuse?', *Doctrine and Life*, 50 (2), 66-71.

Greer, C. (2003), *Sex Crime and the Media: Sex Offending and the Press in a Divided Society*, Devon: Willan.

Hacking, I. (1999), *The Social Construction of What?* Cambridge, MA, and London: Harvard University Press.

Hanson, R. K. (1998), 'What do we know about sex offender risk assessment?', *Psychology, Public Policy and Law*, 4 (3), 50-72.

Hanson, R. K. (2003), *Personal Communication during Annual Research and Treatment*, Conference of the Association for the Treatment of Sexual Abusers, St Louis, Missouri. October.

Hanson, R. K. and Bussière, M. T. (1998), 'Predicting relapse: A meta-analysis of sexual offender recidivism studies', *Journal of Counselling and Clinical Psychology*, 66 (2), 348-362.

Hanson, R. K., Morton, K. E. and Harris, A. J. R. (2003), 'Sexual Offender Recidivism Risk. What We Know and What We Need to Know', *Annals New York Academy of Sciences*, 989, 154-166.

Hanson, R. K. and Morton-Bourgon, K. E. (2004), *Predictors of Sexual Recidivism: An Updated Meta-Analysis*, (Research Report, No 2004 -02). Ottowa, Canada: Public Safety and Emergency Preparedness Canada.

Hanson, R. K. and Morton-Bourgon, K. E. (2005) 'The Characteristics of Persistent Sexual Offenders: A Meta-Analysis of Recidivism Studies', *Journal of Consulting and Clinical Psychology*, 73, 1154-1163.

Hanson, R. K., Pfafflin, F. and Lutz, M. (2004), (eds), *Sexual Abuse In the Catholic Church. Scientific and Legal Perspectives*, Vatican City: Libreria Editrice Vaticana.

Hanson, R. K., Steffy, R. A., and Gauthier, R. (1993), 'Long-term Recidivism of Child Molesters', *Journal of Consulting and Clinical Psychology*, 61, 646-652.

Hanson, R. K., Gordon, A., Harris, A. J. R., Marques, J. K., Murphy, W., Quinsey, V. L. and Seto, M. C. (2002), 'First Report of the Collaborative Outcome Data Project on the Effectiveness of Psychological Treatment for Sex Offenders', *Sexual Abuse: A Journal of Research and Treatment*, 14, 2, 169-194.

Haug, F. (2001). 'Sexual deregulation or, the child abuser as hero in neoliberalism', *Feminist Theory*, 2 (1), pp 55-78.

Haywood, T. W., Kravitz, H. M., Grossman, L. S., Wasyliw, O. E., and. Hardy, D. W. (1996), 'Psychological aspects of sexual functioning among cleric and noncleric alleged sex offenders', *Child Abuse and Neglect*, 20, 527-536.

Haywood, T. W., Kravitz, H. M., Wasyliw, O. E., Goldberg, J. and Cavanaugh, J. L. (1996), 'Cycles of abuse and psychopathology in cleric and noncleric molesters of children and adolescents', *Child Abuse and Neglect*, 20, 1233-1243.

Hoge, D. (2002), *The First Five Years: A Study of Newly Ordained Catholic Priests*, Collegeville, MN: Liturgical Press.

Hudson, K. (2005), *Offending Identities. Sex offenders' perspectives on their treatment and management*, Devon: Willan Publishing.

Inglis, T. (1998, 2nd ed), *Moral Monopoly. The Rise and Fall of the Catholic Church in Modern Ireland*, Dublin: University College Dublin Press.

Inglis, T. (2005), 'Origins and Legacies of Irish Prudery: Sexuality and Social Control in Modern Ireland', *Éire-Ireland: An Interdisciplinary Journal of Irish Studies*, 40, 3-4, (Fall-Winter), 9-37.

Jenkins, P. (1995), 'Clergy sexual abuse: The symbolic politics of a social problem' in J. Best (ed) *Images of Issues, Typifying Contemporary Social Problems*, (pp 105-130), New York: Aldine De Gruyter.

Jenkins, P. (1996), *Paedophiles and Priests. Anatomy of a Contemporary Crisis*, New York: Oxford University Press.

Jenkins, P. (1998), *Moral Panic. Changing Concepts of the Child Molester in Modern America*, New Haven and London: Yale University Press.

John Jay College (2004), *The Nature and Scope of Sexual Abuse of Minors by Catholic Priests and Deacons in the United States, 1950-2002*, Washington DC: United States Conference of Catholic Bishops.

John Jay College (2006), *Supplementary Report. The Nature and Scope of Sexual Abuse of Minors by Catholic Priests and Deacons in the United States, 1950-2002*, Washington DC: United States Conference of Catholic Bishops.

Johnson, J. M. (1995), 'Horror stories and the construction of child abuse', in J. Best (ed), *Images of Issues. Typifying Contemporary Social Problems*, New York: Aldine De Gruyter.

Kafka, M. (2004), 'Sexual molesters of adolescents, ephebophilia and Catholic clergy: A review and synthesis', in R. K. Hanson, F. Pfäfflin and M. Lütz (eds), *Sexual Abuse in the Catholic Church: Scientific and Legal Perspectives* (pp 51-59). Vatican City: Libreria Editrice Vaticana.

Keenan, M. (2006), 'The Institution and the Individual – Child Sexual Abuse by Clergy', *The Furrow. A Journal for the Contemporary Church*, 57 (1) 3-8.

Kennedy, E. (1971), *The Catholic Priest in the United States: Psychological Investigations*, Washington DC: United States Catholic Conference.

Kennedy, E. (2001), *The Unhealed Wound. The Church and Human Sexuality*, New York: St Martin's Press.

Kincaid, J. R. (1998), 'Erotic innocence', *The Culture of Child Molesting*, Durham and London: Duke University Press.

Kitzinger, J. (1999), 'The ultimate neighbour from hell: Media framing of paedophiles', in B. Franklin (ed), *Social Policy, the Media and Misrepresentation*, London: Routledge.

Kitzinger, J. (2000), 'Media Templates: Patterns of Association and the (Re) Construction of Meaning Over Time', *Media, Culture and Society*, 22 (1), 61.

Küng, H. (2003) (second edition), *The Catholic Church. A Short History*, trs John Bowden, New York: Modern Library.

Lane, D. (ed) (1997), *Reading the Signs of the Times. A Survey of Priests in Dublin*, Dublin: Veritas.

Langevin, R. (2004), 'Who engages in sexual behaviour with children? Are clergy who commit sexual offences different from other sex offenders?', in R. K. Hanson, F. Pfäfflin and M. Lütz (eds), *Sexual Abuse in the Catholic Church: Scientific and Legal Perspectives* (pp 24-43), Vatican City: Libreria Editrice Vaticana.

Langevin, R., Curnoe, S. and Bain, J. (2000), 'A study of clerics who commit sexual offences: Are they different from other sexual offenders?', *Child Abuse and Neglect*, 24, 535-545.

Loftus, J. A. (1999), 'Sexuality in priesthood: Noli me tangere', in T. G. Plante (ed), *Bless Me Father for I Have Sinned* (pp 7-19), Westport, Connecticut, London: Praeger.

Loftus, J. A. (2004), 'What have we learned? Implications for future research and formation', in T. G. Plante (ed), *Sin against the Innocents. Sexual Abuse by Priests and the Role of the Catholic Church* (pp 85-96). Westport, Connecticut, London: Praeger.

Loftus, J. A. and Camargo, R. J. (1993), 'Treating the clergy', *Annals of Sex Research*, 6, 287-303.

Lukes, S. (2005), *Power: A radical view*, London: Palgrave Macmillan.

McGee, H., Garavan, R., de Barra, M., Byrne, J. and Conroy, R. (2002), *The SAVI Report: Sexual Abuse and Violence in Ireland. A National Study of Irish Experiences, Beliefs and Attitudes Concerning Sexual Violence*, Dublin: The Liffey Press.

McGlone, G. J. (2001), 'Sexually offending and non-offending Roman Catholic priests: Characterization and analysis', unpublished PhD thesis, California School of Professional Psychology, San Diego.

McGlone, G. J., Viglione, D. J. and Geary, B. (2002), *Data from one treatment centre in USA (N=150) who have sexually offended*. Presented at the Annual Research and Treatment Conference of the Association for the Treatment of Sexual Abusers. Montreal, Ontario: Canada. October. Unpublished paper.

McGuinness, C. (1993), *Report of the Kilkenny Incest Investigation*, Dublin: Stationery Office.

Marshall, W. L. (1996b), 'The sexual offender: monster, victim or everyman?', *Sexual Abuse: A Journal of Research and Treatment*, 8 (4), 317-335.

Marshall, W. L. (2002), 'Historical Foundations and Current Conceptualisations of Empathy', in Y. Fernandez (ed), *In their Shoes: Examining the Issue of Empathy and Its Place in the Treatment of Offenders* (pp 36-52), Oklahoma: Wood 'N' Barnes Publishing.

Marshall, W. L. (2003), *Consulting at the Vatican*. Keynote Address given at the Annual Research and Treatment Conference of the Association for the Treatment of Sexual Abusers, St Louis, Missouri, October. Unpublished paper.

Marshall, W. L. (2004), 'Cognitive Behavioural Treatment of Child Molesters', in R. K. Hanson, F. Pfafflin, and M. Lutz, (2004), (eds)., *Sexual Abuse In the Catholic Church. Scientific and Legal Perspectives*, (pp 97-114). Vatican City: Libreria Editrice Vaticana.

Mercado, C., Tallon, J. and Terry, K. (2008), 'Persistent Sexual Abusers in the Catholic Church. An Examination of Characteristics and Offence Patterns', *Criminal Justice and Behaviour*, 35, 5, 629-642.

Mercer, D., and Simmonds T. (2001), 'The mentally disordered offender. Looking-glass monsters: reflections of the paedophile in popular culture', in T. Mason, C. Carisle, C.

Walkins and E. Whitehead (eds), *Stigma and Social Exclusion in Healthcare*, (pp 170-181), London and New York: Routledge.

Moore, C. (1995), *Betrayal of Trust, the Father Brendan Smyth Affair and the Catholic Church*, Dublin: Marino Books.

Nelson-Rowe, S. (1995), 'The Moral Drama of Multicultural Education', in J. Best (ed), (1995), *Images of Issues, Typifying Contemporary Social Problems*, New York: Walter de Gruyter.

Nines, J. (2006), *Sexuality Attitudes and the Priesthood*. Unpublished PhD thesis, School of Human Service Profession, Widener University.

Noyes, T. (1997), *Broken Vows, Broken Trust: Understanding Clergy Sexual Misconduct*. Unpublished PhD thesis, The Union Institute.

Oakley, F. and Russett, B. (eds) (2004), *Governance, Accountability and the Future of the Catholic Church*, London and New York: Continuum.

O'Brien, C. (2009a), 'Twenty Dead and 6500 At Risk of Abuse: The State's Children Today', *Irish Times*, 23 May, 7.

O'Brien, C. (2009b). 'Lack of Inspections leaves Thousands in Care Vulnerable to Abuse Groups', *Irish Times*, 23 May, 7.

O'Brien, C. (2009c), 'HSE to Review Child Deaths in Care over Decade', *Irish Times*, 6 July, 5.

O'Brien, C. (2009d), 'Children still at risk, says Ombudsman', *Irish Times*, 1 July, 6.

O'Brien, C. (2009e), 'State's Aftercare "Responsibility" for Young', *Irish Times*, 4 June, 8.

O'Mahony, P. (1996), *Criminal Chaos. Seven Crises in Irish Criminal Justice*, Dublin: Round Hall, Sweet and Maxwell.

O'Malley, T. (1998), Opening Remarks, *Conference on Treatment of Sex Offenders*, Irish Penal Reform Trust. Dublin: 14 November. Unpublished paper.

Papesh, M. (2004), *Clerical Culture, Contradiction and Transformation*, Collegeville, MN: Liturgical Press.

Perillo, A., Mercado, C. and Terry, K. (2008), 'Repeat Offending, Victim Gender and Extent of Victim Relationship in Catholic Church Sexual Abusers. Implications for Risk Assessment', *Criminal Justice and Behaviour*, 35, 5, 600-614.

Piquero, A., Piquero, N., Terry, K. Youstin, T., and Nobles, M. (2008), 'Uncollaring the Criminal. Understanding the Criminal Careers of Criminal Clerics', *Criminal Justice and Behaviour*, 35, 5, 583-599.

Plante, T. G. (1996), 'Catholic priests who sexually abuse minors: Why do we hear so much yet know so little?', *Pastoral Psychology*, 44 (5), 305-310.

Plante, T. G. (ed) (1999), Bless Me Father for I Have Sinned, Westport, Connecticut, London: Praeger.

Plante. T. G. (ed) (2004), *Sin Against The Innocents. Sexual Abuse by Priests and the Role of the Catholic Church*, Westport, Connecticut, London: Praeger.

Plante, T. G. and Boccaccini, M. T. (1997), 'Personality expectations and perceptions of Roman Catholic clergy members', *Pastoral Psychology*, 45 (4), 301-315.

Plante, T. G., Manuel, G. and Bryant, C. (1994), 'Catholic priests who sexually abuse minors: Intervention, assessment and treatment'. Paper presented at the 13th annual conference of the Association for the Treatment of Sexual Abusers, San Francisco, CA.

Plante, T. G., Manuel, G. and Bryant, C. (1996), 'Personality and cognitive functioning among hospitalised sexual offending Roman Catholic priests', *Pastoral Psychology*, 45 (2), 129-139.

Plante, T. G., Manuel, G. and Tandez, J. (1996), 'Personality characteristics of successful applicants to the priesthood', *Pastoral Psychology*, 45 (1), 29-40.

Pollock, L. (1983), *Forgotten Children: Parent-Child Relations from 1500 to 1900*, Cambridge: Cambridge University Press.

Quinn, D. (2005), '241 clerics accused of sex abuse over four decades', *Irish Independent*, pp 26-27, 28 October.

Ranson, D. (2002a), 'The climate of sexual abuse', *The Furrow*, 53 (7/8), 387-397.

Ranson, D. (2002b), 'Priest: Public, personal and private', *The Furrow*, 53 (4), 219-227.

Reder, P., Duncan, S. and Gray, M. (1993), *Beyond Blame. Child Abuse Tragedies Revisited*, London: Routledge.

Robinson, G. (2007), *Confronting Power and Sex in the Church. Reclaiming the Spirit of Jesus*. Australia: John Garratt Publishing.

Robinson, E. A., (1994), *Shadows of the Lantern Bearers: A Study of Sexually Troubled Clergy*, Unpublished Doctoral Thesis, Loyola College, Maryland, USA.

Rossetti, S. J. (1990) (ed), *Slayer of the Soul: Child Sexual Abuse and the Catholic Church*, Mystic, CT: Twenty-Third Publications.

Rossetti, S. J. (2004), Remarks made during Conference, *Sexual Abuse In the Catholic Church. Scientific and Legal Perspectives*, Vatican City

Rossetti, S. J. (1997), Personal Communication.

Russell, D. E. H. (1983), 'The incidence and prevalence of intra-familial sexual abuse of female children', *Child Abuse and Neglect*, 7, 133-146.

Serran, G. (2006), Preliminary Recidivism Data from Rockwood Psychological Services, Kingston, Ontario, Canada, presented during Conference, Dublin, to mark the 10th Anniversary of the Granada Institute.

Sipe, A. W. R. (1995), *Sex, Priests, and Power: Anatomy of a Crisis*, London: Cassell.

Smith, M., Rengifo, A. and Vollman, B. (2008), 'Trajectories of Abuse and Disclosure. Child Sexual Abuse by Catholic Priests', *Criminal Justice and Behaviour*, 35, 5, 570-582.

Stone, L. (1977), *The Family, Sex and Marriage in England 1500-1800*, London: Weidenfeld and Nicolson.

Tallon, J. and Terrry, K. (2008), 'Analyzing Paraphilic Activity, Specializations and Generalizations in Priests who Sexually Abused Minors', *Criminal Justice and Behaviour*, 35, 5, 615-628.

Terry, K. (2008), 'Stained Glass: The Nature and Scope of Child Sexual Abuse in the Catholic Church', *Criminal Justice and Behaviour*, 35, 5, 549-569.

Valcour, F. (1990), 'The treatment of Child Sex Abusers in the Church', in S. J. Rossetti (ed), *Slayer of the Soul: Child Sexual Abuse and the Catholic Church*, (pp 45-66). Mystic, Connecticut: Twenty-Third Publications.

White, M. And Terry, K. (2008), 'Child Sexual Abuse in the Catholic Church. Revisiting the Rotten Apple Explanation', *Criminal Justice and Behaviour*, 35, 5, 658-678

Wilson, S. (1984). 'The Myth of Motherhood a Myth: The Historical View of European Child Rearing,' *Social History*, 9, 181-198.

35   The Moralists and the Obscene

Peter Connolly

(*Irish Theological Quarterly*, Vol 32, No 2, April 1965, pp 116-128)

The aim of this article is to draw attention to some literary aspects of obscenity which seem to be commonly overlooked by most of the moralists – whether secular or religious – who deal with the subject. The neglect or otherwise of these literary considerations must affect the moral evaluation of obscene writing in various ways. My primary interest here centres on the morality or moral theology on which law depends for its foundation and support – the canon law of the church more immediately than the civil law of states. The many problems of legal machinery posed in the practical sphere by the need to control obscenity lie outside the range of this article and the legal approach itself will be touched on only in so far as it is relevant.

Canon Law

At the present moment it would be quite untimely to speculate on the Roman Index and its legislation. It is due for major and perhaps drastic revision in the reforms emerging from the Ecumenical Council. One fact, however, may be noted from its practice up to the present. As a list of prohibited books its attention has been limited very locally to Mediterranean Europe and it has made no pretence of coping comprehensively with the vast continents of modern print or even with those areas of it marked obscene.

Behind the Index, however, stands a general ruling on obscenity binding all Catholics everywhere. Something corresponding to Canon 1399, 9° is bound to survive in any system of general legislation in the church. For that reason among others Canon 1399, 9°, when viewed in the contemporary context, focuses some interesting problems of interpretation.

It does no more than prohibit – *ipso jure* – though subject to permitted exceptions – a general category of books: 'books which *ex professo* treat, narrate or teach lascivious or obscene matters'. (*Libri qui res lascivas seu obscenas ex professo tractant, narrant, aut docent.*) The Code does not provide a legal definition of the obscene: it simply offers the word 'lascivious' as a synonym. But the canonists who interpret this canon offer no definition either and devote their whole attention to the other words in it. This is all the more surprising in view of the increasing attention given to the phenomenon of obscenity in the civil law of many countries and the consequent evolution of its meaning over the last fifty years.

In the absence of such commentary we have to fall back on some general principles within the Code which govern the various particular canons. As regards its subjects (those whom it binds) Canon 21 lays down that *leges latae ad praecavendum periculum generale urgent, etiamsi in casu particulari periculum non adsit*: so the prohibition in C.1399 applies to individuals who would not be bound in this matter by the natural law alone in the absence of positive law. On the other hand, as regards what it imposes it comes under the rule of C.19 which says that laws restricting the free exercise of rights are to be interpreted 'strictly' – i.e. their sense is not to be broadened but restricted. Moreover, C.18 says that laws (such as C.1399) are to be interpreted according to the proper meaning of the words considered in the text and context and, if that remains doubtful and obscure, one is to have recourse to parallel places (if any) in the Code, to the intention of the legislator, and to the purpose and circumstances of the law, i.e. to the broad historical context in which it functions. Here is a warrant in the Code for taking account of the meaning assigned to a term like 'the obscene' by common usage in a particular culture.

Canonists hitherto have taken the phrase *ex professo* in a restrictive or minimum sense. Abbo-Hannon for example (*Theologia Moralis* II, p 638, Herder 1952) says informational or scientific books on sex do not come under the latter phrase. Pernicone (*The Ecclesiastical Prohibition of Books*, p 73, Washington 1932), Noldin (*De Praeceptis*, p 658, 1926 Ed), Bouscarin-Ellis (Canon Law, p 716, Bruce 1946) – all agree that *ex professo* does not refer to transient or incidental obscenity but 'indicates the principal purpose of the author or the principal scope of the work' (Bous.-Ell.) … '*ut ex tota eius indole appareat intentio scribentis lectorem de peccatis turpibus instruendi et ad libidinem excitandi*' (Noldin). More liberal commentators still (e.g. Pennachi, Perier) maintain that *ex professo* requires something more than simple obscenity (sensual seduction) however deliberate or systematic but indicates rather the more complex 'obscenity' which is propagandist or doctrinaire, justifying or vindicating immoral attitudes to sex.

Civil Law (England and USA)

Far from diverging (as one might assume) from the spirit of canon law and Christian morality, the civil law of obscenity in England and the US for example corresponds for much of the way with the elaborations of the canonists on the other terms of Canon 1399. The basic notion of obscene matter itself has not changed over the last two centuries. It is the 'prurient or lustful appeal' of the writing in the US; 'the tendency of the matter … to deprave and corrupt' in England. In both systems 'the general tenor (or dominant theme) of the material taken as a whole must appeal to prurient interest' and this must be verified on the reader's side by 'the average adult applying contemporary community standards' (*Roth v USA*, 1957).

Along with these specifications both legal systems 'take account of literary merit', the British system more formally since 1959 when the testimony of literary experts was first incorporated into trials for obscene matter. In this new emphasis, and in the stress on contemporary community standards, the civil law in these countries is moving ahead of canon law, though of course it has only begun to grapple with the literary clause. These are at least significant pointers for the thinking of Catholic moralists and canonists.

Theological descriptions

More important for our present purpose is the fact that in all this mainly legal commentary a theological notion of obscenity is implied and assumed. In fact it is so much taken for granted that further investigation does not seem necessary. Noldin merely glances at it in his phrase *'de peccatis turpibus instruendi et ad libidinem excitandi'* and Vermeersch in an analogy with painting or sculpture (*Theologia Moralis* IV, p 94, 1926 Ed) *'non omne nudum dici potest obscenum. Sed vulgo dicitur obscenum nudum allectans; et dici potest: turpis in nuditate manifestatio animi vel solicitatio'*. A panel of theologians at the ninth annual convention of the Theological Society of America (*Proceedings* 1954, New York) summed up this tradition in their descriptive definition of the obscene: 'The obscene is that which in its general tenor invites or excites to venereal pleasure by appeal to the sensitive appetite.' Gerald Kelly SJ and Harold C. Gardner SJ clarified this by adding that venereal pleasure in the strict sense involves *per se* genital commotion and that this is occasioned normally not by ordinary sense-pleasure or sense-pleasure based in the spiritual appetite but only by 'carnal-sensitive' pleasure the psychic tendency of which is to pass into the venereal. The psychological model used here may no longer be very acceptable but in these distinctions and the partial descriptions hinted at above lie most of the elements of a fuller morality of the obscene which still remains to be worked out.

The subjective morality

All attempts to define the obscene comprise subjective and objective elements: *allectatio* and *delectatio*, a tendency inherent in an object (lustful or prurient appeal) which is in turn determined by reference to the subjective reactions of somebody who contemplates it. Apropos of the latter the recognised morality has been the theology of occasions. So in virtue of the natural law the degree of sin or guilt is said to be proportionate not so much to the objective tendency of the work read as to the likelihood of this or that reader taking harm from it. For pastoral purposes this may be quite sufficient.

The obscene may be handled in terms of subjective moral risk alone. If not reduced to manual form, this procedure can be as subtle as the circumstances of the individual are complex and variable, provided it takes into account his age, motives, psychological condition, educational level and range, moral maturity, and the whole society and cultural context in which he lives. A judgement which balances prudence with fortitude on the basis of past experience and some self-knowledge can estimate such subjective moral risk with a fair degree

AN IRISH READER IN MORAL THEOLOGY

of moral certainty. Unless it is applied in a mechanical or static way this morality of effect is open-ended and dynamic enough to allow for growing experience and knowledge. It has the advantage too of covering obscenity both in the strict and extended senses noted by theologians: sensual description which may excite the appetite to venereal pitch here and now or in the proximate future (simple obscenity), and 'thematic obscenity' which may undermine orthodox moral attitudes to sex on a long-term basis. (Most contemporary bannings on the Roman Index, e.g. those of Gide, Moravia, were directed against the latter kind of obscenity.) In this way it broadens out beyond the obscene into a general morality of reading, whatever the material or ideas in question.

Objective criteria?

The subjective approach then is workable enough even though in theory it separates too sharply effect (of the reading) from function (of the work). It is mentioned here only that it may be left aside at this point and taken as said in all that follows. The rest will be confined strictly to the objective side of the question. For the descriptions of the obscene noted above from the theologians seem to be rather lacking on the objective, i.e. literary, side. The moralists referred to merely bring obscene writing under the general heading of occasions of venereal pleasure or sexual corruption as if such writings were exactly on a par with alcohol, loose company, or brothels. As 'occasions', therefore, they are inadequately specified. Whatever certain kinds of reading may lead to, either in the short or the long run, they operate first in the realm of imagination and fantasy. We may ask then what makes any piece of writing obscene? And whether all obscenity is of the same kind? And if not, whether we can discern any differences of innate tendency between them – in the way their intrinsic designs enter the mind? In seeking some clarification along these lines some objective criteria of obscenity are available to the moralist from the traditional genres and styles of fiction.

The obscene as a literary category

On the basis of sociological and anthropological studies, the obscene is understood today to represent inversely or negatively a standard of social propriety in sexual matters. It is the convention which marks the limits of acceptable or tolerated expression of these matters in public.

The etymology of the word (*ob-scaenum* = not for the stage) is only probable but this was the meaning it undoubtedly acquired in traditional usage – something or other improper or shocking on the public stage, i.e. for presentation to the sight of others. Clearly it denotes the public circumstance or manner in which some act, gesture, or word was performed, represented, or uttered. We may infer that no human act, function, gesture, or word is in itself (or intrinsically) obscene; that depends on a public context which makes it obscene.

The relatively modern machinery of law applied to control obscene writing can lead to a common misunderstanding. When the law declares a book 'obscene' or 'not obscene' it does not decide on the absolute presence or absence of a particular quality. It really declares that for this community in this time or place the book is too obscene or not too obscene. In the records of literature the obscene is but one of the constant elements among many others which crops up in various guises and various degrees. It includes the shock of such moments of sadism as the torture of Edward II in Marlowe's play or the blinding of Gloucester in *King Lear* and the moments of blasphemy in Webster, Tourneur, Joyce, or Genet – but for convenience the directly sexual obscenity need only be considered. Even when its sadistic and blasphemous offshoots are left aside the sexually obscene itself displays a number of sub-varieties.

Literary v subliterary varieties
The current task for 'literary experts' is to draw firmer and clearer lines between obscene literature and pornography. At present in legal contexts they are referred to confusedly as if they differed only in degree whereas, judged by literary standards they really differ in kind ... (To anticipate briefly – pornography is a sub-literary product which only mimics the creative imagination.) It is more helpful to contrast these two as 'incidental' and 'total' obscenity provided these are not taken to be terms of quantity – a source of further confusions. The primary difference is one of quality – of the informing spirit which animates the sexual material being presented.

Three literary varieties – bawdy, scatology, erotic
Before the pornographic genre can be more sharply isolated, the traditional varieties of literary obscenity must be recalled for these have been lost sight of or confounded by the legal-moralists. At least three types need to be disentangled – the bawdy, the scatological, and the erotic. In practice of course these distinct strains are not always found apart or totally unmingled but on the other hand one or other tends to predominate in this or that author or in different works by the same author. All three are 'literary' in so far as they represent ways of handling and interpreting human experience but they spring from different attitudes to it and so the psychological drive or direction in each case when translated into words on the page results in a different innate tendency in the work.

The bawdy imagination selects the coarsest physical aspects of human sexuality, dwells on them with gusto, is moved to ribald laughter, and so issues in farce, comedy, or comic satire (e.g. ranging from the old fabliaux to the bawdy of Chaucer and Shakespeare, to Merriman's *Midnight Court*, to passages in Joyce and Nabokov). Its literary forms draw on the earthy gusto and unconscious innocence of the folk-imagination. To see the ludicrous side of sex is obviously one of man's oldest needs –a therapeutic and a moral need despite its apparent dissociation from overt moral standards.

The scatological imagination links human sex more explicitly with the excremental, is stung by the paradox (*inter faeces et urinam nascimur*) and presents it in a repellent or disagreeable light. So it issues generally in savage satire or invective (e.g. much of Swift, much of Pope, the emetic episode of *Nighttown* in Joyce's *Ulysses*). Clearly it is based on a reaction against this aspect of human sex and attempts to exorcise disgust, horror, or fear – to work them out of the system through 'rime's vexation' or any search for a vocabulary adequate to these feelings.

Those two modes of the imagination would sustain a lot more analysis leading off, however, in other directions. For our present purpose it is enough simply to note that the *allectatio* of the moralists (the lustful or prurient allure) fits neither variety. Both counter *aphrodisia* and each in its own way provides violent or explosive release from sexual tension. Neither should raise the sort of problems presented by the erotic – an imaginative attitude which pervades the love-poetry, romances, novels, and dramas of the western world. This kind of writing certainly places the sexual dimension of human experience in an alluring or seductive light. On the one hand, comparison with bawdy and scatology shows it to belong to the same genre of literary obscenity. Unlike them it does build up erotic feeling and does not provide so obvious a catharsis or purgation as the other two varieties. Nevertheless it orders, controls, and contains this feeling in its own more complex way. For it transcends and often includes the other two varieties to sex by interpreting that area of experience from a more sophisticated standpoint. On the other hand, comparison with pornography brings out an ambiguity in the notion of 'allure'. For this may be towards either the physical or the spiritual. Pornography can be shown in fact to be a verbal counterpart to lust, whereas erotic writing in the West has become a literary correlative for the state of romantic love as it evolved in that tradition. If it can be shown that the two genres face in opposite directions from the psychic point of view then they can be correlated with the theological terms 'carnal-sensitive' and 'spiritual-sensitive'. Pornography will then present no problem because it is the only one of the four obscenities which corresponds exactly and totally to the theological definition: *ut ex toto eius indole appareat intentio scribentis lectorem de peccatis turpibus instruendi et ad libidinem excitandi*. On the other hand, erotic writing will demand a more complex moral appraisal.

The erotic
It is unfortunate that the label 'erotica' should have been so often misapplied to certain brands of writing from the classical and renaissance periods which really served as the esoteric pornography of the few. But Eros, even from its classical origins, stood for a spiritual-intellectual love which included within itself as a lesser part of itself Venus – the carnally or animally sexual element. Eros as passionate romantic love ('passion-love') is a later variation and com-

plication – a product of the Christian West from the tenth century onwards. It makes no sense outside that context – in the East for example, just because it represents a unique effort to spiritualise love between the sexes. At the same time of course passionate love outside marriage clashed notoriously with the Christian morality of sex and to this day it stands as an unresolved contradiction at the heart of the Christian culture which has tried only sporadically to assimilate it (cf D. de Rougement, *Passion and Society* – the most exhaustive study). However much secularised, this is the archetypal pattern behind the love-poetry of Donne or Yeats, the novels of Richardson or Graham Greene, the drama of Claudel or O'Neill and is to be found woefully diluted in a thousand popular novels. The ambiguities and dangers in the notion of passionate, romantic love are legion and are rightly to be feared, but they should not be misplaced. As C. S. Lewis showed (*The Four Loves*, 1960) the older theologians assigned the dangers of Eros almost entirely to the carnal element within it – just as they tended to ascribe to marriage a soul-destroying surrender to the senses. But it remains in its basic impulse and direction a myth of spiritual desire – desire for the whole person of another human being – which does not merely aggravate the sex-appetite but reorganises it on a higher level by shifting it from self-centred need-pleasure to other-centred appreciation. Its real danger in fact lies in its spiritualising drive which on the impermanent basis of passionate love tends to erect a rival absolute to the divine love (agape) – for which nevertheless it provides the closest human analogy. These seminal ideas of modern eroticism, commonplace as they are, cannot be ignored in this context – for while theologians are trying to incorporate its 'personalist' aspects into the theology of marriage, their atomic or piecemeal approach to fiction shows they do not recognise there the very cultural myth which supplies the challenge.

Erotic realism
However, the myth of erotic love not only shapes the storyline or plots of so much modern fiction but expresses or works itself out in the whole texture of the writing. The elaborate techniques of the realistic novel have come to be applied to the traditional erotic patterns now hugely swollen by the psychological awareness of the present age. The result is the erotic realism of so much modern fiction. Moralists of all schools are hard pressed to distinguish this from pornography, especially as the two styles seem to converge and to resemble each other more and more with every decade. Market considerations have indeed tempted some writers to mingle the two wilfully but the fact remains that they cannot really be crossed out, only placed side by side, and the two streams of contemporary fiction remain distinct – that which exploits and that which explores the modern consciousness of sex. Most moralists still tackle the problem in quantitative terms, trying to decide by the amount, number and fre-

quency of sexual details whether these are 'necessary' or 'unnecessary'. This mathematical method is too mechanical for imaginative fiction in which style is the only key to meaning and for which consequently the test is the quality of the detail. The same details, in the same situation (sexual initiation or intercourse, rape, etc) may be treated in either of the two ways. Thus erotic realism, however obscene, is distinguished from pornography not by any difference of subject-matter but by commitment in depth (e.g. the material of *Lolita* or *Lady Chatterly's Lover*). Erotic realism differs from the pseudo-realism of pornography in being precisely an attempt through language to order, control and interpret the sexual experience of man in the present age. (The interpretation judged finally by Christian standards may of course be muddled, astray – as Lawrence's was – or hopelessly inadequate – but the searching dynamism which drives it is all that is at stake here.) So in itself – granting all along the likelihood of its pornographic use or abuse and prescinding from such possible effects – erotic realism as a literary technique or style challenges the reader to at least a minimum ordering and control of the material.

Style as test and norm
It would take more than the available time and space to demonstrate in satisfactory detail how the two genres are antithetical, despite their superficial resemblances. Until very recent times, literary criticism could take this so much for granted that it had no need to substantiate it. The most available piece of practical criticism is perhaps on pages 218-21 of Richard Hoggart's *The Uses of Literacy* (1957) where he analyses and contrasts a typical passage of pornography with a passage in Faulkner's *Sanctuary*, describing Temple Drake's introduction to Miss Reba's brothel by her raper Popeye. His method could be applied with similar results to relevant parallel passages from say *The Carpet Baggers* and *Catch 22*, Edmund Wilson's *Memoirs of Hecate County* and Grace Metaliou's *Peyton Place*, Lawrence's *Lady Chatterly*, with any title by Micky Spillane, Durrell's *Justine*, with any book by John O'Hara. Similarly it offers the only genuine clue to threading one's way through fiction which may include encapsulated sequences of pornography such as Henry Miller's 'Tropic' books or J. G. Cozzens's.

By love possessed
By way of illustration, here are a few extracts from *The Carpet Baggers* (1961) by Harold Robbins set beside two passages (not used by Hoggart) from the same book of Faulkner's *Sanctuary* (1931). This book is chosen again because in it Faulkner comes nearer to pornography than anywhere else in his fiction. On the other hand, *The Carpet Baggers* is fairly 'stylish' pornography, not at first sight the most glaringly perverse kind, and the pornographic core is well wrapped up or disguised in other kinds of 'interest' – action, adventure, period,

and social setting – all mere props but masquerading in 'imaginative' dress. So if the difference of genre can be spotted here it will be much easier to discern as a rule. Italics are added to words and phrases which seem to illustrate the centripetal and centrifugal tendencies of the two genres – taking the 'centre' in this test to be physical sex heading for orgasm.

The Carpet Baggers
p 153 (a) I sipped at the drink as she came over to me. 'You don't have to take a bath on my account', she said. 'That smell is *kind of exciting*'. I put the drink down and walked into the bathroom, taking off my shirt. When I turned to close the door she was right behind me. 'Don't get into the tub yet', she said, 'it's a shame to waste all that musky maleness'. She put her arms around my neck and *pressed* her body against me. I sought her lips but she turned her face away and buried it in my shoulder. I felt her take a *deep, shuddering* breath. She moaned *softly* and the heat came out of her body *like steam from an oven*. I turned her face up to me with my hand. Her eyes were almost closed. She *moaned again*, her body *writhing*. I tugged at my belt and my trousers fell to the floor. I *kicked* them aside and backed her towards the vanity table along the wall. Her eyes were still closed as she leaped on me *like a monkey climbing a coconut tree* ...
p 227 (b) (After two pages of teasing 'play' between brother and sister): 'You bitch', he said, *tearing* his belt from his trousers. He raised her arms over her head and *lashed* her wrists to the iron bedpost. He picked up the half-empty bottle from the bed where it had fallen ... The bottle flew from his hands as she *kicked* it away. He caught at her legs and *pinned* them against the bed with his knees. He *laughed wildly*. 'Now, my darling little sister, there'll be no more games'. 'No more games', she *gasped*, staring into his eyes. His face came down and his mouth *covered* hers. She felt herself begin to relax.

Then the fierce sharp pain *penetrated* her body. She *screamed*. His hand came down heavily over her mouth, as *again and again* the pain *ripped* through her.

And all that was left was the sound of her voice, screaming silently in the confines of her throat, and the *ugliness and horror of his body on her own*.

The last phrase is a particularly good example of ostensible moral reference which is implicitly denied by the whole texture of the writing up to this point. The 'interior scream' as cliché here may be compared with the one below ...

On page 280 a lesbian event – less assault and more mutual seduction – is worked out in a similar limited set of stock or cliché verbs: parting, brushing, touching like hot iron, burning, shivering, giving way.

The rape of Temple Drake in *Sanctuary* is described at least four times from four different points of view as the novel advances. Here is a long paragraph from the first account given in the narrator's person (p 82) followed by a paragraph from Temple's own three-page account much later in which she recounts the flinching fantasies of that moment 'with a sort of naïve and impersonal vanity, as though she were making it up'.

AN IRISH READER IN MORAL THEOLOGY

(a) He waggled the pistol slightly and put it back in his coat, then he walked towards her. Moving, he made no sound at all; the released door *yawned and clapped* against the jamb, but it made no sound either; it was as though *sound and silence had become inverted*. She could hear silence in a thick rustling as he moved towards her through it, thrusting it aside, and she began to say Something is going to happen to me. She was saying it to *the old man with the yellow clots for eyes*. 'Something is happening to me!', she screamed at him, *sitting on his chair in the sunlight, his hands crossed on the top of his stick*. 'I told you it was!', she screamed, *voiding* the words *like hot silent bubbles into the bright silence* about them until he turned his head and the two phlegm-clots above her where she lay tossing and thrashing on the *rough, sunny boards*. 'I told you! I told you all the time!'.

(b) I could feel my mouth getting fixed to scream, and that little hot ball inside you that screams. Then it touched me, that nasty little cold hand, fiddling around inside the coat where I was naked. It was *like alive ice* and my skin started jumping away from it *like those little flying-fish in front of a boat*. It was like my skin knew which way it was going before it started moving, and my skin would keep on jerking just ahead of it like there wouldn't be anything there when the hand got there. I hadn't eaten since yesterday at dinner and my insides started bubbling and going on and *the shucks began to make noise it was like laughing*. I'd think they were laughing at me *because* all the time I *hadn't changed into a boy yet* ...

In the total design of the novel Temple's rape and hysteria are as much invited and self-induced as forced on her. It is enough, however, to notice how the vitality of simile, metaphor and verb makes the physical details contribute to her whole psychological condition and this in turn keeps the lines open to other times, people, places, and states of her being.

Hoggart's pioneer effort showed how the verbal texture of each sexual episode – and not merely the plot-sequence – in a pornographic work isolates physical sexuality from every authentic context of emotion or spiritual feeling and imprisons the mind in a world of genital stimulation. On the other hand, the prose texture in Faulkner shows his language stretching and straining to meet the demands of a complex and varied perception responding to the episode at several levels and so preserving moral perspective simply by its continual reference to a larger pattern of life outside the immediate obsessive scene. To 'work' at all, pornography must of course achieve a certain narrow power which excites the nerves during the recurring moments of sexual action or violence. But its limited aim does not allow it to develop beyond this crude efficiency. The hack talent it requires should not mislead us with the illusion of a 'literary' pornography. In fact it needs no more than a mechanical skill in narrative and a verbal competence which manipulates shock. The absence of organic vitality betrays itself over the course of such novels in secondhand descriptive cliché, characterisation to formula, and faked morality. Hence the fact that every pornographer is driven back by compensation to rely on mere situation, and so on the inevitable stock-structure of a series of venereal contests arranged in ever more rapid sequence.

Joyce, generalising beyond the present subject, hit on the essence of pornography. All writing he claimed was 'pornographic' or 'impure' which overflows or spills over into the world of action; the creative imagination by contrast, being non-kinetic, attains and invokes a state of contemplative stasis. Pornography then is a direct solicitation to the *action* of lust whether within the mind or outside it. Erotic realism certainly appeals to and builds up sensual and erotic feeling but *contains* it (literally) in solution. Moralists often observe that the greater the art the more profound and lasting the impression it makes on the mind – which is true – but they conclude that in this domain art is more dangerous carnally than the inferior product. The fallacy here consists in forgetting that the 'impression' made in the first case is of a different order entirely.

Although Vermeersch's analogy with the visual arts quoted earlier must allow for the differences in the non-verbal media, it is still a useful one when developed along similar lines. The nude is again the most challenging case because it holds such a high degree of sexual and erotic content in solution. The so-called 'nudes' of striptease or commercial pornography are in fact photos of naked women – the body merely stripped of its clothes – and can do no more than arouse lust – or fail to do so according to taste. But the naked transformed into the nude in art embodies a psychological and ultimately spiritual attitude to the carnal. It is, of course, more liable than any other genre of painting or sculpture to arouse the initial prurient curiosity in the uninitiated but its whole design – its intrinsic tendency – resists the stare which lust directs at the isolated detail and insists through its lines of interior tension on leading the mere gazer or spectator to contemplate the relations of body and spirit. Whether these are seen in harmony or disharmony, as capable or incapable of reconciliation, the artist's vision witnesses to a need and desire inseparable from our civilisation.

In this article I have attempted in a very general fashion to clarify the various literary meanings of the obscene in the belief that it is an artistic or literary category in the first place before it can be taken up by lawyers and moralists and incorporated into their categories. This seems to be the only genuine starting point from which to begin constructing a more exact morality of the obscene[1] – one which, allowing the law its own peculiar functions is still not too legally structured, but leaves room rather for the dynamic and dialectical function of creative fiction.

Part Nine
Celibacy and Single Life

36 Sexuality, Chastity and Celibacy

Fergal O'Connor OP

(*Doctrine and Life*, Vol 18, No 3, March 1968, pp 128-141)

One cannot discuss the problem of celibacy without placing it in the wider context of ideas to which it belongs. It is obvious that celibacy is in some way connected with sexuality just as marriage is. Without sexuality we could have neither marriage nor celibacy. A full understanding of Christian celibacy would seem to demand a complete understanding of sexuality. We need to be reasonably clear about what it means to be sexed, and what it means to develop one's sexuality. Like marriage, celibacy is a way of developing one's sexuality or of using one's sexuality. They are distinct but complementary ways of realising a certain human value, or perhaps a range of values.

When we ask, what is sexuality? the answer is not at all clear. It is fairly obvious – a truism in fact – that in the human species we just don't have persons as such. In our language we have two specific words to signify differences between the two great classes of human persons – 'men' and 'women'. There are also adjectives associated with these differences, like 'male' and 'female'. These adjectives are, however, also used of the animal world. But the expressions 'man' and 'woman' are specifically human.

We are all aware that there are differences between men and women, but so often we are inclined to think of these differences in a purely physical sense. By physical I mean both the structural differences which are obvious and also their different biological roles. Women are bearers of children. Men are generators of children. But anyone who would seek to define men and women in terms of their physical characteristics or in terms of their biological roles, and seeks to build up an understanding of men and women on these terms will obviously meet with difficulty. In fact, what he will have to say about them will be little more than what he has to say about the male and female of other animal species. Conversely, any attempt to define the human person without reference to sexuality can only lead to a very imperfect view of human life.

There is therefore much more to human sexuality than the mere physical aspects and much more to human personality than its spiritual nature. The human person is sexed and there is a personal dimension to human sexuality which transcends and transforms the merely physical. Sexuality touches on the very depths of human nature, creating mental, affective and emotional differences which make for different sorts of persons. In fact the differences in bodily structure which we tend to regard as merely superficial should be seen as signs of more profound personal differences.

There is a good deal of humour about the mental differences. Men are prone to regard women as illogical, unreasonable and irrational, precisely because women do not think in the way men do. Being prone to a superiority complex, men regard this as a defect in women. On the other hand, women regard men as stubborn, pig-headed, over-logical, pedantic, and for this reason also unreasonable. In fact if we observe closely how they both think in concrete instances, we begin to see that there is a different way of thinking, even when they are thinking about the same thing. As a result, they see and judge the world in a different way. In a word, they *experience* differently.

These differences can be a deep source of conflict between men and women, but they need not be. Rather, they should be seen as the basis of their complementarity. In fact, neither has the complete approach to truth, and therefore neither can hope to have full understanding. Together they have complementary approaches, complementary pictures, and here we find the true notion of complementarity.

There are also affective differences. By this we mean that men and women love in different ways. It isn't easy to find words to describe these differences, but anyone who observes a father and mother loving their children will notice that the mother is much more instinctive and affectionate in the way she loves the child. The mother loves her child not so much for what he is but just because he is her child. In a sense it is an unconditional kind of love, an unconditional kind of giving, and usually it is totally loyal even when such loyalty is not deserved. On the other hand, the father is much more remote in his way of loving; he stands back, as it were, and is not spontaneously and automatically involved with the child. A father's love is not given in the unconditional way that a mother's is; it has to be merited. If you like, the father's way of loving stresses the personal aspect of love. More generally we can say that men and women get involved with other persons in quite a different way. A man establishes a relationship with a person, while a woman drifts into it. He chooses a relationship; it happens to her. It might be said that men tend to engineer involvement while women tend to accept it. To say this does not imply any relative imperfection; all we are saying is that they love differently and because of these differences men and women speak different languages of love. How they enter a relationship, how they develop such a relationship, and how they express the love content of that relationship differs greatly.

The third level of difference which we talk about is the emotional, and all we want to say here is that men and women suffer emotions in a different way. They are happy or sad in different ways. Great moments of emotional crises affect them differently.

Now if we put all these differences together we can say that men and women are different sorts of persons, and because they are different sorts of persons they are different sorts of agents. They do things in different ways; they have different perspectives, different approaches and different responses. They create meaning and value in different ways. To return to the starting-point, this means that sexuality can be defined as that complex of psychological factors which makes for the different classes of human persons that we call men and women. In a sense, therefore, one is sexed through and through, one is a sexual being and one's being is conditioned by one's sexuality. This is a basic fact about human nature. To ignore it is to ignore a great area of truth.

Of course this is not the whole story about human sexuality. There is also in human sexuality what we might call an appetite side; it is a physical appetite rooted in physical sexual faculties. It is of course entwined with the whole emotive, affective and mental life of the person, but there is a sense in which it is true to say that human sexuality is an autonomous appetite. It awakens in us at a certain stage in life which we call puberty and once it awakens it poses problems for us, problems of growth, problems of maturity. Sexual life, in this sense, is often in conflict with our personal choices and decisions. The reason is, quite simply, that it is not of its nature integrated with our personality; it is not automatically subordinated to the personal side of our sexuality. In a sense the sex appetite has a kind of free-wheeling life.

But it can and must be integrated into our personality. In this sense sex is a challenge to the person, a challenge the nature of which is conditioned both by the sexual nature of the particular person and by the quality of life of the appetite. The basic need here is control, which is not given. It is something which must be acquired by constant discipline, of thought, desire and action. Acquiring this control implies the integration of the appetitive side of sex into the personal. The biological urges and tendencies must be personalised. The behavioural expression of this achievement – the personalisation of the appetite – is shown when a man or woman behaves according to their moral beliefs and standards in matters of sex. They are neither the victims of their sexual desires and urges, nor prevented from performing those patterns of sexual actions which their vocation in life demands of them.

Obviously, sexuality creates specific problems for human beings, and for that reason it is the concern of a special virtue. In the first place, being a man is something quite different from being a woman. In each case something more than just being a person is involved. In other words there is a sexual modality to every human value. For this reason it is not preposterous to suppose that there is a general virtue whereby men and women cultivate their sexuality in its widest sense, whereby the individual man or woman cultivates in his or her own sexual way those various forms of human goodness which every human being must acquire. To put it more concretely, men and women need to acquire the various virtues according to their own sexual pattern of behaviour; they are generous or just in a different way. It isn't always easy to describe these specific differences, but in virtues like courtesy, graciousness, humility, and love in its widest sense, we can begin to notice them. Now the virtue which takes care of the specifically sexual aspect of human goodness we call chastity.

AN IRISH READER IN MORAL THEOLOGY

St Thomas places the virtue of chastity within the context of the virtue of temperance. For him temperance is a virtue which is concerned with the proper use of the material world. In particular, it is concerned with the way we use our bodies with regard to food, drink and sex. It is the purpose of this virtue to enable us to use these gifts, and the pleasures derived from them, in a proper human way. Like all virtues, temperance has two sides. On the negative side, it prevents abuses; the great danger with regard to sex, food and drink is that we should indulge in them selfishly. The positive side of temperance is the capacity to use these things well, and through them to achieve fulfilment. By fulfilment we mean nothing more than we become human to a certain degree. After all, every action qualifies or affects a man as a man. Every action which he performs flows from him as a free moral agent, and for that reason his actions affect his total being. To apply this to the particular context, the temperate man is a man who in and through his actions both shows forth the particular human quality at stake and simultaneously acquires it.

More profoundly, although temperance and the virtues associated with it are discussed in the context of specific appetites, the human values associated with these appetites are qualities of the whole man. It is I who am chaste. It is I who am abstemious. Let us try to elaborate the deeper significance of this notion of virtue and apply it to chastity.

Each virtue implies three things. It implies knowledge of the human value which is at stake and knowledge of those patterns of action by which the value is acquired. Secondly, a virtue implies a certain degree of commitment to a particular form of human goodness and to the performance of the pattern of actions through which this goodness is acquired: a virtue is a particular way of being good. In more practical terms it is a particular way of loving others because each virtue describes and prescribes a pattern of actions designed to relate us to others in a loving way. Finally, moral virtues imply a certain discipline. By discipline we mean the capacity to act in a certain way and the emotional control which enables us to carry out specific patterns of action. In the case of chastity these three requirements concern the sexual dimension of one's total attitude to the world.

Take the first requirement – that of knowledge. The chaste man must understand himself as a sexual being. This means understanding what it means for him to be a man in the full personal sense of that word i.e. understanding that specific modality of all human values which we refer to by words like manly or manliness. He must know also how he is to fulfil himself sexually and what sexual fulfilment means. He must understand the role of sex in his life, the values implied in sexuality, and in particular he must know how the appetitive side of sexuality is to be integrated into his life. He must know in fact how to cultivate himself sexually in the fullest sense of that word. Chastity is a dimension of this understanding of himself in the world of things and persons.

The other two requirements, commitment and control, are of course more related to actual performance, related, that is, to the capacity to do something. Without commitment to the specific area of goodness which we refer to by the word sexuality, a man is unlikely to endeavour to acquire the values at stake. Without control and discipline he is incapable of following through the judgements which he makes about his own sexual fulfilment. If we put these three aspects of virtue together we can say that they spell out the necessary and sufficient conditions for achieving sexual maturity, when the virtue in question is chastity. These three requirements (i.e. knowledge, love, discipline) will of course be possessed in greater or less degree. Some people will have a high level of each, others not so high, and we may have the knowledge without the other two.

Fundamentally, chastity is the measure of our capacity to love as men and women. By that we mean that it is the measure of how we treat others precisely as men or women. Negatively this demands that we will never use them selfishly. Positively it means that we know in detail how to respond to another person in varying circumstances. Responding to another person means opening up to him or her in such a way that love in its wider sense grows between us. In a true sense, therefore, the chaste person is the person who has a good grasp of the language of love. More particularly, the chaste man is one who is skilful in expressing love in a sexual way; he has the capacity to respond totally as a man to a woman or to another man. Because the chaste man is not distracted by uncontrolled desires or thoughts or feelings, he is capable of much greater openness towards others, much greater commitment to others, and he is incapable of abusing others for his own selfish interests. Chastity gives us that stability of mind and will which guarantees the constancy of our love of others. It gives freedom to the human heart, allowing it to follow its loving desires to their fullest, without fear of loss or error. It is chastity which puts all our acts of love in focus and ensures that they are a sincere gift of self to others.

If we integrate this understanding of chastity with the Christian concept of virtue, we can say also that acquiring chastity in this sense is part of what is meant by redeeming ourselves. In acquiring chastity we are putting on Christ in a certain way; we are becoming Christlike. We are, in fact, restoring to human nature something of the integrity which was lost in the fall of man. We are beginning here in time to take possession of the resurrection of Christ. We are beginning to put on something of the glorification of Christ.

Now, there are two great ways of exercising chastity, two great ways to sexual fulfilment. They are marriage and consecrated virginity, and we cannot understand them in isolation from each other. Today the sacramental and redemptive significance of marriage have become much clearer. No longer do we think of marriage as a kind of second best. We see it as one of the great signs of the Christian sacramental structure set up by God, to redeem, not merely those who enter into this way of life, but also the whole world for which it is a sign. The vocation to marriage is a call to redeem human sexuality through sexual love and it is as central to the life of the church as is consecrated virginity. Chastity therefore plays a central part in married life, precisely because the specific character of married life is sexual, and chastity is the virtue by which we cultivate our sexuality. Married love and chastity go hand in hand. Indeed, we can say that the measure of the degree of love of which two people are capable is given by the degree of chastity which they possess. Therefore, growth in married love moves step by step with chastity. Every valid use of sexuality in marriage is at once both an act of chastity and marks growth and development in that virtue.

The second way to sexual fulfilment is consecrated virginity. The virgin, like the married person, is seeking to fulfil himself or herself precisely as a man or as a woman. There is no question of virginity implying a denial of sexuality, a running away from sexuality or a refusal to undertake the task of cultivating one's sexuality. Marriage and consecrated virginity are alike in this, that both are concerned with the full sexual development of men and women. They differ only in the kind of commitment which they imply.

The married person seeks fulfilment through a unique and, to that extent, exclusive love of another. The married person seeks to show forth Christ to the world by his or her dedicated love of a partner, of the children which they undertake to bring into being and of those many others who form the family circle. The virgin on the other hand seeks to fulfil himself or herself, not by this unique dedication to one, but rather by a total and complete dedication to all men, usually of course in some specific area of service determined by his special vocation.

If, therefore, we want to understand the full meaning of celibacy, it is perhaps best to see it as a form of life parallel to that of marriage. By parallel I mean that it makes a contribution to the welfare of the church and society which is similar, though still different, to that made by marriage. If marriage is meant to be creative of human personality, particularly from its sexual aspect, so too must celibacy be. A celibacy which tends to frustrate or stultify anything good in the human personality would obviously be defective. It is one thing to say as a matter of principle that celibacy is a parallel way of developing sexuality, but it is another thing to realise it in fact. This gap between ideal and fact is no less peculiar to celibacy than it is to marriage. Not all men achieve sexual fulfilment in marriage in the personal sense in which we have talked about sexual fulfilment. So too we must expect that there will be celibates for whom celibacy does not lead to sexual fulfilment. In both cases the causes for this lack of development are manifold, but here I just want to mention a few that are relevant.

Obviously, a wrong understanding of sexuality, or a wrong understanding of chastity, will affect adversely both the celibate and the married person. If either brings to their respective states a view of sexuality that sees it as something to be suppressed or indeed as something to be sublimated (when sublimation carries the connotation of sanctifying or glorifying something evil in itself) then of course meaningful sexual development will be very difficult and may even prove impossible in some cases. More specifically from the point of view of the celibate, it is important for him to realise that the object of his dedication includes both men and women. The celibate is not a celibate just for men. His mission is to all mankind, both men and women. To this extent he is in no way different from any other person except that he has explicitly assumed a responsibility to all. In Christian terms he has undertaken to love all with whom his work brings him into contact; to love them, not in an abstract, cold, distant sort of way, but to love them with all the warmth, affection and generosity that is part and parcel of genuine human love. What his celibacy demands of him is both the preparedness of mind, the willingness of heart and the real capacity to give the love that he is asked to give.

Celibates have also suffered from a rather negative moralising about the place of friendship in their life, whether the friendship be with their own or the opposite sex. It is often suggested that a celibate should not need friendship, even with his or her own sex, while friendship with the opposite sex is something to be frowned upon always. As a result, celibates are often given a negative view of human love and their relationship with their opposite sex, with inevitable stunting of their affections and emotions.

It may be well here to recall some fundamental facts about human beings. One of the most essential things in human life is love. From what we have been saying, all love is basically sexual love i.e. it is either the love of a man or a woman. The term is always a sexual being. In particular, every human being needs that highest form of love which is friendship, and unless we subscribe to the weird philosophy of Plato in this respect, friendship must usually be bisexual. By that I mean that every individual person needs friendship with both men and women. In a word, he or she needs friendship with the opposite sex. The example of Christ should reassure anyone who doubts this. Among the apostles he had special friends, and the evangelists seem to go out of their way to tell us of his love for women in general and for a few in particular.

This immediately raises a question. In what precise way should that friendship be conducted? What precise forms of affection should be shown between them? Clearly the answer to these problems will be given in terms of the standard moral theology of sexual behaviour for those who are unmarried. Basically, the same principles with some modifications apply to celibates and to the unmarried where heterosexual friendships are concerned.

The kind of moral theology which we absorbed and taught over the last hundred years about this matter is scarcely relevant today. The kind of language which moral textbooks used about the patterns of action which can be used to express love can no longer be accepted. When we say it can no longer be accepted we are not saying that it is out of date simply because it is old, but because the deeper understanding of sexuality which we have, both as an appetitive faculty in man and as a potentially personalistic thing in man, makes possible a whole new theology of sexuality and its associated values. The classical moral theological textbooks revealed a rather dubious attitude to the human body and some suspicion of the power of Christ's grace to redeem and sanctify sexuality. They gave little hope that the appetitive side of sexuality, which is and can be so disorientating for certain individuals, could be integrated into a personal love for another man or woman. It is true of course that the practical norms given to the unmarried were – for the greater part – effective in that they achieved the negative purposes of chastity. But they were not practical in another sense, because they did not, when followed, help to build up those qualities of mind and heart which were so necessary if two people were to grow and develop sexually in their marriage. I might put this another way, by saying that where a boy and a girl are preparing themselves for marriage they are inevitably drawn towards deep and profound expressions of their love. These expressions of love are mostly by means of bodily patterns of action. We must remember that the person is both body and soul and that what I am loving is either a man or a woman, not just a soul or a mind. In a very real sense, human love needs to express itself in a bodily way. We see this very clearly in the relationships between parents and their children, particularly in the relationship between a mother and her baby. To put it in more theoretical terms we can say that the language of human love is partly a bodily language. It is through bodily actions that we foster, cultivate and develop any form of love for others, even God. The liturgy is a concrete proof of this.

What we need to teach boys and girls is not just the kind of things they should not do, so much as the kind of things they ought to do if their love is to grow to maturity. We can do this only if we teach them the values that are at stake in this relationship, values like love, tenderness, care, concern, chastity, gentleness, refinement, and indeed a whole barrage of values which can be summed up in the word 'aesthetic'. Aesthetics are very important where sex is concerned. In a sense aesthetics – the sense of beauty – about sex is a kind of musical background to all sexual relationships. It acts both as a protector and a fosterer of certain other values. This is why there is a real meaning in the idea of modesty of dress as a factor in chastity.

Now in a similar way, when we are training young people to be celibates, we must point out these facts to them also. We must try to teach them the positive values in heterosexual relationships and friendships; we must try to teach them the kind of actions that foster them, the kind of actions that destroy them. Certainly any moral teaching that seems to imply that there is no place in the friendship of celibates for the whole range of emotional affective responses is more likely to do harm than good. To put this more concretely, the celibate has, as I have already said, undertaken to love all men and women with the greatest possible intensity. His aim therefore must be to try to cultivate as gentle, as refined, as affectionate a relationship with them as possible. The celibate is not dispensed from the positive demands of chastity. If anything, he is more committed to them.

Against this background we can see the sacramental role of celibacy much more concretely. The celibate shows us that sexual love is first and foremost a personal thing and must be grounded on personal relationships. He shows that a man can have a deep relationship with a woman without that relationship being sustained by all the physical expressions of love peculiar to married people. He stresses for us the ennobling aspect of sexual love. In this way he helps both the married man and the unmarried man. For the married man must learn, in advance of marriage, that married love is not just confined to sexual intercourse. He must learn in fact that sexual intercourse is just one word in the language of married love and that it is as rich or as deep as the richness and the depth of the language of which it is part. By establishing (in a very personal sense) close and intimate relationships with women, the celibate thus teaches men, both married and unmarried, how they should relate to women.

It is only when he is doing this that the various theological significances of celibacy have application. We are told that consecrated celibacy manifests and makes clear the virginal love of Christ for the church. This, of course, is the statement of an ideal. It must be made fully real by the celibate's own life of love and dedication. In other words, the people must see in him the virginal love of Christ for the church, and this means the virginal love of Christ for men and women. Another theological meaning, which is grounded on this same fact, is the eschatological significance of celibacy. Celibacy shows forth in time and history something of the condition of being which is proper to those who share fully in the resurrection of Christ. We are told that in the resurrection they are neither married nor given in marriage but are like angels in heaven. Celibacy attempts to proclaim that truth here on earth in time, in history, in the place where the celibate is. It is important to stress that these are ideal statements and must be given flesh and blood in the actual living of celibate life. Unless the celibate is really a man who is dedicated to the love of other people, a man given utterly and completely to all in his care in the way a married man is meant to give himself to his wife or a wife to her husband – unless he is this kind of man – then the sign value of his life is going to be dimmed seriously, just as the sign value of Christian marriage is dimmed when in fact true Christian love is not realised within it.

We hear a great deal of talk about the fall-away in vocations to all forms of celibate life. It is difficult to discover the real reason for this decline. There are of course many, but one is never sure which operates in the mind of any would-be priest or religious. But it seems fairly safe to say that the celibate life does not appeal as strongly as it did. There are two reasons for this. One is very much to the credit of the church, namely the new positive theology of marriage which is being developed and preached and has already filtered down into the minds of young people. As a result, they feel that they can serve God in a very real way in marriage. At the same time they can serve their fellow-men, particularly the less fortunate in the developing countries, by taking to them some particular human skills like medicine, economics or science. To the extent that this is a cause for the fall-off in vocations, the church has no reason to worry. But it is probably true that the fall-off is also due to the fact that the image which celibates present to young people is by and large not an attractive one. They may not be seen as men and women whom young people admire; men and women whose lives inspire young people to follow them. If this be so, then it would seem that the kind of image which the celibate presents is either an imperfect or an inauthentic one.

We have already indicated that part of the reason for this may be the wrong moral teaching about chastity, friendship and love as they affect the celibate. It is essential, therefore, that we set about offering a positive theology of love, friendship and chastity for those who undertake celibacy. With such a positive theology we could make celibacy a more attractive thing to young people, and thereby prevent them from abandoning vocations purely as unattractive. But the theology must be lived. If the celibate is to attract others to his way of life then he must be, and must be seen to be, a really great lover of men and women. If he is the sort who fears women, who sees women as a temptation to his celibacy, then a great area of fruitful work is cut off for him. Or if, as so often happens in religious life, he even fears friendship with his own sex because of some false theology of religious life, he is likely to become stunted and withdrawn into himself. The outgoing warm approach to both men and women which seems to have characterised Christ's relationship with others is certainly lacking. We read in the gospels how Christ loved Martha, Mary and Lazarus; how he wept for them. We read how Mary sat at his feet. Here we have an indication of the gentle tenderness which Christ showed towards women at all times. Such gentleness and such tenderness are not to be found in someone who fears women and friendship with them, for one reason or another. Is it any wonder that he lacks the power of Christ to draw others to him?

Still the bad theology seems to prevail, especially the kind given to religious sisters. In many convents it is still taught that particular friendships between sisters are destructive of community life. This attitude is often a generalisation of dangers which lie in those friendships at certain stages of adolescence. If community life means anything at all, surely it means that those who form it live together in love and particularly in the highest form of love which is friendship. We know of course that friendship is not possible with everybody, though the religious should and will strive to achieve as high a degree of intimacy as he or she can. But a community which is linked together in a network of close friendships will always be a happy community, because each will have someone to whom it is possible to turn as a genuine friend. Without this friendship religious life becomes little more than a formal community – a group of people held together by the bond of external rules with very little soul or love. Those who condemn close friendships in religious life do not understand the fundamental basic need, particularly among women, of close affection. Why must we be suspicious of affection or of emotion? Surely if celibacy means anything at all, those who practise it should be models of all these qualities of human love? In them we should be able to find an example of how to cultivate friendship, how to maintain friendship, and how to sustain friendship against all odds and all difficulties. Clearly if celibates are to fulfil this role they must practise true friendship with all its joys and sorrows. Coldness, aloofness and emotional indifference to those near us have no place in virginal chastity. The celibate must be a model and a master in the whole field of personal relationships.

Whatever one's attitude to the present debate on clerical celibacy, it is clear that the celibate life will always be cherished by the church, because of its practical and theological significance. The controversy about priestly celibacy must not blind us to the fact that it is only one of many forms of celibacy within the church. The church certainly needs celibacy and the world needs it too. The witness of the celibate cannot be allowed to perish, since the values he seeks to realise and proclaim are basic human values – generosity, care, concern, affection, loyalty and total dedication. As yet we do not have a surplus of men and women who realise these in a high degree. In any case the world can never have too many such people.

The great task facing the church today is to ensure that a meaningful form of celibacy survives. This will not be accomplished just by legislation. We need a profound renewal in our thinking and teaching on all matters concerning sexuality, and on marriage and celibacy as ways of redeeming it. Only then will young men and women understand it and, understanding it, see it as an authentic way of serving mankind and the church and of achieving personal sexual fulfilment.

37   A Christian Spirituality of Celibacy

Donal Dorr

(*Time for a Change*, Dublin: The Columba Press, 2004, pp 126-146)

One of the most striking things about the gospel accounts of Jesus is that they give no suggestion that he had an intimate sexual-genital relationship with anybody. This raises the major issue of a spirituality of celibacy. I will argue a little later that the example of Jesus is a crucial element in a Christian approach to celibacy. But, before coming to that, I want to make some more general observations about the vocation to celibacy and the celibate lifestyle.

In trying to work out a spirituality of celibacy, it is necessary to take two different situations into account. The first is where a person chooses celibacy as a value in itself; I propose to treat this topic at some length. Then I shall comment briefly on the other situation, which is where a person accepts celibacy not for its own sake but simply as part of 'a package' such as priesthood, or life as a member of a religious community.

In relation to the choice of celibacy as a value in itself, Sipe makes an important preliminary point. 'Celibacy', he says, 'is one way of being human' (Sipe 32). He stresses the fact that it should not be defined in purely negative terms but rather in terms of a commitment 'to live for the good of others' (42). He puts a lot of emphasis on the word 'altruism' (61) and argues that there is even a biological basis for this: in the animal kingdom there are many species which have members that 'are sexually nonreproductive and/or not sexually active, but they serve the group by fostering the well-being and survival of others' (22). Furthermore, the notion of celibacy as a religious value is not confined to Christianity. It is accepted also by Hindus and Buddhists (35).

Solidarity versus individualism

All this raises a very significant point. In our Western world today it is almost taken for granted that, when we look for meaning and purpose in life, we think first of all in terms of the person in isolation. However, this is a very individualistic way of thinking which only emerged in Western cultures over the past few centuries. In earlier times, people experienced themselves first of all as part of a community. This sense of being in solidarity with others (including those who have gone before us and those who will come after us) is characteristic of most non-Western cultures even today; and it is quite taken for granted in the biblical world. A crucial part of the development of spirituality is a recovery of this sense of community solidarity. It does not mean the abandonment of our Western sense of the uniqueness of each person; but it does involve moving away from a purely individualistic conception of human fulfilment.

The difference between these two different approaches becomes very evident in regard to sexuality. The modern Western approach leads one to assume that each individual has a right – and almost a duty – to have personally fulfilling active sexual relationships. The 'solidarity' approach takes it for granted that different individuals can have very different roles in the community – and that this applies in the sexual sphere as well as in other aspects of life. Within this way of thinking and feeling, it is much easier to accept that some individuals, who are not sexually active in the genital sense, can make an important contribution to the community – and that they can find personal fulfilment in doing so. I think we need to make this shift away from individualism in order to accept Sipe's claim that celibacy is one way of being human and that it is not unnatural (22 and 59).

Taking this a step further, we need to recognise that meaning in life and personal fulfilment can be found in devoted service of others (cf Sipe 100). Oddly enough, we tend to take this for granted in regard to working for justice or caring for the poor. But we find it more difficult to accept that this is also true in the sphere of sexuality – for here individualism comes to the fore. This is such a strong cultural prejudice in our presentday Western world that theoretical arguments are not very effective in challenging it. What carries much more weight is the living witness of people like Dorothy Day or Mother Teresa of Calcutta. And of course the outstanding model is Jesus. The gospels present him as one who obviously had intimate friendships with various people, but who lived a fully human life without having a genital relationship with anybody.

Psychological and theological basis
Even though the witness of celibate people is more convincing than any theological argument, nevertheless we do need some intellectually satisfying account of how celibacy can bring human fulfilment. I think it is best to build such an account on a careful reflection on the very nature of sexual love. In my account of the unfolding of sexuality, I tried to bring out the fact that eros is not a static reality. It leads one on naturally from the stage where it is focused on personal fulfilment (through possessing the other and being possessed) to later stages where it involves very high degrees of self-sacrifice. So it is a serious mistake to set personal sexual fulfilment over against generosity and altruism as though they pulled us in opposite directions.

Of its very nature, love has two dimensions – the personal and the universal (Kimmerling 1986:461-3). We humans cannot at first hold both together in full degree. So most people start with a deeply personal relationship to another person. If their love develops properly, they progress after some time to the more universal dimension, starting with the birth of children and eventually moving on to a point where 'the stranger' can be welcomed. (I described this pattern in a previous chapter.) However, while this is the usual pattern, it is

AN IRISH READER IN MORAL THEOLOGY

not the only one. Celibates start at the other end. In their journey of exploration into love, the first dimension to emerge is the universal aspect of love (Kimmerling 1986:463; 1993:88).

Loving concern for refugees, or the poor, or abused people – all these are obvious examples of the universal dimension of love. But the primary object of celibate love can also come in other forms. A passion for justice in the world, or a burning concern about preserving the tropical forests, or some other aspect of ecology – these too can be instances of universal love. If we take seriously the fact that all aspects of human life and endeavour have a genuine value, then we can see how the total dedication of a person to art or mathematics or science can also be manifestations of the universal aspect of love.

What I am saying is that, for some people, the primary focus of love is commitment to a sexual partner, while for others it is care for the poor, or a commitment to justice or art. Does this imply that married people cannot be as devoted to the poor, or to justice, or to art, as a celibate person? Not at all. In referring to the primary focus of the love of different people, I am not making a direct comparison of the love of the married person with that of the celibate. It would be an impossible and pointless task to try to weigh up how much love each of them can give. I am simply noting an observable fact – that some people, at a particular point in their lives, or even for their whole lifetime, are so single-mindedly devoted to, say, caring for the poor or working for justice that they do not in fact take the time and energy to nurture a loving sexual-genital relationship with another person.

Superiority?
We need to get away, once for all, from the false idea that the celibate vocation is intrinsically superior to that of the person who opts for a sexual partner. We are dealing here with two different vocations, each of them uniquely personal. Because each person is unique, we cannot compare two different people and decide that one person or one call is superior to the other. Each individual, however, does have to look at his or her own personal options and decide which way of life is right for him or her. Those who are advising or facilitating a person in making this personal choice should not suggest that one way of life is objectively 'higher', or superior in principle, to the other.

It would even be wrong to suggest that, in responding to the more universal aspect of love, the celibate is manifesting a greater degree of generosity or nobility than the person who chooses a sexual partner. As I pointed out above, there is a natural progression by which sexual love, which is at first narrowly focused on one person, tends subsequently to broaden out to the wider community. So married people, having already exercised enormous generosity in caring for their children, are normally drawn to broaden the scope of their generosity by reaching out to serve the poor or to work for justice.

Of course, there are some married people who refuse to broaden their horizons; they do not let their love blossom outwards to the wider community. They cling on to the personal dimension of love at the expense of its universal dimension. The temptation for those who choose the celibate path is the very opposite. Starting with the universal dimension, they may fail to realise that love can never be fully itself until it becomes deeply personal. So they remain rather distant in their care for orphans, or the poor, or refugees. In the case of those whose devotion is to justice or care for the earth, their commitment may degenerate into angry fanaticism. In this way, their love fails to blossom; it becomes dried up.

In recent times, unfortunately, we hear of various situations where celibate people fell into this trap. Appointed to run institutions for the care of deprived young people, they gave priority to organisational values. So they were perceived as heartless and cruel, rather than kind and loving. It is evident that this sad failure arises mainly from the unconscious adoption by these celibates of one or other of the various stratagems described in the previous chapter for escaping the shame attached to sex. In the more extreme cases of abuse or cruelty, the 'attack other' pattern is very evident. But the other escape patterns (avoidance, withdrawal, and 'attack self') have also been operative and have done a lot of damage – not only to the celibates themselves but also to the children in their care. If celibates are to develop into warm and caring people, they need to 'own' their sexuality, and devote time and energy into developing the more personal dimension of love.

Because the celibate style of life is not the normal or spontaneous way sexuality develops, it is very likely that, at some point in their lives, those who have opted for celibacy will have to face up to difficult questions about how they are handling their sexuality. Are they trying to escape from acknowledging their sexuality through a pattern of 'withdrawal' or 'avoidance' in the technical psychological sense I outlined in the previous chapter? Are they dealing with their internal tensions by attacking those around them physically, verbally, or psychologically? Have they turned in on themselves, allowed their love to remain coldly impersonal, or to become desiccated through burnout? Or have they, on the other hand, developed an attitude of loving openness to other people – and of genuine interpersonal intimacy with one or more close friends? If all their relationships with others remain distant and impersonal, then there is a serious lack in their human development, no matter how much good work they are doing in other spheres.

Contemplatives
What about those celibates who devote themselves to the contemplative life? Should we say that the distinctive feature of their choice is that they give priority to their love of God rather than to any human love? That may well be

how they experience and articulate it. But I think that, from a theological point of view, it is not fully accurate. God the Creator (as distinct from Jesus) is transcendent, beyond our world. So whenever we direct our love to God, it always has to be 'carried' through some agency within this world. For some people the primary 'carrier' of love is commitment to a sexual partner; for others it is care for the poor or the sick; for still others it is devotion to art or science; and, finally, for other people it is living a contemplative life of prayer and meditation. We cannot say that any one of these is, in principle, superior to the others. Any one of them may be the best and highest way for a particular person, depending on that person's individual call.

Sexual energy is not excluded or ignored in any of these different ways of life, since sexuality is a fundamental aspect of our human existence. But that energy can be channelled or focused in one direction or another. The usual way of doing so is through love of a partner and family. But some people find themselves so passionately drawn to meditation and prayer, or so concerned about the poor or the environment, or so deeply immersed in art or science, that they channel all their energy – including their sexual energy – into that passion. For them, the way forward is the celibate life, freely chosen.

Christian celibates who opt for a life of meditation and contemplation are choosing to sublimate their sexual energy in a very specific way. To outsiders it may seem that they are opting out of the world, becoming indifferent to all the concerns of those who have to face the daily round of family difficulties, tensions at work, and political upheavals. But the reality is generally different. Quite commonly, those who successfully choose the contemplative vocation have a deep and burning concern for the world and its peoples. In them the universal dimension of love burns bright – but not at all at the expense of its personal dimension. They may restrict their contacts with the outside world; but they make up in quality what they have given up in quantity. Their hours of prayer enable them to bring a depth of compassion and understanding to those they meet. And even those who seldom communicate with other people are relating to God and to Jesus in a deeply personal way which is nourishing their humanity and bringing an energy of personal love into the environment.

Supports

I have already referred to Sipe's insistence that celibacy is not 'unnatural'. However, it must also be said that those who opt for celibacy are not following the usual or 'normal' pattern. They are going against a natural biological dynamic that is built in to each of us, and has been inherited from our animal ancestors over millions of years. This means that the initial choice of celibacy is not easy. Furthermore, it means that celibacy involves an on-going series of choices. For the dynamic of eros remains; and those who have opted for celibacy may find in themselves, on various occasions during their lives, a strong sexual attraction for some person; so their option for celibacy has to made over and over again.

For this reason it is necessary for celibates to build a support structure which will enable them to remain true to their commitment – and to experience their celibacy as a source of personal growth rather than a burden. Perhaps the most important support for celibacy is a regular practice of meditation and prayer. Sipe puts this very strongly:

> In studying religious celibacy for thirty-five years, I have never found one exception to this fundamental rule: Prayer is necessary to maintain the celibate process. A neglectful prayer life ensures the failure of celibate integration … Prayer means facing ourselves as we really are in the safety and privacy of our hearts. (54-5)

A second major support is to talk about one's sexuality with at least one other person in a completely open and honest manner. Once again Sipe makes the point strongly and clearly:

> Honesty is a necessity, not a luxury or an option … Social isolation can encourage us to overidealise sex and maintain fantasies that sexual activity alone can heal our loneliness. It cannot. Fearless self-knowledge and reality sharing are invaluable correctives to ignorance, naiveté, and natural vulnerabilities. (97)

The person with whom the celibate talks openly may be a friend, or it may be a counsellor or spiritual director. It may be that what is best is to talk quite honestly with both a friend and a counsellor or spiritual support-person.

The third major help that is needed to live a fruitful celibate life is to have a culture or sub-culture which provides an atmosphere of understanding and support. Such support can come from a group of colleagues who are at ease with the living out of their commitment to celibacy. By giving a living witness that this life can be fulfilling and fruitful, they help each of their members to persevere in the commitment through the dark times or difficult patches which are likely to arise.

But the sub-culture created by a group of celibate colleagues can be a hindrance as well as a help. It will be a hindrance if the members of the group generally adopt a selfish and easy-going lifestyle. For the choice of celibacy is a renunciation which does not make sense unless it is part of a wider commitment to frugal living. The whole point of the sexual renunciation is undermined, and the witness value of celibacy is cancelled out, if the celibate tries to make up for the loss of a sexual relationship by indulging in luxuries of various kinds (the best motor-car, expensive holidays, etc.).

Solidarity with Jesus
For very many Christians who choose to live celibately, by far the most powerful motivation and support is the example of Jesus. They feel strongly called to discipleship and they want to live as Jesus lived. For many of them, the desire

to come ever closer to Jesus is so clear and strong, that it becomes the primary driving force of their lives. Everything else seems of secondary importance to them – and that applies even to the very natural urge of eros, which in other circumstances would impel them to look for a sexual partner.

There is a danger that apologists for celibacy would read too much into the fact that Jesus did not get married or engage in a genital sexual relationship. I do not think that the fact that Jesus did not get married proves that celibacy is a higher calling or a more privileged or effective way to come close to God. But it certainly suggests that it is not necessary to be sexually active in the full sense, in order to live a fully human life. As I pointed out in a previous chapter, this challenges the assumption in most Western cultures that sexual intercourse is an indispensable part of living a fully human life; and it also challenges the assumption in primal cultures that anybody who has not generated a child is not yet fully human.

Suppose somebody tells me that the reason why he or she has chosen celibacy is in order to follow Jesus, or to live like Jesus. This answer leaves me somewhat dissatisfied. I need to hear more. When Jesus chose to live celibately what was the positive value to which he was giving witness? The best answer I have found to this question is given by Rolheiser (199):

> … when Christ went to bed alone at night he was in real solidarity with the many persons who, not by choice but by circumstance, sleep alone.

I think about two friends of mine in this situation. One is a widow, a young woman who recently lost a very loving husband. The other is an even younger woman, a gifted and loving person who for some reason has never yet managed to find a boyfriend. Both of these people – and millions of others – are truly deprived. Each of them is tempted at times to think that life has played a cruel trick on her, preventing her from having her heart's desire – the joy and fulfilment of a loving intimate sexual relationship.

I do not know whether it is any consolation to these women to know that Jesus chose freely to live as they are forced to live. But I can see how some followers of Jesus might wish to join him in such a renunciation as an act of solidarity with people who are sexually deprived, as these two women are deprived. I think people who choose celibacy would be very unwise if they were to claim that their way of life is a proof that those who do not have an active sexual relationship have nothing to complain about or are not really deprived! But, whatever about their words, their witness in living a fulfilled and loving life could perhaps bring some consolation and be a sign of hope to people who are unwillingly deprived of a loving sexual relationship. But, quite obviously, this could only happen if these celibates succeed in living a full and love-filled life. If they can meet this challenge successfully then the witness of their lives can be a very valuable ministry to others.

Celibate love and intimacy

Celibacy is not an alternative to intimacy but a different – often a more difficult – way of achieving intimacy. Anybody who is celibate must make a commitment to developing a love that is deeply personal as well as universal in its
scope. This applies, not just to those who choose celibacy as a value in itself,
but also to those who accept celibacy as part of the 'package' of priesthood. It
applies also to those who find themselves celibate because they have failed to
find a suitable sexual partner or because their partner has died or left them.

In a previous chapter we saw that intimacy involves holding an open space,
in which there is relevant and truthful disclosure, and a presence to the other
with transparency and trust. It is very difficult for one to grow in intimacy
while holding oneself physically at a distance from everybody. That is because
the primary language in which intimacy is learned is the language of touch.
(The reason for this presumably goes back to infancy or even to the pre-birth
situation when the link between mother and child was primordially a bodily
bond.) How, then, can a celibate person grow into intimacy?

Certainly not in the manner laid down in old-style programmes of formation, where physical contact (except in sport) was actively discouraged. And
certainly not by the kind of 'withdrawal' I referred to earlier, where the person
effectively closes off the whole sexual area of experience. We cannot grow to
full maturity and full humanity unless we acknowledge the sexual longing and
sexual attractions, and even the falling in love, which are part of the human
condition. But that does not mean that we have to act on all our sexual im-
pulses, or seek to become the sexual partner of the person with whom we fall
in love.

We can develop a close friendship, and learn to express that friendship in
ways which involve some degree of physical intimacy, but which do not go 'all
the way' into sexual intercourse. It is not an easy road to choose, and there is
no general roadmap which is suitable for everybody. It may seem at times that
it is wrong to practise restraint, to hold back from allowing the natural dynamic
of intimate touch to find its culmination in sexual intercourse. But Kimmerling
points out that sexual intercourse is 'just one means of expressing love' and
that 'the celibate person discovers that while the need for love has to be met,
the desire for sex does not.' (1993:93). She goes on to say:

> Though sexual intercourse may be the most intense form of touch it is not
> the only form of touch which can transform, liberate, and redeem us. Any
> caring touch can heal us and open us up more fully to God and to others.
> (1993:95)

A rather obvious question arises: how far can one go? It is not possible to
give any general answer to such a question. Indeed the question itself is not
helpful because it suggests that one is thinking in terms of rules – and of stretching the rules as far as possible. The question each person needs to ask is: 'What

AN IRISH READER IN MORAL THEOLOGY

is the most appropriate way in which I can express my intimate relationship with this person, while at the same time enabling both of us to keep in mind that I am committed to celibacy?' The answer to this question is very personal; it will differ from one person to another; it may be different on different occasions; and it will depend not merely on one's own situation but also upon the other person's response.

An alternative approach

In all of what I have written here about celibacy I have presumed that it involves abstinence from full genital sex (sexual intercourse). However, Ó Murchú, in his account of the vows taken by members of religious orders (as distinct from the commitment to celibacy taken by priests), defines celibacy quite differently. To put it more accurately, he maintains that 'we ... need to abandon the traditional language "[vow] of celibacy" and adopt the phrase "[vow] for relatedness"' (1999:49).

In order to do justice to Ó Murchú's approach it is important to take account of his overall position. He believes that about 10,000 years ago 'the many sexual hangups that prevail today seem to have been largely unknown'. At that time, there was worship of the Great Mother Goddess which brought a 'wild and often uncontrolled exuberance [which] was quite overtly sexual' and was marked by playfulness (1999:46). But with the coming of patriarchy, at the time of the agricultural revolution around 8,000 years before the Christian era, there came various distortions and 'hang-ups' in relation to sexuality. Ó Murchú believes that one of the more important tasks of those who take religious vows is to rescue us from the guilt and 'hang-ups' associated with sexuality. The aim would be to help people of our time to recover a sense of playfulness in sexual relationships and an awareness that 'sexual ecstasy is at the core of divine creativity' (45).

It is against this background that Ó Murchú says: 'The vow for relatedness is a call to engage with the emerging issues of psychosexual relating in the contemporary world ...' (49). He maintains that the person who takes this vow needs to remain unmarried in order to make this engagement in a countercultural way. Then he goes on to make this very controversial statement:

> Whether or not the celibate should totally refrain from sexual genital intimacy, in a world where such intimacy is no longer tied exclusively to marriage, it has at least to remain an open question. (1999:51; cf 1998:112)

There can be no doubt that Ó Murchú is right to emphasise the importance of relatedness, and the need to explore different forms of intimacy and appropriate ways to express it. But I am not convinced that it is wise to suggest that the possibility of genital intimacy remains an open question for celibates. It is of course true that life is larger and more complex than any set of rules we devise to cover all the options. But to suggest that there may be special circumstances in which one can transcend the normal rules seems to me to be establishing a further 'rule' – a category of unusual or exceptional cases where the usual rule does not apply. In effect, then, to say that this issue is 'an open question' may well be taken by some as approval for sexual experimentation, on the grounds that the situation is exceptional.

In seeking to answer the question whether celibates might be entitled to engage in genital intimacy, it is particularly important to take account of the experience of women. By and large, women tend to feel more 'bound into' a sexual relationship once it is established, more inclined to see it as involving commitment on both sides. A woman is therefore more likely to feel betrayed and abandoned if her partner moves on to somebody else – and to feel cheated and let down if the partner refuses to make a binding commitment to her. Furthermore, there is the most obvious argument against Ó Murchú's position, namely, that contraception is not 100% effective, so the possibility of pregnancy cannot be totally excluded if the woman is of child-bearing age (unless the woman is prepared to bear a child or to use abortion as a back-up in case of the failure of contraception). In the present culture, which still retains notable elements of patriarchy, intercourse by somebody committed to celibacy could easily lead to further exploitation of women.

It is true that many people today engage in sexual intercourse as a sign of intimacy, or warm friendship, or strong sexual attraction – but with no intention of making an exclusive, life-long commitment to the other person. But it has not at all been proved that this more 'liberal' approach marks a real breakthrough to a more human way of relating. It may well involve a de-valuing of sexual intimacy. Moreover, Ó Murchú's account of sexuality in the pre-patriarchal era seems unduly idyllic. Should we really see the attitudes and sexual practices of that era as a model for the future? And is it wise or realistic to call on vowed celibates to lead the way to such a future?

Finally, there is the issue of whether it is legitimate to replace 'celibacy' with 'relatedness'. To do so seems such a radical re-definition of celibacy that there is little, if any, continuity with the past, or with celibacy as practised in other religions. It leaves us with an understanding of celibacy as a renunciation of marriage and family but not necessarily a renunciation of genital sexual activity. I think we need to face the question of whether or not there can be a real value in the total renunciation of genital activity 'for the sake of the kingdom'.

Renunciation and transformation of energy
Celibacy is a form of asceticism, namely, a renunciation of genital activity. If it is to be fruitful, this 'letting go' has to be transformed into positive energy. The first and more obvious way of doing this is one familiar to football coaches. They advise their players to 'hold back' from genital activity before a big match, in order to build up a reservoir of energy which can then be 'harnessed' during

the match. In somewhat the same way, the celibate can re-focus the sexual energy which is not channeled into genital activity. That energy can be re-directed to any one of a variety of activities – for instance, campaigning for a just and sustainable society, or caring for refugees, or dedication to science or the arts, or commitment to a life of meditation and prayer.

There is a certain risk in this re-focusing of sexual energy. If it is done in a way that lessens one's commitment to intimacy, the celibate becomes 'dried up', no longer open, trusting, sensitive, and vulnerable. This kind of celibacy makes one less than fully human. So it is important that the person committed to celibacy takes practical steps to avoid this danger, by developing and nourishing deep interpersonal relationships with at least a couple of close friends.

Hindus, Buddhists and Christians have all had a tradition of linking celibacy with meditation and contemplation. What seems to be involved is a refocusing of sexual energy. Mark Patrick Hederman maintains that various meditation techniques are used to train the body, so that the need for sexual gratification is lessened. The energy is redirected 'to the base of the spine and allowed to travel upwards towards the area of the brain' (Hederman 1999:46). I do not doubt that such a refocusing of sexual energy can take place, but I think it is important that those who use these techniques to help them meditate should not try to de-sexualise themselves.

There is a further way in which the abstinence from genital activity can be re-directed into a positive energy. This renunciation is a kind of fasting. It has something in common with fasting from food, or giving up coffee, or chocolate. Suppose I decide to give up coffee for the sake of my health. Each time I refuse a cup of coffee I am likely to feel a little stab of loss. I may develop a habit of allowing that 'stab' to remind me of why I am doing without coffee. And on each occasion I may then 'harness' the energy I expend on the renunciation, to strengthen my commitment to becoming a more healthy person.

The situation of those who commit themselves to celibacy is somewhat similar. They are likely to experience a certain feeling of loss whenever they refuse an opportunity to engage in genital activity, or perhaps when they see the children of their friends. They can develop a habit of using this sense of loss as a reminder of their purpose in giving up genital activity. For the Christian celibate this purpose is to be more like Jesus whose renunciation of genital activity was linked to his single-minded commitment to his ministry, to his utter devotion to prayer to God, to the way he allowed himself to be constantly led by the Spirit, to his compassionate and sensitive reaching out to those with whom he came in contact, to his warm and intimate relationship with his friends, and to his solidarity with the poor and deprived – including those who are sexually deprived in one way or another.

Because the celibate remains a fully sexual person, and because sexual energy is not given its 'normal' expression in genital activity, there is likely to be a certain build-up of sexual tension. This will manifest itself in sexual attraction or sexual imagery and fantasy. So the celibate will have no shortage of 'reminders' of the cost of renouncing genital activity. Each of these 'reminders' can then be made an occasion for renewing the commitment to follow Jesus in his celibacy – and for deepening one's faith that this is an authentic way to live a fully human life.

Part of 'A package'
Celibacy is such a specialised and personal call that it is not wise – and in my opinion not just – for the Catholic Church authorities to insist that everybody who wishes to become a priest in the Western church must take on celibacy (apart, of course, from previously married Anglican priests). But that is the present discipline in the Catholic Church. It has given rise to serious questioning and grave reservations among very many priests who bought 'the package' when they were young, but who now feel that they did not choose celibacy in full freedom and with full knowledge of the demands it would make on them.

This issue is made more serious by the fact that, until quite recently, Church authorities and theologians maintained that celibacy was a higher state than marriage. This incorrect theology was applied not only to the priesthood but also to the vowed religious life. Consequently, present-day questioning of the value of celibacy is not confined to priests. Quite a number of members of religious congregations – women and men – now wonder whether, in taking their vows, they were misled by a false theology which presented celibacy as a vocation superior to marriage.

That false theology of sexuality has now been quietly dropped. But, unfortunately, the church authorities do not seem to have replaced it with a more satisfactory justification of celibacy. The result is that there are many in the Catholic Church who think of themselves as 'stuck with' a celibacy which they chose many years ago and about which they now have serious reservations. They feel now that they were 'cheated' when they were told long ago that the more perfect way to follow Jesus was to take a vow of celibacy.

There is no easy answer for those who find themselves in this situation. Some of them have chosen to give up the priesthood or the religious life. But they have felt it a choice they should not have been asked to make. Some of the most 'priestly' people I know have reluctantly relinquished a fruitful priestly ministry because they became convinced that they were not called to celibacy. When they applied for laicisation, many of them were angered and alienated by the attitude of the church authorities, as reflected in the documents they were asked to sign. These documents give the impression that the authorities see a close analogy between an application for laicisation and an application for a declaration of nullity of a marriage: in each case the key thing to look for is a defect in the original intention of the person. But many of these priests hold that there was nothing seriously wrong about their original intention in choosing to be a priest. They look back on their time in priestly ministry as a fruitful period of their lives. Now that they have chosen to get married, they do not want to repudiate their original choice of priesthood.

Church authorities need to change the present practice. At a very minimum they need to couch the application form for laicisation in more acceptable terms, and to adopt a more sympathetic approach to those who now wish to leave the active ministry. This is a matter of justice and respect, especially in view of the fact that the theology of celibacy which was taken for granted up to quite recently is now seen to have been mistaken.

In the light of the seriousness of this mistake, there is a very strong case for a much more radical change – for a process which would offer an opportunity for those who left the priesthood and got married, to explore again the possibility of returning to active ministry. Not all of them would wish to do so; and the character or circumstances of some of them would preclude their return, at least on an immediate basis. But the church authorities are being unduly rigid, and are depriving the Christian community of a rich resource, if they continue to refuse to open the possibility of welcoming back to active ministry priests who left to get married.

Some of those who chose celibacy as 'part of a package', and who now feel trapped by that choice of many years ago, have opted reluctantly to stay in the priesthood or vowed religious life. They have rejected the old theology which told them that celibacy was 'a more perfect' way of following Jesus. But they have not found a satisfactory theology of celibacy to replace the old one. So they may drift along, living celibately but not making any serious effort to 'harness' its energy in a positive direction.

For them, it may perhaps be helpful to reflect on the celibacy of Jesus as an act of solidarity with the many people who, for one reason or another, do not have a satisfactory sexual relationship. Such a reflection may lead these 'reluctant celibates' to believe that they can have a helpful and fruitful ministry to those who, against their will, are sexually deprived. In order to do so they would have to decide that the best practical choice they can make is to continue to accept 'the package', including celibacy; and they would have to choose wholeheartedly, however reluctantly, to live celibately with generosity and love. By doing so they would give a witness to others that it is possible to live a fully human life even if circumstances do not allow one to have a fulfilling sexual relationship. They could in this way give a positive value to their reluctant celibacy by linking it to their ministry.

Education for celibacy

In a rather striking phrase, Sipe maintains that the Catholic Church operates 'a system that demands celibacy but does not educate for it' (78). One might wish to qualify that statement by noting that, in recent years, a lot more attention is paid to the development of personal maturity in candidates for the priesthood and the vowed religious life; moreover, applicants to seminaries and novitiates are generally screened much more carefully than in the past – and this usually includes professional psychological tests. Furthermore, Vatican guidelines for formation now put a heavy emphasis on the importance of personal growth and maturity.

Nevertheless, it remains true, by and large, that positive education for celibacy is quite inadequate. I think there are two main reasons for this serious lack. Firstly, church authorities, and many of the staff in houses of formation, do not themselves have any very convincing theology of celibacy. They are still rather ambivalent about whether celibacy is 'a more perfect state'. They probably do not proclaim openly that celibacy is a higher value, but they are part of a system which was built around this assumption. This causes a general uneasiness in those who staff the system; and the most convenient way to deal with this uneasiness is to say as little as possible about the subject. Teachers of theology tend to leave the topic of celibacy to spiritual directors or to those who give spiritual conferences or retreats. Consequently, celibacy is dealt with in a rather 'pious' way, rather than as a theological subject which can be probed and debated with some intellectual rigour.

Closely related to this is the second reason for an inadequate education for celibacy. It is that church authorities, by insisting on the inseparability of celibacy and priestly ministry, are demanding too much of a theology of celibacy. As I indicated above, the fact that Jesus chose to be celibate provides a sound basis for linking celibacy with some aspects of ministry. But it is simply not possible to 'prove' that any minister should opt for celibacy. In the present quite repressive church climate, it is not easy for theologians to say this openly. And if those who teach theology in formation programmes did say it, they would be opening up a debate about 'compulsory celibacy' – a debate which church authorities have forbidden. All this gives rise to a great reluctance to deal openly with the topic.

There seems to be a general hope that those in formation will somehow 'grow into' celibacy by living a celibate life. The trouble is that there is no longer the kind of widespread unquestioning atmosphere which would allow this process of 'osmosis' to take place. Those in formation are exposed to a great deal of critical comment in the media and elsewhere about celibacy; and the church does not seem to be providing any clear theology and spirituality of celibacy which would counteract this.

What is probably much more serious is what happens when people in formation look to those who have gone before them. They find very few who are willing to share openly about their positive experiences of living a celibate life. For the most part there is a silent 'getting on with the job', with an occasional critical or cynical comment. Every now and then, the word goes round that 'so-and-so' is leaving to get married. What is worse, it occasionally emerges that somebody is not leaving, but is quietly ignoring the rule of celibacy, either through a one-to-one sexual relationship which is incompatible with celibacy, or through more promiscuous sexual activity.

There is no easy solution to this issue. One element of a way forward should be an honest acceptance by church authorities that it is unjust to make such a rigid link between celibacy and priestly ministry. If that link were loosened, it would open the way for a more free choice of celibacy by those who are really willing to take it on.

A second, and much more immediate, step that is required is that those who live a celibate life share openly with each other their experiences of celibacy (cf Sipe 117). In fact, this is by far the most effective education for celibacy that can be undertaken. This alone can break down the wall of silence, of reserve, and of embarrassment which surrounds the topic. Furthermore, it will provide the raw material for a new and more grounded theology and spirituality of celibacy (and indeed of sexuality) to replace the old theology which we now see to have been both dualistic and unrealistic.

I conclude this chapter by expressing the hope that open sharing of experiences of celibacy – difficulties as well as consolations – will help to take this important spiritual value out of the shadows and back into the mainstream of Christian life. If this is done, it will be major service to those who have already taken on a commitment to celibacy, and to those who may wish to do so in the future. But – just as importantly – it will also provide a great enrichment to the overall theology of sexuality, and will be of immense benefit to all who wish to make their sexuality an integral aspect of their spirituality.

Books and articles referred to:
Cozzens, Donald B. (2000), *The Changing Face of the Priesthood*, Collegeville, Liturgical Press.
Crowe, Frederick E. (1989), 'Son and Spirit: Tension in the Divine Missions', 297-314 of *Appropriating the Lonergan Idea* (ed Michael Vertin), Washington DC, Catholic University of America.
Hederman, Mark Patrick (1999), *Kissing the Dark: Connecting with the Unconscious*, Dublin, Veritas.
Hederman, Mark Patrick (2000), *Manikon Eros: Mad Crazy Love*, Dublin, Veritas.
Kimmerling, Ben (1986) 'Sexual Love and the Love of God: A Spirituality of Sexuality' (a series of three articles) in *Doctrine and Life* 1986: 300-8; 363-7; 454-465.
Kimmerling, Ben (1993) 'Celibacy and Intimacy' in *The Way: Supplement No 77* (Summer 1993), 87-96.
Ó Murchú, Diarmuid (1998), *Reframing Religious Life: An Expanded Vision for the Future*, (revised edition) London and Maynooth, St Pauls.
Ó Murchú, Diarmuid (1999), *Poverty, Celibacy, and Obedience: A Radical Option for Life*, New York, Crossroad.

Rolheiser, Ronald (1998), *Seeking Spirituality: Guidelines for a Christian Spirituality for the Twenty-First Century*, London, Hodder & Stoughton. (A US edition of this book was published in 1999 by Doubleday, New York, under the title, *The Holy Longing: the Search for a Christian Spirituality*; the pagination in this US edition is slightly different.)
Sipe, A. W. Richard (1996), *Celibacy: A Way of Living, Loving, and Serving*, Dublin, Gill and Macmillan

AN IRISH READER IN MORAL THEOLOGY

38   Celibate Clergy: The Need for a Historical Debate

Thomas O'Loughlin

(*New Blackfriars*, Vol 85, November 2004, pp 583-597)

One recurring theme in almost every discussion of Catholic Church's ministry is a call for a debate on what has been one of the most carefully fostered aspects of the image of the priest: that he is without a wife.[1] This usually has attached a strange historical twist that this discipline is either 'simply canonical' with the implication that it can be changed easily; or that it is a most 'ancient tradition' – often with a passing reference to the Synod of Elvira of 306[2] – and the argument's implicit thrust is that a change is either difficult or well-nigh impossible.[3] Since the first group often see no reason to appeal to history they are not my concern here as an historical theologian. For this group, the argument is simply that a change in discipline can be demonstrated now to be good for the church, its ministry, its task of evangelisation, whatever. If anything assists in these tasks, then that outcome is sufficient justification for change. Others who argue the discipline can, or should, be changed, see the historical commitment to celibacy as posing little difficulties. The argument is that whatever reasons were offered in the past, their impact on a present decision cannot be too serious a matter: there have been, *de facto*, married priests in the Latin tradition (both in the past and today) who were not inhibited in the *usus matrimonii*, so what is the problem?

For those, however, who support the present canonical discipline of the Latin church, history appears to be of great moment. Indeed, it is, as witness the work of Cardinal Stickler or his protégé Cholij,[4] the bulwark *par excellence* against change. The assumption is that when the evidence is laid out, then it is 'clear' that clerical celibacy has an ancient lineage, is to be seen fundamentally as a discipline based within the essentials of Christian spirituality, and, hence, it was a matter of legitimate 'development' that it should be codified in law.[5] Moreover, this clamour that history demonstrates the depth of the significance of celibacy, also produces the call that any change must be justified historically. An example can be seen in a statement by John Wilkins: when making a call for a debate on compulsory celibacy felt obliged to add 'But there is a tradition of celibacy which goes right back to the early years of the church to contend with'.[6] It is this 'twist', namely that there is a major historical case to answer, that is my concern here: how significant is this 'objection from history', and, more importantly, what is its nature.

'Tradition' and 'History'

In any investigation of the 'history' of an aspect of the belief/practice of the Christian church where that discussion is deemed to have relevance to current practice, a first step is to clarify how 'history' and 'tradition' are to be distinguished. For much of the past two millennia such a distinction would not even have been understood. History, understood as the past activities of the church, and tradition, that which linked the present to the past, were almost identical. This was ably expressed by Vincent of Lerins in the fifth century: the rule of doing and believing was what was always done or held, by everyone, everywhere.[7] The past of the church was a seamless robe whose true activities were immune from the ravages of decay and so past action was a guarantee of present action. Hence 'churchly history' (*historia ecclesiastica*)[8] could be seen as doctrine teaching by example. So much were 'tradition' and 'history' related as concepts, that for the sixteenth-century Reformers to argue that the church had become corrupt in its recent history was tantamount to declaring that tradition had no authority: if the historical church could be corrupt, then tradition could err, and so have no force greater than custom.

The key assumption in this view are that past and present form an unbroken continuity, and the whole history of the church can be seen as a single historical epoch.[9] With this view of the past one must expect consistency and continuity in decisions and one enters the metahistorical *hodie* of canon law,[10] and the realm of the systematician who can cite papal statements of long ago along with quotations from long-dead theologians as part of single argument. And, moreover, doctrine becomes predictive for history: if the infallible church makes a decision 'now' (e.g. at the time of Trent), then that must have been reflected in some way in the past if we could only find it! Hence the older manuals of historical dogmatics which, for example, could not say that auricular confession of sins to a priest did not exist in the church until the medieval period, but rather used the, seemingly more precise, form: 'no evidence has survived of ...' which left open the possibility that it had happened! This pattern of obfuscation had begun in the nineteenth century in the face of the rise of history as a discipline when theologians latched on to 'inchoate anticipations' ('it does not look like what we are talking about but it was there') and the *disciplina arcani* ('it was there but they did not want anyone to know') to preserve the continuity of practice between then and now.[11] Such a model of tradition and history begins with the assumption that the present is an ideal, and if it can be shown to have a past, then it is tradition and so belongs to that deposit which must have a future. History is now the methodology, and a sub-section of the argument, that shows a practice was there in the past and so the present discipline is not a novelty. Ideally, the practice should be everywhere and at all times, but it suffices to show a range of items from as early as possible – hence the recurring citation of the Synod of Elvira.[12] These items do not show that it was *the* practice of the church, but merely an approved practice for they are not historically *tesserae* from which an historian wants to create a larger picture but legal precedents for current discipline.

AN IRISH READER IN MORAL THEOLOGY

The assumptions of the modern historian, and so what is usually referred to as 'history' when it is the product of historians, stand in radical contrast to those who identify 'tradition' with 'history'. The assumption of the historian is change and difference between the present and the past. The present does not need a history, and the past needs one only because the activities, lifestyle, and worldview are different. The historian's equivalent to the Vincentian dictum is that 'the past is a foreign country, they do things differently there!' The historian follows the changes and seeks to explore the impact of changes and, when possible, to follow the sequences of changes interacting with one another. The past needs a history, it does not simply have one nor is the past and history identical. History is the way we in the present view the past, hence each present re-writes the historical narrative asking different questions and highlighting different aspects of the past. That history is a current activity, and not simply rooting out obscure information about the past for its own sake, can be seen by noting how quickly works of history become dated.[13] Pick any historical work – no matter how critically excellent, e.g. Duchesne's *The Early History of the Church*[14] – from before 1960 and look at a chapter at random: while the dates and details may be the same, the chapter itself feels as if it belongs to an alien world with its concerns, debates, and its overall vision of the topic.

Our history describes to us the past, or a past, as it can relate to us; as such it is not an ancient snapshot (anything that has survived from the past, e.g. a text like the canons of Elvira, is but a datum for history, grist for the historians' mill – it is not itself 'history'), but a *genetic explanation of our present*. History answers the basic question: how did we get to where we are now – and, as the historian knows better than most, where we are now is always changing. History, therefore, when studying theological issues or issues of church practice, can be, depending on the locus of the historian asking the questions, a theological discipline in its own right in that it is a reflection on the nature of Christian action and belief now in terms of how it has come to have the shape it has. It is not simply that the systematician or canonist can use 'history' in doing theology,[15] but history enquiry becomes another method of theological questioning. History, as a human science, is a matter of present understanding, not a collection of background information; and its purpose is to estimate the present in terms of how it has come about: as such it does not seek 'to recover the past' (which is impossible except as a romantic illusion) nor to mimic it as if one could live today as a Christian within the same world as a millennium ago.[16]

Tradition as community activity

So what is tradition? Tradition is the process within which we live and which allows for the changes that history studies: if history seeks a genetic explanation of the present then much the past is the result of a 'handing on' of practices, memories, and ideas, and that handing on is what produces connections between people and generations in the past. Human beings in living in societies live within traditions and it is this human contact that makes the church a community of people rather than a religious club. But any single practice or idea that is handed on within the community cannot by that fact be assumed to represent an ideal. There is no perfect Christianity of which communities are reflections – such notions when produced by systematicians or preachers are only abstractions – but only the real continuity of the communities that stretch back to the first Christians.[17] It is their vicissitudes, knowing some things, forgetting other things, emphasising in one community, ignoring in another, becoming confused on one aspect, growing stronger elsewhere that makes up the collective experience of the Christians. These growths and declines operate for good and ill over the history of the church; and if we want to know the range of Christian action then we access this vast pool of experience by interpreting it as part of what made us what we are today and placed us, again for good or ill, where we are today. But it is the tradition that makes us a real community over time, linked by human bonds to the Christians of the past, and with a sense that as we have received from the past, so we must induct others into the experience of discipleship. In this handing-on, history helps us judge where we have got to and may help to alert us to the contingency within which we live: things have turned out this way, but they could have turned out very differently! And as an awareness of history points out that the past was different, so an awareness of existing in a tradition should make us aware that the future will be different to today for each day presents a fresh situation. As Picasso is reputed to have remarked: acting in a tradition is not putting on your grandfather's hat, but having a baby!

Beginning with this distinction between 'history' and 'tradition', then the original question posed in this article is radically transformed. One does not look back to history as a series of obstacles to be overcome, as if the tradition were a chronological collection of legal precedents[18] that have to be set aside or worked around so that we can change and yet not look as if we have erred in the past; but rather it is an acknowledgement of where we are today in terms of how we got here, what factors were influential in bringing us here, what limitations were operative in that course of time, all the while noting if the paradigms of ministry and holiness used in past times are different to those of our own time as investigators – for they may have done things in the past that we could not countenance today, simply because the past is a foreign country.

A possible history
So what would an historical review of celibacy, from the standpoint of a genetic explanation of the present western discipline look like? Here is a sketch, without footnotes, of an approach.[19]

In recent centuries, the image of celibacy as ancient and valuable has been built-up by the church's administration as an essential part of its own *esprit de corps*. Moreover, since clerical scandals in mid-eighteenth century France, the authorities have perceived in celibacy a badge of identity for its officers and presented it as representing a willingness to pay any price for the survival of their religious system. Popes have spoken of it as 'the jewel in the crown of the priesthood'. And some, notably Pope Gregory XVI in 1832 and Pius IX in 1846, have suspected that there was a vast conspiracy to undermine Catholicism by attacking celibacy. Gregory was quite certain that 'their' strategy was to promote the abolition of celibacy, for once priests were married they would no longer have the energy to resist the larger conspiracy of those who wanted to destroy the church.

Until very recently clerics on recruitment drives in schools used more robust language and presented celibacy as leaving the priest without ties and attachments: ready for worldwide deployment at a moment's notice. The celibate priest was a hybrid between a spiritual Red Adare and the Marine Corps of the army of Christ. If this B-movie romanticism ('I've no family at home, I'll get the message back through the lines!') seems far-fetched, then study the old seminary anthems such as this from All Hallows, Dublin: 'in lands afar – for Christ our King – our comrades bravely fight – for to teach the nations to bear – the banner of the Lord'. Meanwhile, nineteenth-century defenders of celibacy to the general population, realising that the local clergy had neither the energy of a Red Adare nor the mobility of the marines, presented a different image of one who was always ready to go 'on a sick-call', the ally of the outcast, the friend of children. This image, fostered by nineteenth century French religious writers such as Lacordaire, while not ignoble was certainly fanciful as repeated episcopal legislation demanding minimal availability of clerics in their parishes makes clear. The bishops' concern was that priests had, after their sacramental duties had been carried out, little to hold them to account with regard to pastoral care. And, as transport and the possibilities of travel improved, so did the complexity of the attempts of diocesan synodal law to keep them on the job.

Parallel to this official promotion of celibacy there was always a grim realisation that it caused serious and widespread problems: not just the drunken priest problem, but a range of situations which if public would be scandalous. Other problems such as men leaving the active priesthood were quietly ignored, such that many believe that 'priests leaving' was a phenomenon first encountered in the 1960s. The best evidence for this awareness is to examine what was covered by law – not only in the universal law, but more tellingly in provincial and diocesan synodal regulations. This ranged from the excommunication incurred by a priest who absolved his sexual partner, to regulations forbidding a priest to let a woman sit in the front seat of his car if she were travelling with him. If we want to see celibacy's effects on the church we should not look to theological tracts or sermons given to seminarians, for they may not be based in the actual experience of Christians, but to the minutiae of the pre-1917 corpus and diocesan regulations – but study them as historians wishing to see the society they reveal, not as canonists anxious to justify their contemporary legislation.

First references to celibacy

From what can be gleaned from the scanty references to ministers in the earliest Christian documents, it is clear that there was no notion of celibacy; indeed, the positive evidence runs counter to any notion of a *disciplina arcani* type. The first Christian ministers were married and took this for granted. 1 Cor 9:5 and Mt 8:14 provide the clearest evidence. In later times, under the need to demonstrate the antiquity of celibacy (at that time already seen as an ideal of apostleship) both these references would be controverted: in the case of Paul 'wife' would be translated as 'woman' (cf the Vulgate) in the sense of a helper/housekeeper, or more recently that Paul was a widower; in the case of Peter that he was a widower at the time he became a follower of Jesus – but, significantly, there is no early evidence for these added elements and both references were taken at face value to imply wives. We know that late first-century Christians rejoiced that Peter's wife was a martyr (Eusebius, *History* 3, 30 ,2) although her name did not survive in later martyrologies. Eusebius also tells us that the apostle Philip had four daughters who were important leaders in the Syrian church in the second century (*History* 3, 31, 4). From the late first and early second centuries we have a collection of texts (included in the New Testament under the name of Paul) which specify some qualities of bishops and priests: they should have shown skill in running their own families and be monogamous (1 Tim 3:2 and 3:12; and Tit 1:6); and indeed, there is a general warning on those who forbid marriage on religious grounds (1 Tim 4:3). From slightly later we know that Clement of Alexandria (c.150-c.215) did not like having unmarried clergy in his church lest it imply approval for a rejection of marriage. For Clement marriage was a central plank in Christian spirituality and he exhorted his flock to look to the example of the apostles who were married – and especially Peter and Philip who fathered children, and Paul who had a living wife. Here we see Clement using history as a genetic explanation of his present: he did not agree with those who rejected marriage as 'belonging to the devil', so he showed that position as a deviation from the practices of the churches.

Yet, by the fourth century something had changed. Then we see the first signs of disquiet about the compatibility of marriage and priesthood. For example at a local synod in Spain (Elvira, c. 306) it was decreed that any cleric who would not undertake absolute continence should be deposed. But when a Spanish bishop tried to get a similar law given general acceptance at the Council

AN IRISH READER IN MORAL THEOLOGY

of Nicea (325), which intended its law for the whole empire, he was rejected. An Egyptian bishop Paphnutius, who felt he could speak with authority as he was unmarried, thought the idea imprudent, difficult in practice, and objectionable as it reduced a personal choice of celibacy to a regulation. Recently, Stickler has gone to great lengths to show that this speech was not part of the 'official' *acta* of the council – but this is not an historian's objection, but a lawyer's. The issue is not whether one can 'cite' Paphnutius as a 'legal precedent' but whether that debate reflected part of the Christian story that might help us understand what has happened in our past.

But elsewhere things were afoot. First, there was the growth in monasticism and the notion that this was, with its implicit celibacy, the ideal of a Christian and holy life. Second, a group of influential writers, notable Jerome (c.347-419) and Ambrose (c.339-397) held that celibacy was a higher spiritual condition than marriage and that the cultic purity of the priest required abstinence from sexuality. For these writers, marriage was an earth-bound reality, but celibacy was angelic, and if the priest was to be involved with the holy he could not be involved with a wife. Jerome's phrase that 'while marriage peoples the earth, virginity peoples heaven (*matrimonia terram replent, virginitas autem paradisum*) captures the second-rate value placed on marriage – and it became a dictum repeated in law-books and writings on the religious life until the Reformation. This notion that sexuality was (a) incompatible with holiness, (b) destroyed cultic purity, (c) was somehow lower in the scale of things, dirty, and (d) connected with Original Sin, has complex origins. But, what is interesting is that it appears repeatedly in different guises until well into the last century – although since the Reformation, official praise of celibacy has usually attached a warning-phrase like: 'but no one should understand this as a denigration of marriage'. Third, during the fourth-fifth centuries the clergy emerged as a distinctive group in the church, with a developing theological identity – the notion of 'orders' and of a divide between clergy/laity emerge at this time. Likewise, in civil society the church, first a legal and then the official religion, and the clergy had a new public profile (distinctive dress is mentioned for the first time) and a corporate identity that was defined in law. Celibacy set the cleric apart as a leader in society, and spirituality sanctioned the separation in lifestyle as holiness. But for most bishops, priests, and deacons of the period – who combined ministry with earning a living – such ideas were far from their lives. We know that in the late fifth century in Britain the clergy were the inheritors of the Roman administration and that ministry usually passed from father to son (e.g. the father and grandfather of St Patrick), and it was these clergy that truly made Christianity the grassroots religion of the Latin world.

We see these forces favouring celibacy coming together in a series of legal documents. Pope Damasus, a friend of Jerome writing to some Gallic bishops (c.380), his successor Siricius writing to a Spanish and some African bishops (c.

385), Innocent (early fifth-century) to several bishops, and Leo I, some fifty years later to several bishops, said priests should be continent, even if married, or at least periodically continent (i.e. before saying Mass) – clear evidence that part of the rationale of celibacy is a notion of cultic purity which implies that women are unclean and a source of unholiness. Similar laws can be found in a series of local councils (mainly from southern Gaul) from the fifth and early sixth centuries. They envisage that only celibates be ordained, and those ordained should cease having sexual relations with their wives either permanently or for the night before they say Mass. Needless to say, given that almost all clergy were married in the areas affected by these decrees, legislation on matters like sleeping accommodation, maids, women (other than mothers) living in the same house, begins to appear at this time also. One other feature of this legislation should be noted – it recognised the dangers of church property being alienated by passing to a wife on the death of a priest.

This early body of legislation is often appealed to as evidence for the antiquity of the practice of celibacy. But it is nothing of the sort: all it shows is that one small, influential, group believed it should be mandatory. The decrees were all local in intent, and had little or no effect for they are often repeated verbatim from one council to the next. All they indicate is that among some administrators the idea of celibacy was in the air. In reality, the clergy (monks apart) were married, and in most places there was no hint of disapproval. The best evidence that these early laws were not considered universal, and had little impact, is that when in the eight-century the first great systematisation of church law took shape, this legislation was not included. While these law-books praise monasticism and virginity using Jerome and others, celibacy is not mentioned in their laws on clergy, and their marriage law does not exclude clerics. For example, one of the most complex of these books, from Ireland, the *Collectio canonum hibernensis* (early eighth-century), assumes that clerics marry, quotes 1 Tim 3:2 on monogamy and well-regulated households, and is concerned about church property. But while those early decrees had no effect in reality, the idea that the ideal priest was a celibate had been born.

Conflict and reform
The next phase in the development of the practice of celibacy comes in the eleventh century as part and parcel of what medievalists call 'the investiture struggle' and church historians call 'the Gregorian reform'. Again several factors come together. The first issue is power. Whose law, imperial or papal has primacy in church administration, to whom do clergy owe first loyalty, and who has the power to make appointments? The issues are usually discussed in terms of the precedence of pope or emperor: is the pope the imperial chaplain, or the emperor the pope's secular administrator? But the dispute was also fought at parish level. Celibacy first enters the conflict in 1018 when Benedict

VIII issued a series of decrees all of which were primarily aimed at avoiding the shift of property from church control. This continued with Leo IX (1049) and Nicholas II (1059) who sought to reduce priests' wives to the status of servants and held that people should not attend Mass from inferior (i.e. married) priests – *sotto voce*: do not support them with your contributions. It was clearly seen that in a conflict about the church's rights and property, a celibate clergy would be far more tied into the canonical administration and so be far more likely to look to the papacy than to local rulers for their maintenance and advancement.

Second, in this period there was a general movement for a new style of organised religious life, which was presented (using a ninth-century notion) as a 'reform' (i.e. there was once a 'perfect age' of the church; so anything thought of as an improvement on the present situation was, therefore, a 'going-back' (*reformare*) to that perfect age). And, a 'reform' of the church meant a 'reform' of the clergy: but what was the ideal? This ideal was not constructed historically: there and then they had ideal Christians and ideal priests: the monks. Therefore, the monk-priest was the model for every priest. And, as the new 'reformed' monasteries founded from Cluny, and later Citeaux, began to spread across Europe, and became a source of 'reforming' pro-papal bishops, they presented a new ideal of the priest – formed not on an analysis of the priest's role in the ordinary community, but on the pattern of a monk. For example, when St Laurence O'Toole, a monk, became Archbishop of Dublin, in 1162, one of his first acts was to 'reform' the canons of his cathedral by insisting on celibacy.

Third, linked to this 'reform' movement, a new theoretical understanding of the priesthood, marriage, and sexuality began to emerge in which celibacy became a value and a virtue of outstanding worth in itself. Many, such as Peter Damian, now argued along lines like this: if the church is Christ's bride, and the priest is devoted to Christ and represents him, for him to be married is to be an adulterer to Christ. Those who opposed his extremism, or suggested he was getting mixed up in his metaphors were condemned (e.g. Bishop Ulric of Imola by decree of Gregory VII, 1079). These theological developments have been well-named by Christopher Brooke as 'the cult of celibacy'.

Fourth, this period saw a massive growth in the scope and detail of canon law; the age of the lawyer-popes had arrived. The men involved in supporting the papal position, those interested in reform, and many who were particularly interested in celibacy, such as Peter Damian, had all one thing in common: they believed the way forward to success on all fronts was that of law. A comprehensive legal structure, drawing on every ancient precedent that could be found, coupled with an efficient legal system in the service of the pope, would make him the appeal court of Christendom, enhance his prestige and influence, and create a highly structured clergy that looked towards Rome. Celibacy was part of this as it would help create this new clergy and administration, and would prove that at the heart of 'reform' was the papacy. For all its political expediency, the attempts to impose celibacy sprang also from a genuine desire for the good: what could be more noble in 'reform' of the church than to want ideal priests, and – in their eyes – any priest who engaged in any sexual activity had to be less holy than one who was celibate; so, if spiritual 'reform' can be effected through law, then make it law. And this is exactly what they did.

In a series of synods leading up to two councils held in Rome, First Lateran (1123) and Second Lateran (1139), the marriages of clergy were declared not only unlawful, but null and void. The law stated that anyone in Orders could not marry, and someone married could only become a priest if the marriage were set aside (i.e. they no longer lived as husband and wife, but the wife could not re-marry). However, on the ground little changed. While we think of councils having effects rapidly around the world, this was not so in the twelfth century, even the notion of an 'ecumenical council' did not yet exist. These decrees were from an important council, were agreed by the bishops there, but no more than that. They would only take effect where individual bishops decided to enforce them, and even then any change would be slow and random. As ever, if such a law was applied to cathedral canons and the important clergy in towns, it was a very different matter in rural areas far from episcopal interest.

Gratian and the Law Schools
The up-surge in interest in celibacy might have petered out, were it not that it occurred in a stream of developments in canon law. Canon law's importance as an instrument of power and doctrine had been steadily increasing since the eleventh century, and reached a new height with Gratian (died before 1159). He brought together over 4000 legal decisions, for the earliest times until the Second Lateran Council, in a new organised format that presented the church's law in a systematic and coherent body in one book. Now, the laws on celibacy were not just a jumble of decisions, some pro and some anti, but a structured position: the papacy had legislated, so other laws and precedents should be understood in conformity with this. Gratian presented canon law as systematic, coherent, internally consistent, and in perfect continuity from the earliest times to the most recent. His *Decretum*, was an immediate success. It became a standard reference and textbook in universities, was a model for other subjects such as theology and philosophy, and formed the base of the church's legal system until 1918. Since Gratian included Lateran II's decrees, these were guaranteed an influence and publicity their framers could not have hoped for. And, from then until the Reformation, they would be commented on, added to, and gradually given effect among the clergy.

By the sixteenth century a situation had emerged where everyone knew the law, in many places (perhaps most – we do not know) it was adhered to, while in many places it was ignored or by-passed. We know this from bishops who arrived in their dioceses with new brooms. Usually their first complaint (and the proof of the uselessness of the former regime) was the 'awful morals of their priests' which means that 'house-keepers' were in fact – and all knew it as they had children – the priests' wives. This is also seen in cases presented to Rome by priests asking that their sons be legitimated, so that they could inherit or so that these sons could themselves be ordained. Incidentally, not only were these requests very common, but were looked on most favourably by the Roman Curia as they were among the most expensive dispensations to be had, costing 12 Gros Tournois. Finally, in sixteenth-century tax-returns from Germany we find that a sure guide for assessing the spread of the Reformation is to look at how clergy describe those who share their living quarters. In many cases, while he considers himself in union with Rome, we find, beside a woman's name, *ancilla* (house-keeper); when the actual break comes and he considers himself Protestant, beside the same name is *uxor* (wife). Little, but the formalities, seem to have changed.

Luther marks the next stage in the story. He argued that something one does, for instance making a vow or being celibate, could not add to one's holiness (1522). Later, he condemned celibacy as the creation of canon law, itself the work of the devil (1530) and held that for fallen men, burning with passion, marriage was a necessity if they were to avoid sin (his understanding of 1 Cor 7:9). Luther himself married in June 1525 and died the father of a large family. His position on celibacy was, in broad outline, that of the other reformers as well. For example, Calvin held that some are called by God to celibacy, but that it should not be prescribed by law and nor be considered a more spiritual, nor higher, vocation than marriage. Significantly, his is the best historical scholarship of the period. Commenting on references to marriage in scripture, he recognised that Jerome's position could not be sustained with its extremely corrupt view of sexuality, and indeed, not one shared by the New Testament. He further recognised that it was Jerome's hang-ups about sex and virginity, rather than scripture, that influenced law and ordinary theology textbooks. Jerome was to be used with caution, and this comes from Calvin who, on other matters of interpretation and linguistics, had Jerome as his hero.

The opposition of the Reformers sealed the fate of celibacy for the Roman Church. Trent declared that celibacy was possible, founded on scripture, and that it was heresy to say that virginity / celibacy were not objectively superior to marriage (1563). If the Protestant ministers were married, the new men of the Counter-Reformation would be celibates, trained and organised with a precision and uniformity unimaginable to medieval clerics. Moreover, the continuing Protestant/Catholic divide gave Trent an impetus to enforce its law unlike any previous council. Celibacy was to be a badge of the priesthood, and every priest trained in a special way and in a special place, the seminary. The distinction between the priest in the parish and the priest-member of a religious order further disappeared. A good priest was a member of a spiritual elite formed on a pattern designed for monks and friars. It took many decades for Trent's vision to inform practice; but where Catholicism remained the religion, it gradually replaced older forms and attitudes. Variations certainly continued in reality, but they were increasingly seen as 'irregularities' and 'occasional lapses'.

Celibacy is a classic example of how an idea from one period, if it gets lodged in law, can become self-perpetuating and eventually be seen as an ideal. When a law is repeated over a long enough period it justifies itself even if it does not accord with reality or the larger values it claims to serve. Once the law provides the norm, it is reality that is judged defective, and any attempt to change the law is taken to reflect on the authority of the law in general and those who administer it. To say the law erred regarding celibacy was to suggest that the law was not the will of God, or that the papacy had been making erroneous decisions for years. Such prospects abhorred those who spent their lives in administration, and (as another lawyer said of a another clash of law and reality;) 'it opens an appalling vista' that a whole system could be wrong on something like celibacy – on which it had expended so much effort. In this situation anyone who questioned celibacy had to be marginalised as in error or disloyal, or, as Gregory XVI believed, part of a vast conspiracy against God and his church.

Soundings

Given the range of the Christian experience over two millennia, the historian can rarely take more than soundings on how Christians have linked their practices to their desire to be disciples. But even a few soundings shows that certain factors have played major roles in bringing the Roman western church to its present position.

Clearly, on many occasions in the past there was a fear of disloyalty from clergy and a belief that this is somehow increased if they are married. This fear may still be present today in those who argue that celibacy allows greater 'freedom for service'. This point is never tested empirically by those who make it. For example, most of those who have put their lives on the line in the twentieth century have been married; and comparisons of the work output of celibate clergy with that of married clergy of other denominations have been made by American sociologists of religion without showing any particular benefit from celibacy.[20]

Secondly, there is a tendency to link priesthood – which is primarily presiding at the Eucharist with a community of Christ's faithful – with vocation to the religious life (most often exemplified historically by monks). If this form of life becomes the pattern for the priesthood, then its demands become by extension the demands for a priest. But perhaps this nexus needs to be formally broken to free both the religious life and the priesthood from being identified and confused. Cassian famously said that monks should flee women and bishops as both could destroy the monk's calling – perhaps monks have not been as successful at fleeing the latter as the former.

Thirdly, there is in Latin Christianity – despite what was said at the Second Vatican Council – a legacy of seeing marriage as second best with regard to the things of God. This makes it hard for Christians brought up with a celibate clergy to imagine religious dedication and marriage in the same person.[21] This implicit down-grading of the discipleship of the majority of Christians may be the hidden price of placing a religious value on celibacy – as Clement of Alexandria recognised in the late second century.

Does history help?
History provides an explanation of where we have come from and reminds us of the Christian experience that has been valued and ignored in the past. It alone cannot decide any issue – to assume that it can is the essence of fundamentalism – but it can enrich the debate on how the Latin church should address issues relating to the Eucharist and the wider topic of ministry. That church's position appears to be one more area where what has been presented as a 'fundamental value of the priesthood' is the product of particular and accidental aspects of its tradition. As a feature that has been open to radical change in the past, it can be open to equally radical change in the future.

Notes:
1. Cf C. N. L. Brooke, 'Gregorian Reform in Action: Clerical Marriage in England, 1050-1200,' *Cambridge Historical Journal* 12 (1956) 1-21.
2. For the text of the canons of Elvira, set in context, see S. Laeuchli, *Power and Sexuality: The Emergence of Canon Law at the Synod of Elvira* (Philadelphia 1972).
3. See T. O'Loughlin, 'Priestly Celibacy and "Arguments from History",' *Doctrine and Life* 49 (1999) 411-22.
4. See A. M. Stickler, *The Case for Clerical Celibacy: Its Historical Development and Theological Foundations* (San Francisco 1995); and R. Cholij, *Clerical Celibacy in East and West* (Leominster 1988).
5. Once anything is codified in law, it is automatically related to precedents and so becomes part of the 'seamless robe' of law – in all such cases to then argue that the law is a legitimate 'development' is virtually to argue in a circle.
6. *Tablet*, editorial, 4 May 2002.
7. *Commonitorium* 2, 5 (*CCSL* 64, p 149); cf T. O'Loughlin, 'Newman, Vincent of Lerins and Development,' *Irish Theological Quarterly* 58 (1991) 147-166.
8. Early Christian historians did not write 'church history' in the sense of a specific branch of the discipline dealing with one aspect of society (e.g. as 'military history' deals

with soldiers; so 'church history' deals with believers' societies); rather they saw it as the history of communities of Christians acting as churches.

9. Cf J. J. Contreni, '"By lions, bishops are meant; by wolves, priests": History, Exegesis, and the Carolingian Church in Haimo of Auxerre's Commentary on Ezechiel,' *Francia* 29/1 (2002) 29-56 which not only deals with this sense of today being the whole age after Christ, but also deals with the systematic relegation of marriage to an inferior spiritual state, and hence one that is not truly suitable for those who are pastors.

10. See S. G. Kuttner, *Harmony from Dissonance: An Interpretation of Medieval Canon Law* (Latrobe 1960), passim.

11. Cf T. O'Loughlin, 'Medieval Church History: Beyond apologetics, after development, the awkward memories,' *The Way* 38 (1998) 65-76; and idem, 'Theologians and their use of historical evidence: some common pitfalls,' *The Month* 261 (2001) 30-35

12. In the 1922 edition of H. Denzinger's *Enchiridion symbolorum* (ed 14 by C. Bannwart and J. B. Umberg; Friburg) the first appendix (p 1*) was entitled *De coelibatu clericorum* and (surprisingly in a work dedicated to papal degrees and councils judge to be 'ecumenical') supplied the relevant canons from the local synod of Elvira.

13. On the changes in history writing, see W. H. C. Frend, *From Dogma to History: How Our Understanding of the Early Church Developed* (London 2003).

14. The English translation of the three volumes appeared in London, 1901-1922; for an appreciation of this monument of early critical scholarship in history by a Roman Catholic, see Frend, op. cit., pp 108-143.

15. However, such a relationship of dependency can even be seen in those who pioneered the modern discipline of church history such as Duchesne.

16. See R. Taft, 'The Structural Analysis of Liturgical units: An Essay in Methodology,' *Worship* 52 (1979) 314-329 at 317-8.

17. See T. O'Loughlin, *Teachers and Code-Breakers: The Latin Genesis Tradition, 430-800* (Turnhout 1999), pp 39-72.

18. Such were the first collections of canon law.

19. It should be noted that there is still no detailed modern history of celibacy, hence one must still look at H. C. Lea, *History of Sacerdotal Celibacy in the Christian Church* (2 vols, London 1907) which is hostile in tone and argument, uncritical in the way it uses many sources, and dated in its theological assumptions.

20. See D. R. Hoges, *The Future of Catholic Leadership: Responses to the Priest Shortage,* (Kansas 1987).

21. See C. Broohe, *The Medieval Idea of Marriage*, (Oxford, 1989), Chap 3: 'The Cult of Celibacy'.

AN IRISH READER IN MORAL THEOLOGY

39   Towards a Theology of the Single Life

Gerard O'Hanlon

(*The Furrow*, Vol. 41, No. 5, May 1990, pp 267-276)

> Every spinster should be assumed guilty before she is proved
> innocent, it is only common civility (Muriel Spark, *The Mandelbaum
> Gate*).[1]

This is the wry thought of the fictional Barbara Vaughan, heroine of Muriel
Spark's novel. Barbara is a good person who is tired of being taken for granted;
she knows that there is a lot more to her respectable appearance than meets the
eye, and sees that ironically an air of guilt would make her life as a single person more interesting to others. Single people within the Christian Churches
might be forgiven a similar longing to shock the rest of us into some recognition
of their true worth. Within the Roman Catholic Church in particular there has
in recent years been a very welcome renewal of interest in lay married and family life, to put alongside the traditional esteem accorded to priesthood and the
religious life. But what about the lives of single lay people, without vows and
without the support of religious community life? Both pastorally and theologically those single people are, for the most part, neglected, and when considered
at all they tend to be described negatively in terms of being un-married or non-
religious.

What follows is an attempt to raise our consciousness about the lives of single people and to explore their theological significance. In the first part some
indication is given of the reality experienced by single people; the second part
is a theological reflection on this experience. There is very little literature available on the subject.[2] I have been helped mainly by the many single people,
known and anonymous, who were so generous in sharing their experience with
me in order to contribute to this theological exploration.[3]

The Reality and Experience of being Single

The term single refers to a variety of categories of people and to a variety of reasons for belonging to a particular category. Our primary focus is on the person
who has always been single (and may or may not be open to change). Nonetheless we also include those who are divorced or separated, widows and widowers,
and single parents. We note that single people may be hetero- or homosexual,
and that they belong to different classes in society. There are some who are single
by positive choice, and wish to remain so forever or not. Others are single through
circumstances, and again, may or may not change their status if these circumstances change. These circumstances themselves are various: looking after aged

or ill parent(s); never having met the right partner; being in transition from priest-hood, religious life or another relationship; psychological incapacity to sustain a committed relationship, and so on. Underlying our assumption, then, of a certain homogeneity in the use of the term single we acknowledge the variety – and indeed uniqueness – of single personal lives, and we will try to be aware as we go along of the crucial differences and limitations which this variety introduces to our sketch of what is proper to a theology of the single life.

One of these limitations becomes immediately evident as we examine the experience of single people based mainly on a non-scientific questionnaire, answered mainly by people who were always single, the majority being women and from a middle-class background. Yet the findings of the questionnaire do tally with much that is found in the general literature on the subject, has the advantage of coming from the Irish context, and does give an impression at least which the reader can then assess for him/herself.

The great positive advantage to being single for a huge majority of respondents was that of freedom – to develop oneself, to travel, to manage one's finances, to serve others, to stay on in bed reading on Sundays (!), and so on. Conversely the great disadvantage for the great majority of respondents was loneliness – expressed in terms such as having no one special to share moments of both sorrow and joy, and in more mundane terms such as having no one to turn to when the car breaks down, or to meet one at the station when returning from a journey. To this loneliness was added sometimes a fear of being on one's own in old age. The most concerted response came to a question concerning the attitude of society and the church to single people. Almost without exception, and while admitting some progress in this area, respondents complained perceptively, sometimes humorously and often passionately, about how they experienced themselves in the eyes of non-singles. The words used are telling – 'society makes me feel second class'; 'I feel people don't give me a chance, they make me feel it's awful to be single and there must be something the matter with you not to have found someone, and so you are left feeling you are out to trap someone'; 'make you feel inferior'; 'left on shelf'; 'pity from friends, although I'm happy with my life'; 'what's a nice girl like you doing on your own?'; 'one must either be a nun, or a career woman, or living it up wildly to get respect as a single woman'; 'I feel I'm a threat to marrieds'; 'the expectation is that most "normal" people get married'; 'I feel I don't belong'; 'am invisible'; 'stigma'; 'failure'; 'oddity'; 'they think I'm a-sexual and ignorant of human need/experience'; 'contempt, lack of interest'; 'missed the boat'; 'viewed with suspicion'; 'I feel like a freak'; 'old maid'; 'spinster'; 'the church assumes family to be the context of all'. One could go on and on. The long replies to this question, expressed with deep feeling, give a very negative view of how single people experience the attitude of society and church (which is said most often to mirror that of society, sometimes to be better or worse but only marginally so).

The experience of the single woman is crucially different from that of the man, as the respondents to the questionnaire and the general literature indicate. Overall there is more tolerance extended to the single man by society – the connotations of the term bachelor, in contrast to the word spinster, which so many women hate, already alerts us to this. Apart from the negative (in our Irish culture) occasional suspicion of homosexuality, one expects the bachelor to have fun. A single woman on the other hand is very often still expected to look after others, can have difficulties borrowing money from financial institutions, can feel the need to be aggressive in the workplace in order to avoid being pushed about, can be seen as a threat in relationships with men, and in most cases in Ireland makes what is often the great sacrifice to many women, of going without children. All this is so despite the changed socio-economic circumstances in which women at least in principle may enter the workforce as equals, through contraception have control over their own fertility, and are thus potentially in a position to be single in a less defensive way than before. With regard to the church's response to single women, one woman noted how she was struggling in a secular, couples-oriented male world to be a single Christian woman and was getting very little help from the church in the process.

There are some other observations worth making about the experience of single people, whether male or female. Being outside conventional family or community life, many single people find that relationships with others have to be worked at – they don't just 'happen' or get thrust upon one as they might in other circumstances. Similarly there is often more time for solitude and silence, with the threat and opportunity these bring – the occupational hazards for the single person of becoming either selfish or overly active are recognised by many. At a very ordinary level, there is the experience for many singles of preparing and eating meals alone; of not having anniversaries to celebrate; of a peculiar aloneness at occasions very much associated with families – for example, Christmas time, weddings, and so on. There may be the gradual realisation that this is the life that suits me, or a reluctant acceptance that this is how it is – or active resentment that such is my fate. And there are huge cultural differences in the experience of being single – the African experience is clearly different from the Irish or American one, but in ways less easy to see it may be supposed that the working class Irish experience is not the same as the middle class one.

It is obvious, finally, that many single people are happy with their lot and see themselves as having much to contribute. However, it is also obvious that most, whether happy or not, feel that the rest of us regard them as inferior and do not recognise the contribution they can and often do make. This is a real challenge for the churches in particular. One woman humorously noted the categories available in the liturgical calendar to describe her state – virgin and martyr were, she objected, too spectacular to encompass her everyday existence! More seriously, another person hinted at the church's attitude by suggesting that 'I don't think the church understands my type of selfishness.' Tired of being ignored or being referred to in what they experience as a token way in homilies and episcopal pastoral letters, many single people are crying out to have their voices heard in the church, as the long and often impassioned responses to the questionnaire indicate. There is the added problem, of course, that many single people are not happy with their lot, are living lives of quiet desperation, and some of their unhappiness at least may be due in no small measure to their internalisation of those appallingly negative attitudes towards them which they perceive society and church to hold. The church can remedy the injustice of simple neglect and give more pastoral and theological attention to single people. It may be more difficult, at first at least, to change fundamental attitudes and to develop a theological understanding of the single life which goes beyond attention to acceptance of this life on an equal basis with other ways of Christian living. May one, for example, talk about a vocation to the single life? May one see the single life as one of the traditional states of life? It is to this exploration of the single life that we now turn. In doing so, it is well to be aware of our own spontaneous attitude to single people – deep-down do we really wish they were married or in priesthood/religious life? It is at this deep-down level that the challenge to ourselves may become clearest.

Theological Reflections on the Single Life
Theological value: Single people who are Christian share with all Christians the baptismal commitment to participation in the life, death and resurrection of Jesus Christ, as well as the vocation to holiness and perfection that comes with this commitment.[4] These baptismal vows are the generic basis within which the specific theological value of the single life may be sought.

In particular, then, the existential solitude or aloneness of the single person (known by the single man Jesus) points very well to the uniqueness of each human person. We speak quite properly, but perhaps too easily, of the intrinsically relational nature of personhood – this has to be complemented by an appreciation that the persons who relate are unique, are different, and that without this difference reality is dissolved into bland uniformity and, ultimately, philosophical monism. The single person, particularly when committed to the single life, is a clear pointer to that uniqueness which is intrinsic to the Trinitarian, relation life of Jesus. Secondly the inherent insecurity of the single life, its lack of roots in the institutions of family, priesthood or religious life, invites a reliance on God which is peculiarly similar to the radical obedience to the Father of the man Jesus. The single person and, in this instance, one whose singleness is experienced as provisional and temporary, may often be without too many external markers to indicate his/her way into the future. As such, he/she is called to a radical openness to the future, grounded in a discernment of God's action in the present. This is life within an eschatological horizon, an invitation to experience the first fruits of the decisive in-breaking of God into the present of historical time. Both these values of uniqueness and openness to God are rooted in that peculiar aloneness of the single person, which need not be interpreted simply in terms of psychological introversion, but may rather signify a way of living which of its very nature is conducive to an opening to the transcendent. For the single person who does not simply drift, the very state of being single jolts one into the realm of mystery. Thirdly it is clear that the freedom of the single person may be assessed positively ('my type of selfishness'!) when it leads to the self-development of the mature adult who is involved in service of others. Single people themselves are very aware of the pitfalls here – once again a discerning wisdom is needed to negotiate the contrasting but related evils of narcissistic self-indulgence and a neurotic kind of activism which feels under compulsion to be at everyone's beck and call. But so many single people are maturely heroic in their service of others without this being properly recognised by the church in particular: here is surely an area of potentially immense apostolic value, and an area too which shows clearly that single people are gifts and resources to the church, not just people in need. Fourthly, in a culture which finds commitment difficult, and in which a hedonistic, *mé féin* ethos can encourage styles of living that are privatised, promiscuous, cynical and careerist, the counter-cultural witness of the Christian single person is valuable. It is so because such a person, who feels the negative pull of the culture, has a healing effect in opening up other possibilities of responding to those pulls in line with his/her fidelity to the call of Christ. In this, as in the previous points, the single person will experience the reality of the cross of Christ while living in hope, and with the first-fruits, of his resurrection.

A problem: commitment and the single life

There is one important objection to any attempt to give equal theological value to the single life. The objection focuses on the human and Christian value of permanent commitment to a way of living; most single people lack this commitment. Hans Urs von Balthasar urges this objection strongly.[5] He wishes to retain the three traditional states of life (religious, priestly and lay), characterised by their specific and definitive self-giving in either celibacy or marriage as our participation in that unique self-giving of Christ which found its highest expression in the cross and is basic to our generic commitment in baptism. In this context for Balthasar (unlike Suarez) there are two basic states, marriage or virginity, and there can be no third state for single people.

While Balthasar's position may be somewhat severe, it is important to appreciate the genuine issue which underlies it. He is afraid that by describing the single life as a third basic theological state one is threatening the radical nature of the two basic states whose 'yes' of the vows is, like the model of Christ on the cross and the grain of wheat that must die, a gift that is not to be taken back. Sexuality touches the innermost being of a person and by taking up a basic attitude of permanent commitment (marriage/celibacy) with regard to one's sexuality, one is participating in the mystery of that 'losing of self' which was characteristic of Christ's self-giving. This point is developed in a broader way by Sandra Schneiders[6] who notes that for various cultural and historical reasons we live at a time when permanent commitment is difficult. Yes, Schneiders argues, it is eminently human to promise, to be faithful, to take up a position with regard to our future. The human self-transcendence involved in permanent commitment is sacramental in mirroring and realising the fidelity of God in his/her covenant with humankind. Schneiders notes that relationships in depth, the trust that is involved in a proper use of freedom, prosper within the time and ethos that permanent commitment allows – as, once again, mirrored in the life of Jesus who 'having loved his own who were in the world, (he) loved them till the end' (Jn 13:1).

How is one to respond to this objection? First it is important to acknowledge and treasure the threatened value of permanent commitment, along the lines that Schneiders and von Balthasar indicate. Secondly, it is clear that all single Christians do share in this value by virtue of their baptism and to the extent that they live faithful Christian lives in accordance with their baptismal vows. Nonetheless (with the exception of perhaps a small minority who do make a permanent commitment to the single life) it may be admitted that typically many single people do lack a commitment to a permanent way of life corresponding to their baptismal status. This lack may be compensated for in different ways. One such way is the radical openness to God's will which we have already adverted to as a characteristic possibility of the single life. Another would be greater acceptance by the church itself of the value of the single life. This would supply somewhat the lack of institutional support which the life of permanent commitment enjoys. Existentially too it seems to be the experience of many single people that while in early life, in prospect, there was a lack of clarity about the concrete way to live out the baptismal commitment, later on what seemed uncertain and temporary falls into a pattern in which God's providential guiding is more apparent, and in which indeed there was a kind of retrospective and real permanence. We need to know more about the experience of single people to come to a clearer understanding in this whole area. And we need to acknowledge the real risk of drift and loss of nerve that can be a connivance with the cultural temptation to avoid permanent commitment. Nonetheless I would suggest that, within the values and disvalues that have been referred to, the balance favours an understanding of the single life that acknowledges its intrinsic difficulties and impoverishments but recognises its objective human and Christian validity too. In particular it may be argued that

AN IRISH READER IN MORAL THEOLOGY

there are no pure instances of chance, good or bad 'timing', or exceptions within God's providential love of each individual, and that the divine call to the single person may and often does result in just as radical a self-giving as obtains within the more clear-cut state of permanent commitment in the lives of the vowed celibate or married person. It may be proper linguistically and in accordance with tradition to avoid speaking of a single state of life: this should not stop us, however, ascribing equal theological value to the vocation[7] of the single way of living, with its complex relationship between temporary and permanent and its underlying radical openness to God's will.

Singles in relationship

One of the examples of overlapping that occurs between different ways of life is precisely the fact that single people too (even though not married or living in religious community) are obviously open to a wider range of significant relationships of a temporary or permanent nature. Angela Lewis[8] writes perceptively of the lack of support that single people feel in exploring the role of sexuality in particular in such relationships. She suggests the need single people have to explore and establish their own boundaries in this area, within a context which accepts the validity of intimacy and of sexual expression in a non-genital, non-exclusive way. Once again the value of discernment (and with it the advice to be in spiritual direction of some kind) is highlighted. Here too it is clear that we need a theology of the body, of friendship and of sexuality which is not limited just to the real gains made in recent times within the theology of marriage. Of help here would be a more frank exchange of experience between people in different life situations, as well as the more recent discussion of this area within the theology of the celibate life.[9] This is another area in which respondents to the questionnaire complained of a lack of ecclesial support, some ascribing this bluntly to fear.

Singles and option for the poor

If justice is indeed a seamless robe, and poverty more than just economic, then it would seem clear that the ordinary single person within the church is marginalised in a way which means that the theology of the single life involves that option for the poor which is so central to Christian consciousness nowadays. This is even more true of the single person who is single for 'non-respectable' reasons – the homosexual, the person who fails in relationships or who is also poor economically. The danger of paternalism and a self-indulgent victimology approach is to be avoided here. It has already been made clear that so many single people have a huge amount to contribute in very obvious ways: that God is close to the brokenhearted, that those who fail share in the sufferings of Christ, ought to persuade us that the less obviously gifted single person gives far more than he/she receives. In all cases the desire of Jesus to give us life to the full, and his particular concern to do so to the marginalised, reinforce the validity of this exploration of the theological value of the single life.

Conclusion

The term exploration has been used several times and deliberately to express the nature of our attempt here. There will be other ways of theologising about the single life, and these ways will be better if they are based on more listening to the experience of single people themselves. This must be our starting point. These people are longing to speak and will do so to all our advantage if and when they are given a proper forum. In principle the church now gives explicit recognition to the laity, to married people. We need to be more explicit in our recognition of single lay people. In doing so, we will do well not to over- or under-estimate the value of the single way of life. In particular, we will do well not to domesticate it, to take away its quality of otherness; better perhaps to question ourselves if we describe this otherness as oddness and if we find it threatening. A pastoral response goes hand in hand with this theology of the single life. The nature of this response will only become clear once the issue is acknowledged, and may involve (among other possibilities) a more serious attention to singles in homilies, the invitation to contribute personal resources, the search to provide a forum within which single people may speak, and perhaps even the upgrading of the Easter renewal of vows to ensure that all adults, single and other, are given an opportunity to make and renew a serious baptismal commitment. The church is greatly impoverished, and its treatment of its members unjust, so long as this pastoral and theological task remains neglected.

Notes:

1. Penguin, 1967, 152.

2. See S. Muto, *Celebrating the Single Life* (New York, 1985); M. Niemann, *The Single Life* (Missouri, 1986); S. Brown, *The Art of Being a Single Woman* (Eastbourne, 1989); P. Walsh, *The Single Person* (Oxford, 1979).

3. I am particularly grateful to Clare Bowmann and Carmel McBride; to many single friends; to the 1988-89 post-graduate Theology of the Spiritual Life class in the Milltown Institute of Theology and Philosophy; and to the eighty or so anonymous single people who returned the questionnaire referred to in Part One and which formed part of the course on the Theology of the Single Life conducted with the 88-89 Milltown group. Of course the theological position that follows is my own. I can only hope that it reflects to some extent the concerns of those consulted.

4. See M. Guite, 'What Do We Mean by Vocation?', *Doctrine and Life*, 39, 1989, 396-407; also, *Dogmatic Constitution on the Church*, Vat II, 32, 41 and 42.

5. See H. U. von Balthasar, *The Christian State of Life* (San Francisco, 1983) (tr Original 1976), 236-243; 312-313.

6. See S. Schneiders, *New Wineskins* (New York, 1986), 193-206.

7. For an indication of the legitimacy of the wider reference and usage of the term vocation in modern times see M. Guite, op. cit., *passim*.

8. See A Lewis, 'Experiencing the Heart-Space', *The Way*, 28, 1988, 222-30.

9. See Schneiders, op. cit., 114-136; 207-235; B. Hoban, 'Priesthood: The Celibacy Factor', *The Furrow*, 40, 1989, 195-203. For a non-conventional approach to the issue of homosexual friendship see .J Cotter, 'Homosexual and Holy', *The Way*, 28, 1988, 231-243 and A Pastoral Minister (name withheld), 'What are we doing to our Gay People?', *The Furrow*, 1990, 27-33.